REFLECTIONS
WITHOUT
MIRRORS

An Autobiography of the Mind

Louis Nizer

REFLECTIONS
WITHOUT
MIRRORS

An Autobiography of the Mind

DOUBLEDAY & COMPANY, INC.
Garden City, New York 1978

Grateful acknowledgment is made for use of the following: material adapted and abridged, with permission of Farrar, Straus & Giroux, Inc., from *This Timeless Moment: A Personal View of Aldous Huxley*, by Laura Archera Huxley. Copyright © 1968 by Laura Archera Huxley.

Material written by Edward Balmer, Igor Cassini, and Jacqueline Susann, all used by permission.

CONTENTS

Dedicated
to
The Dedicated
to Law
and Justice

REFLECTIONS
WITHOUT
MIRRORS

An Autobiography of the Mind

BEGINNINGS

There are few men important enough to recount their lives. Almost everyone, however, has some experience worth telling. If an autobiography of such selected experiences could be written, there would be profit, learning, and excitement for all of us. Is this not the secret of the novelist? By a combination of events from his own life and those of others, he constructs a single story. His observation enables him to write an imaginative autobiography, enriched by the texture of many lives. The historian and philosopher employ the same device; without simulating the origin of time and persons.

I have shunned writing an autobiography, considering such an enterprise an arrogant exaggeration of ego. But I have toyed with the idea of a selective series of incidents and my thoughts about them, which might contribute something to an understanding of man and his times. Indeed, in *My Life in Court* and *The Jury Returns,* I wrote such a selective autobiography of a few of my experiences as a trial lawyer. But no man's horizon is limited by his profession. A full and turbulent life, and this I have led, sweeps one into the presence of great men and women, famous men and women who are not great, and sometimes great events. Coincidence is more fascinating than planning, because its consequences are beyond expectation. I shall recite some of these in the following pages. But I do not justify this book by such unique accidents. Experiences which may appear mundane become significant and universal if a sharp eye and a memory-filled pen can re-create them; especially if they are interpreted by reflection, the gift of time. These abound.

So I shall eschew the usual trappings of autobiography. The fact that I was born in London on February 6, 1902, is of no importance, even to me; but the fact that I have a vivid recollection of Whitechapel Road, on which my mother carried me when I was one year old, is of some interest because it deals with the mystery of the mind and its computer recordings. Since I emigrated to the United States at the age of three, my parents used to ascribe my recollection to descriptions I may have overheard in later years from them. But when I filled in detail, which even they did not recall, and which was confirmed by their friends, such as that of a pub at the end of the walled street, at which a bobby in a chin-strapped high cup hat would regularly have his ale, or the horse detached from his wagon which was fed outside the market nearby, they were less skeptical though still confused about the indelible imprints which the mind can make before even a semblance of maturity has begun.

Similarly, my description of what I wore when I arrived with my mother at Ellis Island, the entrance funnel to the United States, was so accurate that only a daguerreotype, taken of us in London on departure and later found, demonstrated that I was not inventing. Invention, it would have seemed, considering that I had on a blue velvet Lord Fauntleroy suit, across the front of which ran a pink brocade cord ended by a whistle, high button shoes needing only two buttons for my size, and all topped by a Napoleonic hat, with a huge pompon on the front. The only accouterment in the photograph which I did not recall must have been a photographer's prop, a tennis racket, which lent the final incongruity to the whole attire. Yet, my mother was certain that the enigmatic smile and knowing eyes which peered from the photograph indicated that I was amused by the outfit and was already demonstrating the trait of being above such nonsense.

But when the blond curls which hung underneath my emperor's hat ultimately had to be cut off at the ripe age of six, my alleged insouciance abandoned me. I joined my parents in tears, though I grew to hate those curls, for they were framed under glass and hung over the living-room door for years and years. (What makes hair so hard to grow and so indestructible when severed?)

These early recollections indicate that every scene and word is recorded (perhaps programmed is the word) in brain cells to be released when we know how to do so. But how? For we use only 10 or 15 per cent of our capacity (whatever it be, as determined by the genes and chromosomes at birth). If we could more effectively explore our inner selves, perhaps we might improve human nature so that we could cope with our scientific achievements. Then we would not be in the desperate plight of creating forces so great that they ought to belong only to God, and putting them in the hands of man, still bedeviled by his own inadequacies.

The miracle of brain storage has been demonstrated by hypnotism. When it emerged from the entertainment world into the medical, we learned that men under hypnosis could repeat the foreign language which, at the age of five or six, they had learned from their nurses, even though when out of hypnosis they could not recognize a single word. When one also considers the physical feats of which the body is capable under hypnosis, such as holding up heavy weights with extended arms, controlling pulse, withstanding pain, stiffening the spine so that the body can be supported by head on one chair and heels on another while carrying a man's weight on the stomach, and much more, it becomes evident that we have not begun to exploit our potentials either of mind or body.

I learned this lesson in a peculiar way when I was about thirteen years old. My father owned a cleaning and dyeing store on Sumner Avenue in Brooklyn, New York. For some reason I do not yet understand, it was called the California Cleaning and Dyeing Establishment. Perhaps it was an augury of my later designation as counsel to the Motion Picture Association of America, Inc. which made Hollywood a laboring vineyard.

My father had emigrated a year ahead of us from London to the United States and quickly saved enough to send for my mother and me, greeting us in a bowler hat, which sailed off his head as we flew into his arms to be smothered with kisses, tears, then laughter and more kisses. He had also saved enough money to buy a steam pressing machine. He worked eighteen to twenty hours a day, and during holiday rushes, all twenty-four hours at the machine, disappearing every few seconds in a cloud of steam as the foot lever closed the jaws of the contraption and made a huge pants sandwich. He seemed proud of the steam explosions, and the hisses which announced them because they represented not only progress over the old-fashioned hand iron, but also his progress in being able to afford it. I vowed then, although I considered it a child's fantasy, that I would free him from his slavery. Before he was fifty years old, I was able to fulfill this dream. At my insistence, he retired. Thereafter he tried to use up his enormous energy in household chores, trimming lawns, stripping fruit trees, and shopping. I was never sure his "freedom" wasn't a burden to him.

But back to my early lesson about the body's untapped skills. We lived in one room behind the California Cleaning and Dyeing Establishment. Later we prospered enough to lease a few rooms above, and ultimately to buy the building, although heavy mortgages made ownership a verbal concept. To meet the added burden of the mortgages, my mother and I worked nights at home for a nearby manufacturer, scalloping the edges of laces with small scissors. We grew so adept at maneuvering the curves that reams of laces flowed from our hands and piled high on the floor. Since we were paid a few cents for a specified number of yards, speed was of the essence, and we sang songs of quick tempo to stimulate the rhythm of our flashing blades.

Behind the room in the rear was a yard. How can I call it that? It was paradise. To me it was a park. We planted flowers there. A tree on the property beyond spread its burdened branches across the fence, and we were grateful for the intrusion.

So after school, I retreated to this paradise, playing with my dog Nellie and enjoying reveries in this wild outdoor, fifty yards in length and twenty-five yards in width.

I took to bouncing a ball off a side wall. Probably this training later made possible my being on the handball team at Columbia College. One day a slat of wood broke in a wooden door of that wall. It left a small lateral opening, barely big enough to have a ball go through. To amuse myself, I invented the game of hitting the ball into that slot. At first, it took forty or more bounces before I could score. With practice, this came down to thirty, and then twenty. Finally, I could hit the ball through that slot every second shot, and frequently would score in one shot. When I invited my friends to play, they were astonished by the proficiency which endless practice had produced. There is no limit to what the human body can achieve in dexterity and accuracy. Sharpshooters, who hit bull's-eyes looking into a mirror and aiming over their shoulders, acrobats who leap and tumble in incredible fashion, balancers who spin plates from sticks resting on their chins, soccer players, basketball stars, pitchers and fielders, football runners who dodge and twist while changing speeds, and, of course, golfers, who allow for wind and terrain and club a ball to within a few feet of the hole, two hundred yards away, all attest to the artistry of the muscle.

Many years later, when I represented Robert Young, the railroad magnate, he invited me to play golf at Greenbrier Country Club, a resort in West Virginia owned by the Alleghany Railroad Company. Sam Snead was the golf professional there and we played a foursome. I oohed and aahed as he shot a 68 (he replied, "But can I write a brief?"). When we finished, it was pretty dark, and Young followed the happy tradition of inviting us to the "19th hole"—the bar. Snead excused himself. He headed for the practice tee to hit his 5 iron because it was "not crisp enough." The stories are legion of Ben Hogan practicing six and eight hours a day, until he could place a caddy at an instructed distance for each club, and hit directly to him.

Aside from the body's untapped capacity, I learned a far more critical lesson on the streets of our tough neighborhood. It was to remain with me for life. It dominated my legal work. Curiously, it was learned in a fistfight.

The Williamsburg gang was headed by a brutal kid only fifteen years old, called Leo. He had climbed to the top because of his prowess as a fighter. He was short, but had the torso of a man at least a foot taller. His muscles bulged out of the short-sleeved shirt he always wore, undoubtedly to exhibit them and add to the terror of his hoarse voice. His crew haircut, a novelty then, a flattened nose, and a slit where his lips should have been made him look like a powerful gnome. He later turned to professional fighting.

He was not content with his domination. A cruel streak in him required that he beat up one of his adherents whenever there was the slightest sign of disobedience. Sometimes when obeisance afforded no opportunity to vent his rage and skill, he would provoke or invent a grievance and then punish the imagined offender. To widen his domain, he took to bullying every child in the neighborhood, forcing him to join his gang, and always attending to the initiation personally by exhibiting his punching prowess. Parents complained. Police pulled in Leo once or twice. But revenge was meted out to those who had complained. Ultimately, the neighborhood was cowed by this one bully. What a microcosm this was of the future Hitlers, Mussolinis, and Stalins, although we did not realize it then.

Like others, I wanted nothing to do with Leo or his gang. I kept out of their way. I sought no heroic confrontation. I was afraid of them.

But my turn came. Leo waited for me one day, as I went on a mission to the grocery store. He blocked my path, and demanded that I report to his gang that evening in front of the pool parlor. I told him I could not come. Immediately, a group of his "soldiers" formed a circle around me. Leo was so eager to administer a beating he did not wait for my possible change of mind. He leaped into action with his fists. Within seconds, a gash over my eye sent hot streaks of pain through my body. Then my lips were split and felt a foot wide. A pleasant warm feeling on my face and neck turned to horror when I saw the blood. I was repeatedly knocked down but got up again and again to be rewarded for my audacity by being pelted with blinding blows. Leo's grunts as he belabored me added terror to the attack, like the karate fighter, who utters piercing screams to stun his enemy for a fraction of a second, thereby delaying the defensive move. I felt weak. A blow in the stomach folded me in half and a blow on the top of the head felt as if I had been hit with a hammer. There were hissing noises in my throbbing head, which made the onlookers' wild yells sound distant. Although I was semiconscious and staggering, the outrage of it all released an uncontrollable flood of anger. It was an anesthetic which made me impervious to pain. I charged him furiously. If nothing else, my blood smeared over him and gave the illusion of a contest. My right eye was completely closed, but I kept coming at him the more I was pummeled.

He grew tired punching me. His grunts were no longer auditory attacks but signs of exhaustion—as I continued to rise after each knockdown. Occasionally, I reached him with wild flailing fists. Since I would not stay down, Leo decided to take further measures. He reached into his pocket for brass knuckles. I seized his wrist, twisted it, and as they fell to the ground, I kicked them away. In so doing, I staggered and fell. He came forward and kicked me, but nothing hurt anymore. I got up again and as I weaved toward him in slow motion, I looked into his eyes. They were different! Instead of the squint of joy at the punishment he was handing out, they registered fear. It was as clear even to my one usable eye as if a film had obliterated the satisfaction of cruelty and written doubt on them. The bully, true to his character, began to cringe and for the first time backed away.

I have read that the most vicious animal will not attack man unless he shows fright. A steady look will keep even a lion at a distance. In the case of animals, they probably smell fear. I saw it. The effect was the same, however. It released a new charge of adrenalin. My hands, which had been so heavy that I could not lift them, suddenly became light. My dragging feet took on speed. I clenched my teeth behind the puffed lips and redoubled my effort. The fear in his eyes grew. I rushed him again and I could almost see his disintegration. Panic was written all over him. Within seconds, although really not hurt, he fell from a blow which ineptitude made a shove. He remained on his knees shaking his head helplessly. He was unbloody but bowed. Even through the thumping noises in my head, I realized that silence had descended on the scene. We all remained frozen in our postures, like a motion picture which has turned into a still. After minutes, only Leo moved, looking up as if expecting pity for his plight.

The gang around him, which must have had mixed feelings of satisfaction as well as astonishment, lifted him and restrained him, as he wished, while he pretended he wanted to continue.

I had to be carried home. One of my ribs was broken. There was a huge gash on my scalp which required stitches. The scar remains to this day. I was in bed for a week, attended by a doctor. My parents were furious at me. Love can create anger as well as sweetness. My father threatened to administer a thorough thrashing if I ever got into a street brawl again. They saw no humor in my comment that if I did the thrashing would be administered in advance.

The police hauled Leo in again. But his real punishment was the abdication of his Fuehrer's role. A junta of three ambitious toughs took over. Leo disappeared from the neighborhood. Many years later, I read that he had been convicted of murder and died in the electric chair at Sing Sing.

But I had learned the lesson—he who will not be beaten can't be beaten. Sheer *will* can triumph over great odds. In later years, I saw my contest with Leo on television dozens of times. The contestants were different but the story was the same. In those days, Friday night was fight night on television. It is a cruel sport that should be barred, but I must admit its fascination, a token of the belligerence, if not cruelty, in each of us. Time and again, some inferior fighter would receive a trouncing but would refuse to surrender. My father and I always rooted for him, calling his opponent Leo. Indeed, few fighters are ever knocked unconscious for the count of ten. It is their determination which gives out and paralyzes them with fear. Then they are really helpless, like the hypochondriac who really suffers from his imaginary disease. Of the dozens of ring contests I have seen on television, I think of only two fighters who were actually knocked senseless, Ingemar Johannson by Floyd Patterson and Rocky Graziano by Tony Zale.

A determined will can hold off even death. The stories are not apocryphal of men doomed to die in hours, who lived for several weeks until they could complete some task or duty they had set for themselves. Conversely, those with a good chance to survive, but who give up the fight, die quickly. There can be a will to die as well as to live.

During a matrimonial contest between Marquesa de Portago and her husband, I attempted an amicable resolution and arranged to see the Marquis. He was about twenty-five years old, and as dashing as his reputation foretold. He had a Spanish nobleman's brooding, dark face with a long nose, high forehead, an aggressive mane of black hair. His eyes were deep and shone brilliantly and his flashing white smile gave an appearance of gaiety to an otherwise somber and diffident appearance. The over-all impression was that of vitality. He was proficient in all sports, but was particularly eager to win the top prize in auto racing. No one could have given a better impression of the will to live and live fully.

But when I discussed financial terms, he startled me with an unexpected answer. "As you know, I am entering another race in Mantua, Italy. You may not have to worry about these things." His casual, unheroic manner removed the melodramatic implication of his statement. The next week, we read that the Marquis de Portago had been killed on the last lap of the Mille Miglia race. I believe he had willed to die.

My father had a surfeit of determination—we called him obstinate—and he had successfully weathered surgery at the age of seventy-four. But he was tormented by continuous tests which were not only painful but frightening. One Saturday night, during my visit at the hospital, I watched a procedure which couldn't have been calculated to be more alarming. A huge needle, looking like a thin dagger, was plunged into his chest to draw some marrow or fluid from his breastbone. I barely suppressed a scream as the dagger went in. I saw my father's eyes open wide with horror as if he were being stabbed to death. The doctors made light of it. It hadn't even required an anesthetic. They later declared the test negative. Oh, these tests! Is there not some better evaluation of whether the anguish exceeds the necessity? Or must every book procedure be applied to make sure like a new toy that must be used. When our pallor had subsided, I did everything to cheer him up. Then I left saying, "See you tomorrow, Pa." Instead of the smile and happy wave of the hand, which usually greeted these words, he merely shrugged his shoulders in an unaccustomed gesture of "What's the use of all this torture?" Fright was still frozen in his eyes. That night unaccountably (?) he died.

Long before the emergence of psychology as an independent science, philosophers recognized the peculiar power of the "will to live." Nietzsche wrote, "He who has a *why* to live for, can bear with almost any *how*."

Just as some species will persevere to produce young and then die, there are people who wish to complete tasks for posterity and expire when they have fulfilled their mission. Goethe believed in this theory. He also exemplified it. He began to write Faust when he was in his twenties. He finished it when he was eighty-two years old, and died the next year before it was published. It can also happen at an early age. Mozart and Raphael, being prodigies, achieved their mission early and each died at thirty-five.

It may be significant that prisoners in camp who expected that advancing Allied armies would free them by Christmas, 1945, died in greater numbers than previously when their deliverance did not eventuate.

On the other hand Winston Churchill observed the phenomenon of survival when London was blitzed:

I feared that the long nights for millions in the crowded street, shelters . . . would produce epidemics of influenza, diphtheria . . . and what not. The fact remains that during this rough winter the health of the Londoners was actually above the average. Moreover, the power of enduring suffering in the ordinary people of every country, when their spirit is roused, seems to have no bound.

Dr. Arnold Hutschnecher presented the extreme thesis that "We die only when we are ready to die. If we truly wish to live . . . then no matter how sick we may be, no matter how close to death, we do not die."

History presents no more vivid illustration of "finis" when the task is ended than the death of Thomas Jefferson and John Adams on July 4, 1826, the fiftieth anniversary of the Declaration of Independence. Or was it a coincidence?

Court trials, being contests, depend upon will, courage, or determination—call it what you wish, even though they are battles of the mind, rather than brawn. In every trial in which I have ever participated, there is a revelation which destroys the topography of the original plan. Despite the most thorough preinvestigation, some unknown document or unexpected witness shows up. I do not recall a single trial, among the hundreds I have been in, where this does not happen. After all, it is not so surprising. Complicated court battles involve periods of time from two to twenty years, thousands of documents, and thousands more of conversations. The lawyer is like an archaeologist who must exhume the past. But what archaeologist can ever be certain that his diggings have uncovered *everything* in the locale of a great find?

So, as I tell my assistants, they may be sure that sooner or later, no matter how smoothly things are going, "we are going to be hit over the head." I feel this warning may insulate them against the inevitable shock, so that they will not facially register their distress in the presence of the jury. For jurors may be more affected by the impact upon counsel than by the damaging evidence.

In every trial there is a moment, sometimes many, when sheer will must see us through. Often it turns out to be a psychological rather than a factual crisis, because every new development leads us by the very rule of probability to further facts which may reconcile it with the original plan. It is unlikely that a long train of events which we know about would have taken place if there was a preceding contradiction. Usually, what has happened is that a missing segment in the mosaic has turned up, and because the segment is not complete, it appears to be inconsistent with the rest of the structure. It becomes our duty to uncover the rest of the missing data so that the mosaic may be complete, and present a fuller picture of the truth as originally conceived.

Absent the determination to see it through, the unanticipated revelations can be fatal. There is a rush to surrender, usually in the form of settlement—that graceful disguise of defeat. I have seen many sacrificial settlements made because resistance and persistence had been unnecessarily undermined. So the rule should be, "In smooth sailing keep a careful watch of the horizon; in a gale keep a careful watch of your own head."

It is not only in trials, but in the more peaceful pursuits of commerce, that the same quality of never giving up pays off the largest dividends. Time and again an acquisition of a company or a merger arrangement is stymied by antitrust laws, SEC regulations, unyielding union contracts, required approval of two thirds of the stockholders, prohibitive financing demands, accounting restrictions, or, worst of all, the choice of predominant management among executives each of whom considers his business a child he has reared through infant's diseases to virile manhood, not to be lost by adoption by a stranger.

Time and again, one reads that such transactions have fallen through, although the insuperable obstacles are seldom listed. The formal announcement is as uninforming as the customary statement of voluntary resignation of a government official, together with profound regrets and compliments from the President, who has fired him.

But it is rare that the obstacle to the deal cannot be overcome by resourcefulness and will. The latter is always more important. Not to brook defeat is more than half the battle.

When Thomas Edison was searching for a filament that would not burn out in the electric bulb, he attempted by empirical means to test various metals and other substances seriatim. After ninety-odd experiments had failed, his discouraged assistants regretted that they had not learned anything after weeks of sweaty work. "Wrong," was Edison's undaunted answer. "We now know ninety-four substances that won't work."

His will ultimately lit the world.

IT DOES NO GOOD FOR SHEEP TO PASS RESOLUTIONS IN FAVOR OF VEGETARIANISM WHEN THE WOLVES THINK OTHERWISE

There was another lesson to be derived from my combat with Leo. I was a pacifist at heart. What good did it do me?

When I read of the peace marches, and the noble sentiments expressed by the speakers, who chant "Let's make love—not war," I reflect on the futility of unilateral peace drives. As long as there are Leos in the world, whether individuals in the neighborhood, or nations preying on their neighbors, is there any alternative to defensive violence? Only man's emergence from the animal's lust to kill the weaker of the species can free us from the horror of killing the attacker in order to survive. That emergence may be hastened artificially at least so far as nations are concerned by restraints imposed through international force. I refer to a revised United Nations charter which will substitute pre-emptive collective force for *post hoc* resistance.

The foremost advocate of pacificism in the Western world was Bertrand Russell. He advocated surrender to brute force rather than waging war even in defense: "It is better to be Red than dead." But when Hitler ravaged Europe and appeared on the verge of worldwide conquest, Russell thought World War II to resist was justified. Then what happens to his principle of pacifism? If war becomes justified, depending on subjective judgment of the pacifist, then aren't most wars justifiable according to the differing evaluations of their moral objectives? Or may only Russell and his disciples decide for us which wars are indefensible?

If we contract the lens, the issue of violence becomes more clearly focused. Hundreds of times each day, decent citizens are mugged and robbed on the streets or in their homes. No longer does the marauder wait for the protection of darkness or the isolated path. He operates in sunlight and in the most traveled areas. His brutality is indescribable. Old men and women are stomped to death. Others are stabbed dozens of times in frenzied attacks. It is surmised that dope addiction is responsible for such sadistic outbursts. However, in many instances, when the attacker is apprehended, the explanation is not so simple. Men can be incredibly cruel while in full possession of their faculties. They are driven by devils, which cannot be identified by the name of poverty, environment, or lust for excitement.

Well, shall we of the community be pacifists? Shall we surrender to nihilists because we are above their tactics? Must we not resist even if to do so means more violence and bloodshed? Even Woodrow Wilson, who was elected on his pacifist pledge to keep us out of war, ultimately found that one cannot always be "too proud to fight." The moral imperative which motivates the pacifist may operate in reverse.

I have proposed a "Good Samaritan Law," which would make it a criminal as well as a civil offense not to come to the aid of one in distress. If a child was drowning in a lake, and a good swimmer walked by without helping him or throwing him an available life preserver; or if a child was playing on railroad tracks and someone saw a train approaching but didn't warn him; or if a worker was backing into the jaws of a dangerous machine and was not warned by a fellow worker who saw the impending tragedy; or if the captain of a ship failed to give aid to a man adrift in a small boat; should not such passivity be deemed a crime?

Van Heflin, the great actor, was walking in Central Park on a bright Sunday afternoon, when he was blocked and surrounded by a group of hoodlums. Dozens of people saw his predicament but did not protest or intervene. Having once served in the Navy, Van Heflin knew a few tricks of defense. He kicked one assailant in a vulnerable spot, and got away. No one near him had even cried out for help.

In the well-known Catherine Genovese case thirty-eight persons heard the cries of this twenty-eight-year-old girl when she was knifed to death, but they did not even call for help. In another case an eighteen-year-old secretary was stripped, raped, and beaten in broad daylight in the Bronx. Forty witnesses watched silently and did not even telephone for the police.

Who can approve such pacifism? We have no right to require martyrdom. An unarmed citizen has no duty to attack a criminal who brandishes a gun or knife. Reasonable standards must apply.

This proposition is not entirely novel. In 1945 France amended its penal code to provide that anyone who was able to prevent bodily harm, without risk to himself, and failed to do so was punishable by three years imprisonment or a fine of twelve to five hundred thousand francs, or both.

If we adopted the crime of violating the dictates of humanity, yes the crime of passivity, we might ultimately apply it to the international scene.

Voltaire expressed the principle eloquently: "We must not be guilty of the good things we did not do."

A GOOD TEACHER'S INFLUENCE AFFECTS
ETERNITY

Of all the teachers before whom I sat, two left indelible impressions upon me. While all others have disappeared from memory (I hope their teachings haven't), these two are as clear in my mind as if I had spent a lifetime with them, although I took only one course of several months with each fifty-nine and forty-seven years ago.

Undoubtedly, this is due to the impact an unusual personality makes on an impressionable mind. It has nothing to do with teaching as such. Others whose names I cannot remember taught more effectively. Still others like Professor John Dewey, Professor John Erskine, Professor Thomas Gifford, Dean Harlan F. Stone of Columbia University were world-famed authorities. But they never made their subjects exciting stimuli which inflamed the mind and produced a quenchless curiosity.

I remember Mr. Bishop (the first name *does* escape me), who taught geometry and trigonometry at Boys High in Brooklyn, New York. He was about forty-five years old, and bore no mark of distinction in his thin face. He was sallow, with deep, heavily lidded eyes, a short, roundish nose, and a slightly jutting chin. His voice was unresonant and inclined to fade off in a whisper. It had a matter-of-fact quality perfectly suited to the uncompromising logic of mathematics, as if, of course, the result was Q.E.D.—*quod erat demonstrandum.*

All of this should have made him the most forgettable character I ever knew. But no. When he taught, the unimpassioned lucidity of demonstrations created sheer beauty in the triangles and logarithms. He was continuously voted the most popular teacher in the school. Perhaps kindness had something to do with it. A pupil who failed to understand was led tactfully onto the right path, as if it was the most natural thing to have missed originally, and how bright he was to arrive at the corrected conclusion.

The writer who later influenced me most was Emerson. His elegance and grace of diction added verve and beauty to his thought. As Judge Benjamin Cardozo once observed, style cannot be separated from substance. An argument well phrased is more persuasive than the same argument prosaically phrased. Substance can titillate the mind, while style thrills it.

I refer back to Emerson, because Bishop had the same quality in explaining figures which Emerson had in explaining thoughts. We felt a fire built under us by this quiet man's expositions. We could not be certain how the fire was lit. Was it skill with which the problem was dissected so that the solution seemed to burst upon us with the excitement of a mystery unraveled? Was it the purity of mathematical logic, the beauty of which caressed the mind? Was it Bishop's own dedication and concentration which set higher ideals for us than his instructions? Or was it that supreme gift of all great teachers, a fatherly concern for their pupils which accompanies the joy of teaching? Whatever the mystery of personality, there was no doubt about Bishop's achievements. At reunions for a half century—only one teacher was remembered affectionately. It was he.

The second teacher who left his mark on a whole generation of students, including myself, was Professor Thaddeus C. Terry, who taught "Contracts" at Columbia University Law School.

Curiously enough in almost all physical respects and personality, he was the opposite of Bishop. He was about sixty-five years old. He had a clubfoot, and his limping and later use of a cane had developed powerful shoulders, which malformed him, since they jutted out horizontally. His face was so ugly that there was almost beauty in its rugged asymmetry. He was in the penultimate stage of complete baldness, only a few strands holding out. The heavy flesh over his eyes made them look slanted. His nose could not make up its mind whether to be hooked or flattened, so it was both, and looked no better from wearing an unrimmed pince-nez with a black ribbon which shivered down to his vest. Each of these features, which could have aspired for predominance, was put into shadow by his mouth. It was a thick-lipped wide permanent scowl and the red glistening inner skin, which showed when he talked, completed the ferocious face. As one would expect, no sweet voice could emanate from that face. A deep baritone sound came forth, and its resonance was constantly squeezed by sarcasm. Such sarcasm. He was a master at it. When he called out your name, it sounded as if you were an illegitimate child who had adopted a false name to disguise the bastardy.

Instead of Bishop's kindliness, there was unremitting cruelty. He humiliated. He taunted. He ridiculed—but how he taught! How he made you understand the majesty of the law and its philosophical striving for justice. In his hands, the law was "a sorcerer's wand which created a new world of equity."

He used the Socratic technique, asking questions, never giving answers. You had to find your own way, but he deliberately led you into byways so that you would learn your own way back and really understand the terrain. No matter which way you answered, a barrage of questions threw doubt on your conclusion. Sometimes you were compelled to change your mind. Then the questions pushed you back to your original conclusion. At the end, you knew that the law was not a precise science, but a process of reasoning in which diverse answers might all be right depending on the perspective and social objectives which subjectively provided the greatest moral satisfaction.

So he would begin with the most elementary lesson in contract.

"Mr. Nizer, what is a contract?"

"It is a meeting of the minds, sir."

"Is a meeting of the minds enough?"

"I don't understand, sir."

"If you and I agree who should be President, is there a contract?"

"No, sir. There must be an offer by one party which for a consideration is accepted by the other."

"Does the contract come into existence the moment when the minds meet?"

"Yes, sir."

"Oh, it does, does it?" The snarl that accompanied this question was like the sudden appearance of dark clouds preceding a storm.

I was silent.

"Suppose A offers to sell his car for $3,000 and sends his offer in writing to B, who is in another city. Suppose that B writes his acceptance and puts it in the mail. Is that a contract?"

"Yes, sir."

"Why?"

"Because their minds have met on the deal."

"Even despite the fact that A has not yet received B's letter of acceptance?"

Hesitantly, "Yes, sir."

"Suppose that A has changed his mind and sent B a telegram withdrawing his offer and the telegram is received by B before his letter of acceptance reaches A? Is there a contract?"

"Yes, sir. Their minds had met when B mailed his acceptance."

Angrily, "Their minds had met on *what*?"

"On the offer made by A."

"How could the offer be accepted which has been withdrawn by telegram? What was there to accept?"

"But B had already mailed his acceptance," I reply with a little acerbity.

"Doesn't the meeting of the minds require communication of acceptance? How can the minds meet if A doesn't know that B had agreed?"

"I suppose that's right, sir."

"Has not the offerer the right to withdraw his offer before the contract has been consummated?"

"Yes, sir."

"Then doesn't it follow that A's offer having been withdrawn by telegram, there was nothing to accept, and that B's intention to accept was ineffectual?"

"I can see that, sir."

"So you would change your previous answer, Mr. Nizer?" The name was pronounced so as to be synonymous with dunce.

"I believe I would. Yes, sir."

"And you would now say the opposite of what you previously said, namely that there was no contract under the circumstances?"

"Yes, sir," spoken with the resignation of one who permits his shoulders to be pinned to the mat.

Professor Terry stared at me for a long time. Then he called on another student.

"Mr. Thomas, do you agree with Mr. Nizer's last answer?"

"Yes, Professor Terry."

"Why?" The challenge was flung at him as if nothing had happened in the past several minutes.

"For the reason you gave, sir."

"I gave no reason. I asked questions. Stand on your feet! I have asked you why?"

"Well, the offer being withdrawn by telegram there was nothing to accept."

"But hadn't B already accepted when he wrote that he did?"

"But his writing had not been received by A."

"Why is that necessary?"

"Well, until received, there was no meeting of the minds."

"Where do you get that idea from? If I hold out a proposal to you and you agree, even without mailing such agreement to me, haven't our minds met at the instant you accepted?"

"Sir, I might agree one moment and then change my mind the next."

"In the hypothetical case I gave, B's acceptance was not a mere mental concept. He wrote it out and placed it in a mailbox, beyond his power to control. Would that make a difference?"

"Yes, sir, perhaps it would."

"Perhaps? It would, wouldn't it?" The booming voice sounded like an explosion of a cannon shot, reverberating around the room.

The mental and physical assault was intimidating.

"Yes, sir, it would."

"Furthermore, if each party must learn that the other has agreed, wouldn't A's receipt of B's acceptance have to be communicated to B? And then would A have to learn that B got it? Wouldn't it be an endless chain which would prevent a contract from ever being consummated?"

"Yes, sir," almost inaudibly.

"So you would say that the withdrawal of the offer was too late, because the minds had already met as evidenced by the overt act of mailing the acceptance, is that right?"

"Yes, sir."

"And you would go back to Mr. Nizer's original answer, which he changed after questioning?"

"Yes, sir. I would."

A long stare. "Mr. McGraw, who do you agree with—Mr. Nizer's *final* answer or Mr. Thomas' *final* answer?"

The word "final" put the spotlight back on Thomas and me, just when we were recovering in the darkness of inattention.

"I think there is a contract when B mails his letter of acceptance. Nothing thereafter can change that fact."

McGraw's jaw jutted out. His voice was angry as if in anticipation of the harassment he was about to endure. Having seen the fate of his predecessors, he was determined to take a position and stick to it. If he had to go down, he was going to do so with flags flying, not in a surrendering whimper. We could sense the impending battle.

"Nothing can change that?" asked Professor Terry, his voice slow and ominously sweet. He smiled at McGraw for what seemed hours. We could see McGraw quiver, as Terry finally turned angry and the red glistened from his inner lower lip.

"Suppose two minutes after B has mailed his letter of acceptance, he calls up A and says, 'I've decided not to buy your car. By the way, I mailed a letter of acceptance to you a short while ago—just ignore it when you get it.' Is there still a contract?"

McGraw was defiant and definite.

"Yes, sir. When B mailed his acceptance, A's offer ripened into a contract. The fact that B called later can't change that."

Professor Terry's face lit up, announcing to one and all that the trap had been sprung.

"Suppose then that A, having received the telephone call from B, sells his car to C—Can B sue A for breach of contract?"

"Well—"

"Well—what?"

"I don't think he can. After all, he told A he was not buying. So A had a right to sell to someone else."

"But if the offer had 'ripened into a contract'—nice phrase Mr. McGraw [the compliment could not assuage the distress on the recipient's face]—then no call thereafter could wipe it out—wouldn't you agree?"

"No."

"Didn't you say a few moments ago that when a contract comes into being nothing can change that?"

"Yes, sir."

"Well, if nothing can change it, isn't B entitled to sue A for having breached his contract by selling the car to someone else?"

"I suppose so."

Terry turned away in disgust.

"Mr. Harrison, do you agree with that?"

It didn't matter which position Mr. Harrison took. He was run down just as mercilessly. And this was only the first and most elementary lesson. What fireworks awaited us, as the really involved problems of contract law were explored.

It eventuated that all our answers were right. Some states follow one rule, and some the other. What would be held to be a contract in Massachusetts would not be in New York. That was why one of the courses still to be taken was called "Conflict of Laws." Which of the conflicting rules applied under varying circumstances? For example, does the rule of the forum where the case is tried prevail, or the rule where the contract was consummated? So, even in the very first session, we learned that the law was not an exact science. It was a philosophical pursuit of moral precepts, and the logic used in the quest was not irrefutable. We were to become sculptors molding the law to desirable ends, and we would thus be engaged in an art not a science.

Entering Professor Terry's classroom was an adventure, and a frightening one. We studied with particular care the cases he had assigned the previous day. Yet we knew that if called upon we would be stripped mentally and compelled to stand nude and foolish in the presence of witnesses. We dared not laugh at our neighbor's discomfort because we knew our turns would come, and the exposure would be as inexorably embarrassing.

Despite our fear (which we did not experience in any other course), we were thrilled by the intellectual exercises Terry put us through. If we had more such teachers, students wouldn't want to turn to pot and LSD for excitement. We literally trembled as we entered his class. And later, for hours, we would talk among ourselves about the brilliance of the technique which made us turn somersaults, as if we were animals being put through our paces by the trainer. Only then could we afford to laugh at ourselves.

Strangely enough, Professor Terry's uncompromising pressure, which often seemed tinged with viciousness, did not make us bitter toward him. A deep affection set in for the man. We understood that he was dedicated to us; that he was determined to equip us for our profession, not by drumming some rules of law into our heads (for anyone can go to the library and find them), but by developing our reasoning powers, so that we would rule the law and not the law rule us; so that we could become interpreters of the law, not its reciters; so that we would be historians of the law who would divine its future; in short, so that we could achieve the highest standard of the profession to be wise enough to be *advisers*.

Professor Terry encouraged discussion with him after the lecture, as if he recognized that a runner who had run a hard race could not stop suddenly, but must taper off. So we crowded around him continuing the discussion. Then for the first time, we knew he was our friend, and that the punishment he had meted out was for our own good. And when in the course of that more informal exchange at the podium he put his hand on our shoulders, we felt as if we had been knighted. Finally, he would limp off while we stood around in small groups too stimulated to leave.

Professor Terry became a legend at Columbia Law School. Thousands of students who passed through his classroom over the years remembered him above all other teachers. But our class was privileged to participate in a special event, which revealed a dimension no others had seen.

He announced his retirement. Dean Harlan F. Stone and the faculty decided to give him a farewell at which an oil painting of him would be hung in the library. Terry asked that the students be invited. We crowded into the library eagerly, but had no inkling that what would happen would be so startling that it would become the most moving experience of our young lives. But, then, that was Professor Terry.

Seated on a raised tier, with the professors, was a lady all in brown. Even her lace collar was dark brown. A beautiful young girl is an accident of nature, but a beautiful old woman is a work of art. She was a work of art and inexpressibly beautiful. Her perfectly proportioned features were enhanced by gentle curving white hair which added aristocracy rather than age to her face. Her neck was long, and she held her head regally high, but without a trace of hauteur. She sat motionless and attentive, a faint smile on her lips, which did not fully disguise her emotions. We wondered who she was. All eyes were upon her until the ceremonies and speeches drew attention away. When they were concluded, with grace and not a little solemn dignity, Professor Terry rose to speak.

He stood motionless for a long time. We observed that his face was different than we had ever seen it before. It had lost its severity. It was flushed and looked pink and kind. The mouth was not a snarl. One could actually see his lips as if they had finally triumphed over the scowl which had suppressed them. He took off his ribboned glasses, which we knew he needed, and placed them slowly in his vest pocket, as if he wanted to remove anything which would interfere with direct eye-to-eye communication. His voice, too, was different. It was soft without a trace of belligerence or sarcasm.

After expressing gratitude for the painting "which would keep memories fresh of the torture I have imposed," he explained that he loved the law, and he had the feeling that every student who had committed himself to the greatest of all professions was his son. He could best express his love to his many sons by training them for excellence. The law deals with every facet of human experience, and cannot brook mediocrity. There is enough of that wherever one turns. One who aspires to be a lawyer must recognize his obligation to become a social philosopher, a leader of thought, a cultured and cultivated man worthy of his profession. For he becomes a minister of justice—justice, "the bread for which the nation hungers." Therefore, out of *love*, he had been remorseless in his training. The mind can only grow if it is challenged, if it must exert itself. Then, in self-defense, it calls upon the reserves of imagination and resourcefulness. These were the reasons he used the Socratic method, always asking, never answering. The student must find his own way as he will have to do in the outside world. That was why he was abrasive. The world outside would be more abrasive. He could not afford to be tolerant with anything but the best that was in us. His great satisfaction in life was to see his students later become brilliant lawyers, judges, and public servants, giving leadership to a society which sorely needed it. He continued in this vein, an unaffected outpouring of idealism. He put into words the high purpose which had motivated most of us to enter the law, but which we never mentioned because it would be striking a posture of nobility, and, therefore, suspect, like the soldier who spoke of his exploits in battle. So he continued, for the first time in declarative sentences instead of questions to fill our minds with inspiration. Our hearts were next.

He expressed his gratitude to the dean and the professors who had been his "intellectual colleagues and personal friend all in one." He said good-bye to the law school, speaking of it not as a building of red bricks, marble, and rooms, filled with student chairs which had one swollen arm to make place for notebooks, but as a huge person throbbing with exertion, and sharing emotions with him over the decades. In my dimmed eyes, there was a picture of tiers of bookshelves drooping in sorrow, the walls waving good-bye to him, and the oil paintings in the alcoves turning their heads toward their new neighbor to greet him for posterity.

Then the unexpected happened. He took one of his long pauses, which had been so meaningful in the classroom, like an exclamation point of silence. He turned toward the beautiful woman in brown:

"I have been expressing my gratitude to you, my students, my colleagues, and my school. But it is all only a very tiny portion of the gratitude which fills my heart. I cannot bid you all good-by and leave unsaid that which is the most important thing in my life."

He took a deep breath and continued, his voice hoarse with emotion.

"At the age of twenty, I met the most beautiful girl I had ever seen, or seen since. Looking at her, no one could be certain whether her charm, warmth and brightness of mind and spirit made her beauty unique, or whether her breathtaking beauty deprived us of the appreciation of her other qualities.

"I was stunned and in love with her immediately. I am sure every other young man who saw her felt the same way. But I considered her unattainable for one such as me. Nature had not endowed me with any of the graces of appearance."

He looked down at his foot and continued.

"I dared not even contemplate the audacity to befriend her, and certainly not to confide my feelings to her. Most impossible of all was to dream of her reciprocal love. I was happy just to think of her, and this gratification I indulged in day and night.

"But she ordered events so as to bring us together. She overcame the inarticulateness which my awe and worship of her created. With delicacy and sensitivity, she told me that she knew how I felt about her, and that she had to tell me, she was more in love with me than I could possibly be with her. I have been blinded by ecstasy ever since.

"Through the years which followed, we have reared a family in supreme happiness. She has dedicated her life and her love to me without reservation or pause even for the vicissitudes of life. I have functioned in the aura of her love. Teaching, writing and practicing law at times, have been temporary absences made bearable only because I knew I was returning to her. Every thinking moment has had the silent musical accompaniment of her presence."

His voice grew hoarser as he struggled to eliminate the quiver which was entering it.

"So, although it is farthest from my nature to discuss the most private of all emotions in public, I cannot in this leavetaking do other than tell you that I owe all my happiness to her, that she has—"

He turned his head toward her and his eyes completed the sentence, as if words could not possibly convey the depth of his feeling.

Tears were running down her cheeks, but she did not move. Her eyes were clear despite the streams and she looked steadily at him. Their gazes met and locked in long silence. Then without another word, he sat down.

No one applauded. We just sat there. After a few moments, everyone got up slowly and left.

The phenomenon of attractive women falling in love with unattractive or older men is not as mysterious as it seems. The answer is power; not because of power itself but because of the energy and brilliance required to achieve it. Energy is all attractive. It connotes sexual power, protective power, and security. I have sought common characteristics among people of great accomplishment. There is only one common denominator—energy. Whether it be the business tycoon, the great painter, or dramatist, the performer, the professional man, the political leader, they are as different in personality as infinite variations of color and form in nature's creations—except one. They are alike in their boundless energy.

I recall seeing Pablo Picasso, his friends, and wife, young enough to be his granddaughter, in Juan les Pins. He was close to eighty years of age, tiny and bald. But his round black eyes blazed, and impishly he led the others in singing songs, among them, surprisingly, *Hatikvah*, Israel's anthem. Even if one did not know who he was, he would have been impressed by the sheer energy which spurted from him.

So the question "What does she see in him?" may be answered by "Perhaps nothing, but she feels much in him." Some cynical people rush to the conclusion that such women are calculating, rather than in love. Undoubtedly, there are such. But more often there is real love, engendered by a captivating power. For many women, despite their declarations of independence, want to be dominated, and only the powerful man, not the handsome man, or the noble one, or the considerate one, can gratify this secret and sometimes unconscious yearning. Sometimes the power involved is an evil one. Nevertheless, fine women have been unable to resist it and have devoted themselves to criminals. Great wealth also gives power, but if it has not been earned, but merely inherited, the qualities which accompany the acquisition are lacking, the power is not real, and the disillusionment is as cold as the metal.

All this may explain many divorces which to the outside eye are perplexing because the fine and handsome husband is dropped for one not nearly as attractive. I shall not supply the names of many public figures who have been involved in such mysterious "changes for the worse."

So, Professor Terry, despite his razor-sharp mind, had missed the real point of his wife's love. It was no miracle, as he considered it to be. He need not have been self-deprecating, despite his ugly countenance and clubfoot. She had been overwhelmed early by the power which he ex-uded and which made him the most unforgettable teacher and man to almost two generations of students.

Professor Terry's farewell outpouring was as beautiful as it must have been embarrassing to him and to her. I can well understand that she chose not to reply or was unable to do so. But I imagine that if she had she would have added still another dimension to his joy, for she could have told him that it was she who was fortunate to have him confer his deep love and passionate nature upon her; that she had made no conscious choice for which her judgment and discretion should be honored with gratitude; that she could do no other than love him, for he had captured and captivated her—and it was she who was grateful.

Maybe, if she had so spoken, the circle of revelation would have been completed, and we could have emerged from our stunned condition to cheer them both.

The journey from sentiment to science is sometimes short. The inspirational stimulus in education is more valuable to building character than acquiring knowledge.

As for learning—the science of absorption—we are as backward as the Neanderthal man's rock is to a hydrogen bomb. The vista before us is so immense that even though we have learned that science has erased the word "impossible" from the dictionary, what will soon be here would be deemed an insane fantasy.

The impending miracle began with the epoch-making discovery of the cryptic DNA code, which explained the building blocks of life itself. This new science of molecular biology has now taken us to the brink of molecular neurology, the innermost secrets of the brain rather than the body generally.

Were it not for the credibility of renowned scientists like Dr. Francis O. Schmitt of M.I.T., Dr. Holger Hyden of the University of Göteborg in Sweden, Dr. James V. McConnell of the University of Michigan, Dr. Allan L. Jacobson, and Dr. David Krech of the University of California, Dr. Georges Ungar of the Baylor University College of Medicine, Dr. William L. Byrne of Duke University, Dr. David Samuel of

Israel's Weizmann Institute, Dr. D. Ewen Cameron of the Veterans Administration Hospital in Albany, New York, Dr. Alexandre Monnier and Dr. Paul Laget, researchers in France, and a brilliant synthesis of their achievements by David M. Rorvick, what is now projected as a new method of acquiring knowledge would be incredulous to the most hardened science-fiction writer.

It appears that man's brain has a capacity for storing knowledge exceeding several million miles of magnetic tape of a computer. The brain accumulates a million billion bits of information in a lifetime. How? The molecule responsible for storing memory is nucleic acid, called RNA.

Can this stored memory be transferred? Little worms known as planarians were taught by electric shock to avoid certain parts of their training mazes. Later, they were chopped up and fed to untrained planarians. These unschooled cannibals were able to learn the maze, avoiding "forbidden" turns in far fewer trials than other planarians. They had eaten their education!

The next experiment was with rats and hamsters. They were taught certain skills. Then they were killed. RNA was extracted from their brains and injected into untrained rats and hamsters. They acquired the same skills with extraordinary speed. For example, Swiss mice were taught to ignore loud noices which would normally make them cringe in fear. Protein-like molecules from their brains were injected into unconditioned mice, who thereupon became completely unmindful of noise.

Cautious experiments have now begun with man. First, there was the effort to strengthen or restore memory. RNA was extracted from yeast and administered to patients who, due to age, suffered from extreme forgetfulness. There was marked improvement, although it did not last when the treatment ceased. Since then, magnesium pemoline, a chemical designated as Cylert, has been very efficient as a "memory pill." It works by stimulating a brain enzyme which is vital in the manufacture of RNA. Patients who could not remember how to turn on their television sets or how to tie their shoes were able again to play bridge after taking Cylert.

All this presages the transfer of accumulated knowledge directly into the brain by injecting specific RNA memories into the bloodstream. This could be done by using benign viruses, which are nothing more than protein-coated RNA, and which would easily "infect" the brain. Given time, synthetic RNA is virtually a certainty, thus facilitating the development of transferring memories.

Since memories are the receptacle of knowledge, we can foresee learning French, algebra, organic chemistry, music, law, and athletic know-how by taking a pill, or an injection no more painful than a polio vaccination. Indeed, the development of genetic engineering may make it possible to be born with a college education, fulfilling J. B. S. Haldane's prediction that someday our children will come into the world "speaking perfect English."

The minds of great savants can be made imperishable and immortal. To cornea, kidney, and heart "banks," we may add molecular memory libraries. They would consist of synthetic copies of brain molecular RNA extracted from leading men of arts and sciences. The originals would be preserved in vaults. A scholar who wished to benefit from the genius of a predecessor could go to a library for an appropriate pill or injection. This possibility would also overcome the fear that because the most ignorant people breed freely, we are doomed by the survival of the least fit.

The transfer of memory even crosses the line of different species. This is due to the fact that DNA is common to all life on earth. So rats were able to acquire new skills from the RNA of hamsters and vice versa.

If the species barrier can be overcome, then man may be able to acquire the memory and knowledge of a leopard or dolphin. As David M. Rorvick says, such experience would surpass the most profound hallucinogenic "trip." When one speaks of "acid" in the future, he may be referring to nucleic acid.

The science of "grafting" memory onto the brain also makes possible its erasure. The RNA factor can be reduced by an antibiotic called puromycin, which halts the synthesis of protein molecules. Experiments have been conducted with goldfish who were trained to ring bells in order to obtain their food. When puromycin was injected into their brains, they completely forgot this intensively conditioned skill.

If more refined drugs could be developed to selectively blot out crippling memories, what a boon this would be to neurotics and psychotics. Thus, the pattern of chemical cure for mental disease is revealed again.

So there lies before us, and not too far away, the possibility of a new and instant education of man. For centuries, we have been told that only education will lift us out of animalism to humanism. Civilization was the slow process of learning to be kind—but oh how slow. Pedagogic sciences crept along with imperceptible gains. We had to learn to substitute patience for frustration, and hope for failure. Now, suddenly, we face what was once thought to be the millennium, man's emergence from the wilderness of ignorance.

Most significant is the fact that this scientific achievement is different from all previous ones in that it has a built-in *moral* factor.

In the last fifty years science has made more "progress" than in the one million years of man's supposed existence on earth. Indeed, if we made a list of all the great scientists who have ever lived, 90 per cent would be alive today! That is how acceleratingly dominant science has become in this half century.

Yet has man's nature improved similarly? Of course not. We need only look at the prevalence of wars during the very period of scientific accomplishment. Fifty-five million people were killed in World War II. Professor Friedrich Foerster once observed that German virtues—industriousness, obedience, efficiency—were all put in the service of the devil. Similarly, modern science has been put in the service of the devil. We are constantly improving the techniques of slaughter, so that even hydrogen bombs seem obsolescent for most effective killing. Gases, bacteria, laser rays, neutrons, and a concoction of electronically controlled multiple-delivery systems which can attack any point of the earth's surface, from the sky or from the depths of the sea, threaten the annihilation of two hundred million people in a half hour, and perhaps man's extinction in one great suicidal holocaust.

This gap between science and humanism is the greatest dilemma and challenge to mankind. How can we improve man's inner nature so that he will provide moral direction to the forces now available to him? How can we reverse the trend in which the more powerful the vehicle, the more insane the driver? Until now science equipped us, but did not guide us. Science illuminated our path to the farthest star, but left our hearts in darkness.

Even when science was beneficent, prolonging life by eliminating disease, providing food by eliminating pests, creating the highest standard of living if not yet *for* living, increasing the American national product in one year to a trillion dollars—even then we now find resulting heavy entries on the other side of the ledger sheet. For just as Einstein discovered that there was one unifying equation which explained magnetism, electricity, time, and space, I suspect that there is one central explanation for what appears to be disconnected and variegated crises of our century, such as population explosion, race antipathy, pollution, poverty pockets, and war. The central link is that amazing technology descended on man before he was ready to absorb it.

Smokestacks were once the proud symbol of a burgeoning city. Now we suddenly realize that they destroy oxygenization. Jet planes, buses, and automobiles were the wonderful shrinkers of time and space. Now our admiration turns to disgust as we watch the trail of poison they dump into our air.

Large cities were the triumph over the loneliness and hardship of farm life. Now the very crowding of masses of people in close proximity creates nervous tensions greatly responsible for the fact that one out of every ten Americans occupies a bed in a mental hospital at some time in his life. (Experiments with animals have demonstrated that those living in a large cage remain normal, while those living under the same conditions but in confined quarters become neurotic, violent and attack each other. Perhaps restricted space alone is one of our somewhat hidden problems, and yet in many places in the world we are facing geometric increases of population.) The hustle and bustle of city life was once deemed a necessary stimulation, now we discover that boundless and continuous noise alone can disrupt our nervous systems. Even though we marveled at the Concorde, which has made the previous jet planes look slow, we worried about our ears. We forbade it to land in New York City, thus provoking an international crisis and court review. The extension of life's span was medicine's proudest boast. Now we find our mental institutions, our hospitals for the incurable, our welfare and medical rolls jammed, while we struggle with the population explosion.

Even when we attain the objective of technology—leisure—it presents a new problem. For what will non-Renaissance men and women, who have no cultural and versatile interests, do with time on their hands? The treasure of leisure turns into corroding boredom, and some psychiatrists predict we may ultimately start wars for excitement. Already we see the lure of violent movements, permissive and distorted sex, and drugs. The pace and tensions of a speeded-up technologically improved world have made millions of men and women escapists. In the United States, we consume annually $320,000,000 worth of tranquilizers, $280,000,000 of sleeping pills, 350 million gallons of hard liquor, and a billion dollars of drugs. In New York City there are 200,000 drug addicts. The need to escape from life has even infected children, who still in their teens turn to LSD and heroin, dying by the dozen before they have even become mature enough to savor the beauty of life. Machines have made it unnecessary to use the body fully. There is an alarming state of unfitness even among our young, as we discover when they are examined for army or other service.

We were proud of our technological genius in agriculture, which gave us abundance of all good things and enough to feed a large part of the world. Now we find that DDT and other sprays which have killed "harmful" foliage and pests have fouled our streams, killed our fish, eroded our soil, and even put poisons into the delicious technologically produced fruits and meats we eat. New words become universal. Ten years ago, it was gerontology. Now it is ecology. We have a new concern, but the source of all is the same, a burgeoning technology before man was conditioned to accept and absorb it.

Just as we were despairing that every new scientific achievement moved us farther away from man's control of his own belligerency, envy, and greed; just as scientists, recognizing the nihilism of their own inventiveness, were beginning to boycott their own creation, along come scientific achievements, hypnotic induction, subliminal learning, and neurological biology with none of the defects of the past to offer possible solution for its own evil.

In a sense it was inevitable. The gap between science and humanism had to be filled by science itself. Instead of drawing away in an increasingly uneven race, science had to teach humanism how to keep pace. Frankenstein, because of his power, must tell his master how to bring him down to size.

Man only uses 10 to 15 per cent of his capacity. If by new scientific techniques we can teach him to utilize more of his untapped capacity, and even utilize the capacity of others, what a new world awaits us.

THERE IS NOTHING IN THE WORLD SO MUCH LIKE PRAYER AS MUSIC

Back to my childhood and an essential phase of any education—music.

I was the fortunate inheritor of a great Jewish tradition in music. Most Jewish children learn the violin or piano. I can only speculate whether such concentration among a relatively few explains why so many of the great concert pianists and violinists are Jews.

My parents were too poor to provide such training for me, but not too poor to sing. The voice is an instrument which need not be paid for in installments, and it is mobile. I cannot remember talking to my father in my early years, but I clearly remember singing with him from infancy on. It was a customary means of communication, and since song frees the spirit, it was a dialogue of beauty and joy.

Memories are like paintings and each one of us has his own gallery. One such indelible scene is the Seder on Passover night. My father is dressed in a white robe and high satin skullcap worn by cantors. A sofa laden with white pillows has replaced his chair, so that he may recline in kingly fashion as the Haggada requires. The table is filled with gleaming dishes and wine-filled glasses which shine like huge rubies. The matzohs are covered by a gold brocaded satin cloth. The lit candles, over which my mother has waved her hands in prayer, flicker back and forth as the rush of song bends them. My father holds a silver chalice and sings the *Kiddush* so exuberantly that the wine flows over his hand and upon the spotless white tablecloth. With his other hand, he leads all others to sing "amen" at appropriate places.

There is magic and joyousness in the air. The room is transposed into a golden palace. The ceremonies require the youngest to ask the four questions, *koshis*, which are preceded by the introductory question, "Why is this night different from all other nights?" "Why on all other nights do we eat matzoh and bread, but tonight we eat only matzoh?" "Why on all other nights do we eat other vegetables but tonight we eat

bitter herbs?" "Why on all other nights do we simply eat food but tonight we dip it into bitters and salt water?" "Why on all other nights
do we eat either sitting upright or in a reclining position, but tonight
we eat only in a reclining position?" I ask these questions in Hebrew in
appropriate intonation. Then I translate into English for the assembled
guests (for it is a tradition to invite even some strangers to the feast—
to symbolize that all men are brothers).

The answer to the questions is read from the Haggada, the bible of
the occasion. It is a historical recital of the bondage of the Jews under
Egypt and the miraculous achievement of their freedom, and re-establishment of their country.

During the reading the symbols of the events are partaken by the
guests. My father hands out pieces of matzohs, which he has dipped in
harosess (apples chopped with nuts and soaked in wine) to denote the
sweetness of life; matzohs with sharp horseradish to denote the bitterness of life; and lamb to denote sacrifice.

The children are fascinated by the ritual. When the text describes
the ten plagues which God visited on Pharaoh and those who killed
each firstborn son of the Jews, we spill a bit of wine from the cup ten
times.

At one point a child is directed to open the door so that "Alya
Hanuva," God's invisible visitor to every Seder, may enter and sip the
wine. A special glass for him stands in the center of the table, and the
children's eyes open wide as they "see" the wine in the "becher" go
lower. I remember this when many years later I am in Italy and am
pushed by thousands of devout peasants who have trudged many miles
to the Cathedral of Naples on St. Gennaro Day. There, in a semidark
corner behind an iron gate, stands a statue of St. Gennaro and the cup
in his hand fills with Christ's blood on this holiday. We peer through
the gate, to pierce the darkness, and in the fierce heat created by the
throng, we see moisture on the outside of the cup and a glistening
within. Women faint. Men try to fall on their knees and pray, but cannot because they are wedged in by others who cry out hysterically. Yes,
not only is seeing believing. Believing is seeing—something I remember
when I cross-examine witnesses.

The Haggada is divided into two "acts." The intermission is dinner.

First, my mother brings a pitcher of water and a large bowl. All in
turn pour water over their hands and recite a prayer of cleanliness.
Then follow the *gefilte* fish, chicken, and *tsimmes* (cooked carrots and
prunes).

There is one unique Passover dish served on no other occasion. It is
soup, consisting of salty cold water. Into it a whole hard-boiled egg is
placed after peeling the shell at the table. It is sliced in the "soup," no

mean feat as it slips around. Small pieces of matzoh are crushed and sprinkled into the water, like croutons, to give it body. The taste is deliciously exotic. Gourmets vow that it is better than the finest hot soups and superior to cold soups like gazpacho or vichyssoise.

Invariably someone asks why in the world we don't make this dish during the year. Always the answer is that "it only tastes good on Seder night." Either superstition or forgetfulness has prevented us from ever testing this explanation. I don't know of a single instance where it has been tried on more prosaic nights. Before I am through I intend to engage in an extreme act of daring by ordering a plate of cold water, salting it, and cutting a hard-boiled egg into it. If it tastes as bad as it sounds, I won't scoff at Passover superstitions anymore.

After dinner a prayer is read silently in thanksgiving for the bounties of life. Then follow the Haggada songs. They can be disposed of quickly or made into a lengthy "concert" by skipping no verses and teaching the assembly by sheer repetition to become a choir and give orchestrated effect to the rhythms. Of course, my father followed the path of most persistence. We caught the spirit and sang until two or three in the morning. The children enjoyed not only the escape from customary bedtime, but the harmonies which they learned to create. The elders simply had a rip-roaring singing time, for here was their initiation into jazz, rock, and soul singing, long before these words were known.

The melodies for "*Adir Hu,*" "*Ekhod Mi Yode-ah,*" "*L'Kho-af-L'Kho,*" "*Khad Gadyo,*" and others are centuries old. Yet they contain rhythms and tempos more modern than anything sung by the Beatles or pop groups, including skipped beats and inventive varying pace. It is not surprising that Irving Berlin made his breakthrough in "Alexander's Ragtime Band," or that Al Jolson, the son of a cantor, produced the rhythm within a rhythm in "Mammy," or that there are so many Jewish composers of popular music, from George Gershwin to Burt Bacharach. They came by it through long inheritance. Examine Gershwin's "Get Happy" and you will find a well-known chassidic melody and rhythm. Phil Baker adopted an identifying melody for his television program which my father used to sing Friday nights before *Kiddush.* "The Anniversary Song" is a melody sung by Jews in Poland a century ago. This is not to decry the originality of modern composers. Their inventions stem from a memory stimulated by their talents. But the genre is as traceable as a Chinese song is distinct from Western music.

My father was not content with his own gusto. He beat a spoon against any glass object near him, creating beats in different pitches. Sweating and joyous in conducting, he drove everyone to participate, his hands waving toward those whose voices were timid, until they rose with him in swelling sound. When the sopranos had the upper hand, he provided the bass accompaniment, sometimes with humorous gestures. When the harmony was lacking, he turned tenor, or even soprano. And when the notes were false, he held his ears in pain, while the children burst into laughter. My mother sang too, she wouldn't dare not to, but her eyes roamed around the room observing the scene knowingly and happily.

The Haggada service always concluded with the singing of "My Country 'Tis of Thee" or "The Star-Spangled Banner." The contrast between the ancient religious ritual with its Hebraic rhythms and the American anthem was sharp and telling. We were transported from history and imagery to the reality of today. But there was one constant, the emotion of gratitude for freedom.

My father sang this paean of dedication to the United States with eyes closed and deep feeling in his by then hoarse voice. Those who immigrated here have by their choice evidenced an appreciation for our country which those born here may lack because they take its opportunities for granted. This was certainly true of my parents. My father worked sixteen hours a day for a pittance in London and seldom saw me awake as an infant. The contrast with life in this country caused his gratitude to overflow. He was unreservedly patriotic. I recall him posting a huge American flag in front of our summer home in Bethlehem, New Hampshire, every day. Even after his doctors cautioned him against exertion, he insisted on climbing a ladder at sundown to remove the flag and fold it tenderly for the next morning's display. When he died, we found in his will the most unusual provision I have ever seen. No one who had been a communist could be buried in our family mausoleum.

My musical education was not entirely homegrown. It stemmed from a great religious tradition. Synagogue music is as distinct and developed an art as that of opera or ballet.

The rabbi was vested with the formal conduct of the services and delivered the sermon. But the cantor was the musical exponent of the prayers. He was chosen because of his great voice as well as his interpretive skill. Like opera stars, cantors came from all parts of the world. The eastern part of Europe produced many of the famous ones. As their fame spread, they were invited to the leading synagogues in Kiev, Warsaw, London, and ultimately the United States.

Here they were eagerly awaited by the cognoscenti. So Cantor Sirota, he of the golden Caruso voice, Cantor Kwartin, whose pure tones shattered chandelier globes, Cantor Reutman, famed for the sweetness of his lyrical tenor, Cantor Koussevitsky, and others were invited to occupy the singing pulpits of leading synagogues in the United States.

Some of the American cantors like Richard Tucker and Jan Peerce became Metropolitan Opera stars. Others trained in Jewish musical lore, like Robert Merrill, also joined the Metropolitan. However, despite their careers, Rosh Hashanah and Yom Kippur services were performed by Richard Tucker, Jan Peerce, "Leibele" Waldman, and other concert or opera singers who returned to their earlier profession on the holy days.

The most famous cantor to arrive on our shores was Josef ("Yosele") Rosenblatt. He had scored triumphs throughout Europe. His arrival in the United States was awaited in Jewish circles with the same breathless anticipation as balletomanes welcome a Pavlova, Fonteyn, Nureyev, or Baryshnikov, or opera buffs greet a Chaliapin or a Sutherland.

Like all supreme artists his performance exceeded the exaggerated claims made for him. He was immediately signed by RCA Victor Records to record his religious renditions, and his platters broke sales records all over the world. In a sense he was a freak, but what a magnificent freak. He had three voices, a most beautiful hearty and distinctive tenor voice of clarity and power. Also, he could sing in the baritone range, and his tones were just as pure as they were deep, even descending to a basso range. But most astonishing of all, he could transfer to a falsetto soprano of incredible beauty.

Enrico Caruso used to play and replay one of Cantor Rosenblatt's records because he was fascinated by the sheer virtuosity of what seemed to be an impossible vocal feat. Rosenblatt recorded a prayer in which he performed a vocal exercise beginning with a low baritone note and rolling in coloratura style up the scale, until he reached the tenor range, which he passed into without the slightest break, continuing to ascend until he shifted into the soprano range, where he engaged in trills which would have made Tetrazzini, Galli-Curci, or the modern Beverly Sills proud; then without a pause or taking a breath, he descended through the tenor and baritone ranges, concluding with a vibrant basso tone of profound purity.

I heard about all this when I was a child because I sang in a choir and the sensational stories of Cantor Rosenblatt's brilliance were bruited about in all Jewish circles, as indeed they were recognized by lovers of music everywhere.

An essential part of the cantor tradition was the development of great choirs. The directors of these choirs also became well known, and their names were featured with those of the cantors. Their art was as distinctive as that of a motion picture director in his medium. Often they were composers of devotional music. Two of them, Joseph Rumshinsky and Abraham Ellstein, later became leading musical comedy composers of the Jewish theater. They produced the shows which starred Molly

Picon and Ludwig Satz, and many of their songs, like *"Bei Mir Bist du Schoen,"* have since acquired English lyrics and become popular American standards.

Usually the "basement" auditorium of the synagogue was filled with worshipers, who had to be content with the performance of a gifted *gabbay* or a rabbi who could intone the prayers without vocal virtuosity. To reduce the unpleasantness of the monetary distinctions which entitled some to enjoy the great cantor and choir, while others had to express their religious devotion in more prosaic style, the rabbi would repeat his sermon to the congregation "below." At least the mental stimulation was equalized.

Great cantors, like stars in other fields, were highly paid. So were choir directors. On high holy days, those synagogues which featured a famous cantor and a choir under a well-known director assessed members for the privilege of maintaining their regular pews for what was not merely a service but a unique religious concert. For others tickets were at a premium. A private police guard was usually placed at the entrance to control the crowd, which was motivated by musical appreciation rather than by religious devotion.

Jews had a sense of humor about all this. A favorite joke was about the man who sought admission without a ticket because he "must talk to his brother, for only a minute." The guard finally yielded but warned him, "Don't let me catch you praying."

The money problem in religious activity was solved in ingenious ways. It was the practice at an intermission in the formal service to read portions of the Torah. Members of the synagogue and visitors were called to the pulpit and were honored by reciting a brief passage from the holy scroll. After the reading, they could donate money to the synagogue, the rabbi, the cantor, and others. Eighteen dollars was a favorite contribution because the Hebrew word for eighteen is *chay* which also means life. Thus charity and long life were linked—a happy symbol. Since it was forbidden to write or to handle money on the Sabbath, gifts were recorded by using prepared cards for various denominations or by other devices. So a pragmatic approach was found for financial support of religious institutions, even though a collection box could not be passed around to parishioners.

Choir directors had to find fine voices to achieve effective musical ensembles. So tenors and baritones who aspired to be cantors or concert or opera performers first rendered their services in leading choirs. Children with beautiful alto and soprano voices were in particular demand. If they were vocally gifted, they were trained by the choir director and his assistants in private and group sessions. They were taught to read music, to place their voices correctly, which meant to produce tones not

merely from an open throat, but in such a way as to create the resonances from the cavities in the head and chest, to understand the
nuances of rhythm, and to express feeling.

A few were gifted enough in voice and talent to become soloists. The
cantorial art permitted alto and soprano solos to contrast with the
cantor's broad tenor and the symphonic arrangements of the choir.

I qualified as an alto soloist and received my training under Cantor
Isaac Kaminsky, who occupied a post in a leading synagogue in Brooklyn, New York.

Cantor Kaminsky was a distinguished composer of devotional music.
His choir and cantor compositions were sung all over the world. Since
he was more talented as a musician than as a singer, he trained and led
his own choir.

So I went to a special kind of musical school and was taught by a
master. I learned to read notes. I learned the variations of harmonies
and, above all, the importance of rhythms, which Kaminsky broke,
changed, and restored with such skill that the listener thought his own
pulse was adjusting to the momentum of each change.

During services, I watched Cantor Kaminsky closely. With limited
vocal equipment, he created a thunderous voice. This he achieved by
singing softly, and then approaching the climactic note with gradual increase of volume until the listeners' anticipation supplied the effect
when the final note was taken.

Later, I stood in the balcony at the Metropolitan Opera House and
heard Enrico Caruso use the same technique to give an enlarged effect
even to his naturally powerful voice. Listen to his record of the fisher-
man's song "*Sur le mer*" for a perfect illustration of this technique. The
drawn-out, ever-increasing, but slow approach to the high note lifts
you out of your seat and you are actually relieved that the destination
has been reached.

Also, I observed Kaminsky's knowledge of the physical aspects of producing sound. By twisting his mouth and forcing the voice to rever-
berate against the roof of his mouth, he created resonances which were
deceiving in their volume.

The by-products of any education are sometimes as important as the
formal training itself. That is the principle of gestalt philosophy—the
total exceeds the sum of its parts. This is particularly true in music. A
symphony conducted by Toscanini is not merely the sounds which emanate from the individual instruments. A by-product of my studies was a
realization of the entirety of a composition. I was taught the alto part
and it sounded unmelodious and strange. Later, when I heard the
prime melody to which my contribution was addressed, I perceived the
beauty of the continuously varying harmonies, sometimes due to the

even more grotesque basso thumping or the baritone's single note holding through a series of variations.

After a while, I could detect the whole composition merely by studying the alto section. My ear and imagination supplied multiple constructions. I became bold enough to suggest some of these to Kaminsky. Even when he didn't adopt them, he was struck enough by my attentiveness and understanding to call me affectionately, "my little artist." He composed special duets for us, one of which was so entrancing and modern in conception that I hope to reproduce it in his name, if I ever fulfill an ambition to write the lyrics and music of a musical comedy.

I am grateful to Kaminsky, not only because he opened a new horizon of the joys of music for me, but because his training has been greatly responsible for such forensic skill as I have. For speaking is also a form of music. About this—more later.

The schism between Orthodox and Reform Judaism is typical of the differences in other churches. The Orthodox synagogue permits voices but no instrumental music. However, in Reform temples, organ music may be played. In Orthodox synagogues, men must keep their heads covered with hats or *yarmulkahs* but not in Reform temples. Women may not sit with men in truly Orthodox synagogues. Their distracting influence is avoided by seating them in the balcony or in a separate section in the rear.

The psychological aspect of somber dress being a sexual reminder is interesting in our current drive toward nudity. The designer Coco Chanel was not being prim when she turned to basic black. Women covered to the neck in satin and black lace can be more enticing than in the most revealing minis. So when women dress decorously for religious functions, whether to have an audience with the Pope or to attend church or synagogue, they draw special attention to their charms. The practice in the East of women covering even their faces with veils adds mystery to sexual curiosity. Perhaps it is the posture of innocence which is exciting. What is more intriguing than a gold cross or other religious symbol resting in the shadow of a low-cut gown?

So the Orthodox practice with respect to women in the synagogue is only one of many with which the Reform Jewish temple disagrees. In most religions, the divisions and sects multiply, each being certain that its form of worship is more consonant with God's will.

For example, on Chanukah, a gay holiday observance, even Orthodox Jews permit instrumental music. So Cantor Kaminsky, his choir, and a full orchestra, which he had rehearsed for weeks, gave a three-evening concert. By this time, I was featured as a soloist in the announcements.

The "dirigeant" of Cantor Rosenblatt's choir had heard of my performances and sent for me. I was auditioned by him and the great cantor himself. With Cantor Kaminsky's blessing, since he was proud of his handiwork and did not wish to stand in my way, I was engaged for the high holidays to sing in Cantor Rosenblatt's choir.

So I met Cantor Rosenblatt, a legend in his day, and more, I was trained to sing several duets with him, as well as solos on my own.

The cantor was a short man, about five feet five inches in height. He was also surprisingly slight, without the broad chest which is the chamber for most great singers. That is why women opera stars who slim down to meet theatrical standards suffer in voice production. Vocal chords cannot stand diets, no matter how good they are for health and the rest of the body. One can tell on the telephone by the hollow voice that the person on the other end has lost much weight.

Cantor Rosenblatt was respected for his religiosity as well as for his voice. He followed the true Orthodox practice of not shaving. So his ascetic beautiful features were almost completely hidden by a black beard which left only his blazing black eyes and a small portion of his pink cheeks visible. When he sang, he was immovable. Only his mouth formed a circle as if suddenly an opening was discovered in his hirsuteness. And from that dark opening, miraculous sounds poured out. Only when he engaged in his soprano coloratura did he close his eyes as if to add prayer to the angelic effect of his incredibly pure trills.

Then after a suitable pause, he opened his eyes and concluded with a most lionesque tenor high C.

It is the tradition of a synagogue service, as in all churches, to have the audience repeat in unison the prayer uttered from the pulpit. But when Cantor Rosenblatt had concluded one of his renditions, one heard not the responding chorus of the worshipers but a widespread gasp, then a chuckle of wonder, and finally, as if collecting themselves, a disorganized reading. Often his prayers were so moving that one heard sobs in the audience.

Yet he was a naïve and simple man. I was amused when we were in the dressing room, where the cantor's and choir's robes were put on, and he asked me for a cherry drop from my five-cent box. This was how he treated that precious voice. Later when he sang, I saw the red dye from the cheap candy on his tongue.

The Metropolitan Opera House tried on numerous occasions to engage him, but he would not shave his beard or agree to sing on Saturdays, and no amount of persuasion or money could induce him to do so.

Instead, he gave himself freely to charities of all kinds. He sang for the Police Benevolent Association, and they rewarded him with an engraved police whistle. This was the pride of his life. He showed it to all who would listen, and blew it frequently. His manager, who took care of his frequent recording sessions to meet an insatiable and growing demand, was beside himself, bemoaning the fact that any organization could save itself $10,000 by giving him a token toy instead.

His naïveté ultimately ruined him. He was induced to go into a large Jewish publishing venture. He lost his enormous earnings, and in addition was obligated on notes totaling almost a million dollars. He would not think of bankruptcy. He decided to accept a vaudeville and concert tour, where he could retain his beard and not sing on the Sabbath, to earn the money to pay his creditors in full. Also he performed marriage ceremonies, and although the fee was $2,500, he was besieged with such engagements. Many a bride and groom mistook the crowd which filled the synagogue or ballroom, and overflowed into the street, as a tribute to them.

The strain of his concert tour not only affected his voice but drained him of his energy. I went to hear him at the Academy of Music, in Brooklyn. The huge auditorium was filled to capacity. Since his audiences were non-Jewish in large part, his program was arranged accordingly. First, he sang Jewish lieder, such as the moving description of a rabbi teaching the Hebrew alphabet to his pupils:

Afn pripetshik brent a fa-ye-rl
Un in shtub iz heys
Un der Rebbe lernt kleyne kinderlekh
Dem Alef Bes.

Zogt zhe kinderlikh gedenkt zhe ta-ye-re
Vos ir lernt do
Zogt zhe nokh a mol un ta-ke nokh a mol
Kometz—alef—"O"!

Az ir vet, kinderlekh, elter veren
Vet ir aleyn farshteyn,
Vif'l in di oysyes lig'n trern
Un vif'l geveyn

In the fireplace a fire burns
And the room is hot,
And the Rebbe is teaching
Small dear children the Alef Bes [Hebrew alphabet].
[Refrain]
Say now children, remember dear ones
What you are learning here.
Say now and repeat again
The vowel *Kometz* together with
The letter *Alef* is pronounced "O"!

When, dear children, you become older
You will understand on your own
How many tears lie in these letters
And how much weeping.

Then he sang a song for the Irish in the audience. His accent destroyed the lyrics of "Mother Machree."

> "I luv the dear sil-vaire dat
> shines in her hair."

But his voice overcame all. The audience cheered in never-ending ovations for the lonely little black-bearded figure with skullcap on his head,
who stood next to a piano on a huge stage, too dignified to bow. He
walked off awkwardly, and when he was dragged back on the stage by
his manager, he shuddered at the screams which his appearance evoked.
Unsmiling, he stood for a minute and sauntered off again.

He learned to sing encores, which he gave freely not only because of
his generosity but because it was the best escape from the embarrassment of applause. (In synagogues, it was forbidden to applaud, and
the repressed feeling was expressed in head wagging, tears, and mur-
murs of appreciation and wonderment, which, when multiplied, I
learned to recognize as a special form of applause.)

After he had paid his indebtedness, rescuing his honor with his
throat, Rosenblatt went to Israel to replenish his spirit—or perhaps he
went there to die. For sudden death came to him in the Holy Land at
the age of fifty-two.

Fortunately his recordings, reorchestrated like Caruso's, to give them
the utmost background fidelity, are available, so that his unique talents
survive. Thanks to the accidental discovery by Edison when a dust-
encrusted point scratched one of his turntables covered with wax, death
no longer stills the voice.

Cantor Kaminsky also came to a sudden and tragic end. When he
had retired on meager means to Florida, he came to New York to visit
his friends and two of his alumni. I was one. General David Sarnoff,
who had preceded me in his choir, was the other. The General loved to
talk Yiddish, and Kaminsky's visits afforded an excellent opportunity.
The cantor was also an amusing companion, being an excellent storyteller. His timing and long pauses, derived from his musical talent, were
expressive enough to cause gales of laughter, before the punch line produced a second explosion of merriment.

By this time the cantor's blond Vandyke beard and mustache had
turned grayish. His fine features prospered with age—except his eyes.

He had trouble with his eye ducts, and I was never sure when his characteristic blotting of his eyes with a large white handkerchief was to wipe away tears or was an emotionless gesture.

One day, he stepped off a curb in Miami Beach and was instantly killed by a speeding car. Little notice was taken of his passing, but Sarnoff and I grieved for our teacher.

Most talents develop with age, but a child's voice is the victim of its own growth. The last time I sang in public was at my high school graduation exercises.

I doubled in brass. I was to deliver an address and later sing John McCormack's famous ballad "I Hear You Calling Me."

My voice was changing. I had no trouble with the lower register, although it had acquired unaccustomed heavy shading, but when I reached the high notes, which once flowed so easily, my vocal chords, growing thick, resisted. I was almost in panic, but strained and got by, though not without a telltale crack in what was to be the glissando finish.

Vocal experts told me to be as silent as possible for a year, so that a mature singing voice could develop. One cannot predict for a caterpillar what its coloring will be when it turns into a butterfly. The voice is just as mysterious. One doesn't know whether the change in structure will produce a tenor or baritone, or what distinctive colorations the new voice will have; indeed, whether any singing voice will develop at all. So the voice doctor, like other doctors, depends on nature to supply the answer. He counseled the avoidance of strain so as not to interfere with the process.

I had entered Columbia College and had ambitions to be an athlete. Since I was very small, I qualified to be coxswain on the crew. Weight was a handicap and I fanatically trained by running from the campus to Grant's Tomb and back several times a day until I got down to a hundred pounds. I made the crew.

Running in freezing winter, and then practicing in the shell on the Hudson River, screaming counts to the crew through a megaphone were exactly what the voice coach had not ordered. Nor did the periodic dunkings of the coxswain in the ice-cold Hudson or Harlem River, a tradition after crew races, help the changing voice. But such are the values of youth. I would have sacrificed much more than my voice to make the crew.

While I lost whatever singing voice I was destined to have, the law of compensation—or is it of averages?—rewarded me with a satisfactory speaking voice. I feel fortunate, for what is more disconcerting than a scratchy, cracking, or high-pitched, nonresonant voice?

A whole army of motion picture stars discovered this tragedy when

sound came to motion pictures. Almost all of them disappeared overnight. The impression of heroic men and alluring heroines disappeared
the instant they spoke. Their voices registered weakness, and their diction betrayed their breeding. It was ludicrous to have the virile hero talk
up in a squeaking voice. Just as suddenly actors who had fine speaking
voices, like Conrad Nagel, became stars.

Nature has played tricks in real life, too. The redoubtable Jack
Dempsey shocked you the first time you heard his high-pitched voice.
Political figures, too, depend largely on their vocal chords. Thomas
Dewey and President Nixon were fine baritone singers, and always
spoke as if they were producing recitative in an opera. Roosevelt had a
bell-like voice which was distinctive and beautiful. Who besides Coolidge, with his nasal twang, and Truman ever achieved high public
office without an appealing voice?

So despite my foolishness in college, I did not lose the voice instrument so necessary for my life's work.

While I regret not having learned the piano or some other musical
instrument, a skill which would not have been lost at puberty, my musical training has afforded me an enjoyable avocation.

For years while traveling on vacation, I would compose songs about
the places I visited. Several of these, "Hawaii" and "Jamaica," were
published and my wife and I had the pleasure of dancing to them when
they became popular on the islands. Some of my songs, under a fictitious name, were bought by Paramount Pictures for one of its pictures,
and by a television producer for his series.

Since then I have composed songs for each of our grandchildren.
These were published, and RCA made a record of them under the title
"Songs for You." It was interesting to watch a child listening to a song
bearing his or her name. The universal reaction was one of embarrassment, shyness, and pleasure. Perhaps this was the evolution of the
ego drive—shame at being so self-centered, but lured by the pleasure of
adulation.

So I am a member of ASCAP, The American Society of Composers
and Publishers, and the small checks I receive periodically for my compositions seem very large and gratifying. Doesn't every comedian want
to play Hamlet, or is it too conceited to say, and vice versa?

Fates decreed that I should be trial counsel for the motion picture
companies to defend them in an antitrust suit brought by seventy-one
composers on behalf of their class for 300 million dollars in damages. Neither our opponents nor I considered my standing as a composer serious enough to constitute a conflict of interest. It was an insult
I gladly bore, rather than be disqualified.

HE TOOK SUCCESS LIKE A GENTLEMAN AND DEFEAT LIKE A MAN

Two mayors have become famous national personalities. Municipal government being closest to the people but also to the local political boss, it has demonstrated the best and worst in democracy. The electorate has swung from one extreme to another in the same city. Can anyone imagine a greater contrast in appearance, personality, and devotion to duty than James J. Walker and Fiorello H. LaGuardia? Each represented the true mood of the city at a particular time. But conditions changed. That is why Walker could easily defeat LaGuardia the first time he was challenged by him, and then lose decisively to him in his second attempt, though the issues were the same. Since I had the opportunity to observe both from an intimate vantage point, and become an adviser to one of them, it is worth describing and evaluating two unique political characters on the American scene.

If an artist with great insight had to personify New York City during the gay twenties, he would have drawn Jimmy Walker. He was never a mayor. That was only his title. He was Mr. New York, jaunty, fun-loving, and not bothering too much about standards or morals while entertaining himself and the populace. He loved. He drank. He spoke wittily. He flaunted his sybaritic nature at the expense of dreary municipal caretaking. He took care of his friends, and we shall see that they didn't reciprocate. He was loyal to the worthy and unworthy alike.

He was emaciated as well as dissipated-looking, and he made a virtue of both. Being frail and narrow, he specialized in carefully tailored suits which hugged his waist and made his shriveled frame look dapper—that was the word applied to him. He wore his fedora hat with brim turned down rakishly on one side. He skillfully made his contrived appearance look like devil-may-care casualness. As if to make up for his sunken chest, his dark blue or black shiny satin ties, thinly knotted, curved out at least three inches before tucking into his pearl gray vest.

Obviously, he was the bane or envy of well-built men, whose bulging muscles prevented stylish fits, while his clothes clung to his skeleton frame, as if they were "poured on." All this was made consistent by his face. It was puckish. He had a thin nose which tipped upward roguishly at the very end. His black hair was flattened down in shiny precision and contrasted with his eyes, which were light or dark blue depending on the colors of his suit and tie. They really twinkled. Indeed, he laughed with them, while his lips would purse in comical appreciation. His most robust feature was his voice—low-pitched, distinctive in its half-hoarse, half-resonant quality, with variety of shadings, used as skillfully as an organist plays his keys to surprise and please the ear. Just as effective as his voice were his silences. When making a speech, he would not hesitate to pause for twenty or thirty seconds before the conclusion of a sentence, shaking his head slowly up and down, challenging the audience's anticipation of the jest or point he was about to make. Audiences would respond to his long silence with laughter and applause. He would finally utter the conclusion, in which event there was a renewed burst of appreciation; or not end the sentence at all shrugging as if to say, "Need I say more?" Then he would nod his head in *his* appreciation of the audience. This brought forth another sally from those who now felt they were participating in the speech. He made every speech a two-way affair. It was unique milking of an audience.

Of course, it could only be carried off by one who had supreme self-confidence. A long silence usually breaks concentration and the listeners' attention wanders off. Only masters can make silence a continuation of thought processes. Like telegraphic communication, dashes as well as dots fill out the message. It is all called timing, but very few can practice the art. The only actor I ever saw who dared to be silent for long stretches and not lose his audience was George M. Cohan. He applied the same technique on the stage that Walker did on the dais. I recall his performance in Eugene O'Neill's *Ah, Wilderness!* There was a scene in which the father explained the facts of life to his son. When the son asked a question, Cohan did not follow the author and reply. He inserted his lengthy silence, looked quietly at the boy for what appeared on the stage to be hours, while occasionally nodding his head as if weighing the question, and gazing again intently into the child's eyes. The audience was forced to appreciate his embarrassment and imagine the impending reply. The audience became the author. There was laughter and suspense. His reply was matched against the audience's anticipation and set off heightened reactions as the guessing game was played out. It became dialogue not only between the characters on the stage, but between them and the audience.

Most performers feel that they must be doing or saying something to hold attention. They act as if a pause represented forgetfulness. Comedians, particularly, practice a frenetic delivery to keep momentum going. But silence properly used is part of momentum, because it provides contrast and opportunity for appreciation. Comedian Jack Benny claimed that the most sustained laugh he ever received, in his many sketches depicting himself as a miser, was when a stickup man confronted him with "Your money or your life"—and there was an endless radio silence, while the laughter mounted at the mental struggle he was going through in making his decision.

Walker was cut out to be an actor, not a statesman. His talents ran to writing songs and exuding charm. Unfortunately, he had studied law, the most arduous and exacting profession, and totally unsuited to his aversion to drudgery. His disposition was to savor the final achievement if the effort necessary to attain it could be evaded. Someone should have told him that this is about as possible as winning the Nobel Prize for Literature without writing a word. Shrewd Tammany leaders decided to exploit his personality politically. He became a senator in the New York State legislature. His nimbleness of mind enabled him to read only the title of a proposed bill and make a creditable speech for or against it as party dictates required. He did not hesitate to be cryptic. Once, in opposing a censorship bill, his oration consisted of thirteen words: "I have never heard of a girl who was ruined by a book."

He had the gift of pleading guilty in such a way that the sins of all were epitomized by him, thus evoking sympathy for the many, not merely himself. Once, when he was Mayor, and his escapades with Betty Compton were reaching scandalous proportions (his limousine bearing the No. 1 license plate was continuously parked overnight in front of her apartment, an available target for newspaper photographers of which he never deprived them), Cardinal Hayes summoned him and appealed to him as a Catholic heading the greatest city in the world to be more upright in setting an example for others. He replied, "Your Excellency, there are dozens of confessional booths in St. Patrick's Cathedral. They can't all be for me."

When critics attacked his neglect of city business, he replied, "I don't understand this. You can see lights burning in my office hours after I leave."

He understood that he was violating political psychology, but he was delighted because he could get away with it. He said, "My wisecracks rose many times to plague me, but I couldn't help laughing, even though I well knew that the public does not trust a banker who is gay, a clergyman who smiles, or a politician who forgets to frown at the news camera."

He made a virtue of what others would have hidden. "I've read not

more than fifteen books from cover to cover. What little I know, I have
learned by ear!"

Al Smith once said to Walker, his protégé, "Why can't you be like
Jim Foley? His light is burning late and he studies. While you . . ."

"I'm lit up, too, Al, at that hour."

But he was the perfect mayor in extending the city's hospitality to
the world's celebrities whose greatest reward was a ticker tape parade
down Broadway. So Lindbergh and channel swimmer Gertrude Ederle,
General Foch and Babe Ruth, Queen Marie and Bill Tilden, President
Coolidge and Red Grange, King Leopold and Jack Dempsey, and
dozens of others in the limelight received their ultimate glow when he
bestowed his luminous presence and felicitous praise and wit upon
them on City Hall steps, while newsreel cameras recorded and spread
the event to the far corners of the world. Wherever people saw his slim
figure overshadowing the celebrities he honored, they recognized the sophisticated good will of New York City. He was the symbol par excellence of a teeming cosmopolitan center, prosperous and joyous.

It seemed in those worriless days that the city belonged to the world
and that its main function was to be a port of celebration for those who
had achieved fame, even of a transitory nature.

Some countries exist on tourism. New York City, under Walker, was
the forerunner of the United Nations, apparently with no more difficult
task than to honor headliners. This function was so important that
there was an official greeter, Grover Whalen, aristocratically mustached
and carnation buttonholed, who added the Old World touch before
presenting the guest to Jimmy, the king of the New World. Walker's
greetings became a feature of newsreels shown around the world. To
Guglielmo Marconi he said, "It is gratifying that you did not send a
wireless but came in person. Here we do not know much about trans-
mission but we have fine receptions." And when he was invited for reciprocal visits abroad, which he eagerly accepted with the comment
that "A Mayor is not fully performing his duty until he leaves town,"
he charmed everyone there too. He was shown on a newsreel talking to
a woman in Paris who asked him whether he spoke French. "Fluently,
madam," he replied, "but the ignorance of these natives is deplorable.
They can't understand a word I say."

Of course, no ballroom dinner was complete unless adorned by
Mayor Walker. Here his official status and special gifts melted perfectly. He attended all the important ones. Sometimes this meant seven
nights a week and two or three a night, not to speak of cocktail parties.
If only he had been as conscientious about his other duties.

The reason for the plethora of testimonial dinners was the discovery
that the easiest way to raise funds for any cause was to select a guest of

honor who could command a large attendance at twenty-five, fifty, or a hundred dollars a ticket. This resulted in some peculiar guests of honor. The head of a buying concern for department stores, like John Block of Kirby, Block & Company was a surefire bet to sell a thousand tickets. He was the most frequently honored guest in New York. Fortunately, he was a fine man, who understood that he was lending himself to charity, and his only difficulty was changing his acceptance speech to express differently his awareness that he was merely the bait to bring in the fish. Often a good cause would be enhanced by $100,000 or more derived from these functions.

However, there were many occasions when distinguished men in science, literature, art, and government, some from abroad, were honored. Curiously, the attendance was in inverse proportion to the importance of the man. When the grand ballroom of the Waldorf was not filled, a fact disguised by leaving a large dance floor space in the center (as if discriminating guests needed more *lebensraum* than the hoi polloi when they danced), one knew that the attendance was voluntary to honor the guest, and not just to raise money. To correct the imbalance of attendance, the price of a ticket was modest, just to cover the cost of the occasion.

Since charitable causes abound, and New York City attracts the great, there was not and is not an evening when the ballrooms of the large hotels are not being used by Heart, Cancer, Cerebral Palsy, Psychiatry, Catholic Charities, Federation of Jewish Philanthropies, Protestant Big Brothers, Greek Relief, Old Age Homes, and dozens of other charity organizations.

Irrespective of the cause or personality involved, it became the custom for entertainers, officeholders, important business executives like Bernard Gimbel, sport figures, and writers to bestow their presence on these occasions. The gregariousness of men and women of accomplishment is not of the ordinary kind. Except for a few so introspective that they cannot bear exposure, they enjoy being introduced from the dais, hearing the gasp of recognition, and the following salute of applause to express appreciation. It is the only direct confirmation that someone out there likes them.

So there were large daises to seat the attending celebrities and sometimes two tiers of them. What better symbol of brotherhood is there than a city composed of more Italians than in Venice or Genoa, more Jews than in Jerusalem or Tel Aviv, more Irish than in Dublin, more Germans than in Bonn, and huge black, Puerto Rican, and other ethnic groups living side by side. Until recent outbursts, huge metropolitan centers like New York were a living example of a world community living in peace and mutual respect. The multiple daises at these dinners were microscopic reflections of this reality, and of something else. Democracy and tolerance applied to achievement, as well as race, religion, or color. Of course, all were not to be evaluated equally, but the prizefight champion Jack Dempsey sat next to author John Gunther, the Metropolitan Opera star Martinelli chatted with the chief executive of the J. C. Penney Company, James Farley, once a political manager for Roosevelt and later a Coca-Cola executive, conversed with Dr. Schick, whose findings eliminated the scourge of diphtheria. Judges of the highest courts sat next to nationally famous pop singers. Governors, senators, members of the Cabinet rubbed shoulders with concert violinists or pianists. The dais was a melting pot of talents as well as races. Propinquity can create warmth as well as distrust.

Jimmy Walker often acted as toastmaster, or if Harry Hershfield, George Jessel, Eddie Cantor, Milton Berle, or later Bob Hope or other stars presided, he would be a speaker. In order to give the entertainers fuller scope, and add a more "dignified" touch to the proceedings, nonentertainers with some felicitous gifts were invited to be toastmasters. Authors like Fannie Hurst and Quentin Reynolds, judges like Ferdinand Pecora, laywers like myself served this function.

Over the years, I introduced Walker and he me at these dinners dozens of times, interchanging our roles as toastmaster and speaker. Since honesty is the best policy in speaking as well as in conduct, I never alluded to him as a great or even competent public official. He did not mind. Few would have believed me if I had claimed he was. On the other hand, exchanging witticisms with him, for he never failed to reply effectively, pleased him and titillated the audience. And one could go as far as one wished in praising his charm and warm qualities, symbolic of the good heart of New York, without straying one iota from the truth. He was less discriminating when the time for reply came. For he indulged in lavish introductions of me (usually involving the name of Judge Benjamin Cardozo, probably because he knew I hero-worshiped him and despite the fact that coupling Cardozo's name with those of men far more worthy than me was still preposterously inappropriate).

There are a few traditional annual dinners which bring out the foremost citizens in the land, including the President of the United States—for example, the Al Smith dinner. One such occasion, requiring a triple dais, was the annual McCosker-Hershfield dinner for a cardiac home in their name. The cause was good but hardly pre-eminent. However, Alfred McCosker, who was the president of a radio network, was a most popular and charitable man, and Harry Hershfield lived up to his unique billing, "He walks with the highest and is loved by the humblest." Except for a dinner greeting a Churchill or De Gaulle, no function regularly attracted more "celebrities" from every walk of life than this one. The attendance overflowed each year, filling the Waldorf-Astoria's tiers of boxes and flowing into the corridors. People reserved tickets months in advance. The foremost entertainers and artists from the concert and operatic stages came forth to volunteer their services, and many were resentful because they were not invited.

The perennial trio at this function for twenty years were Jimmy Walker, Bishop Fulton Sheen (then Monsignor) and myself as toastmaster. Sheen and Walker contrasted and complemented each other in an extraordinary way. Walker, with his ubiquitous wit, graciousness, and charm, and Sheen with his hypnotic eloquence. He fulfilled the classic definition of an orator—the flashing eye and philosopher's brow. He could emotionalize the simplest aphorism and move the audience to tears (for example, his description of a muddy pool on a dirty street; but God shines the sun on it, purifies it, and lifts a single drop triumphantly out of the stagnant pool to His heart).

But there was a day of reckoning—literally. Moneys were missing. While the Mayor was fulfilling his social duties brilliantly, greedy contractors, bus operators, and others serving a teeming city were gaining control of the captainless ship of state. And they did not steer it in the direction of the public's interest. Scandals spewed from many city departments. Now Walker's amber-lit romantic goings-on suddenly had ominous green lights cast upon them. There were recitals of Betty's expensive jewelry and contrasting reference to the Mayor's salary. Rumors spread that there was a bagman with more than a million dollars held for Walker in a sort of dis-trust fund.

An investigation was ordered by Governor Franklin D. Roosevelt, and Judge Samuel Seabury, formerly of the highest court in the state, acted as counsel, really prosecutor, before a State Legislative Committee headed by Samuel H. Hofstadter (who later became a judge in the State Supreme Court and upon his retirement after thirty years of scholarly service joined my law firm).

If a dramatist reveling in contrast had invented two contestants, he could not have excelled the diversity between Judge Seabury and Jimmy Walker. The judge was stocky, heavy, white-haired, and white-faced from study, dressed in the most conservative old-fashioned clothes, dignified to the point of stiffness, aristocratic in bearing, humorless, courteous even when irate, severe even when friendly, impeccable in speech, but neurotically paying a price for his rectitude by a most annoying automatic clearing of his throat between words, as if his larynx stuttered.

Of course, as we have seen, Walker's trimness, dark Irish countenance, advance-style clothes, wit, easy bearing, and felicity made a perfect foil. When they confronted each other on the stand, Walker evaded, parried with humor, respectfully mocked the Judge, and squirted charm all over the hearing room. But Seabury had documents in his hand; bills for jewelry and expensive gifts, contracts granting franchises to friends, some of whom were not distinguished for honorable conduct, millions of dollars of deals approved by the Mayor about which he had no knowledge, and so on, like dripping water which seemed to make a louder and more unbearable noise by sheer repetition.

"There are three things a man must do alone," Walker said, "Be born, die, and testify."

The contest was uneven even though Seabury never raised his voice and Walker was brilliantly flamboyant. But as Walker himself once said, "If you must fight, never choose the quietest person in the saloon —the little fellow sitting in a corner minding his own business. The chances are he is the ex-welterweight champion of the world."

Governor Franklin D. Roosevelt was not unmindful of the co-juncture of official duty and political opportunism. Rumors from authentic sources indicated that he would remove the Mayor from his post. Walker resigned. Worse still—since Seabury's relentlessness might have resulted in criminal action, Walker exiled himself by leaving for London with Betty Compton, his last gesture of defiance, loyalty, and love.

Ironically, the Democratic convention for the selection of a nominee to succeed Walker was taking place. Powerful political leaders pleaded with Walker to head home at once, saying that he could be nominated and elected. Like Mayor Curley of Boston, he probably could. But Jimmy did not wish vindication. He was pleased to be rid of responsibilities, which constricted his life, interfered with his pleasures, unless the public was ready to enjoy them vicariously. Reformers had made this impossible. The price of the spotlight he loved had become too high because it followed him even when he sought the darkness of privacy.

Much later, I was taking an annual European trip with my friend Jack Alicoate, the publisher of a motion picture trade magazine called *Film Daily*, and we decided to visit Walker, who was living in Dorking, a suburb of London. We were astonished to find him, Betty, and her mother in a typical country squire's home, with thatched roof, rose garden, hedges, and gravel road leading to the fenced-in grounds. Walker was wearing an English tweed jacket with leather elbow patches (I have never understood this style. Do English gentlemen lean more on their elbows than others—doing what, playing chess, drinking, or thinking?). Jimmy was delighted to see us. His exile must have been particularly painful because of the contrast between his former turbulent life and the quiet countryside. Our presence made the memories of New York more real. He grasped my hands with fervor. For a moment, I thought I saw his eyes glisten with a tear. But instantly, they changed into that familiar laughing twinkle, while his face remained solemn, and he advised us that soon the vicar was to arrive and we would all have tea and crumpets. Jimmy Walker, the vicar, and tea and crumpets! He enjoyed our chuckles. Later, the vicar did come, and Walker acted the part of a well-bred English gentleman as if he were to the manor born. And he did so delightfully, without making fun even subtly, but causing everyone to fall into the gentle mood of religious good will and warmth.

Alicoate and I urged him to come back to New York. He asked me in mock melodramatic voice whether the coast was clear. But he meant it. Friends had told him that he better let more time intervene, or he might face trouble (the euphemism for criminal indictment). He confided in me that he was broke and that he lived on the beneficence of Betty's mother, whose house it was. I believed him. I did not think he was merely refuting the stories of the million-dollar bag money he was supposed to have accumulated.

Later in October 1935, he did come back to New York. He was hailed affectionately by almost everyone. There was no talk of any retribution. Once more, he became the darling of the dais. He did not need the title of Mayor to give him status on the public platform.

He talked to me about earning a livelihood. It was obvious that the stories of his secret booty were a myth. He did not have a cent. He had done favors for friends, acquaintances, and strangers, but not for personal aggrandizement. They had profited. He and the city had lost. The city owed him no gratitude, and those who did had no interest in him at all.

He was a lawyer. Emissaries came to suggest that he be taken into my law office and that almost any salary would do. But he had never practiced law and the slurs on his name further disqualified him in a profession requiring supreme character as well as competence to match it. Charm never hurt a lawyer, but where it is the chief reliance, he better look for other weapons. Surely, it would have been more appropriate for Walker to be engaged in some corporate good will mission where his popularity could overbalance his shortcomings. But no such proposal came from any of the myriad of "friends" whom he had freely served at so high a cost to himself.

I wanted to be of help. There was the possibility of his obtaining a post as impartial arbitrator in the garment industry to determine disputes between employers and the union. I sent word to President Franklin D. Roosevelt of Walker's plight and the possible solution. He appealed to the president of the International Ladies' Garment Workers' Union, David Dubinsky, who complied with the request. Walker had a job at a salary of $25,000 a year.

It was Walker's idea that Roosevelt, of all people, would help him. Why? Because he had never criticized or attacked Roosevelt for his hostile conduct toward him. Indeed, he had spoken favorably about Roosevelt when he ran for President and thereafter. All this was due to Walker's philosophy, which he once expressed to me in this way. "The worst thing a politican can do is get acid in his blood. When he developes a hate for his enemies, it will ultimately destroy him, not them. One can never tell in diplomacy, politics, or for that matter other relationships, when yesterday's enemy must become tomorrow's ally.

"Look at Al Smith," he continued, "he got sore at Roosevelt, whom he considered his protégé, for not consulting him when he reached the top. He got acid in his blood. It made him come out for Landon when he ran against Roosevelt. He didn't hurt Roosevelt. He destroyed himself. Al never had any influence after that, and he died a bitter man.

"I never bore a grudge against Roosevelt despite what he did to me. After all, what else could he do under the circumstances? Ruin his career by standing up for me? Roosevelt's friends have told me how he appreciates my attitude and is sorry that things worked out as they did —and that he is very fond of me."

I never forgot his "acid in the blood" philosophy and I have seen its truth demonstrated time and again; John Lewis, the powerful labor leader, condemned his benefactor, Roosevelt, and lost his unique hold on the labor movement; or farther back, Teddy Roosevelt was so galled by his protégé President Taft that he formed the Bull Moose Party and ran on a third ticket, thereby preventing Taft's re-election and squeezing in Woodrow Wilson as President. But also thereby ending his own career. Taft wasn't destroyed. He went on to be Chief Justice of the Supreme Court of the United States.

In less portentous situations, the same principle holds true. Wives or husbands who get "acid in their blood" in divorce preceedings pay a price in ulceration and nervous exhaustion. The tragedy of a broken marriage is thus elongated, so that later their visits with their children at graduation, marriage, and the event of grandchildren become hateful confrontations, the only amelioration of which is avoidance. Without "acid in the blood," time heals the wound, and pleasant memories of early love make it possible to share the joy of its consequences.

I have urged husbands to make property settlements on their wives in settlement of the matrimonial controversy even where courts have no power to do so, because, aside from tax and other advantages, such a gesture of affording security to the wife pours balm upon exacerbated feelings and prevents the acidulous grudge. If a doctor or psychiatrist could measure the injury to health from a protracted contest which is filled with frustration and hatred against the money differences which separate the disputants, he would find that the cost in health (and ultimately the doctor's bill) often outweighs the money over which the quarrel persists. Indeed, there is such a medical condition as a litigation neurosis, which manifests itself in all sorts of nervous disorders or other malfunctioning, and disappears the moment the litigation is ended. I once tried a case for a woman whose hand was convulsed into a "clutching hand" by an injury. Foremost specialists for both sides examined her and pronounced her condition permanent. They agreed it was not a form of hysteria. Nevertheless, the moment the suit was settled, her tendons relaxed and her hand opened up. She and her doctors were as surprised as we were. Mysterious forces which had responded to her deep anxiety about the outcome of the suit had similarly unlocked her hand when she derived inner peace from the end of the litigation. We suspect the result would have been as Lourdes-like even if she had lost the suit but knew it was over.

In other types of litigation, the same phenomenon can be observed. After a controversy has been decided, the contestants prosper physically. They sleep better, eat better, and recapture their perspective and balance.

Time and again, women who refuse to give their husbands a divorce, which would only free him to marry the proverbial blonde, have insisted that they are not condemning themselves to permanent spinsterhood. "You may be sure," they say, "that as soon as I meet someone I can fall in love with, I'll grant the divorce and reconstruct my life." But curiously, they rarely fall in love, while psychologically they consider themselves bound to their straying husbands. However, when they yield to advice not to have "acid in their blood" against their husbands, but think of themselves and end a meaningless marriage, they frequently marry shortly thereafter. In the same mysterious way, their emotions which have clutched tight open up, when the anxiety and frustration of a legal holding operation is ended.

One day, I invited Walker and Betty Compton to my home. On announcing to my wife, Mildred, at the last moment, as was my inconsiderate custom, whom we would have for guests that evening, she expressed her dissatisfaction, although, unlike the Russians, she never exercised a veto. It wasn't the belated notification which bothered her. Long experience had inured her to this injustice and the maids were always ready with extra plates and would have been stunned by reasonable notice. No, it was that Mildred didn't care for the Mayor. She had never been impressed with celebrities as such and she said some plain words about his frailties as a public official.

It was an interesting test of Walker's prowess with people. Within five minutes after he arrived, not only Mildred, but Alberta and Nora, the cook and maid, the doorman, the elevator man were completely charmed by him. Here he was no platform personality.

His affectations which were so effective had become second nature to him, and therefore appeared to be natural. Thus, he salvaged their charm and yet eliminated the irritation of their artificiality. He could posture and be sincere, all at the same time. He was chummy with the help without the slightest condescension, and he was respectful to his equals or superiors without pretended servility. And when, as the evening warmed up, he sat down at the piano, and played and sang his own well-known composition, "Will You Love Me in December as You Did in May," everyone melted.

Throughout all this Betty sat silently, like a beautiful poster of a composite show-girl beauty, unemotional and uninvolved almost to the point of aloofness. She did not, like other women, fawn over Walker, or reflect the glow he gave out. Her manner was almost a challenge to him, unintended, I am sure, that he better do something more if he wanted her adulation. Some men are intrigued by such resistance. Bobo Rockefeller, in the marital strife with her husband, revealed that when she first met him, he asked her, a coal miner's daughter, for a date, she refused. Aside from her beauty, which had won a prize, and her other qualities, it was the beginning of his pursuit.

Jimmy's dissipation in his early years invaded the later period of his good habits. He gave up drinking because of his ulcers. "Just when a man can afford a steak, his doctors put him on a milk diet," he said. Arthritis plagued him. His frail body became even more boyishly thin, but his posture and hesitant walk gave away his age.

He took sun lamp treatments every day to hide his sallowness. When I saw his ruddy face and commented on how well he looked, he replied, "I am like an old house that is painted on the outside, but the plumbing is no good."

I introduced him at the last public dinner he ever addressed. It was a function to aid a charitable cause, and the guest of honor was Ben Sherman, of the A.B.C. Company, which owned the candy machines installed in theaters and elsewhere. So, still responding to the loyalty one owed to a friend, the first commandment in Walker's decalogue, he got out of a sickbed against doctor's orders, to confer his unique luminosity on the occasion. He had been told, and rightly enough, that his presence would "make the dinner."

The poor man was in pain, which at times doubled him up. The audience appreciated his being there. They sensed the sacrifice he had made. When he was introduced, he received a standing ovation that seemed endless. Perhaps they intuitively realized that it was the last time he would hear applause. Men and women cheered and some cried as they did so.

He was tremendously moved, but in characteristic fashion, he hid his embarrassment with wit. When the pandemonium, which had several lives, rising to a new crescendo each time it seemed to have subsided, finally yielded to his finger-to-the-lips gesture for silence, he began for the tenth time, "Ladies and gentlemen." There was a hush. There he stood bent over from arthritis, but his head jaunty and his eyes looking sideways mischievously. It was signal enough, like a comedian's funny hat, that he was not going to respond emotionally. But what he said surprised everyone:

"You will forgive me for being bent over this way. [long pause] After all, why should I at this late stage of my life start going straight!"

The explosion of merriment turned into another ovation, to assure him that they believed in him and loved him.

A few weeks later he was dead.

ONE WHO BRAGS THAT HE IS A SELF-MADE MAN RELIEVES GOD OF AN AWFUL RESPONSIBILITY

The pendulum swings. The Mayor who succeeded Walker was Fiorello H. LaGuardia.* Democracy is not a perfect system, but it is a self-correcting one. It is the forerunner of the computer which miraculously detects that one of its parts is not functioning, announces the fact, and sometimes corrects the defect. Where the pendulum is fixed, as in a dictatorship, there can be no swing to reform, only to force and revolution.

How could the people have reversed themselves more completely than in choosing LaGuardia? In every way, he was the antithesis of his predecessor.

He was chubby, tending toward the roly-poly type. He was so small that Napoleon could have seen the top of his head. Like other ungainly men (Heywood Broun and Thomas Wolfe, for example), he made a fetish of being careless about his clothes, which were baggy and ill-fitting.

He had a thin, shrill voice, which reached shriek proportions when he was excited, and that was almost always. His chunky head squatted necklessly on his shoulders. He was swarthy, and his eyes blazed with blackness. Instead of poise, he had fury.

His most outstanding characteristic was the way he spoke. His mouth would open wide and one could see his tongue forming the words. The impression was that his mouth was filled with tongue. It gave him an unusual accent. It was not Italian. It could not be identified, except that it was LaGuardian or tonguish. There is a psychological reason for speech mannerisms. Usually, as in his case, it is to hide an accent. Boris Morros, the Russian composer of "The Wooden Soldiers," who later

* The unfulfilled term left by Walker was filled in by Joseph McKee and John O'Brien.

became head of the music department of Paramount Pictures, tried to disguise his accent by whispering. Only when he spoke so softly that he became inaudible did he succeed. The tongue has more muscles than any other part of the body, but early training is not easy to overcome. Some speak dialect with an accent. The French and English are proud of their accents and make a special effort to preserve them. If the word charm is ever applied to Italian and Jewish accents, perhaps they too will struggle not to eliminate them.

LaGuardia's squeezed high pitch and labored pronunciation made him instantly identifiable. He recognized early the power of radio and whenever he appeared there could be no doubt who was uttering the words.

He had come up the hard way, courageous flier in World War I, interpreter at Ellis Island, and Republican congressman in a Democratic district. His restlessness spilled over party lines. He had frequently changed political parties, at one time running as a Socialist. Appropriately enough, he wound up combining all on a fusion ticket.

Having no funds and no political support from the leaders who detested him, because he railed against them, he practiced all the arts of showmanship to attract attention. Although he had enormous ability and a piercing intellectual mind, he was not above demagoguery. He believed in F.D.R.'s political primer, "First, you must get elected. Then you can carry out your idealistic program. A candidate who sticks to his principles even though they defeat him at the polls has betrayed his own mission and his opportunity to serve the people." Political death, like other death, is permanent silence. What good is it to the community to be defeated if you have something good to give it? When Roosevelt was accused of having clay feet, he chuckled. It was not an insult. He deliberately maneuvered politically to be in power.

LaGuardia once said to me during a hot campaign, "Louis, if they try demagoguery, I'll out-demagogue all of them." He could, too.

As a congressman opposing the Volstead Act, he stood on the steps of the Capitol eating grapes, and announced that they would ferment and produce alcohol in his stomach, and he defied the law enforcers to prevent the process. The newsreels (the forerunner of television news) asked him to repeat the performance. So did the newspaper photographers. He ate bunches of grapes for all of them.

On another occasion, he conceived a way to dramatize the high cost of living. He brought a chunk of raw steak into Congress, slapped it on his desk, and announced the price. Again, he drew national attention.

He ran for Congress against a Jewish opponent in a predominantly Jewish neighborhood. As the last week of the desperate campaign arrived, a mysterious handbill appeared, charging that LaGuardia was anti-Semitic. His answer was characteristically unique. He hired a hall and challenged his opponent to appear for a debate. There was only one condition. Both must talk Yiddish. His Jewish adversary couldn't, and failed to show up. LaGuardia, gifted in five languages (and drawing on his Ellis Island experience), addressed his audience in Yiddish and won the election.

It was the era of stunts. The law produced its own practitioner. William Fallon, the criminal lawyer, defended a husband accused of poisoning his wife. A vial of poison in his valise, identical to the poison in her body, was the prosecution's prize exhibit. In summation, Fallon, timing his conclusion to precede the lunch recess, charged that the vial did not contain poison at all, and that the prosecutor had engaged in an outrageous hoax. To prove his point, he picked up the exhibit, which experts had testified was deadly, withdrew the cork, and slowly swallowed its contents, while everyone looked on in horror. He sat down smiling. The Judge was barely able to rap his gavel for recess. Fallon walked out into a nearby empty courtroom where doctors were waiting to pump his stomach, which had been readied previously with special oils for the poisonous invasion. The jury acquitted Fallon's client.

Of course, public relations representatives considered stunts especially suited to their talents. Harry Reichenbach was the acknowledged master in this field. His thick gray hair and hard-lined face gave him a magician's looks, but did not reveal his pixie imagination. Some of his ingenious schemes became legendary guides for his profession. But when reaction set in against his unscrupulous devices, and laws were passed making their repetition a crime, his career ended and with it the stunt era.

One of Reichenbach's exploits was to publicize a visiting Hindu princess by leaving her clothes on the edge of a lake and announcing her disappearance. The authorities dragged the lake for the body. The public followed the tragedy of the missing princess in daily newspaper stories until she suddenly turned up well and hearty, explaining lamely that she had gone for a swim and had returned in a robe leaving her old clothes behind. An ordinance was enacted making it a crime to cause the city huge search expenses through deceptive publicity schemes.

Reichenbach similarly obtained free front page notice for a circus which was coming into town, by ordering two hundred pounds of raw meat to be sent to a suite in a leading hotel, registered in the name of T. R. Zann. When the manager investigated, he discovered that a lion had been smuggled into the hotel in a huge trunk. Of course, dispossess proceedings were instituted but not without the piquancy of the story drawing laughter and reams of newspaper space for Reichenbach's client.

Twice I had to tangle with him legally, once, when he was employed to publicize a motion picture called *The Great Gabbo,* a ventriloquist theme, with Erich von Stroheim. He conceived the idea of a huge sign at Forty-fifth and Broadway, on which scantily clad girls would cling to the iron bars and wave their legs in Roxyette fashion at the gaping crowds below. The live sign stopped traffic at Times Square. The city declared it a nuisance and ordered it to be abandoned. I advised compliance. Reichenbach was in a fury. He insisted that I bring an injunction proceeding against the municipal authorities. "Of course, you will lose," he comforted me, "but we'll get the darnedest front page story you ever saw, and everyone will be talking about *The Great Gabbo.* I told him that the law directs the publicity department and not vice versa, and warned the president of the company, Harry Thomas, that Reichenbach might lead him to jail as well as to higher receipts.

On another occasion, Reichenbach was miffed at William Fox, the motion picture tycoon for not rewarding him adequately for his services. He decided to demonstrate his powers in reverse. He spread the rumor that a new Fox theater was built on sand, and might collapse if too many patrons attended. If a plague had been announced in the environs, the theater could not have been more shunned. I forced Reichenbach to retract the falsehood, and with the aid of Building Department announcements restored attendance. But Reichenbach amused his friends by estimating the cost Fox had incurred, which exceeded the amount in dispute between them many times over.

Perhaps the most original stunt Reichenbach ever pulled resulted from sheer pride in his resourcefulness. He made a bet with an incredulous friend that he could elevate any ordinary girl to a $2,000-a-week booking at the Palace Theater in New York City, the very summit of vaudeville achievement and the dream of every vaudeville entertainer who ever set foot on a stage. To win the bet, he employed accomplices. He had the famous Dolly Sisters drive through the Garment District on the Lower East Side of New York. While halted in a narrow slum street by a flat tire, they heard a nightingale voice floating from a window of a factory. It was of such extraordinary beauty that even the annoyance of the car's breakdown could not deter them from climbing the rickety wooden stairs of a decrepit building to find that the incredible tones were emanating from a dark young girl twisting cloth in all directions under, appropriately enough, a Singer sewing machine. They hurried the bewildered genius into their Rolls-Royce, and ensconsed her in a magnificent suite at the Pierre Hotel, where, as fate would have it, the story broke in the next day's newspapers. The background material was not very backward. Co-workers asserted that they had been lulled into heavenly trances by the girl's tones. Never in musical history had such a natural talent been hidden from the world for so long. The question was whether the Metropolitan Opera House could capture this phenomenal voice whose pristine beauty ought not be despoiled by formal training.

The publicity was nationwide. Reichenbach's agents saw to it that the Palace Theater would have the first opportunity to let the public hear the miracle of the golden throat. Of course, tryout was out of the question. Would anyone insult Tetrazzini or Caruso by suggesting an audition before a vaudeville house booker? She was engaged at several thousand dollars a week for an extended engagement. If one had judged by the thousands who stormed the box office at the first performance, she still would be singing there. But the sewing girl reaped as Reichenbach had sown, and she was pulled off the bill the second day. All but Reichenbach, who collected his bet, were indignant, although on reflection a few were amused by his ingenuity and their own gullibility.

Reichenbach's devilish talents played a part in Jimmy Walker's successful first campaign against LaGuardia. During most of the contest, Walker never mentioned his opponent's name. This is an ancient tactic followed by candidates who are decisively favored to win. Why publicize their opponent? It is always the underdog who demands face-to-face debate. Television has put more pressure on reluctant debaters. Programmers find confrontation between opponents exciting and, therefore, offer free time. In view of the effectiveness and high cost of political advertising on this medium, rejection of such offers gives strong hint of fear to face an opponent. And, of course, the adversary exploits this inference and makes the matter a political issue in itself. So it was that after the Nixon-Kennedy debates, which were generally credited with Kennedy's narrow victory, Nixon refused to debate Hubert Humphrey, and the latter charged his opponent with violation of the democratic principle of open discussion of the issues.

However, LaGuardia's taunts and sarcastic effectiveness got under Walker's skin. He told his advisers he was going to take on LaGuardia and give him what he deserved. All the political pros warned him against it. "He hasn't reached the public, but he seems to have reached you," they said. "Just ignore him. He hasn't got a chance."

Walker would not listen. It was not merely his honesty and ability that were being impugned. He might have stood for that. He was being pilloried with wisecracks. That was his game. He would fix the little so-and-so.

Unable to restrain him, Harry Reichenbach, Jimmy's public relations adviser, made a deal with him. "If you must reply, will you let me guide you how?" Walker was relieved to be unleashed, and consented.

"When you have finished your speech on schools tonight, as usual without mentioning his name, announce that you have a question to ask Fiorello H. LaGuardia, 'Why did he leave Bridgeport in 1915?'"

WALKER: "What have you got on him? Why did he leave Bridgeport?"

REICHENBACH: "Nothing. Just do as I tell you."

Walker did. Reporters excitedly rushed to LaGuardia. At last the Mayor had acknowledged his existence. Now the campaign would come to life. LaGuardia contemptuously swept the question aside. "I don't remember ever being in Bridgeport. What has this got to do with the issues? The Mayor better address himself to the terrible conditions in the city. That's what the people are troubled by."

The next night Walker, prompted by his gray-haired Iago, had the following peroration to his speech.

"Yesterday, I asked Mr. LaGuardia a simple question. 'Why did he leave Bridgeport in 1915?' His answer was he didn't remember ever being there. Now my opponent has demonstrated a remarkable memory for all sort of fact and statistics about the city's affairs. But on the subject of my question, he doesn't remember. I think we are deserving of more forthrightness from a reform candidate. I repeat my question: 'Why did Fiorello H. LaGuardia leave Bridgeport in 1915?'"

Now LaGuardia's voice was two octaves higher. He bounced as he screamed that the Mayor was trying to engage in red herring tactics instead of discussing the terrible conditions in the city. "This is all nonsense. I had no reason to leave Bridgeport or any other city. If Jimmy Walker knows any let him state it, instead of engaging in dishonest insinuations. I'll match my record of honesty with him or any other Tammany politician. This is no game. Let's talk sense. Let's discuss the issues. I challenge him to a face-to-face debate."

WALKER: "At first, he didn't remember being in Bridgeport. Now he admits he was there but doesn't remember any reason for leaving. I think it is time Fiorello H. LaGuardia came clean with the people of this great city. No more evasions, Mr. LaGuardia. I still have had no answer to my question, 'Why did you leave Bridgeport in 1915?'"

So it continued. LaGuardia was driven to distraction, the people were amused, Reichenbach laughed, and Walker was elected.

When LaGuardia ran for mayor again on a fusion ticket, he asked me and four others to act as his kitchen cabinet. I agreed. His headquarters were in the Paramount Building, where I had my law office. He would dash into my office unannounced and unmindful of other activities, and throw himself on a couch, bouncing once or twice, thus contradicting his claimed exhaustion (I never saw him tired or subdued). Then he would talk out loud about the next speech he had to make or the proper tactic to use in meeting the usual hourly crises of a political campaign.

What I suggested had to be interlaced with his continuing diatribe in which he rejected, modified, or accepted the proffered idea, as if he were just talking out loud to himself all the time. He was either too proud to accept advice, or it was part of his volatility to absorb outside voices into his thinking process without the usual station stops to listen and acknowledge that a dialogue was taking place.

He won the election. I had arranged for him to appear first at The Motion Picture Club, since our Entertainment Division for LaGuardia had rendered yeoman service for him. We went to the Bond Building, where the club was situated. It was a very cold night. All but the new Mayor wore winter coats. He traveled in his suit. It was not bravado. His wife, Marie, confided in me that he had no coat. A few of us chipped in and the next day she presented him with an overcoat. It was a symbol of his penniless condition. That was the way he left the office. He was fanatically scrupulous about money. There could be no Seabury investigation of *his* regime.

There was such a crush at The Motion Picture Club that he disappeared in the crowd and had to be rescued by two burly police captains who had already been assigned to him. But his dramatic ingenuity made him one of the most visible public officials this country ever had.

He brought to his mayoral task a feverish dedication to city business. Aside from being a good administrator and delegating duties to others, he strove to be a one-man army. He was everywhere. When fire engines sirened their way down the streets, he was speeding after them in the fire chief's car, making a clanging racket greater than theirs. Newsreels delighted in shots of him, in a black raincoat, water from the hoses pouring down on him, while he peered up from under a fire hat many sizes too large for his head.

If a murder occurred, there he was with the inspector of police, giving directions.

Suddenly, he would appear at eight-thirty in the morning in one of the magistrates' courts, and, finding no judge there at the opening hour, he would exercise his right as Mayor to sit as magistrate, dispose of cases in his unique way, threatening "a tinhorn gambler," bawling out "a punk," appealing to an alcoholic and sending him to a rehabilitation center while inviting the wife and children to come to see him at City Hall. Finally, when the magistrate arrived a half hour late and found to his surprise that court was functioning, LaGuardia would publicly admonish him that he owed a full day's work for the city's pay, and if the unfortunates and the police could be there on time, so could he.

No department was safe from such flying visits. He set a personal example of conscientious service, stimulating, driving, threatening, imploring, and generally raising hell, because the people were entitled to be served. The city was too large for such physical personal direction, but he stormed to his task as if by his own energy he would do the job tens of thousands were assigned to do. He was King Canute standing at the foot of the ocean sweeping back the waves of inefficiency and neglect, and by sheer dint of a furious broom keeping a little of the water from flowing too high on the sand.

But he also understood the importance of obtaining the foremost experts to man the departments. He scorned selections from political ranks, and often went out of the city to bring in a competent executive.

It was interesting to watch him lure a specialist into city service at reduced salary. Suddenly, his imperious manner was gone. Butter would melt in his mouth. He flattered. He cajoled. He subtly held forth promise of national recognition—and perhaps a cabinet post. He appealed to the ideals of the reluctant expert. Didn't he want to demonstrate his theories in real life rather than in a classroom or in a book and do something for the suffering people? If he came from another city, didn't he want to apply his unique talents in the biggest arena of all? He suggested that the acceptance would be heralded across the nation as a breakthrough in city management, and precipitously called in his secretaries to have the newsreels and newspapers alerted for a special announcement. He told the now wavering executive that he would be his personal confidant, and at the center of a great new experiment in civic reform. He offered cigars (for a new baby was coming into the administration); he brought in coffee and personally poured it like a solicitous hostess and inquired how much cream and how many lumps; he had a city car (of whose use he was most sparing) to be at the beck and call of the soon-to-be Commissioner. He was jovial, earnest, respectful, and even sycophantic (the most difficult of all roles for him) until he got his man. I doubt that any woman could have resisted such consummate wooing.

In this way, he induced Professor Russell Forbes, who taught at New York University, and had written a book on municipal purchasing, to become the head of the City Purchasing Department, and he imported Health Commissioner John L. Rice, Correction Commissioner A. M. McCormick, as well as Park Commissioner Robert Moses, the most redoubtable builder of them all. Had the law, which forbids raiding of corporate executives, been applicable to him, he could have been subject to wholesale suits.

But when the conquest had been achieved and the stunned victim had been personally ushered out with an intimate shoulder hug, he astonished those present by a lightning reversal. His easy, gracious tempo of but a moment before became a bouncing fury of action, as if a picture in slow motion had been turned into high speed. His dulcet ingratiating tones disappeared, and one heard the shriek of a football coach on the sidelines commanding his players to perform beyond their capacity. He was rude to any show of slowness or incompetence, and he didn't give a damn about hurt feelings. I heard him humiliate a high police official, who had brought him a sandwich to gobble, because the dressing was wrong and he did not even know how to fulfill such a simple order correctly.

Yes, his personal force and leadership verged on the dictator complex. Mussolini had once been a Socialist and reformer, but found his boundless energy too strong for subservience to democratic processes. Lenin, Castro, and other revolutionaries also had programs to free the people from oppression, and wound up enslaving them so that they would not resist the good medicine *they* prescribed. The path of idealistic movements often continues right on to a police state, without a detour.

Perhaps I do him an injustice, for it is only a psychological reading, but, given other circumstances, I can imagine LaGuardia, honest and devoted to high ideals, believing that he could do better if unrestrained by a system of checks and balances. He had the impatience of a strong leader.

This is a constantly recurring phenomenon. The weak executive lives under the shadow of the legislative and judicial branches. The strong executive chafes at the restraints and delays they impose. The people are protected in both instances by checks and balances. Democracy rejects the notion of the elite, not because it may not produce brilliant results, but because there is no assurance of its constancy or that with all good intention it won't abuse its power. We prefer less spectacular achievement with the guarantee that the people will determine their own fate. Still our constitutional structure permits the Chief Executive to be strong. Indeed, there are very few leaders in the world who have the powers of our President. But power tends to be absolute and this we never permit.

I am partly led to the surmise of LaGuardia's propensity for personalized government by an incident which ought not to be taken literally because he was not above playing games to achieve results. He didn't float balloons. He pushed them up like kites, and he knew that kites rise only against the wind.

"The March of Time" was a popular motion picture documentary which treated with personalities and issues very much like the special documentary on television does today. It chose LaGuardia for one of its subjects. It was a compilation of newsreel shots of his varied roles, combined with personal interviews with him and others about him.

It showed the full dimension of the man. It jumped from the comic and colorful to his genius for serious administration. There he was, the midget fireman, or cutting Tammany leaders to shreds with his sharp tongue (fully visible as always), the futile replies of the politicos (if they were dignified, they lacked manliness in the face of his tirade; if they were angry, their bad English betrayed them and caused laughter); and then scenes of him closeted for a full week with sheafs of documents higher than he was, working on the city budget, his sleeves rolled up, his shirt collar open and dirty, and his hair disheveled (he dramatized the event as a personal ordeal), looking up sleepily and telling the interviewer, that he was determined to take the fat out of each department, to relieve a long suffering public. Then he was shown addressing a large group of the nation's accountants at the Bar Association Building in New York, and without a note reeling off dozens of figures of the city's budget, funding, interest, bond, and other complex financial plans, with such profound grasp of their complexity that the conservative audience of professional men stood and cheered the tour de force they had just witnessed. All in all, the film was a fascinating document. It was booked into the Radio City Music Hall.

The only trouble was that election time was approaching. Tammany Hall, which was supporting William O'Dwyer, was horrified by this special pleading for the opposition. It felt that the reel was a campaign document and that it was unfair to project it at that time. "Show it after election," they urged, "but not now, or else equalize the situation by showing a Democratic document we'll supply." Great pressure was put on the Music Hall to discontinue the showing of the film. At the end of the week, and before the feature picture had completed its run, the "March of Time" reel was taken off the program.

The next day, I got one of the panic calls from LaGuardia. They were never less than extremely urgent. The fact that he wanted to discuss something immediately elevated it to an emergency.

When I arrived at City Hall, he did not greet me. His first words were, "Louis, who is Leo Spitz?" I was taken back at the inquiry. "Why, he is president of R.K.O. Pictures," I replied, searching his face for the significance of the question.

"He is a gangster!" he yelled. "He is a Chicago gangster!"

"Oh, come now, Fiorello, Spitz is no gangster. He is a distinguished Chicago lawyer, who became president of the R.K.O. motion picture company. I know him well. He is a fine man. What is this all about?"

"He is a member of a Chicago gang. He is a mobster!" His fist banged so heavily on the desk everything on it bounced. Then he leaned over as if he was going to let me in on an important confidence.

"R.K.O is distributing 'The March of Time' subject about me. The crooks in this city have gotten the Music Hall to take it off the screen. The gangs know how to go about these things. They got to their Chicago bums and Spitz pulled the picture. Now, I tell you what I want you to do. You go to Leo Spitz and tell him they have thirty-eight R.K.O. theaters in this city. They are full of violations, fire violations, building violations, sanitation violations. They are rat traps. Tomorrow morning, the inspectors of these departments are going to serve notice of violations on every single one of them. I am going to close them up! Now you tell Leo Spitz that he better retain you to keep those theaters open, and that he authorize the putting back of the 'March of Time' into the Music Hall. And what's more, I want that 'March of Time' to play in the R.K.O. circuit and all the other circuits in this city!"

He paused breathlessly. I leaned back and smiled. "I am not going to threaten Spitz with violations of his theaters. Of course, I am not going to ask him to retain me. Furthermore, Fiorello, if I said I was going to do all these things and started out of this room, you would stop me. You know better. You're just sore and you are letting off steam. I will find out the facts. I'll get them from Spitz himself."

I went to see Spitz and in a friendly way inquired about the matter. He confided in me that Tammany Hall was so aggrieved at the partisan stunt, as they called it, that they threatened through various building and other departments they still controlled to take it out on R.K.O.'s theaters by filing wholesale violations. I did not dare tell him where I had heard of this idea before. A compromise was ultimately effected whereby those theaters which were friendly to LaGuardia would play the reel if they wished to do so, and those which didn't could abstain.

LaGuardia's skill in dramatizing events knew no bounds. He was as resourceful in publicizing himself and his program as he was devoted to making the city the finest in the country. When there was a delivery strike of newspapers he decided that the children would miss the Sunday comics and he would read them to the tots (and, as if he didn't know, to their parents) over the radio. The resulting newsreel shot of this effort became a classic and was shown throughout the country. It depicted him in a white shirt, horn-rimmed eyeglasses perched on the tip of his nose, describing the panels of the cartoons and reading the balloons with such intensity that even the elders were frightened by the goings on. When the picture had the words "crash!," "bang!," LaGuardia shrieked these words hysterically while his open hand smashed the table, knocking over the microphone and causing more "crashes" and "bangs" than the cartoonist had planned. When the villainous animal approached the young boy stealthily, LaGuardia hunched over, almost shrinking to cartoon size, and in breathless hushes frightened the hell out of the kids as no professional actor could have done.

Suddenly, when his pantomime and portrayal of a hundred moods had ended, he straightened up, took off his glasses, and, looking emotionally into the camera, sermonized in as measured and low a tone as he could muster, "And what does all this prove, my dear children? It proves that those who do wrong are punished and end up unhappy, but that if you live an honest and good life, you will be rewarded." He had turned a cartoon entertainment into a Sunday school lecture. He was John Barrymore, the Big Bad Wolf, and Billy Sunday all rolled into one.

On another occasion, he was faced with a serious crisis. The Nazis had booked Madison Square Garden for a rally. They had applied, as was necessary, for a license from the city to hold the meeting. When word got out of the impending fifth-column gathering, a storm of protest broke over the city. The general hatred and contempt for the Nazis was heightened by the presence of so many Jews and Catholics, who were their special victims. The rally was a provocative challenge to the sensibilities of almost all the people. Yet, a great division of opinion existed as to whether the meeting should be barred. Foremost liberals and anti-Nazi leaders asserted that in a democracy the gathering, no matter how despised, should be permitted.

LaGuardia called me. This time his urgency was real. I skipped lunch and rushed down.

"What do you think," he asked, "should I refuse the license?"

"Yes," I replied.

Before I could say another word, he rose from his desk in a fury, pranced up and down the room in a hopping movement and screamed, "How can you, a liberal, say such a thing? Suppose the next week the Republicans or Socialists want to hold a meeting, can the Democrats stop them? Must I refuse a license to the Catholics because the Protestants don't like their meeting?" It reminded me of the Goldwynism "For your information, I will ask you a question."

I let him expend himself for a while and when the purple receded from his cheeks, I interrupted, "Did you call me down to abuse me or ask my opinion? If you will be good enough to listen, I will tell you my reasons."

He looked at me disdainfully and sat down.

"You have two reasons to reject the license. The first is clear and simple. The second is a philosophical reason which you probably won't accept and I won't blame you. It is strictly a minority view."

"Go ahead, what are they?" he said with a gesture, as if he were granting me permission to speak when I deserved to be dismissed.

"The first reason is that a Nazi meeting in the heart of New York is likely to stir a riot and bloodshed. It presents a clear danger of a nuisance. There are many legal decisions which give a city the right to prevent a provocative act which is likely to cause disorder. No clearer case than a paramilitary meeting of Nazis, in the midst of a populace that is feverishly opposed to them, can be given to bring the preventive riot rule into effect."

I took advantage of his reflective silence and continued.

"The second reason is that we liberals have misconstrued the liberal credo. Voltair's 'I disapprove of what you say, but I will defend to the death your right to say it' is sound but can't be universally applied. It has misled us at times into martyrizing the finest among us. That precept is true for all those with whom we disagree, but who would give us the same right to be heard, if they were in power. But when the Communist and Nazi program, which you can buy for ten cents, asserts that if they ever win, they will kill or imprison all 'counterrevolutionaries,' their phrase for minority dissidents, then the battle is uneven. Ultimately, we must die. For we may win a thousand times and protect their right to oppose us. But if we lose once, they will destroy us.

"Look at Germany. The liberal democratic government threw police cordons around Hitler's gatherings to protect his right to rant. When he won, he killed them all.

"Every philosophy must have the seed of survival in it. If it leads to its own destruction, then it doesn't deserve to survive."

"What happens to the Bill of Rights?" he said quietly.

"I contend that legally the right to assemble has one inherent exception. It is not granted to those who themselves proclaim that they won't grant you the right to assemble."

"And you would say the same for the right of free speech?" He didn't look up.

"Yes," I said. "The right of free speech is guaranteed to anyone, no matter how detestable his views, unless he tells you himself that if he ever succeeds in being in power, he will deny it to you. There are recognized exceptions to the right of free speech too, you know. You can't yell fire in a theater, or run a sound truck in the middle of the night, or libel someone. I know you won't agree with this," I hastened to add. "It is a radical departure from the traditional view, but I have thought this through. More accurately, Fiorello, I have felt it through. Whenever my mind tells me what I must do but my heart aches, I re-examine the proposition. There must be something wrong with it. I would be mortified to have to insist that the Nazi Bund, which has been conducting military drills in our suburbs for months, should be permitted to meet at Madison Square Garden and spew their evil in our midst. I don't think democratic principle requires it. And even if I am a minority of one on this among liberals, that is my opinion. However, you don't have to struggle with so contentious a proposition. You can refuse the license on the first ground. You ought to do so."

For the last few minutes of my "speech," he seemed inattentive and lost in reverie. As if he had concluded his own thinking process simultaneously with my conclusion, he said, "No, I am not going to do that. I have another idea."

Knowing his propensity for startling dramatics, I expected a surprise. But I never anticipated one so unique that it would appear on the front pages of newspapers all over the world.

LaGuardia called in the Commissioner of Police and asked how many Jewish police officers and patrolmen there were on the force. Since the Jewish members of the police force have a social benevolent society called The Shomrim (Watchmen), it was not difficult to provide the answer. There were hundreds, including inspectors and captains. A huge number of police would be necessary outside and inside Madison Square Garden. LaGuardia granted the license, but ordered that only Jewish officers and patrolmen should guard and protect the Nazi meeting!

So it came about that protest marchers all over the city were kept in order by Jewish police. Mobs outside the Garden were fenced off by Jewish police. And dozens of Jewish police stood stiffly on guard inside the huge arena, in the midst of Nazi uniformed troops marching to the platform, while the "Horst Wessel Song" blared hoarsely from loudspeakers. (Why is it that Nazi speeches or songs always had an eerie animalistic hoarse sound?) Swastika flags draped the boxes and hung under searchlights from the rafters, and speakers, interrupted by "Heil Hitlers" and thousands of stiff arms pointing upward, like flesh bayonets, harangued the audience with adulation for "The Fuehrer," which would have been too lavish for God himself.

LaGuardia's solution for the dilemma did not meet the principle involved head-on. But his ingenuity turned indignation into ridicule. It broke the tension. People laughed at the Nazis, and the photographs of Nazis protected by Jewish police appeared in hundreds of newspapers all over the world. They caused mirth or consternation depending on the reader's point of view.

LaGuardia's method of controlling crime was similarly inventive. He knew that the police knew who the leading criminals in the city were. They could not be jailed because it was difficult to prove their criminality "beyond a reasonable doubt." He decided that the best he could do was contain them. So he ordered the police to bring them to City Hall in small groups. Sullen chieftains of crime were brought before him. They summoned their attorneys and were ready to assert their constitutional rights not to speak. Also, they were confident nothing could be "pinned on them."

To their surprise, he told them just that. He had no proof against them. He was not going to ask them to say anything. But he had something to tell them.

"I know you bums and tinhorns are the heads of criminal gangs. As long as you stay below Fourteenth Street, we will not do anything to you, until we can prove what lice you are. But if a single one of you, or your lousy gang steps foot across Fourteenth Street, we're going to pull you in as vagrants. We'll keep you in jail until you can prove how you earn money to drive Cadillacs, have swell homes, molls, and the rest. Now, I've warned you! Stay behind your line. We'll get you anyhow. But if you show your face uptown, in the jug you go, immediately. Now get out of here!"

In this way, he kept the major criminals out of the business and lucrative districts of the city. A gang leader didn't even dare to go to the theater in Times Square. The police knew who they were and they were quarantined.

Similarly, he did not attempt to eliminate prostitution establishments. He regarded them as an inevitable evil, but he confined their number and territory. However, no ladies of the evening marched the streets. Unlike most reformers, he recognized the limitation of the cleansing process. He allowed for the impossibility of perfection and tried to protect the public in a realistic and reasonable way.

This rule of pragmatic compromise did not apply, however, to city employees. He pounced upon any policeman who took graft from prostitution or gambling houses or any building inspector who overlooked a violation.

He understood the temptation to which low-earning city employees were subjected. He didn't depend on moral lectures alone. He continuously shuffled the police force to prevent improper alliances which were made more likely by propinquity. He could not eliminate graft, but he reduced it to the lowest ebb in municipal history. The cynical doctrine that one must accept petty dishonesty in a bureaucracy was rejected by him with such vehemence that hands outstretched for a take, for the first time, trembled.

He developed a resourceful policy for dealing with the race problem in Harlem. While on the one hand he strove mightily to obtain funds from Washington and Albany to build new housing, give relief funds, and eliminate the squalor, starvation, boredom, and humiliation which existed there, this was a long-range program. On the other hand, he devised techniques to control crime and riots which were the immediate consequences of the festering conditions. He went to Harlem and formed co-operation committees of black ministers, writers, businessmen, athletes, stars, and other influential citizens. If anyone whose voice might count resisted, he would be subjected to the LaGuardia tear in the eye—bent knee—wringing-hand treatment, and he didn't have a chance. After all, it was true that the chief victims of disorder were black citizens and businesses. Aside from its preventive function when trouble started, LaGuardia and his squad of black leaders, using bullhorns, would drive through the streets appealing for order and directing the people to go to their homes. He augmented this strategy with the use of black police almost exclusively in black neighborhoods, and, in addition, gave strict orders to use weapons sparingly, if at all. It was the first experiment in compassion before arrest rather than in punishment. Because of extremists in later years, the fruits of this leniency have not been good, but in his day, it was a successful maneuver to keep the kettle from boiling over.

Whatever his views about approximating justice rather than insisting on its absoluteness, he was uncompromising in his personal standards.

He carried his crusade of honesty to extreme lengths. No matter how just the request or recommendation, if it was made by a friend, he rejected it. Only a stranger or enemy received consideration. When I was asked to submit the name of some very worthy candidate with a fine record, for a judgeship, I would refuse, saying that my recommendation would be fatal. I wonder if the sponsors believed my explanation or thought it was an evasion. Dr. Stephen S. Wise, the noted rabbi, and president of the American Jewish Congress, who was an ardent supporter of LaGuardia, as were Dr. John Haynes Holmes and other clergymen interested in a clean city administration, once said to me, "I don't know what's the matter with Fiorello. He will consider recommendations from anyone but those who worked with him and have his interest at heart. He is losing out on some fine people."

I suppose he feared that if anything went wrong he would be charged with yielding to influence. He had denounced political bosses so long, because they exacted tribute for their support, that he would not risk being accused of paying off even to his dearest friend.

Once he appointed a magistrate on the recommendation of strangers. The new judge turned out not only to be incompetent but to have once made a speech expressing his respect for Nazis! Hostile newspaper reporters descended on LaGuardia en masse. They felt they had him. He was not going to squirm out of this one. Why hadn't he investigated the appointee's background more carefully? Who had recommended him? Once more, they underestimated his ingenuity and genius for public relations. He triumphed by uttering only nine words. Before they could begin their assault, he said, "Gentlemen, when I make a mistake, it's a beaut!"

This explanation became famous. Again he had turned indignation to laughter. He had ridiculed himself, and the people joyously accepted the admission of vulnerability from one who had striven so fanatically for high standards.

Just as he personalized his own shortcomings, so he personalized his enemies. When he attacked corporations in his weekly broadcasts, he addressed them as if they were individuals. "Look here, Mr. Western Union," or "Let me tell you something, Mr. Con Edison." He needed personal confrontation to be effective, not the vagueness of corporate enterprise.

I wondered whether he ever slept. He had an eighteen- to twenty-hour schedule, and his pace increased as if to banish tiredness by acceleration. Though his day often started at five or six in the morning (he could be seen inspecting garbage-collection procedures before the sun rose), he also spoke at most of the formal dinners in the evening. Unlike Walker, his day did not start at night.

He was extraordinarily facile at these functions. He had had no time to prepare. When I was on the dais, he would sit down next to me and say, "What are we selling tonight, Louis?" I would brief him in verbal shorthand:

"They are building a new wing at the Bronx Home for the Aged.

"They need two million dollars.

"The guest of honor is Max Schneider, president of the bank— You know him.

"In New York State there are now 1,200,000 people over the age of sixty-five. Most will reach eighty-five.

"There are no facilities for them. The city can't do it alone.

"This home is unique. It has apartments, not cells.

"There are paintings and pianos in some of them. There are no inmates. They can come and go as they wish.

"But there is a communal dining room for those who want it.

"There is a medical and dental department. Gerontology and geriatrics will be two of the most important words in the next generation." I defined both.

"In the new home to be built, old people will be able to *live* out their lives, not *die* out their lives."

"What is that last phrase?" he asked, for he was continuously being interrupted by greeters. I repeated it.

Then, when he arose to speak, usually early, so that he could appear at another function, he would deliver a twenty-minute address, skillfully blending the information he had soaked up into an emotional appeal. The audience must have thought he had prepared himself assiduously for the event. This "instant speech skill," combining a smattering of information with boiler-plate paragraphs previously used dozens of times, often is acquired by public officials and candidates. When listening to television interviews, one can sense that the "personality" interviewed has struggled through a few improvised sentences and reached the secure plateau of excerpts from his previous addresses, citing statistics and ringing conclusions. Sometimes the preprepared data is dragged in although not pertinent to the question. But LaGuardia was extremely felicitous and sufficiently original and inventive to make his speech completely applicable to the event.

I learned from him how to deal with men and women who stream toward the dais to shake hands and speak with the celebrity of the occasion. Invariably, the visitor holds out his hand and says, "I bet you don't remember me?"

"Yes, I do. Glad to see you."

"What's my name?"

"Well, I don't remember it right now, but I do recall you."

"Where did we meet last? Can you remember that?"

This cross-examination continues, while the celebrity loses ground, being trapped by his own kindliness. I have seen Presidents, Governors, Nobel Prize Winners, and dozens of other dais sitters unable to escape this ordeal. I used to think political figures played this losing game because they did not wish to antagonize a constituent or potential voter. But no, famous men in other walks of life are similarly cowed by dais visitors. I suppose the flattery of being approached prohibits a rebuke. So out of goodness of heart they evade, fumble, and pretend, while the person holding their hand in a secure grip remorselessly pursues his inquisition.

LaGuardia was the only one who knew how to deal with this kind of dais pest. To the ubiquitous question "I bet you don't remember me" he replied quickly, "No, I don't. What's your name?"

Taken back by the counterattack, the visitor would give his name and make one more try. "Do you remember where we met?"

"No, I don't. You know how many people a mayor sees. Glad to see you." He would turn to his neighbor and continue his conversation, thus dismissing the visitor, who would linger bewildered for a moment and then leave. It worked like a charm. I wondered why none of us had thought of so simple a device, or, more accurately, why we hadn't had the courage to use it.

LaGuardia was too impatient to have a five-year plan for the city. He had a daily plan and it extended to land and air. He built the first great municipal incinerators (not knowing then that they would be large contributors to the pollution problem and might have to be shut down). He brought in engineers to take advantage of the Catskill Mountain ranges, so that New York City would have the purest and best-tasting water in the country. He contracted for new kinds of mechanized garbage-collecting trucks, which required almost no lifting of cans, and thereby reduced hernias and the city's sick and hospital expense for sanitation workers. He ordered a new kind of snow-removal equipment, firefighting apparatus, and established new police car and communication systems. He believed in mechanization, provided those in charge never became calloused to duty because their labors had been reduced. In his eyes, leisure was just another opportunity to work. He resented those who when they got a job stopped looking for work.

One had to see him testing a new piece of equipment to determine whether it met specifications. He was like a woman in a market who knows quality: touching, smelling, squeezing, examining on all sides. He would work the new machine himself, over and over again. The contractor who had been forced by LaGuardia to outbid his competitors, until his profit margin was tissue paper thin, was nevertheless held to the highest standards. If the equipment was not perfect, LaGuardia would cajole the manufacturer into another effort, and Lord help him if he resisted. He was subjected to a public blast that lifted him into the next county.

He resorted to one of his stunts to improve airplane service. One day he flew from Washington to New York. The plane, according to schedule, arrived at the Newark Airport in New Jersey. LaGuardia refused to get out.

"My ticket says 'Washington to New York' and I want to be taken to New York."

Airline executives pleaded with him to evacuate the plane. He settled back tighter into his seat, closed the safety belt, and ordered, "Take me to New York. That's what your contract says." They did not dare evict him forcibly, especially since by this time photographers were swarming over the plane recording a traveler's sentimental plea to be taken home. He won his point. The plane, with one passenger, arrived at Mitchell Field in New York, and the first citizen of the city stepped out. The event was not unrecorded.

Appropriately enough, the air terminal he later built was named after him. It is a fitting memorial. When one sees the planes roaring in and out of LaGuardia, one is reminded of the restlessness and power which drove him frantically in all directions to achieve a better city.

The mayoralty of New York is generally conceded to be the second most difficult executive post in the United States. Like the presidency, it challenges one human being's capacity to survey, reflect, and decide hundreds of complicated problems in varied fields, any one of which would warrant years of concentrated study. Any decision at all is only possible by dependence on others, who, in turn, delegate to still others. The dilution is dangerous. Final resolutions may be based on the opinion of those far down the line, whose names and competence are not even known at the top. Little wonder, then, that any analyst can demonstrate contradictions, inconsistencies, and duplications among the various departments of government.

We are turning to miraculous computers to reduce the scope of this problem. Time saved in fact analysis, and even recommendations based on hard statistics, are invaluable. Even though experience is thus mechanically supplied, the input and output are still subject to judgment factors—another name for wisdom. As the government enlarges its activities to care for the individual citizen, yes, as it becomes paternalistic, reorganization of our government structure becomes essential. Even our constitutional demarcations, so brilliant and simple for the needs of that day, need overhauling. Some, like Professor Rex Tugwell, have suggested a new Constitution, preserving its imperishable spirit and freedoms, but restructuring the three departments of government to deal with new functions. For example, he proposes that a President and four vice-presidents be elected for a nine-year term and that various streamlined departments report to different vice-presidents. He also proposes that one house of the legislature be appointive and serve for life. Amendments to the Constitution would be facilitated. It is not necessary to evaluate the soundness of these and other proposals. It is significant that the Constitution, resulting from a long series of compromises among the quarreling delegates of that day, is not so holy a writ that it doesn't permit revision to meet exigencies never contemplated by those who drew it. As a statement of general principle, it turned out to be an inspired document (although it didn't forbid slavery). But our phenomenal growth required resort to regulatory agencies, economic control through antitrust, SEC, labor, and a host of other laws, and the curtailment of states' rights in favor of central power, all of which were as unforeseen as our nuclear or space sciences or our involvement as a superpower in international affairs. The Supreme Court established supremacy over the legislative branch, and is interpreting the constitutionality of enactments not defined or remotely envisioned by the generalities of the Constitution. Certainly, it was not anticipated that the President would be required to carry the weight of international and domestic anxieties which today challenge the strength and wisdom of mortal man.

LaGuardia was the last executive who strove by sheer superhuman energy to participate in every function of the city. His irascibility and temper were not due to exhaustion, but rather to his fierce determination that everyone measure up to the highest standard. He was a fanatic for good government. Of course, such torrential effort on so many fronts made him appear impetuous and so quick of judgment that his box score of errors and unjust statements was high, and some of them were "beauts," but, when compared to his accomplishments, his average ranked among the highest for a public official in several generations.

At one time there was much speculation that he would be a vice-presidential candidate. This was quite possible. President Roosevelt was a great admirer of LaGuardia and met with him frequently. Roosevelt suffered in the presence of boring people even though he used their competence. He was refreshed by exciting personalities, and where, as in LaGuardia, ebullience was combined with great talent, Roosevelt was fascinated. Probably he also appreciated LaGuardia's dramatizing ability (opponents would call it demagoguery) especially when it was employed not to deceive but to achieve. Roosevelt, generally, was attracted to intellectual mavericks, like Harold Ickes. LaGuardia's political genealogy was the same. But geographic considerations (Roosevelt and LaGuardia both were from New York) as well as other political factors (after all, LaGuardia wasn't even a Democrat) deprived the speculation of fulfillment.

A favorite fantasy bruited about in Hollywood was that when Cecil B. De Mille, the motion picture producer and director, died, he went to heaven (if that is where movie moguls go). He immediately organized a large corporation to entertain the angels. He ran into only one problem, and that was when he proposed that God be first vice-president.

LaGuardia, whose credentials for admission were excellent, would have reorganized the various departments, and might have encountered the same problem, but we can be sure that under his aegis, things up there would be like heaven.

When one contemplates the two most famous mayors in New York history, the intriguing idea presents itself: isn't it too bad that the city didn't use the unique talents of both; Fiorella LaGuardia as the chief executive, and Jimmy Walker the social mayor? It would have been a gay time in the old town tonight, and an efficient one, too, every day and night.

WHAT WE ARE IS GOD'S GIFT TO US. WHAT WE BECOME IS OUR RECIPROCAL GIFT TO GOD

Interviewers who have made a close study of public curiosity and cater to it have a series of ubiquitous questions. For performers: "What was the most interesting role you ever played?" "What attracts you most in the opposite sex?"

There is a similar catalogue of questions for lawyers: "What is the most exciting case you ever tried?" (I dodge this with "the next one"); "What was the most humorous incident you ever experienced in a courtroom?" In this list of questions, presumed to hold attention at least until the answer is given, is one that deals with "firsts." "What was the first case you ever tried?" is a prototype. Ordinarily, the truth would be, "I don't even remember," or "Really, it was of no significance." What else would one expect from a neophyte?

It so happens, however, that my first case was unique and with unusual consequences. To understand the reason for its being at all, one must understand how a lawyer enters into his profession. Without this background, the painting in the foreground loses meaning.

There are two general branches of law, substantive and adjective. The first deals with the philosophy and principles of law. The second with procedure. For example, adjective law is concerned with which courts have jurisdiction over certain disputes, the form of a complaint or answer, what motions can be made to elucidate the pleadings, within what period of time certain legal steps must be taken, and the like. Since each state has different procedures, set forth in Civil Practice Acts, the bar examination, which each graduating lawyer must take to obtain a license to practice law in the state, concentrates heavily on adjective law of that state.

On the other hand, leading law universities place almost all their emphasis on substantive law. While a course in procedural law is given, it is general and illustrative, because the students come from many states, and one cannot concentrate on any particular state. Furthermore, it is prosaic, technical knowledge, not worth pedagogic emphasis. So, adjective law is left for special bar examination courses outside of the college, given by specialists for the state where the student will seek his license. He pays for this course (and it is a lucrative field for teachers who know how to give a cram course in two weeks. Judge Harold Medina, when he was a teacher at Columbia University, gave such a private course).

So, it comes about that students of the best law universities are least trained for the bar examination of their state, and must seek help in adjective or procedural law before subjecting themselves to the test. When the bar examinations were divided into substantive and adjective parts, many passed the substantive law test with flying colors, but failed the adjective law section and consequently had to take that phase of the examination over again the next year. Chief Justice Charles Evans Hughes flunked his bar examination (of course on adjective law only) three times. Other famous lawyers and judges stumbled once or twice. These historic debacles have been a comfort to thousands of students who fail to pass their bar examinations. Indeed, they get to believe it is an omen for their future eminence, because they are following very large footsteps. The mind is capable of all sorts of ego-salvaging operations.

It is true, of course, that no great lawyer ever achieved high standing by proficiency in procedural law. The great law colleges properly stress the substantive law. However, there are smaller law schools which are local and chiefly attract students who intend to practice locally. These give extensive courses in the adjective law of that state. Their graduating students do not require a special preparatory course for bar examinations. They have had it in their regular studies. So, it eventuates that graduates from the smaller law schools have higher bar examination success than those from leading universities.

Bar examinations are unimaginable ordeals. Students have prepared themselves for seven years of college and law school training, met the severest tests of excellence and have finally graduated with honors. Then their right to enter the profession depends on one lengthy bar examination divided into substantive and adjective law questions.

Having sharpened their reasoning powers, rather than their memory or accumulative skills, they are at a great disadvantage in facing a test in which knowledge of rules of law is a requisite. So they must refresh, review, recapture, and recall years of learning in a few weeks in order to be prepared for a few questions which may be scattered over wide domains of law. I took Professor Harold Medina's cram course.

Preparation must exceed necessity. So it is later in the practice of the law. I have studied and absorbed for weeks the testimony printed in the record of a trial, because on the argument of the appeal one of the judges may ask a question, the answer to which lies buried in some remote part of the record. Uusually these extensive preparatory efforts are wasted. The judges either sit in silence or their questions are addressed to the mainstream of the argument. But, occasionally, the court inquires whether there was any proof on some offbeat matters. Counsel can, of course, reply that he does not recall whether such testimony appears in the lengthy record, and not lose any ground thereby. But if, by heart, he can refer instantly to the page on which the subject was treated, the favorable impact upon the court exceeds the significance of the answer itself. Counsel's mastery of the record instills confidence in the rest of his argument. At such a moment, all the tedious hours of "unnecessary" preparation are fully rewarded. The lawyer tries to hide his exhilaration, as if the feat he had just performed was nothing at all, but he can see the glint in the eyes of the most stony-faced judge, reflecting acknowledgment of the virtuosity he has just witnessed.

There is no greater anxiety than that which the aspiring and perspiring candidate experiences while awaiting the results of the bar examination. It is almost as if after careful hoarding of his resources for a decade, he put all his money on one throw of the dice. Yet, when the bar examination is passed, and several years of practice follow, the ordeal completely disappears from memory. It is an early lesson that anxiety makes mountains out of molehills and perspective makes molehills out of mountains. The crisis of the moment most often is an insignificant incident when viewed through the glasses of intervening time. Of course, it is not always so, but experience proves this to be true in such a large number of cases, that it is wise to anticipate that possibility, and not permit immediacy to act as an artificial enlarging glass.

Harry Hershfield used to tell the story of the coal miner who slaved twenty years in the dark, cold, and wet underground, and saved up $5,000 by frugal living. Then he goes to Las Vegas for a celebration, puts the entire sum on one number, loses, and sighs, "Well, easy come, easy go."

After the bar examination has been passed, and the character committee has found no flaw, the great moment arrives for the swearing in before the Appellate Division. As I stood there on the threshold of a new world I had dreamed of entering all my life, there stirred within me such deep emotions that I could not hear either the encouragement or admonition which came from the bench. Once, I dared turn my head and saw my parents crying unashamedly. It had been a long struggle for them, and all the waiting had suddenly come to one moment of happy climax. And, of course, profound joy is giddy enough to lose its way and indiscriminately trigger tears as well as laughter.

My wandering thoughts were brought to a halt by awareness that the candidates had all raised their hands. I raised mine and repeated the oath being administered, with all the fervor in my being. Then we were given our certificates. In one magic second, we had become lawyers, although we did not realize then how frail the parchment in our hands was in the steel and iron combat we were about to engage. I have not failed to make this point when I address incoming lawyers before they are sworn in.

The courage essential for future engagements was necessary at the beginning simply to overcome the disappointments which beset a beginner. We could not even get jobs. Despite qualifications which were not unimpressive, there seemed to be no opportunity open anywhere. I searched the law journals for positions, put my own ads there, applied to the placement bureau of the law school, and had friends arrange interviews at law firms. But this was 1925, and there were few openings. Many turned away in disgust from the profession, and entered business or other fields.

I was sorely tempted myself by a business offer. During summer, I had done odd jobs, like working for the Intertype Corporation, which manufactured Linotype machines. The job was thrilling because the office was at Court Street in Brooklyn, two blocks from the Supreme Court Building. So I would skip or curtail lunch hour and gravitate to the Court House, where I peered through the oval-glassed green leather doors into the wondrous land within. Someday, I was determined, I would be inside that arena.

Another summer job was for the Carbona Company, which manufactured a cleaning fluid. It was simply a chemical called carbon tetrachloride, and an excellent cleaner. All the owners did was bottle it and give it the trade name Carbona. I was given a small salary and a commission on sales. I talked my heart out to managers of chain stores, and did fairly well. One day, I discovered by accident that Carbona cleaned typewriters. Since it evaporated quickly, the impressions left by the carbons on the platen could be removed and the typewriter used immediately thereafter. I opened up a new and successful market for Carbona. I then dared to approach steamship companies to buy large quantities for cleaning pistons and other equipment. The small bottles of Carbona customarily made were too expensive for this purpose. The new sales field and need for a wholesale cheaper-priced gallon container brought me to the attention of the president of the Carbona Company, Mr. Weintraub. It turned out that he had a son who, as sons so often do, disliked the business, and thus shattered his father's dream of ultimately turning over his company to him. Instead, Mr. Weintraub must have found my enthusiasm and dedication the very qualities he had hoped his son would have. It may have been this transference, or a guess by the old gentleman, that an investment in me might not be a bad gamble.

So he called me into his office, before my last term in law school, and offered me a contract for five years to begin at a salary of $100 a week and going upwards so that by the time I was out of law school I would be earning $200 a week. Two hundred dollars a week! This was more than brilliant young lawyers earned after five years or more. In addition, I would ascend through various titles to the presidency. My legal training would be helpful, but the Carbona Company didn't need a counsel. I was being offered a business career.

Although I knew what my decision must be, I, of course, discussed this proposal with my parents. My heart was heavy. Might they see in this a desirable career and advise me to enter it? Of course, I should not have underestimated them. There was not a moment of hesitation. My father commanded (I could have hugged him for his anger, and I did), "You finish law school. You are going to be a lawyer. What kind of nonsense is this? If Mr. Weintraub offered you a thousand dollars a week, would you quit school and give up the profession you were cut out to follow since you were born?"

He was getting so angry my mother soothed him, "Zindel-leben [our dear son] isn't going to take it. He just wants us to agree. Of course we do. Money isn't everything." As an afterthought, "And besides, who says you can't earn more if you become a great lawyer?"

So I declined the offer, and was told to return at any time that I had a change of mind, if not of heart.

However, when I could not obtain employment as a law clerk, I began to notice Carbona signs and billboards, to which I had never paid attention before. Finally, one day I answered an advertisement for a law clerk and was hired. It was the office of a woman lawyer, a rarity in those days. Her name was Miss Emily Janoer. She had an office on Fourteenth Street, in Manhattan, which I thought was a strange location, until I found out that her chief occupation was real estate, and that my main function was to serve dispossess summonses on defaulting tenants in buildings she owned. My salary was seven dollars a week. The only indication that I was in a law office were a few lawbooks and the daily *New York Law Journal*. These comforted me, but the $200 a week offered by Carbona was like the beautiful nude temptress which lay herself before St. Anthony to distract him from his duty and holy mission.

My parents were bewildered but not disheartened by the early tough going. "Water always finds its own level," my father said. He didn't finish the thought, as if it was preposterous not to realize that that level would be extremely high. "Just stick to it. Everybody will realize your ability someday." My mother just smiled her assenting opinion.

THE PUSHCART CASE

It is against this background that my first case came to me. One evening (yes, it was night, for I had no office or even a shingle), my mother announced in a voice registering excitement and perplexity that several men were at the door asking to see Counselor Nizer. Could they be clients!

They were ushered into our dining room, but not before the green oilcloth cover on the table was hastily replaced with our finest white tablecloth with the fringes and tassels hanging on the sides. My mother immediately busied herself brewing tea, which, according to her London training, was served not only in the afternoon, but as a pacifier for any crisis, small or large.

Although my heart was pounding, I greeted the visiting dignitaries casually as if this were just another conference in a busy day. The spokesman, Mr. Jacob Bassuck (how could I ever forget his name?), told me that he and the three gentlemen with him were property owners on Ellery Street, in Brooklyn, which was part of a public market area. Pushcarts with all sorts of produce and products were lined up on one side of these blocks. They were not permitted to be stationed on the west side of the street. Consequently, shoppers abounded on the pushcart-lined sidewalks. Stores on that side prospered. Property was valuable.

But my visitors owned buildings on the opposite side. There was little traffic. The stores did little business. Many were vacant. Property values were down in sharp contrast to the buildings facing them across the street. Could anything be done legally to see that pushcarts would be permitted on their side of the street?

I had always thought of discrimination in terms of people. It had never occurred to me that the injustice of discrimination could attach to something as inanimate and prosaic as a pushcart.

"Who forbids the stationing of pushcarts on your side of the street?" I asked.

"The city," replied one of the men. "The Commissioner of Market," added another, narrowing the target.

"Does he give any reason?"

"Sure, lots of them. He says Public School 24 is only a few blocks away and there must be clear sidewalks for children going to school. There is also a firehouse nearby and the street must not be closed in on both sides by pushcarts, or they couldn't run through easily."

"Have you asked him to alternate pushcart placements, one week on your side and the next on their side?"

"Look, we've asked him everything. He won't listen. Go fight City Hall!"

The other members of the committee looked askance at the speaker's tactlessness. Was this the way to encourage the young lawyer to try his hand at an impossible case?

"Certainly, you can fight City Hall," I replied, calling on my vast fund of political inexperience and naïveté. "There is a proceeding called mandamus. It is the remedy used to compel a public official to do his duty properly. We could apply to the State Supreme Court for an order directing the city official not to discriminate against you."

My assertiveness must have stirred the conscience of Mr. Bassuck. "I must tell you," he said haltingly, "that we have been to other lawyers, and they all said nothing could be done." Continuing his confession, he mentioned their names, all well known and able, including Emanuel Celler, who was congressman from that district and who later served for half a century in the House, rising to Chairman of the Judiciary Committee.

It was quite obvious that I was not only not a second, but a last choice. (Like the political leader who told the applicant, "You are my second choice." "Who is your first?" "Anybody.") Apparently, some members of the committee had heard me speak, and on such slight evidence had urged a final try. What did they have to lose?

I was not embarrassed by the revelation that, unlike Abou Ben Adhem, I did not head the list. Instead I was stirred by the challenge. Fools step in where fools have stepped before, but I had not stepped anywhere yet. I was unafraid.

"I think you have a meritorious case," I said. "If you want me to undertake it, I would like to spend a few days investigating the facts thoroughly, with your help, and then we can proceed."

They agreed to pay disbursements and, if I remember, five hundred dollars for my representation.

A lawyer who only knows his own side of the case knows little about it. He must anticipate the defense and be prepared to demolish it. What would the city argue if I attacked? The doctrine of discretion. There is a rule of law that where a public official performs a duty which involves his discretion, the courts will not challenge it, even if they disagree with him, unless—unless there is a clear abuse of discretion. So, for example, a judge who decides a case and specifies that it is not purely a legal matter, but that it involves discretion, is virtually immune on appeal. The burden on the appellant is overwhelming. He must demonstrate either that the matter was one of absolute right and did not involve the exercise of contrary discretion, or that the discretion was so bizarre as to fall within the rule of abuse of discretion. The same, of course, applied to the Market Commissioner. We could be sure that the word "discretion" would permeate the defense, to create an impenetrable shield. The Corporation Counsel of the City might, for purposes of persuasion, even strike a generous pose that he, himself, or the court might have acted differently, but that didn't matter. The Market Commissioner had exercised his discretion, based on many surrounding circumstances, and no court should, under well-established law, substitute its discretion for his. The cases supporting this proposition were legion. Undoubtedly, this was the reason that other lawyers had refused to take the case. Perhaps some of them had another reason more visceral than scholarly—they just didn't think there was a future in suing the City of New York.

I prepared myself by preparing the city's argument. With all the force which I could summon, I constructed the corporation counsel's argument; school access, fire engine lanes, consumer advantage, traffic considerations, and all the rest. Then with these contentions ringing in my ears, I set out on foot to visit other city markets, examining the surrounding territory, wresting a fact here and there. I drove my clients (what a wonderful word when used for the first time) to help me investigate the facts. My objective was definite and limited. It consisted of one word—inconsistency. To me this was equivalent to abuse of discretion. If the Market Commissioner had acted differently under similar circumstances, he could not argue that he had exercised his discretion honestly. Mistaken or not, he could only hold his feet if he had acted the same way in the exercise of his discretion. But if he had not, the suspicion arose that there were other factors which accounted for his conduct, and this negated reasonable exercise of discretion. It spelled out "abuse of discretion."

The task was further complicated by the fact that varying circumstances in each market area might justify varying decisions. This would contradict the charge of inconsistency, and restore his claim that he had exercised his discretion honestly, whether wise or not.

So I not only had to find inconsistent conduct, but eliminate factual distinctions by demonstrating that they were too thin to overcome the accusation of abuse of discretion.

This was my first enlistment and for life in the army of "thorough preparation." The demands of such service (should I say servitude?) are enormous. They had driven me to perilous rooftops to peer down a shaft in which an elevator fell; to a barge cutting through icy water to watch divers looking for a metal box in a murder case; to laboratories making atomic tests of paper to determine its origin; to French archives searching for reports in a plagiarism suit; to a secret attic equipped with electronic devices and hundreds of recordings; to a search of an abandoned villa where a missing diary was found behind a bookcase which the wife had thought was thoroughly emptied; to many countries to persuade a knowledgeable witness that it was his duty to give his testimony in a deposition which would be taken in the local embassy; to a hazardous walk on an elevated railroad to find the hole from which a bolt had plummeted onto a man's skull; to a university's records to find a psychological test taken by a student (killed in a railway accident) to establish damages based on his potential earnings; to chemical tests of textiles in breach of warranty cases; to poring over hundreds of Arabic translations in an oil case, or thousands of clippings from a German newspaper to demonstrate Nazi affiliation; to tedious examination of corporate minute books, or accountant statements in SEC cases; to countless interviews with doctors, psychiatrists, surgeons, economists, geologists, public officials, workers, janitors, teachers, executives and all manner of people, young and old, who the fates had decreed should have been present at certain events or heard some words which needed to be reconstructed so that truth, so easily faded by time, could be salvaged from oblivion.

I have adverted to the slavery of preparation, but oh, its rewards! They exceed the windfall from the largest lottery. Many millions of dollars, and more precious rights than can be measured by money, result from a fact or two unearthed by dedicated research. Not least is the exhilaration from triumph over knave or dupe, and the reassurance that justice is attainable in this imperfect world.

If I needed encouragement for the precept that preparation equates with proficiency, my first case provided it. Treading through the sometimes nonaromatic lanes of the city's markets, I discovered practices totally inconsistent with those in my clients' area. Official duty which compelled discretionary manipulation of pushcarts in our market was not applied with similar fervor in others. Some of them also had nearby schools, and firehouses. Of course they would. These existed in all neighborhoods. Yet pushcarts were permitted on both sides of the street. There was enough lane left for vehicles in streets which measured the same or even narrower than ours. Children coursed over the sidewalks on their way to school, without being impeded by the purchasers at the curb. Why only in our market need there be precautions taken for a one-sided use?

My suspicions turned me to an investigation in the County Clerk's

records of the owners of the favored real estate. Yes, among them were
the names of some who were influential in Tammany circles. One was a
political small-wig in the party. This could not be used in the litigation.
It was too remote by properly protective legal standards for an accusation against a public official. But it didn't diminish my clients' skepticism about the city's declarations that only considerations of public
welfare lay behind the regulations.

When I had prepared the affidavits and exhibits (which included
photographs to give visual support to the discrimination), we sued City
Hall. Mayor John F. Hylan, Market Commissioner O'Malley, and the
Board of Estimate were all joined as defendants in a mandamus proceeding. It was strange that this form of action, so unique and rarely
encountered, and which we learned in law school as a sort of esoteric illustration of the law's comprehensiveness, should be the first vehicle for
my ride to court.

Justice James C. Cropsey was sitting in the State Supreme Court,
Kings County, where the argument would take place.

God takes care of the innocent. He was a Republican. I would not
have thought that the rules of law would be applied differently because
of the Judge's political adherence before he was elected. How can there
be a Democratic or Republican rule of law? That was and is as unthinkable to me as if the Ten Commandments were tampered with. But my
clients were not so trusting. They breathed with relief when they heard
that a Tammany judge would not preside.

Judge Cropsey had a reputation for fanatical rectitude. He was the
severest judge on the bench. A witness who was an obvious perjurer
would be melted in his seat by the verbal lava which the Judge poured
over him. Any lawyer who overstepped his bounds was subjected to a
scathing denunciation.

The bar feared and admired him at one and the same time. His righteous indignation was a purifying factor in a calloused world. But his
temper made him impetuous, and it could be triggered too easily.
There was little compassion in the man. He seemed always poised to
strike. That is why no judicial system is perfect. It reflects the frailties
of those who administer it, and which judicial robes can neither hide
nor eliminate.

Lawyers are often good psychologists. Hard experience trains them to
be. It becomes well known that in arguing before a judge like Cropsey,
it was extremely important to have the opportunity of speaking first.
Once he caught fire, it was almost impossible for the defendant to
quench the flames of his conviction.

I had all these advantages; a judge who would be outraged by official misconduct; and the right to open the argument because we were the plaintiffs.

Knowing that Judge Cropsey was a legal scholar, I planned to catch his fancy by a daring maneuver. I announced early in the argument that the city would rely on the rule of discretion, and I conceded that no matter how right we were on the merits, it would not avail us if we could not demonstrate a clear abuse of discretion; that this was a heavy burden I had to meet; that I accepted it and would address my entire argument to demonstrating that never in the history of the city had there been such a clear case of executive favoritism; that every excuse offered by the Commissioner of Markets for his discriminatory conduct was hypocritical, and so proven by his own inconsistent conduct. I continued in this vein in the very introduction to indicate at the earliest moment who was on the side of the angels.

I could see the gorge rise in Judge Cropsey as I proceeded. His smooth, angular face became more florid as the heated words reached him. When he looked at the black and white photographs attached to the papers, they seemed to cast a red light on his features. Suddenly, he could contain himself no longer. He interrupted me in the middle of a sentence and announced in a tone reserved for sentence of death, "I'll hear the other side." This was accompanied by slamming the sheaf of affidavits on his desk, with a gesture of anger and disgust.

The poor City Counsel. He knew very well that "I'll hear the other side" was a challenge, not an invitation, and meant he would be given little opportunity to speak, and that it was he who would be listening to a tirade. So it was. He was not aided by his lack of resourcefulness. The situation called for an improvised beginning which might delay the imminent explosion from the bench; some soothing words and promise of a developing argument which would encourage patient withholding of judgment. But he had no such flexibility. He had carefully prepared an address based on an exposition of the rule of discretion, and an analysis of the cases which defined "abuse of discretion." That was his speech. His notes were before him. He stuck to the text as if nothing had happened to make such an approach hollow.

"I know the law," screamed the Judge. "Mr. Neezer [the mispronunciation was innocent] has conceded it. Stop wasting time. What have you to say to the demonstration that the city has applied a standard here not used in any other market?"

When the city's lawyer sought to make distinctions, the Judge furiously rejected them as pretense. It was the first time I was to enjoy the experience of the Judge acting as advocate for our position. It is a comforting feeling. There is no one there to overrule him.

The decision was foreshadowed. The Judge wrote a blistering opinion in a style which Judge Cardozo once described in his book *Law and Literature*, as pronouncement from on high. No careful balancing of conflicting claims, no dissecting of the logic to demonstrate a crack here or there in its façade—just stentorian tones of an inviolate judgment— as if it was being read from engraved tablets handed down from the Mount of Justice. He issued a mandamus order directing the Commissioner of Markets to permit pushcarts to be placed on both sides of the street, or, if he wished, he could alternate them for equal periods and without any discrimination of days or hours from one side to the other. All city officials, including the Mayor, were enjoined from interfering in any way with this direction, and the order explicitly applied to any subsequent Commissioner of Markets. In other words, though the order was personal, it was made to attach to the office, like a covenant running with the land in real estate.

My clients read the newspapers with special pride. They had brought about a miracle. City Hall had crumpled. A lowly pushcart had brought it down. They preened themselves on having picked a lawyer who, because he knew little, had entered into awesome battle unafraid. They considered the victory a greater testimonial to their shrewdness than to my skill. When they came to celebrate and congratulate me and my parents, I acted calmly, like a battle-scarred veteran, and warned them that appeals lay ahead. The city would not take such a defeat docilely. There was the Appellate Division, composed of five judges, and the final Court of Appeals in Albany, composed of seven. The gamut had to be run. We passed the Appellate Division and then on to Albany.

Only few cases reach the Court of Appeals. Many lawyers practice a lifetime without an occasion to appear there. Yet, here I was in my very first case standing before the court of last resort in the State of New York.

What made the occasion paralyzing was that the Chief Judge, Benjamin N. Cardozo, presided. There he was in the flesh.

To understand the impact, one must imagine a musician who has worshiped Beethoven's genius and studied his works all his life. Then, he must appear to perform before a group of masters, and by some miracle, there sits Ludwig van Beethoven also, peering down at him. The analogy is not too fanciful. Some men have such immense reputations that we consider them historic figures. We, therefore, associate them with other geniuses who are dead. One forgets that although by reputation they are already in the pantheon, they are still alive.

Cardozo, like Einstein, Picasso, Edison, and Freud, belonged to this group of assured immortality in their fields. In law school, we had read his precedent-making opinions with awe reserved for Coke and Blackstone; except that their styles were flat compared to his. He was a master of prose, a great writer. One has only to read *The Nature of the Judicial Process* to be fascinated by the grace of diction, the symmetry of structure, the musical acceleration of pace, the flowering of emotion out of fact, the humor used to invade a resistant mind, all adorning profound thought and incredible learning. He was the supreme legal philosopher, and since the law encompasses all social sciences, his philosophy extended to domains as broad as life itself.

It seems unfair to engage in such lavish evaluation without supporting illustration. One has only to turn to any page of his writings for it. I select a few passages from an abundance of riches, choosing these particular ones only because they deal with less involved professional problems.

In *The Growth of the Law* he writes:

Judges march at times to pitiless conclusions under the prod of a remorseless logic which is supposed to leave them no alternative. They deplore the sacrificial rite. They perform it, none the less, with averted gaze, convinced as they plunge the knife that they obey the bidding of their office.

We should know . . . that magic words and incantations are as fatal to our science as they are to any other . . .

Here is his comment on the enormous number of precedents which now confront the lawyer and the judge:

The fecundity of our case law would make Malthus stand aghast. Adherence to precedent was once a steadying force, the guaranty, as it seemed, of stability and certainty. We would not sacrifice any of the brood, and now the spawning progeny, forgetful of our mercy, are rending those who spared them.

He discusses the compartmentalizing of the law with this observation.

One line is run here; another there. We have a filigree of threads and cross-threads . . . We shall be caught in the tentacles of the web, unless some superintending mind imparts the secret of the structure . . . The perplexity of the judge becomes the scholar's opportunity.

His reputation was international. Legal scholars everywhere recognized his eminence. When other courts, whether the Supreme Court of the United States or courts in foreign countries, cited cases he had decided, they made a special point to mention that he was the author of the opinion. That gave it unique authority. He was quoted by courts, law journals, and legal writers more than any other judge in history, and invariably his words cast a light on the text, and gave velocity to its thought.

How had his genius developed? There might have been a psychiatric impulse. His father was a judge in the State Supreme Court and became involved in a scandal of dishonesty. Young Cardozo must have determined to make amends, and restore the honor of his name. This might explain his fanatical dedication and even his distorted ascetic life, but not his brilliance, fecund mind, and felicitous pen.

Judged by other mortals, he lived at least two lives in one lifetime. He concentrated on law to the exclusion of all else. He never married. He lived with his sister all his life. He never went to the theater, to a concert, or even to a social event unless it was a legal occasion. Since he required little sleep, he read and studied law eighteen to twenty hours a day. He was familiar with legal periodicals written in French, Italian, German, and Spanish. Since law is all-encompassing, and he never compartmentalized it, he also studied philosophical and sociological works of foremost authorities, and mastered economic theories, scientific developments, and political tracts. His cultural curiosity embraced the widest domain.

More remarkable than all this was that his mind never became stuffed with the enormous intake. He synthesized, eliminated, and sorted everything in orderly fashion. His learning complemented a liberal mind and a perspective of infinite horizon. Stimuli from hundreds of sources were refined by him and then poured out into his opinions. Little wonder they had breadth and scope, which gave them the stamp of authentic wisdom.

In discussing the philosophy which molds the law, he once wrote:

We do not need to spend pages in an attempted demonstration that Gesetz (law) is not coterminous with Recht (right), that la loi is narrower than le droit, that the law is something more than statute. We are saved from all this because in action every day about us is the process by which forms of conduct are stamped in the judicial mint as law, and thereafter circulate freely as part of the coinage of the realm.

Here is a remarkable observation, confession, and objective squeezed into two sentences:

The inscrutable force of professional opinion presses upon us like the atmosphere, though we are heedless of its weight. How shall we make the most of it in service to mankind?

Cardozo's manner was benign. He was a kind man. Civilization being the slow process of learning to be kind, he was on that and other grounds perhaps the most civilized man of our era.

It is the man who gives distinction to the title, and not the title to the man. When Judge Cardozo presided over the Court of Appeals in New York, it was the most honored court in the land. Ultimately, his distinction caused a clamor for his appointment to the Supreme Court in Washington. Although he was ineligible by geographic and religious standards (two of the judges on the court were from New York and one Jew was already on the bench), his reputation transcended such considerations and he was appointed by President Herbert Hoover to acclaim from judicial authorities and intellectuals all over the world.

He was reluctant to take the post. He was ensconced in Albany in his ascetic way of life, and moving to Washington tore up roots of habit and subjected him to a new environment with accompanying demands to be resisted all over again. But he yielded, and for a long time was unhappy on the highest court. He was even subjected to anti-Semitic crudeness by Associate Justice James McReynolds, who ostentatiously read and rattled a newspaper when Judge Cardozo discussed a case in conference. But he wrote a brilliant chapter in the all too short time of six years he served before his death in 1938 at the age of sixty-seven.

Paintings and statues of him abound. One portrait hangs on the ornately carved light wood wall of the Court of Appeals in Albany, parallel with the lectern where counsel speak, as if he were looking gently at them, as he once did from the high-backed center chair. Another hangs in the study next to the Supreme Court chamber. But no painting can capture the ivory-white pallor of his skin and its translucent quality. He had a shock of white hair which by contrast gave his face faint color. His lower lip protruded ever so slightly and formed a graceful curve with upward indentations at the ends affecting a gentleness which looked like a smile. His chin was large and determined. Some accident or arthritic condition had shrunk his neck, so that his shoulders were high. To diminish the distortion he wore high collars.

The over-all effect of his face was one of complete repose. He seemed spiritually above the din of contentiousness. His voice was soft and nonresonant, almost like a whisper without sibilance. No man I have ever met, whether pope, priest, chief rabbi, or guru, seemed more saintly than he.

Considering my belief in a full and vibrant life, there is no man I would less emulate than him, and no man whose mind I have admired more.

There is an anecdote about a young lawyer appearing before the Court of Appeals and expounding a simple legal proposition at length. Judge Cardozo apologized for interrupting him and in a characteristically noncritical manner said, "May I suggest that you need not use up your limited time on that point. I hope you will give this court credit for being familiar with as elementary a rule as that."

"Oh no," replied counsel, "that's the mistake I made in the lower court."

My dilemma was similar. What could I possibly present that was not known to Judge Cardozo and the six other judges on that bench? The answer was—the facts. An answer which applies to most appeals. Counsel usually bear down on the legal authorities and the distinctions among differing cases. But these are often known to appellate judges, or can best be read in the briefs. A mere indication of the legal umbrella under which the client seeks shelter is sufficient. Quotations at length from prior decisions are boring and rarely productive.

The realm about which the judges know nothing—and are not sensitive to the assumption that they are ignorant—is the facts.

The art of advocacy is to demonstrate that the facts warrant the application of a particular rule of law. The adversary often concedes the legal proposition, but argues that it does not apply to the facts in the instant case, because they are different from those in the case from which the rule stems.

In short, it is the factual terrain on which the battle is customarily fought, and it is here that the lawyer should concentrate his fire. He wastes his ammunition by shooting in other directions.

So I cast my argument before Judge Cardozo and the other judges in terms of a recital of the facts, so interwoven that they exuded the city's unwarranted partisanship, favoritism, and discrimination in favor of one set of property owners, and to the injury of another group of citizens deserving of equal treatment. Here and there the facts bounced off the rule of abuse of discretion, making their own dissonant clangor.

A few months later, Judge Cardozo addressed the Bar Association of the City of New York. As always, when he appeared, the huge amphitheater was fully seated long before the lecture. His talks were literary gems, destined for publication. The script was before him and he read it. Of course, as I have indicated previously, this was bound to make a weak presentation. However, we knew that when we would read his talk someday we would appreciate it fully. Then we could pause over its passages, and savor them to derive fullest pleasure. Some sections would need concentrated attention and absorption. They had passed by teasingly when he pronounced them in even gait and went blithely on. But the audience composed of judges and lawyers was thrilled by being in his presence and watching him closely as he delivered the paper.

His talk was followed by a reception. Although the decision in my case had already come down, I approached him hesitantly. I hoped he would remember me. To my surprise, he took my hand warmly and said, "I would like to see you." I did not know whether this was an invitation to visit him in chambers or to wait. I stood aside.

After a while he approached me. He complimented me on the argument before the court, referring in light detail to its persuasive formulation. He asked me how long I had been practicing, and in view of my choked condition, it was fortunate that the answer was necessarily curt. Then he put his hand on my arm in a half gesture of intimacy, and gave me encouragement for what he hoped would be a distinguished career. He concluded with a deliberate air of casualness to suggest that I should feel free to visit him in his New York City or Albany chambers. He must have seen how moved I was by what to me was the conferring of the Nobel Prize of friendship, even though the only words I could summon were, "Thank you, sir."

Through the years, I did visit him and developed a warm acquaintance. I cannot say friendship, for I doubt that with the exception of perhaps one or two, his immersion in thought and work permitted such a relationship. However, I achieved enough rapport to indulge in a privilege which only close friends can enjoy, to be silent together.

So in my very first case I had sued City Hall and met the legendary Cardozo. What a leap from Emily Janoer on Fourteenth Street to Chief Judge Cardozo in Albany.

My father became a philosopher. "Lawyers in fancy neighborhoods don't get pushcart cases," he said.

Every success breeds an opportunity for another. Clients began to appear with regularity.

I received an invitation to join Louis Phillips' law firm. By one of these strange coincidences, he had known my parents in London, and he was prone to tell everyone in later years that he had once held me on his knee when I was an infant. This gave some the false impression that we were relatives.

Phillips was attorney and executive secretary of the New York Film Board of Trade, which represented the leading motion picture companies. He had the privilege of practicing private law. So the handsome quarters of the trade association and his law office were combined in an impressive suite at 1520 Broadway on Times Square.

I had thought of asking him for an association when I graduated, but this would have been imposing on his acquaintance. I was determined to make my own way. Phillips, on the other hand, had needed a clerk, but he guessed correctly that I might want to be independent and avoid favors. However, word of my progress encouraged him to invite me, for now an offer of a job was recognition of my worth, not friendly condescension.

I came to see him, walked over the plush carpets of his office and into the hushed library with its huge oval table covered with stacks of lawbooks. This was a real law office. I was fascinated by the surroundings. I like Phillips' enthusiasm for law, which I was to learn for the next quarter of a century was his predominating trait. He was happy only when he could talk law. All else in life was interstitial.

So I eagerly accepted the job. But by this time, I had a practice, and it was agreed that in addition to my salary of twenty dollars a week, I would receive 50 per cent of fees derived from my own clients.

Within two years, my fees grew large enough for him to offer me an equal partnership. More important, we realized in each other spiritual brothers-in-law. So the law firm of Phillips and Nizer was founded in 1928, and has grown ever since.

Louis Phillips had a love affair with the law. He was so dedicated to his work that it consumed his every thought, his every minute, whether in the office or out of it. When he visited me for a social evening, he would beg off from the other guests for ten minutes to discuss a legal problem with me. It was not urgent, but his mind was filled with it and there was joy in legal exchange.

His professional excellence was given nobility because it was rooted in integrity. That is such an abused word. It is not likely to convey its ripe meaning as it should when applied to him. He was reared in the orthodox Jewish tradition of right and justice. It was the core of his deep religious feeling. True religion is the life we lead, not the creed we profess. I have never known anyone whose life was guided by purer concepts of honesty, decency, and justice. These were not to him esoteric concepts to be uttered in a house of worship, or paid obeisance in conversation. They were his daily applied standards of conduct, and he never, never deviated from them no matter what the exigency. He would not accept the permissible exceptions established by precedent. On this subject he was quietly fanatical. He would brook no compromise. But there was no holy self-consciousness about this. On the contrary, he would hide his embarrassment about his extreme standards with a jest or the Jewish expression "*Es past nisht*"—"It just wouldn't be nice."

What a wonderful canon of ethics "*Es past nisht*" makes. What a guiding rule for a fine life it constitutes. Particularly for one of his tender sensitivity, it was a severe standard. If anything made him feel uneasy or just slightly embarrassed, or gave his delicately attuned conscience the slightest twinge, why, that was enough. So he would not take a case against someone whom he knew and liked even though he had never been his attorney and was not ethically barred from the retainer. He often pleaded with me to reduce fees to clients. He turned down lucrative retainers because the client or his cause did not fully appeal to him.

His exquisite sense of right and wrong motorized his legal conduct. "Where is there any book of law so dear to each man as that written in his heart?" asked Tolstoy. As general counsel of Paramount Pictures Corporation, he was subjected to an annual checkup by the company's physician, Dr. Leon Warshaw. The doctor was alarmed. All signs indicated extreme agitation and nervousness.

"What is the matter, Mr. Phillips? Is anything troubling you particularly?"

"Not really, but I have been somewhat upset by a company problem. I must admit I haven't slept recently."

"What is it?" asked the doctor, scanning the abnormal blood pressure, pulse, and other readings.

"Oh, I have asked for increases for the lawyers of my staff and due to an economy drive, they have been refused."

"Is that all?" asked the doctor. "And you are so upset?"

"Of course, do you realize what these lawyers have to face in increased living costs for their families? And they have worked so devotedly for the company. I will give them increases from my salary, but that won't be enough."

When Dr. Warshaw got to the checkup of the president of the company, Barney Balaban, he said, "If you don't want Louis Phillips to die of a heart attack, better approve his request for increases."

They were granted.

Laughter came easily to him. He had an eager gaiety of childlike exuberance. But tears also came readily, as he was swept by emotion. Anyone's misfortune, no matter how removed from him, would send him into hushed depression. I learned to control my alarm when he telephoned and spoke in almost inaudible sadness, for it often turned out to be nothing more than that some virtual stranger had suffered a broken leg, or that a preliminary motion had been lost in a North Dakota Federal court. There was no terminus to his great capacity for feeling, and he felt so deeply that one could not distinguish the sad from the truly tragic. To see his face lit up dazzlingly with happy excitement, or to see its funereal caste and hear his shaken voice, was to experience only partly the range of his pure emotionalism.

The only sadness he ever caused anyone was when he died.

I enjoyed the practice of law more when we were a small firm with one clerk. Each client received personal attention at all times. There were no departments to which he was sent for specialized advice to be ushered back to the senior for final decision. But the complexity of society has revolutionized law offices, just as it has the medical profession and business.

Today there is barely a legal service that may not be affected by tax consequences. So there is a tax department—lawyers who have made a life study of the tax laws and their kaleidoscopic changes from year to year.

Modern business is not content with internal growth. Acquisitions and mergers are resorted to for accelerated advancement. So there is an acquisitions department—manned by lawyers who understand the applicable regulations and procedures of the Securities and Exchange Commission.

On the other hand, growth can run afoul of the antitrust laws. So there is a department knowledgeable in the law of monopoly.

The public is now the largest of all corporate investors. So stockholder minority suits and proxy battles for control abound. There is a department trained to defend or conduct such contests.

So it is with wills and trusts, copyrights, divorce, real estate, libel, international law, and myriad other problems a law firm must solve to give a client a full rounded professional service. That is why, unfortunately, the individual practitioner or small law firm is at a great disadvantage. That is why law firms today are composed of fifty, a hundred, and even several hundred lawyers under one firm name and under one roof.

The process is not dissimilar to that which has occurred in business, where the small enterpreneur is at an ever-increasing disadvantage against the chain or huge competitor.

Even in medicine scientific advances make medical complexes with available laboratory services, and specialists in various branches, superior to the individual practitioner. How is one doctor to keep abreast of all the progress daily recorded?

Sometimes people introduce themselves and tell me they are clients of my office. I am always humiliated by such an incident, because I consider the role of adviser and counsel uniquely personal. But a complex society separates us from intimacy. There was a time when if your neighbor was ill, you would bring him soup, a hot-water bottle, and your personal solicitude. Today we live in huge cement cubicles and we do not even know who our neighbor is, though he may reside a few feet away.

I cherish the anecdote of the family doctor in a little town who has delivered children, treated them during infancy and maturity, and brought their children into the world. He has taken care of all ills from surgery to mental disease, and his intimate knowledge of the patient and his forebears have given him insights which no contemporary analyses alone could provide. Having grown old and tired from caring for an ever-increasing flock, he heartily welcomes a new graduate who has come into town to practice medicine. He hopes the young doctor, superbly trained, will relieve him ultimately of his responsibilities, but he soon learns that the newcomer does not intend to be a general practitioner. He will be a specialist. "Of the stomach?" the old doctor asks. "Oh no, that is too large a field for one man to master."

"Of the ears, nose, and throat?"

Of course not, there has been such an accumulation of knowledge in these areas that he cannot hope to absorb it all.

The old practitioner can contain himself no longer.

"What nostril do you intend to specialize in?" he asks.

Despite the growth of legal domains, I have striven with might and main to keep direct contact with each client. For I firmly believe that the psychological comfort which a client derives from his lawyer or doctor is of immense importance. A man or woman in trouble needs more than advice or even ultimate relief. There is the intervening period of deep anxiety which must be bridged. It is unnecessary torment, because it contributes nothing to solution, and enervates the victim, whose cooperation is necessary. I consider it the lawyer's duty to address himself to this problem as much as to the pure legal problem presented.

The client, like a patient, who is in trouble is highly sensitive to the demeanor of his adviser: a smile and confident manner are great therapy. A furrowed brow or pursed lips strike terror in the heart of the troubled. The attorney or doctor may only be gesturing unconsciously about a minor aspect of the difficulty, but to the overwrought, disaster is being registered. Scowls should be reserved exclusively for the adversary. Whether the condition is physical or mental, the body does wonders to ease the suffering, if given a chance.

Of course, the truth cannot be tampered with even to assuage suffering. But what is the truth and how is it to be presented? I tell the client that the problem is serious, and that I do not take a Pollyanaish view of it, but I am confident that it can be solved, that far worse has been overcome, and that he may be sure all our energy and resourcefulness will be applied to correct the situation. This is combined with a direct appeal to leave his worries on our doorstep. If he will realize that the ogres he dreams about are exaggerated shadows cast by him standing in his own light, he will understand that they are not real. Some peace of mind then becomes possible.

There is also the matter of "client relationship." Often lawyers are too busy and harassed taking care of the client's battles to worry about informing him or her of developments. What is more cruel than such suspension? Even adverse news is preferable to the imagined disasters conjured up by silence. Frequently there is no news, nothing but delay, but this is no excuse for not reporting—not if the attorney is sensitive to the client's fears. A telephone call or personal report of developments, even if they are thin or nonexistent, is tonic for the client's nervous system.

In short the lawyer or doctor who ignores the psychological areas of his professional duty is as unfaithful to it as if he were guilty of malpractice. Indeed it is humanistic malpractice to be unaware of the client's or patient's suffering when it is possible to alleviate it.

To overcome the impersonal aspect of a large law office, and mindful of the importance of knowing the client profoundly, I adopt what may be considered an inefficient procedure of inviting the most junior associate who may assist in a case to sit in at the very first conference with the client. The young lawyer is not assigned to a cubbyhole to prepare pleadings or bills of particular, or to research in the library, on the basis of an abstract presentation of the problem. He is introduced to the human side of the law, literally and in person. He hears the original, perhaps disjointed, and self-conscious description by the client, with all its telltale emphasis, evasions, or irrelevant excursions. He observes the client's candor, sometimes significantly burned at both ends. If he is perceptive, avenues for further factual research may open up, and may lead to resourceful legal ideas.

Also, empathy for the client is likely to be created (if it is distasteful, he should be taken off the case quickly), and this stimulates the effort, just as hostility dampens it.

I recall a matrimony case in which my associate dedicated himself at all hours on behalf of our client. However, when we discussed developments privately, he laughingly doubted her protestations of virtue.

The client repeatedly pleaded with me to have a junior, who was assisting in the case, assigned to her. She paid tribute to the talents and devotion of the associate, but she was enamored with the talents of the junior, not half as able.

The associate was flabbergasted by her ingratitude. I suggested that his private opinion of her had come through to her. He remonstrated that this could not be, he was fond of her and had never indicated his skepticism. It was difficult for him to realize that there are emanations which cannot be disguised.

My association with Louis Phillips opened up a door to the motion picture industry. I sat in at meetings of the New York Film Board of Trade. In those days there was a compulsory arbitration system whereby disputes between theater owners and motion picture producers and distributors were arbitrated before boards consisting of exhibitors and distributors evenly divided. I was entrusted to try these cases for the producers. They presented complicated industrial problems of clearance (the number of days of exclusive showing of a picture before the second and subsequent run theaters could show it), and copyright infringements (the showing of a picture in a theater for which it had not been licensed). This was called bicycling because that is how the motion picture print was transported to the theaters in the chain which did not pay for it. It was said that in the early days, a Charlie Chaplin print would not be returned for months. It rode the bicycles. Later the techniques became more sophisticated. Motorboats, and even planes, were used to rush the prints to unlicensed theaters.

To stop this practice, I urged that the damages be not merely the license fee which should have been paid, but damages under the Copyright Act, which were a minimum of $250 and a maximum of $5,000 a showing. Arbitration boards handed down awards of thousands of dollars for the illegitimate exhibition of a newsreel which could have been licensed for $2.50. In one case in Boston, the board awarded $26,000 damages for a film whose license fees ran only in the hundreds of dollars.

There were many other industrial disputes, such as conflicts of booking and deceptive advertising. I tried these cases throughout the country. Later the Government challenged the right of motion picture producers to own theater chains. This was claimed to be a vertical monopoly garnished by conspiratorial division of theater territories, scratching each other's backs in supplying films to each other's theaters, and other practices which were charged to be abuse of power. It was a lethal blow aimed at the motion picture structure. I was too young to be chosen for the defense of this action. Giants of the legal profession were retained—John W. Davis (who had been a Democratic candidate for the presidency), former appellate judge Joseph H. Proskauer, and Fred Wood, a lawyer's lawyer. But they lost.

The Supreme Court directed the motion picture companies to divest themselves of their theater chains or of their producing activities. They could not engage in both. This was called divorcement—a quaint domestic reference to corporations, who were compelled to live apart not because they quarreled but because they did not.

The aftermath was worse than the defeat itself. Dozens of theater owners brought antitrust suits against the motion picture companies, relying on the finding in the Government suit that the producers had violated the antitrust laws. I defended the companies in many of these involved litigations in the federal courts of many states. The risk and responsibility were great. The antitrust laws provide for treble damages. Many millions of dollars were at stake in each contest.

Although each plaintiff had the advantage of the finding of monopoly in the Government suit, he could recover damages only if he could demonstrate that he was injured in his theater operation. He could not throw the cloak of the Attorney General around his shoulders to claim damages he had not suffered. That was a Government privilege, but in a private suit, the plaintiff had to demonstrate that he had been victimized and how badly.

I lived for months in Chicago, Philadelphia, and other cities where these protracted cases had to be tried. We were rewarded for our exhaustive efforts and fared extremely well.

When Louis Phillips was offered a counsel post by Paramount Pictures Corporation, I suggested that despite the tempting offer, he should refuse it, unless he was granted permission to continue the private practice of law. He would agree to give his personal time exclusively to Paramount, but he could remain a partner in our law firm. This was an unprecedented request and it resulted in an unprecedented consent. The battle for independence had been won.

I have never veered from this principle. Later, when my law partners, Robert S. Benjamin and Arthur Krim, took the chairmanship of the board and the presidency of United Artists Corporation, the same reservation was made. They remained partners in our law firm. Their salaries were deemed fees earned for our firm—but not their equities. These were just as deliberately reserved for them, and excluded from our firm.

I never owned a single share of stock in United Artists or in any other motion picture company, directly or indirectly. My personal principle has been that an attorney should have no investment which may cut across his complete objectivity in representing clients—particularly where they are competitors in the same industry. He is necessarily entrusted with confidential information of the highest order and like Caesar's wife he must not only be pure, but avoid any act which may give even a suspicion to the contrary.

Of course, a reputation for absolute integrity is the final assurance to a client. I was retained at different times to represent Metro-Goldwyn-Mayer, Twentieth Century-Fox, and Columbia Pictures in proxy contests for control. These retainers and the struggles which ensued involved intricate maneuvers and confidences. But the clients knew that they were inviolate from disclosure even to my own partners at United Artists. So it was with all other types of litigations in which competitive data came to my attention, when I represented motion picture companies in other suits. This is the norm in our profession. The sanctity of confidence is as honored as that of the confessional booth or the doctor's office.

I shall not detail here any of the cases which I fought—whether they involved the lives and fortunes of corporations or individuals. I have depicted a small number of them in *My Life in Court* and *The Jury Returns*.

This being a more personally focused chronicle, I go back to my point about independence. I believe that any lawyer who casts his lot with one client, usually as corporation counsel, makes a serious error. He may rise as he often does to an executive post, even the vice-presidency or presidency, but his tenure is subject to the uncertainties of corporate control. Time and again, I have seen counsel for large companies displaced not because of any deficiency of their own, but because new interests took over and brought in their own lawyers.

The tragedy is that such counsel have become experts in the specialized field of the corporate enterprise, and, when let out, find very few, if any, similar posts available, where their expertise could be applied. Also, though very competent, they have been away from the general practice of the law so long that they are worse off than a beginner, because their distinction and high earnings are handicaps to new training. "A used key is always bright."

I, therefore, advise young lawyers to join law firms, not corporation staffs, so that when they have earned partnership, they are in professional business for themselves.

On several occasions, partners in my own firm were lured by attractive offers made by companies I represent. In each instance, the earnings were much higher, and the proffered title flattering. I would not stand in their way. Indeed, I had introduced them to the client and developed the relationship. But I advised against acceptance, because the shelter of a law firm is secure, while that of a corporation is subject to all the vicissitudes of changing business climate, absorption by acquisition, growth by merger and new faces at the top, and, of course, proxy battles which, when successful, result in new management and the unceremonious ousting of the old. I have been involved in these battles of corporate democracy and seen the defeated regimes lose power just like defeated officeholders when they lose an election.

I have myself been the recipient of proposals to abandon the general practice of law, in favor of exclusive corporate service. I recite one such offer because it was so unusual. An executive of a large company urged me to quit my law office and become his counsel and personal adviser. He made an offer which he thought I couldn't refuse. He would put two million dollars in a trust for me and pay an annual salary in any amount my conscience would permit me to suggest.

I did not give this an instant thought. My rejection was all the more difficult because he and his wife are charming companions. But my principle held fast. I am willing to be enslaved by each case, but do not wish to be a prince in one man's domain.

CURIOSITY AND ABSORPTION

In my junior year in college, I qualified to teach English to foreigners in night school. It was another way to eke out some money for my own education. But I enjoyed it so I should have paid for the privilege. In the first place, the class consisted of mature people, some of them graduates from the gymnasiums of Europe (what a curious transposition of meaning the word gymnasium involves—exercise in thought, not physical exercise). One or two of my students had doctoral degrees. Furthermore, they were eager to learn.

However, they all had one severe handicap—tiredness. They worked during the day and were exhausted at night. Not all had the energy which I had inherited from a long line of ancestors. I was brimful of enthusiasm for the task. The common experience in night school was that attendance dwindled. Students flocked to the opening sessions. A class consisted of forty to fifty. Within weeks there were only twenty or thirty. Toward the end of the term some classes had only five or six attendees. There were even instances where the course had to be terminated because nobody showed up.

Good resolutions rarely have long lives. There is a large drop-out among those who sign up for exercise courses, diet regimes, nonsmoking cruises, correspondence courses, encyclopedia purchases, and the like. The night students had a better excuse for quitting than others, because some could barely keep their eyes open, and without great concentration it was difficult to learn a new language.

The Board of Education trained its teachers in certain techniques. These were set forth in guidebooks. I disagreed completely with them, so I ignored them and followed my own ideas. They worked. Attendance not only remained steady throughout the term, but actually increased, as other classes declined. Furthermore, I arranged a final debate which demonstrated a mastery of English by students who could barely utter a phrase when they entered the course.

The authorities at the Board of Education used attendance figures as an index to effectiveness, as well they might. They were startled to find one class which had a drop-in instead of a drop-out record. What was going on there?

One day an assistant superintendent and two other dignitaries of the Board of Higher Education paid me a surprise visit. They introduced themselves and said they would like to sit in during the lesson. All seats were taken; indeed one or two were doubled up. The principal brought chairs which were placed in the aisles.

What they saw first was that the two large blackboards were filled with material which I had written and printed a half hour before class was to begin.

The contents were startling. Acting on the principle that memory depends on concentration, and that concentration results from aroused interest, the material on the blackboards had nothing to do with the customary techniques of learning a language. There were no lists of nouns, verbs, or adjectives. There was not a word about grammar, parsing, tense, vowels or consonants. I considered these as dull as the Official Instruction Guides which prescribed them.

Instead the first item was headed Health Hint. Each night a useful suggestion was set forth, so presented that it contained words and usage built on the progression of past lessons.

Then followed in succession an interesting history item, a statement by one of the world's great philosophers, a joke, a science curiosity, an unusual biographical fact about a famous composer, or painter, or writer.

For a full half hour, I read slowly from the boards, explaining, repeating, and restating everything in simple form. I did all the talking. I did not call on a student.

This also violated the guidebook. Its theory was that the student should be compelled to speak as much as possible. This seemed to me to be psychologically unwise. A student called upon to express himself when he is not ready to do so is embarrassed before his audience. Every mispronunciation or wrong word causes a gale of laughter. He feels he is being ridiculed. He dreads the ordeal of being exposed.

In my class he knew he was safe. Only when he volunteered would he have to perform.

I believed in teaching through the ear. Over and over again I repeated a question and answered it. I jested. I walked among the students making comments which became familiar to them by sheer varied repetition. I never used a foreign language to explain. But I permitted them to help out each other with translation. Their curiosity stimulated them. Those who understood the joke on the blackboard laughed, and those who didn't would lean over to a friend to get a definition of a word. One could hear the delayed giggles as comprehension reached some students in installments. This reminded me of a story about Adlai Stevenson when he watched a comedian who performed in Hebrew in an Israeli night club. Stevenson joined the others in hearty laughter. Someone asked him whether he understood Hebrew. "No, but I trust these people," he replied.

As the different items were read from the board, curiosity and excitement spread among the students. Once a brilliant student who had studied astronomy in Berlin challenged my astronomy fact on the board. His expertise compelled him to express himself. I helped him with his English whenever he lapsed into German, so that he could complete his argument. Then I asked him whether he would mind repeating his contention solely in English, because I was proud of his effort, and stood corrected on astronomy.

As the informal atmosphere developed, students began to talk to me and, at times, excitedly to their neighbors. "In English," I always reminded them. With a little help, they would utter whole sentences and laugh at the way their compulsion to express themselves had made English words tumble out of their mouths—usually words which had been absorbed from my constant talking to them.

There were times when the subject matter caused disagreement among the students. They forgot that they were in a class and debated with each other. I never interrupted them, except with the stricture "In English—please—only in English," and when their eyes turned pleadingly to fill in a vacuum in their vocabulary, I supplied it, repeated the sentence with it, expressed the thought still another way—and then turned them loose again.

The students were having such a good time (isn't that the best way to learn?) that I could not help showing off and asking whether they would like to stay longer. They voted for another half hour. The dignitaries from the Board of Higher Education had to stay after school.

After the session I met with the visitors in the office of the principal. He reminded me that I had ignored all the rules, but his superiors were far more friendly. They commented that while my individualistic style might work for me, they doubted that it could be applied generally. I thought it could. I quoted Robert Hutchins: "The purpose of education is to inflame the mind." The corollary was even more important: intense interest was essential to learning. A dull lesson could not penetrate a tired mind. These students were grownups. They were intelligent and mature. They would come alert and concentrate if the content was stimulating. Also, language was similar to music. It literally had a tune. One could learn it better by listening. Of course the ultimate goal was to have the student speak. But premature insistence on his practicing out loud was self-defeating. Self-consciousness wiped out his sparse vocabulary. Why not try a new approach?

They asked whether I would volunteer to help write a new guide-book. I did, but it was compromised down the road by conventional technicians. Still it was an improvement.

I cherished the friendships which developed with some of the students, and which lasted for many years. To this day I receive an occasional letter which begins, "Perhaps you remember me. I was a pupil in your class in night school." The gold pen and pencil presented to me by my last class out of their meager earnings was the most touching gift I ever received.

Next to law and medicine, I would have preferred teaching as a profession.

I have continued to teach sporadically. I give law lectures annually on "The Art of a Jury Trial" or some other subject at Columbia, Yale, Harvard, and other universities. I also have presided at moot court trials at various law schools. On each occasion I meet with the students in private seminars after the talks and engage in a dialogue, which is, I hope, as useful to them as it is to me.

Some years ago, I thought I would share my love for law with teaching. I accepted an invitation to give a law course at Yale Law School to be given only on Fridays. I thought this was manageable. But before it could begin, I was retained to try an antitrust case in the Midwest. I was away for months. The law is truly a jealous mistress. I have only succeeded in stealing a day here and there from her, to address students across the land.

Great developments in pedagogic science have not dented the simple principle that stimulation of the mind increases its receptivity and retention.

THE COSMIC SHELL GAME

For some strange reason, trivial incidents, which ought to pass by in a flash, impress themselves on the mind permanently. Something about them digs so deeply into our consciousness that they survive as pressing and sometimes oppressive memories for the rest of our lives.

For example, I recall a minor incident, when boarding a bus. I was late and eager not to miss it. I rushed up the steps, heedlessly pushing an old man aside, unintentionally, I am sure. He remonstrated loudly at my rudeness, and gave me a deserved dressing down in front of the crowd of passengers. I apologized, but to no avail. He condemned me as one of the younger generation, who had no manners or respect for anyone. I finally thought he was overdoing it, but not the audience he was addressing. Some of them mumbled their disapproval out loud too. It was a fleeting instance, but the man's face and his castigation remain indelibly in my mind. Why this psychic scar, when so many worse transgressions have been obliterated by time?

I am sure everyone has experienced a brush with death or injury. I have had a number of such traumas—a plane whose motor has fallen off, a near-drowning incident in a lake, and other perils. But one minor escapade is vividly haunting to this day. I was walking across Times Square in New York City on my way to lunch at the Algonquin Hotel, where I would "preside" over the Round Table.

My mind was still trailing behind on a legal problem I had wrestled with in my office. Absentmindedly, I stepped off the curb. A huge truck, traveling at irresistible speed, passed by me so closely that it ripped a button off my overcoat and smashed it to bits. I was startled, of course, and blew a sigh of fright, but continued to lunch. There I sat as usual with the writer Konrad Bercovici, publishers Martin Quigley and Jack Alicoate, humorist Harry Hershfield, columnist Dr. Frank Kingdon, owner of the hotel Ben Bodne, and one or two visiting celebrities. The table talk was witty, stimulating, and warm. It did not even occur to me to mention the incident. Hadn't we all gone through the same near accidents many times? But the thought that a few inches forward and my life would have been snuffed out never left me. It is as if my subconscious had registered the imminence of death from which soporific nature protects us otherwise.

Well, two incidents of completely different character left the same deeply etched impression on me forever. They also gave me a better insight to other people's sensitivities, and in that sense have been instructive as well as painful.

The first occurred in 1928. In the New York Film Board of Trade there was an executive who took care of the trade association functions. His name was John Cronin. He was about sixty-five years old, having "retired" to this job after being Mayor of Peekskill, New York. He was a very devout Catholic, with impressive bearing, being tall, gray and not convex in the middle. His slightly bulbous, veined nose (not due to drinking) did not detract from his dignity.

Cronin must have been starved for decent conversation. With my advent in the office, he found the opportunity for discourse. I liked him and was stimulated by his knowledge and his fine mind. So whenever the opportunity presented itself, he would wander into my office, inquire whether I was too busy, and sit down to chat, no matter what the answer was.

I found lunch hour most easily sacrificed. So we got into the habit of ordering a bite at my desk and talking about "life" and all its vagaries.

Of course, we reached religion. He entered into this discussion with zest. He did not fear any inroads of logic, because he had faith, which is the ubiquitous bulwark against the finite powers of the mind.

So in the same innocent and friendly spirit in which I had assailed some of his economic or political views, I challenged what I described as the "superstitions" which abound in all religions. These made for lively if inconclusive discussions. He seemed to cherish and enjoy them and indeed invited their continuation.

One day, he brought up the tenets of his religion. Not without sensitivity, I went at some of them, exploiting what I thought was the intellectual atmosphere which pervaded our discussions. I was sure he knew of my respect for his religion, as he had for mine. I merely took an agnostic view about some of the "miracles" which pervade religious lore, whether it be the splitting of the Red Sea or the Immaculate Conception. I recall the playful manner of some of our exchanges, such as my reference to the quotation "I am an atheist, thank God." However, his face became flushed during our argument, and since he had high blood pressure, I changed the subject. He would not detour. He remained chained in thought to the "cross-examination" to which I had subjected him. My words now passed him by. Suddenly, he interrupted. His face was contorted as if he was suffering physical pain, and in a low voice he said slowly, "Please, don't do this to me."

These words and the incident to which they are attached are engraved permanently in my mind. Cronin was a sophisticated man who had undoubtedly been through many discussions about Catholic dogma. He was very able and could give better than he received in any debate. He also had a sense of humor which gave him imperturbability. His profound religious convictions were therefore impregnable, I would have thought. Yet something had happened which threatened to breach his faith. It was a sin to do this. I never felt more guilty in my life.

Nor could I ever forget his abandonment of the verbal contest to plead for mercy. It was so uncharacteristic of him, and revealed the depth of his anguish.

My apologies exceeded my embarrassment, but every disclaimer of intent to offend his sensibilities only emphasized the injury, since it had been inflicted despite good will. Like a rent garment, the more one fusses with it, the worse the tear becomes.

Every person builds shells around himself to protect the inner core. In Cronin's case it was a shell which protected him from the extinction of death and assured him everlasting life.

Others surround themselves with an idealistic shell. They would sacrifice everything for a better world. I can think of nothing more tragic, for example, than one who sincerely believes in the Soviet Union as the perfect society, and gladly makes all sacrifices for his belief, only to discover its corruption and Mafia-like leadership, as evidenced again right from the bear's mouth—Khrushchev's book.

It is only when one cannot build a shell because he hates himself that he is really sick. Hating others may be detestable and foolish because every minute of hate is sixty seconds of possible happiness lost. But hating oneself is permanent unhappiness. The inner core cannot be protected.

There are certain areas where change of mind is not disruptive. Indeed, it is part of enlightenment to explore one's beliefs. Ideas transplanted in other minds grow better. A mind stretched by a new idea never returns to its original size. But one must recognize the difference between opinions which can be shaped or discarded and those protective shells which are vital to survival.

I thought I had learned my lesson. I used to have delightful talks with Martin Quigley, a lay leader in the Catholic Church. He was a Jesuit scholar and it was unnecessary to spare his feelings, because his keen mind could thrust as well as parry. His best weapon was an enigmatic smile as if to say, "It is too bad you don't understand, but after all, how can a finite mind comprehend the infinite?" Nevertheless, we jousted on politics (he thought Roosevelt's financial profligacy would bring about a Fascist state), the arts (he was the founder of the original motion picture code, and considered the mild permissiveness of those days the beginning of the ruin of the industry), on civil rights (we agreed on its universal application), and on religion (he recognized my own religious feelings and used them to combat my own questions). Though he didn't need solicitude, I treated him tenderly, after the Cronin episode.

But many years later, I repeated my error. I was off guard, because the subject was in a different direction. It involved my sister-in-law Cora.

She and her husband were students and followers of the esoteric philosophers Gurdjieff and Ouspensky.

Through their precepts they sought higher consciousness. Cora, who was goodness itself, nevertheless struggled all her life to improve her soul, to prepare herself for the endlessness of all forces. It is always so. The pure seek purification; the clean bathe most frequently.

Cora also believed in reincarnation. As a result of her intensive studies, she became not only an exemplar but a teacher. She and her husband traveled to many countries, where groups of followers practiced these philosophies. Part of the ritual involved intricate dances and exercises, like those of Indian dervishes, to achieve higher concentration and free the mind for nobler spheres.

On one occasion she sought to enlist me and my wife, Mildred, in "the movement." This was, of course, intended as a compliment, for only those who were capable of banishing negative thoughts could aspire to these teachings. Out of curiosity, I attended a meeting at which Gurdjieff presided.

He was a fat, totally bald Russian, with a flowing white handlebar mustache and an unbelievably insulting manner toward his own followers. I was aghast at the supine subservience of his students. I witnessed a microcosm of a tyrannical domain and was revolted by it, even though I am ready to accede the brilliance of his writings and, particularly, those of Ouspensky, who wrote the highly regarded mathematical work *Tertium Organum*. I expressed some of my resentment with a lowly pun. While lecturing and cursing, Gurdjieff had eaten the head of a sheep, tearing it apart with bare hands. I referred to his huge belly as Sheepshead bay.

Years went by. Cora took the place of esteemed leaders in "the movement" who had passed on. Unlike some of them, she was a model human being, kind, sensitive, and striving ever to be more worthy.

A part of her duties was to give talks. She feared them, and sought my help. This, and her general interest in my activities and opinions, led to friendly discussions. I expressed my skepticism about much of her philosophy. Of course, there was some truth in the precepts she held. There is in every "movement." Christian Scientists, Religious Scientists, Quakers, Mormons, Seventh-Day Adventists, Jehovah's Witnesses, Chasidim, Yogis, all preach some psychological truths. It is presumptuous to concede the same for the dozens of religions and sects. The area of doubt begins when these limited truths are extended into full-blown credos, every tenet of which is required to be accepted.

In any event, I argued out my rejection of some of her theses, from reincarnation, with its familiar argument that child geniuses, like Mozart, can only be explained thereby, to higher consciousness in preparation for soul-like existence.

At one point, she paused and looked at me a long time. I thought she was thinking through a reply. Instead, she said in a voice whose change of octave and vibrancy connoted deep emotion, "Lou, live and let live."

It was an echo of Cronin's plea. She had devoted her life looking for its higher meaning. Like hundreds of philosophers who had preceded her, she could not accept the brief cycle of life and death as a fleeting moment to no purpose. So she searched. And she thought she had found. Now all her dedication at great sacrifice to mundane joys of the unthinking was being challenged. Words were reaching her which threw some doubt on the certainty which sustained her. If the shell of spiritual preparation would be loosened—if the great truth might be an illusion after all, of what avail the years spent in study, teaching, and believing? "Live and *let live*" was a literal cry.

I had assaulted a precious shell. I vowed never to do so again.

I can only hope that her untimely death several years later has solved the great mystery for her, and that she now hovers over this page smiling at my foolish skepticism.

IF A SPEAKER DOESN'T STRIKE OIL IN
FIFTEEN MINUTES, HE SHOULD STOP BORING

I have made thousands of speeches and never used a script or a note. This does not mean that I improvise or am not thoroughly prepared. On the contrary, the preparation is intense. I would no more address an audience without exhaustive preparation than I would try a case without advance mastery of the facts. The "secret" of public speaking, like that of successful trial work, is preparation. In lectures to law schools, I have attempted to impress this on memory by creating a "scientific" equation: I.Q. (Intelligence Quotient)$+$W.Q.^{2} (Work Quotient squared)$=$S. (Success).

I would rather try a case against the most famous lawyer, who by virtue of age and success depends on his assistants for preparation, than against a neophyte, who has slaved to learn every factual and legal facet of his case. As Benjamin Franklin put it, "Never was one glorious without first being laborious."

Unfortunately, the opportunity to triumph over the brilliant but unprepared veteran rarely occurs. For he, too, knows the secret of his success, and he is not likely to abandon it. Sir William Osler once stated this principle felicitiously:

> There is an old folk lore legend that there is some mystic word which will open barred gates. There is, in fact, such a mystic word. It is the open sesame of every portal. The great equalizer in the world, the true philosopher's stone, which transmutes all the baser metal of humanity into gold. The stupid man it will make bright, the bright brilliant and the brilliant steady. With the mystic word all things are possible. And the mystic word is "work".

Yes, the trial lawyer has many opportunities to improvise, to triumph because of a sudden inspiration, to balance like a gyroscope in a storm

—but all of these are subordinate planets. The sun around which they orbit is thorough preparation.

The same is true in making a good speech. It is arrogant for anyone to take the time of an audience with unthoughtful improvisation. The least one owes to any occasion is thorough preparation so that some ideas may be projected which will be stimulating to the audience.

So much has been written about public speaking. I have contributed a book myself—called *Thinking on Your Feet*. What is generally overlooked is that the overwhelming requirement for a speech is profound thought. Communication has come to mean the process of transfer, instead of the thought which is transferred. Ideas transplanted in another mind seem to grow better. But original thinking is the rarest to come by—and no amount of forensic skill can substitute for it. Technique is an adornment of substance. It is never a substitute for it.

That is why people groan when the program announces a long list of speakers. We have learned from experience that there is not a thought in a carload, and we do not wish to suffer through bromidic exhortations.

However, if the speaker is thoughtful enough to have an original idea and has made a special effort to develop it, the evening can be exhilarating and informative. But where are they?

Dozens of times I have sat on committees to select speakers. The occasions were important enough to warrant acceptance by the most famous men and women in the nation, not excluding the President of the United States. Yet we have struggled to find a suitable speaker. We usually turned to celebrities instead of thinkers, to pique our curiosity rather than to stretch our minds.

This probably explains a unique American phenomenon which assumes that achievement in one field qualifies a man to be an expert in others. The industrialist makes speeches on international affairs; the nuclear scientist on mores; the novelist on the state of the economy, and the motion picture star on politics. Brilliance in one field is rarely across-the-board versatility, and we traverse arid areas with an impostor.

Henry Ford once sued the Chicago *Tribune* for libel, claiming one million dollars damages. The cross-examiner, aware that Ford was brilliant to the point of genius in his field, sought to bring him down from his pedestal by changing the subject.

"Who was Benedict Arnold?" he suddenly asked.

"He was a writer, I think," replied Ford, thus setting off a laugh which reverberated around the nation for many years. It is doubtful that his error was due to confusion with Matthew Arnold. Even that name was probably beyond his ken. More likely he was thinking of Horace L. Arnold, who had written a shop manual for Ford workers.

Charles Lindbergh similarly revealed that his unique competence as a flier could not be transferred to the political and military arenas. He announced his belief that the Nazis would triumph. He headed an isolationist movement. He had earned the world's adulation for his historic flight, but would many want to shower ticker tape upon him for his other views?

We have become cynical about all this. The public takes it for granted that elected officials do not write their own pronouncements. Experts prepare speeches for them, and even the President can claim no more than that he exercises editorial judgment in adopting one view given to him rather than another.

There is not even an effort to disguise this sorry fact. Official announcements are made that two economic advisers are preparing a policy paper which the President will deliver to the nation in a few weeks.

Granted that the complexity of government requires research and advice of experts, but this does not mean abdication to the opinions of unknown men who never submitted themselves to the electorate.

One had only to learn how Churchill, Roosevelt, and Stevenson made every speech their own, irrespective of what material was prepared for them, to understand the difference between an independent intellect digesting research and a weak executive adopting another's thoughts, and sometimes faltering over the delivery of them.

Having stressed substance as the irreducible requirement for any speech, I turn to the art of delivery. Cardozo once pointed out that form is not a protuberance on substance; it is part of substance itself. An argument or speech well made is not the same as the identical argument or speech poorly made.

Perfectionism requires that no speech be read, and that no notes be used. Why? Because the rhythm necessary to absorption of the spoken word is completely different from that of the written word.

All one has to do to verify this is to use one's ear attentively. Listen to any conversation. It is slow, halting for a thought, full of pauses, and then a sudden torrent of words as the idea develops. Often anticipation by the listener makes it unnecessary to finish the sentence. The parsing is faulty. Speech, which is the conveyor belt on which the thoughts are carried, is slow or fast depending on its comprehensibility. Often a word, clause, or sentence is repeated as the speaker senses that the pace is too fast for the complexity of the thought. In short, the delivery is irregular, adjusting to the absorptive capacity of the audience. The listener cannot do what he does with a passage in a book which confounds him—read it over again or put it down for another occasion. If he cannot follow the speaker *instantly*, he deserts him. That is one of the reasons audiences are lost when speeches are read from a script.

There is the jest, all too true, of the speaker who began, "My duty is to speak, and yours to listen. But if you quit before I do, please let me know."

On the other hand, that which is intended to be read rather than heard should never be dictated to a stenographer or on a machine. It should be written or typed, because the rhythm for the words which are read is different from the rhythm when words are heard. The construction can be more involved and more polished. The style more graceful. Short sentences can be balanced against longer ones; declarative ones against questions. Interest can be created through contrast and coloring of diction. The grammar and rhetoric should be impeccable, and enjoyment can be derived by the reader from the beauty of construction as well as thought. There is almost a mathematical construction, like in music, which, although unnoticeable, creates a rhythm which affects the emotions.

So the firm rule is: a speech should be delivered without a single note, the speaker looking his audience in the eye and timing his delivery to match its immediate comprehension.

A book or document intended to be read should never be dictated orally, but written or typed personally by the author. I have followed these precepts. All my platform speeches have no written crutches lying on the podium. All my writings, as this very page, are written out longhand by pen or pencil.

The only exception I make is to have a quotation or statistical data before me when I use them in a speech. These too are in my mind and I do not need the notes, but I deliberately resort to them to assure the hearers of authenticity. Audiences are so skeptical about memory that they may distrust the accuracy of a long quotation. So I make a special point to read them—putting on my glasses, to be sure this part of the delivery is distinguished from the rest.

Is this the rule for all who make public speeches? Of course not. A busy executive called upon to address a group of his pretended peers may not have time or inclination to reach for perfection. He may not even aspire to be a public speaker. He is content to share his expertise from a written script. But let him not pride himself on an art which he does not practice. And when he is complimented by a request that his talk ought to be printed because it was so good, he might suspect that the audience couldn't follow it orally.

Professor John Dewey drew large classes at Columbia College because of his eminence, but he suffered the highest absences. He was as dull orally as he was profound in his writings. Professor Albert Einstein did not need the aid of his accent to be incomprehensible. His eyes were buried in a script. His words in monotone emerged haltingly from behind his mustache, losing volume as they were sifted through hair. Audiences rushed to see and hear him, and after they had satisfied their eyes, they closed their ears. Ultimately, they turned to small talk among themselves while the great man droned on. His best oration was at a commencement exercise where he was one of the speakers. He arose and said, "I do not have any particular thoughts to express today, so I wish you all success in your future years." Then he sat down. If only others who had nothing to say would follow his example.

The speaker must see his audience, look into their eyes, observe their facial expressions, and communicate directly to them as participants.

Even a stripper, like Gypsy Rose Lee, knew that it was eye-to-eye contact that was important to hold attention. In one of the Follies, she was gowned in Ziegfeld's abundant silks and satins, with a flowing train, and a hat as tall and as shimmering as a fountain. As she made her way down the bejeweled circular stairs, she learned that she had to keep her eyes on the audience to hold their attention. The scene was not for stripping, but the risk was tripping. She dared not look down to ensure a safe journey because it would break eye contact.

This principle is responsible for the wise practice at public dinners to put the most brilliant lights on the banquet room when the speaking program begins. That is why the art of public speaking requires experience before an audience. The more frequently the speaker appears, the more at ease he will be. A speaker's nervousness or distress is the most communicable disease in the world. An audience is immediately infected and suffers with him.

One who has not addressed an audience from a platform, dais, or stage cannot possibly imagine the shock from the unexpected surroundings. There is a sea of faces. The eye can only take in a few at a time. They are moving, talking to one another, or looking up challengingly (it might even appear mockingly). A spotlight on the speaker blinds him and the audience becomes blurred. There are all sorts of noises emanating from the front. Applause or laughter does not sound like individual expression, but like a cumulated roar from some huge beast. If the speaker is inexperienced, and becomes overwhelmed by the terrifying surroundings, there is quickly added to his discomfort a competitive conversational buzz throughout the room which signals him that he is being ignored. If he attempts to shout over it, the noise accelerates just enough to make him unheard. He is like a greyhound chasing a rabbit and he cannot win the race for attention. Only his own poise and "presence" could have compelled attention in the first place. This can come only with practice—not in the home, but before an audience.

It is the old vicious cycle when one seeks experience. He is disqualified because he has none. And he can't acquire it until he has some.

Like the inexperienced applicant for a job who demanded a larger salary than his experienced competitors, because "it is much harder work when you have no experience," the aspiring speaker must pass through a much tougher ordeal than the experienced one.

There is a compensating principle. Each appearance before an audience reduces the fear. It is not a gradual descension from panic to self-control, but a progressive one. Ultimately, the speaker learns not to play the game of obliterating the audience's presence in his mind in order to achieve inner peace. Ultimately, he reaches the sophisticated level; when he can look at their faces and observe their reactions to him without being distracted; when awareness of the audience's presence is a stimulation to him; when he is master of his audience; when the "beast" in front knows the assurance and strength of its rider, and is not tempted by his very panic to challenge him. Only then has he become a public speaker.

Even then appearance in front of an audience must be frequent. A long lapse will cause self-assurance to atrophy. Like exercises for the muscles, there is no lasting benefit without slavish repetition. Know-how in some activities is never lost—driving a car, riding a bicycle, or swimming. But in others, like golf, one begins all over again, after a lapse. The greater the psychological demand upon performance, the less self-replenishing it is. So, the more often—the better.

I was fortunate, therefore, to gain speaking experience at a very early age and to accelerate my appearances over a lifetime. In elementary school, I was selected to recite the Pledge of Allegiance at each morning's assembly gathering (a procedure now challenged in our highest courts on the ground that compulsory patriotism is a violation of individual rights. I have always thought that, irrespective of the legalism, this was a rather humorless approach. Children reciting in unison enjoy their self-expression like their elders enjoy a communal sing-in, and entirely apart from the lyrics. But, unfortunately, good causes often ride on a solemn horse. Is that not why people yearning for a light mood sometimes vote sinners into public office?).

At the age of ten, I had become a soapbox orator. In the Brooklyn district where I lived, the Socialists were making their first advances from proclaimers of a better world to election in the State Assembly. There, they learned that their blueprints, as beautiful as bluebirds, were not easily transferable into reality. The defects in dreams are never visible to the dreamer, only to the interpreter. "Where is the money coming from?" was a question that resisters asked, and while there were many answers, the reformers had thought least about such things and were the least competent to pragmatize their visions.

Still, how could one's heart not beat faster as sincere radicals railed against the evils in our society, and called for a better world.

The leader of the local Socialist party was Morris Hillquit, a mustached intellectual whose calm demeanor and uncharacteristic soft tone made him palatable to the average voter. Only when one saw the fierce light in his eyes was it evident that the revolutionary fire within him was disciplined, not dampened. He ran for Mayor of New York City on a Socialist ticket against a Democrat, John F. Hylan, and polled extraordinarily well. His successful campaign pulled in for the first time several Socialist assemblymen.

Morris Hillquit and Eugene Debs became the heroes of the Socialist movement, and their followers predicted the ultimate triumph of the Socialists in American political life. Fate decreed that they should be virtually eliminated from the political scene. But they did not fail entirely. They were to be the catalysts for recognition by Government of direct, not vicarious and remote, responsibility for the welfare of the people. Except for their extreme notion of Government ownership, their program was not rejected. It was adopted by their opponents. Al Smith, a Tammany-dyed Democrat, built a brilliant career from the sidewalks of New York to the State mansion in Albany and to the threshold of the White House, by putting into law most of their demands. When Smith proposed a Child Labor Law, he was denounced as an IWW (International Workers of the World, scornfully translated as I Won't Work), a more deadly appellation than "Communist" in Senator Joseph McCarthy's day. Later, President Franklin D. Roosevelt's New Deal was, in large part, the old deal of the Socialists, a fact which his bitter opponents did not hesitate to hurl at him. Yet, Republican and Democratic conventions in later years both accepted in their official platforms the whole catalogue of "radical" proposals, such as the National Labor Relations Act (the bill of rights for the "working class"), Government insurance of bank deposits, minimum hourly wage, child labor laws, Social Security, Medicare, Tennessee Valley Authority (Government ownership of utilities), civil rights laws, income tax ("confiscatory" taxes on high income), and more and more. Every new effort was denounced, like its predecessor, as the last blow which would destroy capitalism. Yet books appear regularly in which noted economists demonstrate that Roosevelt saved capitalism, because he lifted the people out of despair caused by the great depression and proved that freedom and welfare could be wed without destroying the sacramental authority of democracy. Yes, the Socialists were like spiders which impregnate and die in the process.

Well, my reputation as a boy orator spread. I rejected the suggestion of the powerful Republican leader John Crews to devote my energies to his club, situated enticingly on Sumner Avenue, opposite my home, and accepted the call of none less than Hillquit's emissary to speak on street corners for the Socialists. I always drew a crowd. Few had political interest. They were mainly neighbors who were intrigued to hear Joe Nizer's son hold forth. They reported back to my mother, who beamed because I had made "a good speech," even if it had been on the subject of cruelty to horses (which if too old or sick were shot on the street by a policeman. Those were the days when horses, not cars, were towed away. That is where the old joke stems from about the policeman who could not spell Koscuisko Street, and therefore reported a dead horse on Bushwick Avenue).

My harangues about poverty and an unjust society were not drawn from personal experience. True, my parents were very poor, but the terrible thing was we were happy. I would wake up in the morning in a cold flat, where the defective window permitted the snow to drift in and form icicles on the inside. I shuddered to get out of the bed, and drew the puffed-up huge feather *perineh* closer around me until I disappeared in its billows. My mother encouraged a courageous venture into the cold world by warming my socks on the stove and handing them to me under the quilt, and throwing a warm sweater, as well as her arms, around me as I emerged. (It does not take a skilled analyst to understand why even in my warm penthouse apartment today, my electric blanket is turned on nearer to high than low.)

True, food was not plentiful. My mother tried to hide the fact that the egg which could be spared was given to me. I knew despite her protest that it was not her lack of appetite which caused her to put up her nose at dairy products while urging me to eat because it was good for a growing child.

True, my mother and I worked evenings scalloping laces, but I could hardly inveigh against child labor, because we sang and joked, to the accompaniment of the scissor blades, and often I felt as if I was playing with a toy.

True, I ran errands for the local Regal Shoe Store in the heat of summer to earn a few dollars, but the romance of a job at that early age was as fascinating as my walking across the Brooklyn Bridge to save a nickel, or eating only rice pudding because it cost only a nickel.

True, my clothes were limited to one outfit, as if it were a uniform which discipline decreed must not be changed. But when, as a birthday gift, I received a shiny black leather raincoat and attached hood, like that worn by heroes in motion picture storms at sea, I got up at dawn each day to scan the skies in the hope of a downpour which would justify such stifling garb against the fierce elements. Finally, the dastardly good weather exhausted my patience, and on a slightly cloudy day, I ventured forth in my new regalia, buttoned up to choking. I chose to regard the stares of passers-by as admiration rather than wonder at my anticipation of a second Noah's flood. But I was happy.

"A happy home," says the Bible, "is an early heaven." Try as I might, I could not build my speech upon my own suffering. So I soaked up the Socialist literature of the working class's grievances throughout the world. From the oppression in Siberia to the "exploitation of the masses" in remote regions of the world. I soon learned that mass statistics and generalizations were not the road to persuasion. They were devoid of emotion. Audiences were held by the novelty of a youngster in knickerbockers holding forth from a short triangular stepladder which provided a precarious platform. Later, as the crowds increased, I was provided the back of an open truck, and still later "stardom" brought me the luxury of an open Ford.

There were no microphones, and outdoor speaking was a challenge to the voice because there were no confining walls to bounce the sounds back. So I had invaluable training in the production of sound which could reach a large audience (they grew to hundreds) in all sorts of weather, including winds and rain.

But an attentive audience did not mean a persuaded audience. Huge crowds stormed to hear the great orator Williams Jennings Bryan, but they voted for his opponent. He ran three times for President because his party could not believe that his popularity as a speaker could not be translated into votes.

Persuasion, I learned in those early days, was a two-layered structure —a solid foundation of fact topped by an emotional appeal. Curiously, fact or emotion alone had the same defect—it was interesting but not moving. But the two combined turned their inactive ingredients into explosive persuasion. "When Brutus speaks, everyone says 'what an extraordinary oration!' When Caesar speaks everyone follows him."

But in that early practice, I also observed that there were gradations of emotional appeal. Fist-waving exhortation, so customary to political harangue, had least impact. There were some orators who literally tore their shirt collars open, screamed until their voices cracked in breathlessness, while their eyes almost popped out of their head. Their delivery was bathed in sweat—while the audience remained quite dry and more fascinated than stirred. There is an epigram which reads "when you're in the right you can afford to keep your temper and when you're in the wrong you can't afford to lose it."

On the other hand, if the emotion flowed from an inner well and shone with sincerity, it could set the audience to weeping and it even helped if the delivery was restrained. Apparently, conviction was achieved in inverse ratio to the frenzy of the speaker, because sincerity was blurred and distorted by hysteria. If a speaker cannot control himself, he has little chance of controlling his audience.

The surest way to an effective peroration was to test oneself. Was I moved? Was I so stirred with emotion that my own difficulty in controlling articulation deepened the sincerity of the statement? I decided early that until this test was met, the task of moving an audience was insuperable. That is why I never resort to the most frequent of all elocutional flourishes, a poem. It is too calculated, too esoteric, too contrived.

So I went to the library and searched for vignettes, aphorisms, epigrams, or historical analogies which made a deep impact on me. Later, I created them myself.

For example, to conclude a speech on a high religious note, I depicted a library late at night when the master had retired to sleep. The books begin quarreling among themselves as to which is the lord of the library. The dictionary proclaims that it is because without it, there would be no words or library at all. The book of science angrily retorts that it is the king of the library because without it there would be no printing press or techniques of publishing. The aristocratic gold-embossed novel insists that it depicts life and gives insights necessary to man's progress. The book of philosophy asserts loudly that it is the lord of the library because it has given meaning to man's existence and purpose. The book of poetry argues that it gives surcease to the master when he is troubled. So the noise mounts as the angry contestants insist upon their pre-eminence.

When the din and contentiousness are at their peak, a small voice is heard. It comes from a frayed, brown-covered book lying on a table near the master's armchair. It is heard to say slowly and in a low, vibrant tone, "The Lord is my shepherd. I shall not want . . ."

All the noise in the library ceases. There is a hush. For all the books know who the true lord of the library is.

By the time I was fifteen I had transferred my speaking appeals to charitable rather than Socialist causes. The United States had entered World War I. There were Liberty Loan drives, and the Government enlisted speakers to make appeals for the sale of these bonds. I was chosen to use my skills in this patriotic endeavor. I was eager to shift my speech from the bonds of slavery to the bonds of freedom.

I was assigned to large motion picture theaters like the Brooklyn Fox at Myrtle Avenue and Keith's Bushwick. The flood of pledges following my appeals impressed somebody up there, and I was told that my next talks would be at the New York legitimate theaters on Broadway.

I had never stepped foot on Broadway, so it was bizarre that my introduction to it should be in front of the footlights on the theater row. I stumbled over the paraphernalia, cables, and ropes backstage to the repeated warnings of stars, or curious chorus girls, to be careful. Then, as if I had emerged from a thicket to a beautiful clearing—there was the stage set, incongruously neat, orderly, and beautiful. However, the curtain was down, for these appeals were made at the end of the intermission. The lights dimmed as if the next act was to begin, but instead of the curtain rising, I stepped in front of it.

I had honed my appeal to present the most interesting facts about our war efforts (how did I know they were interesting? Because they interested me. Everything else I eliminated). The speech accelerated to the sacrifices of our soldiers, their needs and our obligation to make moneys available to meet those needs. "I would not demean you by telling you that in buying a Liberty Bond, you are making a good investment at good interest. You must respond for a higher reason. We are all depressed by the brutality and sacrifice around us, and here is an opportunity to lift your arms as if they were wings and do something to ennoble your spirits!"

I had also learned that the mind's lens could not take in too large a scene and maintain definition. Talking of thousands of soldiers dying or being wounded would make an audience shake its head or cluck its tongues in horror, but they really didn't feel it. But if one soldier could be descriptively isolated and made identifiable as an individual, so that in a few brief strokes the audience got to "see" and like him, and then they were told that this boy's legs were cut off by a shrapnel burst, the emotional impact was heightened by identification with the victim.

The patriotic and humanistic peroration reached a climax. Audiences often stood and cheered. I stopped them and pleaded that the only applause which meant anything was at the end of their fountain pens as they filled out the pledges to buy bonds. The usherettes were showered with pledges—and their baskets overflowed. It became the practice of artists backstage to come out on the stage and announce their pledges, which they gave to me. Being naturally emotional as their professions required, some stood on the stage, tears streaming down their cheeks. Some hugged me, much to my embarrassment. The emotion communicated itself to the audience, and a new wave of pledges ensued, some shouting that they were doubling or tripling their purchases. Some pledges were thrown from the boxes onto the stage and floated like heavy confetti into the pit. The musicians in the orchestra handed up their pledges. Excitement reigned. Government assistants made quick calculations and announced approximate totals. They reached hundred of thousands of dollars, and precipitated new enthusiasm.

There was a story of a midnight Liberty Bond rally at Times Square in New York. A record was established. However, they included five-hundred-million and billion-dollar pledges. Hopheads, alcoholics, and derelicts who had gathered had responded with uninhibited patriotic fervor. If they were going to aid their country, they decided to do so in grand style.

While there was always a percentage of defaults, especially where the pledger had overstepped himself when carried away, the audiences at the legitimate theaters were responsible and we had no fear that the unprecedented pledges would turn out not to be genuine.

The Government awarded me a certificate of merit in acknowledgment of my services. My father, whose intense patriotism I have already alluded to, was prouder of this award then any other honor or even honorary degree I ever received thereafter. He had it framed in finest silver and it hung in the most conspicuous place in our home, a token of his vicarious contribution to his country.

My development as a speaker continued through high school and college. At Columbia, I entered the competition for the Curtis Oratorical Award. This required the contestant to write an original composition and deliver it. Wisely, both the content and the style of declamation were evaluated as a whole. During the year, eliminations were held, judged by a group of professors. Four finalists were selected. The finals were held in the evening at Earl Hall, in the presence of faculty, students, and visitors. It was a formal occasion. The judges were distinguished citizens.

I made the finals and this created a sartorial crisis. White tie and tails were required. My father would not hear of renting the outfit, even though the occasion for ever wearing them again seemed remote. A fine tailor, judged more carefully by my parents than I was to be in the contest, prepared the "costume." My parents thought they must be equal to the occasion too, but practicability, which did not apply to me, took over. My father rented a tuxedo, and my mother bought a blue lace gown.

Among them in the audience sat the judges, Governor Al Smith, Charles Evans Hughes, and Nicholas Murray Butler, president of Columbia University.

I was already a veteran at facing audiences, but the splendor of the event and its significance made me nervous. The sharp edge of the wing collar cutting into my neck and the tails flapping behind didn't help.

I delivered an address on disarmament (forty years later, nations are still negotiating on the subject while the armaments have grown infinitely more potent and the will to curb them more feeble). It would be unfortunate for this chronicle if I had not won, and indeed I did. The

Curtis Oratorical Medal was presented to me. It was a huge oval medallion (later inscribed with my name) in an eight-inch leather box so constructed as to please my parents because it could become a stand for display. The program, which described the medallion, stated that it contained one hundred dollars worth of silver. Although its real worth to my father was incalculable, he surprised me with his greeting. He kissed me but said, "The fellow who spoke last was better than you were." My mother waved him aside with a condemnatory "Oh, Joe!" which expressed shock at such an outrageous judgment, and hastened to assure me that everybody in the hall thought I was best. As they walked away to wait for the congratulatory line to end, I overheard him protest that he wanted me to do still better because he knew I could, and that she would spoil me by her adulation.

Later, when he laughed about his unsuccessful effort to prevent me "from getting a swellhead," he referred to my mother's assurance, based on her neighbor's expressions, and told the joke of the concert pianist who was approached by a member of the audience, with no such benign purpose as those who preceded him had. He told the pianist that he had given a terrible performance, weak in interpretation and faulty in execution. The artist's manager, standing nearby, was horrified by the insult. Quite flustered, he comforted the pianist. "Pay no attention to him. He doesn't know what he is talking about. He just repeats what he hears around him!" My mother's eyes twinkled, but she pretended to be serious. "You can be sure I repeated what everybody was saying about Louis."

The next year, the Curtis Oratorical Contest came around again. Professor Brander Mathews, who taught public speaking (and who had given me an unprecedented A+ at the end of the semester, announcing that he doubted such a mark had ever before been given a student at Columbia), urged me to enter again. I thought it might be unseemly, but he insisted that the rules did not forbid it, and even though I would be handicapped as a prior winner, I ought to try. I did. Again, I made the finals.

The white tie and tails outfit became useful again. This was typical of my father's unreasonable stubbornness. Time and again, he turned out to be right after all, but it never discouraged us from making a new but hopeless stand, as when he bought the property on which our store was situated though he had no funds and undertook to pay an oppressive mortgage by working still harder, as if that was possible; or when later he bought our home in Bethlehem, though hotels abounded for our summer vacations at modest rates; or still later when he built an $18,000 marble mausoleum with the name NIZER inscribed on its

Grecian façade, probably to perpetuate our name in some way, since I was the only child and had no children of my own.

This time I put wax on the wing collar to dull its cutting edge, and I wore the tails as if every week was Curtis Oratorical time.

I chose for my oration the subject of capital punishment. Even then it was a classic debating subject. Yet it remained current until the United States Supreme Court, fifty years later, decided the struggle between humanism and severe punishment in a crime-ridden society. I was to encounter the problem in my professional work (I have described one such struggle in detail in the Crump chapter of *The Jury Returns*).

I presented my original composition, constructed on the two layers of fact and emotion. I won again, and presented the first medallion with a mate.

This time my father left his prophylactic skepticism at home. He embraced me unreservedly though not as profusely as my mother.

From that day on, he was uninhibited in his praise and I found this far more difficult to bear than his critical approach. But my mother reveled in his conversion.

How does one go about memorizing a half-hour speech? The memorization is not of words, but of sequences, with felicitous phrasing or climactic sentences as landmarks in the journey.

If a speech doesn't memorize easily, it is because the structure is wrong. If the logical development of sequence is correct, each suggests the next with no effort. When I review a speech in my mind and find my memory fails me at some particular point, I know that the fault is not my memory, but the defect in the correct chain of ideas. Speech memorization is not, as the memory experts tell us, based on association of ideas. For if the association is out of kilter with logic, memory lapses. It is logical sequence which controls memory.

One can check a speech like one can check the addition of figures. If logical sequence inevitably leads to easy memorization, then the structure is sound. The audience will find it easy to follow, because its anticipation will be gratified.

The techniques of memorization may differ with each individual. Like writing practices, they depend on each writer's personal idiosyncrasies. Joseph Conrad wrote in a bath. Perhaps the thick cigar smoke and water made him feel he was viewing the Indian Ocean. Dostoyevsky wrote his psychological studies in the midst of night. Beethoven soaked his hands in ice water before composing. Balzac and Leibnitz prompted the muse by consuming great quantities of coffee, while many, including Shakespeare and Edgar Allan Poe, preferred goblets of wine. Mark Twain wrote best when reclining in bed, which I find the most sensible because I practice it myself. Some write best in the morning. Others through the night. Some concentrate best with music in the background. Others must have silence. Some like beautiful surroundings, others a blank wall. The variations are infinite and sometimes bizarre, like Schiller's insisting on the smell of rotten apples.

I recall selecting Sun Valley for a writing vacation, because there was a balcony outside the room overlooking an idyllic pastureland with a cool shaded lake in the center. I set myself comfortably in this soothing atmosphere with pencil sharpener handy for frequent use. Then I found myself gazing at the sleek, bronze-skinned horses, their necks stretched twice their size toward the grass, while geese skimmed effortlessly on the lake, giving no hint of the furious paddling beneath. When I looked up at the sky there were faded apple green colors melting into blazing orange and red patches, contrasting with fuchsia and violet streamers running in and out of pink-white clouds. I turned my chair around and spent the rest of my writing endeavors looking at the imitation log cabin wall one foot in front of me.

Some speakers prepare by writing out their talks, because the visual and mechanical process in so doing engraves the words on their minds. I disapprove because the writing procedure, even if only as a preliminary to memorization, distorts the proper rhythm. However, each to his own. Therefore, I do not prescribe my own method as the one suitable to others, but I set it forth. I memorize by walking.

Having gathered my research material and thought through my general thesis, I put on comfortable slippers, and begin walking up and down an isolated room, talking the speech out loud.

As I hear it, I reject, add, and develop, but all with an "eye" to my ear. Does it sound clear? Is it easily comprehensible? I become the audience, reacting to my own words. This sentence is only mildly interesting, even though the thought is acceptable. It must be phrased so as to excite attention. Perhaps an epigram or colorful phrase will give it the necessary emotive power. That sentence is too involved and therefore dull. It must be shortened and simplified. These sentences are clear and interesting, but their rhythm is too even and therefore sleep-inducing (the ear, as well as the eye, is the entrance channel for a hypnotic spell). The tempo must be changed, sometimes only by vocal emphasis.

So the process continues, as if I were an editor blue-penciling my own oral script. Each time I begin over again, like a conductor tapping for order, making a suggestion, lifting his baton to say, "Now, from the beginning." The repetitions cause memorization even though I do not strive for it. It is best to be "loose," phrasing the thought differently when the mood dictates. In this way a lapse will not cause a collapse. A word-for-word memorization is dangerous because it enslaves the speaker. If he forgets a sentence, or even a word, the whole sequence disappears and he is left gaping. He must be master of the content and substance, improvising until he reaches the next logical passage in the chain of thoughts.

A speaker who has memorized his speech word for word has a crowd of critics in front of him. They will notice his mechanical reproduction, his distress when a word fails him, and silence suddenly substitutes for the easy flow. The embarrassment is painful to audience and speaker alike, because the singsong cadence of a memorized delivery is revealed in all its artificiality as a pose without inner feeling or thought. Children rushing through a memorized poem, and suddenly gaping at their parents, whose proud smiles turn to shamed prompting, are the familiar prototype of memorization risks.

However, since speech rhythm, like music, requires ascendancy and contrasting climaxes, there should be an emphatic conclusion of every major point. This should be memorized. Here, the speaker may indulge in the luxury of emotional statement. Such statement must be striking and moving—a sort of summation exclamation point. For example, if the point is that violence cannot correct the evil of prejudice—"Civil wrongs can't make civil rights"; or if the thought is that democracy is based on a scientific principle too little observed—"As you multiply judgments, you reduce the incident of error. Two heads are better than one; a thousand better than a hundred; and on a question of right or wrong (not science or mathematics, in which event I would rely on a scientist or mathematician), I would rather trust two hundred million Americans than the ten most brilliant professors in the world!"

These memorized passages are like landmarks in the topography of the speech. They cue in the speaker to the next sequence. So I find that interstitial memorization of specific sentences, combined with a general mastery of the subject matter, provides the best of all worlds for the speaker. He is thinking on his feet, communicating with his audience as he looks into their faces, and improvises the language of his well-prepared argument. At the same time, he reaches memorized plateaus which give epigrammatic, aphoristic, allegoric, or other felicitous emotional appeal to his words. Even if he is occasionally awkward when he is improvising the phrasing, it matters not. Thereafter, the impact of the memorized sentences will be all the greater, because they will be cloaked with the inherited mantle of spontaneity.

I have seen gifted speakers bring a previous unruly audience to rapt attention within a minute. Even those who have lingered too long and eagerly at the preceding cocktail bar will grow silent if the speaker has "presence," another word for self-assurance and direct contact with the audience. No test is too severe. I recall addressing a gathering in Yuma,

Arizona, immediately after the air conditioning broke down in the banquet room and 120-degree heat took possession of the crowded room. Though I felt the trickles and then streams of perspiration flow down my body, even the waving of menus as improvised fans ultimately yielded to attentiveness. Let no one who aspires to be a speaker ever blame an audience for not being in the mood to listen. It is always the "orator's" fault if he cannot gain silence.

I would not belabor this subject if it were not for my conviction that how a person speaks privately or in public provides the quickest and surest insight to his intelligence and personality. Thought, diction, and the skill of expression are X-rays of intelligence, knowledge, and wisdom. How else is a civilized man to be judged? There are a few exceptions—as there always are: the profound thinker who cannot articulate well. But usually muddled expression reveals a confused mind. One has only to watch the dozens of television talk shows, in which the speakers fumble and mumble "you know's" as a stalling device several times in each sentence. It used to be "you know what I mean," a ludicrous question interspersed between words, since what preceded it could have been understood by a cretin, like "I walked into the room, you know what I mean?" or "So I looked at him, you know what I mean?" The modern contraction "you know" is just as vapid, and because of its brevity permits more frequent use, so that every sentence is filled with stuttering irrelevancy. Those who aspire to be leaders reveal their capacity or lack of it on the public platform.

A partial answer to Jimmy Carter's miraculous ascendancy to the presidency is his excellent selection of words, best demonstrated in press conferences during the give-and-take after the prepared text. His syntax is correct, unlike that of President Eisenhower, who mangled it. His sentences are not only properly completed but lucid. He has none of the artificial mannerisms of Nixon, who covered his uncertainty about his next thought by assurance that it was "perfectly clear," and whose sonorous, dignified delivery contrasted terribly with his talk on the tapes.

Although President Carter tries to give the impression of an ordinary, a very ordinary, citizen (he even signs his letters "Jimmy"), his diction reveals an orderly and cultivated mind. Combined with a simple and low-key delivery, there is an impression of sincerity and ability. The resulting confidence in him may well be the answer to the riddle of how an unknown figure triumphed over his famous political adversaries. Such is the power of speech.

I recall a New York State Democratic dinner at the Waldorf-Astoria preceding the 1952 presidential election. All the aspiring candidates were invited to speak. It was as if they were on display for evaluation not only by several thousand sophisticated faithful, but by the nation's political leaders, who controlled the vital delegations. It was in a sense a preview of the convention struggle. Conscious of the importance of the event, each candidate had prepared his best.

Senator Robert Kerr made a brilliant political address, whipping the audience into frenzied applause by his epigrammatic denunciation of the opposition, his partisan sallies capped by clever phrasing and slogans. His clear, ringing baritone voice rang out in eloquent cadences. But even while one applauded and laughed, there was no great admiration for the man himself. It was a fine performance, but not a profound statement. It was appreciated as political attack geared to a partisan rally, but left everyone in the dark as to the leadership qualities of a man who might be President.

Senator Estes Kefauver spoke. His thin, tall presence and matter-of-fact drawl, deliberately employed to make a virtue of a nonoratorical approach, were more impressive even though less applause-provoking than Kerr's delivery. There were no eloquent flourishes. One felt dedication to good causes, but awareness of the resistance in his home territory of Tennessee, requiring him to surround his convictions with a layer of ambiguity. The raccoon hat which he had selected to hover over his head as an invisible symbol announced during every word he uttered, "Remember, I come from a region which won't accept some of my beliefs, and please allow for my difficulties as you evaluate my statements." Poor man. Like other Southern statesmen, he was imprisoned by prejudices, slowly being eradicated, but which were still strong enough to make him politically dead if he were honestly read.

Senator Lyndon Johnson spoke. His Texan height and congressional record were equally impressive. He spoke in deliberate formal tones, as if to negate the informal explosiveness which one easily sensed beneath the surface. He seemed to be engaging in an exercise of self-discipline, to create the impression of solid judgment, although the passion he suppressed would have revealed the man to much better advantage.

Senator Hubert Humphrey spoke. How unfortunate that his sincerity and mental equipment were beclouded by volubility. Like the great director who destroys his achievement because he is in the forefront of the magic he weaves, Humphrey detracted from his excellent statement of ideals by unwittingly featuring his own fluency and felicity.

Senator John F. Kennedy was introduced. His record in the Senate was undistinguished and afforded no stimulus for any special burst of applause. But no one could fail to admire his handsome presence. His youthful appearance was not an asset in the eyes of the politicos who sought presidential stature. Perhaps—perhaps, the murmur went—he might be a vice-presidential candidate, never more. Another evidence that experts are experts only as long as we assume their superiority and make their predictions come true.

Others spoke. Franklin D. Roosevelt, Jr., presided. Unlike Jimmy Roosevelt, he did not have his father's voice, but he did offer visual reminders of that elegant head, with the discolored skin beneath the eyes revealing the torment of muscleless legs, while every tantivy movement of his head conveyed the gallantry and bouyance of his spirit. He introduced the Governor of Illinois.

Few in that room had ever seen or heard Adlai Stevenson. He arose to a smattering of applause. He was terribly short, bald, and unimpressive in face or voice. Within literally three minutes, the audience was spellbound. Magic had suddenly spread across the room. He began with some witty comments about the rumors that he and Mrs. Roosevelt (who sat next to him) were romantically joined. He treated this sensitive subject so farcically and with such becoming self-deprecation and adulation of Mrs. Roosevelt that the charm and humor made the women's eyes moist, and the men's hearts warm. After some original spontaneous reactions to the speeches which had preceded him, inoffensively poking fun at the political necessities of the occasion, he got down to his message. He spoke of the new challenge to our generation, of the destiny of our country, of the sacrifices and new horizons of thought which would be necessary to meet a social revolution spreading across the world; of the pressures on the prosperous, whether individuals or nations, to correct the injustice of inequality, economic as well as social—I refer the reader to his published addresses in *Call to Greatness*—of which this was one.

As he spoke, he grew in size, as if a giant bestrode the podium. The audience was entranced. In less than twenty minutes, the great qualities of the man filled the air. He was no longer short. He was no longer bald —it was a noble shining head we saw. His voice was no longer squeezed and thin. It had a philosopher's cadence. When he finished, the audience stood to a man, woman, and child and cheered and clapped in an unending ovation. Everyone knew that if the hour called for a leader, he had appeared. All this in a few moments. Yes, speech is an X-ray of a man.

I was just as moved. Little did I know then that I would have the privilege at his invitation to work intimately with him in losing elections and winning causes. As for that—later.

THREE GUNS

When I first began tangling with powerful adversaries, my mother tried to persuade me not to take such "hard cases." Although she pretended that she was worried about my exertions, she revealed her true concern by asking, "Isn't it dangerous to fight such terrible people?" I assured her that no one would dare harm an opposing lawyer, and gently chided her for believing motion picture melodramas in which the villainous gang wreaks vengeance on the district attorney. But, children, Mother was right. On three occasions my life was threatened.

The first was when I represented a group of retail butchers who refused to pay tribute to a gang operating a racket under the guise of a union. I sued the outfit, among whom were a number of notorious gangsters with criminal records. I sought an injunction which would strip them of their bogus union and prohibit the compulsory exaction of "dues." The complaint was a weighty document supported by dozens of affidavits by the victims. The answer was weighty too. It was supported by a bomb thrown into the establishment of one of my clients (Ben Danziger was his name), which destroyed his business and almost his life.

The day arrived to argue the application for a temporary injunction. I had no assistants in those days, but as I ascended the steps of the Supreme Court, I suddenly discovered that I had two companions, one on each side. They fell into step with me, looking straight ahead, in correct Warner Bros. style, and one of them said, "If you argue this case, you won't come out alive." They disappeared as I reached the entrance, sending me on my way, as they must have believed, to request an adjournment, if laryngitis would permit me to speak at all.

I cannot analyze my emotions at this late date. It may have been a swimming head, or more likely a conviction that I hold to this day, that those who openly make threats do not execute them. (The dangerous attack comes from those who do not forewarn.) In any event, I proceeded to make a lengthy, impassioned argument. The court may not have known the true reason for my tremulous voice. But my exit was devoid of bravado. I waited for groups to come out of the courthouse, and slunk into the center, like the halfback who runs behind a phalanx of blockers. Then I dashed down the steps of the nearby subway, and I am sure that if there were such an Olympic event, my time would still stand as a record.

The injunction was granted. Deputy Attorney General William Donovan indicted the entire group of sixty-odd defendants. It resulted in the largest mass criminal trial ever held in this Federal district. They were convicted.

Since no ghost-writer is involved in the present telling, it is obvious that the true author came to no harm.

The second instance was mercifully briefer. A chain of theaters owned by one of the major motion picture companies had a labor dispute with the projectionists. Although I was counsel for the New York Film Board of Trade, this matter did not come under my jurisdiction. Nevertheless, a nonrepresentative of Local 306 did not appreciate such niceties. He decided to visit me.

My practice has always been to keep an open door. I resent secretaries putting those who seek an appointment through a drill to determine whether they may enter the holy sanctum. It reflects badly on the king within. It is at best impolite and at worst arrogant and conceited. Even the telephone test which some executives require their secretaries to make: "May I ask what is the nature of the matter you are calling about?" is irritating. When I am so grilled, my equanimity is most disturbed and I regret not replying, "It is none of your business."

Of course, a policy of easy access results occasionally in my being subjected to kooks and salesmen. It is also a time waster, which I am sure the manual of executive efficiency decries. But it pleases me to amend the declaration that all men are created equal with the corollary that they should have equal access. There are 25 million stars in our galaxy and many galaxies. That should give each executive a better sense of his own great unimportance. Besides, one learns even from meeting the strangest characters, and the day is more interesting if also more aggravating.

So, it was that without any ceremony or advance notice a name was ushered in. He was short, swarthy with sleepy lidded eyes, but despite a studied casualness, he was intense. He approached my desk with quick steps. Then he reached into his breast pocket as if he was about to take out his eyeglasses. Instead he pulled out a snub-nosed black revolver, which he handled familiarly, placed it in front of him on my desk, sat down, and said, "I came to talk to you about my men in the booths."

I had never before had such a calling card. My reflex reaction was to deal with this situation as if he had insulted me by boorish conduct. I buzzed for my secretary, Miss Cunningham. She was a slight blond girl. Obviously her entrance was neither protection nor a threat. Psychologically, however, her frailty was just right. A burly male secretary might have caused the visitor to reach for the little cannon he had added to my desk equipment. Instead, he sat impassively for a moment.

Calling on my need to improvise the proper script for such a ridiculous melodrama, I said, "I don't talk to people who threaten. I want you to leave at once. Miss Cunningham, show the gentleman out and take that damn thing off my desk."

Like all who must retreat, he salvaged his pride by assuring me that I wasn't going to get away with this. I wasn't going to get away with what? Under other circumstances, we might have laughed at this prize non sequitur. But his statement was akin to that of the lawyer who after a defeat announces boldly that he will appeal, or, during a trial when the judge rules against him, proclaims angrily, "Exception!" even though it is no longer necessary to use this magic word to preserve one's right on appeal. Why deny the defeated the balm that comes from defiance?

So, the gentleman with the gun left quietly, escorted by a shaking little figure who needed the day off after her unaccustomed service. I never heard from him again.

The third incident was the most dangerous. On behalf of Paramount Pictures, Warner Bros., and Metro-Goldwyn-Mayer, I had obtained a judgment of $27,500 against Nat Steinberg, the owner of the Grand Theatre in New York City, New Dyckman Theatre in the Bronx, the Liljay Theatre, and the Palchester Theatre in Parkchester. The charge was that he had violated the contracts with these companies by playing their motion pictures on more days than licensed for. Motion pictures are copyrighted property and, as I have indicated, the companies were therefore entitled not merely to a proportionate added license fee, but to statutory damages ranging from $250 to $5,000 for each violation. Congress has enacted these heavy damages to protect writers and other artists from having their property stolen by unauthorized showing.

So it was that in the case of Steinberg's theaters, the court had awarded copyright damages which were far larger than what the owner would have had to pay had he contracted for the pictures honestly.

The theory of the copyright law is that merely to recover what the contract fee would have been would not stop the practice of stealing the author's works. It would simply be returning the stolen property.

(There is the story of the jury which found a defendant not guilty of having stolen a mule, but directed him to return it. The Judge rejected the verdict and insisted on a proper one. They returned, "We find the defendant not guilty and he may keep the mule.")

Damages which are not realistic are considered penalties, and in civil actions are illegal. They can only be imposed in criminal proceedings. To get around this the copyright law provides that its high scale of damages "shall not be deemed a penalty."

Nat Steinberg did not appreciate all this. Simplistically, he reasoned that had he bought the right for extra showing in the first place, he could have done so for a few hundred dollars. Now, he had lost his case and there was a judgment of ten times that amount. He didn't understand why his dishonesty (even if he thought of it as such) should be so disproportionately assessed. Unlike most clients who blame their own lawyers when they lose, he turned his venom toward me. He had heard my impassioned plea in court justifying the copyright law, and its wisdom in recognizing that tens of thousands of dollars of stolen time go undetected. The proven infringements are only the tip of the iceberg, and even statutory damages probably constitute a small portion of the unjust enrichment. How else but by severe damages in the case proven at great expense would the practice be stopped which deprived authors, sculptors, painters of the just rewards for the creations of their minds?

Steinberg blamed me for his disaster. So, one day he visited me. He had been a professional wrestler. His muscles pushed his suit away from his body, making him look more ungainly than he was. His sallow cheeks fell in toward his mouth, as if his face had to pay the price for his body development. He was totally bald (perhaps he had completed the process by shaving the surviving fringe). Athletes either wear long hair, the sign of virility, or affect bald domes, which, combined with general muscularity, give the impression of a missile to be launched. Steinberg's neck was a trunk, undoubtedly developed by bridging during his wrestling matches. He was past his prime, if he ever had one. His eyes were small and squinting and his voice hoarse. He got down to business quickly.

"Mr. Nizer, you have this judgment against me. I came to tell you that if you try to collect it, I'm going to kill you."

He spoke in a matter-of-fact manner as if he was discussing the date of payment.

I treated the matter lightly, assuming that he was exaggerating, and explained that he had had a fair trial, that I had done my duty as a lawyer, and that if he needed time to pay the judgment, I would attempt to arrange it.

"You don't understand. You think I'm kidding. I'm not. I am telling you straight and I mean it. If you try to collect this money, I am going to kill you. I have a gun [he tapped his pocket] and I'm going to kill you. So forget the judgment."

I warned him that he could be arrested for his threats, and that my duty as a lawyer would not be abandoned by such outrageous tactics.

"I am telling you it will cost you your life," he said, as he arose to leave. "Think it over."

An hour later, I received a call from Earl Sweigert, branch manager of Paramount Pictures. Steinberg had just visited him and pronounced the same sentence of death on him if Paramount collected one cent of its judgment.

"He told me he would shoot you too," Sweigert said. "This is a crazy man, Lou. Don't take him lightly. I was told that he beat a neighbor to a pulp over some dispute. The poor fellow had to be taken to the hospital, but he has been afraid to make charges against Steinberg because he might be killed if he did. I know he has a revolver. He really might kill both of us. I think we ought to take this up with the company."

I had no intention of yielding either to threat or entreaty. I have the habit of enlarging incidents into international analogy and getting more incensed because of the principle involved. Do we surrender to the Hitlers of the world to save our skins? Experience has taught us that such roads to safety are strewn with more skulls than result from resistance.

I arranged another meeting with Steinberg, but seated at my desk were Inspector Goldman and a captain from the New York City Police Department. When he arrived, I asked him to sit down, and introduced him to the police officials, advising him who they were.

"Mr. Steinberg, when you were here previously, you told me that if I attempted to collect a judgment which several motion picture companies have obtained against you, that you had a gun and that you would kill me. Is it true that you made that threat against me?"

"I did. Do you want me to repeat it? I will. Take it down, go ahead." Then, looking squarely into the faces of the police officers, he said, "I'm telling you again. I'm going to kill Mr. Nizer if he tries to collect a penny of that judgment. What are you going to do about it? Arrest me? Go ahead. I'll tell it to the Judge. Do you want it in writing? I'll write it out. What can you do to me? Put me in jail? For how long? Ten days, thirty days? When I come out I'm going to kill him!"

The police officials were so flustered by this daring assault that they lost their composure and acted as embarrassed and stuttering as one would have expected Steinberg to be.

"Don't do anything foolish," the Inspector said foolishly. "We're

going to watch you"—another opening of which Steinberg took immediate advantage.

"Go ahead and watch. You can't watch me every minute of my life.
You know that's illegal! No matter what you do I'll kill him!"

He pointed to me with his eyes. His quiet demeanor gave credence to
his threat.

"Do you want to arrest me, or can I leave?"

They told him that he could go, and sent continued warnings after
him which seemed to bounce off his back as he walked out slowly without another word.

The inspector turned to me. "Mr. Nizer, this is a dangerous man. I
have dealt with many cranks who threaten but are harmless. This man
is no fake. I think he is crazy enough to do what he says."

"We can provide a twenty-four hour watch for you, but for how
long? I must be honest with you. I don't think we can protect you if
this man is determined to get you. I would advise you to do something
which would relieve this crazy man's mind."

The Captain spoke up. "Inspector, we ought to look up his record.
What happened today is enough to revoke his license for a revolver, if
he has one."

"Absolutely," said the Inspector, his emphasis indicating that he had
had this in mind all the time. "But that is no protection either. You
know how easy it is for anyone to get a gun."

They were chagrined at their helplessness and I comforted them out
of the office, telling them that I did not intend to yield, but I would
think of something and let them know.

"Please, don't take any chances" were their parting words, a sentiment which Steinberg would have heartily approved.

At the next meeting of the New York Film Board of Trade, the
agenda included an item entitled "Steinberg," although for Sweigert
and myself, it could better have been described as "To Be or Not to
Be."

Sweigert reported that his company, Paramount Pictures, had authorized him to compromise or abandon the claim entirely in his discretion.
It did not consider it his duty to risk his life. Warner Bros. and Metro-
Goldwyn-Mayer, which had part of the judgment, joined in this consent. One of the branch managers who had been a college wrestler said
it would be worth surrendering the money if he could just give Steinberg a headlock and squeeze the craziness out of him, to which another
replied, "How do you think he got that way in the first place?" But
behind the banter was solicitude for Sweigert and me.

I protested strongly, giving all the arguments why it would be coward-
ice to surrender to a hoodlum.

"Suppose you had lost the case, Lou. We would be in the same position," argued one of them. "That would be worse for Lou than if he got shot," suggested another of my friends.

When all views had been expressed, I said, "Of course, you as clients have the right to forgive any judgment. You make contract adjustments every day for business reasons. And, I am bound by your decision. But this is action taken out of fear. True, it is fear for me and Earl Sweigert, and I appreciate your concern for us. In a way, you are paying ransom for our safety.

"It just goes against my grain for you to surrender to a blackmailer, who holds our lives as hostage. So, for the present, I do not accept your instruction. Let me think of some other way. I'll report back to you."

I invited Steinberg again to my office. He came. "No cops today?" he said as he sat down.

"No, just you and me. I have a proposition to make to you. Before I do, let me explain something. Neither the film companies nor I as a lawyer can simply forget about the money you owe. You should understand that. Suppose the people who owed you money told you not to ask for it or they'd kill you. What would you think?"

He stirred angrily, as if he was not going to listen to another rejection of his ultimatum. I held up my hand. "Just be patient, I am not finished. I told you I have a proposition. Hear me out."

He settled back sullenly.

"I understand that you consider this different because the judgment is many times greater than you would have had to pay for the contract rights."

I explained why the copyright law exacts such larger sums, and rhetorically asked him whether he hadn't gotten away with many other copyright infringements, which had put thousands of dollars in his pocket. So the judgment against him wasn't as exaggerated as he thought. It was just delayed justice. Then, I suddenly shifted to a question which was so irrelevant that it startled him.

"Do you ever give charity?"

He looked at me a long time as if to make sure he had heard me right. I repeated the question.

"Sure I do," he said.

"Well, that's my proposition. You do not pay one cent to Paramount, Warner's, or M-G-M. But you give the $27,500 in three equal parts to Jewish, Protestant, and Catholic charities."

When his silence ultimately turned to questions, I knew the shooting was over, so to speak.

How long would he have to make the contribution? Would his license for a revolver be reinstated? (He explained that he needed a gun when he took his receipts to the bank, and, I thought, also when he canceled his debts.) Would the gifts be solely in his name? (The film companies must not get any credit.) When he reached the point of arguing that a larger proportion should go to one charity rather than another (he lost that one, too), I knew this strange negotiation was going to be successful. It was.

Within eighteen months, the Federation of Jewish Philanthropies, Young Men's Christian Association, and Catholic Charities each received beneficences from one Nat Steinberg. They never knew the evil origin of the good deed.

It is said that when God examines you he does not look for medals. He looks for scars suffered in doing good deeds. I doubt that Steinberg will ever get credit for this particular charity.

This was the paradoxical solution. The film companies did not collect the judgments, but Steinberg paid them.

HE WHO STEALS MY NAME

It wasn't until the seventeenth century that the law recognized that you could assault a person with a weapon called words. Until then only physical blows entitled the victim to a remedy. Concepts of honor and reputation were cherished long before, but they were supposed to be vindicated by violence. Duels on the field of honor, not courts, were the forum for satisfaction.

Of all the remedies the law has fashioned to redress grievances, the libel law ranks among the noblest. It provides a judicial means to salvage a person's dignity; to recapture the esteem in which he has been held by the community; to restore the victim to his profession and business, and to his family and friends. In addition the libel law provides for a triple-tiered damage structure; actual money loss suffered from loss of job or business or professional activity; recompense for pain, suffering, and humiliation; and if the libel was motivated by malice, punitive damages to teach the perpetrator a lesson and discourage others from similar misdeeds. Indeed libel can also be a crime. The effect of inflammatory words can be so severe that it causes riots. Interestingly enough —under the common law and still in many states—even truthful words can constitute a crime if they are maliciously designed to arouse passions which cause violence. Why not? Much less, like loud music all night, or sound tracks blaring at unearthly hours, has been held to constitute criminal nuisance. Despite the philosophers, truth doesn't justify everything. It, too, must accommodate itself to the peace and safety of the community. Here we begin to see the impending clash between the libel laws and free speech, which I shall discuss later.

Although libel laws do not distinguish between a minor hurt and a serious one, I have always felt that it was good discretion not to launch a suit for every lie uttered. The highest estate which a lawyer can reach is not to be a brilliant technician but to be a wise adviser. Not every grievance should result in a lawsuit. In a crowded competitive world, people will step on each other's toes literally and figuratively. But we ought not to rush into court every time we have been jostled or an angry cussword has been spoken. Legal warfare is expensive and harrowing. It should be resorted to only when there is real damage, not merely high sensitivity to a slur.

The exception, of course, is when an important principle is involved. Then the damage is subtle. It may not injure the individual, but he becomes the vehicle through which the rights of many may be asserted. Sometimes the reputation of the person maligned is so firm that it is impervious to libel. Nevertheless, the target, though unscathed, may recover punitive damages.

Most often, however, the grievance is narrow. It affects one individual and no one else. The air is filled with vituperative gossip. Columnists are more short of material than that devouring monster, television. So in desperation for items, columnists pick up rumors, hearsay, and even invented "information" cloaked in anonymity—"What famous Hollywood star has left his home and board because of a redheaded starlet who has a minor part in his new picture?" I discovered on one occasion that the author of the titillating item had no more idea of the answer than the reader. This procedure is encouraged because reporters consider their source sacrosanct. Unless there is a state statute which gives the same immunity to a reporter as to a doctor, priest, or lawyer, such privilege does not exist. There is much to be said for the protection of newspapermen by means of such laws because the serious reporter might not be able to obtain information if, later, he could be forced to reveal his source. However the unwritten law of silence, which has caused reporters to martyr themselves and go to jail rather than speak, also shields the irresponsible gossipmonger.

Is it not always thus? Every law is like a disc—recorded on two sides. The virtuous purpose is stated on one side, but if we examine the platter on the other side dissonances appear. The libel disc has two sides too. One, the idealistic judicial tool to avenge injury to reputation by civilized means, the other the use of such tool to attack for every petty, inconsequential slight.

As a lawyer I have been engaged in lengthy court battles of the first genre, but on the other hand I have probably discouraged and prevented more libel suits than most lawyers.

Let me give several illustrations. Truman Capote, he of the talented pen and gossipy tongue, made disparaging remarks about the writing ability of Jacqueline Susann, the author of *Valley of the Dolls*, *Once Is Not Enough*, *The Love Machine*, and *Dolores*. (Capote insists that all artistic writing is gossip, citing *War and Peace* and Dostoyevsky. This is a shaky thesis which depends on a contrived definition of history as accumulated gossip.) Capote's comments about Susann were made on Johnny Carson's "Tonight Show," thus assuring an audience of millions for his contemptuous views. Opinions are not generally subject to libel. They may be wrong, but not untruthful. They express the critic's frame of mind accurately, and the reader knows that he is receiving an evaluation, not a statement of fact. If, however, a critic writes that an actor's performance was defective because he was drunk, and he was not, that would be libelous; indeed, as the law says, libelous per se because the libel demeans one in his professional capacity. There is the anecdote of Heywood Broun's review of a play in which he stated that the star gave the worst performance ever seen in a theater. He was sued for libel. A year later, while the suit was pending, the same actor appeared in another play. Broun was cautioned by his lawyers not to write anything which would aggravate the situation. He reconciled his critical integrity with his lawyers' admonition by writing about the star whom he had previously impaled that "his performance was not up to his usual standard."

Although Capote's less than enthusiastic view about Susann's artistry was not libelous, the battle of words was on. Carson, like any interviewer, was not averse to controversy and he invited Susann on his program. She was ready. When asked whether she had heard Capote's comment, she surprised everyone by doing a remarkable takeoff of him. Whatever one might think of her writing, there was no doubt she was a great mimic. Capote lends himself to that art. He is very short, pudgy, puffy, baldly blond and talks in a high-pitched, nasal, slow Southern drawl which outrageously exaggerates his homosexuality. He is like a cartoon of himself. It is only respect for his fine writing talents which prevents audiences from laughing at him. Nevertheless his rolling eyes, giggles, squeaky voice, pursed lips, and feminine gestures provoke stifled laughter even from those most attentive to his views.

Susann captured all this prefectly. Despite her large size and dark visage, she shrank to his gnome-like size, and her whining cadences, interrupted by stretched out "w-e-l-l-s," sent the audience into paroxysms of laughter. It is easy for an imitator to gain recognition of a subject who has one outstanding characteristic. Cartoonists know this well; De Gaulle's long nose, Roosevelt's onesided smile, Churchill's bulldog nose, Nixon's jowels, Carter's teeth (called chiclets by one comedian). But for live imitators, the voice and the musical scale it travels are the trademarks of individuality. They are considered as distinctive as a fingerprint. A gifted mimic can achieve his effect by talking from a dark room. But his virtuosity on the stage includes posture, subtle gestures, and idiosyncratic mannerisms. Susann mastered her subject to the finest detail.

Now it was Capote's turn. He was invited to occupy the same chair from which she had performed and give his rebuttal. His was not the skill of imitation. He was an originator, and he must have given much thought to finding just the right descriptive phrase which would ridicule her and create as much laughter as she had subjected him to. When Carson asked him what he thought of Susann's views, he raised his voice to its shrillest pitch and declared that he paid no attention to her. "A-n-y way, she looks like a truck driver in drag!"

Words are like chemicals. Some combinations fizzle. Others explode. The laughter which burst across the nation drove her and Irving Mansfield, her husband and gifted partner in the dissemination of her works, right into my office. They insisted on an immediate suit. I advised them that in my opinion a slander had been committed. Aside from the falsity of the literal description, the innuendo expressed the animus of the words. What is an innuendo? It is the law's device to spell out the intended vicious meaning of what might otherwise appear to be innocent. So, for example, if one writes, sarcastically, "Oh, sure, he is an honest man," one can sue for slander if spoken, or libel if written, and plead the innuendo that such words meant that he was dishonest. So, the innuendos to be ascribed to "A-n-y way, she looks like a truck driver in drag" were many. One was that she was a lesbian of masculine inclinations, or that she was so unfeminine that she was more like a man who, because of perversity, dressed up as a woman, or that she was as ugly as an uncouth truck driver who aberrationally disguised himself in woman's clothes—all clearly slanderous.

I recognized the anguish the words had caused her, her husband, and many friends. She had been ridiculed. She had been made a laughingstock particularly in those quarters where envy is the by-product of success. We are hero-worshipers but paradoxically we like to see the mighty fall. It levels us, creating the illusion that we have risen somewhat, rather than those we looked up to have descended. That is why we cheer the champion and yet thrill at his defeat.

So, although Capote's comment was in my opinion libelous (television broadcasts have been held equivalent to written publications and therefore libel rather than slander), and although I was not unaware of the hurt and humiliation they had suffered, I advised against suit. It seemed to me that what was involved was an unfortunate exchange not worthy of the fees, exhaustion of time in extended pretrial depositions, ultimate lengthy trial, and probable appeals. Furthermore, there would be no actual damage. Wasn't she still on the best-seller list? Did she really believe Capote's snide comment would affect her popularity as an author? I saw no principle involved. Also, there had been some provocation, which in law is deemed to ameliorate damages.

All this fell on unsympathetic ears. We are blind to what we do not want to see and deaf to what we do not like to hear. They were determined to attack. Fees were of no consequence. She was fabulously successful. She wished revenge. She wanted to see the day when "the little worm would squirm under cross-examination."

I was losing the battle of persuasion rapidly. In the course of the friendly argument, I learned that they were leaving for Germany to attend a book fair, in which her book was featured. I seized the opportunity to gain time.

"You are leaving in a few days. A complaint cannot be prepared in such a short period. Why don't you wait until you return? We'll confer again. Perhaps you will view this differently by then."

They were well aware of the ruse. For the first time, their tense demeanor changed and they smiled.

"You are not going to talk us out of this," Susann said. "We'll be back," she announced with MacArthur determination. "We expect you to prepare papers. Please, please, we want you to sue the nasty little ——." She used a heavenly phrase not intended to be angelic.

Their visit to the bookfair in Frankfurt was a triumph. Her books were featured. She was honored. International recognition is particularly gratifying to an author. It gives the impression of historic appreciation.

When she and her husband sat again in my office, she was glowing with pride, and he reflected hers as well as his own. Her description of her trip set a different stage for the discussion. There was no longer single-minded insistence prompted by desperation.

I redoubled my effort to have her drop the matter. By this time, recollection of the ridicule to which she had been subjected was less painful. I reviewed her acceptance by the public at large, her increasing invitations to appear on forums and television interviews, her husband's prideful citation of the phenomenal sale of her books, the inescapable jealousy such success produces, including possibly Capote's (this pleased her most), the protective callus an author must develop against the inevitable blows from critics, an experience not unknown to her (unanimous praise is almost impossible), and therefore she ought to rise above the taunt in a television exchange. I felt it was my duty to protect her against an improvident litigation, but if she disagreed, I knew there were many able lawyers who would undertake the matter. They insisted that they would only proceed with me, and resignedly, though good-naturedly, the matter was closed.

So we thought. But we counted without Capote's penchant for gossip and pursuit.

A short time later, the following appeared in a publication called *After Dark*:

"It was Capote who took advantage of television exposure to get in an effective gut-stab at another highly vulnerable 'writer,' Jacqueline Susann. On the 'Tonight Show,' he told the world that she looked 'like a truck driver in drag.'

"It didn't take long for Miss Susann, who isn't exactly a novice at verbal self-defense, to announce she was suing Capote for a million dollars.

" 'Had to drop the whole suit,' Capote says, chuckling with victorious pride. Had to! She and her lawyer, the famous Louis Nizer, went to NBC to watch a replay of the program which they watched and watched, and finally, Louis Nizer turned and said, 'Jackie, forget it. You don't have a case.' She went into a rage and screamed, 'A case? Whaddya mean? It's right there in living color. Libel if there ever was libel!' 'And then Nizer told her that all my attorney would have to do was to get a dozen truck drivers and put them in drag and have them parade into court and that would be all. So, no million-dollar suit from Miss Jacqueline Susann.' "

Immediately thereafter, and as surely as inventive venom begets retaliation, I received a brief note from Susann.

Dear Louis—
Now the little 'capon' has put words in your mouth—it's really wild? What do you think?

Best
Jackie

The restrained tone of this note was undoubtedly due to her belief that she now had an ally. She knew that Capote, by repeating and enlarging the libel, and fictitiously drawing me into the suit to confirm him, had made it difficult for me any longer to plead with her to be forgiving.

Her previous gesture of forbearance had resulted in a gloating repetition of the attack on her. I would have to act. She was right. I sent the following letter to Capote.

My dear Truman Capote:
In the May issue of After Dark you are quoted as describing my rejection of Jacqueline Susann's request that I represent her in a libel suit against you because there was an invulnerable defense; our viewing the broadcast at NBC, etc.

Every statement attributed to you is incorrect. I did not advise her and her husband that she had no cause of action against you. On the contrary, I thought you had libelled her. I did not view the broadcast. It was not necessary.

The reason I persuaded her not to sue was that it is my policy to discourage libel suits unless there is very serious injury to the plaintiff and his or her career, or an important principle is involved (as in the Faulk or Reynolds-Pegler cases). There is always hurt to sensibility, but not every injury, at least in my judgment, warrants a legal war.

I had hoped that my judgment in dissuading a suit would be justified by lettting the matter die with only the sacrifice of hurt feelings. However, you have chosen to revive the matter, claiming to know of the confidential conference between myself and my client, presenting completely false reason for your not being sued, and one which incomprehensibly has me confirming your libelous statement. Thus you involve me too. In addition you give further evidence of malice towards Jacqueline Susann.

I may have to reconsider my decision to discourage litigation even though there was a cause of action. My decision may well depend on your reply. In all fairness I would expect and appreciate a prompt correction of the matter.

Sincerely yours,
Louis Nizer

Truman Capote answered with characteristic verve and wit. He flattered me by saying that he found it impossible not to answer a charming letter from a lawyer even though the burden of the communication was to sue him.

But the point of the letter, all said in good humor, was that he did not see how he might have libeled Miss Jacqueline Susann. He remarked that in the give and take of interview language he had commented, off the cuff, that she bore a striking resemblance in some of her publicity photographs to a truck driver. This he felt was "bitchy, yes; malicious, no." He was of the attitude of one professional to another with admiration for what she did in her field of literary endeavor although he reserved judgment on the virtue of the field itself.

The matter of whether or not I was with her at the screening of a Carson TV show, he covered with clever grace full of artful guile. Maybe it was someone else from my office; maybe the meeting was all fantasy . . .

He then turned his attention to the fact that Miss Susann had made some remarks about him in West Coast interviews that might be reviewed. She had repeatedly referred to him as a homosexual which accusation he turned off with the comment, "Big news." He felt that she had also accused him of sloth and that she suggested that he was green with envy of her energy. This accusation seemed to bother him not at all. That he was unhappy about the quantity of her output compared to his he found totally without merit; as far as he was concerned she could win the world's major literary prize and it would not disturb him.

He was gracious in acknowledging the fact that I had told him about one or two magazine and newspaper interviews of whose existence he was not aware. He did tell me about a specific interview and where it ran.

Once again he thanked me for such a delightful scolding letter and pointed out that correspondence was something he indulged in so rarely that he suggested that I keep his letter for my heirs to sell at some far later date at a literary auction.

It was the kind of letter that brightens one's day and suddenly, by his magical writing ability and disarming candor, he had removed the heat from the whole situation.

Susann was completely appeased by this disarming letter. She had received an apology, been told that he respected her "as a very professional person," had conceded that his comment about her was "bitchy" and confirmed her charge that he was homosexual, by chiding her that she had hardly made a new discovery. She laughed about the whole thing and might even have been charmed by his wit.

But the real reason known to few, that she now saw the matter in better perspective, was that she had been advised that she had cancer and had only one year to live. If we could sense the imminence of death one year or twenty, would not most quarrels subside?

Celebrities are of course the special victims of libels. Also they are more sensitive because thousands and sometimes millions of readers consider them vicarious friends, and wag their heads about some revelation to which they wouldn't give heed if it were about a private person they really knew.

So it comes about that most entreaties for suit come from famous people in one field or another. They are written about most often and their skins are the thinnest.

Two illustrations: Cary Grant was distressed because a magazine quoted him as saying he had never loved anyone. It was a garbled version of an interview in which he commented that he had never "left" anyone. His constancy had been turned into emotional sterility. It would be merely a funny transference of meanings (like the nervous editor who featured the homecoming of a "bottle scarred veteran," and hastened to correct the error by changing the type to battle scared veteran) if it were not so humiliating.

The false item was piquant and therefore carried by U.P.I. and reprinted in many newspapers. Grant was furious. He had been sought out by every motion picture "love goddess" to play the lover's role. His handsome face, charm, and acting skills would have been enough. But there was an added dimension which made him the most famous star

in Hollywood. It was his sincerity, an abused word—applied even to inanimate objects, but essential in lovers' roles. It could not be completely simulated. Fine actresses rarely shed glycerine tears. They feel
the emotion they are projecting and really cry. Powerful love scenes are
made possible by real passions. In acting, the less counterfeit, the better
the result, another way of saying that the great actor acts least.

All one had to do was watch one of Cary Grant's love scenes on the
screen to realize that in real life, too, he loved. Close-ups, catching
every shortened breath, hoarsened voice, trembling lips, and above all
the glistening eye (not always the lighting man's trick of having the
pupil reflect a shimmering beam) lent unmistakable sincerity to the
scene.

Furthermore, he had virtually abdicated from his screen kingdom to
devote himself to his nine-year-old daughter. She, too, would read of
the false accusation.

Still, I told him it was a misprint of a word, worthy of correction but
not a suit.

On another occasion, I instituted a libel suit despite my original advice to abstain. The issue was too close to deny the client. A motion
picture magazine of no particular standing had featured Elizabeth
Taylor on the cover. This was a usual circulation gambit. Her beauty,
dazzling in its even simplicity, and her adventuresome life guaranteed a
minimum sale, even if there was nothing else inside. The cover test
preceded the polls as a measuring yardstick. For years after President
Franklin D. Roosevelt died, his picture, or Mrs. Roosevelt's, on a magazine cover boosted its circulation throughout the world. Elizabeth was
accustomed to being featured and exploited. She knew it was the reward and sometimes the penalty for being the face which launched a
thousand stories each week. Why then her unmollifiable anger on this
occasion? What had turned her violet eyes dark with rage?

It was the appearance of her two children alongside her and a teaser
headline which read, "Elizabeth Will Lose Her Children." When one
turned to the designated page for the story, there was an ill-written
"Psychological" analysis of how children of famous parents break away
from home when they grow up, to live their own lives. It was an obvious fraud. Those who bought the magazine because of the promise of
sensational revelation would have had the right under consumer laws to
demand their money back. But who bothers to do so? And the magazine cared not a whit about alienating the reader, since it was a fly-by-
night corporate venture which might be destined for a few issues at
best, to resume under another name.

I explained all this to Elizabeth and tried to discourage her from incurring the expense and harassment of a suit against an irresponsible publication of no account.

But she was adamant, and I had to respect her logic. "I don't care what they say about me, true or false. You know I have been silent despite many printed lies. But I will not stand for having my children pictured and exploited. The whole thing is a fake. I don't care what it costs, and I understand that I will never collect a cent. But I want to put them out of business, and I want the world to know that they must leave my children alone."

Her statement of principle overcame the pragmatic considerations. There must be a limit to sensationalism and the line is best drawn at the children. So we sued, won, and the magazine was shut down, never to appear again. Elizabeth was content, even though, as anticipated, there was no one from whom to collect.

Even when the libel is serious enough to warrant suit, there are other reasons not to do so. There is wisdom in the old saw "I take it from whence it comes." The source of the article may be so disreputable and limited in circulation, and the prominence of the victim so great, that a suit would only provide wide dissemination of the lie. Also, it would confer the fame of the plaintiff on an otherwise unknown sheet. There are many such instances. I cite only one.

Dorothy Thompson was the most famous woman political writer of her day. Her column appeared in the New York *Herald Tribune* opposite Walter Lippmann's, whose influence she also shared. She was frequently listed among the most important women in the world. Her columns against Nazism were fiery polemics which won a worldwide attention.

Nature, too, had not disappointed her. She looked the part. Even though she wore the weight of fifty-odd years, as well as some extra poundage, she was beautiful as well as distinguished, from her blue eyes and florid cheeks to her crown of gray hair, which tossed with vehemence when she held forth.

She used to attend private gatherings in my home on election night to celebrate the assured triumphs of Franklin Roosevelt, "again and again." It was interesting to see the inevitable grouping around her. Men and women literally sat in a circle at her feet, while she, in a lounge chair, with a martini in her hand, fascinated them with incessant brilliant talk. To hold a conversation, you must let go once in a while. She rarely did. She lectured and we learned and enjoyed it.

Dorothy was also an activist. When the Bund held a Nazi meeting in Madison Square Garden, which was desecrated with swastikas for the occasion, she appeared in person as a reporter. Fritz Kuhn, Hitler's American leader, recognized her. There was an enemy in their midst.

He ordered her ejected. She refused to leave, announcing that she was there to describe the whole obscene conclave for her newspaper. It took an army of shock troops to carry her out physically. The incident was pictured and reported on the front pages of the world's press. It was ludicrous to see storm troopers, puffing from lack of condition, their gritting faces registering supreme effort, as they heaved the rolling woman inch by inch out of the building. Czechoslovakia was easier to conquer.

Dorothy had been married to Nobel Prize winner Sinclair Lewis. Many years later, a murder mystery played by Elmer Rice called *Cue for Passion* appeared on Broadway. To add spice to the plot, two leading characters were a Nobel Prize author married to a famous columnist. It was as difficult to guess their identity as to answer the quiz "What countries were involved in the Spanish-American War?" Since there was no rhyme or reason for their inclusion in the play; they might just as well have been any suburban couple caught in a murder mystery. Dorothy insisted on an immediate injunction.

Otto Preminger was the director. The play was in rehearsal, about to open in a few days. I prepared the affidavits and proposed order to enjoin the play from opening. But my heart went out to the author, director, and cast. There were enough natural hurdles for a play opening on Broadway to surmount without visiting an injunction disaster upon it at the last moment. I explained to the panicky company that my client's objective was not to destroy the play, but merely to remove the identification of herself and her former husband from participation in a murder mystery plot. Why not rewrite the scenes involving them so as to make them as fictitious as the rest of the play and thus save the production? I offered to withhold the injunction application, and even help in the last minute rewriting. This proposal was accepted, but the required changes were not simple. The author had played with the relationship of the famous couple, deriving humor from their rivalry and self-centered dispositions.

I devoted myself to the needed surgery which would remove Dorothy Thompson and Sinclair Lewis from the scenes while preserving whatever virtues the play had.

A bizarre scene followed. The author, Preminger, and I sat up through the night rewriting the play, while the actors, who always grumble when revisions necessitate new memorization, had a special reason to do so. Sleeplessness was not conducive to a keen mind. The play opened on time.

It would be nice to report that not only was the client's mission fulfilled, but that the play enjoyed a long run. Alas, it was not so. While I cannot, therefore, preen myself on having made meager contributions which catapulted the work to success, I am certain that if the main characters had been disguised as a President in a wheelchair because of polio, and his wife as a peripatetic traveler with an ascending high-pitched voice who wrote a column called "My Day," the run of the play would not have been any longer.

Dorothy Thompson, unfortunately, was also an activist in her personal life. She fell in love with an able Czechoslovakian painter, Maxim Kopf. He was married. His wife refused to give him a divorce. Dorothy resented this. She wrote a letter in longhand to Mrs. Kopf upbraiding her for holding on to a loveless relationship. She denounced her attitude as immoral. She advised her that Max and she were in love and that a thousand Mrs. Kopfs could not stand in the way of their happiness. It was indecent of Mrs. Kopf to interfere. She lectured her as she was accustomed to doing with awed admirers.

But Mrs. Kopf was not an admirer. She suddenly had in her hands not only written proof of her husband's infidelity, but a document which might destroy his mistress. For this was in the 1940s, when the bonds of matrimony had not yet become so loose that they slipped off readily. Also sexual freedom was still called licentiousness. Public figures particularly bore the burden of "setting good examples for the young." It was part of the price of fame, that the peccadilloes overlooked in private life would not be tolerated for them. How could we be sure that Mrs. Kopf, embittered by her husband's desertion, and burning for revenge against the woman who had destroyed her marriage and life, might not use Dorothy's letter as a retaliatory weapon? We might call it blackmail, but a scorned wife would consider it nonpoetic justice.

Dorothy was a controversial figure at best. Now her enemies would be joined by moralists, and even those who might not disapprove would be disgusted with her cruelty. I could see her ousted from her column and stunned by public denunciation, the possibilities of which she seemed totally unaware.

I arranged a meeting with Mrs. Kopf and her attorney. Despite Dorothy's insistence, I forbade her to be present. Brilliant woman though she was, she hadn't any understanding of the human problem. She wanted to confront Mrs. Kopf, with Max at her side, and convince her that her dog-in-the-manger attitude would be of no avail. She was going to shame her into granting a divorce, as if a woman's pride and lost love could be stormed by force.

Instead I adopted a sympathetic attitude toward her, one which I sincerely felt. Only one thing could be more painful to a woman than to lose a husband she loved, and that was to be rejected in favor of another identified woman. To assuage her anguish, the abandoned wife often convinced herself that her husband still loved her but that he was "sick." She expects the illness to be brief and then "he will come to his senses again." This rationalizes her refusal to free him. She will wait until he recovers from his insane infatuation.

That is why it is well nigh impossible to obtain consent for divorce from such a wife. Her obstinacy is strengthened by conscious and unconscious motivations. On the one hand she hopes to outwait his fever until normalcy returns him lovingly and apologetically to her side. On the other hand she is determined not to free him so that he can marry "that whore"—isn't she always that to a betrayed wife?

Still there are countermoves of persuasion. They are effective because they are true. The most important is that the husband has other alternatives to obtain a divorce. If he establishes a genuine residence in another state and sues for divorce there, the wife is in a terrible dilemma. If she appears in the action to defend herself, she confers jurisdiction on the "foreign" state, and she is bound by the decree. If she refuses to appear in the action on the ground that it is brought out of the jurisdiction in which they have lived most of their lives, her husband may obtain a divorce by default. If his residence in the foreign state is held to be genuine, the divorce is effective. Particularly people of means have little difficulty in establishing other residences. For example, Winthrop Rockefeller, in his contest with Bobo Rockefeller, actually built a large home in Arkansas, voted there, joined a local club, obtained local driving and hunting licenses—all to establish a genuine residence. The graft of residence took root so well that he became a leading citizen of the community, entered politics, and was elected Governor. Indeed, he had real residence. It was at the Governor's mansion.

The combination of Kopf and Thompson could well achieve a residence in Vermont, where they lived, and he could bring a divorce suit there. Then Mrs. Kopf would have to take the risk of going to a foreign state to defend, or default. Neither was an enviable choice. Even if she won, there might be small alimony because Kopf was not a large earner.

On the other hand if she yielded to her husband's request for a divorce on legal grounds in the state in which they lived, she would receive appropriate alimony and even a lump sum settlement, not obtainable in most states.

The law could not restore her husband's love, but the least he could do was to provide her with reasonable financial security. This he would do if she consented to a divorce.

These were the hard dollar facts. But there was something more important. She ought to stop thinking about him and Dorothy. There were understandable hate feelings. But they would injure her, not them. She ought to consider her own welfare first and foremost. Holding on legally to a fleeing husband was self-defeating. It bound her but not her husband and Dorothy. The sooner she freed herself emotionally, the sooner she would rebuild an independent life. To lose a man she loved was a tragedy. But vindictiveness was not the remedy. For her own sake she ought to look at her terrible loss in true perspective. It was not the worst evil that had ever befallen a human being. People are resilient. They survive the death of their dearest, and their own crippling diseases. She ought to build a new life. At the moment she could not conceive of a happy existence without him, but it would happen.

I asked her to confer with her lawyer privately, and determine whether this wasn't the best course for her.

After a number of sessions, she agreed. Satisfactory financial terms were worked out. Then came the most difficult task. I wanted Dorothy's handwritten letter returned to me, and a written agreement that no copies had been made or issued, and that nothing would be said about it, at least until after Dorothy's death. Violation would bring about financial sanctions under the divorce decree.

Having been persuaded that venomous pursuit of either Max or Dorothy was stultifying, she made this final gesture.

So the Kopfs were quietly divorced. Dorothy and Max married and lived happily in Vermont.

I won custody of the letter.

Against this background of Dorothy Thompson's assertive personality, I turn to a libel suit she insisted I bring, and which in her interest I refused to do. An inconsequential half-newspaper, half-scandal sheet, attacked her. It is always possible to find an ugly photograph of a much-publicized person. One can often tell a newspaper's view of a candidate by the kind of photograph it selects for the news story. From thousands of snapshots one can always select a handsome exhibit or a repulsive one. The malicious intention toward Dorothy could easily be discerned by the picture accompanying the article. It caught her mouth wide open, eyes distended, hair standing straight up as if lifted by electric shock, copious breasts without a waistline so that they became part of a protruding stomach, and a clenched fist on top of a trunk-like arm to add an extra touch of belligerence to the pose. Beautiful Dorothy looked like an ogre. She could have tried out for the freak fat lady in a circus.

As if this wasn't enough, the article, as puerile in expression as it was venomous, had a phrase about her which even Capote would have been proud to have coined. It said she was "having her menopause in public."

"Isn't this libelous?" she raged. Of course it was. I could have filled five pages of a complaint with innuendos. But was it wise for her to sue and cause a feature story in hundreds of newspapers which would repeat the ugly phrase? The offending publication was too unknown to be quoted. As it turned out the devilish description had motive power of its own and was circulated widely, but surely it was not advisable to give it the propulsion of an announced litigation by the famous Dorothy Thompson. She insisted. I resisted. It was a curious battle of wills, because our common objective was to protect her. She was fair enough later to appreciate my defiance. I was not the kind of lawyer who asked the client what advice he wanted and then gave it to him.

This is an illustration of why, before a libel suit is launched, the relative positions of the involved parties should be evaluated. An unknown publication with limited circulation can do little damage to a prominent individual. But if the victim loses perspective because of hurt feelings and strikes back, the ugly story is given wide currency and the injury is enlarged in the very course of seeking a remedy.

What better example of this principle can there be than the despicable item some time ago in an Italian magazine that the Pope was a homosexual. Let alone, only a relative handful of people would have read the item, and most of them would disregard it in view of its irresponsible source. But the Vatican chose to issue an official denial. It was published throughout the world. The respectable press had no reason to resist a statement by the Vatican. I read it in the New York *Times*. Millions, perhaps tens of millions of people, were thus made aware of the charge. The Pope needs a good lawyer.

And so did President Lyndon Johnson. His sensitivity to press criticism was a weakness which even his tumultuous years in political life could not eradicate. If an editorial in a remote and small newspaper attacked him, as he felt, unfairly, he would telephone the publisher or editor, or communicate with someone close to them to protest. On one occasion when Mildred and I were at the White House, I heard him chide Senator Magnuson for not replying to an unwarranted criticism of him during a Senate debate. "Why don't you fellows get up and defend the President?" He sounded like a football coach rallying his players to greater effort.

In view of the controversies which swirl around the presidency, I am not surprised that he had a heart condition. Although he was a courageous man who I am sure would risk his life for his country, he could not face criticism. This vulnerability makes understandable why the gale of Vietnam opposition blew him out of office. His was not an Achilles' heel, it was tenderized skin.

For the most part, the American people have chosen complex and neurotic men to be their presidents. Occasionally simple men like Calvin Coolidge or Gerald Ford, who didn't grow, or Harry Truman, who did, come to power; but in each instance through accidental ascendency from the vice-presidency. Our deliberate choices, while varied, have one common denominator—involved personalities. Witness Lincoln, Hoover, Wilson, the Roosevelts, Kennedy, Johnson, and Nixon.

To see Johnson sitting in an armchair in the West Hall next to a cabinet with mysterious equipment which enabled him by stretching his arm to communicate with the leaders of the world, or press buttons which might start air and sea armadas moving thousands of miles away, or, heaven forbid, release the power to powderize the planet, was to get a glimpse of the joy of power.

He made no secret of it. His face aglow with satisfaction, he called attention to the circular cabinet and then reveled in a description of the first use of the Hot Line from Kosygin to him during the six-day Arab-Israeli war. He led to the climax like a good storyteller. The war had broken out. Russia was threatening to intervene on the side of the Arabs. Naturally her objective was to control the Middle East.

The President inquired how far the Seventh Fleet was from the battle shore. It was steaming in the opposite direction, but could be there in two days.

"How long will it take Russian submarines to report that the ships have turned around and are headed toward the war zone?" the President asked.

"About two hours," the high command informed him.

"Order the Seventh Fleet to head back full steam!"

Several hours later the Hot Line telephone rang. The President beamed. The script was going according to plan. Kosygin offered to stay out of the conflict if Johnson did too. (I noticed that the conversation was personalized. It was not Russia and the United States. It was two Herculean individuals pitted against each other.)

The President turned from the recital, as if he had put his hand over the phone and was commenting on his reasoning before he replied.

"I was willing to bet on my horse and let him bet on his."

Then back to the phone, "All right, Mr. Premier, in the interest of containing the conflict, I am willing that we both stay out. That's a deal. You have my word."

His enactment was so real I could see him hang up the receiver and chuckle at the outcome.

The penalty for love of such power is that a day comes when it no longer exists. The loss is excruciating. Singers who entrance audiences and then lose their voices to age; athletes who thrill millions with their prowess and suddenly (to them) find that their bodies do not respond; actors and actresses who captivate millions with their beauty and talent, and who have to retire to character parts or else completely retire; and political leaders whose every word and action affect the course of events and then are relegated to private citizenry, all suffer deeply from the removal of the spotlight. They cannot bear the darkness of anonymity into which they are pitched.

Little wonder that rulers struggle to maintain power, even if they must turn dictatorial and kill to do so. And similarly, little wonder that artists, athletes, and politicians almost never gracefully quit the scene of the triumphs they can no longer repeat. Power is an addictive drug. That is one reason why it corrupts. That is why politicians are forever running. They cannot stand the withdrawal pains.

When Jack Valenti became president, and I counsel, of the Motion Picture Association of America, we took our first trip through Europe to visit the heads of nations. (Motion pictures are our country's foremost good-will ambassadors as well as export. Every foreign government is interested in the cultural economic aspect of the American movie.)

In France we visited André Malraux, Minister of Culture under De Gaulle. I had looked forward eagerly to meeting this great writer and activist. We had to wait. He was ill, and wouldn't be in his office for another week. We returned. There he was in the ornate office Napoleon had occupied, with gold-edged carved wood, chandeliers which glistened without light, hand-pressed glass windows, and all the other trappings of authority and power. One could read Napoleon's ambition by looking at this room. It was that of an emperor, not a general. One could read Malraux too.

He was still ill. He had become an opium addict during the Chinese Revolution, in which he fought. When he overdosed, he was away for weeks. There he sat, pale, dark eyes staring, and his clenched fist tight under his chin to keep his head from shaking. While we conversed, many questions passed through my mind. They involved the mystery of power. The radical who had volunteered to fight in foreign wars had become an ardent supporter of De Gaulle, the supreme nationalist. Undoubtedly he rationalized his role as one who would restore art to its high French estate. Even his execution of an edict that important buildings be steam-cleaned was a symbolic gesture of patriotic purity. But he clung to his title of Minister of Culture even though he had earned more important recognition internationally as a writer.

I had an opportunity to observe this clutching to power close up with Lyndon Johnson. After I addressed the University of Texas, Mildred and I were invited to spend a day with the ex-President and Lady Bird at their nearby ranch on the Pedernales River.

During the entire morning Johnson was straining to get out and tour the ranch. At last lunch was over, and we proceeded to a large jeep. Because of his heart condition, the President had been forbidden by his doctors to drive. Mrs. Johnson, with great tact, took the wheel, chatting away to relieve the President of the embarrassment of his incapacity. For him not to be in the driver's seat was about as acceptable as if someone had suggested while he was in office that the Vice-President preside over a cabinet meeting while he sat by.

He made up for it by being a front seat driver. In sharp commands he told Lady Bird where to go and where to stop. She didn't mind. It was his way of defeating the doctors.

Also he had a shortwave radio speaker system, and he barked out his orders to the superintendents and workers in the field. (He was communicating with faraway lands.)

"Jim, why are there no deer out there? I wanted Louis and Mildred to see some. The fence must be broken and they have gone through. Get to it. Find the hole and fix it!" (Turn the Seventh Fleet back!)

"Yes, sir, right away," came a voice from an invisible spot. (The Hot Line telephone was working.)

"Harry, the brush fire is smoldering. It will spoil the patch. Clean it up!"

"It is out, Mr. President. It's only the smoke you see."

"Well, snuff it out!" (We don't want alibis from our commanders. We want results.)

In his mind, Johnson had never ceased being President. He had simply transferred his authority to the vast acres of his ranch (it wouldn't have surprised me if a map showed them to be the shape of the United States).

He, too, had had a dream. It was to achieve a better life for the people. "The Great Society" was not a platform on which to ride into office, but one to stand on while in office. He aspired to be the greatest benefactor of the people who had ever resided in the White House. His sincerity could not be questioned. He strove to lift the underprivileged whether black, yellow, or white, to improve their health, and see that their pursuit of happiness would not be too long a chase.

The Vietnam involvement, which others began and he sought to bull through by half measures (a contradiction in terms which assured defeat) cast a pall of smoke over his achievements. But history may "snuff out" the smoke sufficiently to appraise him justly.

Truman, too, had suffered megaton criticism for use of a new weapon which we now regard fearfully only as a symbol of terror. History is a selective eraser, rubbing out faults, and thereby emphasizing the virtues of its subjects. Otherwise, Washington, Jefferson, and Lincoln would not have fared as well as they justly do.

Johnson was too impatient for long-range appraisal. He smarted at criticism, no matter how minor or unimportant the source.

One Saturday night, while Johnson was President, Eddie Weisl, a distinguished lawyer, Mildred, and I were at a formal dinner for a charitable cause in the Grand Ball Room of the Waldorf-Astoria in New York. A Waldorf official approached Weisl and myself breathlessly. "The White House is calling Mr. Nizer. The President would also like to speak to Mr. Weisl." This is one of the miracles of White House telephone efficiency. Anyone can be traced anywhere.

We were led to a special telephone. The President was too angry to engage in any introductory formalities. "Louis, I want you to start a suit Monday morning against *The Saturday Evening Post!* An article written by a damned liar quotes me as saying, 'If these niggers want it, I'll give it to them!'

"Now you know I have done more for civil rights than all other presidents combined. I want to teach these lying sons-of-a-bitches a lesson they'll never forget. Sue them for everything they've got. Let's put them out of business."

I made the mistake of starting my cooling down campaign too soon. I should have known that he was too furious to listen to reason in a hasty telephone conversation.

"But Mr. President you can't sue—"

"Why not? It's false. Isn't that a libel?"

"Of course it is, but if you, the President of the United States bring a private suit, it would be a front-page story all over the world. You'll spread the lie and its filthy connotation. On the other hand—"

I was interrupted sharply. "Put Eddie on the phone!"

Weisl, who was a close friend of the President, didn't have a chance even to say, "Hello." He listened to a lengthy tirade, and then said, "I'll tell him."

He hung up and said, "He insists that you start a libel suit immediately."

"But it is not wise to do so," I remonstrated. "Even though *The Saturday Evening Post* is a reputable magazine, how many people do you think will read this article, notice the quoted phrase, or most important, believe it? Everyone knows Johnson's record on civil rights. The article is an obvious lie. But can you imagine the front-page stories, followed by editorials, and special features which a libel suit by the President will provoke? The author of the article, rejoicing in the opportunity to joust with the President, may claim he can substantiate his story. Political enemies will quickly point to lies they claimed the President told Congress about Vietnam. 'How do we know this denial now

isn't a lie?' So it will go, about a phrase which won't see the light of day
if the President ignores it.

"Furthermore, there will be many who will acknowledge that the article is false, but will attack the President on the grounds of free speech.
They will condemn him for trying to muzzle the press. They will insist
that it is better for the President to suffer criticism, even false criticism,
than use his power to make publications shy of writing about him."

Weisl interrupted with a gesture which indicated he didn't need to
be convinced. He had his eye on the complex personality of the President.

"You must wait until he calms down. Come to Washington Monday
and we'll talk to him."

"Do you think by then he will be ready to say, 'Come let's sit down
and reason together?'" I said, referring to his favorite quotation.

The aftermath was that the President needed little persuasion to
drop the matter. The enormous burdens of office, and perhaps a host of
other items, distracted him. So far as we could learn, no one paid attention to the quotation which had so riled him.

The irony of it was that without our push, *The Saturday Evening
Post* went out of business. I do not consider this a coincidence. I have
observed that magazines which are in financial trouble attempt to hype
their circulation by sensational stories. When a flood of libel claims
suddenly appear against a particular publication, I sense a desperate
effort by the editors to salvage their failing enterprise by sensationalism.

All these illustrations of abnegation do not mean that there are not
times when libel suits must be brought, when they are the most appropriate and noble means to right a terrible wrong. They cannot only provide justice. More than almost any other legal remedy, they can actually save lives.

During the McCarthy era, artists such as Mady Christians, Philip
Loeb, and a number of political figures committed suicide because their
reputations and means of livelihood had been destroyed. We shall
never know the full cost.

That wonderful woman and gifted artist, Margaret Webster, had
been designated the American representative of an International Meeting of the Theater in London. The State Department refused her a visa
because she had come under the poisonous cloud of McCarthyism. She
was so depressed that she wrote me a lengthy letter in which she at one
point said she was contemplating suicide. I was frantic with the responsibility of speedy persuasion. Fortunately her threat might have been
the expression of her disgust with the stupidity of the world rather than
a resolve to flee it.

She survived, and went on to brilliant achievements in presenting Shakespeare throughout the nation. She was chiefly responsible for making the Bard one to be enjoyed by the populace rather than merely revered by name. She also directed Metropolitan operas, removing the stiffness from the joints of traditional posturing. But how near she and many others came to destruction because "He who filches my good name makes me poor indeed."

So I use the libel sword wherever it is necessary. I shall advert here to two illustrations: one of a private citizen, and one of a public official.

Alfred Strelsin was a successful businessman known only to a small circle of friends and acquaintances. He had never sought nor attained any public notice.

In three minutes one night, his name came to the attention of millions of people. It was not fame which was bestowed upon him by the miracle of television. It was contempt. He was cast in the role of a despicable person. The suddenness and unexpected nature of his debacle made it even more devastating.

It came from a news broadcast on a national Metromedia network. Interspersed with the news was a gossip commentary by Rona Barrett. Its relationship to news was similar to the relationship between a gossip column and the editorial page in a newspaper. Its purpose was to relieve the strain of thinking by tickling the mind. Rona Barrett specialized in stories about Hollywood stars, congressmen who sinned at government expense, and those who used their own money, couples who were heading for "splitsville" and those for "church bells" (with batting averages, her second, his third), and since there are more divorces than ever before, there was no lack of fill-in material. What was needed was sensationalism.

The style was breezy. Posing in a three-quarter profile and adopting a saucy manner, she brought the most unimportant, but titillating, items of the day to the attention of her listeners. Any scandal was precious. Rona Barrett had heard something about Strelsin, or so she claimed. She spurted it out on the network as follows:

First Party givers were those fabulous trillionaires [to Rona Barrett millionaire was not impressive enough], Dorothy Strelsin, singer extraordinaire [etc.] and husband, Al Strelsin who once admitted to friends that he sold guns to Hitler during World War II."

The daring nature of such an accusation gave it verisimilitude. Would anyone risk saying such a thing if she wasn't sure? Everyone knows that network lawyers check the broadcasts to prevent libel suits.

The fact that this statement was passed by counsel indicated that some proof of its accuracy had to exist.

Even Strelsin's friends must have experienced some doubts. Was this a skeleton in his closet no one had known before. Was this how he had amassed his wealth?

Strelsin was Jewish. His brother had died fighting for Israel. He had been active in Jewish as well as other causes. This made the perfidy of his accused conduct even greater.

As a friend of Donald Nelson, the head of the War Production Board under Roosevelt, during World War II, I knew that Strelsin had been designated by him to serve in the economic division of the Board, to prevent strategic materials from reaching Hitler. The destination of such items was scrutinized and traced so that indirect deliveries by other countries would not be made. Also vital goods produced by foreign countries were bought up by the United States, so that they would not fall into Hitler's hands. I have reason to believe that this economic warfare did not stop at peaceful means. Any investigation, which I do not suggest, of our activities in blocking strategic materials from reaching Hitler might provide a saga of unsuspected violence.

So to say of Strelsin that he shipped guns to Hitler was also to charge him with being a traitor to the United States. For his mission was to prevent guns or even cotton or food from arriving in Germany. Also the moral dereliction of aiding the Haman and Hun of the twentieth century to slay his kinfolk was so vile as to make Strelsin an inhuman beast.

When Strelsin came to see me, he had aged perceptibly. He literally trembled as he described the blow which had just befallen him. His sleeplessness and torment made him look ill.

I advised immediate suit. "We'll examine Rona Barrett before trial under oath. We'll find out who in the network had approved the script and on what basis. We'll demonstrate the falsity and recklessness of the inflammatory broadcast."

This was not the kind of libel to ignore in the hope that like a wave it would dissipate itself and roll in harmlessly. His reputation had been destroyed, his health undermined. His business might well suffer the same fate. He had no choice but to fight back, hard and immediately.

We served a complaint on Rona Barrett and the network. It was insured against such claims and experienced counsel appeared. They challenged New York jurisdiction over Rona Barrett, who resided in California. We attached her funds in New York to obtain jurisdiction in rem (of her property if not her person). Then we moved to examine Rona Barrett before trial and under oath.

In a libel suit, the phrase "the moment of truth" is not a mere idiom.

It is the literal point of time when the defendant must demonstrate that he is not a liar.

At that moment, the defendants sought settlement.

We wrote a hard ticket. The money request was substantial but not prohibitive. The defendants would have to pay Strelsin's counsel fees, allowing a punitive sum to Strelsin for satisfaction purposes. But more important, we demanded that Rona Barrett read on her regular broadcast a retraction and apology which I would compose. I made it clear in advance that it would confess gross and inexcusable error and contrition and be as strong as my mastery of language would permit. Not a word was to be changed. Also she was to make a tape of it, so that we could listen to it in advance to be certain that her delivery of it would be as sincere and emphatic as the words required, and that no facial expressions or slurring of words would detract from its effectiveness. Finally, we were to have the right to publish her retraction in any newspaper we chose, or mail it to stockholders of Strelsin's companies or to others, with an accompanying statement of the suit, the surrender and the admission of falsity.

Churchill's precept "In victory—magnanimity" appeals to me, and I derived no joy from insisting on such humiliating demands. Indeed, I thought they would not be accepted; that the defendants would rather subject themselves to a trial and damages, seeking to ameliorate the amount by admitting error, but denying malice.

However, the defendants felt denuded of any defense. The accusation was completely baseless. Rona Barrett claimed that she had heard it at a cocktail party from some unidentified source. Even a drunken man could hardly have had the inventive wit to make up such a whopper. Those who were supposed to check such broadcasts must have had hangovers themselves and been too bleary-eyed to read. Otherwise how could such a story have passed them by?

The defendants had the usual Hobson's choice. Either they accepted "unacceptable" settlement terms, or they risked a disaster at trial. They chose the former.

I wrote the statement to be made by Rona Barrett. No script writer ever had a similar task, to write that which would make the star most uncomfortable. We tested the tape. To her credit, she delivered the lines with sincerity and due emphasis. It was not easy for her. Crow tastes more bitter to columnists than to others. Making a mistake is understandable for businessmen and politicians. But pundits, whose stock in trade is purveying inside news, can lose their influence and jobs, if they are exposed as panderers of fiction.

Strelsin notified as many people as possible to listen to her broadcast at the appointed time. They and millions of others saw Rona Barrett, still in three-quarter profile (but now it looked as if she was turned aside partly in embarrassment) say:

"Some time ago, I broadcast over this station a serious charge against Mr. Alfred Strelsin, one of America's leading industrialists, attacking his patriotism. Unfortunately, I found out too late that the charge was totally unfounded. Tonight Metromedia and I want to set the record straight.

"I have found that Mr. Strelsin's record of distinguished service to our government is unquestionable, including top-level government assignments during World War II. He is a dedicated philanthropist with a record of honor and distinction. There was not and is not the slightest basis for the charge I broadcast against him. I retract it fully and offer my and Metromedia's sincerest apologies to a distinguished American, Alfred Strelsin."

In addition she wrote him a lengthy letter dictated by me, saying that she recognized "the severe anguish and distress my erroneous broadcast has caused you . . . I offer my sincere apology for the injury caused by this unfounded broadcast. I authorize you to make such use of this letter in the future as you may find necessary." Metromedia Inc., whose president, John W. Kluge, had demonstrated his integrity in support of correction, also wrote that "the charge was totally unfounded. We regret that our staff failed to detect and delete this false statement from the Barrett broadcast before it was made."

Another illustration of a libel suit which had to be brought involved a public official. It will introduce a subject which has troubled the Supreme Court more than almost any other conflict between constitutional rights.

Governor James A. Rhodes of Ohio was one of those rare men in public life who appealed to the people so strongly that he rose politically with rocket-like vertical propulsion. He had been Mayor of Columbus four times, and then was selected in 1962 to run against the popular Democratic Governor Mike DiSalle. Ordinarily this would be an invitation to disaster. But Rhodes won by the largest majority ever in an Ohio election. The fact that he was a Republican who had swept a Democratic state brought him to the attention of the nation. He was re-elected for another four-year term, and as it was ending, there were plans to run him for the United States Senate, and then for national office. Already he was prominently mentioned for the vice-presidency and even the presidency.

At this moment of increasing momentum for a brilliant career, his future was cut off as if by a single sharp knife stroke. *Life* magazine announced on its front cover a feature story, entitled "Scandal Overtakes the Governor of Ohio." Inside, a two-page spread had the caption "The Governor and the Mobster." Photographs have innuendos too, particularly their placement. One was of Governor Rhodes opening the baseball season in Cincinnati. "He has been mentioned as the next Baseball Commissioner." Immediately alongside were two "mug shots of Thomas (Yonnie) Licavoli, taken in 1934," side and front view, to make sure that their dishonorable origin was clear. On the opposite page was a dramatic photograph of Licavoli taken thirty-five years later, in a stretcher, being wheeled out of Riverside Hospital to return to prison, after he "had reportedly suffered a massive heart attack." On the next page were photographs of four gangsters.

The chief accusation was that Governor Rhodes had commuted Licavoli's life sentence for murder in the first degree to second degree. This turned out to be on the unanimous recommendation of the Parole Board, whose decision the Governor accepted. This made Licavoli eligible to apply for parole. But the article did not reveal this. A subheading in the article gave the flavor of the charge. "Plenty of Money Floating Around to Set Yonnie Free." The innuendo was unmistakable. There were references to $250,000 being available to free Licavoli and that in the past there had been overtures to previous officials to free Licavoli. They had rejected the proposed bribes, although there was a vacuum in the article as to why they had not reported the matter to the criminal authorities. The clear implication was that Rhodes had yielded to temptation.

Life magazine was so proud of itself that it took full page advertisements in various newspapers announcing its scoop. One such advertisement appeared in the New York *Times*. Nine tenths of the page was a huge photograph of Governor Rhodes. Underneath was a large head line: "Ohio's Governor and the Mob." I noticed immediately the subtle change from singular to plural. The *Life* article referred to Mobster. The *Times* advertisement to Mob. The accusation, like amoebas, had multiplied itself in the course of transition. "To top it off," said the rest of the ad, "*Life* presents evidence showing that, while in public office, Governor Rhodes 'has engaged in high handed manipulation of political funds.'"

Governor Rhodes and his executive assistant came to see me at once. He was calm on the surface, although I was sure he was seething with anger. It was quickly evident why he was a popular and effective official. He was sincere, gracious, and charming but very firm. It was quite a combination. My partners, Judge Hofstadter, Vincent Broderick, and Paul Martinson, who sat in at the conferences, had the same high impression of him. At the end of one session, Judge Hofstadter commented, "If he survives this, he can go on to be a presidential figure."

As in every matter, we examined the evidence with deliberate skepticism. Indeed, we cross-examined him and his executive assistant as thoroughly as our opponent would ultimately do. No questions were barred. All were answered frankly and satisfactorily. Whenever we requested supporting data, it was sent immediately. We were convinced that the accusations in the article were completely false.

Licavoli had been convicted of conspiracy to kill two people. Since he was not charged with the actual shooting, the jury recommended mercy. He was sentenced to life imprisonment. His confederates were sentenced to be electrocuted.

The mercy recommendation entitled Licavoli, after he had served twenty years, to apply to the Parole Board for commutation to second-degree murder. If the Board did so recommend, the Governor could commute. The Parole Board then for the first time had the power to hold a hearing and grant or refuse parole. On one occasion the Parole Board recommended commutation, but Governor Rhodes rejected it.

Later, after Licavoli's thirty-fifth year of confinement, and serious illness which was certified by doctors, the Parole Board repeated its recommendation to the Governor for commutation. This time he gave it more consideration. Licavoli had written a personal plea to the Governor in which he said:

"I have a daughter who was born three months before I came to prison. Now she is married, with two lovely girls and a little boy of her own, and none of them have ever seen me except behind bars. My first-born daughter was killed, along with my father, while they were on their way to visit me one day."

For four years Licavoli had been under the psychiatric care of Dr. Anderson. During this period he received commendation from Warden Henderson for initiative and action beyond the normal call of duty on three separate occasions:

(1) When I climbed the outside of "C" cellhouse wall, 80 feet above the ground, and saved a man attempting to commit suicide;

(2) When I entered the cell of a demented inmate who had set his mattress on fire—at this time I had to fight the inmate and ended up losing 90 per cent of the sight of my right eye from an acid burn as a result;

(3) When I overpowered another homicidal inmate who was attempting to kill a guard (Mr. Helles) and was struck with an iron bar by the psychopath, 12 stitches being required to close the wound.

Looking back I realize that it was during this period that my rehabilitation began. I began to think about other people more than myself and my own troubles.

Warden Alvis entrusted him thereafter with narcotics of all kinds which were used on the psychiatric ranges. The trust was never violated.

One of Licavoli's confederates, sentenced to death, had had his sentence commuted and was paroled by a former governor without any fanfare.

Governor Rhodes had attempted generally to apply new humanitarian principles in dealing with the penology. He had ordered a list to be prepared of all prisoners who had served lengthy terms and were over sixty-five years old, that he might give special attention to parole applications. He had reduced the number of inmates in one prison by 50 per cent, saving the state money, but, more important, rewarding those who had undergone rehabilitation. He employed at the Governor's mansion trustees, some of them sentenced to life.

In Licavoli's case, he also received a plea from Chaplain Theodore Gratjohn:

Tom Licavoli is assigned to work as a nurse in our Tuberculosis Ward and has done a commendable job in performing his duties . . .

I am certain that he is neither the type man, nor individual that many would like to picture. Instead I knew him as a truly repentful soul, who is deserving of another chance before his fellowman.

Rhodes, aware of the previous rumors about attempted bribes to spring Licavoli, took the precaution of having a careful check made by his executive assistant, John M. McElroy. He requested and received a letter from Mrs. Licavoli which stated that neither she nor any other person to her knowledge "had paid or promised anything of value to anybody," to assist in obtaining a commutation. Inquiry was also directed to the prosecutor's office which had convicted Licavoli. The Attorney General of the state, Paul A. Brown, in commenting on the commutation wrote that "Governor Rhodes has acted justly and with high moral courage in an area always fraught with the risk of misunderstanding."

The basic fact was that the Governor had not pardoned Licavoli. He had merely accepted the seven-man Parole Board's unanimous report to commute his sentence to life imprisonment for second-degree murder. Thereafter a parole application was made and in view of the press furor it was denied. Licavoli remained in jail. He was one of the victims of the false rumors.

What is the purpose of imprisonment, revenge or rehabilitation? We must make up our minds. All would agree that society's objective is to protect itself from repetition of crime and deter others. So unless the prisoner is truly rehabilitated and becomes safe to society, his sentence should run its course. But in the rare instances in which real rehabilitation has occurred, the prisoner is no longer the same man who was sentenced. We ought not keep him in jail indefinitely if he is no longer a threat to society. It would be as wrong to do so as to keep an insane man confined after he has recovered sanity.

Such a policy would not open the door wide for incorrigibles to be let loose. Genuine transformation of a personality is somewhat of a miracle, and does not occur often. I have had occasion to write about one such extraordinary case, that of Paul Crump. He was a vicious, illiterate killer, who like the beautiful flower which grows in the mud of India, became a literate good man while in jail. He proved it by his deeds. So did Licavoli. Wasn't such a man, who paid his debt for thirty-five years and was old and sick entitled to a few years with his family? Why the outcry? There was not one scintilla of proof that money or influence played any part in the unanimous recommendation of the Parole Board or the Governor's acceptance of it. Indeed, even though the Governor's commutation made it possible for the Parole Board to act, it did not do so. Licavoli remained in jail.

If revenge is the purpose of penology, then let us kill convicted murderers, rapists, and kidnapers and perhaps any repeater of a violent crime. Why not also punish lesser offenders, by cutting off arms, legs, blinding some and cutting out the tongues of others? This is still done in some Arab countries. We could all become Nazis in spirit and revel in torture. We shy away from going all the way, because a civilized society must act decently even when attacked and injured. Otherwise there would be no Manual of War. Prisoners would be shot, women raped, and the enemy's cities plundered.

Life's article piled a few additional charges on the wild claim of mob association. These involved improper use of political slush funds, and income tax involvement, accusations which had been raised and found baseless in the 1962 campaign, when the voters rejected them and lifted Rhodes into office with a massive heave of votes.

The multiplication of falsehoods created a picture of a vile, unscrupulous hypocrite. Our indignation rose at the outrageous attacks. Who could be safe, if such tactics succeeded? But once again we asked the Governor to satisfy us, as counsel, by documentary proof. His accountants forwarded a cent-by-cent analysis refuting every accusation. We advised Governor Rhodes to issue a public statement, setting forth the assets of his wife and family. He did so in detail.* After more than twenty years of public service, he had wound up virtually impoverished. His reward had been the honor of high office and the regard of the people for him. Now even these were taken away.

Rhodes was at the time involved in a primary contest for the Senate with the redoubtable Robert A. Taft, Jr. We could not bring him relief in time to overcome the accusations of corruption and Mafia association which *Life*'s article announced. He nevertheless asked that he be permitted to announce a libel suit immediately.

"Governor," I said "I would like to ask you a blunt question. Is it your main purpose to institute suit in the hope of salvaging the primary campaign, or, even if you lose the primary do you intend to pursue the suit to vindicate your honor?"

"Mr. Nizer," he replied, "I want to nail their lies, which will probably defeat me in the primary. But that is a small part of it. I have a wife, children and a host of friends, in my state and throughout the country. I do not want to go to my grave with a cloud of dishonor over my head. I must clear my name for their sake, even if I never hold a public office again in my life."

I was moved by his statement. Who wouldn't be? Factually, there would be no problem. The article was an atrocious lie. We would prove it. But there were unique legal obstructions. I knew he understood them because before he consulted me, he had issued a public statement in which, after denying every accusation with emphasis which only innocence and sincerity could command, he said, "Whether I intend to sue for libel, I have not decided. Under United States Supreme Court decisions, it is almost impossible for a public official to win a libel suit. These decisions make it plain that it is all right for a publication to lie about a public official so long as there is no malice. I will not sue just for political purposes." I explained that we would endeavor to prove malice, by equating recklessness with malice. This was a difficult undertaking, and the Supreme Court had not yet given even this thin cloak of protection to a public official. Why? First Amendment. The need to protect the press from harassment even when it is mistaken.

The risk of obtaining relief was therefore great. But we believed that the Governor was supported by moral considerations of impelling na-

---

* "I own no corporate stock.
I own one $1,000 bond.
I own no mutual funds.
I own no real estate—not even a home.
I am not the beneficiary of any trust or foundation.
Over the years, I paid into the Public Employee Retirement System $24,867.83. All other assets, including those of my wife, myself and my youngest daughter, come to approximately $40,000. I want to make it emphatically clear that I have paid all my taxes."

ture. We were willing to try. We instituted suit. The complaint set forth the evil innuendos to be drawn from the *Life* article: that Rhodes "had acted in collusion with Licavoli and the Mafia"; that he had been bribed "by Licavoli or the Mafia"; that as Governor "he had finally been exposed in a scandal involving flagrant corruption on his part."

It then asserted that *Life* had made these false statements "with reckless disregard of whether they were true or false," and had done so "maliciously." The defense stressed the special immunity given to the press, in the absence of malice, and asserted that *Life* had no malice toward Governor Rhodes.

In the meantime the Governor lost the senatorial primary to Robert Taft, who then lost the election. Ohio turned Democratic.

The legal struggle continued. Supreme Court rulings worsened our position. New decisions put heavy emphasis on the freedom of the press, even where what it published about a public official was untrue. Only malice could sustain a suit.

The legal war heated up. We moved to examine the writers and editor of *Life* magazine to demonstrate the recklessness with which the false accusations had been made. The defendants sought to examine the Governor, and advised Federal Judge Harold R. Tyler that they might consider moving for summary judgment.

As counsel met to arrange the legal duels on the field of honor, the possibility of ending the lawsuit arose. Would *Life* in writing remove the taint on Governor Rhodes's integrity? We stated that, aside from the legal problems, damages were not our goal. The restoration of Governor Rhodes's reputation was. If this could be achieved we would forgo our determination to take the matter, if necessary, to the highest court, to review the restrictive rule which made public officials open targets for published lies.

The editors were decent men and may have regretted the excesses of the publication. An arrangement was concluded. It protected *Life* against the humiliation of open confession of misdeed, and protected Governor Rhodes by withdrawing the charge or innuendo that he had any association with "the mob" or had been bribed or influenced improperly in his conduct.

By agreement Governor Rhodes issued a press release which stated:

"Life magazine has now acknowledged that it did not state or intend to state that I had acted illegally or dishonorably in commuting Licavoli's sentence. Its attorney has written my attorney, Louis Nizer, that 'you are correct that Life did not state in its article that Governor Rhodes commuted the sentence because of any illegal involvement.' Thus Life has withdrawn the charge which motivated my bringing the lawsuit.

"Under the circumstances, my honor has been vindicated and the cloud over my children and family has been removed."

The litigation was withdrawn without prejudice to Governor Rhodes.

Later, the real verdict was given by the citizens of Ohio. They elected Rhodes to be Governor again.

Life magazine suspended weekly publication soon after. Had the magazine been in trouble and reached out for circulation and the stimulation of advertising? We find a clue in the very full page advertisements headed "Ohio's Governor and the Mob." Underneath the largest photograph of a face I have ever seen in a newspaper (it now seemed to bear a triumphant look) appeared the following copy:

"All this week, advertisers, large and small, share the tension and excitement.

"Again, the vitality of the magazine rubs off on the advertising. The things we put on our pages help sell the things *you* put on our pages."

This unabashed linking of the Rhodes exposé with advertising supported the Nizer rule that there is an equation between daring sensationalism in a publication and its imminent expiration.

In any event Governor Rhodes is politically alive and flourishing. *Life*, the weekly magazine, is dead.

I am appalled by the renewed popularity of capital punishment, and the Supreme Court's decision that, if consistently applied, capital punishment is not a violation of the Eighth Amendment of the Constitution, which forbids "cruel and unusual punishment." Could anyone who actually witnessed an execution of a human being, whether by noose, which breaks the neck, by gas, which asphyxiates, or by electricity, which breaks the lenses of the eyes and cooks the body until the skull emits smoke, say it is not a cruel and inhuman act? "In every one of us," wrote Arthur Koestler, "there lurks a little furry animal who cries out for blood." But we do not want him to make the laws of the land. Understandably, we hear him when we are horrified by an outrageous crime, whether by the Manson killers or the assassination of the Kennedys. There is no doubt that each one of us, if he could have reached Hitler, or the murderer of someone dear to us, would want to destroy him with our bare hands. But this is just the time to resist the little furry killer within us. It is the test of emergence from animalism to a more civilized state. Those who believe in the punishment of death cite the Bible, "An eye for an eye and a tooth for a tooth." I believe a fair interpretation of this phrase is that the punishment should fit the crime, not the literal interpretation that we should poke out a criminal's eye. The Bible in many passages expresses its indictment of the taking of life under any circumstance. The civilized and Christian philosophy is best expressed by St. Augustine, who, when the heretics murdered the Christians, said, "We do not wish to have the sufferings of the servants of God avenged by the infliction of precisely similar injuries in the way of retaliation. Not, of course, that we object to the removal from these wicked men of the liberty to perpetrate further crimes, but our desire is rather that justice be satisfied without the taking of their lives or the maiming of their bodies . . ."

If we do not recognize the possibility of rehabilitation in an individual, what hope is there for all mankind, which also must be rehabilitated or we will continue to murder millions in war?

I detest capital punishment not because of sympathy for the killer, but because it degrades and demeans us. The usual arguments, pro and con, rage around the question of deterrence and the possibility of irrevocable error. These are not the crux of the matter. Our self-respect is. However, I don't believe executions deter. If we really thought they did we would hold our executions in broad daylight in the public square and invite children. They are chiefly the ones to be deterred. But we don't do that. We subconsciously are ashamed of the act and sneak away at midnight in a closed room to commit the deed.

Our uncertainty as to whether we wish revenge or rehabilitation results in self-defeating practices which have made our prison system as obsolete as ancient dungeons. For example, we do not permit conjugal rights, as many other countries do. Men and women deprived of their sexual satisfaction are virtually driven into homosexuality and lesbianism.

Since many serve limited terms, they are freed to join their families, having first been emotionally crippled by their prison experience.

Since I believe in the good sense of mass opinion, how do I reconcile my view with the growing popular approval of capital punishment? Many states are passing enactments to authorize the supreme penalty, particularly if a public official, policeman, or prison guard is killed. I believe the reason for this wave in favor of extreme penalty is due to the public's outrage with crime in the streets which seeps into our homes as well. We dare not walk at night on thoroughfares even in "good" neighborhoods. Muggings occur in broad daylight. Our homes are invaded. Store windows require iron sheaths. Purses are torn from women's arms. Our parks are no longer havens for relaxation. For a few dollars men are killed in the streets. During the 1977 blackout of New York City, the darkest traits of man emerged with looting and burning. I believe that our disgust with this lawlessness has evoked the "kill them" reaction.

However, this criminal plague is not of the usual variety. It is drug addiction crime. When addicts are arrested, many of them inform the authorities that they must mug and steal seven or eight times a day to accumulate one hundred dollars needed for the drug shot. That explains the nature of the petty crimes; a television set carried out of a home and sold in desperate haste for ten or fifteen dollars; a typewriter taken out of an office and sacrificed at one tenth its worth; a purse snatched or a man mugged to obtain a few dollars, and if he has no money, perhaps killed in the frustration of the nerve-screechy addict who is minutes away from unbearable craving.

There are reputed to be two hundred thousand addicts in New York. If only one half of these engage in multiple crimes to pay for the day's drug need, it accounts for a minimum of half a million crimes each day. The problem is proportionately the same in other cities throughout the land. This is the explanation for the new kind of crime wave which has terrorized the population.

The antidote is not stiffer penalties. A drug addict driven by inner devils would kill his own mother at the moment of extremis. He would not be deterred by the threat of capital punishment or even by a guaranteed burning in purgatory.

The solution for this unique problem is to provide free heroin and other addictive drugs under governmental and psychiatric auspices. Heroin, for which the addict must pay one hundred dollars a dose, costs the government only two cents. The by-product of such a free drug program would be to drive the drug racketeers out of business. Its chief virtue would be to reduce if not almost eliminate the chief cause of terror in our society.

Unlike other programs to reduce crime, there would be no interminable delay in obtaining relief. Education, improved social conditions, welfare, and unemployment funds are admirable but long-range programs. We are not resigned to suffering in the meantime. Impatience increases our sense of hopelessness and contributes to wild swinging at the enemy.

If the addict did not have to turn criminal to relieve this uncontrollable urge, we might well have instant peace in our streets, homes, and parks. This would not eliminate the usual type of crime, which has a history as old as mankind and unfortunately a future too. But the special scourge of drug addiction crime would be reduced very substantially overnight.

We might profit from England's experiment of supplying free drugs to addicts. The program suffered because it was under private doctors' supervision, and therefore more subject to the canny ingenuity of addicts in obtaining double dosage and other violations. When the program was put under direct governmental control, it worked.

The resistance to this idea comes chiefly from those who argue that it would make "permanent addicts" and even induce others to try drugs. I do not see much correction of addiction under present conditions, or even the reduction of the disease. If anything, such a program would discourage pushers, who would have to compete against a free product. This ought to reduce the number of new addicts. Finally, even if government and psychiatric supervision did not cure a single addict, our choice must be made between these poor incurable devils and the safety of citizens on the streets. It is not a hard choice, and it ought to be enthusiastically supported by the "severe" advocates, whose concern rightly is the protection of the innocent.

In short, capital punishment is the wrong solution for the problem. Entirely apart from the moral aspects, a policy of hatred would make it impossible to run our prisons, unless we had an armed guard for every prisoner. Caged men, deprived of sex, embittered by crowded conditions (which experiments with animals have shown create hostile neurotic tendencies), fed unpalatable or boring food in mess surroundings, and harboring grievances against society on the theory that "it prepares the crime—we only commit it," are difficult enough to control. Riots, burnings, maiming and killing of guards are frequent occurrences. It is the lure of reward for good behavior which makes discipline possible.

The need for freedom is not a mere political slogan. It is a rule of nature. The mockingbird, learning that its young has been captured and put in a cage, will bring poisoned berries to it to end a life of wingless agony.

THE UNBALANCED SPHERES

Being happily married to lovely and loving Mildred for almost forty years might disqualify me as an authority on why the marriage institution is dissolving before our very eyes. But considerable experience in dozens of matrimonial contests, and observations and analysis (the experience of the mind) encourage me to offer an explanation.

The stark statistics are that in one hundred years between 1860 and 1960, the divorce rate in the United States increased eighteen times.[*] In the 1970s there were 437 divorces for every 1,000 marriages over a twenty-five-year period. This rate, close to 50 per cent divorce of all marriages, must be enlarged to include broken marriages without divorce; husbands who just leave their wives, or vice versa, and even those who continue to live under the same roof in what sociologists have termed "empty shell families." It is significant that divorces occur in the early years of the marriage. Thirty per cent occur in less than four years; 40 per cent in less than five years, and 66 per cent in less than ten years.[†] At the same time there were fewer marriages in 1975 than in the preceding six years.

When as ancient an institution as marriage fares so badly in the modern world, there must be many reasons, but also a basic cause. I believe there is, and that it is identifiable.

The poetic vow which binds two people is translated in law as a marriage contract. But it is not an ordinary private contract. It is a contract involving public interest to build and preserve the family. Each party to the arrangement has a function to perform. Traditionally, the husband's function was to be the provider and the protector. The wife's function was to rear children and take care of the home. As long as

[*] Adams, Bert, ed., *The Family: A Sociological Interpretation*, Rand McNally, 1975, pp. 452–53.
[†] Professor, Judith T. Younger, "Love Is Not Enough," in *The New Republic*, June 19, 1976.

these two spheres of action were accepted, there was marital balance. It was subject to the various infirmities of marriage, the irritations of illness, unemployment, sexual maladjustment, personality clashes, and the daily conflicts of proximity. So there were always divorces despite the joys and warmth of love and growth. But basically there was a balance of spheres, which gave over-all permanence to the marriage institution.

Then came great changes. They were chiefly on the wife's side. The husband still remained the provider if not the protector. But women sought to change their "subordinate" role. Those who could afford it thought that cooks, maids, and nurses could well substitute for their traditional services, and many who couldn't sought jobs so that they could. This was the first liberation movement, although it occurred without books or fanfare. Millions of women, freed from "menial" tasks, sought to realize their potentials out of the home. They entered the business, professional, artistic, and even sports worlds.

The figures show the extent of this migration. In thirty-three years between 1940 and 1973, 50 per cent of married women who had no children under six years of age got jobs even though their husbands worked.* Many who did not take paying jobs gave vent to their restlessness by engaging in philanthropic, social, and, ultimately, political activity. But the home was no longer the exclusive center of interest.

This emancipation from home work was ideologically, as well as economically, motivated. Ibsen foretold it in *A Doll's House*. When Nora was warned by her husband that "before all else, you are a wife and a mother," she replied, "That I no longer believe. I believe before all else I am a human being as much as you are—or at least that I should try to become one."

The notion that self-fulfillment was primary and the shaping of a family secondary has blossomed into a full-fledged movement. Its banners announced that marriage must not inhibit the woman's role as a member of society. Some denounce marriage itself, charging that it "causes premature deaths of mind and soul through sexual rot and plays for power."†

The movement away from marriage gained momentum from the success which women achieved in their new occupations. Instead of being "protected" by their husbands, they became competitors, often outdistancing them in achievement and earnings. The ugly word "emasculation" came into prominence. The transition was too sudden to permit suitable adjustment. It was inevitable that a political women's libera-

* *Statistical Abstract of the United States*, U. S. Government Printing Office, Washington, D.C., pp. 336–41.
† *Marriage Is Hell*, Kathrin Perutz. William Morrow & Company, 1972.

tion movement would follow. It would demand freedoms already partly
won, and equality, where women's superiority had often been established.

Like all revolutions, it was not gentle. Man became a "chauvinist
pig," the oppressor, from whom long-denied rights were to be wrested.

The issue is not women's rights to equality. That is about as debata-
ble as whether they should be veiled again and walk seven feet behind
their husbands. But the progressive achievement of these rights has
disrupted the respective functions in the marriage and thrown them
out of balance. It is another instance in which an inevitable revolutionary reform has had unexpected consequences. Marriages are crumbling faster than ever before.

The process was hastened by foreseeable corollaries. If many men for
centuries practiced a double sexual standard, then why should not
women too? Curiously the drive was not always for monogamy, but for
equal freedom from it. Technological advances played a part. The pill
had wiped out one of man's "self-justifications" for a double standard.
Add a dash of philosophy about the freedom to enjoy, and the marital
arrangement of sexual loyalty received another serious blow.

More than this, sexual freedom actually acquired some respectability,
thus eliminating the hope of religionists that we were dealing only with
a fad. Children in high school, and, of course, in college, entered into
relationships with no intention of "death do us part" permanence.
Sometimes they did ripen into marriages. The pressure of parents and
community was still a factor. But with increasing frequency, there was
no shame in convenient temporary alliances. The New York City Department of Health has issued instructions to all secondary schools on
what to do if a pregnant student went into labor or gave birth in
school. The Department notes that in 1969 there were 2,487 unmarried
pregnancies among seventh to twelfth graders. There has been a steady
increase since then.

Even more startling was the readiness generally to bear children out
of wedlock. Celebrities, who used to set the fashion for dress, set them
for immorality. That last bulwark of the marital institution, "You want
to have a child, don't you?" yielded to a flood of illegitimacies.

Nationally, more than one in twelve children born in 1967 were illegitimate. In four years between 1964 and 1967, 1,187,400 illegitimate
children were born in the United States. The number so born in a ten-
year period from 1961 through 1970 was sufficient to populate a city as
large as Los Angeles, and, in the five years preceding 1971, to populate
a city as large as Detroit.*

* Harry D. Krause, *Illegitimacy Law and Social Policy*, Bobbs-Merrill Company,
1971.

So we are witnessing not only the corrosion of marriage by ever-increasing divorces, but the defiance of the rules of legitimacy which provided a foundation for the marital institution. The increasing number of illegitimacies is tending to make us a nation of bastards.

Unable to change these developments, we have resorted to new laws which eliminate the stigma of illegitimacy. Many states, like New York, prohibit birth certificates from revealing that the birth was out of wedlock. The theory is that it is the parents who are illegitimate, not the child. Even inheritance laws have been tailored to wipe out the distinction between legitimate and illegitimate children. The Supreme Court of the United States ruled that "illegitimate children are not 'nonpersons' . . . but 'persons' within the meaning of the Equal Protection Clause of the Fourteenth Amendment. . . . Why should the illegitimate child be denied rights merely because of his birth out of wedlock? He certainly is subject to all of the responsibilities of a citizen, including the payment of taxes and conscription under the selective Service Act."†

This is society's way of conceding its inability to maintain the historic structures of marriage and legitimacy. By eliminating the disgrace and financial consequence of out-of-wedlock births, we record our helplessness to prevent the crumbling of the marital institution.

The impact of all this on our social structure has yet to be realized. It portends a greater change than political or economic upheavals. It challenges the precepts of all religions.

The disintegration of the marriage institution may contribute to another phenomenon, the extraordinary increase of suicides, particularly of children. The shattering of family unity has added to the psychic pressure of a frenetic age. "When I'm alone, I stop believing I exist." This appears to be a rule of nature. Experiments among rhesus monkeys indicate that if one is separated from the family for only a few weeks, despondency sets in. Biologists call partiality to relatives in the animal world "kin selection." When ants are accidentally isolated from the group, they circle in a suicide mill until they march themselves to death.

Human suicide is the fourth largest killer among those between the ages of fifteen and forty-four, reports the World Health Organization. Suicide is the second leading cause of death among adolescents (accident is first). The increase is extraordinary—more than 200 per cent in recent years.

These figures are deceiving. Actually the percentages are much higher. Many suicides are not recorded. Deaths caused by firearms, drownings, and poisons leave doubt as to whether they were accidental

† *Levy v. Louisiana*, 391 U.S. 68.

or intentional. Children's suicides are often deliberately disguised by
those who fear they may be blamed. Also self-destruction by slow, deliberate methods, like drugs, is not deemed suicide, although Karl Men-
ninger calls it "chronic suicide." In Great Britain, France, Germany,
and Japan there has been an enormous increase in deaths from drugs.
The suicidal intention is indicated by the proportionate decrease in the
previous suicide methods of hanging, drowning, jumping off heights,
and violent self-destruction.

Experts estimate that the reported suicide rate is understated and
should be substantially increased to reflect the true rate. Many sociologists attribute the dramatic rise of suicides among the young to the
breakdown of the home and church. That the religious "hold" on a
child may be an important factor is indicated by the fact that more
Protestant youths commit suicide, fewer Jews, and fewest Catholics.

Of those who attempted suicide unsuccessfully, almost 90 per cent
felt that their families did not understand them. Doesn't divorce, which
is the suicide of a marriage, often begin with a similar charge by one of
the parties against the other? Both involve alienation.

A recent study showed that 71 per cent of young suicides came from
broken homes. Some felt "responsible" for their parents' divorce. A
much larger number came from "disturbed" homes, in which families
quarreled, had severe financial problems, where one parent was absent,
alcoholic, or institutionalized, or where conflict arose with a step-
parent.

All this would indicate that the breakdown of the marital institution
may have unexpectedly caused an epidemic of suicides. Is it only a coincidence that in foreign countries there is a relationship between the
rate of divorce and the rate of suicide, particularly among the young? In
Europe, the countries with the lowest divorce rates, Italy and Greece,
also have the lowest suicide rates. Sweden, which has ten times as many
divorces as Italy or Greece, has five times the suicides of those countries. Denmark's high divorce rate corresponds with its suicide rate.
Norway, which has the lowest divorce rate among Scandinavian countries, also has the lowest suicide rate.*

It is impossible to accommodate ourselves to suicide, as we do to illegitimacy. There, we can by law forbid the recording of the illegitimacy
and preserve inheritance rights. We have tried to deal with suicide legally, by making its attempt a crime. But this is inherently silly. We
threaten an unsuccessful suicide with a jail term when he is eager to
inflict capital punishment upon himself.

To fully grasp the enormity of the suicide phenomenon, one must
remember that it runs counter to the most basic principle of self-preser-

* *United Nations Statistical Yearbook,* 1975.

vation. A psychiatrist in the Nazi camps reported only four suicide attempts of a group of three thousand persons living under terrifying circumstances. Generally the suicide rate in concentration camps was extraordinarily low, despite the indescribable tortures to which the inmates were subjected. It is not external misery which provokes the death wish, but rather inner psychological collapse. Living things struggle to the last gasp (a doubtful description for a microbe) to avoid final oblivion. The occasional exceptions of lemmings drowning themselves in mass suicide, or insects and fish, like the salmon, expiring after their mission of propagation has been fulfilled, are part of nature's mysterious scheme, probably to avoid overpopulation. But a human being's yearning for life is so intense that many attempt by their last testaments to stretch out their hands even after death to direct their property among the living. We have had to prevent this by laws which limit the validity of such directions in wills, to two lives in being plus twenty-one years. If old people use such artifices to give them longer "life," what shall we say of children, bursting with energy, and propelled by nature's forces to growth and fulfillment, who nevertheless want to die before they have even tasted life?

Another consequence of the family unit's destruction is juvenile delinquency. If children grow up "without strong personal attachments, without a consistent structure of discipline, the result is likely to be an inner emptiness for them and increasing violence for society."* This is tragically borne out by figures as cruel as their deeds. Between 1960 and 1974, the number of arrests of juveniles increased astronomically for every type of offense. The percentage of increase during a fifteen-year period by offenders under eighteen years of age was:†

Murder	224 per cent
Rape	147 per cent
Robbery	307 per cent
Assault	221 per cent
Prostitution	372 per cent
Drug offenses	3,777 per cent

So we have surveyed the wreckage from the disintegration of the marriage institution. It is as if a train engine collided with new mores and the cars behind it were derailed, causing painful injuries of illegitimacy, juvenile delinquency, drug abuse, and suicide.

Of course, my theory of "unbalanced spheres" can at best be a partial

* *The Fractured Family*, Leontine Young, McGraw-Hill, 1974, New York.
† *FBI Uniform Crime Reports*, 1974, U. S. Government Printing Office, Washington, D.C.

explanation of divorce. No social revolution ever lends itself to simplistic analysis. For a long time I believed that sexual incompatibility, which does not mean only physical incapacity, but, in most cases, declining sexual interest, was the chief cause of marital disharmony. Where the sexual quotient in the marriage remained high, all other grievances seemed to be overcome. No matter how many reasons were offered by husband or wife for their difficulties, ultimately a frank answer to a sensitive question revealed that sex had failed to rear its beautiful head. But if one pursued the matter further and asked what caused the passions which united the couple to dissipate, the "unbalanced spheres" theory threw a meaningful light on the subject. It encompassed many social phenomena. These ranged from the disruption of the couple's traditional roles to a new consciousness of freedom of action for all human beings.

Women had more ground to make up and were therefore more impatient and aggressive. The impact on the sexual relationship was profound in many ways: a new kind of jealousy, centering on achievement rather than sex; women's realization of equality or superiority in various activities, which sometimes diminished their respect for their husbands, even to the point of contempt; and an evil circle of retaliation by one or the other until sexual feeling was dulled.

Also, men and women in their new quest for independence mistakenly rejected mutuality of feeling as if it were the enemy of their freedom. Love of self cannot really be achieved without dependence on another's love. There is an "inborn Thou," wrote Martin Buber. "The single, solitary being is meaningless." When emancipated men and women considered pleasureful isolation essential to their credo, they further upset the marital arrangement. For that matter, they entered a road of emotional nihilism which depressed them, no matter what their status.

This provides another insight to the suicidal trend, and also why it is not mainly the poverty-stricken, the very ill, or the failing students who are the victims. On the contrary, the statistics show that the well-to-do, the healthy, and the high-grade students supply the highest number of casualties. It is not a paradox that the most intelligent often destroy themselves. To cite only a few of the artists who have killed themselves: John Berryman, Anne Sexton, Hart Crane, Virginia Woolf, Sylvia Plath, Ernest Hemingway, Marilyn Monroe, Vincent Van Gogh, Mark Rothko.

In many instances, those who had won the battle for independence, which they equated with antipersonal dependence, found that the victory had left them with empty lives. They then turned their hatred against an "unjust world" inwards toward themselves. Alienation had become disorientation.

I shall illustrate with a case history. Of course it is atypical. Case histories always are. They are the individualistic combination of facts, moods, and neuroses as different as most fingerprints are from each other. But the roots of atypical cases are typical.

This was a marriage broken by the wife's discovery of her rights and the husband's bewilderment at a new relationship. Her background conditioned her for the ultimate assertiveness. She was a brilliant student and earned her Ph.D., but in the course of her studies, several teachers "made a pass at her," and she felt victimized. Her experiences later made her cry out to her husband, "Because I have a vagina, it doesn't mean you have a right to enslave me." The endearing words of love were replaced by the now banal epithet that he was "a male chauvinist pig."

She joined women's groups in England, where they lived for a while, and then in the United States when they returned. Theoretical conflicts gave way to real life ones when a child was born. She insisted on equal turns in the care of their son and in household chores. "I diapered him this morning. You must this afternoon. I shopped yesterday. It is your turn today." "I washed the dishes last evening . . ." I could only wonder what the demands for equality were in the marital bed.

The strain became so great that the husband, in a fit of frustration, smashed a plate over his own head. Thereupon she claimed she feared that his violence might be outward the next time and insisted that he visit a psychiatrist. She had been a patient of one for a long time. The psychiatrist set forth his principle that a divorce was better than strife and its effect on their child. So they came to see me.

As always, the first effort was for reconciliation. They were two fine people of good breeding and character. The little son was a delight to both of them. I talked to each separately. I told her that the women's liberation movement, to which she was fanatically dedicated, was just in principle, in civic and economic rights, and in equal opportunity in all directions. But how could one derive happiness from a life lived with an abacus, counting each service and deed in a love relationship?

"You say you love your husband. Then it would be no sacrifice, when he is sound asleep and tired, for you to care for your son when he cries at night, even if it is his turn. Similarly would you consider it a lack of affection, if you have a headache, but he insists it's your turn to wash the dishes!"

What I thought was a simple statement of accommodation in a love relationship infuriated her. She didn't vocally assign me to the pig family, but she said I was partisan and lacked understanding. She dashed to her psychiatrist, and when he agreed with me she quit him too.

I do not believe that her fanaticism tells the whole story. He was not blameless. Was there ever a marital dispute in which the cause and effect were not uncertain? The lines for responsibility in a marital breakdown always run in circles. The initiation and the reaction vary according to the perspective of the litigant.

The significance of the case history is only that whatever provoked the wife's "liberation philosophy," the marital spheres were disrupted. They were divorced.

Only one inconsistent note arose in the financial settlement. The wife, or perhaps it was her lawyer doing his proper duty, insisted on alimony and child support in accordance with traditional law, protecting women. She did not protest this relief on the ground that it violated her principles.

The centrifugal force of whirling divorces has cast off family unity. I have recorded some of the observable consequences, but no one can foresee the ultimate events. Will men and women be happier without the classic bonds which have existed for many centuries? This depends upon the value judgment of the word "happiness." Women will derive "happiness" from achievements in fields previously pre-empted by men. Self-fulfillment in other ways, including sexual freedom, may also give them "happiness." But these are in a sense negative factors. They result from contrast with old conventional standards, the satisfaction of fighting for and winning their rights, more than from the glow of the rights themselves.

Will men be happier in the new estate than when they were the binding force in the family unit? My conclusion is the same. They will not be. They will not have to be as surreptitious about their polygamous tendencies, but they will be deprived of the satisfaction of presiding over a growing family, nature's intimate demonstration of the maturing life process until death.

The impermanence of a flitting life is its own defeat. Even the sorrow and disappointments which often beset the family unit are part of the living process. Marriage is not merely a man- (or now, man- and woman-) made convention, but a response to nature's cosmic scheme of herding its inhabitants in units for physical warmth and psychic security. "The true morality is remembering and making visible the tradition that gives you form," wrote André Malraux.

We cannot go back to the old balanced spheres.

The change which has occurred is irreversible. Women's involvement in activities which were previous male monopolies was inevitable. It resulted in part from universal education. Did anyone expect that we would send our daughters to college, broaden their horizons of life, stimulate their cultural ambitions, and then have them follow the confined paths of their grandmothers? Entirely apart from economic motivation, women felt suffocated by the roles assigned to them in marriage.

So a new balance of spheres will have to be accepted by partners in marriage, if the institution is to survive. Men will have to recognize and enjoy the new role of women in society, without considering it an abandonment of their duty to home and children. Women will have to recognize that their independence is not inconsistent with their dependence on the strength of their husbands, and that their "rights" may well be voluntarily sacrificed in sufficient measure to devote themselves personally to their children, for their psychological health, as well as that of the marriage. It has even been suggested that the Government should aid by giving tax benefits and child care allowances to working mothers, to encourage direct parental guidance. Other adjustments will be found, just as we must find them in a new technological era which has severed old customs and traditions in many other fields.

My guess is that the new moral structure will lose the glamour of its sophisticated order, and that we will somehow find our way back to the family unit tradition. The glories and beauty of its commitment cannot be found in any other way. "Repetition is the only form of permanence that nature can provide," wrote Émile Zola.

Even the old horrors were less than those which accompanied the escape from confinement.

AND A CHILD SHALL DESTROY THEM

This is the story of a man who was convicted of sexually abusing a child.

Although I have been involved in all manner of litigations, this case created more emotional impact than almost any other I can recall. It also presents the old question, what is justice? Do we take the hard road of protecting the accused by insisting on his innocence unless overwhelming evidence is presented, or the sympathetic road of protecting the accuser even though his testimony is uncorroborated? How does the law deal with a child who accuses? What is justice in such a case? Does the jury system go wrong at times? If so, how can it be corrected? Do those who cannot afford outstanding counsel and appeals have a remedy? These and other vital questions in the judicial system were all raised in the melodrama which follows.

John Bateman (I shall call him) and his wife and three young sons lived in their own comfortable house in a suburban area. They were a model family, a unit of what economists and orators proclaim "the great middle class, the backbone of the nation." Bateman was employed by a large corporation situated in the city, and one could tell the precise time of the day by the train he caught every morning, after his car had been parked at the station. Consistent with this American apple pie picture of life was his hobby. He loved baseball. There was devotion to the home teams which exceeded that of their owners and players. He knew batting averages better than they knew attendance figures and receipts. This and a sense of service to the community led him to be active in Little League baseball.

He became president of it, an honor his neighbors conferred upon him because of his dedication to the venture and his fatherly supervision of the kids.

One day, a bomb destroyed his house. It was not a dynamite bomb, but the effect was even more devastating. It was the appearance of two policemen who arrested him on the felony charge of having sexually abused a young boy.

What is more sensational than an accusation of sexual perversion? It has all the ingredients of a Jekyll-Hyde story—the normal-looking man, but inside him lurks an evil creature. It is the oldest mystery and the oldest plot. Appearances are not what they seem to be. Since all of us have suppressed yearnings, we are ready to believe the worst in people.

Perhaps they are enacting what some of us have only thought. That is why rape stories seem more believable to men than they should be, and why the victim is looked upon with skepticism by women, when the rapist says he was enticed. While this is not as true of sexual abuse of a homosexual nature, except to the relatively small minority of men with homosexual leanings, the general inclination to believe in animalistic tendencies, under the civilized veneer, creates a prejudice in all sex cases.

The charge against Bateman jumped from the police blotter to the front pages of the local newspapers, and from there to the large circulation city press. The story received lurid touches as if a monster had been discovered in the midst of a normal community.

The Bateman house, which previously was unidentifiable in a uniform row, suddenly stood out alone in the spotlight of publicity. The glare enveloped Constance Bateman and her three children. It had the numbing effect of a shock ray. It dulled them to pain for a while. Then continuous tears washed away the narcotic impact and they were immersed in shame and humiliation. Constance struggled to prevent a nervous collapse. The terrible revelation was the topic of conversation in every home and store, and was carried in sonorous or hushed tones by radio and television announcers. To the Batemans, every head on the street became a wagging head; every gesture, a pointing finger. It was a relief not to sleep because nightmares of jail cells, ruin, and death were thus avoided.

A local attorney was retained. He assured the Batemans that the prosecutor's case was flimsy. Without any preparation in depth, he answered ready for trial.

The prosecutor requested that all witnesses be excluded from the courtroom. This was granted. The theory is that witnesses should not be able to accommodate their own testimony to what they have heard from others. In criminal cases particularly, this precaution is taken.

The prosecutor called the accusing child, Walter, to the stand. He was ten years old, blond, handsome, and well spoken—a very appealing witness. Despite his youth, he was sworn in, because he understood the meaning of an oath. Then under guidance of the prosecutor he told his story.

He had gone to watch his father umpire a championship game between Little League clubs. After the game, he made arrangements with Bateman's son to come to the Bateman home and stay overnight. This was a customary practice in the community. Children slept over in the homes of their friends.

Walter's father drove him to the Bateman home about seven-thirty in the evening. Mrs. Bateman called his mother to be sure she approved of Walter's night out. She did. Walter was invited to have dinner with the family, but he had already eaten. So, he watched television, and then played Ping-Pong and ran a train set with the Bateman boys.

The time came to go to sleep. He and one of the Bateman boys shared the same room in separate beds. Before putting the crucial question to the young witness, the prosecutor asked him if he could identify the defendant in the courtroom. The boy pointed unerringly to Bateman. It was the smallest but most damaging finger among the many which actually or in his imagination Bateman had faced. Then came the question:

Q: Now, tell us what you recall about what happened after you went to bed?

A: Well, we went to bed and I was just dozing off. Mr. Bateman came in the room and he came over to my bed and he pulled down the covers and pulled down my pajama bottoms and touched my bottom.

Q: What do you mean by your bottom?

A: My backside.

Q: Please continue.

A: Then he kept touching my forehead like this.

Q: For how long?

A: I don't know—seemed like a pretty long time.

Q: Had he said anything to you or did you say anything to him at this point?

A: No.

Q: What happened then?

A: He pulled my pajama bottoms partially up and kept the covers down and went out of the room.

Q: What happened then?

A: He came back in the room.

Q: What happened then?

A: He came in the room, did the same thing. This time, touched my penis.

Q: What did he do with his hand?

A: Just rubbed it.

Q: For how long?

A: I don't know. Seemed kind of shorter than the first time.

Q: What happened then?

A: He touched my forehead again. He kept touching it, touching my penis. Then he left the room.

He came back a third time but left without coming near him. In the meantime, the Bateman boy was sleeping peacefully in the other bed.

In the morning, Walter ate breakfast with the Bateman boy and was driven home by Bateman.

Q: Did you say anything to Bateman when he asked you how you slept?

A: I said fine.

That was it. The prosecutor called no other witnesses.

The defense called Mrs. Bateman to the stand. Warnings by her own attorney to keep her voice up indicated the nervousness verging on terror that gripped the poor woman who had to defend her husband, her three children, her home, and their future.

She and her husband had "tucked the children in" and together gone to their bedroom for the night. She had shut the door and locked it.

Q: Mrs. Bateman, was there some particular reason why you locked the door?

A: Yes.

Q: What is the reason, Mrs. Bateman?

A: We purchased a king-size bed that was delivered that morning, a gigantic bed and we had discussed all day the fact that as soon as the kids went to bed, the first thing we wanted to do was to go to bed.

Q: Now, Mrs. Bateman, did your husband leave the room?

A: No, he did not leave the room.

The new bed continued to play a part in the story. The next morning, Bateman, his boys, and Walter rode to the local dump to drop off the old mattress and spring. Walter drove back to the Bateman home, and played with the children. There was no accusation or protest made by him for what he later claimed was an unwarranted "touching." Bateman drove him home.

Q: Mrs. Bateman, have Walter's parents called you at any time after this occasion?

A: No.

Then the defendant himself faced the jury. He gave his age, thirty-five, the ages of his three children: ten and a half, nine, and six and a half. Even during these preliminaries he was trembling. "Keep your voice up," he was told. Later, "You have a tendency to drop your voice and the jurors will not hear you." He and his wife tucked in the children, kissed them, said good night, and went to their own room. "I believe I even remember telling Walter the bathroom is down the hall if you have to use it."

Q: Did you go down and pull down the covers and pull down his pajamas?

A: No sir. I did not.

Q: Did you touch his buttocks and his penis?

A: No sir. I did not.

Q: Mr. Bateman, did you leave your bedroom after you went into it that evening?

A: No sir.

Q: Did you have—did you do anything that particular night, Mr. Bateman?

A: Yes, we had intercourse.

So, the new bed, waiting to be tested, played its role for the defense. Natural passions kept the defendant in his room. It made it even more unlikely that Bateman would go wandering downstairs for new sensations.

Bateman's testimony about Walter's behavior when he rode him home the following morning was so inconsistent with the accusation that someone had to be inventing a fanciful tale. He testified that Walter said, "Thanks a lot, Mr. Bateman, I had a great time."

The prosecutor sought to extract a conversation which Bateman had with one Armstrong, to whom he was supposed to have said that Walter did not hate him, thus implying forgiveness or consent. They fenced a long time about this supposed conversation, and then:

Q: Are you able to quote Armstrong precisely? What did he say about this matter?

A: I am able to quote him precisely.

Q: Quote him.

A: He said this whole thing is a "Crock of s—t."

It was on this inelegant note that the testimony ended.

After summations and the Judge's charge, the jury retired to deliberate. An hour and fifteen minutes later, it returned.

THE COURT: Mr. Foreman, would you please announce your verdict?

FOREMAN: We find the defendant guilty.

Later, after a probation report, Bateman appeared for sentence. He said to the court, "I absolutely never touched that child or any child in my entire life."

Because of his previous impeccable record, he was sentenced to "probation for one year, on condition that he undergo psychiatric evaluation and treatment as deemed necessary."

There are cases in which the degree of sentence doesn't matter. Condemnation as a child abuser deepened the tragedy. In a sense it was a life sentence. It would have been easier to wash away bloodstains than the stigma of a jury verdict. Unless he and his family fled the community to seek anonymity in some distant place, how could they ever escape the shame with which they had been branded? The compulsory psychiatric treatment only confirmed his perversity. If he complied and took treatment, he would be confessing his illness.

The Batemans were as desperate as they were numb.

It was at this point that the president of the company for which Bateman worked appealed to me to look into the matter. The fact that his employer for ten years had faith in him, and made an emotional appeal to save him and his family, impressed me.

So it was that Bateman and his wife sat in front of my desk. Their faces were drained and drawn. Their eyes half closed from swelling. Their voices quivered and broke so that they couldn't talk. It was a heartbreaking scene of noncommunication. I asked for the stenographic minutes of the trial, which request gave them hope. After ministering to them with assurance that no problem was hopeless and that they must not permit the enlarged shadows of their own fears to undermine their ability to resist, I asked them to return after we had studied the record.

When we reviewed the trial in cold type, we discovered a number of startling things. For the first time, we understood what had gone wrong.

It began with the selection of the jury, a process called the voir dire. The prosecutor's examination of would-be jurors took sixty-five pages of the record. The defendant's counsel did not ask a single question. He left this critical phase of the proceeding entirely in the unfriendly hands of the District Attorney.

So, it came about that a jury was selected which was predisposed to convict Bateman. The technique used by the prosecutor was to challenge any juror if he indicated that he would examine a child's testimony with care. This, as we shall see, is the law.

Nevertheless, the prosecutor excused seven out of fourteen jurors who as a matter of common sense expressed such caution. One juror said "it would be truthfully hard" to convict anyone beyond a reasonable doubt solely upon the testimony of a child. She was out. Even though another conceded that he would convict if he "firmly believed" the boy, the "firmly" was too much risk for the prosecutor. He excused him. To make matters worse, these jurors were excused "for cause." There was no just cause, such as admitted prejudice, acquaintance with the parties or lawyers, or refusal to follow the law as directed by the Judge. The prosecutor could only have exercised a "peremptory challenge" against such a juror—namely without cause but for psychological reasons. Peremptory challenges are limited to three—sometimes as high as four or five. Challenges for cause are unlimited. In this case the prosecutor exercised an excessive number of peremptory challenges by falsely designating them "for cause," all without an objection by defense counsel. The enormity of this process was capped by the following question put to the jurors by the prosecutor:

"Do I have your assurance that if you find there is a failing of proof or the defense does not meet the law, that you will find Mr. Bateman guilty? Do you all understand that?"

Still no objection by the defense to this garbled and inaccurate statement.

What a jury. It was about as impartial as the juror who was asked whether he believed in capital punishment. "Generally no," he replied, "but in this case, yes."

The selection of jurors should be as much a "contest" between the lawyers as the testimony of a witness. Prejudices are thus detected and eliminated, not perfectly, but substantially. But for one side to default in the choosing of a jury is to distort the process as much as if one side defaulted on all testimony offered by the other. It is even worse, because the jurors are the judges of the facts. Bateman was doomed before the trial began.

To add oversight to neglect, the defense did not call a single character witness. In view of the fact that Walter, ten years old, was the only witness for the prosecutor, and his credibility was thus pitted against that of Mr. and Mrs. Bateman, what could be more helpful than to have leading members of the community speak highly of the Batemans' probity?

The issue was simply who was to be believed? This is the classic reason why, in criminal cases, character witnesses are permitted. The philosophy is that the reputation for truthfulness, which the accused has earned during his life, is a proper weight in the scales of justice. Since the defendant must be proven guilty beyond a reasonable doubt, character testimony may just tip the scale in his favor.

The other approach to the battle of credibility is to attack the accusing witness's reputation for veracity. Nothing was done about this, either. So the defendant did not utilize his weapons in the duel of truthfulness. He neither buttressed his own story nor attempted to undermine the accuser's. The irony of it all was that there was brilliant opportunity for both.

When we announced that we would undertake the appeal, we sought to tap the community's support. The very process of approach and open inquiry cleansed the atmosphere. No accused person should slink away. I advised him to conduct himself as he always had; go to business, to the theater, and keep social engagements. Even if one is innocent, this is hard to do. The sensitive have shame. They believe that appearing in public is brazen and calloused. Nevertheless they must overcome their hermit-ism. Human beings, like other animals, smell fear, and conclude guilt therefrom. The public responds to those who are not crushed by adversity. It is difficult to instruct a client how to look when he emerges after a not-guilty plea. Should he be jaunty? Then he is not sensitive to his plight. Should he look solemn? Then he may register the pressure of guilt. Should he just smile, indicating confidence? This is usually best, but it depends on the person who must carry off the mood so as to be natural.

The Batemans' sensitivity caused their friends to avoid them. Probably it was out of a desire not to force themselves upon them in their hour of distress. What looked like walking on the other side of the street when they saw him turned out to be an effort to avoid the embarrassment of confrontation. It is an open question whether expressions of sympathy do not deepen the wound. Cripples resent being given special privileges. It makes them conscious of their infirmities. What is more humiliating to a proud man than to be told how sorry everyone is for his plight? So when Bateman and my law partner William Reilly frontally approached Bateman's neighbors and asked them whether they would submit affidavits giving their opinions of him, they responded eagerly. The expressed relief that they could assist him because to a man, woman, and child they did not believe a word of Walter's accusation. We gathered in sixty-five pages of affidavits by twenty-six leading citizens of the community. Their laudatory statements about Bateman's integrity and honesty of word contained such words as "impeccable," "top-drawer," "outstanding," "spotless," "excellent," "100 per cent," "superb," "very good," "of the highest." Some who knew him well praised him as a good father and family man. Ten persons stated that despite the conviction they had no hesitancy in permitting their children to stay overnight in the Bateman home. What better vote of confidence could be given than that?

Immediately after Bateman was indicted, he resigned as president of the Little League. The directors hesitated to accept his resignation, but were pushed hard by interviewers who provocatively wanted to know how a man accused of molesting children could hold such a post. The directors evaded the challenge by giving assurance that they would "do the right thing." However, deriving courage from the community's favorable response, the directors rode the momentum to the following resolution by a vote of twenty-two to three:

> We firmly believe in John Bateman's innocence and feel we are compelled by our consciences to support him and retain him as our president.
>
> We consider that a conviction based on the uncorroborated testimony of a ten-year old is insufficient ground for Mr. Bateman's removal. We believe John Bateman will be vindicated, completely and irrevocably.

It is difficult enough to restrain the "mob spirit" of condemnation after an indictment, but to receive such an accolade after conviction was a unique tribute to Bateman. What character witnesses could have been paraded at his trial!

This acceptance of Bateman's credibility was automatically a rejection of his young accuser's story. There must have been reason for this, too. We turned our search in the other direction. What was Walter's history? Interviews with the neighborhood's children and parents resulted in affidavits that he was considered by many of the youngsters to be "weird," "strange," a "kook," "a bully," "liar," "cheater," "troublemaker," and "flaky." He was known to be extremely hot-tempered. Some parents would not allow their children to play with him.

On one occasion, "Walter put a rope around the neck of a boy in front of him in the classroom and pulled it with both hands, resulting in a visible mark on his neck. The teacher sent the injured child to see the school nurse."

So this was the angelic child whom the jury believed!

Even a jury prejudiced in his favor might have thought twice had these facts been developed on cross-examination and by affirmative testimony. Without the ugly colors filled in, the youngster appeared lily white.

Not all clues are physical. Great detectives achieve their triumphs from psychological insights. But the law does not recognize inferences drawn from speculation. It insists on hard facts. Our investigation turned up an incident, which though remote and irrelevant in a legal sense, revealed Walter's possible motive for telling an elaborate lie.

Several weeks before he slept over at the Bateman home, a child had been molested in a nearby supermarket. The attack caused a sensation in the community. The molester had escaped, but his victim, to those who knew who he was, became the center of sympathetic attention. He was a schoolmate of Walter's. Is it possible that this planted a seed in

Walter's mind that he could become "prominent" if he made a similar claim?

After the complaint was filed against Bateman, the police called him to a "lineup" for possible identification as the molester in the supermarket. He was completely cleared by witnesses, but he suffered the ignominy of the suspicion that he was a repeat offender on the loose.

When our investigations were completed, we faced the question of how to use them. If what we discovered was new evidence, a motion could be made to open the case. But it was not.

To qualify as new evidence, it must not have been previously available. If a reasonable effort would have discovered it before trial, then its use was forbidden to obtain a new trial.

Typical illustrations of new evidence are the discovery of a witness whom no one had heard of, but who turns up with vital knowledge after the trial; or a document found in a vault, which no one knew anything about, but which comes to light after the trial.

In the Bateman case, there was no doubt that diligent effort could have resulted in obtaining for use at the trial the testimony we elicited after the verdict. Therefore, what we had was informative and provocative but it was not new evidence in the legal sense. The neighbors were known. Their children were known. No one had sought them out. The new affidavits could not be used.

This is not technical folderol, as some laymen might suspect. Unless such a rule existed, it would pay to withhold important evidence in every case. If one won on the limited evidence presented, well and good. If not, there would be a second trial, and perhaps a third and fourth, by trotting out evidence not previously offered, and calling it new evidence. To prevent two or more bites at every trial cherry, the test is "Wasn't this evidence reasonably available to you originally? If you were too confident or too careless to prepare more thoroughly, that is not the court's fault. There must be an end somewhere to a litigation. As it is, the judicial process is extended enough."

But justice finds wondrous ways its miracles to perform. We had a plan to overcome the obstacle. It consisted of three steps.

First, the record of the appeal had to be enlarged to include the affidavits. Otherwise they could not even be mentioned. Appeals are limited to the original testimony. Counsel cannot go "outside the record." He cannot present evidence which was not ruled upon by the original trial judge. If the testimony was not in the record and subject to cross-examination, it is out. The reason is similar to that for newly discovered evidence. Why struggle to present a full case in the lower court if you can augment it on appeal? Also the trial judge's rulings on dismissal, based on the testimony at the trial, could not properly be reviewed on appeal if one could add new testimony at the appellate level which the lower court did not have before it. So, to assure ourselves of having the trial record properly broadened for appeal, we made a motion for a new trial based on our affidavits. When this motion was denied, we appealed *both* from the original jury verdict and the motion denying a new trial. The record was thus enlarged so that the affidavits were in the printed record.

Second, we argued on appeal that even if the affidavits did not qualify as new evidence, they ought to be considered because there was an exception to the new evidence rule. It was this: if trial counsel's carelessness or ineptitude was of such magnitude that a great injustice may have occurred, the courts would disregard the customary rule. We told the appellate court, "We are loath to criticize trial counsel's inadequate representation of his client," but the issue was justice, and in this case an accumulation of errors had resulted in an injustice. There must be a remedy. It existed in the exception we cited. The affidavits should be considered and evaluated.

The third step in our plan was to contend that the guilty verdict must be reversed as a matter of law and irrespective of the facts.

This led us to a discussion of the law. What should the rule be concerning sex offenders of children? Should any person be convicted of a morals charge on the uncorroborated testimony of an infant? The answer is, no. Some corroboration, some substantiation, in addition to the infant's word, must be presented.

Otherwise, none of us would be safe from the imaginative and sometimes malicious irresponsibility of infants who are generally disposed to inventive lies. Child psychologists consider fantasizing, stimulated by budding sexual urges, quite normal. Walter might have had an erotic dream and ascribed "the rubbing" to Bateman. Or he may have masturbated after Bateman tucked him in and associated him with the act.

No man or woman who permitted a child to sleep over would be safe from a child's uncorroborated story of immoral tampering. The law considered the risk too great. So the highest appellate court in New York had held that "no conviction for impairing the morals of a child may validly rest on the uncorroborated testimony of the child victim" (*People* v. *Porcaro*).

We must remember that we are not dealing with an ordinary claim, but with a criminal charge which, because it involves sexual abuse of a child, is particularly inflammatory and evokes feelings of horror. The degradation of the accused is so great that it may well destroy him and his family. Any criminal accusation must be proved beyond a reasonable doubt. How can the unsupported word of an infant satisfy such a standard?

We cited cases in which the evidence was more substantial than that against Bateman, but which the courts held did not meet the test of "proof more than usually clear and convincing." So, for example, in one case (Churgen), the court commented that the ten-year-old female complainant "told a logical, sensible story, and told it well. She was not contradicted the least bit on cross-examination. Except for the age of the child, I seldom have seen a better witness." But there was no corroboration. The conviction was reversed.

Children can be persuasive liars. Their innocence and open-eyed guilelessness can be misleading. Their imagination becomes reality to them and constitutes truth. Their story is therefore less vulnerable to contradiction than the conscious lie of a mature person. Also, a child's malice can be more virulent than a mature person's because it is not inhibited by the tolerance of experience. One court expressed it this way: "There have been countless instances in which children have been known to invent morals charges against individuals who have never been near them." In another case (*People* v. *Oyola*) the court wrote: "It is time that the courts awakened to the sinister possibilities of injustice that lurk in believing an infant witness without careful psychiatric scrutiny."

A leading textbook on evidence (Professor John Henry Wigmore) comments: "The most dangerous witness in prosecutions for morality offenses are the youthful ones (often mere children) in whom the sex-instinct holds the foremost place in their thoughts and feelings. It is just such witnesses that often throw suspicion recklessly on the most worthy persons."

Judge Stanley Fuld, a former prosecutor under Tom Dewey, commented on this quotation, "Anyone who has had experience in prosecuting this type of case can document this observation with graphic illustrations."

The enlarged evidence demonstrated that Walter might well be a "disturbed" young boy. Wasn't the conviction of Bateman solely on this infant's testimony a perversion of justice?

The appellate court unanimously held that it was. It not only reversed the verdict of guilty, but dismissed the complaint in its entirety as unworthy of a new trial.

The District Attorney's office announced that it would not appeal. It even made some amends for its prior pursuit of an unworthy cause by consenting to eliminate the record from the files, so that there would not remain a trace of the disgrace.

I once had a client who became rich by taking waste sludge remaining after oil was refined, and, instead of dumping it in the marshes, mixed it with oils and used it for paving roads, making boards and other products. The residue turned out to be almost as valuable as the original product.

I think of certain trials that way. There were frustrating residues from the Bateman case, but with thought they have instructive value. A number of questions raised about the judicial system are exemplified by that case. Can a good case be lost by a bad lawyer or a bad case won by a good lawyer? Unfortunately the answer is "yes." If a trial was God-ordained and controlled (as the priests thought who determined guilt or innocence by putting the accused's arm in boiling water, and after incantation seeing whether there was a burn), then human intervention by the lawyer would not affect the result. Justice could be self-executing. The truth would prevail. It would not be subject to the vagaries of diligent preparation, and the myriad insights and skills of the art of persuasion. But since our judicial system, like any other enterprise, is administered by men and women, whatever robes they wear, it is subject to the frailties which beset all human activity.

Consider the jury. It is a magnificent device to determine the facts. Its common sense is as good a guide as we have ever found. But its decision can only be sound if the critical evidence is presented on both sides. If one litigant or the other fails in his duty to put vital evidence before the jury, its decision will be a distortion of the truth. The verdict may be a correct reading of the scales, and yet be unjust because many weights were missing.

The Bateman case is a good illustration. The jury was subjected to limited stimuli. Its decision might have been right, based on what it heard. But how much it had not heard! Also, we have seen how in the selection of the jury the defendant's counsel sat back in silence while the very balance of the scale was being tested.

Since the jury is the microcosm of democracy, the lesson learned here can be magnified to throw some light on the national scene. The voting public is a jury. If the crucial facts are put before it, its decision is as reliable as any which can be attained by any other method. But if because of illiteracy, or demagogic exploitation of literacy, or imbalanced presentations, the public-jury has inadequate or mangled information, its verdict can be correctly erroneous; correct on the facts known to it, and incorrect on the total picture. Fortunately this is as infrequent in elections as it is in jury trials.

This view of democracy also indicates why it cannot prosper in soil unprepared for it. It is a sensitive mechanism requiring sophisticated preconditions. It cannot be imposed on emerging countries which haven't a minimum base of education and experience in self-government. Tried too soon, it can result in pillage and rape.

Can we eliminate the defect of partial presentation either in the court or in the political arena? Never. We can only minimize it and thus achieve an approximation of justice. We must have tolerance for that amount of failure which is unavoidable in the human condition. While at the same time we can fulfill our idealistic yearnings by closing the gap between "the impossible" and "the attainable."

Although democracy is far from perfect, it has functioned brilliantly. Witness the two centuries of our country. Despite the nation's infant and mature diseases, scandals from Grant to Harding to Nixon, and enormous growth with its attendant complexities, we have preserved our liberties while becoming the most prosperous and powerful country in history.

Similarly, with all of its faults, our judicial system is still as good, if not better, than any other in the world.

We can attain the most civilized view of any issue by confessing the defects of what we praise, and praising the virtues without resigned satisfaction.

Striving for improvement is gratifying even if unsuccessful. That is why those who sacrifice for a cause are almost never defeated. The effort makes them feel noble and becomes an end in itself. This explains why we will never lack idealists. They are involved in a guaranteed enterprise.

In this spirit let us acknowledge and resolve:

Perfect justice—impossible. Approximate justice—acceptable. Efforts to make justice more perfect—always.

FRIENDLY INEFFICIENCY

There is understandable disdain for people who visit a remote country, like China or Russia, for a few weeks, and return experts. But this does not mean that their observations are valueless. I liken such a trip to a photograph sent by wireless from overseas. It is composed of hundreds of dots of dark and light shades which form a face. If the picture is enlarged sufficiently, one can actually see the dots, in their meaningful formations.

In 1971, as counsel for the Motion Picture Association of America, Inc., I accompanied a committee of stars and executives to a film festival in Moscow. For so many years, I had read about and discussed Russia, "the riddle wrapped in a mystery inside an enigma." Now I was there. Surely the vastness of the land and profusion of hard and soft curtains behind the Iron Curtain made impossible any profound conclusions. But each moment my eye detected a dot. Ultimately there were many dots. They formed an image, even if vague because not complete. I record these dots through these words.

Upon our arrival in Moscow, we, like so many other visitors, were immediately impressed with what would stamp every moment of our stay in Russia—its inefficiency. Although there were interpreters, the porters were endlessly confused about our bags. It took many hours to move out of the airport. We were confronted with similar delays in registering at the hotel, getting into the room, or doing anything else. Some friends who had arrived earlier gave us the password: "Be patient and smile." It was not too difficult to practice this advice, because the colossal waste of time and confusion were not due to hostility or laziness. It was pure, sweating, friendly inefficiency.

In the prime old Moscow hotel, the Moskva, the room was dingy with a bare wooden cupboard of a closet and beds that looked like wooden cots. One wouldn't mind their hardness (there was only some kind of an imitation of a mattress), but who wanted to sleep on a *curved* hard board? The quilt was enclosed in a white sheet with an oval cutout which permitted the color underneath to make a design. This was apparently deemed to be fetching, because in the brand new Rossiya Hotel, the same hard beds and cutout quilts were used. Perhaps it was not a matter of style but of necessity. But even in the Rossiya, the new carpets in the hallways looked like billows. They didn't know how to lay carpets. Someday when there have been some accidents, they will probably import an expert.

The Moskva favored hanging electric bulbs rather than chandeliers, but it had a prize in the "bedroom-parlor"—a television set. Its screen was eight inches and its wooden box was exactly like the oldest Amos and Andy model of a radio when it first appeared in the United States. Sound sometimes mysteriously came out of the set even when it was turned off. This heightened the uneasiness of the bugging in each room, about which we had been fully warned. That rooms are bugged was no illusion. I had the occasion to speak to several Russian artists and newspapermen. They pointed to the ceiling and motioned silence, then took me to the street. The cumulative, depressing effect of this, upon one accustomed to privacy in his home, must be experienced to be fully realized. And this was the new, liberalized Russia.

The bathroom had a huge tub, but we had been advised to bring our own stopper. For some reason, they didn't supply them. But there were two large rough brushes for shoes. This might be a holdover from the days of muddy streets and caked boots. The soap, a luxury not supposed to be there, was a one-inch square which looked like red wax and was unusable. The plumbing worked infrequently, but made up for its delinquency by tremendous noise.

The hotels had no central switchboard. Each room had its own telephone and separate number. Unless one had everybody's individual room number, it was impossible to connect. Whether all this was due again to inefficiency or for reasons of security was hard to figure out. But it may help to know that upon leaving your room, you had to leave your key with a woman at a desk which guarded the entrance to each floor. Thus, your absence from your room was at all times known. When you returned, the woman could not understand the number of the key which you requested. But here was the first sign of business ingenuity. She had a list with numbers on it, and you pointed to the number of your room. This was one of the shortest operations in my stay in Russia.

The telephone was generally a nightmare. This was not so merely for foreigners. Our embassy officials who talked the native language motioned with resigned exasperation, subdued by long experience, when they hung up again and again because the busy signal a second ago was followed by no answer, and then busy again. It could take fifteen minutes to a half hour to make an ordinary telephone call.

On entering the country, one had to declare all currency and jewelry, and account therefore meticulously when leaving. One bought coupons which were used as currency to pay for meals. The result was another maddening delay while the waiter computed the bill and translated the price into coupons. Frequently, he brought an abacus to the table to help him make the addition. It did no good to offer an extra coupon or two, to avoid the delay. Earnestly, he figured away, while sweat broke out on his brow, and good-naturedly he told you he must finish. So every lunch or dinner was delayed an extra half hour or more to go through the mathematical gyrations.

The menu, in all but a few special restaurants, was the same: caviar or sturgeon, borsch, hot or cold, fish or chicken, black bread, fruit compote served in a glass, ice cream, and tea or turkish coffee. The food was edible but not good, and one soon learned that the best thing to order was an omelet. Even the caviar and vodka were not of the best, because the prime quality was shipped out as an invaluable export. The ice cream was exceptionally good and this brought about the question, why? In the 1930s when Anastas Mikoyan visited the United States, he tasted ice cream for the first time. He became a devotee of it and ate pints at a time. He arranged for an expert to come to Russia, build a plant, and provide the formulas. So, the ice cream in Moscow was better than in London, Paris, or Copenhagen. It was universally popular. Stands on the streets sold ice cream to the multitudes, who walked along sucking their cones.

I wandered out at night and within a few blocks came across Red Square in front of the Kremlin. Whether it was the hugeness of the cobblestone square which was so impressive or the recognition of the familiar site which newsreels had depicted year after year, filled with endless arrays of marching soldiers, ponderous tanks, and missile carriers, I could not be certain. My imagination filled the empty platform above Lenin's tomb with figures of the past, Malenkov, Timoshenko, Beria, Malinovsky, Mikoyan, Stalin, Khrushchev, and others whose ill-cut suits were topped with fedora hats, which looked too large contrasted with the military splendor below. To the right of the tomb were white rows of low horizontal benches, not wide enough to sit on. They acted as markers for prominent standees.

The square and streets were deserted, except for a bundle of people who had gathered in front of Lenin's tomb. I soon learned the reason. It was almost midnight, and a ceremony was about to take place in which two guards, facing each other stiffly at the entrance, were to be replaced. Suddenly, I heard tromp, tromp, tromp. Three Russian soldiers, two in front, one behind, were approaching from the tower, about a hundred yards to the left. To my surprise, they were doing a perfect Nazi goose step. Their legs shot out in a straight line as if they had no knees, and came down with tremendous force on the echoing stone. They carried guns with gleaming bayonets in their left hands, while their right hands swung in an automatic semicircle across their stomachs and back again. When they had made a left angle turn and marched to the tomb's entrance, one soldier stood tight against the door. At that precise moment, the clock on the tower struck twelve. The two guards were replaced and the three goose-stepped back, hammering their heels into the stone so that the clanging noise again echoed through the square. The two new guards had become part of the immobile stone façade. On another day, when I visited the tomb, I noticed that an overseer wiped the sweat off the nose and forehead of one of the guards, who could not move, nor even blink an eye.

Why the Russians should adopt the Nazi goose step, which evoked the memory of 22 million of their people killed by Hitler, or why they should engage in a royal ceremonial for the father of the proletariat regime, which made the changing of the guard in London an informal affair, were among the enigmas which abounded in this land.

The knot of people who had watched the ceremony untied and disappeared. But my attention was attracted to a woman dressed in white party clothes, with a bouquet in her hands, exchanging shrill words with a Russian policeman. He had fined her for some transgression and she was protesting. Her two friends, dressed like her, and with bouquets in their hands too, were trying to mollify her, but she would have none of it. Another policeman appeared. She was put in their car and driven off. Before we had completed the circle of the square, the car was back. A large black police wagon had arrived. She was now thoroughly subdued, as she was transferred into it, and her two friends were taken along for good measure. I wondered what would happen to them.

The courts in Russia were presided over by a judge and two laymen who flanked him. However, if the charge was of a political character, the judge sat alone. He was then acknowledgedly not objective. He became the arm of the government and was virtually the prosecutor.

Still I was heartened by the woman's audacity. In Stalin's day, could such an incident have occurred? Even this little zephyr of protest pointed to the relaxation of the former absolute tyranny.

At the end of Red Square was St. Basil's Cathedral. It was built by one of the czars to commemorate the victory over the Tartars when they were driven out of the land. The war consisted of nine battles, and so there are nine chapels in the church. It is the outside of the structure which is fantastic. It consists of turnip-shaped towers, one above and beside the other in haphazard architectural imagery. Each turret is striped with curved gold and green lines, in barbershop design. The top of the Byzantine array is a dome covered with gold which shines blindingly in the sun. At night it is favored by dozens of spotlights which light the square. The effect is as if Disney had built a fairy church for one of his cartoons. It is garishly beautiful. The Russians use their night lighting effectively. The huge red star over the highest tower in the Kremlin against the blue-black sky and St. Basil's sparkling turrets create a magical scene of colored moonlight on the empty square.

The next day I visited Lenin's tomb. It was vacation time and a million Russians come to Moscow each day. The chief attraction was to see Lenin in the flesh. To understand the impact of this event, imagine that we had been able to preserve the body of Washington or Lincoln, and you could see them as they were on the day they died. Even this fails to convey the emotion which gripped the visitors. For Lenin was more than the father of the revolution and of the state. In a country where "religion is the opiate of the people," he had taken on the role of a god. To many Russians, looking at Lenin was almost as profound an experience as if a Christian could see the face of Christ.

The single line of viewers was like a rope which snaked its way through many bustling city blocks and finally reached Red Square. Tourists, accompanied by an official guide, were cut into this line at the outer end of the square. It was then only a half-hour wait as the rope slowly moved into the tomb.

Originally, the tomb was constructed of wood. Later it was replaced by a dark red marble structure built in severe, modernistic simplicity, in contrast to the curving colored spires of St. Basil.

Finally, I was inside the semidark building. A hushed silence enveloped me, except for the noise of shuffling feet, as I descended several small flights of steps. The day was hot, but the temperature dropped precipitously as I approached the crypt itself and it was quite cold. As I followed the barely discernible figures in front, I suddenly saw suspended above us in mid-air (the dark marble on which it rested could not yet be seen), the glass-enclosed body of Lenin, brilliantly lit by spotlights within. The stairs led up to the level of the body, across a short platform and down a flight toward the exit. This afforded a view of Lenin from all sides. Dimly I now discerned at the bottom of the pit on both sides four soldiers guarding the glass coffin.

Lenin lay in formal dark clothes, his head on a red pillow. His pate and face were a healthy pink and white color. So were his hands, the only other flesh visible. They lay on his thighs, the fingers of his left hand straight and those of his right curved under in graceful pose. His beard was neatly trimmed. He was expressionless and the glowing flesh belied the inertness of death. Even allowing for the cosmetic skills of an embalmer, it was a miracle of preservation. It aroused skepticism. Why had no other important person been immunized from decay? Why haven't wealthy Russians used the technique to achieve one of man's fondest dreams—permanence of body? Or was the Lenin we saw a wax statue, while underneath lay his decayed remains? Why was the tomb kept noticeably at cool temperature? Perhaps some enterprising writer will pierce the mystery of this preservation of the flesh.

When I emerged, I was in an area between the tomb and the high brick Kremlin wall, which once protected the czars who lived within. It was a graveyard. Buried in this place of honor were great generals, and former officials of the revolutionary regimes. At the head of each grave was a marble column topped by the sculptured head of the deceased. Stalin's grave was at the end of this line, but significantly, his was the only grave without a column or sculptured likeness. Only a bronze plaque revealed his name.

Immediately after his death, he had been placed alongside of Lenin inside the tomb. Soon, however, disenchantment became vocal, when Khrushchev denounced him as a ruthless murderer and madman. Stalin was then ousted from the tomb and buried unceremoniously in the rear. At that he was fortunate. The Russian practice of erasing their fallen heroes from their history books and effecting their nonexistence might still befall Stalin. Obliterating their former leaders is the highest form of ignominy. Stalin's photograph had hung in every office and home. Millions of Stalin banners had fluttered throughout the land. Thousands of statues and busts of him had decorated the squares. One recalled the jest of Stalin's offer of a prize for the best memorial to Pushkin. The winner designed a huge figure of Stalin reading a book by Pushkin.

Upon ascendancy to power, the technique used to be the issuance of banners of Lenin and, in profile alongside him, Stalin. When the royal succession had been sufficiently impressed upon the public, a new banner was issued, Stalin in front and next to him Lenin. Then the final banner—just Stalin. Thereafter, cities, streets, plazas, buildings, parks, rivers, mountains, ships, planes, books—all named after Stalin. Yet now it would be difficult to find a trace of all these. Huge statues of Stalin on foot, on horse, reading proclamations, protecting Moscow with a sword—all have melted into the night and disappeared. On millions of walls discolored squares appear where once his photograph hung. A thirty-year regime has vanished as if it were all a mirage. Probably, future generations will read his name only in foreign books not in

Russia. Mussolini and Hitler went through similar obliteration of their cults heralded by them to be thousand-year empires.

In the Kremlin wall itself, small holes had been cut to contain urns with ashes of other prominent officials who were identified by a covering square bronze plaque. The newest of these was Vladimir Komarov, the astronaut who perished when his capsule's parachute lines became snarled and he crashed.

A tour of Moscow revealed how drab most of the city was. The landscape in the suburbs was scrawny. With the exception of several new housing developments, the buildings were unkempt and candidates for slum status. One soon noticed iron scaffolding of box design around various structures. At first the impression was of a repair operation, but their number (it looked like about 10 per cent of all buildings) elicited an inquiry. One then learned from circumspect sources that, due to defective construction, many buildings constructed in the last ten years crumbled and leaned toward collapse. The scaffolding was a permanent crutch. It was another illustration of Russian inefficiency.

The monotony of the Moscow tour was broken by two sites. The guide registered excitement as she approached them. The first was a huge swimming pool. It was the largest in the world and accommodated thousands. It was shaped like a half grapefruit with quadrants separating one section from another. In the central circle was a high diving board. Each quadrant had its own. On the outer circular edge were roped-off shallow sections. The triangular distance toward the center was also roped. The people paid a small price to enter, and the water was heated in the winter so that even when there was snow on the ground, thousands swam in the pool.

On the road to this circular compartmentalized artificial lake, the guide pointed to hospitals on both sides. One wondered whimsically whether there was a connection between the outdoor winter pool and the hospitals. The Russian people received free hospitalization and medical treatment, in contrast to the punishing costs in hospitals in the United States. In Russia only medicines which were bought outside of the hospital had to be paid for by the individual.

The other attraction of the Moscow tour was the university. It was a large pink brick complex of buildings. We assumed its educational excellence and were impressed by it, but the guide characteristically stressed its size: "If a student went into a different classroom each day, it would take him ten years to get out," she told us triumphantly. Would we think of describing Columbia University or Rockefeller Center this way?

The striving for size was the revelation of the government's struggle to give the impression of a mighty power. Was it motivated by an inner realization of inadequacy? Was it intended to hide the slow progress of a defective inflexible system which could not even solve its agricultural problem in a vast fertile land?

Size. The Russians were completing the largest hotel in all Europe. It would have 3,100 rooms. It was conceded that there was no need for so huge a structure and that economically it was bound to be a disaster. But it was a government project. The public had no right to a reckoning; and the pride in the "largest" was rich reward for a national inferiority complex.

Size. The subway in Moscow had the largest up and down escalators in the world. It took at least three minutes to ascend or descend one at high speed. The guide visibly thrilled as he escorted us on them and observed that we craned our necks to see the bottom or the top, which were so far away as to be out of sight.

Size. Even Russian humor, as Freud would have been quick to point out, stressed the unconscious desire for bigness. The chief comedy routine in the Russian circus was a machine which enlarged anything put into it. One comedian demonstrated it to another by dropping a small comb into a slot. Immediately the other pulled a three-foot comb out of the other end of the machine. Then a small bread roll was placed in it. Out came a four-foot loaf of bread. The astonished comedian had an idea. He ran offstage and to the delight of the audience returned with a small bottle of vodka. The end product was so huge it could not be taken out of the machine. They lifted the entire mechanism to reveal an eight-foot-high bottle of vodka.

What is the explanation for the paradox of colossal inefficiency and a low standard of living side by side with the hydrogen bomb, huge missiles, the largest tank, the most powerful sputnik, the largest jet plane, etc.? The answer is that when the government concentrated all its resources on a particular project, sparing neither expense nor manpower, it could achieve an outstanding prototype. But this did not signal natural growth. There was seldom mass production or simultaneous progress in many directions. If the government could abandon its military concentration, it might solve the fertilizer, tractor, and scientific agricultural problem. Also, size was raw power. Today miniaturization is the key to scientific achievement. The Russians, who were far ahead in space when shooting heavy loads into orbit was the chief requirement, have now dropped out of sight in the "race," because sophisticated complex scientific systems, requiring technological production of the highest order, are the requirement for planetary travel. This they have not got. Indeed, despite the discount which one must give to Egyptian alibis for their humiliating defeat by the Israelis in the 1973 war, one begins to wonder whether there might not be some truth to their claim that the "advanced" Russian military equipment shot shells in parabolas instead of toward the enemy.

The Russians are pragmatists. Those in power are not likely to deceive themselves. Perhaps this accounts for Russia's withdrawal whenever frontally confronted. What greater loss of face in full international view could any nation have suffered than when President Kennedy directed their ships on the high seas to be searched for missiles and sent back, and their missiles in Cuba moved out? They complied. In the June 1967 Middle-East crisis, when there was danger of a direct clash with the United States because of Russia's age-old ambition to control the gateway to three continents, it was Kosygin who used the Hot Line to the White House for the first time, and assured President Johnson he would not intervene directly in the conflict.

To what extent do the controlled news media condition the Russian people against the West? Does impartial news enter the country and filter through to the masses? Even with full investigative powers, it would be difficult to reach a definitive answer. But a number of experiences may be significant.

A short while before our trip, Svetlana, Stalin's daughter, had defected to the United States. Then she had enlarged the gesture of flight by writing a book exposing the tyranny from which she had fled. The Russian Government took the position that the Svetlana defection and book were a plot by the United States to spoil Russia's Fiftieth anniversary celebration of the revolution. Russian diplomats made overtures to our Ambassador Llewellyn Thompson to postpone the publication of Svetlana's book at least until the jubilee year was over. Although Thompson, who was highly respected by the Russians and spoke their language fluently, had assured them that in our country the Government has no power to instruct a publisher what to publish or when, they remained unconvinced and bitter. The official line was that Svetlana was crazy and irresponsible. Kosygin, in his interview following the Glassboro Conference with President Johnson, revealed only two moments of exploding impatience. One involved a question of anti-Semitism, and the other Svetlana, whom he deemed to be emotionally sick. This position seemed to be swallowed without any reflective chewing by every Russian to whom I talked. One well-educated man contemptuously rejected my assertation that the United States Government had no jurisdiction over such a matter. "What would the publishing company do if it received an order from the President?" he asked. "It would go to court and have the order annulled," I replied. "You sue the government?" he exclaimed. "I and others have done it many times, and won," I replied. If I had been Lenin, he would not have believed me. He threw up his hands in a gesture of "What's the use of continuing this discussion when you are spouting ridiculous propaganda and I am talking facts?"

Our guide, an intelligent college student, similarly asserted that Svetlana was mentally sick. When I told him that I had seen and heard her on television and that she was composed and charming, he replied, "Yes, but right after that broadcast, she had to be taken to a hospital." Astonished, I asked, "Where did you get that notion? She was never put in a hospital." "Oh, please!" he said, with an air of great tolerance for my attempt to deceive him.

A Russian newspaperman of great experience, and not without some empathy for the United States, talked earnestly about Vietnam. When I told him that our President had offered to stop the bombing if the Vietcong would come to a discussion table, he demurred, "Then why hasn't he ever said so?" I told him that the President, Vice-President Humphrey, Dean Rusk, and others had on many occasions proclaimed and embraced unconditional talks as a way of ending the conflict; that once the President had unilaterally stopped the bombing for thirty-seven days without a whisper of reciprocation by the Vietcong. His skepticism (to put it mildly) yielded slightly when I offered to mail to him newspaper reports of these events from several countries. He asked particularly for the New York *Times*.

Knowledgeable Americans and others who spend much time in Russia were unanimous in asserting that Voice of America broadcasts were listened to by millions. This was the real penetration of the fog curtain which hides the truth from the people. Those who discovered the factual integrity of these broadcasts, perhaps because they recited adverse news to American interests as well, accepted it and compared it with the monotone of villainy which emanated from Russian radios. Taxis were constantly spouting controlled news. Even if one didn't know the language, he was struck with the continuous use of "Amerikanski." It was obvious that this dinning of hatred of the West into the head behind the wheel, and millions of other Russian heads, could not be easily overcome. Finally, the broadcast turned to music. Ironically it was American jazz and, just coming into vogue, rock and roll. Occasionally, there was a Russian folk song like "*Shatzy*," which was far more beautiful to my ears.

The artistic level was high in all the arts. We had become familiar with the superb verve and freshness of the Moiseyev Dancing Ensemble, and the classical perfection of the Bolshoi Ballet. When they performed in the United States they were hailed by American audiences as incomparable. Time and again they received ovations. The performers, in a reciprocal gesture of warmth, applauded the audience from the stage. The artistic bridge of comradeship had been significant in several ways. When these troupes of young men and women returned to Russia, did they not recognize the official line of unrelieved anti-Westernism as propaganda and a distortion of the truth? Cultural exchange was not only a proper expression of the internationalism of art, but a leveler on both sides of the boundary walls of prejudice and falsity which poison the people's good will. It was significant that the United States cherished these exchanges. The Russians called them off arbitrarily whenever they wished to heat up the atmosphere of national hatred. So, during the Middle East crises, several tours of the ballet were canceled by Russia.

The Russian circus was a stupendous show. Here tradition played a great part. The Russians had for generations been great tumblers and horsemen. Their feats continued to be incredible. They leaped on and off horses which were circling at top speed. They climbed under the horses' bellies and up on the other side. They held onto the horses' tails and dragged in the sawdust, finally maneuvering under and through the horses' hooves. They did not pretend that these were achievements under the revolutionary regime. They dressed as czarist Cossacks, and waved gleaming sabers, displaying the skills of cavalry fighters in days of old.

The trained bear was another extraordinary tradition. In a comedy act, he rode in an auto, which continuously exploded and poured out frightening smoke. The bear was unperturbed, as he fixed a tire, telephoned for help, and performed with full understanding of the fun involved.

Russian acrobats and tumblers began where most others left off. Triple somersaults, side cartwheels of such speed that the performer became blurred, and man-constructed mountains were performed with such ease that they almost lost their theatrical effect.

Poetry and other forms of writing were flourishing in Russia. The advance was in direct proportion to the defiant declaration of independence by the artist. Many go to jail for their audacity (how many dozens would be incarcerated for life in the United States if lèse majesté of President Johnson had been a crime?), but occasionally there was enough protest internationally to release a victim from torture.

The control of the artistic field fell under the heading of political control. Thus, when the 1967 Moscow Film Festival was planned, all nations were invited to participate. Whether tourism or a policy of lifting the curtain a few inches was the motivation, it became advisable to accept on pain of injuring the sensitivity of Russian leaders. It apparently didn't occur to them that prior restraints might have affected the sensitivity of others.

The State Department officially encouraged the American motion picture industry to send as impressive a delegation as possible. It agreed to do so. But shortly thereafter the Middle East crisis erupted. Suddenly the United States was denounced with more than customary vehemence as a vicious imperialistic mad dog. The tap which trickled friendship had been turned the other way and a torrent of abuse gushed forth. There was consternation in the American delegation. Should we call off our visit and thus turn the good-will mission into one of reciprocal contempt? Some artists and executives found it impossible to attend and withdrew. Nevertheless, it was decided to go through with the venture lest we broaden the breach. The secure must cater to the insecure. There were anticipatory tremors. Would the head of the delegation, Jack Valenti, be marked for humiliation because of his prior association with President Johnson?

The trip came off well. On arrival, the head of the Russian film industry, a government official, was at the airport with Ambassador Thompson to greet us. Flowers were presented to the ladies. At the conclusion of the Festival, Sandy Dennis was awarded a prize as the best actress, and Paul Scofield an award as best actor for his role in *A Man for All Seasons*.

However, there were also petty meannesses. The American entry, *Up the Down Staircase*, which was scheduled to be shown in an evening, was suddenly reduced to an afternoon exhibit. The picture starred Sandy Dennis as a teacher in a problem school in New York. She presided over a class which included neurotic juvenile delinquents, one of whom threatened her with a knife and another with rape. The real assault was on her idealism. At one point she gave up the struggle to be a teacher, because she didn't wish to cope with the special problems of a rebellious group. She wanted to teach in a normal school or not at all. Finally she triumphed over the morbid and criminal environment and decided to stay.

There could be no doubt that the school and students were atypical. This was the whole point of the picture. Yet *Tass*, the Russian newspaper, reported "American authorities stated that this was a typical American school." To add ingenuity to mendacity, the next sentence stated that Stanley Kramer (who because of *Judgment at Nuremberg* and other pictures, was popular in Russia), had said that "'Up the Down Staircase' is an honest and true work." Of course, he hadn't subscribed to the first sentence that "it represents a typical American school." Thus, by skillful juxtaposition, he became authority for the original misrepresentation.

At the same time, the Russians at the last moment barred the showing of another American entry, *The Young Americans*. It was a wholesome, gay depiction of America's youth. Ambassador Thompson tried diplomatically to overcome this slur by showing the picture in his embassy home and even inviting Russians to see it.

After each country's exhibit, a party was tendered at which other delegations were invited.

The American dinner and dance took place in the ballroom of the new Russian hotel. The occasion was formal. Robert Mulligan, the director, Tad Mosel, the scriptwriter, Sandy Dennis, the star of the American picture, Jennifer Jones, Sandra Dee, Dmitri Tiomkin, the composer, Stanley Kramer, Anatole Litvak, Abby Mann, George Stevens, Jr., King Vidor, and foreign managers of leading American motion picture companies were present. Ambassador Thompson and his wife attended. So did V. Baskakov, the head of the Russian motion picture industry, who was given a seat of honor.

At an appropriate moment, Jack Valenti, head of the American delegation, made a graceful and eloquent toast to the Russian people. He expressed the genuine good will which motivated the journey. To our surprise, Baskakov did not make a reciprocal toast. Even a cautious word in the most general terms from him would have reduced the strain. His silence was like a roar of unfriendliness. An American producer, who knew Russia and its langugage well, decided to speak to Baskakov. I watched as he led him into lifting a glass of vodka with him and nudged Valenti into clicking glasses. But it was all silent. Indeed a Russian photographer standing ready for any occasion was about to snap a picture of the incident, but Baskakov called him off with a negative wave of the head.

We were subjected to other picayune discourtesies. There were insufficient tickets for the American delegation to attend the showing of the American entry. Finally this mysterious bureaucratic annoyance was overcome.

The French delegation, in co-operation with the Russians, also snubbed us. De Gaulle, having found another opportunity to berate the United States, had joined the Russian camp in the Middle East crisis. Suddenly he, who supported Israel against their surrounding enemies when they were screaming threats of destruction, now declared that the United States was belligerent. This catapulted him into a position of being an ally of Russia in her drive to control the Middle East. His own countrymen, including some in his cabinet, protested his view. All this made France the darling of the Russian Government at the festival. The ill-will toward the United States, which permeated the Russian-French partnership, spilled over onto our delegation. We were the only nation not invited to the French celebration after the showing of its picture.

It was customary for American motion picture representatives to meet with producers, writers, and directors of every country they visited. This furthered the international aspect of motion pictures and our desire to achieve excellence in the art irrespective of nationality. So our delegation sought a meeting with Russian artists. We were refused. Probably when we were originally invited to the festival, such meetings had been part of the program. But there was on each Russian invitation an unwritten postscript, "Subject to change without notice, in the event political expediency so requires."

However, one day unexpectedly, a handwritten note was slipped under my door inviting me "as a writer" to attend a meeting of Russian motion picture writers and directors. I accepted eagerly. English, Mexican, Peruvian, and other artists attended. A picture of Lenin was the only decoration in the room of the writers' union building. The meeting was in the morning, but there were the usual caviar and vodka, which respected no hour. The chief discussion turned to the respective rights of the author and director to credits announced on the film. Writers claimed that the director's billing was overweening and excluded proper credit for the author. This controversy had been raging in Hollywood too. In the course of the discussion, the freedom of a writer to express himself without directors' or governmental interference was bespoken. The Russians listened attentively and obviously sympathetically to my exposition on American freedom of expression. The discussion thereafter was like a fresh ocean breeze which wafted away stifling air. The union of Russian writers (not limited to the screen) had been in a tumultuous quarrel. Novelist Aleksandr Solzhenitsyn and poet Andrei Voznesensky had openly defied and condemned the union for censorship. The poet had recently jumped on the stage of Moscow's Taganka Theater where *Antiworlds* was being performed for the two hundredth time, and despite official disapproval yelled "How shamefully we hold our tongues, I'm ashamed of things I've written myself." Russians were discovering that a little freedom could be a dangerous thing. Once loosed it could gather unstoppable momentum from long-suppressed yearning.

Russians have preserved their lavish past with great relish. The czars' palaces were exhibited to the public, which filed through the incredibly ornate, bejeweled rooms in wonder and pride. Then they trudged through the gardens stretched out for acres toward the lake, which provided the air conditioning of that era. Fountains were everywhere giving frenzied motion to the surrounding flower beds. In some castles there were collections of paintings which outglittered the columns of malachite, onyx, quartz, and lapis lazuli. The Pushkin Museum in Moscow and the famous Hermitage in Leningrad contained rooms which were filled with Rembrandts, Goyas, Rubens, Van Goghs, Cézannes, Matisses, and Renoirs, and in sculpture, Michaelangelos, Da Vincis, and Maillols. In terms of modern values, the greatest growth stock in the world was the art treasures in these museums.

Yet the Russians sometimes built modern structures which clashed with the symmetry of their architectural past. The most glaring example was the 6,000-seat modern theater with a huge stage where the Politburo met on official occasions, and which was used for the motion picture exhibits of the festival. This building was situated inside the Kremlin wall and contrasted incongruously with the czaristic palace and structures which surrounded it. We wondered why it was not built immediately outside of the wall.

There were three million Jews in Russia, and for years efforts to permit their emigration had been thwarted. Disconcerting reports of their persecution under Stalin had been published. Jewish newspapers were forbidden. Synagogues had been closed (as were many churches). During Passover, matzohs could not be imported. Yet the official line was that there was no governmental anti-Semitism, and that the anti-religious policy was universal rather than specific. So, now that tourism had been encouraged, it was natural that visitors should visit the only Catholic church in Moscow, or the famous large synagogue in Moscow. A group of us did so. In the synagogue we spoke to Rabbi Levine in his study.

We asked him how conditions were, not realizing until we signed the visitors' book at the end of our interview that he had been visited by similar groups many times each week, and had been asked the same questions.

He was a patriarchal figure, with brightly penetrating dark eyes which belied the equanimity of his manner and the peaceful gray of his long beard. He delivered a long paean of praise for the Russian Government. "Everything is fine here. No one interferes with us. Those who work, earn a good living. Of course, none of us are rich but we are well taken care of. The government provides free medical service and treatment for all the people. We are repairing our synagogue, as you can see, and making it more beautiful. There are many scholars here who spend their day and night studying and discussing the Talmud . . ."

We interrupted to ask whether Jews could leave the country if they wished. "Of course," he assured us. "Those who want to leave can do so. Indeed, even after Russia broke off diplomatic relations with Israel, hundreds of Jews were still permitted to go to Israel."

We were becoming more skeptical every moment. Perhaps he was talking for the record. Was his room bugged too? When we pressed him on the government's attitude toward religion, he replied, "The powers that be are generally against religion. That means all religions, not just the Jewish religion. Therefore the youth is largely lost to us. It is the middle-aged and the older generation that attend. But on Saturdays, our synagogue is filled and on the holy holidays, the streets outside are filled with Jews who wish to worship."

We called his attention to an incident in the small synagogue on the ground floor, which was used for study and early morning prayer. Two old scholars were seated there as we entered. We had asked them how they were faring. Both had made a forbidding gesture that it was not wise for them to speak. The rabbi seemed alarmed. He disposed of this with a vehement statement: "I am telling you how it is. If you wish to interpret some old Jews' gesture, you may do so. I am telling you the facts."

A few moments later in answer to another prodding question, he exclaimed, "All that we want is peace. Peace in Vietnam. Peace in Nigeria. Peace in Israel. Peace in the Arab world. Peace in all the world."

Peace in Nigeria! By this time, some of us were convinced that the fine man was making his statements for the bugging equipment and simply to protect his flock. We could not be sure, but we believed that we had been dim-witted in pressing the poor man. Recent reports from Russia, which had broadened its attacks on Israel to include Zionism generally, with implications of the revival of the colossal lies about international Jewish plots, and even horrendous analogies of Hitlerism and Judaism, pointed to the dangers affecting the Jewish population in Russia.

The United States followed a policy of patience with Russia. For example, its embassy was housed on the top floor of a ramshackle building, with an old-fashioned elevator which held only two or three passengers and was self-operated. The quarters were inadequate in size and appointments, and contrasted with our beautiful embassy buildings in Mexico, England, France, Italy, and other nations less important in the political strata. Furthermore, the Russians permitted only a limited number of attachés and assistants. The wives and children of the embassy personnel therefore filled in as secretaries and associates to take care of the enormous responsibilities of such a leading outpost. The private home of the Ambassador however, was magnificent. Averell Harriman once bought this palace from a wealthy Russian businessman and presented it to our government as a residence for its ambassador.

One of the most poignant consequences of Russian rejection affected a choral group from Amherst College. Under the leadership of its dean, it was making a tour of Europe, and had been invited to perform in Moscow and Leningrad. However the Middle East crisis had put frost on

American ventures, and their performances in Russia were canceled and forbidden. This fine group of students, typically American in their friendliness, zest, and good humor, found itself barred after a long trip. It performed in the International House for other foreigners, but Russians stayed away. What a waste and souring of good will?

We departed from Russia by plane from Leningrad to Helsinki. The Amherst choral group was on our plane. So were other foreigners who had visited Russia. As the plane roared out of the airport and away from Russia, the passengers spontaneously and without any prearrangement, sang *The Star-Spangled Banner*. I had never heard it sung with such quiet fervor. Thereafter all the passengers from many visiting countries cheered and applauded, expressing openly the relief of leaving the stifled air of an oppressed country and winging toward freedom. It was no ordinary patriotic gesture. One felt in that unique moment the true meaning of liberty and how essential it was to the very essence of man's existence.

When we had been taken through the customs procedure at Helsinki, we waited for baggage clearance. There was a door leading to a sunlit terrace where taxis were stationed. I asked the Finnish guard whether I could step out. I shall never forget his reply. With a smile he said, "Of course, you are in Finland now," and held the door open.

HOW TO TELL A LIAR

Can a lawyer tell whether a witness is lying? Very often yes. He does so by a variety of means, from advance preparation, which enables him to compare the witness's story with contradictory documentation, to psychological insights.

It is the latter which are most intriguing and which I shall discuss. We all use techniques to judge credibility, even though we may not be conscious of doing so. For example, if you are at a dinner party you may tell your spouse on the way home that you wouldn't trust the man who sat next to you farther than you could throw a piano. How did you come to that conclusion? If we had a tape recording of your conversation with him that evening, it probably would be quite innocuous and would not explain your impression. But you didn't like the way he looked at others while he was talking to you, or his affected flirtation with the woman next to him, or his raucous laughter at what wasn't so funny, or his pretense of knowledge which he didn't have; or his voice, eyes, mannerisms, all spelling out lack of sincerity. On the other hand you might form a very favorable opinion of him—again evaluating everything from his clothes to his speech and his persuasive sincerity. The point is that we gauge credibility not merely by what we hear but what we see while we hear it. That is what a jury does when it *observes* a witness intently. That is why there is a rule that an appellate court will not reverse a jury on a question of *fact*, only on law. The appellate judges have only the printed record of the testimony. They have not *seen* the witnesses as the jurors have. They therefore uphold the juror's determination of credibility, even if they disagree with it.

The jurors too apply psychological tests to determine a witness's honesty, whether they know it or not.

Trial lawyers, because of practice in the arena of contest, often develop special antennae to pick up signals from the witness, which reveal that he is not telling the truth.

Let me illustrate some that I have observed.

1. If a witness puts his hand in front of his mouth before he answers, it might mean "I wish I didn't have to say what I am about to say." Of course it might be an innocent gesture. So I go to another subject and return to the same point. If the hand covers the mouth again, I will cross-examine deeply on the subject, assuming that there is vulnerability even though I don't yet know what it is.

On a number of occasions, this "hunch" proved very rewarding. I recall one such witness, later asking me how I knew the secret dug out of him. Like Cavour, who learned how to deceive diplomats by telling them the truth, which they didn't believe, I told him that he had tipped me off himself. I am sure he rejected this explanation and must have though that I had a phenomenal investigator.

2. Nervous gestures such as scissoring the legs or shifting in the seat whenever a particular subject matter is raised is another distress signal sent out by the witness.

3. The eyes. Poets say they reflect the soul. Perhaps so, but they also reflect fear and confusion. The voice may be steady. The manner confident. But that look in the eyes! Like an animal which senses danger. A combination of an emphatic assertion while the eyes reveal doubt is particularly significant.

4. Undue emphasis. Emotions of course affect the voice, but its tremulousness is not very significant. Anyone sitting in a witness chair facing an audience with a black-robed judge on one side, and twelve jurors watching every flicker of his eyes on the other, will be nervous. But it is a *general* nervousness. It is not related to any particular question. However, when a witness who has testified in a certain vocal range suddenly increases his decibels belligerently for no accountable reason, it is a signal. The question must have touched a nerve and caused a vocal explosion.

5. Instant amnesia. Often a witness who has been answering difficult questions with facility will suddenly stop, look up at the ceiling as if beseeching help from the almighty, then, getting no relief there, shift his gaze to his lawyer, as the second-best bet, and finally in a half stammer say, "I d-don't remember." Particularly when the question appears harmless, the cross-examiner is alerted. Is the sudden loss of memory a revelation of Freud's thesis that one never forgets? He is merely unable to reveal an unpleasant fact.

6. Quarrelsomeness. A witness who protests that he is being harassed or tricked by the cross-examiner reveals his sensitivity to the questions rather than the unfairness of the questioner. Under our system of law, improper questions are ruled out by the judge. If the question is allowed but the witness claims he is being persecuted, he is pitting his

own uninformed view of the law against the court's. Why is he indulging in such an unequal contest, unless he fears to answer the questions?

If a lawyer is earning his bread by the sweat of his browbeating, his adversary, not the witness, should protest. Any unfair tactic provides its own punishment, because the judge and jury will resent it. But the witness's role is to inform, not to control the questioning.

7. Negative pregnants. This is the legal phrase for a denial which appears to be complete but is really partial. For example, to the question, "Didn't you try hard to block the deal?" he answers, "No, I did not." Upon further inquiry, he claims his answer meant he didn't "try hard" to block the deal. He just tried to block it. His answer was negative but pregnant with admission.

Whenever a witness engages in such a ruse, the lawyer's antennae pick up a signal not only of slyness, but of an attempt to evade, which may apply to other answers as well.

8. Candor. A mistake by a witness is readily forgiven by a jury if he is frank to admit it. Memory about dates and details of events years old can be faulty. It is when the witness pretends that he didn't testify as he did, or that he didn't mean what he said, or that he is misinterpreted, that his dishonesty is revealed. Curiously, such feigning does the witness more harm than the frank admission that he was mistaken.

A witness who has erred and is caught will, if he is not honest, invent escape hatches. Such improvisation is almost always fatal. He merely creates more opportunities to demonstrate that he is lying. The witness who can under stress invent an excuse which will be foolproof is rare. As he is forced to retreat from his newly dug trench, again and again, his credibility is completely destroyed.

9. Sincerity. There is an imponderable over-all test of a witness's honesty. Does he look and sound truthful? It is a kind of summation of all the emanations which make him believable. It is his face, voice, directness, and above all his sincerity. That is why credibility has no relationship to education or culture. An illiterate cleaning woman may be impressively honest. A refined executive may appear shifty. Character is a letter of credit written on the face.

10. More useful than any of the other tests for detecting a liar is the rule of probability. If the testimony given by the witness does not accord with common experience, it must be false. Unless the witness is unstable, in which event the bizarre becomes normal, it is extremely unlikely that he will behave in a manner which violates usual standards. This rule is universal. In our daily contacts we apply this test unwittingly. We believe what seems reasonable and disbelieve the "tall story." Why is it "tall"? Because we wouldn't have acted that way under similar circumstances. The rule of probability is also used by the

jurors, though they may not know it. Faced with directly opposite testimony, they accept one version rather than another because it complies more closely with their idea of what would be normal behavior under the circumstances.

It is my favorite litmus test in the courtroom. If testimony violates the rule of probability, I will not let up on cross-examination in an effort to expose the witness.

The rule of probability works its miracles in wondrous ways. Recently the Government brought a suit against wholesale tour operators for violating the regulations which forbid low air fares to charter groups unless their members belonged to a genuine club or organization for at least six months. A Government investigator testified that he had bought a low-priced ticket even though he was not a member of a charter group and had not presented any of the required proof. In defending the case, I was struck by the responsibility of the executives. I was convinced they had given proper instructions to their sales clerks not to sell cut-rate tickets to those who were not members of a qualified group. Yet an experienced salesgirl had broken the rule. The explanation that she had just been careless violated the rule of probability. I pursued the matter and discovered that she had taken a weekend trip immediately after the ticket was sold.

When the Government investigator took the stand to testify to the violation, I drew the following out of him on cross-examination.

Q. You told her you were a schoolteacher?

A. Yes, sir.

Q. Of course that wasn't true, was it?

A. No, sir, it was not.

Q. And you told her you were single, didn't you?

A. Yes, sir.

Q. Now, what relevance did it have that you were single when you talked to her?

A. None whatsoever.

Each admission made it more difficult to resist the next. Momentum prevents a sudden stop of revelation.

Q. You told her you liked her?

A. No, sir, I didn't—excuse me, I did. I did tell her she was a very nice individual.

Q. Did you tell her that you would like to go on the trip and you could spend some time with her in Las Vegas?

A. I said that could—could happen, yes, sir.

Q. What did you tell her about being with her in Las Vegas, if anything.

A. I said perhaps we could get together in Las Vegas.

Q. Perhaps?

A. Yes, sir.

By this time it was too late to retreat. He tried to do so, but found it too embarrassing. The ultimate admission finally tumbled out of him.

Q. So you knew that she was arranging for the flight the two of you would be together on?

A. Yes, sir.

Q. Did you ask her to make an exception to the six-month rule? Did you talk to her about the two of you being together in Las Vegas?

A. Yes, sir, I did.

Not much more was necessary to explain why the pretty salesgirl had violated the CAB rules when she sold a ticket to the handsome young Government agent. It came out that they met at the plane and boarded together.

Q. Were you very attentive to her?

A. Yes, sir, I was.

Q. It was very clear to you that she was attracted to you?

A. Yes, sir.

Occasionally in an effort to protect himself he would announce that he had done it all to perform his duty in uncovering an illegal sale of a ticket. This left him even more vulnerable.

Q. When you told her you were single, did you think that was part of your duty for the CAB?

A. No, sir.

Finally she discovered who he really was. It was the oldest of all plots but it had happened. She thought he was in love, or at least liked her, but he was merely a deceiver gathering evidence for the Government.

Q. Did she tell you that it might cost her her job because she had done that for you, because she liked you and she thought you and she were going to have a good time in Las Vegas together?

A. She may have said that.

Q. Did she tell you she liked you?

A. At some point during the trip there I think she did.

Q. And did she tell you that she had sold you the ticket improperly because she liked you and she felt that you liked her. Did she reprimand you for having deceived her?

A. Something like that, yes, sir.

How could the company which employed her be held responsible for the illegal ticket sale when it was the unauthorized act of a salesgirl who had a rendezvous on her mind, not the company's rules? The Judge and the courtroom were astonished to find that in a prosaic CAB case sex, and not avarice, was the villain. The rule of probability had led directly to evidence of entrapment.

In another case, Roy Fruehauf, president of Fruehauf Trailers, was indicted in 1959 for giving $200,000 to teamster president Dave Beck. Even though the money was a loan, it was a clear violation of the statute. I undertook the defense when it was demonstrated to me that the Fruehauf company had obtained no preference from the union in wages, hours, or in any other manner. Also, Fruehauf was no intimate of Dave Beck. Then why had Fruehauf, quite aware of the law, risked his reputation and liberty by making the loan? The rule of probability told me that something vital was missing.

It turned out that many years before, when a proxy fight was launched against the Fruehauf company to take away Fruehauf's control of the company, he had turned to the Teamsters Union for a large loan to buy in his own stock and stave off the assault. The teamsters had millions of dollars for investment and loans at appropriate interest. The loan was formally made and approved by the union's committee and its counsel. Fruehauf had later repaid it in full with interest.

Years later, Dave Beck was in financial trouble in his personal real estate investments. He turned to Fruehauf to make him a loan. Fruehauf felt that he would be an ingrate if he didn't reciprocate in Beck's hour of distress. The $200,000 he lent was also repaid, although part of the interest was still due.

The legal problem was that the prior transaction might afford a moral explanation but was no legal excuse. The statute forbade gifts or loans to union executives—period. It was, as we lawyers say, draconian. Therefore, the early history would not even be admissible. Fortunately, the Government prosecuter was quite willing to admit this evidence, because he felt that it established a chain of financial transactions which were unholy. The jury acquitted Fruehauf.

Even though the case went to the Supreme Court of the United States before Fruehauf could enjoy his freedom, it was the rule of probability which led us to an otherwise invisible defense.

In another case a gifted top executive was accused of neglecting his office for days at a time. He was a dedicated man, and responsible in every way. Yet there were these occasional absences. His explanation, supported by his family, that he suffered occasional illness did not satisfy the rule of probability. He seemed healthy. There were no doctors' certificates. Persistence revealed that he had a drinking problem. Then the improbable had become probable.

What is referred to as woman's intuition is often nothing but the rule of probability. A wife of a philandering husband will sense a change of relationship which the most cogent explanations cannot overcome. The rule of probability nags at her and finally reveals the naked truth.

Science has attempted to provide lie-detector and chemical tests to expose a liar. Unfortunately, they have not been proved to be reliable. We still depend on the psychological insights of the questioner to reveal the truth.

Cross-examination is still the best scalpel to excise the truth from the brain.

A-OK

In 1966, astronaut Alan Shepard asked me to be the attorney for the astronauts in their personal affairs. There were fifty-two astronauts at the time. (The number grew to seventy-three.) Shepard was their spokesman and he had obtained their authority and that of NASA (National Aeronautics and Space Administration) to approach me, but he had two preliminary questions. What fees would be entailed, and would I come to meet the astronauts and NASA executives in Houston, Texas, for mutual approval of the representation?

I told him that out of regard for the astronauts' heroic service to our country, I would be pleased to represent them without fee, and that I, too, would wish to meet with them and NASA's executives to learn in greater detail the nature of the representation, and the Government's attitude.

So it was arranged. On October 3, 1966, I flew to Houston and had lunch with a large number of spacemen. I addressed them, and then spent hours in private conversation with the most remarkable group of "clients" I had ever encountered.

Thereafter, I was taken by Alan Shepard and Virgil Grissom to the offices of Dr. Robert Gilruth, director of the Manned Spacecraft Center, and Dr. George Low, then the deputy director, for further discussion. They were, of course, concerned with the well-being as well as the welfare of their charges, who were training for feats previously envisioned only in fiction and were now to be attempted with the world in attendance.

I saw the need to assure Dr. Gilruth and Dr. Low that, whatever issues arose, it was necessary to accommodate the astronauts' wishes to the approval of NASA. This was the astronauts' duty in any event.

The astronauts approved my becoming counsel, and NASA did too, and made a public announcement of my designation.

So began a rewarding relationship. It was exciting to know the men who in the millions of years of earth's existence would be the first to attempt to free themselves from nature's forces which bound us to our globe and fly in illimitable space to other planets.

Columbus is held in awe because he dared sail on water into the unknown, where he might fall off the flat earth. Lindbergh is heroized because he dared to do in the air what ships had done countless times on water—reach Europe three thousand miles away. What awaited astronauts who undertook to be blasted off the face of the earth with sufficient force to break the gravitational chains and fly out a quarter of a million miles into the nothingness of space, with sufficient technical skill to find and land softly on another planet?

Innumerable obstacles presented themselves and increased anxiety about an "impossible" task. In a weightless condition, how would the blood circulate without the benefit of gravitational pull? How would the organs of the body function? Would the astronauts perish from unknown physical causes? Would meteorites or radiation or other mysterious forces in outer space crush the capsule, or disorient its equipment or the minds of its inhabitants? Could man, in defiance of nature's plan which separates billions of stars, succeed in invading the privacy of the celestial scheme? Even if the astronauts were not killed by the initial explosion underneath their seats, having a thrust of seven and a half million pounds, and even if by the miracle of miniaturized technology and magnified courage and skill, they landed on another planet, would the lifesaving apparatus which was to replicate the earth's conditions be able to sustain them? And how would they come back? If they did, would they be able to overcome the "bends" of another environment? What visible or invisible injury of deformity would they suffer from having forced themselves in and out of an environment not intended for man?

NASA and the astronauts reduced the overwhelming risks by fanatical preparation.

It began with the most stringent physical and psychological tests which could be devised. Every astronaut had to be less than forty years of age (later thirty-five years), less than five feet eleven inches tall, have a bachelor's degree or equivalent in engineering, and in the early program had to be a qualified jet pilot with at least fifteen hundred hours of flying time.

Then he was subjected to an unprecedented five-day physical examination conducted by the Air Force School of Aerospace Medicine at Brooks Air Force Base in Texas. Astronaut Michael Collins described the process with verve:

Inconvenience is piled on top of indignity, as you are poked, prodded, pummeled and pierced. No orifice is inviolate, no privacy is respected.

Cold water was poured into one of his ears causing his eyeballs to gyrate wildly as conflicting messages were relayed to his brain from one warm and one cold semicircular canal.

Your fanny is violated by the "steel eel", a painful and undignified process by which one foot of lower bowel can be examined for cancer or other disease processes. Your eyes and ears are tested with an unbelievable attention to detail, by some of the foremost specialists in the world.

After blood tests requiring repeated bloodletting (which would have satisfied an eighteenth-century physician), electrocardiac sensors which left no privacy for the slightest tick of the heart, and inspections of every joint, muscle, and organ of the body, the five-day ordeal ended, only to usher in the psychiatric tests. The endless search for "normalcy" by abnormal probing caused Collins to turn on his inquisitors. At least he demonstrated his sense of humor, itself a test of balance.

Then the shrinks take over where their more stable compatriots leave off. Thrust and parry. What are inkblots supposed to be anyway? Is one crotch in ten pictures too many? How can I describe the blank, pure white piece of paper? I said it was nineteen polar bears fornicating in a snowbank, and the interviewer's face tightened in obvious displeasure over my lack of reverence for his precious cards.

Michael Collins, *Carrying the Fire*

The simple external tests of a well-adjusted man were not ignored. Was he married? Did he have children? Was he a good family man? Was he religious? Had he functioned well previously? If we were going to send visitors out into the universe, they were to be as perfect as man could be, physically and psychologically.

Their preparation therefore included postgraduate courses never conceived of before.

On one occasion, when I visited Houston, several astronauts took me on a tour. It began prosaically with a visit to classrooms where astronauts sat at desks, while a professor of astronomy sought to make them familiar with heavens in which they might soon be wandering. Other classrooms hummed with the intricacies of engineering, geology, orbital mechanics, rocket propulsion, meteorology, physics of the upper atmosphere, guidance and navigation, digital computer systems, satellite orbits and trajectories, medicine and aerodynamics.

There were unique subjects never before studied by man. The astronauts had to understand each part of the equipment whose development over the years cost twenty-four billion dollars. They had to learn the ingenious technical means of correcting a defect, and the backup of backups for instruments which might fail when subjected to unanticipated stress.

Panel boards, looking like demonstration models for voting machines, but of course infinitely more complicated, were practiced on, to answer questions which assumed a stream of disasters.

From this college of esoteric aeronautics, I was taken by astronauts Ed White and Virgil Grissom to another building and into a simulator. This was an exact duplicate of the capsule which would fly the Apollo missions. It was on crossrails, so that the rolling motions in all directions could be reproduced. There were three narrow cots for the astronauts. How could they rest on such small beds? I asked, regretting my naïveté before the words were out of my mouth. Of course, they do not lie on beds in outer space. They virtually float over them, and the feeling is euphoric. Indeed, sleeping bags were devised in which their arms were taped down so they wouldn't rise and perhaps be injured. Since there is no up, down, or sides in a weightless environment, one can sleep while attached vertically to a wall, like a suit hung up, or even "upside down" on the ceiling.

In the training capsule, the upper left quadrant opened and the trainee saw the heavens, stars, or planets in precisely the way he would see them from his window in actual flight. A motion picture technique was used to create this outer world. One of the inventions in Hollywood which revolutionized the industry was a screen on which any locale in the world could be shown, full of movement, but integrated with the actors in front of it. By this simple device, actors could be seen walking, or driving in any foreign city, without transporting them. Astronomers and astronauts who had previously invaded the vacuum outside the earth had made it possible to produce motion pictures which enabled the astronauts to experience outer space while in the simulator.

But more was required of him. As I sat in the capsule, various indicators of the panel were deliberately knocked out. The astronaut had to restore them. Then, when this was made impossible for him, he had to "fly by the sky," navigating correctly not only through his knowledge of the stars, but by sunrays called airglow. This is the ionosphere. Of course, the moon and earth provide landmarks. All this while the capsule was deliberately pronated, so that it was flying sideways or even upside down.

Still, this was only a fraction of the drills which astronauts made for months on end. They spent from twelve to fourteen hours a day in the simulators.

A single illustration of the intricacies to be mastered is that the zone of atmosphere re-entry is only forty miles thick, and hitting such a target from 230 miles is, to use Collins' phrase, like "trying to split a human hair with a razor blade thrown from a distance of twenty feet."

Each flight afforded invaluable information for the next, thus narrowing the risk of unknown factors. Who can forget the Apollo 8 flight (Borman, Lovell, and Anders), a 147-hour trip with ten lunar orbits and a Christmas reading of the Bible seventy miles from the moon, "In the beginning God created the heaven and the earth. . . ."?

I know that in law, preparation is more important that inspiration. This was the rule for each astronaut. He was subjected to torturous procedures so that he would be ready for the most gruesome eventuality. To simulate takeoff and re-entry, he was whirled in a centrifuge until he weighed eight times his normal weight, and yet was required to speak into a microphone. During launching, the strain on all body organs compressed his lungs and pushed him toward unconsciousness. By experience he learned that he could overcome these effects and function. He was required to throw balls into a basket while sitting in a speedily revolving room to prove that he was not disoriented.

An astronaut who weighed 160 pounds on earth would only weigh ten pounds on the moon. He therefore had to be taught how to maneuver by training in the near weightless world of water at the naval scuba diving school.

Noise was another hazard. The Saturn V booster created 175 decibels, enough not only to destroy the inner ear, but cause convulsions and even death. So each astronaut was helmeted and bombarded by giant microphones to determine how much noise he could bear and still function efficiently.

The cruelest of all tests was devised to train the astronaut how to gain control of the capsule if it began to tumble in space. He was spun thirty revolutions a minute in three directions at once; head over heels, roundabout, and sideways. This stirred his innards and unhinged his body's balance. His eyeballs fluttered, but he had to train himself to pull and tilt his stick until three needles met at zero, thus stopping the wild descent.

One of the original astronauts with outstanding credentials even in that august group was Donald (Deke) Slayton. When first examined, his heart had functioned perfectly. However, after a centrifuge run, preceded the night before by an innocent beer, he registered fibrillations. He was bumped from the Mercury flight. He stayed in the program and because of his special competence became director of Flight Crew Operations. He was treated by Dr. Paul Dudley White, and by Dr. "Chuck" Berry, the space physician. During the time he was grounded, he repeatedly tried to persuade us not to include him in the distribution of money derived from publication of the flight stories, but neither the astronauts nor I would hear of it. Thirteen years later, in 1975, all doubts about his "heart murmur" were eliminated and he was permitted to fly in the Apollo which rendezvoused with the Russian spacecraft Soyuz.

Another example of overcoming a physical handicap was Alan Shepard. He had pioneered manned space for the United States in a suborbital flight. He had thus become the most famous of the original seven and perhaps of the program. But he developed Ménière's syndrome, which, due to elevated fluid pressure in the ear canal, affects balance and hearing. He was grounded. His leadership was recognized by designating him chief of the Astronaut Office.

Shepard hoped the infirmity would disappear, but after five years of frustration he submitted himself to surgery. A tube was implanted from the ear canal to the spinal column. The pressure was relieved and he was declared fit. He captained Apollo 14, which achieved the third successful landing on the moon.

Spacecraft might be defective too. Even the remote contingency that a crippled capsule might land in wild terrain rather than in the sea was not overlooked. Astronauts were taken to a jungle in Panama and taught how to survive. Indians taught them how to capture an iguana and broil it on a skewer to make it edible. The hazards of king-sized biting ants were explained and the astronauts learned to make a meal of coconut milk and iguana chunks wrapped in a leaf "cone." They had a plastic bag device which used the sun's energy to evaporate sea water, condensing pure drinking water from it. Unplanned incidents filled out the curriculum. While receiving intructions in an improvised classroom in the jungle a huge boa constrictor suddenly appeared. It was merely a pet of the instructor, but the astronauts could not discern its amiable intentions as it curled toward them.

The training of the astronauts did not begin when they were selected from hundreds of applicants. Just as our education begins with our parents, so the astronauts' skills began with their previous occupations.

The first seven astronauts were all test pilots for the Navy, Air Force, or Marine Corps (Lieutenant Commanders Alan B. Shepard, Jr., and Walter M. Schirra, Jr., Captains Virgil L. Grissom, L. Gordon Cooper, Jr., and Donald K. Slayton; Colonel John Glenn, Jr., and Lieutenant M. Scott Carpenter).

Actually, being a test pilot was more hazardous than being an astronaut, except for the terror of the unknown. The astronaut's duty was to take no intentional chance. "Abort the trip rather than risk your life" was the instruction. There were redundant safety systems.

In contrast, a test pilot had to take risks intentionally. His job was to bring the airplane to its ultimate theoretical capacity of speed, altitude, and strength of materials. He would try to put stress on the vehicle to find out whether its wings would break or its controls snap. He was ready to parachute if necessary, but there was no assurance he could. It took a daredevil to be a test pilot. Although he flew in the earth's atmosphere, he challenged the fates. The astronauts sought to avoid them.

Yet, despite guidance by control centers and sophisticated equipment, a test pilot, when he became an astronaut, had to steel himself to overcome fear, a fear which could not be identified, because no one knew what there was to fear. So, the most intrepid test pilots registered a sudden rise in heartbeat immediately before launch, as high as double the normal rate.

Eight astronauts died. Ironically, not a single one in flight.

Four astronauts died when their T-38 jet planes crashed, one in a collision with a snow goose. Another died in an automobile accident. I once suggested a slogan for an airplane company. "Of course, air travel isn't safe. You must get to the airport in an automobile."

On January 27, 1967, three astronauts were burned to death in an Apollo spacecraft atop a Saturn 1-B rocket. It was a practice session. The cause appeared to be a spark from an exposed wire, which set off a deadly conflagration in the pure oxygen atmosphere. The victims were Edward White, the first American to have stepped out in space in a previous Gemini flight. The second fatality was Virgil Grissom, who had been on Mercury and Gemini 3 flights. The third was Roger Chaffee, who had not yet flown on a mission.

The nation was shocked by these three deaths, particularly because it had become familiar with the men. Their agonizing cries for rescue as the flames exploded around them gave poignancy to their death.

The astronauts knew that they were brushing death when they left the earth to venture forth into the heavens, but to die in a stationary capsule on earth deprived them of their heroism and daring.

I had gotten to know these men and their families personally and my grief was deep.

The public was not fully aware of the hazards overcome, only that they had been. The circulation of blood in zero gravity might have been a fatal handicap. At first the heart pumped at the same pace as it did on earth. The astronauts' heads felt "full" as if they were hanging upside down in normal atmosphere. Had this condition continued, it might have become impossible for the men to function, and no trip could have been completed. Fortunately, after a few hours of weightlessness the heart "learned" that it was doing more than necessary and adjusted its pumping rate to the new environment.

However, the body's wisdom worked in reverse, too. It did not need as much blood in weightless condition and it manufactured less. The astronauts returned to earth with insufficient quantity. A simple procedure contributed to the solution—drinking more water. Astronaut Lovell recalled how strange it was that among the sophisticated technical instructions from control center was the cry, "Drink some water."

Similarly, their bodies, sensing that there was less need for the bones to be strong in outer space, reduced their calcium. Exercise was the solution, but how in the constricted space of the capsule? Isometric exercises were devised, and later, when Skylab was built, there was enough cubic footage to accommodate a stationary bicycle-type apparatus. The astronauts returned with less affected bone structure and marrow.

To the surprise of everyone, including the brilliant staff of doctors, swallowing, digestion, and defecation were not problems. Urine was expelled and feces were sealed in sanitary bags to be returned to earth.

What did cause annoyance was unexpected. Eye tears would not flow out because of lack of gravity. Being acidic, the retained fluid caused irritation and more need for drainage. There was nothing to do but remove the tears mechanically by blinking hard and rubbing the eyes.

The unexpected could also be as humorous as frightening. On one occasion, Pete Conrad pulled down the shades of Skylab so that he could go to sleep. Later Pete awoke and saw a green-eyed monster moving in the cabin. He pushed up the shades and saw his watch with a luminous dial floating in space.

The astronauts were troubled by contract problems. In 1959 a contract had been made by the original seven astronauts with *Life* magazine, giving it exclusive rights to the astronauts' personal stories under their by-lines. This involved not only their own experiences but also those of their wives and children. Obviously, the strain on their families was a moving story in itself. They watched their husbands and fathers shot into the unknown, perhaps never to be seen again. This agreement expired in 1962, and was replaced in 1963 with contracts with *Life* and Field Enterprises, Inc., under which *Life* agreed to pay $200,000 a year and Field an additional $320,000 a year to the astronauts.

In addition, *Life* and Field agreed to insure each astronaut for $100,000 a year during the four-year term of the contract.

Misgivings about these arrangements had been expressed in many quarters. President Kennedy, Vice-President Johnson, and a number of senators had been confronted with the ethical problem of the astronauts "exploiting" their military duties for private gains. NASA was deeply involved and sensitive.

The question of renewal in 1963 was not merely a legal but a moral one. The issue had been raised with fervor by those who sincerely believed that their objections were righteous. Did the astronauts have a right to sell their experiences for publication? The scales which measure ethical values do not tip readily one way or the other in all situations. In view of our concern that standards of conduct of officials and private citizens should not be demeaned, it is appropriate to analyze the astronaut issue.

Against the sale were two major arguments:

1. The Government financed the space program, and the story was its property, not subject to private sale.
2. The buyer of the story was put in a privileged position not available to the press generally.

For the sale, there were five arguments:

1. Precedent had established the right of public figures through books and otherwise to exploit their memoirs for private gains.
   Eisenhower, Truman, General Bradley, Kissinger, and Churchill and numerous others had done so. Why discriminate against the astronauts?
2. The stories also featured the wives and children of the astronauts. Their reactions were not public property.
3. The astronauts held full press conferences upon their return. The public had immediate access to the men.
4. The astronauts received merely military pay or its equivalent and were grossly underpaid for their special qualifications. Technicians working on boosters at Cape Kennedy received higher salaries. Furthermore, as international celebrities, they had special expenses. An astronaut and his wife told me that they had to outfit the family because President Kennedy had invited them to the White House and they could not afford to do so. Other expenses mounted because they were in the public eye.
5. Finally, their risks were so great that they were uninsurable. Ought we to deprive their families of a little security?

Originally, President Kennedy opposed the astronauts' contracts. However, a presentation to Vice-President Johnson, made him an advocate of private income for the astronauts and their families. When Kennedy learned of the special expenses incurred by the men the nation called upon to be ambassadors of heroism to the world, and who restored the United States to its pre-eminent position of resourcefulness, he shifted his position, particularly when NASA and the astronauts gave continued assurance that there would be debriefing on television for the first full information to the public.

In the meantime, the astronauts voted to divide all income in equal shares. This meant that the newest tyro, who might never fly but who was admitted into the group, received the same as the famous few who had made several flights and landed on the moon. Also the widows of the men who had perished were equal participants. Even when the three men who stunned the world by reaching and cavorting on a satellite wrote a book, *First on the Moon*, the royalties were shared equally by all astronauts.

In 1967 *Life* magazine renewed its contract, but Field Enterprises decided not to renew. The reason that Field dropped out was that it had paid $1 million while the Gemini program, which was to provide readership interest, was delayed. Also, prior to the moon flights, public excitement about "the greatest story in history" was below expectation. This was a mystery to all media. The answer might be the simple psychological fact that perfection diminished suspense and therefore interest. Recently I attended a performance of a Chinese acrobatic troupe which had been hailed for its incredible feats. The performers lived up to their notices with ridiculous ease. The audience applauded politely. Then during the building of a human mountainous structure, one on top of the other, a girl slipped and fell. She was unhurt. They tried again and succeeded. The applause and cheers rocked the theater and were so sustained that the next stunt had to be delayed. Acrobats have discovered this phenomenon and deliberately miss. When they finally "triumph," the audience responds vigorously. That was the trouble, from a public relations viewpoint, with the accomplishments in space. Everything (with one exception) was A-OK, and while we shook our heads in wonder at the pinpointed completion of the space journeys, the excitement was diminished by their very perfection. I could observe this in my own office. When Neil Armstrong visited me, there was a stir among the personnel to see the first man on the moon, but hardly as much excitement as when athletes like Julius Erving, Muhammad Ali, Joe Namath, or motion pictures stars appeared.

The astronauts were simply too successful and they, the public, and we rejoice that they had been.

One would think that men bound together by unique qualifications might have other common characteristics. Not so. The astronauts' personalities varied sharply. Neil Armstrong is taciturn and withdrawn. One of his comrades said that "when Neil says 'good morning' that's a big conversation." He was besieged with dozens of offers which would commercialize his fame, but he chose to be a professor of aerospace engineering at the University of Cincinnati. His home does not display any award or memento of his historic trip.

Charles "Pete" Conrad, the third man to walk on the moon, is at the opposite end of the personality scale. He is full of fun, and as colorful as he is competent. Frank Borman is aggressive and a quick-witted decision maker. Jim Lovell is open, warm, and friendly. "Buzz" Aldrin, the second man to step on the moon, is serious and reflective. So the astronauts are individualistic and as varied a group of men as one can assemble. They shared a common devotion to the space program and old-fashioned values of duty, country, service, and courage, and they were not embarrassed about it.

Tom Stafford, chief of the Astronaut Office, wanted to express his appreciation for the services we rendered to the astronauts. He surprised me by suggesting that if I provided him with a very tiny *mezuzah* it would be taken on the Apollo 13 trip to the moon and presented to me. He was referring to a miniature scroll of scripture which is enclosed in metal, and which many Jews attach to the outer frame of the door of their homes as a religious symbol. Those who are very devout touch the mezuzah with their fingers and bring them to their lips before crossing the threshold. Stafford mispronounced mezuzah, giving it an unrecognizable Oklahoma twang, and it took me some time to know what he was referring to. Even though I would have been gratified no matter what the object was, I was moved by his desire to make it a Jewish religious symbol. I obtained a mezuzah and gave it to him, but when he learned that it had an inner scroll which was inflammable, he suggested, as a substitute, a small metal Star of David. Once more he sought to please me by choosing a religious symbol. I found a tiny star and gave it to him.

On April 11, 1970, Lovell, as commander, Jack Swigert, and Fred Haise took off to the moon on Apollo 13. When they were hundreds of thousands of miles away from earth, an explosion ripped the command module. The mission was aborted, but could the astronauts be brought back in their crippled vehicle? Tens of millions of people watched breathlessly as control center, calling upon the daring, skill, and cool-headedness of the crew, sought to save them from death in a permanent orbit, the first burial in space.

They returned safely. Superstitious commentators referred to "13" as the omen of bad luck, while I chose to consider the tiny metal Star of David the lucky charm responsible for their miraculous return. Lovell sent it to me with a letter which prosaically authenticated that it had been "on board the Odyssey-Aquarius spacecraft during the space flight of Apollo 13 from April 11 to April 17, 1970." Like most heroes, the astronauts were tight-lipped about their exploits.

The qualities and qualifications of the astronauts have not been overlooked. William Anders became Ambassador to Norway; Frank Borman, president of Eastern Airlines; Michael Collins, director of the National Air and Space Museum of the Smithsonian Institution; Charles "Pete" Conrad, vice-president of McDonnell-Douglas Corporation; Donn Eisele, was Peace Corps director in Thailand; John Glenn, United States senator from Ohio; James Irwin, director of High Flight, an evangelical religious organization which he founded; Edgar Mitchell, a student of parapsychology; Harrison Schmitt, United States senator from New Mexico; Thomas Stafford, major general and commanding officer of Edwards Air Force Base; John Swigert, executive director of the Committee on Science and Technology, U. S. House of Representatives; and Alfred Worden, writer of several books of poetry and books for children.

Others will fare as well. They are unique men, but the impression which the public may have had of them as perfectly adjusted supermen is not true. In their midst have been divorces, a nervous breakdown courageously described about himself by Buzz Aldrin, involvement in esoteric studies such as ESP and Eastern religions. They were trained to be as perfect as physical specimens could be, but the frailties of human nature cannot be eliminated by any programs thus far devised.

The greatest resistance to the space program has resulted not from the failure to achieve, but from the question, "Why do we divert so much money, talent, and energy to outer space, when they are so sorely needed on earth?" "Are we guilty of a misdirection?" These are fair questions.

NASA and the proponents for the space program admit that it is a long-term investment, not to be judged by immediate direct benefit to the man in the street. Basic knowledge often results in incalculable gains which were not anticipated. Roentgen was not searching for a diagnostic means when he discovered the X-ray. He was engaged in abstract testing of the effects of electricity passing through rarefied gases.

When the British scientist Michael Faraday was asked what good was one of his discoveries, he replied, "What good is an infant?"

The cost of the space program does not diminish in any significant way the resources for social programs. It cost three billion dollars a year, which is approximately one per cent of the national budget to alleviate poverty, improve health, control pollution, and eliminate hunger.

During the decade which fulfilled President Kennedy's prediction that the United States would place a man on the moon, the program cost $24 billion. During the same period Americans spent four times that much on liquor, more than twice as much on cigarettes, and still more on pari-mutuel betting. Furthermore, the sums spent on the space program were fed back into American industry.

Also with progress, the proportionate cost of the space program is declining. When the first payload in space, Explorer I, was launched in 1956, it cost a half million dollars per pound. Less than ten years later, when Apollo 7 was launched, the cost was only five hundred dollars a pound. With reusable space shuttles by the 1980s the cost will be reduced to fifty dollars a pound.

Where can all this lead us to? Perhaps the greatest boon to mankind. We can get a glimpse of the possibilities by examining past experience. In 1903 the first theoretical study of rocket-powered spaceships was published by Constantine Tsiolkovsky. In that year also, the Wright brothers achieved the first flight in a power-driven aircraft. Would anyone then have thought that only sixty-six years later man would step on the moon?

Only forty years after Lindbergh's flight, twenty thousand people fly across the Atlantic Ocean every day. So his flight in a single-engine plane was not just a stunt of no practical use.

However, we need not wait for unknown future applications of basic knowledge to justify the space program. Its enormous immediate benefits have not been sufficiently appreciated.

Meteorological satellites have expanded our surveys from 20 per cent of the earth to 100 per cent and made weather forecasting more of a science than an art. In one instance, in 1969, they reported Hurricane Camille, the most intense storm to hit North America, and by giving early warning saved fifty thousand lives by evacuation.

Two butterfly-shaped spacecraft called Landsats circle the globe six hundred miles out in space. They detect new oil and mineral deposits and, even more important, hidden sources of fresh water. They can locate schools of fish, and can report pollution and even the source of it.

It is estimated that satellite information of forest fires, crop infestations, and droughts can save more than $5 billion for the United States and as much as $15 billion for the entire world.

Communications satellites made it possible for five hundred million people to see the first moon landing in 1969.

Satellite telephone calls (10 million in one year) have also reduced prices, almost one half from New York to London.

As an educational device the satellites will contribute much to change the world for better. They can beam lessons, as in India, to five thousand remote villages. They are virtually the only means to combat illiteracy in certain areas.

Satellites will, in the not too distant future, make possible audiovisual communications between any two persons anywhere on earth; the availability any place of any volume in any library; or the ability to have the finest doctors or other experts instantly available throughout the world.

How can one evaluate the lives which may be saved by military reconnaissance satellites which are so powerful that they reveal the number on an automobile license plate?

Scientists are studying how to gather solar energy in outer space and beam it to earth by microwave. This is now feasible because we could send up solar energy power stations. There would be no interruptions because of night or inclement weather. Abundant "free" energy would thus be available, and whether it would take thirty years to develop this technique or a shorter time depends on our resolve.

Those who insist that the space program is too far out (symbolically as well as literally) to do any good on earth overlook the industries which space technology has already spawned. The United States has a natural monopoly of every major computer system. This is the result of NASA's stringent requirements and developments.

To cite only two other spin-offs, there is the integrated circuit industry which has created billions of dollars of income, and the structural analysis computer program, which designs trains, bridges, and buildings at a cost saving of hundreds of millions of dollars.

In medicine, the outgrowth of miniaturized solid state circuitry developed for spacecraft has made possible the cardiac pacemaker. Thirty thousand of these lifesaving instruments are implanted each year in the United States and a similar number in the rest of the world. Also NASA's miniaturization requirements have made possible the development of blood-pressure and heart-monitoring systems, which can be inserted by hypodermic needle rather than surgery; remote monitoring systems which enable a nurse to keep continual check on dozens of patients; electrocardiograms by radio or telephone, and the storage of white blood cells and bone marrow needed in treatment of leukemia.

In industry, the space program has given us fire-resistant paints, stronger plastics, heated piping (which we can use to transport oil from Alaska's oil field), super glues, and much, much more.

Theoretical science researchers are rarely aware of their progeny, although later they can trace their origins back to their begetters. Most often they have passed away not knowing that their creations have grown from abstraction to practical everyday miracles.

Even if the space program had not already shown its usefulness in varied ways, we should be confident that the vast new area of knowledge it opens to us will reward mankind in spectacular ways not dreamed of today. It has always been so, when the border of ignorance has been pushed back, and it will be so again.

SICKNESS COMES ON HORSEBACK AND LEAVES ON FOOT

The closest I have ever come to death was in 1947 at the hands of a doctor—and it was a dentist, too.

It began insignificantly enough. A tooth had lost its nerve and died. It could be saved with root canal work. In all fairness, I was warned that the particular molar involved did not lend itself to root canal procedure and there was a risk of infection. But the thought of losing a tooth was in a small way as horrifying as losing a limb. Vanity, not judgment, spurred me to salvage.

The dentist began the drilling operation. In a microscopic way it was similar to the rigs which drill for oil, ever deeper and deeper. Despite all aseptic precautions, it happened. An abscess developed. Concerned, the dentist suggested that I consult a foremost dental surgeon, who taught at one of the universities. He looked his part—white-haired, gray-faced, and with a taut though confident body and manner. He wore gold-rimmed glasses (which didn't matter because special telescopic lenses fitted over them to give him 100-100 vision). An attached blinding light beamed from his forehead as if it was a cyclops' eye.

He was so besieged by dentists who needed his reputation and skill that I had to visit him in the circular amphitheater where he taught. There were no students present, but I imagined the stands were filled with cheering crowds. To get at the abscess, he had to cut underneath the lower jaw, leaving me with a scar for life, not of honor in combat, but a reminder of my indiscretion. He scraped and scraped. Thoroughness in surgery sometimes means doing more than is necessary. Although I was anesthetized, I felt the knife, if not the pain it caused. That was to come later. It was an eerie feeling, like dreams in which one suffers falls or other catastrophes without being hurt, but experiences fear.

Finally it was over. Immense wads of packing filled my jaw. I was directed to stay overnight in the surgeon's private hospital. He would see me in his office forty-eight hours later to remove the packing, and dress the wound.

That night I became acquainted with an old, senile nurse. The poor woman was still dedicated to her task, but she was addled. She wore her nurse's crown backwards. This should have warned me of what was to come. In the middle of the night, she woke me from a daze and somberly announced that she was going to sponge me down. She did this backwards, too. First she dried me with towels, from jaw to foot. Then she sponged me, and when I was thoroughly wet, she left.

I rang the bell. Other nurses came. They knew of their comrade's hard-arteried brain. One of them set up a watch for her, rather than for me. It was a good precaution. The old lady, her spic-and-span nurse's hat, not only backwards but askew, as if she were drunk, returned with a needle, to give me an injection probably ordered for another patient. She was intercepted and led out.

The worst was still to come. I reported to the surgeon, my mouth still agape with cotton. He set me in his unusual chair, which made the electric chair look like a simple contraption. It had arms which collapsed, pedals which rose, a profusion of lamps on extension arms which moved in many directions, water receptacles with fountains which added gurgling noises to the patient's own, and a huge X-ray box which swung overhead and could have crushed the patient, if its supporting arm had slipped from its hinge. Fortunately I do not suffer from claustrophobia. I merely worried that the surgeon would be so hemmed in that he couldn't reach me.

He began to remove the gauze, yard by yard. He looked like a magician pulling hundreds of silk handkerchiefs from an impossibly small container. Suddenly, I felt a rush of warmth fill my mouth. It trickled out of my lips. It was red. The surgeon was shocked. He acted quickly and efficiently to pack the gauze back into the cavity. His nurse hastily supplied a large wad of cotton and helped him press it down hard over the wound. This was no match for the blood which now came in uncontrollable spurts. It washed away the obstruction, like a torrent of water breaking through a dike. It rushed down my throat. Instruments to suck it up were placed in my already crowded mouth and made gasping noises as they attempted to keep pace with the flood. Now towels were shoved into my mouth and pressed down on the gushes. To no avail. They came out soaked.

What had happened was that the surgeon had accidentally cut the carotid artery and when the packing was removed my life's blood began to pour out. In simple words, he had cut my throat.

My mouth was wide open and my head rigid, but my eyes observed the surgeon. As the towels got redder, his face grew paler. I could see that he was panic-striken. He screamed at his nurse to get more cotton. Then after a 180-degree turn, as if he didn't know in what direction to take off, he ordered the nurse to call an ambulance. "No," he countermanded, "that will take too long. Hail a taxi. Hurry."

By this time the alarm had spread. Attendants appeared from all sides. Hasty orders were given to reserve an operating room at Mount Sinai Hospital for immediate surgery. Dr. John Garlock, a foremost surgeon, was called to perform an emergency ligation (tying) of the artery.

A taxi arrived. The chauffeur was unlucky. His car was destined to be a bloody mess. The surgeon and his nurse took me into the cab. The nurse had taken along a handful of towels. They quickly gave out.

I could read in their faces the fear that I might die from the bloodletting before a transfusion and ligation could be performed.

Although I was sick from involuntarily swallowing blood, I decided to do something about the crisis. What? I had to banish the hysteria which surrounded me. Excitement would only make my heart beat faster and accelerate the spurts of blood. I made a conscious effort to be very, very calm. My training as a trial lawyer, who must remain serene in the midst of storms, came to my aid. I deliberately breathed softly (a strange picture came to my mind of Houdini surviving burial by taking shallow breaths). I closed my eyes, and became immobile. I wouldn't even raise my hand to hold a towel. I relaxed every muscle in my body until I was limp. Whether it was an illusion or not, I felt that I had actually slowed my pulse, and that the blood was not gushing with previous fury.

At the emergency entrance of the hospital, a stretcher was ready. A surgeon hovered over me nervously, as I was taken to the operating room. Mildred and my parents had been summoned. Their shocked faces and tears when they saw my ghoulish wide-open mouth packed red challenged my effort to avoid emotional strain. My blood was typed. Nurses were rushing in and out of the surgery room. Doctors with masks were arriving hastily, heightening the impression that I was experiencing a bad dream.

Then Dr. John Garlock arrived. If he was concerned, he hid it like a good psychologist. I was grateful. He smiled, and in a casual tone, as if there was no emergency (I remembered the lecture of a professor to his students, "If a severed artery is not sutured in two minutes, the patient will die. You can do it in two minutes, if you don't hurry!"), he said:

"Louis, I see that they have fixed you up good. Don't worry, I'll take care of it. You'll be all right."

Moving as little as possible, I motioned for a pad and pencil, indicating that I wanted to write something.

He handed me his doctor's notebook and a pencil. I wrote:

I am not alarmed. I feel that the bleeding is slowing down. I really think it will coagulate. Please don't operate. Give me another 15 minutes. It may not be necessary.

His face looked severe as he read the note. Then the vertical lines in his cheeks gave way to a grin, and finally a full smile.

"Anyone who can write a note like this at this time—I'll take a chance on."

He left for a few minutes, to talk with the anesthetist, nurses, and assistants. He had ordered a delay of the surgery, to the dismay of the dental surgeon, who had become so jittery that I wanted to write another note suggesting that he be given a sedative.

Dr. Garlock called for a chair and sat down slowly. I felt he was in tune with my pace. Then he casually held my hand, testing the pulse without looking at a watch. I renewed my concentration on slowing the blood flow. There was no doubt that each heartbeat was no longer accompanied by a gush into the mouth. Dr. Garlock did not want to disturb me even to determine whether time was a healer or a fatal loss. But one could see that the flood had slowed to a trickle. I did not have to write another note. My eyes did the pleading. He gave me another extension, for which I was more grateful than any I had ever received in court.

The bleeding stopped. I was placed in a bed so gently that the pillow hardly dented. Intravenous relief was given. That night, I did not move an inch no matter how uncomfortable it was to lie in one position. We do not realize it, but each of us exercises a good deal during a night's sleep. Our muscles need renewed circulation which can only be obtained by turning and twisting. A good night's rest does not mean what it literally says. It really means some healthy tossing about. So my determination not to move subjected me to a special kind of pain, like that which comes from being forbidden to scratch an itching skin.

Came the day when the packing would again be removed. Would there be another disaster? This time, Dr. Garlock, surrounded by the dental surgeon and nurses, performed the task. His long, stubby fingers, famous for their strength and sensitive dexterity, were applied to the mundane task, usually done perfunctorily by a nurse. He gently, inch by inch, removed the packing. If there was the slightest resistance, he sensed it, stopped, and with faintest movements freed the gauze before proceeding. As the doctors and nurses peered over his shoulder, I had the image of detonating squads during the war removing a pin from a bomb with breath-holding caution. Only this time it was not their lives which were at stake. It was mine.

At last the task was done. There was no mishap. The very blood with which we had struggled became its own healer and sealed the artery. From then on it was nature's process, not knives and sutures, which completed the cure. Of course there was much discomfort, but fortunately it cannot be re-experienced by recollection. Joys can be. Pain can't.

The cure was not perfect. For about six months I suffered from trismus, a partial locking of the jaw. I nevertheless continued to try cases and make speeches. I had to fall back on my singing days, and by forming circles with my lips, I was able to project my voice even though I could only open my jaws two inches. I missed only one early engagement, an introduction of President Truman at a public function at the Waldorf-Astoria in New York. I would have had to talk through clenched teeth, and I didn't want him to think I was a Republican.

The greatest healer I have ever met was a naturopath. His name was Sholem Baranoff. It was by coincidence that I got to know him, but his influence on me, like that of all great teachers, was profound and lasting. To a considerable extent I have followed his precepts for good health, and as much as possible avoided medicines and particularly surgery. I have never taken a headache pill and only on a few rare occasions, in all my life, an aspirin or its equivalent. I shun drugstore drugs like a plague.

My acquaintance with Baranoff started about forty years ago. Mildred and I had returned from a trip abroad which included Israel. There was a white miracle in that land of miracles. It had snowed in Jerusalem. The unseasonable weather caught us with our resistance down. We returned debilitated from our arduous travels and encountered the penetrating freezing cold of a New York winter. We decided to go south. Florida was a natural choice, but Miami and its environs represented the hectic life of its self advertised playground. Was there anything on the west coast of Florida? Yes, Safety Harbor Spa. Every word of the title appealed to me. We tried it.

It was what I had dreamed of, quietly beautiful and isolated. Its feature was a former state building where spring waters of three kinds were bottled. As the state literature did not hesitate to inform, these springs had been discovered by Ponce de León, and might be the fabled fountain of youth. This impressive building had been bought and transformed into a private dining room, the nucleus of the spa. In the center of the room was still a well, from which waters could be tapped. In each room were three large bottles of differently numbered waters, whose taste, after a while, was sufficient identification.

We checked into a simple room, which had none of the grandeur of the state building. Within a few moments, the telephone rang. "Dr. Baranoff would like to see you."

"Who is he?" I asked.

"He is the owner, and you must be examined, so that he can prescribe the food you are to have, and what spa treatments are permissible."

It was the rule. We could not waive it. Reluctantly, we went downstairs and met Baranoff for the first time. The immediate impression was of a slight, thin man with a shock of hair as white as his smock, contrasting with black eyebrows and dark, penetrating eyes. His head was wide on top because his snowy long hair floated sideways but tapered to a triangle despite a strong chin. We couldn't tell his age. Judged by his vitality, he was about fifty, but his drawn, lined face might make him seventy. His kindness and sincere interest in us quickly overcame our resistance.

After a few preliminaries, and before the usual procedure of blood pressure, listing of former illnesses and the like, he carefully wrote down what our eating habits were. He reached for the smallest detail. It was an emphasis, I learned later from his lectures, which was the key to his diagnosis of all ills.

"Your food is the chemistry you give to the body. You are what you eat. But each person is different. Orange juice is excellent Vitamin C for some, but harmful to others. When we discover the needs of your body, we are on the road to good health."

This was not so startling in 1951, but in the early 1900s, when Baranoff first wrote his theories, it was. His other theories, which I shall describe, aroused the scorn of the medical authorities, but he was to live to see many of them accepted by foremost doctors.

After a little while, he ushered me into an adjoining room, where there was a cubicle, to undress. Then he put me on a table and began to press different parts of my body with steel-strong fingers, here gently, there severely. The first words out of his mouth were, "Your thyroid glands are not functioning right."

Doctors had told me after several checkups that my metabolism was low. His accuracy on mere touch surprised me. My lawyer's skepticism came to the fore.

"What makes you say that?" I said casually.

"You winced when I touched you here," he replied, applying a heavier finger which made me jump. "There is a lack of circulation, or you wouldn't feel it any more than when I touch you here."

"Well, I must admit Doctor, you are right. That's the only thing the doctors found that was wrong."

"So, what have they done for you—given you thyroid pills?"

"Yes."

"Of course. And what will that do? They'll just weaken your heart." Angrily, "Throw them away. Has anyone asked why a person as healthy as you are shouldn't be producing sufficient thyroid extract?" Without waiting for an answer, he turned warm and friendly and spoke in a conspiratorial tone.

"I'll tell you what we'll do. I'll give you a simple exercise for your neck which will correct the defect, but only on one condition." He paused. "If you promise to do it every day without fail. O.K.?" He held out his hand to seal the bargain. We shook hands on it. He then illustrated certain exercises which were designed to bring blood to the neck and particularly to the thyroid gland. In my later annual checkups, there has never been a finding of low metabolism.

I was intrigued by his psychological approach, exacting a promise in the interest of the patient. The concern for my well being was an act of friendship which elicited confidence.

"I will write out a diet for you." Studying the notes he had taken of what I like to eat, he prepared a card, which was an instruction not only for the kitchen but for the waitress. His wife, Lisa, was the chief cook. She had to know you, too. Her inquiries were not the mere formal ones, but the gathering of findings, which in consultation with her husband would result in adjustments on the card. Every person at the table was served a different meal, suited to the idiosyncratic needs of his body. We couldn't deviate. The waitress, trained to be polite but firm, would not honor our requests.

This caused some grumbling, but as most victims found themselves feeling and looking better, they yielded to the discipline, while poking fun at it. I induced my father and mother to visit there for a vacation. For many years he had tried to lose some thirty pounds and had been unable to do so. Being a man of will, he tried all sorts of methods. He would fast Wednesdays, but then he caught up with his hunger the rest of the week.

Under Baranoff's regime, he lost weight, but he amused everyone around him by ridiculing the diet. He would look at the plate before him, nine tenths of which was shining porcelain, and announce, "I usually leave more than this," or "No wonder they make money here. There is no expense spared for food." Nevertheless he and my mother were captivated by Baranoff. There was a common old-country tie among them. Baranoff would gather a few aficionados of Sholem Aleichem, or Peretz, or Bialik and in an improvised entertainment he would read some of their writings in English or sometimes in the original Yiddish. All this intimacy was before Safety Harbor Spa became a roaring success, with million-dollar buildings, modern spa equipment from steam to sauna, and from pools to plush paraphernalia.

Occasionally, guests would arrive who knew nothing of Baranoff's dictatorial dedication to their health. We would hear some commotion in the dining room, because they had demanded bread, and the waitress had told them it was against the rules. The Friday night, at his weekly lecture, Baranoff dropped his benign attitude, and pointedly addressed the rebellious guests.

"This spa has certain theories about good health. I have spent a lifetime developing them. Those who come here and want to learn to be healthier live up to these principles. Those who do not believe in them have no right to interfere with the others. They have a perfect right to live and eat as they choose. There are many fine hotels nearby. They are welcome to leave. If they didn't know about our rules, and came here by mistake, we will make no charge for the day they have been here, and we wish them luck and good health."

Each of his lectures dealt with a different part of the body—heart, liver, pancreas, the mind, and why they failed us. The stress always was on prevention, not cure. Underlying all his theories was a simple leitmotif. Proper food intake, which "keeps the blood thin" and therefore circulating freely, and proper daily exercise of a certain kind, which brings the good blood to the vital organs, were the key to health. "A clear flowing stream will wash away impurities. They will never be noticed. But a stagnant pool will sooner or later be filled with rot."

A half century after he first argued this oversimplistic rule, he had the satisfaction of reading to his audience the conclusion of the famous Dr. Paul Dudley White after a lifetime of study and experience, that healthy eating habits and exercise were the best preventives of heart disease and for that matter of other afflictions.

Baranoff was opposed to all diets. He insisted that one must learn to eat properly. Then there would be no need to cut down intake, be tempted back again to excess, and go through the sacrifice again of severe discipline. He saw no need to be deprived at all. Healthy foods were more delicious than unhealthy ones. He had his own way of persuasion.

"When you were a child, and you wanted to paste a picture into a book, what did you use for glue? Flour and water—right? Well, that is what bread is made of—especially after modern processors remove the only nutritious thing in it, the brown wheat. That's the paste that cakes are made of, and they add all sorts of goo on top of it. They are filled with white sugar from which has been removed the only valuable nutrient to make it white, and a chemical added to make it shine."

After a number of such descriptions one was inclined to look at bread or cake as pretty revolting objects. Then he described a beautiful pear, a rose-tinted peach, a ripe purple plum, grapes filled with sunshine, dates and figs bursting with sweetness, toasted almonds and other variety flavored nuts, before he ennobled the taste of a tomato, artichoke, asparagus, squash, and other exotic-tasting vegetables. Finally he turned to the protein family, in which richly flavored broiled pompano, or juice-covered lean meat crowned the meal and delighted the stomach. One had to hear the saliva flowing dulcet tones in which these descriptions were given to understand why listeners developed a love affair with foods they couldn't stomach before.

"Now, when instead you eat highly peppered and salted pastrami and corned beef, inside two thick pieces of bread, and then some ice cream with whipped cream or chocolate cake, what happens to all the paste which you pushed into your stomach? Your digestive process cannot get rid of all of it. Ordinarily a mound of paste would form which could obstruct your bowels and perhaps kill you. But nature protects you. To prevent this from happening, it passes it into the bloodstream, which then spreads it thin along the arteries to which it adheres. For a long time, you don't notice it. But with the years, the coated arteries get narrower and narrower. Your blood supply to the heart and other organs diminishes. They become undernourished and weak, and victims of all sorts of diseases. The doctors fill you with medicines. But the underlying cause not only continues, it gets worse, because of your suicidal eating habits. Then one day, the blood can't get through the artery at all. You get a heart attack and die. The doctors call it an occlusion. Your friends say, 'He was such a strong, healthy person, and suddenly he dropped dead.'

"Suddenly? It took years of stupid eating to bring it about. You were killing yourself surely but gradually. Your body is the greatest doctor you will ever know. Why do you abuse it? Why don't you give it a chance to keep you healthy."

He interrupted with an epigram, "Nature cures and the doctor sends you the bill."

His nontechnical and, I am sure, at times, nonmedical analysis aroused resistance and sometimes abuse from doctors. I recall my partner, Walter Beck, who knew much about medicine (and had tried malpractice cases), reacting to one of Baranoff's lectures. Baranoff had resorted to his homey analogies, which lent themselves to ridicule from sophisticated, medically trained men.

"Your arteries are like the plumbing in your house. Fatty deposits are like rust that close the openings and make the water come slowly, then in drips and then not at all."

Beck laughed at the plumbing analogy. It demonstrated Baranoff's lack of medical knowledge, which had been such a boon to better health. Our longevity span is constantly increasing, he pointed out.

Several years later, CBS network announced a special program revealing the first motion picture X-ray technique. It enabled the viewer to see blood actually flowing through an artery. It looked like a river running through a ravine. A number of famous doctors and scientists were commenting on the improved opportunity to make observations. The same artery was photographed at different intervals, many months apart. One could see a little hill form inside the artery which obstructed the natural speed of the blood. A later X-ray motion picture showed the hill, considerably enlarged, and the adjoining tissue much thicker. A still later picture clearly showed a narrowing of the artery which impeded the flow. The accompanying lecture by the professor explained that it was cholesterol or other fatty substances which were responsible for the closing of the artery, so that in the last demonstration the blood was desperately trying to get through a pinhole in the clogged artery.

Then the lecturer, apparently as a concession to the assumed low intelligence of the mass television audience, decided to simplify the matter for easy comprehension.

"You see," he said, "the arteries are exactly like the plumbing in your house. When rust gathers on them they grow smaller, and one day we have to clean them out or replace them. Well, it is not as easy to remove the fatty deposits which coat the artery, though we have tried, and of course it is even more difficult to replace them. So the lesson is, ladies and gentlemen, avoid food with saturated oil. Stay away from breads, sweet desserts, chocolates and fats."

Baranoff had his own ideas about what he called compatible eating, more accurately, compatible foods. He contended that there were two kinds of digestive systems. Tigers and lions could digest only meat, not grass or carbohydrates. On the other hand cows could only digest grass, not meat. Man was one of those animals who could digest both. However, the digestive juices required for meats were different from those for carbohydrates. Our bodies produced pepsin and hydrochloric acid to break down meat. But to digest bread, spaghetti, or other carbohydrates other juices were required, such as saliva and pancreatic juice. It was incompatible to mix the two. So, if one ate bread with steak, he was eating incompatibly, because the digestive juices necessary for meat were useless to digest bread, and vice versa. Hydrochloric acid needed to break up meat molecules was unnecessary and inimical to carbohydrates. They clashed. This was the cause, he argued, of heartburn, gas, and indigestion. He therefore counseled that it was all right to eat a protein meal or a sensible carbohydrate meal of spaghetti or potato, vegetables, whole-wheat bread, and even ice cream or fruit, but not with bacon, steak, or other proteins. These were incompatible.

"A piece of bread begins to be digested in the mouth. Saliva is essential. It should therefore be fully chewed before swallowing. But a piece of meat, which doesn't need saliva, could be swallowed without injuring the digestive process. Use one or the other of your digestive systems. Don't mix them."

Baranoff did not claim to be the originator of the compatible eating theory. It came from the old Hays diet. I was never convinced of its soundness. Many authorities insist that our bodies adjust to far greater "clashes" of intake. It had one virtue, however. It reduced the quantity of food we ate. If one eliminated bread or a potato from his meat meal, it might or might not avoid digestive incompatibility, but it surely reduced the calorie consumption. This in itself was desirable. On this point he was adamant and I don't believe contradictable. He insisted that our bodies needed much less food than any of us thought, and that by constantly overstuffing ourselves, we compelled the body needlessly to struggle with burning up the food to turn it into glucose. This was a waste of our energy. It was counterproductive to "thin blood" and good health.

"When you sit down to dinner in a restaurant with your friends, what do you do? You have a cocktail. You are hungry. So while chatting and waiting for the menu, you eat a roll, maybe two, with plenty of butter on it. You do not realize it, but you have already eaten a full meal and not a very wise one, either. You ought to get up and go home. Then the waiter arrives, and you begin all over again. If you put a duplicate of everything you ate thereafter into a pail and under the table, you would be ashamed to carry it out of the place."

Another basic, perhaps oversimplistic theory of his was that in essence there was only one disease, toxicity.

"We have many names for diseases. Wherever there is a weakness in the body, the poisons of toxicity cause trouble. If the frailty is in the shoulder, we call it arthritis; in the blood supply to the heart, we call it heart disease; in the lung, pneumonia; in the eyes, cataracts, but the cause is all the same. If the blood is pure from right eating and you circulate it properly with exercise, none of these conditions will occur."

His lectures were never just strictures for health and longevity. They were accompanied by stirring assertions of the joys of living, of being of happy disposition, of love and generosity. He caused laughter, by mim-

icking the sour face of someone suffering from dyspepsia; his nastiness
to his wife and children, his crotchety walk, and his general misery.
Then he enacted a healthy man. His eyes glistened like those of a
young lover. He pranced about nimbly, and held out his arms as if he
would embrace the world. "Which one do you think will succeed in his
business? Which one will be popular? Which one will make everybody
around him happy? Which one will love and be loved?"

I noticed that he eschewed references to the word spiritual. It was
too ephemeral. His convictions were based on physical perfection. He
pored over anatomy books day and night, comparing their learning with
his own tactile observations. He strove for the impossible. One had to
experience his "treatment" on a table. It was chiropractic or osteopathic. It was uniquely Baranoff. His fingers touched, probed, and
explored endlessly. They were as sensitive as the heralded sandpapered
fingers of a safecracker. Patients dubbed them X-ray fingers. When he
thought he discovered a knotted muscle, or a slight swelling, or a lack
of elasticity, his whole body stiffened, like a hunter who senses his prey.
He soon knew. When he touched more deeply there was pain: the
body underneath him coiled and reacted. Then he would massage the
area, ignoring the agonized outcries of the patient. He became remorseless. He would press still harder. It was his only streak of cruelty.
His dedication to the patient's health overcame his sympathy for the
writhing body. Time and again he would return to the same spot.
Each time the pain was less.

"You see, I have forced circulation there and it is bringing you relief."

Sometimes after such a treatment the patient would go to his room
and fall soundly asleep for an hour or two. I had this experience a number of times. Could it be not only that the muscle or tendon had been
relieved, but that the nerves involved in the area also responded?
Baranoff thought so. He claimed that there were "plexuses," or nerve
centers, which fed various organs. If one of these was constricted, he
knew that the organ dependent on it, whether kidney or liver, bladder
or prostate, could not be functioning right. This was his method of detecting that a vital organ in the body was not functioning as it should.
The patient almost jumped off the table with pain when he dug ino a
plexus which was related to the defective organ.

Although Baranoff may not have known it, this theory had ancient
origins. In effect it was related to acupuncture, but without "insulting"
the body with piercing needles. I have heard of it since as "zone therapy," pressing certain nerve ends, particularly in the toes, which indicate by pain that the organs of the body "fed" by them (echoes of
Baranoff's nonscientific explanations) are not functioning properly. A

touch of a specific area of a toe, "connected with the ear," will not hurt one who has no hearing problem. However, another person, troubled with slight deafness in his left ear, will register intense pain from the same touch. To this extent, credence in zone therapy is heightened. Is it possible that we will develop techniques for bringing nerve energy supply to our organs, as we bring blood supply to our muscles to improve them?

I do not know whether the plexus response explained Baranoff's deduction or whether his general highly developed "instincts" about the body informed him. I am sure that he was sincere, and my skepticism was reduced by some extraordinary cures I witnessed with my own eyes. I shall cite only a few, although there were others.

A woman arrived who was so crippled that despite the sympathy she aroused, there was grumbling by a number of guests that they had come for a vacation and not to a sanitorium. She was bent over so low that she used two small canes to prevent her from toppling over. She was apparently a woman of means and had had treatment by foremost doctors and neurologists at leading clinics. They could not straighten her up. It was a gruesome sight to see her practically on all fours like an animal. She had been recommended to Baranoff. Several days later, she walked into the dining room, straight up. At first no one was sure it was she. Then when a murmur went through the room that indeed it was, everyone stood. Cheers broke out. Women cried. Some yelled it was a miracle. It was a hysterical scene. Baranoff had to quiet the audience and address them. He severely chided them for nonsensical talk about miracles. There were none. The human body is a remarkable machine, and when it breaks down, a good mechanic, that's all he was, can sometimes find the defect and straighten it out. "It only proves that despite the fact that we abuse our bodies, it is never too late to make them function right."

Another case was that of a car dealer who had become well known through radio advertising as "The Smiling Irishman." He was Jewish, but I suppose it wouldn't have sounded as well had he called himself "The Smiling Jew" or "The Smiling Italian." Perhaps the compliment to the Irish persuaded them to overlook the deception. He had such a severe heart condition that he had to retire from his business. He was not even permitted to drive a car. Baranoff insisted that he had no heart condition at all. His heart was quite strong. It was a circulation problem. There wasn't enough blood flowing to it. He put the man on a "cleansing" diet, taught him mild exercises, and spent hours kneading him with those X-ray fingers of his. The man recovered. He drove his car again, and went back to his business.

Baranoff had his failures, too, and it was my own senior law partner,

Louis Phillips, who was the victim of one of them. Louis had a family history of heart disease. The inexorable code written in his genes and chromosomes did not except him from his fate. Five years before he died, from hardening of the arteries around his heart, Baranoff detected the condition. He did not want to alarm Phillips, but he told me, "Your partner has a very serious condition. The muscles near his heart are so rigid they feel like stone."

He attempted to dig deeply into them to soften them with blood supply. His powerful fingers cracked one of Phillips' ribs. Understandably, Louis would have nothing more to do with Baranoff. "Let him illustrate how strong he is on somebody else's ribs," he said. But he was tolerant enough to permit his wife, Helen, to go to Safety Harbor, which she continued to do long after Louis died.

Another illustration involved Wilbur Wood, the sports editor of the now defunct New York *World Telegram*. He had a severe case of diabetes and administered his own insulin injection daily. Baranoff disagreed with the medical theory that once the pancreas stops functioning it cannot be revived. He believed that sometimes it can be induced to produce its vital extract. By careful exercises, deep finger therapy, and a special diet in which onions were heavily favored, he stimulated the pancreas, constantly reducing the insulin intake. Finally he told Wood he could give up the needle. Wood was scared. Baranoff invited him to be tested daily in a nearby hospital. The miracle had happened. When Wood returned, his doctors couldn't believe what had happened. They considered it one of those rare remissions which occur even in cancer. I saw the letter one of them wrote to Baranoff, expressing his delight and surprise and asking for information of the treatment.

Baranoff rejected uniformity in exercise as he did in food. Every individual was just that to him, an individual, not a type. He improvised exercises for each person to correct some particular defect. One could see him experiment until he found the movement which would affect the part of the body he "was after."

"Let's see, hold this leg down and move your right leg out to the side." His fingers tested the result. He was unsatisfied. He tried again and again, until he literally felt that the exercise was reaching the desired result. I was round-shouldered. This he explained was due to a "sway" in the spine. He struck a harmless blow with the side of his hand, like a karate chop into the lower spine.

"There's no use working on the shoulders. They are the result of this down here. Now we can straighten that curve a little. Let me show you how."

He made me get off the table. He bounced on, got on his knees, dug his head inward, and then pushed his hands forward as far as they could reach. He asked me to put my hand on his lower back. I felt the convex curve rise and get flatter. He assured me that even at my age the spine could be straightened, provided I did this exercise at least five minutes a day.

"The body is good to you. It never gives up. It's you who give up."

When he lectured on Friday nights, his enthusiasm broke through all formalities. He stressed mobility.

"If you're forty and you walk like this, you're an old man." He imitated a slouching shuffle, which looked very much like the gait of some of the young men in the audience who laughed embarrassedly.

"But if you walk like this when you are ninety, you are a young man."

This was true of arms as well as legs. He said not one of a hundred persons could lift his arms straight up, alongside and touching his ears. He demonstrated. Suddenly, he took off his tweed jacket, opened his tie, and lay flat on the floor, illustrating knee movements to the chest. "This," he would say from a prone position, "is wonderful for your liver." He held up a fist and closed the fingers tight. "That's the effect of bending your knees tight to your stomach. It squeezes the liver. You ought to do this every morning without fail."

He disapproved of typical American exercises, which developed the biceps and other muscles, not needed for the sedentary life we led. In this respect he was in harmony with yoga theories that exercises should be mild and directed toward stimulating blood flow to vital organs. For example, he advised just simple stretching in the morning and several times a day as most beneficial. "Watch a cat or dog after it has slept. It stretches . . ." He pushed out his hands as if they were paws, threw back his head, and registered relief. Then he lay down and stretched his legs as if they were the hind legs of an animal. "This brings the blood to all parts of the body. It is wonderful." He looked so happy we imagined he had grown healthier in our presence.

When he prescribed numerous exercises which I should do every morning, I would laughingly comment that I would never get to the office. He saw no humor in this. With utmost earnestness, he said, "Have you an appointment diary in your office?"

"Of course."

"Well, write in every morning from nine to ten the name of your most important client. It is you."

After his lectures he would invite questions. There was no lack of skeptics in the audience. "Don't you believe in any medicines? Hasn't medical science eliminated many diseases?"

"Of course, I believe in medicines, chiefly those that nature provides.

They are in every food. The water, after parsley is boiled, is a diuretic. Grape juice is nourishing for the nerves. Grapefruit cleanses the blood. Onions stimulate the pancreas and produce nature's insulin. The trouble with synthetic medicine is that you don't know its complete effect on the body. Medicines are necessary when you are sick. But why should you be? Man's natural state is to be in good health. Live right and you won't need doctors' medicines. They will be in your food."

The year after penicillin was discovered, Baranoff included it as a topic in his talk.

"It will save many lives, so it is a blessing. People torn apart in an automobile accident will survive because of it. Mastoid operations may become unnecessary.

"But, I warn you, ladies and gentlemen, it will also kill hundreds of people. Already hospitals report many deaths of people allergic to it.

"Every time a new drug or pill is discovered, we are in danger that later, it will be learned that it caused cancer, or blindness, or lord knows what. No drug is intelligent enough to attack only the virus that we don't like. Before we sing Halleluja about a patient cured by penicillin, we ought to examine the lacy tissue of his kidney and see what happened to it.

"Please, please, don't ask your doctor or permit him to give you penicillin unless there is no alternative to save your life. There almost always is. The oldest remedy is still good. Sweat out the disease. Fever is nature's way of burning up the germ. Don't kill the fever with aspirins. It is a warning signal, and you don't cure the disease by silencing the alarm bell. Medicines often sweep the disease under the rug. That is why colds reappear again and again, during the winter. You have deceived yourself by thinking you have got rid of it.

"If you must take penicillin, be sure to drink a lot of orange juice with it."

Some of his warnings about food provoked challenging questions.

"Why do you condemn eggs and milk? The whole world knows that eggs are a healthy food. If you believe in nature, how about the fact that babies are nourished by milk at their mothers' breasts?"

Almost half a century earlier, Baranoff had written severe criticism of eggs. He did not know the word "cholesterol," but his study of the content of food and, above all, his knowledge of the human body learned by touch, combined with detailed information about the food intake of each patient, made him suspicious of certain foods. Eggs were one of them. He was not a laboratory scientist. His was an empirical approach. He experimented and observed until he reached a conclusion. He applied the Thomas Edison method to health research, using trial and error. Today, the great laboratories have confirmed the high cholesterol content of eggs, seafood, butter, liver, and meats and other foods with saturated fats. So very respectable medical authorities now agree with Baranoff that eggs should be eaten sparingly.

He was opposed to shellfish, chiefly because they were scavengers. He pointed out that scaled fish ate plankton, and not the filth at the bottom of polluted waters. He warned that scavengers would sooner or later infect us. Much later hepatitis, unfortunately, became a well-known word.

As for Baranoff's opinion about milk: "It is too concentrated a food for a mature person. It has a high calcium content. This is necessary for growing children, whose bones are growing. In an older person, it is not needed, and nature deposits the excess calcium near joints. Then you have arthritis.

"Also, notice that while we swallow a glass of milk like water, a child doesn't drink milk. It chews it. It knows instinctively that it is a very concentrated food, not to be gulped down.

"Besides, once we take the child away from the breast, we cut down the concentration in milk. We devise formulas. That is really a way of diluting the milk."

At one time he had been impelled by devotion to principle as well as to purity of food to be a vegetarian. But, as always, he bowed to nature, the final arbiter. Man belongs to that species of animals whose digestive tracts prospered on meat, even raw meat (witness steak tartare). Also, meat has the highest concentration of protein of any food. So be it, then.

There was no liquor bar at Safety Harbor. There were grapefruit bars. At four o'clock, one opened around the pool. Others were strategically placed inside. You also had a choice of apple or grape juice, depending on the instruction on your card. Dull? Surprisingly not. The cold, juicy half grapefrut with a little honey on it hit the spot after a day outdoors and a receptively empty stomach. Still, there was a thrill in sneaking directly across the street where there was a bar, whose owner understood temptation and the excitement of violating rules. He was the kind of man who would build an oasis in the desert. Guests of the spa ran into each other there, and the sinners laughingly exchanged recriminations.

Actually, Baranoff was not opposed to alcohol. He considered it a natural food and a healthy stimulant, preferring scotch to Bourbon because the former tended to dilate the arteries, while the latter to constrict them. When, after several weeks of discipline, we bade farewell to return to New York, he would share a scotch or, preferably, a little brandy with us. "I am opposed to the cocktail hour, not the cocktail," he would say. "It comes at the worst time. Liquor stimulates the appetite, and we do not need such artificial stimulation before sitting down to eat. We eat too much anyhow."

The only time a question embarrassed him was when he was asked about smoking. He said it was a terrible habit. What could be worse than substituting smoke for clean air in the lungs? Smoking had increased lung cancer enormously. It injured the eyes. It caused bronchial conditions and sometimes fatal emphysema.

Then why was he embarrassed? Because he smoked. He explained that once this awful habit had been acquired, it might take more toll of the nervous system to quit than to cut down. He therefore had reduced his smoking to a few cigarettes a day. He sought to mollify his confession with a little philosophy: "Nothing done in moderation can be very harmful."

In a negative way, he had provided another lesson. That a man of his adamant convictions buttressed by an iron will should not be able to give up the filthy weed only demonstrated what a powerful addiction smoking was. True, he had a habit of sixty, perhaps seventy years to overcome. I could tell he came from Russia by the way he held his cigarette between the middle two fingers, so that when he put it between his lips the rest of the hand covered his lower face. I am sure that he also bit a piece of sugar before sipping his glass of russet-colored tea. Age, and I suspect illness, finally freed him from his only inconsistency. In later years, he has not smoked at all.

He was such a blind lover of nature that even when it contradicted him he yielded. After all the interdictory lectures, he would nevertheless say:

"Your body is your best instructor. If you feel a terrible urge to have chocolate, eat some. It means that you need sugar badly. Or if you are dying for pickled herring, have it. Your body may need salt and vinegar. Ordinarily highly seasoned food eats at the lining of your stomach and helps to bring on an ulcer. But occasionally, it will not hurt you. Moderation in everything is your best protection."

I liked this deviation from fanaticism, even if it had not been justified as another rule of nature, because I distrust any theory, whether in religion, politics, economics, or health which holds itself out as a perfect solution. There are no panaceas even in heaven, or why would we need guardian angels?

Baranoff scorned psychiatry. If I have not already subjected him to discredit as a "kook" because of his theories, this should alienate another large segment of the population. He did not believe that the mind was any less physical than the heart or liver. If it did not function well, there was a physical cause. He would have rejected the couplet:

> What is mind
> No Matter
> What is Matter
> Never mind.

If the brain was not functioning normally, it might be due to defective blood supply, inherited weakness of a lobe, physical abnormality in some part of the body which deprived the brain of nerve or blood supply, "a twisted nerve" (again Baranoff's atrocious similes), but he would not accept what to him was a mystical theory that the mind was spiritual and not to be classified in the same way as any physical organ of the body. In response to the flood of criticisms which this evoked from his listeners, he held his ground tenaciously.

"True, shocking news of a sudden death may affect the mind. There is no physical blow, you say, but there is. For example, it will affect the solar plexus, a group of nerves, here near the stomach. That is why such news can cause diarrhea. A shock to the nervous system is the same as a physical blow, and may therefore affect the brain. Often it will shut off blood supply. That is why a person faints when he hears terrible news. Phobias have similar physical causes. The chemistry of the body can be affected, causing disease, or even insanity. But," his voice turned to sarcastic ridicule, "it has nothing to do with tracing how your mother treated you when you were five years old."

He once made a daring experiment in a lunatic asylum, and got into trouble for his pains. He had persuaded the head of such an institution that he could improve the conditions of many inmates, and perhaps cure some of them, by applying simple health measures. Since no surgery or medicines were involved, the open-minded "warden" permitted him to try. Baranoff studied the eating habits of the inmates. What was outstanding was the number of pills of all kinds which they took each day. Most of them were sedatives to calm the unruly population, and really for the benefit of the keepers rather than the residents. Others were laxatives to overcome the sedatives, and there were many others of varying colors and purposes. The inmates were pimply. Their rashes and skin revealed the "poisoning" to which they were subjected.

Baranoff ordered that all these medicines be stopped. Simultaneously he installed high colonics to cleanse them. Then he prescribed food designed to remove toxicity—grapefruit, grape juice, apples, celery, etc.— but with as much individual adjustment as was possible under the circumstances. The result was remarkable. So much so that the state authorities discovered the unauthorized interference by one not even a M.D. but only a "naturopath." The rules had been violated. The head of the institution was reprimanded. Baranoff, after a hearing, was lucky to escape the cancellation of his license. I do not know whether any attention was given to the demonstration, but I suspect not.

Over the years, our friendship grew. A group of doctors, impressed by the results he was getting in healing, and with the possibilities of growth and profits, bought into Safety Harbor Spa. Baranoff neither needed nor wanted much money. His real mission and satisfaction in life were to preach and practice his theories and teach people how to be healthy. He was induced to make the deal not because it gave him and his family financial security, but because he saw the possibility of enlarging his influence in a greater institution.

As in all things in life, there was bad with the good. Magnificent modern buldings were constructed over the years. New spa equipment was installed, featuring an indoor hot jet pool, whirlpool baths, solariums, massage areas in the sun and indoors, jet showers, and all the rest now copied by many spas which have sprouted all over the country.

One was no longer examined by Baranoff alone. He sent you for the customary medical checkup to one of two resident physicians. Lisa was no longer the cook, presiding lovingly over each preparation. She retired. There was a staff which had to be more impersonal with the increase of guests.

Baranoff could only give his special treatments to a relatively few of the new flood of guests. He worked as hard as he could, never rushing, however. But how could he keep up with the growing clientele? Some came who did not even know of him, except for his Friday night lectures. Many skipped them in favor of motion pictures and prize entertainments offered in other rooms. I could see Baranoff growing unhappier with success and prosperity. He was of course making much more money, but this meant nothing to him. Indeed, he was offered far more attractive contracts by other spas which were being built throughout the country, and this despite his age.

What was his age? No one knew. He always taught that there was no reason why people couldn't live to the biblical one hundred and twenty years "at least." Some thought he was approaching that himself. I recall once sitting in a steam room, chatting with a friend of Baranoff's in tones made hollow and echo-like by the visible heat. He knew him from the old country, Russia. He computed his age by disaster landmarks: a collapsed bridge, a fire which destroyed the vegetable shed, an overflowed river which swept away a child on its bank, and other unhappy events which fixed the dates in memory. By such a circuitous route, he was certain Baranoff was at least eighty years old. That was more than twenty years ago, and Baranoff is still tossing bodies around on his table.

Baranoff's relationship with the doctor-owners sometimes created conflicts. There was such a thing as incompatible association as well as incompatible eating.

One Christmas holiday, the professional managers, not imbued with his theories, arranged a children's outdoor party. Frankfurters and Coca-Cola were served. When Baranoff heard of this, he dashed to the scene and condemned the desecration of his temple with the same passion with which Moses had castigated the revelers around the golden calf. The blow was deeper than his new associates could understand. He had dedicated his life to an ideal, and now the children who should be educated early were being led along the same old path which made Americans physically unfit despite the highest standard of living. His fury astonished the staff. They could not quite understand why a frankfurter and a Coca-Cola should cause such turmoil. They did not understand that he felt his life's work being destroyed before his very eyes and in his own home. Nevertheless, they were moved by the purity of his convictions. When the hall where lectures were given to listeners who sat on hard folding chairs was replaced in 1964 by a modern, one-thousand-cushioned-seat theater, rivaling the finest Broadway structure, with a curtained stage, blazing with lights as varied as the moods he depicted in his lectures, the owners voted that it be called "The Baranoff Theater" and arranged a dedication ceremony.

There are men, like Baranoff, known only to limited thousands whom he taught and touched healingly over a long span, but not known to the multitudes. It is one of the misfortunes of a troubled world that "Full many a flower is born to blush unseen."

Many worthy men make their impact in limited circles, while generals, athletes, and politicians, who ought to be proud to stand in their shadows, achieve worldwide fame. The world's spotlight is not very discriminating. Its beam follows the television wave and thus lights on the sensational, the titillating, and the morbid more often than on the scholarly and profound.

The auditorium reflected two groups. Those who knew, and those who ought to have known. Gathered were many of Baranoff's patients who owed either their health or even their lives to him. They had come from all sections of the country. Also, there were his friends in the community, headed by the city leaders of Safety Harbor, Clearwater, Tampa, and other environs, who had recognized him as a good man, dedicated to all worthy causes. Religious leaders of all denominations had come to honor him as a Jew who actually lived up to the Judeo-Christian ethic.

There were also present "new guests" who knew little about him and who were impelled chiefly by curiosity. In the front row on the side sat Baranoff, an effulgent vision, as if a white cloud had settled on his head while his piercing eyes, shaded by black eyebrows, glowed mostly. Next to him sat Lisa, much younger in years, emotionally moved and struggling to maintain her usual smile, nature's permanent make-up for beauty.

I arose to introduce him. I thought it best to describe his life by describing his theories of nature's preventive medicine. After all, the two were the same. His teaching and his life were one. He had only an osteopathic diploma. He had been ridiculed as a freak because of his food and exercise preachment.

However, the scientific mind, like a parachute, functions only when it is open. There were great physicians who overcame their prejudices inculcated by the aristocracy of formal learning, and supported Baranoff. Dr. John W. Knowles, president of the Rockefeller Foundation, had recently said that gluttony was the cause of most of our ills. We spend billions on "after-the-fact medicine" instead of avoiding disease. Last year, the country's health bill rose by more than $14 billion to $118 billion, but less than 3 per cent went toward the prevention of disease. The next major advance in the health of the American people, he said, "can only come from self-imposed changes in the way individuals live." Spoken like a Baranoff, but fifty years later.

So, at last his life had come to fruition. He was recognized in scientific circles and honored for his achievements.

He rose to an ovation, and ascended the stage. He kissed me ostentatiously on both cheeks. He stood still as the applause, like a stormy sea, rose again, each time a previous wave flattened out. He took advantage of the time to try and compose himself. He could not stop the tears, and there was no use pretending they were not there. The spotlights revealed their glistening paths down his cheeks. He wiped them away with a handkerchief, blew his nose, and finally he was permitted to speak.

In a few moments, his quavering voice strenghtened. He was on his subject. I doubt that the audience listened very attentively to what he was saying. Rather, they were intrigued by his vitality and intensity. He forgot the nature of the occasion. He was not conscious any more of the honor being paid him. There was a large audience out there. The opportunity must not be lost. If only he could put each one of them on a table and make them healthier. He pleaded with them to develop new habits which would make them more useful to themselves and to their families. His concern for their welfare was so deep and sincere that everyone in the room felt enveloped by his love. He forgot all about the new theater and its new name. He never mentioned them.

It was the most gloriously inappropriate "acceptance" speech I ever heard.

One day I received confirmation of the theory of self-restraint in eating habits from an unexpected source. It was from Salvador Dali, the great painter. It is sometimes thought that artists, being under great strain, seek release in dissipation. Not so. There are exceptions, but most creative people know that good health is essential to their achievements and go to great lengths to be fit. I would have thought that Dali, noted for his designed "eccentricity," would be an exception, but I learned otherwise.

We were having lunch in my office to discuss a lawsuit in which he was unjustly involved. He was being sued for his failure to deliver paintings to be drawn on the backs of tarot cards used for fortunetelling. He arrived in a purple-satin-lined Russian sable cape. He wore a lavender shirt with a mustard yellow tie, demonstrating that there was no such thing as a wrong color combination. Even during lunch he would not put aside his silver-nobbed cane. His famous mustache, waxed upwards in bicycle handlebar manner to two sharp points which almost pierced his nostrils, gave no hint of his conservative views on health.

He would not touch the rolls and butter before him. He wanted only a simple salad and fruit. He would not even drink coffee. I thought it would be appropriate to serve fine Spanish wine to complement the lunch. He refused it.

"Don't you drink any liquor?"

He held out his hand, pulselessly steady, his forefingers and thumb clutching an imaginary paint brush. He peered steadily with shining eyes into the distance to symbolize the imaginative visions which had stirred the artistic world.

He continued, dropping articles and prepositions as if they were extra luggage. "There are two kinds people, romantics and realists. Romantic thinks if he takes alcohol, pills, marijuana he find artificial heaven. No find. Realist knows here is heaven." For the first time he dropped his tremorless hand and pointed the imaginary paint brush to the earth. "No interfere clear mind and imagination."

When we concluded our conference, I offered to have my car take him to his hotel. Again he refused, adding that he would walk, walk, walk because it was a necessary exercise for him. He held up his cane, not, as I suspected, a symbol of support, but of protection.

During our discussion I had, as is my habit, drawn his head on a napkin. He noticed it and approved. That was kind enough, but he made a Dali gesture. "I sign generously," he said.

I did not know what that meant but I was pleased to hand him the napkin. He drew a long vertical line with a little knob. It was his cane, but it also was the stem of the letter "D." Then in large script which covered three quarters of the napkin, he wrote the rest of his name. The drawing appropriately shrank in size by comparison.

There could be no more incongruous figures than Baranoff and Dali, but I realized by the very contrast how remarkably their creative theories coincided.

LOOKING INTO THE FUTURE

As a lawyer I have trained myself to anticipate the future developments in every case, even appeals which may take place years after the trial. The habit of looking ahead sometimes enables me to present evidence which at first blush might appear irrelevant but which, in the light of later analysis, may protect the original verdict.

Carrying forward this habit, I have thought about the future of mankind in the next seventy-five years.

It is difficult to peer into the future. H. G. Wells in 1901 wrote that an airplane would never be invented but if it were, it could never be a practical conveyance. Two years later the flyer took to the air at Kitty Hawk.

When Fulton's steamboat stood poised on the Hudson River to make its first demonstration, the cynics stood on the bank of the river and said steam could never move a heavy object. When the stack began to breathe heavily with smoke, and the ship began to glide, imperceptibly at first, and then slowly down the river, the same cynic, his jaw agape, yelled, "They'll never be able to stop it!"

So I know that it is hazardous to predict the future, but I also know that in man's battle against reality, imagination is his greatest weapon. And I also know that never in my lifetime have we lived in a time when our doubts were greater than our problems.

Therefore, I hope that by looking into the future we can lift our spirits and regain our confidence. I will therefore engage in an imaginary exercise. Assume that it is the year 2053 and that we are looking back seventy-five years to the year 1978.

In the year 2053 there are no electric lights or chandeliers in our buildings. They are lit by phosphorescent, luminescent walls.

People do not wear suits or dresses. They are draped in comfortable materials which have the property of either warming or cooling them as they wish. No overgarments are needed. Furthermore, these soft, beautiful clothes are disposable, being made of a synthetic paper material.

The tables at which we eat and the chairs on which we sit are at least a half foot higher, because the average height of men and women is seven feet.

One quarter of the people are over the age of 110, since the longevity average has reached 150, and scientists tell us that in another 25 years it will be 160.

Since we have also developed supersleep, one hour will suffice. So we are conscious and active twenty-three hours a day, thus adding to our span of life.

We wear rings which contain microscopic transistors enabling us to telephone from our hands.

We can determine in advance the sex of children. Because of larger brain development, it has become necessary to resort to Caesarean births.

Around our waist we wear a laser-beam fob which enables the brain, the greatest computer of all, to send brain wave messages for short distances.

We travel in invisible capsules with radar equipment to prevent collision, which fly us to our homes, where the walls part to admit us into the landing room. It is next to a huge circular room, the walls of which, at your choice, are filled with knowledge from a central bank of information, with news and with entertainment sent by satellite.

Weather conditions and temperature are determined by our government, based upon farm and environmental considerations. In some areas we travel north for the warm weather.

There is no race problem, not only because we have overcome the stupidity of prejudice, but because scientists have learned how to change the pigmentation of our skin so that people can be any color they choose to be. The predominant choice is not white or black but rather a suntanned kind of light brown.

We have virtually free energy. We now know the secret of fusion as previously we knew fission, so that we duplicate the process of the sun.

We talk of second and third generation artificial organs and limbs as once we talked of second generation computers.

Our food supply is abundant due to the extraction and creation of protein and other essential vitamins from the air, sea, and laboratory, as well as from the earth.

On our wrists are discs which send a record of our bodily functions twenty-four hours a day to a central medical computer. Every morning we read on the white circular wall a report of any deficiency and the precise remedy.

We do not begin functions by singing *The Star-Spangled Banner*, because the United States has become one of 153 states of a World Federation in which the votes of each state are based upon four factors: size, population, productivity, and educational and cultural standards. The nation-states vie with each other to improve their voting power by improving their ethical, cultural, and productivity standards rather than their armaments. We sing the world anthem entitled *A United World Among the Planets*. Next to the flag of the United States stands the flag of the World Federation, which depicts the globe on which all boundary lines are deliberately eliminated. It is surrounded by 153 stars against a blue background.

Does all this seem incredible? Well, make this simple test. Suppose that in 1903 someone predicted that in the next seventy-five years the following would happen:

That antibiotics would be discovered which would eliminate diseases which had plagued mankind for centuries:

that this nation and the rest of the world would be laced with pavements so that horseless carriages by the millions would drive upon them with no visible means of propulsion;

that huge birds would be built on which hundreds of people would perch, and though they weighed thousands of tons, these mechanical birds would lift into the air and fly across mountains and rivers and even across oceans;

that electronic waves, which circle the globe seven times in one second, would be harnessed so that they would go through brick, glass, steel, iron, and millions of human bodies without injuring them, and come out in a little box so that words spoken thousands of miles away could be heard distinctly;

that human beings would be able to see tens of thousands of miles by simply looking into the same box;

that even after a person died, his voice could still be heard by having a needle scratch a piece of wax;

that a surgeon would cut the heart out of a man without killing him, and then sew in another man's heart to preserve his life;

that an infinitely small particle of matter could be broken in two and would release as much power as thousands of tons of dynamite, and that this discovery would be used to destroy two whole cities and one hundred thousand people in a few seconds;

that three men would be placed in a cabinet which would be shot from the face of the globe, and while traveling at fifty thousand miles an hour toward a planet, one of them would step out of the cabinet and walk in space, and that we would sit in our homes and watch these men cavort on the moon.

And a hundred other miracles. Would all of this have seemed more credible than what I have depicted for the next seventy-five years? And yet, those wild predictions have become commonplace in our lives. So take heart. We will not be the pallbearers of the past. We will create a new glorious future.

There is only one respect in which we will not have achieved our goal in the year 2053. That is the substantial improvement of human nature. Darwin wrote that there are tame animals and wild animals, and that man is a wild animal, and it will take five million years of evolution to tame him. We will cut down this prediction by millions of years.

Indeed, we will by the year 2053 have made considerable progress in this direction. There will be an educational revolution, for we will have learned to infuse knowledge into the brain by electronic stimulation. Thus, we will learn instantly. Universities will be discarded as slow mechanisms. They will be used only for discussion and cultural development.

Also, biological engineering of the human personality will be greatly developed by 2053. The secret of matter and life having been wrested from nature, there will be all sorts of programs to change the genes and chromosomes in the hope of improving the human being. There will be sperm banks as well as brain banks, but who shall determine what the standards of improvement shall be?

This will be the great problem of the next century. For we have learned that while science can equip us, it cannot guide us. Science can illuminate our path to the farthest stars and leave our hearts in darkness.

We will have explored the outer planets of space and built colonies on some of them. We will have traveled to the bottom of the oceans in nuclear craft and excavated untold treasures. But we will not yet have succeeded in exploring the inner continents of man himself.

We will have to, in the words of Pindar, the Greek poet, "exhaust the limits of the possible." And everything is possible.

CONSTITUTIONAL CONFLICTS

In sports, it is only close contests which arouse excitement. Clear superiority breeds disinterest. That is why there was the cry about the original Philadelphia Athletics and later the Yankee baseball dynasties, as well as the Green Bay Packers football dynasty. "Break them up." Monopoly of power in sport is more objectionable than in business. Paradoxically, teams which are too successful sometimes attract small audiences.

If this rule was universal, we would be hanging on the rafters over the contest between constitutional amendments. I hope to convey the excitement which not only grips the scholar, but would envelop every citizen if he understood the neck and neck race among the various constitutional rights which compete with each other.

The First Amendment guarantees free speech. The Sixth Amendment guarantees a fair jury trial. The two conflict. May the press reveal in advance of a trial that the defendant has confessed? Suppose that the confession was obtained by duress and is not later admitted in evidence. How can the jury trial be fair where the jurors have been drenched with the prejudicial press report of confession, which should never have been brought to their attention? Or suppose that the press, exercising freedom of speech, reveals that a man about to be tried had a previous conviction.

Under our law, this would not have been admissible at the trial, because it does not prove that he is guilty of the present charge. For all we know, he may have been arrested because of his prior history, rather than because of evidence supporting the charge for which he is being tried. It is only if the defendant takes the stand in his own defense that he can be confronted with a prior conviction (not indictment) and only for its effect on his credibility, not as proof of guilt.

But if the press publishes his prior conviction, then the jury is advised of an irrelevant fact, which prejudices it, even though the defendant does not take the stand.

The same close contest exists between the First Amendment, guaranteeing free speech, and the Fourth Amendment, which guarantees against illegal search and seizure, and the Fifth Amendment, which protects against self-incrimination. There is a similar conflict between the First Amendment and the right of privacy. Every individual has the right "to be let alone." Is this precious right invaded when the press publishes his history even though he is not involved in any current news?

The most vivid illustration of conflict is that between the right of free speech and the right of an individual not to be injured by lies.

Which right shall be given predominance in each of these conflicts? Neither. They are both precious. There must be an accommodation between these conflicting rights. The courts have struggled to find the proper line to be drawn. In its search for a balanced rule, the Supreme Court has veered one way and then another over the years. The issue is still in flux. Choose which side you will cheer for as I trace the close and fierce contest which is being waged between the free press and the individual's right not to be slandered.

For 188 years, from 1776 to 1964, if the press printed a falsehood about an individual, he could sue, and if the press couldn't prove truth, it was liable. This seemed right enough. A citizen could be destroyed by a vicious accusation. He could suffer the loss of his job. His family could be reduced to starvation. His wife and children shamed. The perpetrator of the wrong ought to pay damages, in the same way as if he had crippled the man by negligently running over him with an auto.

But in 1964, the law was changed. It came about because of a hard case, which legal philosophers say often makes bad law. This means that in order to give relief because of special circumstances, we adopt a rule of law which does mischief when applied generally. Such special circumstances occurred in the famous case of the *New York Times Company v. Sullivan.* There, a commissioner in charge of the Police Department of Montgomery, Alabama, won a half-million-dollar verdict against the New York *Times* for merely publishing an advertisement part of which was false. There was no actual damage. The award was for punitive damages. The advertisement, in the name of the "Committee to defend Martin Luther King and the struggle for Freedom in the South," was signed by sixty-four persons, many of whom were well known in public affairs. Three were black clergymen, who were made co-defendants with the *Times.* The Commissioner who obtained the judgment was not even mentioned in the advertisement, but he claimed that the references to the action of the police against protesting students of Alabama State College reflected on him. Even the errors in the advertisement were not gross. For example Dr. King had not been arrested seven times, as the ad said, but only three. The cost of the advertisement was $4800. The *Times* had accepted it at the request of A. Philip Randolph, a responsible chairman of the Committee.

It can readily be seen why this was a hard judgment to uphold. It cried for relief. In this way there was fashioned the doctrine that unless there was malice, a public official could be criticized even falsely, and he would have no remedy.

The public interest, it was argued, required that the press publish without fear of retaliation. The word "press" includes books, television, radio, or any other means of expression. A rationale was given for this departure from the previous rule that the press, like any other individual or corporation operating for profit, was liable if it lied. It was that a public official sought the limelight. He was involved in public issues. He exposed himself to the acclaim of the citizenry, and thus waived the ordinary standards of privacy. His was a public trust, and was subject to scrutiny and criticism not applicable to private citizens. Also he had a better opportunity to have his reply published than a private citizen. Unless the press could be uninhibited in attacking a public official, it could not serve its highest purpose. "Let there be news. Let there be the right to publish without fear." These were biblical type pronouncements for the holy mission of the fourth estate.

This reasoning spilled over into the area of public figures who were not public officials. So the exception was widened and the press received even greater immunity. This came about in two cases decided by the Supreme Court. The first, in 1967, involved college football. An article in *The Saturday Evening Post* charged that Wallace Butts, a well-known football coach and athletic director of the University of Georgia, had fixed a game against his own team by giving to Alabama's coach "Bear" Bryant, "all of the significant secrets Georgia's football team possessed." The article heralded the exposé with these words: "Not since the Chicago White Sox threw the 1919 World Series has there been a sports story as shocking as this one." The rivalry between Georgia and Alabama had the intensity which only pride of students and alumni can generate. Championships sometimes hung in the balance. Adherents of each took loss with despair more fitting for the death of dear ones, and victory with elation which verged on hysteria. In such an atmosphere, one can imagine the scandal created by the story.

What was the authority for such a damning accusation (aside from our old friend, sensationalism to increase circulation and obtain a reprieve from the magazine's death)? It was based on an electronic mishap. An Atlanta insurance salesman, George Burnett, claimed that by error he was cut into a telephone conversation between Butts and Bryant and that "Butts outlined Georgia's offensive plays . . . and told . . . how Georgia planned to defend. . . . Butts mentioned both players and plays by name."

Burnett claimed he made notes, and gave specific examples of the divulged secrets.

The article added the necessary dramatics to what turned out to be a false story. It discussed the Georgia players' reactions to "the frightful beating" they suffered, "like those rats in a maze."

Experts compared Burnett's notes with the films of the game, and his claims were severely contradicted. Also the players' remarks had been misrepresented. Furthermore Burnett had been placed on probation in connection with bad-check charges, and *The Saturday Evening Post* knew this, but trusted his affidavit without independent investigation.

The defense of truth was rejected by the jury, which awarded $60,000 in general damages, and $3,000,000 in punitive damages. This award was cut to $460,000. The Supreme Court held that Butts was a public figure, rather than a public official, and that it would apply the same rule to both. Malice had to be proven. But it found that malice had been demonstrated because the publisher had "vented his spleen." Therefore it upheld the Butts verdict. It said that "the basic theory of libel has not changed, and words defamatory of another are still placed 'in the same class with the use of explosives or the keeping of dangerous animals.' "

Naturally, one could find contradictions in this analysis. The judges of the Supreme Court upheld the Butts decision but differed among themselves as to the right reason for doing so. Seven out of nine agreed that a public figure was entitled to the same protection as a public official, but they split as to whether the test of malice had been met.

The second case involved General Edwin A. Walker, who, in 1967, sued the Associated Press because in describing the riot which occurred when a black man, James Meredith, attempted to enter the University of Mississippi under a court order, it charged Walker with leading the violent crowd. At the time Walker was a private citizen, although he had been in charge of Federal troops, years earlier during a school segregation confrontation in Little Rock, Arkansas. He denied the story. He claimed that he had actually counseled restraint and peaceful protest. The reporter who gave the dispatch was on the scene. He had a good record for responsibility. The situation required an immediate report. There was no evidence of improper preparation or of personal prejudice.

The jury rendered a verdict of $500,000 compensatory damages, and $300,000 punitive danages. The trial court set aside the punitive award because there was no evidence of malice, but permitted the half-million-dollar verdict to stand. The Supreme Court, however, held that General Walker was a public figure and, like a public official, could not recover even if he was lied about, unless there was malice. There being none, the verdict was set aside, and he received nothing.

The logic for bunching public figures with public officials, to protect the press, seemed impeccable on the surface. Public figures, like public officials, have access to the press. They can defend themselves better than private citizens. So, theoretically, can public figures.

The trouble was definition. There is no doubt about identifying a public official. But what criterion is there to decide who is a public figure? How much fame must attach to him? How wide must the public be, local, state, national? The courts soon found themselves in a maze of conflicting decisions on this point.

Nevertheless, an attempt was made to increase the press's immunity even farther. In a suit brought by one Rosenbloom, in 1971, against Metromedia, Inc., the defendant argued that because Rosenbloom had involved himself in a public *issue*, he could not win a libel suit unless he would prove that the false statement was made with malice. The court extended the immunity it had conferred on the press, when sued by a public official, or public figure, to include one who had discussed a matter of public interest.

Let me take a compass reading of where we are at this point. We start with the inviolable proposition of the precious nature of free speech. It is the bulwark of democracy. It is not necessary to ring the bells on this proposition and relate how many have died for this right. (Thomas Huxley's "It is better for a man to go wrong in freedom than to go right in chains"; Thomas Mann's "Speech is civilization itself"; and of course Thomas Paine's "Give me liberty or give me death"). It is as superfluous to augment the point as to defend motherhood. The real question is how to accommodate this right with other constitutional provisions which are just as precious. Edmund Burke said that the foundation of government is compromise. Where shall we draw the line between competing rights?

The philosophical support for favoring the press is powerful, but not conclusive. If public officials can be libeled with impunity, unless they can prove the lie was born of malice, will not our political and judicial ranks be deprived of many outstanding men?

Distinguished citizens usually earn much more than they can in public service. Most men are willing to make financial sacrifices in return for the honor of leadership and the satisfaction of public service. But if instead of honor, they must look forward to the indignities of "dirty politics" and slander, the price is too high.

I cite a personal experience. Although I had been involved in politics "at the top," writing speeches for Presidents and others, I had sought to maintain my independence by practicing law. Judicial and political posts had been suggested if not offered (the technique is to obtain consent in advance). I refused. It was not modesty, but the love of practicing law which guided me. One accustomed to contest in the arena of justice would find umpiring it a tame affair. The judge cannot experience triumph or defeat. He can only impose it. True, he has the exhilaration of scholarship and writing, but these are not denied to the lawyer. Indeed without them he can neither be a successful office lawyer nor an advocate.

George Medalie, a leading trial lawyer of his day, was appointed by Governor Thomas E. Dewey to the Court of Appeals, the highest court of the State of New York. I met him after he had served a year.

"George, how do you like your new duties?"

"I am not sure," he replied. "The trouble is I don't know which side I'm on."

I did not care to don robes which would make it necessary for me to decide to which side my neutrality would yield. Also, the sedate life of a judge did not suit my temperament.

My resolve weakened one day, while I was on vacation in Colorado Springs. President Truman wanted to appoint me to the Federal bench. I received a series of telephone calls from emissaries conveying the honor. With expressions of appreciation, I declined. It was not difficult to do so. But the calls continued. My senior law partner, Louis Phillips, tempted me with the news that he had checked with the Bar Association, and I would be entitled to income from the law firm for at least two years in matters I had handled. This would reduce my financial sacrifice. I told him it was not money at all that governed my declination. When I set forth my real reasons, he countered that I ought to try the judicial post. "If you don't like it after a year or two, you can resign and return to private practice."

Next, my friend, Austin Keough, the general counsel of Paramount Pictures, Inc., telephoned to urge my acceptance. "The chances are you will not remain a district judge. If you are a distinguished judge, you may rise to the Court of Appeals, and perhaps even to the Supreme Court." I laughed. Knowing that Keough was a devout Catholic, I asked him whether he would have entered the priesthood if his father had held forth the possibility of his becoming Pope. I promised to think it over and reply the next day.

Mildred, who always thought I worked too hard, urged my acceptance on the mistaken notion that judgeships are sinecures. How little the public understands that conscientious judges work evenings and weekends studying voluminous briefs and trying desperately to stay afloat on the ever-increasing flood of litigations which inundate them.

Then a coincidence made up my mind. Judge Charles C. Lockwood of the State Supreme Court was also vacationing in Colorado Springs. He was in the dining room having dinner, when he heard me paged to the telephone a half-dozen times within the hour.

"What is the matter, Louis, anything wrong?"

I told him of the judicial offer and my negative view, although I was beginning to have doubts. He asked me to sit down with him. Then he proceeded in the most earnest terms to set forth the reasons why I should accept. He knew, he said, that I could make contributions to the judiciary which it needed, and which would give me greater satisfaction than repeating my endeavors as a trial lawyer. No matter how much one rejects flattery, some of it by osmosis induced by vanity seeps through and becomes conviction. When one has a good opinion of himself, resisting compliments is a losing struggle.

Everyone in the profession had great respect for Judge Lockwood, not merely as an able judge and good man, but because he had the parent of all gifts—sound judgment. I thanked him for his opinion of me and decided to accept the judgeship.

I returned to New York, and with a heavy heart proceeded to end my activities in the office. FBI reports, checking Federal appointments had been concluded. I was informed that the two senators of the state who had to approve and recommend the appointment were in line.

Then I was advised that as a final step I must visit Ed Flynn, the Democratic leader.

"Why?" I asked with naïveté that was more befitting a novice.

"You must have the approval of the Democratic leader, to get the appointment," I was told.

"I have nothing against Flynn. I don't know him. I have been induced to take this judgeship, because it offered a new opportunity for service in a field in which I have some expertise. But if I now have to cater to a political chief to pass muster, I'm not going to do it."

My sponsoring friends were exasperated with my eccentric behavior.

"For God's sake, Louis, no one is asking you to cater to anybody. It takes one visit. It is political protocol. He knows of you. We're sure he will be delighted to meet and approve you."

"I don't want his approval. I don't recognize the distinction between a Democratic and Republican judge, any more than between a Democratic doctor and Republican doctor, or for that matter a Democratic street cleaner and a Republican one. If I must go through the political routine to be a judge, I'd rather not be."

That was the end of my judicial career.

Men of standing invited to run for office must take into account the vicious attacks made on public officials. The honor of these posts, whether executive, legislative, or judicial, is drained by the debased standards of reckless and crude criticism which now pervades the political scene. The Watergate revelations of dirty tactics were more publicized, but were only the continuation of such practices for many years before Nixon.

Senator Joseph McCarthy's successful demagogy had led to two United States Senate subcommittees looking into the problem of campaign excesses. Senator Guy Gillette's committee recommended the adoption of a Code of Fair Campaign Practices promoted by a nonprofit private organization, to be called the Fair Campaign Practices Committee. Candidates for major offices would be asked to sign a pledge "to conduct my campaign in the best American tradition."

The Code condemned "the use of personal villification, character defamation, whispering campaign libel, slander or scurrilous attacks on any candidate on his personal or family life."

It also condemned "creating doubts, without justification" concerning an opponent's "loyalty and patriotism" or "any appeal to prejudice based on race, creed or national origin." Finally, it denounced any unethical practice "which tends to corrupt our American system of free elections."

Every President of the United States has lent his name as honorary chairman of the Committee. I was pleased to serve on it. It is one of the least publicized but most valuable organizations in our democracy. It is as important to prevent the pollution of our political streams as of our natural ones.

Since 1956 this committee has processed hundreds of complaints. It gathered the facts from both sides and publicized them. Some cases were sent to the American Arbitration Association for impartial finding by qualified arbitrators. It is significant that "dirty campaign tricks" have been about evenly divided between the two major parties. In the 1966 campaign, thirty-six complaints were filed by Republicans against Democrats, and twenty-nine by Democrats against Republicans. The total complaints for three elections of 1966, 1968, and 1970 were ninety-six by Republicans and eighty-nine by Democrats. The Republicans won 59 per cent of their complaints, the Democrats 43 per cent. So iniquity, like nobility, is not the monopoly of either of the major parties.

Robert Kennedy involved me in a controversy of unfair campaigning in the New York senatorial contest between himself and Senator Kenneth Keating. It arose from three campaign speeches which Kennedy made in Syracuse, New York, on October 20, 1964. Among other things he charged that Keating had failed to support the Nuclear Test Ban Treaty, which "Averell Harriman, Hubert Humphrey, and Adlai Stevenson labored to make a reality." Keating had voted for the treaty. He therefore filed a complaint with the Fair Campaign Practices Committee, and did not hesitate to publicize that he had done so. The Committee advised Kennedy of the complaint. Keating used a press release that the Committee "was angered and shocked" by Kennedy's distortion. Kennedy's defense was that he was guilty of nothing more than an ambiguity, because although Keating finally voted for the treaty, it was true "that when President Kennedy was fighting for it, Keating never once rose to speak in its favor before the United States Senate." The trouble with this defense was that in one of his speeches, Kennedy had also charged that "Keating ridiculed the Treaty and did not speak out for it until after passage was assured." Keating denied ever ridiculing the treaty.

Kennedy saw my name on the Committee stationery, and called me. He was terribly agitated. He feared that a public exposé of his error and condemnation by a responsible committee might cost him the election. Having been counsel to the McClellan Committee, he knew the impact of a charge which could be misunderstood as deliberate foul tactics.

When people are in trouble, fear, like a hyperactive thyroid, makes the problem grow. Kennedy sounded panicky.

"This kind of thing can cost me my career," he said. "Louis, please take care of this, will you? It was an innocent mistake. Do you think I ought to call Cardinal Cushing?" (who was also a member of the Committee).

I advised against it. It seemed to me that he felt he was in extremis and wanted to appeal to God for succor, but that he would turn to the Cardinal for more immediate results. It was the wrong approach. I presented his explanation to the Committee. It was a candid admission of his overstatement in the midst of a campaign.

The Committee regretted the publication of its letter of complaint to Kennedy before all facts had been gathered, thus enabling Keating to exploit it as if it were a finding. This pleased the Kennedy forces, while the Keating adherents objected that the matter was not properly resolved.

If a mistake is looked upon as a teacher rather than a progenitor for alibis, it can be valuable. The Committee reviewed its faulty procedures and tightened them, so that its very inquiry could not be exploited by either party to the dispute. In the meantime, however, two members of the Committee, Ralph McGill and Cardinal Cushing, had resigned.

Gratified by his extrication, Kennedy asked my judgment about another problem which he was facing. He had been challenged by Keating to a television debate on a Columbia Broadcasting channel. His brother's experience against Nixon had taught the lesson that the underdog had everything to gain and little to lose in such a confrontation.

Bobby was a clear favorite. Why should he confer his fame as a Kennedy and former Attorney General on the relatively unknown Senator Keating? Going by the rules, his committee had decided to reject the invitation.

Keating took advantage of the situation. He announced that he was going through with the debate just the same. An empty chair would represent his absent opponent. He would accuse the spotlight, which substituted for Kennedy in the chair, with lack of courage to meet him on the issues even though Keating was paying for the program. He would point to the chair and quote some of Kennedy's speeches, and reply to them. In effect he was going to make a campaign speech, dramatized by his opponent's "flight."

I had a different view of proper tactics. Kennedy was impressed by it and invited me to his home, where the Committee heads were gathered, to repeat it. There was Stephen Smith, his brother-in-law; Alex Rose, the leader of the Liberal Party; democratic chieftains, speech writers, and workers. They were milling about in every direction amidst a babble of noise punctuated by a distinct word or phrase which rose above the din thereby adding to the incoherence of the scene. It was not a smoke-filled room but it gave me the same feeling of wonder how anything could be decided sensibly in such a confusing atmosphere. Bobby asked me to state my views. I did. I urged that he should appear on the program and smilingly fill the empty chair. It would give a touch of grace and courage to the event, and upset Keating's prepared speech based on the formula of Kennedy's fear to face him. As to the debate, Kennedy had discussed the issues in dozens of appearances. He could hold his own easily against the ponderous Keating. Why not act boldly?

"But it is too late," came the warning from all sides. "The debate begins in an hour and a half. It's down at the CBS studio."

"All the better," I replied. "We'll show up at the last minute. It will take Keating by surprise."

Bobby's long-toothed smile indicated his approval. All agreed, though not with uniform enthusiasm. Kennedy rushed into the bathroom to shave. He asked that I sit with him there for last-minute preparation. He stripped to his shorts, revealing a very hairy chest, applied lather quickly, and despite the grimaces of shaving, which distorted his words, prepared for the encounter as if he were a witness about to take the stand. And I as a lawyer, accustomed to my soft high leather chair, sat on the hard cover of the toilet bowl, an inappropriate throne for the discussion of principles.

The news media had been advised that Kennedy was coming to the CBS station. Television and news cameramen appeared immediately and escorted our small party to the studio. There a large crowd had gathered. Kennedy was cheered and he waved happily, all recorded for the nightly news. He was already ahead. But surprising developments were to come.

Inside the building, we announced that Kennedy was ready to debate and wanted to be taken to the Keating studio. There was little time, and the executives in charge of the event were taken aback by the change of schedule. There were hasty telephone calls back and forth. At last we were invited to the floor where the studio was. Behind the closed studio door, Keating was already seated opposite the empty chair. Word was sent to his assistants inside, that Kennedy was ready and wished to enter. Distressful voices were heard. Then came the answer.

"It is only five minutes to broadcast time. Mr. Keating will not permit a last second change of heart. Mr. Kennedy will not be admitted."

Kennedy needed no prompting. He exploited the situation with professional skill. With television and flashlights pouring on him outside the locked door, he said, "I demand to be admitted. Mr. Keating challenged me to a debate. I am ready. I am eager to discuss the issues with him. It takes only a second to open the door, and another second for me to occupy that chair. There is plenty of time. If Mr. Keating refuses, who is running away? The people will consider his talk to the empty chair a fraudulent act. With one hand he shuts me out, with the other he gestures I did not show up."

From one of his astute assistants came a loud cry. "Bobby, we have reserved fifteen minutes in another studio for reply. Let's pick it up and tell the people how you were locked out!"

"Let's do it," said the triumphant candidate, waving his hand with disgust at the closed door. Turning to the press:

"Gentlemen, you see that Keating doesn't want to debate me." He knocked at the door for the last time. "I ask again for admittance."

"There you are, it is not a silent chair, but a silent Keating we have inside."

We headed for another CBS studio to hear Keating and then reply. Kennedy asked me to appear on the program with him. I agreed. We were hastily "made up," a technique which always makes me feel like a fop, but is justified by the television personnel on the ground that if you don't, the contrast with those who do is horrendous. ("You don't want to look worse than you are?" I was once comforted by a make-up man who needed a Dale Carnegie course.)

We heard enough of the Keating broadcast to improvise a reply. Kennedy and I decided quickly who would answer a particular argument. He took the issues of the campaign, I the personal references to Kennedy. We wrote out hastily Kennedy's opening, which was a vivid recital of how Keating had locked him out of the studio to which he had been challenged to debate. He told how the press had witnessed his demands for entry, and Keating's pretense that it was too late to live up to the original plan. He characterized Keating's broadcast in which he addressed an empty chair as a shabby trick unworthy of a senatorial contest. He was dry but effective. The camera must have caught his eyes, which turned steel gray with anger.

Keating's main thrust had been that Bobby was cashing in on his brother's reputation. I addressed myself to this. I used a technique known in law as "confession and avoidance." What is wrong with emulating a father or brother who had achieved world recognition for his great qualities? Is filial devotion and the continuation of a great family tradition an argument against electing Robert Kennedy? Then I proceeded to recite and analyze the official positions Bobby had held with distinction, his achievements as counsel to congressional committees, as Attorney General, and particularly his wise advice to his brother during the Cuban crisis. The fact that the President leaned on him during those crucial hours indicated that he recognized in Bobby those qualities which the nation needed. Thus I was able to say things for and about him which would have come with ill grace from his lips. Then I passed the baton to him and he expressed movingly his hopes for the people of the state which he wished to represent.

When we emerged, Ethel Kennedy was there to kiss him and thank me. The campaign squad acted as if a triumph had been achieved, and the cameras continued to roll as he pushed his way through a cheering mob, his slight body disappearing at times among the burly bodyguards and then suddenly emerging as if he had come to the surface after a deep dive.

Much later when Bobby was assassinated while trying to pass through a similar wall of adulating flesh, I thought of the scene at CBS. Why must our public men risk their lives in crowds which may include a mad fanatic bent on notoriety through murder?

Despite the salutary restraints which the Fair Campaign Practices Committee, the press, and the public impose on candidates, their eagerness to win drives many to abominable practices. As election day grows nearer, the fever chart shows a sharp incline of reckless and desperate statements. Moreover, the loser's hope for a better day prompts continuing attacks on the victor. A partisan press and disgruntled opponents join the chorus of criticism which often crosses the boundary of decency. The refusal of many outstanding men to enter the political arena as candidates may well be due to their resentment of the abuse which they consider inevitable, and for which there is no remedy. Should there not be? The libel laws had been the traditional tool therefor. Its edge has been dulled. Was it in the public interest to keep it so?

We are all committed to the First Amendment and free speech, but the press, like other valuable institutions, is capable of perpetrating abuse and injustice.

The framers of the Constitution recognized that none of our institutions is so sacred or safe, not the Presidency, not the Congress, and not the judiciary, that absolute power may safely be reposed in any of them. Fear of absolutism dictated the very system of constitutional checks and balances, which is the most important safeguard of all our fundamental freedoms. Should not the press be subject to the check provided by the libel laws?

Thomas Jefferson thought so. He saw clearly the dangers of journalistic abuse. I quote him:

It is a melancholy truth, that a suppression of the press could not more completely deprive the nation of its benefits than is done by its abandoned prostitution to falsehood.

Jefferson believed in absolute press freedom on matters of opinion (the "public judgment will correct false reasonings and opinions"), but he deplored false factual reporting as "demoralizing licentiousness," an abuse of freedom of the press.

Jefferson believed that curbing of the press to prevent lies was so important that he spoke about it in his second inaugural address. After referring to the "wholesome" remedies against defamation he said a citizen "renders a service to the public morals and public tranquillity in reforming these abuses by the salutory coercion of the law"—in other words by suing for libel. This, coming from the foremost champion of freedom of the press, was not a retreat, but a declaration of a balance between the press and the individual's rights.

Benjamin Franklin agreed. With characteristic felicity he wrote:

If by the liberty of the press were understood merely the liberty of discussing the propriety of public measures and political opinions, let us have as much of it as you please; but if it means the liberty of affronting, calumniating, and defaming one another, I, for my part, own my-self willing to part with my share of it . . . and shall cheerfully consent to exchange my liberty of abusing others for the privilege of not being abused myself.

No talk here of the need to prove malice in order to recover for a lie. Unless truth could be proved, the press was to be held liable. Much later the Supreme Court echoed this view when Justice Potter Stewart wrote that "the reputation of a man or woman rises to constitutional dimensions."

We have understandably ennobled the press's service and the priorities it requires for its guardianship of officialdom and its service to the public interest. For example, we will under no circumstances permit an injunction to prevent a newspaper, book, or telecast from publishing a story. Such advance "shutting of the mouth" is abhorrent to free speech. When it is published, and it is actionable, suit can be brought. Otherwise we anticipate a violation, and this may well be a means to cut off permissible opinion or factual criticism. The rule against "prior restraint," as it is called, is firm and should remain so.

On the other hand, how much protection should the press enjoy after it publishes? If we were dealing only with the majority of great journals, we might consider diminishing the individual's rights in their favor, on the theory that such sacrifice would rarely be needed. But there are yellow newspapers, "sensational" journals, pornographic magazines, scandal columns, trade publications which engage in blackmail ("unless you place ads with us, we'll expose you"), and all sorts of vicious sheets to which printing presses are hospitable. They abound in lies which often are motivated not by malice, but by greed. The editors and writers may know little about the victim and care less about him, but they repeat irresponsible gossip published by a similar reckless source, embroider it with invention, and exploit it for "a buck." Malice in the legal sense may really not exist. Avarice does. This brings about a situation in which the very false accusations which ought to be most subject to remedy are the most immune.

"Muckraking," like "ambition," is one of those words in the English language which can connote good or evil, depending on its usage. Usually we shade our meanings with two words. Persistent-good; obstinate-bad. Generous-good; spendthrift-bad. Self-respect-good; vain-bad. Prudent-good; stingy-bad. Confident-good; conceited-bad. Insight-good; self-centered-bad.

Ordinarily we would consider raking up mud about people a pretty unsavory undertaking. But when the digging exposes facts which, in the public interest, should never have been buried, muckraking becomes a

virtue. Then we cherish the glitter, after the caked mud has been removed, and we honor the muckraker.

The trend to teams (in surgery, economics, and politics) has spread
to muckraking. It was such a team that was responsible for the "Governor and the Mob" story.

The Supreme Court has taken note of the "muckraking" technique,
and decided that it indicated malice under certain circumstances. In
the Butts case, the court said:

The Saturday Evening Post was anxious to change its image by instituting a policy of "sophisticated muckraking," and the pressure to
produced a successful exposé might have induced a stretching of
standards. In short, the evidence is ample to support a finding of
highly unreasonable conduct constituting an extreme departure from
the standards of investigation and reporting ordinarily adhered to by
responsible publishers.

Chief Justice Warren spelled it out more bluntly:

. . . an editorial decision was made "to change the image" of the
Saturday Evening Post with the hope that circulation and advertising
revenues would thereby be increased. The starting point for this change
of image was an announcement that the magazine would embark upon
a program of "sophisticated muckraking" designed to "provoke people,
make them mad" . . .
Freedom of the press under the First Amendment does not include
absolute license to destroy lives or careers.

President Johnson must have relished this slap at the same magazine
which made him so "mad." Governor Rhodes must have been interested in the reference to "muckraking," because *Life*, in his case, had
ascribed its story to a newly formed "muckraking team."

And I, noting that the Supreme Court said the motive for the libel
was "advertising revenues," and observing also that both magazines expired, consider this a confirmation of the Nizer theory of relativity.

As the law stands at the present writing, one could say of the President or the Chief Justice that he is a cocaine user, or has been improperly influenced in his official duty. Even though the accusation was
totally false, if the President or Chief Justice sued, a defense could
successfully be interposed that the plaintiff, being a public official,
could not recover unless he could demonstrate that the charge was
made with malice. The defendant would insist there was no malice.
Witness the fact that he voted for the President, or previously wrote an
article praising the Chief Justice. He merely relied in good faith on a

muckraking investigator. The President or Chief Justice could not even obtain a favorable verdict of six cents, thus vindicating his honor. The suit would be dismissed.

This is how far the pendulum has swung in favor of the press and against a public official or public figure. But, I believe the pendulum's arc is at its zenith. Already it is beginning to swing back in favor of the individual's rights. First it reversed its position that a private person involved in a public issue was to be treated like a public official or public figure. In other words, that he too, if lied about, had no remedy unless he could prove malice. At last, the ever-increasing immunity for the press came to a halt. It even moved back somewhat.

The Supreme Court weakened its public figure ruling by redefining what a public figure was. It laid down a narrower test, so that even many prominent persons could not be qualified as public figures.

It did so in a case in Chicago, in 1974, where a policeman named Nuccio shot and killed a boy. He was convicted of murder in the second degree. The family brought a civil suit for damages against Nuccio. It was represented by a well-known lawyer, Elmer Gertz.

The John Birch Society attacked Gertz, in its monthly magazine, as a "Leninist" and a "Communist-fronter" who was in a conspiracy to discredit local law enforcement agencies. He sued the publisher Robert Welch for libel.

The charges were untrue. But was "malice" required before Gertz could recover? If he was a public figure, yes. If not, the jury verdict of $50,000 could stand, even though there was no proof of malice.

The Supreme Court began its opinion with a frank admission:

This Court has struggled for nearly a decade to define the proper accommodation between the law of defamation and the freedoms of speech and press protected by the First Amendment. With this decision we return to that effort.

The effort resulted in whittling away the immunity to the press which had gradually been broadened. The court held that Gertz was not a public figure. Even though he had written three books; had appeared "very frequently" on radio and television programs, had served on various city commissions, and had represented Jack Ruby, who had killed Oswald, the assassin of President Kennedy, he did not come within the court's new definition of what a public figure is:

Although Gertz was well known in some circles, he had achieved no general fame or notoriety in the community. None of the prospective jurors called at the trial had ever heard of Gertz prior to this litigation.

We would not lightly assume that a citizen's participation in community and professional affairs rendered him a public figure for all purposes. Absent clear evidence of general fame or notoriety in the community and pervasive involvement in the affairs of society, an individual should not be deemed a public personality for all aspects of life.

In a recent divorce case, in 1976, the Supreme Court set a still higher standard for declaring a person a public figure. It involved Russell Firestone, the scion of the famous tire company family. He was sued by his wife, Mary Alice Firestone, for separate maintenance in a Florida court. He fought back with a counterclaim which charged her with cruelty and adultery. She denied the charges. There was a lengthy trial, in which venom flowed freely. The court granted him a divorce and engaged in vivid descriptions which such cases sometimes stimulate:

According to certain testimony in behalf of the husband, extramarital escapades of the wife were bizarre and of an amatory nature which would have made Dr. Freud's hair curl. Other testimony in the wife's behalf would indicate that the husband was guilty of bounding from one bedpartner to another with the erotic zest of a satyr. The court is inclined to discount much of this testimony as unreliable.

So the Judge indicated that both parties had exaggerated. He did not find either party guilty of adultery. Nevertheless he concluded that "neither party is domesticated," which was sufficient reason to grant the divorce. "The equities," said the Judge, "were with the husband." He granted the divorce, ordered the husband to pay the wife $3,000 a month alimony.

Time magazine mistook the decision. It reported that Firestone, "heir to the tire fortune," was granted a divorce because his wife was guilty "of extreme cruelty and adultery," and that the "testimony of extramarital adventures on both sides, said the Judge, was enough 'to make Dr. Freud's hair curl.'"

Time was so certain that it had correctly reported the decision that it refused to issue a retraction. Mrs. Firestone then sued *Time* for libel. A jury awarded her $100,000 damages. The highest court of Florida affirmed the judgment.

Obviously it would be difficult to prove that *Time* was motivated by malice. Therefore, if Mrs. Firestone was a public figure, and had to prove malice, she had failed and the verdict would be set aside.

The Supreme Court reviewed the case and held that she was not a public figure. True, she was prominent in the affairs of society, but only Palm Beach society. She had not thrust herself to the forefront of any particular public controversy in order to influence its resolution. True, she was involved in a sensational trial which was characterized by the Florida Supreme Court as "a cause célèbre," but controversies interesting to the public are not necessarily public controversies. Even the holding of several press conferences in the course of the sensational trial did not make either party a public figure. The doctrine would not be extended to such a situation.

So the pendulum has been swinging back toward the individual's rights. In the center of the arc is an uncontested proposition. Ideas are always protected. There is no such thing as a false idea which is not protected by the First Amendment. No matter how pernicious the opinion, we depend on competing ideas to correct it.

Immediately adjacent to this calibration is "fact." Here we are still in the process of finding a proper equilibrium with the First Amendment.

Charles Rembar, a leading fighter for freedom of the press, said in a Bar Association forum in which I recently participated:

We are pushing the First Amendment too far. My credentials are that I happened to try some cases in which the law was profoundly changed in the direction of more freedom of expression. People who have been principally engaged in furthering the scope of the First Amendment . . . are getting a little sanctimonious . . . We have to watch out that we are not the Anthony Comstock and John Summers just on the other side.

We talk of the sovereignty of nations and states, but who talks of the sovereignty of man, for whom all laws are created? Libel is the legal shield of his reputation, the remedy for the invasion of his sovereignty.

The dignity and worth of the individual is at stake, and they deserve the foremost consideration in a civilized society.

The difficulty with the philosophical discussions concerning freedom of speech is that, like all esoteric evaluations, they are bloodless. To understand the issue, one must climb down from the Olympian heights of generalization, and meet a victim of a vicious lie, face to face; see in his bloodshot eyes, his tossing sleepless nights; meet his trembling wife empty of tears, and his children, sullen with sudden maturity, ashamed to go to school; know that friends were calling to give him comfort and thereby emphasizing the injury; know that others were shunning him, and that his employers were discussing how to fire him without giving the real reason—in short, to see him and his distraught family as the world around him collapses.

He comes to his lawyer and explains that he is fighting for his very life. He wants justice. Under the present state of the law, the lawyer must say to him, "I'm sorry. Because of the freedom of the press, you have no real remedy. You are a public official (or public figure) and you would have to prove malice, or your case will be dismissed."

"Even though they lied?" he asks.

"Yes, even if they can't prove truth. The Supreme Court has given the press immunity."

"Press," he says bitterly. "This was an article in a filthy pornographic magazine. But it has a larger circulation than the New York *Times*, the Washington *Post*, and *Time* magazine put together. Yet you tell me that although my family and I are ruined, we have no remedy?"

I hope to contribute something to see that he does.

THE SPARROW THAT TURNED OUT TO BE AN EAGLE

I first met Harry Truman when he was a senator from Missouri. That he would become President of the United States seemed too remote to contemplate. That I would be present at the White House and witness one of his historic decisions was even less imaginable. But it all happened.

The way for a senator to attract a national spotlight was to be chairman of an important investigating committee. Like Hugo Black and Estes Kefauver before him, and John McClellan and Sam Ervin after him, Truman overcame public inattentiveness to the processes of legislation by chairing an investigating committee. It sought to expose improprieties in war contracts.

The role of an active prosecutor-detective was sure melodrama. Phillips H. Lord discovered the device in his television program "Mr. District Attorney." This was no mere desk-sitting official, assigning footwork to others. He was a crusader, going forth with gun and enlarging glass to track down the villains. The program ran five years. I became aware of its potent formula when I defended it against a claim of plagiarism by a writer who claimed he had originated the idea. Ideas are not copyrightable. Only the execution of them, the language and the incidents which covered the idea's bone structure, was protected and could not be copied. "Mr. District Attorney" spawned many surefire television programs, and whether by coincidence or precept, there were many House and Senate investigating committee prototypes. The best of them were actually carried on television and out-Nielsened the fictional ones.

This is a curious phenomenon, because Senate committee hearings are solely for the purpose of formulating legislation. This would appear to be a dry search for the need of a "new or better law." But it was soon learned that sensational revelations might be hidden under the dust-covered stastical data.

Famous scenes abounded. In a Senate committee hearing John Pierpont Morgan and other millionaires testified that they did not have to pay one cent income tax, and to top it off, a midget placed himself on Morgan's lap while he was in a witness chair. The resulting photograph of the somber financial giant who didn't pay taxes, and the grinning midget who did, must still be the most piquant lesson in civics.

The gangster Frank Costello objected, on grounds of right of privacy, to television cameras and lights blinding him as he testified, so they narrowed the focus to his squirming hands. Thereby they made Hollywood directors envious of a most dramatic effect.

Witnesses, yelling the Bill of Rights over the hoots and applause, defied Senator Joseph McCarthy, who cited them and had them thrown out by guards.

As a senator, Truman had worked his way up on the investigating committee ladder from small bit parts, to feature roles and finally to stardom. He was chairman of a subcommittee which wrote the Civil Aeronautics Act of 1937. Then he became vice-chairman of a subcommittee of the Senate Commerce Committee which proposed the Transportation Act of 1940. So far there was no "sex appeal" in his efforts. But when he headed a special committee investigating the National Defense Program, which was called the Truman Committee, the revelations dealt with nothing less than the safety of every citizen.

It was January 1941. The United States was putting its industry to war. Ships, tanks, and planes began to roll off production lines as if we were mass producing glasses or coat hangers. Technology was demonstrating its prolific nature with a literal bang. But the Nazis had prepared their war machine for many years. We had been jolted into a sudden drive.

Truman warned that the defense effort would fail unless thousands of small manufacturers were utilized. He charged favoritism and inordinate profits in granting contracts to large companies. His committee, originally budgeted for only fifteen thousand dollars, was credited with saving the nation fifteen billion dollars by preventing waste and unnecessary expenditures. More important, by harnessing the incredible resources of our producers, small and large, and our technology, often inspirited by individual entrepreneurs, the flood of armaments swept over the Nazis like a tidal wave.

So Truman emerged from the somewhat obscure mass of senators to become, if not a household word, at least a newspaper and radio word. His qualities of simplicity, forthrightness, and no-nonsense personality were attractive. He was the little man fighting huge, unscrupulous forces who were cheating the American people in making war equipment. He represented plain honesty, and undemagogic patriotism as he exposed the miscreants. There was a new shining hero, not on a white horse, but appropriatedly walking fast in that chesty, straight-backed gait, as he gave interviews. He was the forerunner of the austerity school in politics whose graduates later included Governor Jerry Brown and President Jimmy Carter.

It was through a book that I first came in contact with him. The war was coming to an end. Although the night sky in Europe was still filled with lightning flashes from artillery, and although tanks, like huge ungainly bugs, were still lumbering over fallen trees, and planes could still be imagined in front of long white vapor trails, we all knew that we had reached the epilogue. I had made an intense study in anticipation of the question which would soon confront us, and entitled my book with that question, *What to Do with Germany*.

The publisher sent advance copies to those whose opinions would be meaningful. Truman was one. He responded with extremely enthusiastic praise which he authorized to be used as a blurb on the jacket. Still, the publisher, while displaying it proudly there, placed it underneath those of Walter Winchell, Clifton Fadiman, and Rex Stout, although ahead of Somerset Maugham, Louis Bromfield, and Maurice Maeterlinck. Such were the ratings in those days. But Truman's status was soon to change.

Roosevelt had to choose a running mate. Jimmy Byrnes aspired to be Vice-President and thought he was the President's choice. He asked Truman to nominate him. Truman agreed and came to the Chicago convention with a prepared speech. But Roosevelt exercised the President's prerogative to change his mind. Byrnes had been born a Catholic but had converted to Protestantism. This might create a problem. Roosevelt pronounced his verdict: "It's Truman!" It was tantamount to election. He ascended to the vice-presidency. The fact that he was only the proverbial heartbeat away from the Presidency made him a popular invitee at public functions. His was the eminence of possibility. It was then that I met him in person. I introduced him at several dinners. He responded with references to my book, and revealed that President Roosevelt had sent copies to Prime Minister Churchill and the British cabinet.

He invited me to visit him in Washington. He was burdenless, and chatted easily. With self-conscious contradiction he showed me his desk diary to emphasize his busy day.

Then that heartbeat away became a reality. Suddenly (suddenly? We had refused to recognize the slowly approaching death on Roosevelt's drawn and quivering face and the hollowness in his voice as if it came from a subdued echo chamber), the plain man from Missouri was the President of the United States. There is no greater contrast than the emergence from the darkness of the powerless vice-presidency to the blazing prominence of the most important political office in the world.

It took a long while for the people of the world to get used to the contrast between Roosevelt's patrician head, bell-like voice ringing in metronomic cadences, and Truman's average, undistinguished features, his nasal tones, as if in the last stages of a cold, his chopping hand gesture for emphasis, and his plainness, which he showed off because he excelled in it. "Indeed, the eagles," Churchill and Roosevelt, were gone, and "the sparrows," Attlee and Truman, had taken their place. Or so it appeared at the time.

Sudden acquisition of power can paralyze a man with fright, or stimulate him with confidence. No one can know a man's psyche to predict what his reaction will be. Like the mysterious action of a new ingredient on a chemical compound, it can reduce or activate it. Truman actually grew cocky, when faced with immense responsibility. It may have been due to his knowledge of history, which he did not flaunt, because it might give him an intellectual appearance. He felt more comfortable being known for "common sense" than for learning. Nevertheless, from his immense reading, he realized that great leaders in history followed their instincts, acted firmly, and were not torn apart by indecision and worry. He once expressed this to me, offhandedly, shunning profound psychological exposition. He defined it as a combination of judgment and courage. But how does one acquire them and how often are they confused with recklessness?

The President agreed to make an address at the University of California, where he would receive an honorary degree. He chose to speak on the dangers of Communism and asked me to prepare a draft for his talk. I did so, phrasing his own view, which I admired, that we would not interfere with any nation which chose a totalitarian government for itself. It was only the insistence of fanatics, whether on the right or left, that they must subdue their neighbors in order to bestow upon them the blessings of their totalitarian notions, which we would resist. It was the difference between a benign tumor, which was relatively harmless, and a cancerous, metastasizing one, which invaded the other organs of the body.

Looking back now more than thirty years to Truman's words gives one the eerie feeling not only that history repeats itself, but at times that it is a mere extension of the past. He said:

No action by the United States has revealed more clearly our sincere desire for peace than our proposal in the United Nations for the international control of atomic energy. In a step without precedent, we have voluntarily offered to share with others the secrets of atomic power. We ask only for conditions that will guarantee its use for the benefit of humanity and not for the destruction of humanity.

The speech was dotted with epigrammatic passages. Addressing Russia, he said:

No nation has the right to exact a price for good behavior . . . it is possible for different economic systems to live side by side in peace; provided one of these systems is not determined to destroy the other by force.

Truman's earnestness and sincerity were his own brand of nonoratorical eloquence.

The only expansion we are interested in is the expansion of human freedom and the wider enjoyment of the good things of the earth in all countries.
The only prize we covet is the respect and good will of our fellow members of the family of nations.

His address was well received. The New York *Times* reported, "The speech was easily the most important of the more than forty talks the Chief Excutive has delivered so far on this wide-ranging topic."

On another occasion, I was invited through his special counsel, Clark Clifford, to submit a draft for a new address. I went to Washington for this purpose only. It was Friday, May 14, 1948. I did not know that the day would have historic significance. After I was briefed on the subject matter, I thought I would informally greet the President, if he was not occupied at the moment. I was ushered in. The President was in a tense mood. He had known for some time that on that very day Israel would declare its statehood. He had been under enormous pressure for months by conflicting forces concerning the creation of a Jewish state. On one side were England, the Arabs and their oil, even then a crucial factor, the State Department particularly the Middle East desk, which accepted the Arab view. As Truman later wrote in his memoirs:

Like most of the British diplomats, some of our diplomats also thought that the Arabs, on account of their numbers and because of the fact that they controlled such immense oil resources, should be appeased. I am sorry to say that there were some among them who were also inclined to be anti-semitic. (p. 164)

On the other side were a great majority of senators, representatives, and Jewish leaders who bombarded him with pleas to assist in bringing the Balfour Declaration for a Jewish state to culmination. As far back as 1937, Winston Churchill had said to the House of Commons:

It is a delusion to suppose that the Balfour Declaration was a mere act of crusading enthusiasm or quixotic philanthropy. It was a measure taken . . . in dire need of the war with the object of promoting the general victory of the allies, for which we expected and received valuable and important assistance.

Still, when faced in 1948 with Arab threats to attack if a Jewish state was formed, the Balfour Declaration, which had been described as "humanitarian," of "tactical political advantage," and "long range strategic interests," and therefore "an irresistible combination to any imaginative Anglo-Saxon Statesman," ceased to be attractive to Britain, which could not keep order in Palestine with ninety thousand troops.

Truman similarly experienced the conflict between an ideal and the realities which loomed like obstructive mountains to its effectuation. As senator, he had no difficulty with the concept of a Jewish state. ". . . when the time comes," he said, "I am willing to help make the fight for a Jewish homeland in Palestine." Prophetically the time came, and he, as President, more than any person in the world, was in a position to make that dream of Herzl come true. But the Middle Eastern region had become a political hot spot of intrigue, boiling in oil. Truman expressed his exasperation:

I surely wish God Almighty would give the Children of Israel an Isaiah, the Christians a St. Paul, and the Sons of Ishmael a peep at the Golden Rule.

He had vigorously favored the admission to Palestine of one hundred thousand Jewish escapees from the Nazi terror. With unbelievable callousness, England and other countries were rejecting boats filled mostly with women and children, who, through the heroism of the underground, had escaped the Nazi extermination program. The defective immigrant status of the passengers was such an immoral legalism, in the light of the burning ovens which awaited them, that it should have yielded to the ordinary dictates of humanity. Instead, with few exceptions, there was unwitting but real co-operation with the Nazi hunters.

Truman was indignant. In 1945 he so wrote Clement Attlee, Britain's Prime Minister. Truman's grandparents had been displaced persons, uprooted during the Civil War, who had fled to Missouri. He had been moved and fascinated by their reminiscences, of the misery of dislocation. The impression on his child's mind added poignancy to his compassion for the Jews' plight.

When Ibn Saud protested Truman's sponsoring the immigration of a hundred thousand Jewish refugees into Palestine, he received a blunt rebuke. Truman expressed the hope that countries outside Europe, including the United States, would admit the survivors of Nazi persecution. "The United States," he wrote, "which contributed its blood and resources to the winning of the war, could not divest itself of a certain responsibility . . . for the fate of people liberated at that time."

There was no equivocation. That was not the Truman way. He continued, ". . . a national home for Jewish people should be established in Palestine."

What a contrast with President Roosevelt's communications with Ibn Saud. They were so ambiguous that all conflicting parties drew encouragement from them and later denounced them, or vice versa. First, it was reported by Colonel William Eddy, United States Minister to Saudi Arabia, that Roosevelt had given a pledge to Ibn Saud that he would not support any move to hand Palestine over to the Jews. Later Roosevelt confided to James Byrnes that when he mentioned Palestine to Ibn Saud, "That was the end of the pleasant conversation." Congress was assured that American policy for the establishment of a Jewish homeland remained firm.

Nevertheless Roosevelt wrote to Ibn Saud that "no decision will be taken with respect to the basic situation . . . without full consultation with both Arabs and Jews." Thus the Arabs were given a veto. This was the difference between Roosevelt's diplomatic ingenuity, which operated in circled lines, and Truman's straight point-to-point candor.

Although Truman favored Jewish statehood, he became involved in a conflict with his own State Department and with his most trusted and revered adviser, General George Marshall.

Both the Democratic and Republican parties had planks in their platforms supporting the creation of a Jewish state. Congress was overwhelmingly pledged to it.

On July 2, 1945, a petition signed by fifty-four senators and two hundred fifty-one members of the House of Representatives urged his support of the United Nations resolution for partition, a plan which created two independent states in Palestine, one Jewish and the other Arab. But the "striped pants boys" of the State Department, as Truman called them, would not have it.

The conflicting pressures became so painful that Truman resolved to see no one, outside the Government, on this subject. He would make up his own mind, eschewing political and emotional considerations. It so happened that Dr. Chaim Weizmann had come from Palestine to visit Truman. He was the scientist who had increased the effectiveness of explosives to make them more devastating than ever before. This aided the Allies to win World War I, as much later, Professor Einstein's formula led to the creation of the atom bomb, which Truman used to end World War II.

Weizmann had obtained the Balfour Declaration, the charter which was England's promise to support a homeland for the Jews. He was destined to be the George Washington of Israel, its first President. When I later visited him in the President's office in Rehovat, near the great scientific institute named after him, his bearded head, ineffable charm, and humor ("We are becoming a real nation. We haven't any horses yet, but we already have horsethieves.") gave me the impression that Disraeli must have been like him.

Truman stuck by his instruction to his staff, that he would see no one on the subject of Palestine, not even Weizmann, whom he admired. Eddie Jacobson, Truman's former partner in a haberdashery store and friend for thirty years, came to plead for Weizmann's reception. Truman, who had great affection for Jacobson, nevertheless warned him not to talk about Palestine. Jacobson was desperate. He was not a Zionist, and he had never met Weizmann, but he felt it was important for Truman to be informed in a matter which involved the remnants of his destroyed people.

He avoided Truman's injunction by a ruse. He launched on a discussion of Truman's hero-worship of Andrew Jackson; how he remembered him reading about Jackson whenever there was time in the store, and how he had later put Jackson's statue in front of the Kansas City Courthouse. Then he made his point. Weizmann had been Jacobson's hero all his life just as Jackson had been Truman's. Now, Weizmann, although old and sick, had come thousands of miles to talk to the President. How could he refuse to see him? There were tears on Jacobson's cheeks.

Truman thought a while. Then he said, "I'll see him, you bald son of a bitch." To prevent a new flood of visitors, Weizmann was ushered in through the East Gate, without public or press announcement.

Truman saw the creation of a Jewish democratic state in the Middle East, not merely as a moral debt to six million slaughtered Jews, but as an essential part of American counteraction to Communistic designs on the Middle East and its oil. By 1947, Communists dominated Poland, Latvia, Lithuania, Estonia, Rumania, Czechoslovakia, Yugoslavia, and

Bulgaria. Britain had announced that she was ending her economic and military aid to Greece and Turkey. The President announced the Truman Doctrine and, shortly thereafter, the Marshall Plan to prevent further Communist penetration of Europe. The Middle East and its precious oil had likewise to be immunized from Communist take-over, not only to protect Europe, but because it was in itself the gateway to three continents and was coveted by the Soviets.

In this large strategy, a democratic, modern state with outstanding capabilities, in the midst of feudal Arab regions, which were susceptible to Soviet blandishments, was a great gain, if not indeed a necessity. On the other hand, if it resulted in war, the desired stability would be endangered. It was these considerations of Kennanism and Marshallism which concerned Truman, not, as the critics of the day charged, domestic considerations of the coming election.

So he had overruled the State Department and directed that the United States vigorously support the creation of a Jewish state. Even then, through a strange misunderstanding, Warren Austin, our ambassador to the United Nations, made a contrary public statement. In protest, Mrs. Eleanor Roosevelt resigned as a member of the American delegation to the United Nations. Truman refused to accept her resignation. He was furious with the State Department. He had been made out to be a liar to those he had talked to on the subject. The impression in the United Nations and in the capitals of the world was that the United States was confused, vacillating, and incapable of taking a firm position in a situation fraught with danger.

Curiously, the Soviet Union, through its chief delegate to the United Nations, Andrei Gromyko, denounced Warren Austin's "treachery," and urged the creation of a Jewish state. Anything to oust England from Palestine. That was why Russia had previously sent military equipment to the Haganah, Israel's army, aiding it in capturing Haifa on April 24, 1948. It was not until years later that it served Russia's purpose to become Israel's chief antagonist. This is another illustration of the Soviet Union's inconsistent tactics to achieve a consistent objective.

Truman's difficulty with the State Department merely repeated the experience of other Presidents. The State Department considered itself the repository of historical institutional policies. Presidents came and went. It "taught" the President what should be done, and if he was not assertive enough, it contrived to bypass his contrary views by subtle involved instructions to our far-flung embassies. Roosevelt had coped with this problem by organizing his own little State Department at the White House. Nixon and Ford were to use Dr. Henry Kissinger for the same purpose, much to the distress of the Secretary of State, William Rogers, until Kissinger absorbed the office. Truman struggled to establish the authority of the presidency over the entrenched power of the "striped pants boys" as he continued to call them contemptuously. He finally established his dominance in the Israeli issue.

Despite the formidable opposition of George Marshall, who later relented, James Forrestal, Admiral Leahy, Edward Stettinius, Loy Henderson, and others, Truman, with the advice of his special counsel Clark Clifford, who dared to challenge the impressive opposition, gave full support to the Partition Plan in the United Nations. On November 29, 1947, by a necessary two-thirds vote of thirty-three to ten, with ten abstentions, the General Assembly passed the resolution which gave international sanction of the United Nations to the creation of a Jewish state.

On May 14, 1948, the Union Jack was hauled down from the Government House in Jerusalem and the British mandate came to an end. The English commander, General Cunningham, withdrew his troops to the mournful music of Scottish bagpipers. The Jews decided not to lose a moment in declaring their independence as a state. Egypt and other Arab states had threatened repeatedly that such an act would bring immediate attack. This did not deter them. Fearing an Arab air raid which might snuff out the infant state before it was born, the founders arranged a meeting with great secrecy at which the momentous announcement would be made to the world. The site was designated to be the Tel Aviv Museum and was revealed only one hour before assembling. Soldiers with Sten guns guarded every approach to the building. There, under a picture of Theodor Herzl, the Austrian Jew who fifty years earlier had founded the Zionist movement, Ben-Gurion banged his gavel with the same power with which he had split the rocks on the desert and declared, "We hereby proclaim the establishment of the Jewish State in Palestine, to be called Israel." Then in a frieze tableau, as if staged for reproduction for centuries to come, they stood to the strains of *Hatikva*, the national anthem.

Word of the new state fled on radio wings to every man, woman, and child in the land, setting off hysterical jubilation. The screams of elation were suddenly suppressed. It was Friday evening. The Sabbath had begun and would last until sundown the next day. It was a time for prayer, not for shouting and dancing. So with superhuman restraint, they disciplined their fervor and turned it into reverent silence and prayer.

But the next day, as soon as the sun dipped into the Mediterranean, Hassidic joy burst forth with violent abandon. Men hugged each other, kissed women, whoever they were, formed circles and danced the hora. Individualists ran into the circles with waving arms and high-prancing feet to add to the frenzy. Young boys and girls, many of them in the army, marched in file in and around the swirling masses, singing patriotic songs. Old religious Jews sang their odes to God to express the holy joyousness of Hassidic belief. Their vigorous whirling dervish spins defied their age, and their long satin caftans flew high in the opposite direction of their feet as if they were wind-borne. Flags and flaming buntings appeared everywhere waving the revelers on, and in cafes and homes toasts rang out. At times the fury was stemmed momentarily by tones of the *Hatikva*. But its patriotic solemnity could not long quench the wild joy of the populace.

The name Israel had been chosen because of the legend in Genesis (32:24), according to which the Patriarch Jacob and an angel engaged in an all-night wrestling match. Jacob triumphed and extracted from the helpless angel the mysterious blessing, "Thy name shall be called no more Jacob, but Israel; for thou hast striven with God and with men and hast prevailed."

The emotions of the historic birth, which was a reincarnation of a nation two thousand years old, were understandably overwhelming. For centuries, one of the prayers in every Jewish service throughout the world was for the re-establishment of the Temple and a Jewish state. "If I forget you, O Jerusalem, let my right hand wither. Let my tongue cleave to the roof of my mouth." At last a nation had risen from ashes laden with sacrificial bones. The prayer had come true. To Jews it was the fulfillment of God's grant, set forth in the Book of Genesis.

On that day a covenant was made with Abraham that said to your children I shall give this land from the River known as the River of Egypt until the great river Euphrates. (15:18) And I shall give this land to your children after you; the land of sojourning; the entire land of Canaan as eternal inheritance. (17:8)

The land authorized by the United Nations was only a sliver of the Bible's promise, but it fulfilled a biblical promise of the creation of a state.

The prosaic political task of choosing a form of government and filling its contours with men and women was still to take place. Truman had received notification on the letterhead of "The Jewish Agency for Palestine" (the nation did not yet have its own stationery) that "The State of Israel had been proclaimed as an independent republic . . . and that a provisional government has been charged to assume the rights and duties of government."

It advised him that "The Act of Independence will become effective at one minute after six o'clock on the evening of 14 May 1948, Washington time."

It expressed "The hope that your government will recognize and will welcome Israel into the community of nations."

The letter was signed by Eliahu Epstein, "Agent Provisional Government of Israel."

Truman had several alternatives. He could withhold recognition entirely. He could grant *de facto* recognition to the Provisional Government. He could wait for the finalization of the Government apparatus and grant full *de jure* recognition. Or he could, in anticipation of the formal completion of the Government, grant immediate *de jure* recognition even though there was only an interim "provisional government."

Truman leaned to recognition. But to blunt the opposition in the State Department and the possible criticism that he was acting hastily, he was inclined to await the formal election of an Israeli parliament (the Knesset) and the election of a President. Then he would grant *de jure* recognition. This would give him time, because, as he knew, it would take many months to achieve such a status. Actually, it took six months. Not until January 25, 1949, was a duly constituted Israeli Government completed.

It was about five o'clock, Washington time, Friday, May 14, 1948. In about an hour the Provisional Government of Israel would be announced in Tel Aviv.

It was in this atmosphere that I found myself at the President's desk in the oval office. Clark Clifford had been urging the President to grant full recognition to Israel immediately. He thought this might deter the Arabs from executing their threats to attack the new state. Moreover, this would fulfill the American promise, continuously expressed in the platforms of both the Republican and Democratic parties, supporting the creation of a Jewish state. Truman had given his word. That was enough.

Truman rose agitatedly from his desk and walked to a globe of the world which Roosevelt had kept in the office. He twirled it and indicated the refueling ports and bases for our Navy, and said that Admiral Leahy had warned him that antagonizing the Arabs might deprive us of essential support points and distant oil depots for our ships.

I commented that even if this was so, would it not be advantageous to American security to have a democratic bastion of loyalty in the Middle East with its own shoreline, to offset feudal Arab rulers who were notoriously undependable. Communist expansion in the area would also be discouraged by an Israel which could not be turned into a Soviet satellite.

Truman returned to his desk and gestured with his thumb toward the State Department Building, saying that Secretary of State George Marshall and the rest were firmly opposed to recognition. He would take care of that but he was inclined to wait until Israel was a formally constituted government entitled to *de jure* recognition.

Clifford had urged him to act immediately, pointing out that there was a strong likelihood that the Soviet Union would recognize Israel during the weekend, and thus be the first nation to do so. He was right in his warning. The Soviet Union and Poland recognized Israel the very next day.

Truman spoke reflectively, like a man who was appealing to himself rather than to his hearers. He expressed his profound biblical conviction that Israel's emergence was the fulfillment of a prophecy. I commented that he was in a unique position to make that prophecy come true, and that history would remember him for the historic act he could now perform, perhaps more than for any other thing he would do in his life. He was deeply moved. He authorized Clifford to draft a recognition *de facto*.

Clifford, who during White House meetings that week with George Marshall, Robert Lovett, and State Department officials had stood up to the opponents of recognition and relieved the President of replying to their intemperate statements, had met with Bob Lovett for lunch the day before. Lovett had had a change of heart, and in anticipation of the catapulting events, he and Clifford had drafted a formal recognition statement. Clifford was ready. Eleven minutes after Israel's declaration of independence, the following statement was released by the White House:

May 14, 1948

STATEMENT BY THE PRESIDENT

This government has been informed that a Jewish state has been proclaimed in Palestine, and recognition has been requested by the provisional government thereof.

The United States recognizes the provisional government as the de facto authorized of the new State of Israel.

Although a copy of this announcement was sent to the Secretary of State, none of the United States delegates to the United Nations knew anything of the decision in advance. There were consternation and surprise in the diplomatic fraternity. Many were dumfounded, since they were still engaged, as they believed with United States support, in a debate for trusteeship, the opposite of the creation of a Jewish state. Some thought the report was a joke. Dr. Philip C. Jessup, of the

United States delegation, checked the report and assured the delegates it was true.

The Washington *Post* commented that:

Diplomats were shocked because the United States flipflopped from a policy of confusion and indecision on Palestine to a positive act taken in unprecedented haste.

There was precedent for Truman's action. The United States had granted full *de jure* recognition to the Soviet Union in 1917, even though it was only a provisional government. It had recognized *de jure* the provisional government of Poland after World War II. So that Truman's granting only *de facto* recognition to Israel was unusually cautious. The United States was the only country in the United Nations, except South Africa, which did not grant *de jure* recognition to the Provisional Government of Israel. It finally did so in January 1949, when Israel completed its constitutional procedures with presidential and parliamentary elections.

However, Truman's instant recognition of Israel after its birth, even though *de facto*, was deemed by the Israelis a glorious and unforgettable chapter in their two thousand years of struggle.

It did not deter Egypt and four other Arab states from carrying out threats to invade Israel. The nation had been born in agony and would have to survive infancy against overwhelming numbers of antagonists. The people were calm and inured to strife. An anecdote illustrates this. One evening, a fierce storm broke. Jagged daggers of lightning seemed to pierce the clouds to release torrents, accompanied by tremendous peals of thunder. The next morning, a mother asked her five-year-old son whether he had been frightened during the night. "No," he replied, "I thought it was guns."

Within hours after the pronouncement of the state, Egyptian bombers struck a bus station in Tel Aviv killing forty men and women. The blood which flowed from them was to spread through the small nation.

On Friday nights, it had become a happy custom for Mildred and me to visit the well-known couturier Maurice Rentner, his wife, family, and other guests for dinner. It was a quasi-religious occasion, with candles on the table and a traditional feast. But it was very quasi. After dinner, the candles and dishes were cleared away, leaving only fresh pineapple and plates of candies for the gin players who took over. I was due there as usual that Friday evening.

When I left the White House, I stopped to telephone Mildred at the Rentners' in New York, to tell her that I would be late for dinner. More important, I was bursting with the news that Israel had just been recognized by the United States. The Rentner guests included outstanding executives of department stores and other enterprises. They were quite knowledgeable and apparently as incredulous about the story as our own delegates at the United Nations. They turned on the radio and television sets, and by the time I arrived, the news had flashed across the wires. Yes, a radio wave goes around the world seven times in one second, and the whole world knew that a new state had been born, and that it, the youngest democracy, had been recognized by the oldest modern democracy.

I delayed the dinner further to call my father and mother. They were in their summer home in Bethlehem, New Hampshire. They had just returned from the synagogue situated down the slope on Strawberry Hill. Sensitively my father caught the excitement in my voice and was alarmed by it. "Is anything the matter?" "No," I replied, "it is wonderful news." I gave it to him. "Bella!" he cried out. "Come here, listen to what Zindel-leben has to tell us." She listened and all she could say in a choked voice was "God bless you." I learned later that they had alerted the rabbi and many of their friends who gathered in our home. My father led the singing and schnapps flowed freely. The celebration in Tel Aviv had an echo in a town in New Hampshire appropriately called Bethlehem.

It must have had similar echoes in gatherings throughout the world, many of them among non-Jews, for a biblical prophecy had that day come true.

Truman was a student of the Bible. He had read the St. James Version twice while he was a young man. He had evidenced a special interest in history of the Middle East and had spoken movingly about it on many occasions.

A year after the recognition of Israel and after it had repulsed the invaders, the patriarchal white-bearded Chief Rabbi Herzog of Israel visited Truman. He had previously been the Chief Rabbi of Ireland and spoke with a thick Irish brogue. He expressed the sentiment I had offered to the President on the fateful recognition day. But he did it with mystical eloquence. He said to the President:

"God put you in your mother's womb so that you could be the instrument to bring about the rebirth of Israel after two thousand years."

THERE ARE MANY ECHOES BUT FEW VOICES

It has been my good fortune to be engaged in politics at the top. During the first Eisenhower-Stevenson campaign in 1952, I was invited to introduce the Governor at a number of meetings. I did not resort to the usual political hyperboles. Instead I analyzed the needs of the hour and the qualities of the candidate, as if destiny had offered up the man to suit the occasion. Each introduction carried this theme farther, making a series of political expositions whose connections were not evident to separate audiences but did not escape Stevenson's perception. He told me that they virtually outlined a campaign theme, and invited me to elaborate on them and submit them to him.

Of course, he eliminated the references to himself, although candidates usually unashamedly speak of their own capacities and accomplishments in the most laudatory terms. Somehow the theory has developed that a candidate who is modest about himself forfeits the electorate's support, because then he has no business aspiring to powerful office.

Even John Kennedy, whose grace and taste were impeccable, deemed it politically wise to retort to President Truman's comment that he was too young and inexperienced to seek the presidency, by proclaiming that he was fully qualified and ready to assume the highest office. I was surprised not only by the unabashed declaration of his own ability, but the asperity with which it was announced. He commented sarcastically that apparently no one was qualified for the office unless he obtained the approval of Truman.

But Stevenson could never engage in a gauche gesture irrespective of political dictates. He continued to be self-deprecating and there was more sincerity than humor in his attitude. This did not mean that he held himself in light esteem—certainly not when compared to the rivals on the scene. Rather it evidenced his recognition of the enormity of the problems our generation faced and the inadequacy of any man to cope brilliantly with all of them. His modesty was the expression of a fact of life, not lack of confidence to do as well or better than any other man. But could the people sense those distinctions?

The same problem was presented by his thoughtfulness. He knew that only a demagogue could be sure about solutions for century-old problems made more complicated by rising nationalisms and the developments of science. So he weighed both sides. He pondered. He admitted his doubts. He wanted more information and the opportunity to reflect. This was nothing but an intelligent approach. It didn't mean paralysis of thought or inability to make up his mind. Indeed, he was firm as a rock when he had reached a decision. Who could have been more direct and aggressive than he was with the Russian representative at the United Nations when he demanded that he say "Yes" or "No" whether Russia had placed missiles in Cuba. When the representative paused to gather his thoughts for an evasive answer, Stevenson pushed him with "Don't think—just answer, did you or didn't you?"—and "I am ready to wait for your answer until Hell freezes over!" Did this come from a vacillating man who could not make up his mind?

Yet during the campaign, and until this day, one hears that Stevenson had a Hamlet defect, forever asking "To be or not to be" and never coming to a conclusion. Men who reach decisions carefully and after searching their souls are more resolute than impetuous executives who give the appearance of strength but veer readily under pressure. Woodrow Wilson is another example of a "slow to conclude, but hard to dislodge" (I almost wrote dis-Lodge) type of personality.

I am convinced that Stevenson would have been a strong and decisive President.

Most public men have two personalities, or at least shadings which are different in their public and private appearances. President Johnson, for example, immediately became a different man when he appeared on television. It was as if he put on a cloak of deliberateness and dignity, and temper and passion were washed out of the picture. Unconsciously, he revealed his notion of his ideal by using over and over again the quotation from Isaiah, "Come, let us reason together." In action, he was the opposite. For a good cause he would twist arms mercilessly. Pressure, not reason, was his technique when he was leader of the Senate.

Hubert Humphrey once told me the amusing story of his experience when he first entered the Senate. Senator Johnson called him to a caucus meeting to line up the votes for a bill. Humphrey indignantly announced that he had been elected senator by the people of Minnesota, and would exercise an independent judgment on every piece of legislation. He was not going to be instructed what to do, even by the President himself, let alone the leader of the Senate.

"Of course, of course, Senator," said Johnson. "I merely thought it was a good bill and you would want to be told about it."

Later, there was an opportunity for a junior senator to be appointed to one of the Senate committees. Humphrey was passed over.

On another occasion, he was summoned to a caucus meeting. Again he declared that only his conscience would guide him. "I might vote for the bill when I study it, but I don't want to be pushed," he declared. Again the leader understood, but when a post office had to be built in Minneapolis, the project was held up.

So it went. Finally Humphrey said he realized that he had voted for every piece of legislation proposed by the caucus. The next time he was summoned, he laughingly announced "I am with you, Senator." A great friendship began which ultimately made him Vice-President but cost him the presidency.

On another occasion President Johnson described to a group of visitors, who met in the Cabinet Room, how he wanted the president of one of America's great corporations to serve on a committee with a labor leader and a public representative to control inflation. The executive replied that he would have to consult with his board of directors, and called later to decline. The President gathered some facts and called the executive again. "I hope you will reconsider," he said, and reeled off the precise amounts of payments made to his company under government contracts in the past several years, and the current applications pending.

"Would you believe it," the President smiled mischievously, "this awakened his duty to render some public service, and he accepted the assignment without even going back to his directors."

"Come let us reason together"—indeed? One certainly can't be angry at such use of presidential power for the public weal, but unlike Truman, who bragged of such tactics, Johnson's public demeanor negated his true and often better personality. So did Eisenhower's. But Stevenson's charm, warmth, humor, reflectiveness, and felicity were precisely the same whether on the platform or at the dinner table. He laughed readily. He was flattering, and sincerely so, to others when his generous spirit caused him to believe they deserved it.

Above all he had a large perspective. Some call it a historical sense. To hear him discuss any subject was to be lifted immediately above shallow consideration and see the problem in full dimension. Thus his deliberation for a solution began where others had ended, since they had not even perceived the depth of the difficulty.

Another extraordinary quality was that he would not compromise with himself. "To thy own self be true," was a natural and unshakable principle by which he lived. Despite frenzied pleas by his political advisers, he would not cater to voters by ambiguous statements or subservience to the wishes of a particular group. It was in Madison Square Garden, at an American Legion convention, that he delivered a talk on true patriotism. Those who read his speech in advance had a fit. They feared he would be hooted out of the hall. They knew he wouldn't cater to any jingoistic spirit and cause the rafters to ring with a Fourth-of-July oration. But why couldn't he save this speech for the Civil Liberties Union or the Americans for Democratic Action? Why risk offending an audience which represented a huge following, when it was so easy to sing the glories of America and its flag and bring the house down?

Stevenson would not budge. It took courage to deliver that speech because he might have been hissed off the platform, and the campaign would be lost before it began. He said:

"Consider the groups who seek to indentify their special interests with the general welfare. I find it sobering to think that their pressure may one day be focused on me. I have resisted them before and I hope the Almighty will give me the strength to do so again and again. And I should tell you, my fellow Legionnaires, as I would tell all other organized groups that I intend to resist pressures from veterans also."

He told me that he was not being defiant. He believed in the American Legion. He believed in their constituency. They were the American people, conservatives and liberals. There was no reason to trim his sails.

He was right. The audience recognized his greatness, and even those who disagreed with some of his pronouncements stood and cheered. It was an ovation and gave impetus to the campaign instead of destroying it.

So it went. It was to labor that he talked on the excesses which disserved their best interests. It was to businessmen that he talked of responsibility to the public and the shortsightedness of a greedy policy in a modern world. It was to the South that he talked of the brotherhood of man which could not be abnegated by color, and to the North, that hypocrisy in civil rights was a sin against the Constitution as well as against blacks.

He talked where it did some good for the nation's welfare, not for himself as a vote getter.

Compare Eisenhower's posing for a picture with Senator Joseph McCarthy, whom he detested. When the senator took advantage of the opportunity by putting his arm around the General's shoulder and hugging him like a buddy, Eisenhower nearly spit. He warned his clever political strategists that if McCarthy ever did that again, he would punch him in the nose. But even his unfailing good instincts had yielded to political expediency. He was like the lawyer who found out what advice his client wanted and then gave it to him. It was impossible to conceive of Stevenson in this light. He abhorred political pap. It offended not only his cultured appreciation of our language, but his integrity. "A politician," he jested, "is a man who approaches every question with an open mouth." He insisted on "talking sense to the people." He respected them too much to treat them like fools or infants. In this sense there was no self-sacrifice in his "highfalutin" campaign. The people would understand. They deserved nothing less than the best. That is why he would polish every word of his speeches to its highest gloss, while his assistants were driven to distraction, waiting for the script to be put through the vast communication process.

Four sentences in his acceptance speech at the convention revealed the exquisite qualities of his mind and his deep feeling. "The potential of the presidency for good or evil now and in the years of our lives smothers exultation and converts vanity to prayer. I have asked the merciful Father to let this cup pass from me. But from such dread responsibility one does not shrink in fear, in self-interest, or in false humility. So, 'if this cup may not pass away from me, except I drink it, Thy will be done.'"

He was doing more than running for President. He was lifting the national spirit, appealing to the ideals which he knew were responsible for American's greatness, setting before the people moral standards toward which they could repair from all directions, thus enhancing their unity without obliterating their differences. He aroused their conscience. To be complacent in the face of injustice was to be guilty of indecent composure. Had he been President, he would have utilized the moral power of that office to better effect than any other Chief Executive with the exception only of Lincoln.

The fact that he lost did not disprove his faith in the democratic process. He himself recognized the wisdom of the people in choosing Eisenhower. In intimate discussion, he expressed the rationale for his own defeat. The great problem facing the nation was Russia, and the selection of the victorious general in history's greatest conflict provided an invaluable power symbol which would command Russia's respect and caution. Eisenhower had used his authority to create good will. He was a friend of Marshal Zhukov and other Russian military figures. He was better known than Stalin to the peoples behind the Iron Curtain.

In contrast, Stevenson was an unknown figure internationally, and indeed hardly known to the American people. The Russians might be tempted to test him, as later they did Kennedy—a probe which brought us nearer a holocaust than we have ever been before or since. So the people, in electing Eisenhower, were buying insurance. The premium was reasonable. He had a kind heart and an ingratiating smile. He had demonstrated his diplomatic skill. He was not a martial figure like Mac-Arthur, who was admired as a general, but would have been unthinkable as a President. Indeed, Eisenhower's later valedictory warning against the military establishment corroborated Stevenson's analysis of him as devoid of military impetuosity or arrogance.

Thus, Stevenson rose above his own defeat to understand and justify the wisdom of the people.

Why then did he run a second time against Eisenhower? I participated in that decision, though I was a minority of one. Stevenson invited me to attend a meeting in his law office in Chicago in 1956. Present were his most intimate advisers and friends—among them Colonel Jacob Arvey, his law partners William M. Blair, Jr., and Newton Minow.

Arvey was recognized as the man who had brought Stevenson into the political arena. He was properly honored for his acuity and high-mindedness in attracting such a star into a firmament which usually shone with lesser lights. He, too, however, suffered from the unorthodoxy of his candidate. He told, with a mixture of exasperation and pride, how Stevenson turned down a large contribution from a union when he was running for Governor of Illinois. Every cent was precious, but when the visiting committee requested a promise that, if elected, he would appoint their candidate for Water Commissioner, he respectfully dismissed them.

"Mr. Stevenson, here is his record. He is the best qualified man for the post. Look into it."

"I will," he said, "and perhaps I will appoint him, if I am lucky enough to be elected. But I will make no advance promises."

They withheld their contribution. "He is one of those impracticable idealists," they told Arvey. "He will never be elected dog catcher."

But he was elected Governor. Later, he did appoint the union's choice because he was the best man on the merits.

On the other hand, his principles compelled him to support a member of his administration even though there were rumors of a scandal about him. An opposition newspaper threatened to expose him, unless Stevenson dismissed him. The evidence was circumstantial and did not convince the Governor of guilt. "If I had to appoint him today, I would not do so. There are those about whom there are no suspicions. But I will not dismiss him, and thereby brand him for life."

The headline broke. Stevenson would not budge. Nothing was ever proved, and the accused served well and honorably the rest of the term.

Since then he had become a national figure. It took the exposure of a presidential campaign to lift him to recognition.

I recall the shrewd words of the motion picture pioneer Adolph Zukor, whose hundred-year celebration I attended. Carried away by Stevenson's campaign, I predicted that he could win over Eisenhower. "Never," said Zukor. "You have the best actor but he is unknown. He is running against a star, a Clark Gable. Wait until you see the box office returns!"

But now as a new election approached, Stevenson was no longer an unknown actor. If he wished the Democratic nomination again, there was no doubt he could have it. The question was, should he accept?

Those around the table agreed on two propositions. First that the Governor should run. He was the strongest candidate the Democrats had. If he withdrew, the party would never forgive him. He would be dead politically. If he ran and lost, he would still have to be reckoned with in the future. The most politically knowledgeable men there pronounced this proposition with a certainty that one would ascribe to a logarithmic axiom. When my turn came, I demurred. It was evident that President Eisenhower was a more formidable opponent than he was the last time. Economic conditions favored him. The foreign scene was reasonably quiescent. His much-discussed fatherly image had matured into a more lovable grandfather image. Why court defeat a second time? If the Governor sat this one out, he would be a powerful, perhaps inevitable choice to run four years later, when Eisenhower would not be his opponent. The chances are that after eight years of Republican rule, a Democrat would win, and Stevenson would be an overwhelming choice, over any other Republican than Eisenhower.

As for the political shibboleth that a candidate owed his party the duty to lead it even if in defeat, I confessed my amateur standing in such a matter, but I could not understand why it would serve the party or the Governor to destroy its foremost personality by another defeat when he might well be salvaged for victory in the next campaign.

Everyone turned to Stevenson. He said he had given the matter long and earnest thought. He described his distaste for campaigning. It was an ordeal he would wish to avoid if he possibly could. Even the presidency was not worth it to him. It put a premium on stamina rather than thought. The hoopla, the posturing, the handshaking, the ubiquitous need to beg for support, the humiliating fund-raising functions, the pull and tug to be everywhere and cater to every influential politician—all violated his sense of propriety. Nevertheless, he felt he had to accept the nomination if it were tendered to him.

The reason was somewhat different from that urged upon him. He recognized Eisenhower's increased popularity. He foresaw the great possibility of defeat. If he refused to run, it would appear that he was running away from the battle. He could not act in this cowardly way. He would lead the party as ably as he could if it wished him to do so.

I could not agree with his conclusion. It seemed to me to be based upon a concept of chivalry rather than upon higher and more realistic considerations. But the political experts and the idealist agreed. Such a parallelism was impressive. I kept my peace.

The discussions then turned to the kind of campaign Stevenson should wage if, as seemed a foregone conclusion, he was nominated. Once more, I found myself in a minority of one.

Everyone urged with varying degrees of tact that the Governor should change his campaign style. In effect, they were saying that he talked "over the heads of the people," that he must stop appealing solely to intellectuals; that instead of a few carefully prepared addresses, he ought to make ten to twenty short talks a day to small groups at whistle stops, at shopping centers, and to any whirlpool gathering which a candidate attracts; that he was a warm human being and he ought to communicate this quality by mixing with people, shaking hands, making small talk and seeking out the leaders of the local community. Less humor wouldn't hurt either. Levity and statesmanship don't go together, according to public relations experts.

Of course, there would be the opportunity for important pronouncements on television and at great rallies, but even here, he ought not to write speeches for enshrinement in political literature. He ought to talk to the people in their terms.

It was evident that these were not improvised suggestions. They seemed to be carefully worked out plans for a "down to earth" campaign which would reach the masses, and which would give him a chance to win.

I expressed my dissent, but far more vigorously this time. Often a man's strength is also his weakness. Stevenson's intellectual, idealistic, and felicitous appeal made him a unique figure on the political scene. True, it was not the customary mass appeal. That may have been its weakness. But he had polled more than twenty-seven million votes against a national hero and the most popular candidate of the century. So there must have been considerable comprehension of his stature even if not always of his words. Also his personality had evoked an enthusiastic following rarely seen in political annals. The people loved Ike, but those who admired Stevenson were fanatical about him. Such dedication and loyalty ought not to be sacrificed, which it would be if the gold of idealism turned to the dross of political stratagem.

History has proved that "intellectual candidates" can win and "people's candidates" can lose. But one cannot be transposed into another. The people called Roosevelt, "Teddy"; Smith, "Al"; Truman, "Harry"; Eisenhower, "Ike," but no one called Wilson, "Woody"; Hoover, "Herbie"; or Hughes, "Charlie." Indeed, Stevenson had not done too badly by this test of public identification. They had cheered "Adlai," even though no one would scream at him, "Give 'em hell!" as they affectionately did at Truman.

Furthermore, even if the "humanizing" tactic were wise, it could not be carried off. We had already heard how distasteful the knockabout bruises of campaigning were to him. If he quickened the pace and ran an even more frenzied schedule, without the opportunity for rest and thought, he would become dull, and his infectious zest for a debate of the issues would be drowned in the trivia of public relations gimmicks.

I concluded by turning to Stevenson and saying, "Governor, if you start kissing babies, you'll be embarrassed and so will the babies. It just isn't your style."

He threw back his head, a little like Roosevelt, and laughed heartily. There was no decision on this point. It was considered premature. The matter had been aired. That was sufficient for the time being.

When he was nominated, he gave no hint in his magnificent acceptance address that he was acting out of loyalty to the party. On the contrary, in a typically gallant and witty passage, he said that last time he had been reluctant to accept the nomination conferred upon him, but "this time you may have noticed, the honor was not entirely unsolicited by me."

Weeks later the nation was shocked by the announcement that President Eisenhower had suffered a heart attack. He had been rushed to Bethesda Hospital. The world's attention was focused on the daily bulletins which were issued from his bedside. Affection and alarm were the prevailing mood. Vice-President Nixon was filling the vacuum of the presidency, while announcing that the President was still at the helm and being consulted on anything of major importance.

Whatever the medical outcome, it seemed certain that the President could not run again. The ordeal of a campaign and the burdens of the Presidency were taxing enough for a well man. How could one stricken do justice to the office, and how could he expect the people to take the risk? How could an enfeebled President be trusted to react in a crisis?

Such are the uncertainties of life in general and political life in particular. Like a tropical storm which comes with such suddenness that the sun is still shining as the black clouds drench the land, the Republican Party was inundated by despair at the very moment when the shining countenance of its invulnerable son was at its brightest. There was no other candidate who could beat Stevenson. In one tragic instant, he appeared certain to be the next President of the United States.

"My God, my God," I kept saying to myself. "Suppose he had been talked out of accepting the nomination." I was never so grateful for having lost an argument.

However, Eisenhower's recovery was more startling than his illness. And his courage in staying in the race exceeded both. So desperate was his party to retain him as its candidate, and so confident of his hold on the people, that he even announced the restricted schedule of his activities in the future. With admirable candor he was telling the nation that, if elected, he would be a part-time President.

Here was a new clear-cut issue. Could the nation afford to take the risk of a sick President and perhaps worse? Stevenson decided as a matter of principle that he would not even discuss the subject. He admired Eisenhower as a man, and he would not indulge in morbid speculation about his short life expectancy, or his possible incapacity. He conducted the campaign as if the shadows over the President's health were nonexistent. As always, his punctilious instincts were right. But he abandoned them on the closing night of the campaign. I shall come to this.

It was clear then, and even more so in retrospect, that Stevenson's second campaign was far less effective than the first. He resolved the strategy dispute in his office by adopting both views. He would stick to the high road. Nothing could perusade him to abandon that. His speeches were still sculptured elegance. He still sought perfection as he made last-second changes in the television studio, while his assistants clamored for a finished version. He still put his personal stamp on every paragraph, no matter what the staff handed him.

At his request, I prepared a talk on the Middle East. It was an analysis of Russia's penetration into an area which Napoleon once said was the key to world domination. Despite his feverish schedule, he had somehow found the time to rewrite and improve on my best effort.

So he had rejected the plea to talk down to the people. He would not compromise with excellence whether it be thought or diction. Yet in an effort to make a more pervasive campaign, he had also accepted the advice to appear more often, make improvised, short speeches, which could be repeated ad nauseam to small groups, shake hands, and generally be more a man of and with the people than above them. He had weighted the alternative of limiting his campaign in the main to television, even though that meant relatively few appearances. He asked me whether stumping in person had not been made obsolete by technology. I told him that experience in motion pictures proved the opposite. The more a star's image appeared on the screen, the more eager audiences were to see him in person.

I believe it is a false political concept of democracy that its leader must be reduced to the common denominator (if not the lowest common denominator) in order to be accepted by the people. They look for humaneness in their representative. In this sense he must be one of them. It is a wise insistence because without it he can govern but not lead. But the American people aspire to high estate in whatever occupation they are in, and are flattered that from their midst can arise an exceptional man. They admire and honor men of achievement in art, science, music, business, and sports. They are natural hero-worshipers. They certainly expect their President to be a uniquely gifted man, whom the world can admire and respect. Mediocrity in the White House reflects adversely on the American people and they are chagrined by it.

So it is an error, when one has as sensitive and brilliant a man as Stevenson, to gripe about his articulateness, and worry that he is not performing the rituals to make him a regular guy. I have commented on the lawyer who seeks favor with his client by matching cussword for cussword with him. He may have the illusion that he is effecting a closer tie, but I believe the client would prefer to look up to his lawyer as a cultured man. So, too, the electorate and their leaders.

Nevertheless, Stevenson drove himself in all sorts of nonsensical gyrations to do his duty as an energetic candidate. He mixed with the people, but I saw him wince every time someone slapped him on the back to demonstrate approval or familiarity, neither of which he needed. His schedule was so frenetic that he had no time to think—and this was as necessary to him as breathing. He was pummeled, shoved, lifted, and cranked, until his arm ached from being squeezed, his feet from standing, and his voice from shouting above the din which surrounded him. He made so many appearances in such rapid succession that he did not know whether he was arriving, leaving, or had been there. Cars sped him to unscheduled destinations, because some committee had requested his appearance, and the local managers thought they could squeeze it in.

Some public officials are refreshed by crowds. Truman, Kennedy, and, especially, Johnson reveled in crowd commotion and excitement. Johnson's secretary would come home and collapse from the strain of watching him go through a tumultuous day. But the President was stimulated and stayed up talking or dancing late into the night.

Others, like Stevenson, are dulled by noise. Every conversation used up part of his attentive capacity. It eroded his energy. He related to people. He could not go through the motions without expending himself. Unlike the judge who said he could look a lawyer in the eye for a full hour and not hear a word he said, Stevenson never mastered that art.

The result was that he became numb. Numb with tiredness, with boredom, and with an election process which seemed to him to have been corrupted into a circus. The inner spark of the man, which lit every word with feeling, burned low. He was like an actor who recites his lines from memory but without emotion, and therefore cannot create any in the audience.

I introduced Stevenson to several audiences toward the end of the campaign. One was a huge rally of women. When he arose to speak, they screamed their adulation for Adlai for, at least, five minutes. I thought this might arouse him from what almost appeared to be torpor as he was crushed by the guests on his arrival. Even the police could not extricate him from the pawing men and women who sought his hand, slapped him on the shoulder, sometimes by error a little too high, and yelled their support close into his ears. I thought he looked dazed, having just come from several other such affectionate, crushing exhibitions.

So I tried to shield him for a few minutes while the traditional chicken and cold peas were placed before him on the dais. But it was impossible. A crowd gathered and almost pushed the table over upon him. Each one told him of his or her work in the campaign, or asked for his autograph, or made a twenty-second critical analysis of one of his speeches.

There was only one moment of comic relief. A lady, who perhaps had attended the preceding cocktail hour a little too early, said, "Adlai, I'd put my slippers under your bed any time." He looked startled for a second, then laughed heartily and said, "You might want to use them sooner than you think." When she was led away, the line behind her continued with more dignified and more boring approaches. Some pleaded for autographs for their children and insisted on dictating what he should write on them. He pretended not to hear, or perhaps he really didn't. Certainly the crowd didn't hear or obey when the chairman announced that no more autographs would be given.

Stevenson didn't eat. He couldn't. And so the ovation which greeted his introduction was only more noise to burden his spirit.

He spoke like an automaton. His opening jests, which usually sent a receptive audience into spasms of glee, got only a titter. Nothing is funny when the speaker is uncomfortable and the words fall tired from his lips. His serious comments were memorized recitals without inner feeling. When he finished, he received respectful applause, which was like a dim echo of the ovation which had greeted him.

A few officials approached me and asked what was the matter with

Stevenson. I explained that he was simply exhausted. One of them advised that he go to bed for two days, so that he could wind up the campaign with spirit. I passed on this recommendation, but the howl of protests from those loyal workers who had arranged "wonderful schedules" for him every hour of the day and night almost blew me out of the room.

Perhaps it was his tiredness which put him in a noncombatant mood one night. "The trouble with this campaign, Louis, is that there is nothing we can tell the people about Eisenhower which they don't know. And they're still for him."

How true this was. Even before his illness, every one knew that Eisenhower was not doing his homework. Time and again this would be revealed at his press conferences. A question would be put about a matter which had been on the front pages for days. Despite last-minute preparatory cramming, he would look blank and then begin by saying that he was not aware of the incidents involved in the question. Before he could go farther, a friendly correspondent would tip him off that the fact had been officially reported. Eisenhower, always honest, would then state that unfortunately he was not familiar with it and would reserve judgment until he had looked into the matter.

If delegation of authority is the sign of a good executive, he was the greatest executive the White House ever had. Dulles made and executed foreign policy. So it went with all other departments.

When he did take the helm, his customary good judgment would often yield to impetuosity which only his illness could explain. Heart conditions often trigger bursts of temper. I recall that Federal Judge Archie O. Dawson, who had been a mild and kind man all his life, suddenly developed a fearful temper after he had "recovered" from a heart attack. The outburst was over in a flash. Without warning his fist and voice would explode without any apparent provocation. Then he was contrite and sometimes offered an apology. I cite this illustration because I think it explains Eisenhower's noted temper tantrums. Of course, they affected policy.

In a quick move in July 1958 Eisenhower sent marines to faraway Lebanon to counter a threatened take-over of the government. Fortunately, we didn't get mired in a long struggle, but it is an interesting commentary on Republican criticism of Democratic involvement in Vietnam without congressional approval.

Also, Eisenhower's reputed rude instruction to Prime Minister Eden to "get the hell out of Suez" was uncharacteristic of his proven psychological skills in dealing with disparate forces.

Now, after a serious heart seizure, it was even more evident that he would spare himself. Even if he were not an invalid, he would give only part time to the presidency. Yet, the magnificent symbol of power and goodness remained, and the people accepted it despite all handicaps.

At the very end of the campaign, extraordinary news came to Democratic headquarters about Eisenhower's health. The source was absolutely reliable. I do not identify it because it resulted from a professional leak which might involve the doctor in an ethical violation. A man of Eisenhower's age who had suffered a by-pass ileitis surgery had only a few years of life expectancy. If on top of that one added the specific kind of coronary he had since sustained, the life expectancy shrank alarmingly. The precise figures were given. It meant that, according to the most authentic medical opinion and longevity tables, Eisenhower could not finish his term in office if he were re-elected.

This information was forwarded to Stevenson. The question was whether his sensitive silence ought to yield to the national interest. It was no longer a matter of Eisenhower's illness in general terms. Now there was scientific evidence which made the previous fears a high probability, if not indeed an inevitability. Was it fair to the people not to know that they were electing Nixon and not Eisenhower for a part of his term? The President could not be faulted for keeping this information from the public. Obviously he could not be informed of the fatal news. But why had those high in the party councils, who must have known the facts, permitted him to run? Was it now the duty of the "loyal opposition" to speak the truth in a matter of such importance? Stevenson struggled with the issue. It was more bizarre than the hackneyed plots of duty versus love, or honor versus loyalty. It presented a novel question of the public's right to know versus heartless revelation about the President's heart.

If his exposure of the facts might not also benefit his campaign, the decision would have been easier. What caused him anguish was that he would be accused of exploiting the issue for political gain. This was the very reason he had previously refused to mention the subject. But now the medical portent was so ominous that he felt as a citizen, as well as a candidate, it was his duty to warn the people of the tragic facts. He could have dodged the dilemma by having someone else break the story. But he would not play games. The responsibility was his. Having decided to accept it, he would speak of it himself at the only opportunity he still had—on his election eve telecast.

So in that broadcast he said: "And, distasteful as this is, I must say bluntly that every piece of scientific evidence we have, every lesson of history and experience indicates that a Republican victory tomorrow would mean that Richard Nixon would probably be President of this country within the next four years." It was too little, too late, and too vague. Executed in such a halfhearted manner, it lacked persuasion and seemed to be nothing more than a political ploy, and a dirty one at that. If the revelation had to be made, it required scientific verification, and a decent opportunity for reply. Then, the motivation for so daring a statement might have become clear. But too much delicacy and restraint in such a matter were self-defeating. Better not to have touched it at all. Problems are like illnesses. The worse they are, the bolder the solution must be. One cannot be delicate with a cancer. Extensive and dangerous surgery must be used. Poultices, or just a little cutting to be considerate of the patient, won't do.

Another factor which militated against the strategy was the timing. Unfortunately, the news had come to Democratic headquarters at the last minute. This may not have been accidental. Troubled consciences may have been responsible for the "leak," and they must have been subjected to the same struggle in which Stevenson became engaged. Imminence of disaster puts an end to indecision. So no time was left. But it has always been considered unfair to make a serious charge on the eve of election, when the opponent cannot reply. Stevenson could not have afforded less opportunity for rebuttal than to say what he did at eleven o'clock at night preceding the next morning's voting.

This was not by design. Such sharp tactics were not in him. But he should have considered the appearances. The surrounding circumstances were incriminating. For months he had not referred once to the health issue. Now, at the very last instant, he abandoned his principles and indulged in morbid predictions of his opponent's life-span. If he considered it his duty to give warning, why didn't he do so earlier? The answer, which could have been given, was not supplied. If he knew how serious the matter was, how could delicacy have prevented him from speaking out a long time ago? Again, the ready answer was not given.

It may well be that Stevenson's exhaustion contributed to the error of making the attack, and the greater error of making it in an inadequate and half-baked way.

He would have suffered a bad defeat anyhow, but many experts believe, and I agree, that this incident cost him millions of votes. It appeared to be a revelation that the idealism and high spirit of the first campaign, which made it a glorious enterprise, irrespective of the outcome, was tarnished in the second campaign by political expedients.

The irony of it all is that the scientific data, which had come from the most reliable sources, was completely wrong. Eisenhower not only lived out his term but survived to put his golf instruction on the White House lawn to full test in the Palm Springs sun and elsewhere, as he so richly deserved.

In 1968, twelve years after the dire prediction, a new series of heart attacks struck him. He lapsed into coma. The medical reports indicated that the end was near. Obituaries lay on editors' desks ready for instant use. Headlines reported "Ike sinking." Again the doctors were wrong. He pulled out several times in what were described as "miraculous recoveries." He sat up, received visitors, and left the hospital.

Finally he succumbed. He had been first in war, first in popularity, and perhaps first in the hearts of his countrymen, but far from first among the Presidents of the United States.

The final irony was that Stevenson, who was only fifty-six years old at the time of the second campaign, and in good health, fell dead while walking on a London street. He, who had warned against Eisenhower's fate, died four years before Eisenhower.

This is the trouble with mortality tables and averages. They never apply to the individual case. If they did, they would not be averages. Family counselors succeed in healing broken marriages in less than 5 per cent of the cases, but for the lucky couple in that statistic, there is a 100 per cent result. The local philosopher who was asked what the death rate was in his town, and replied one to a person, was not so foolish. Particularly unreliable are statistics about span of life when applied to a single individual. There are mysterious life forces in each of us which defy prediction, at least by the scientific evaluations available today. Inheritance factors, which are unmeasurable, seem to play an important, perhaps decisive role. We do not yet know what they are. Nor do we know to what extent dissipation or health habits reduce or enhance our inherited treasure.

We are all concerned with longevity, but insurance companies have business reasons to learn as much as possible about it. Theirs is a "life and death" business need to know the answer. Their profits or losses depend on accurate guessing. In the past, medical examinations were the guiding test. How did the heart, kidney, liver function?

But more and more, we have learned to rely on the "life force." It is the mysterious "x" factor in the equation. Many decrepit people live long. Many healthy ones suddenly die. The vitality to overcome disease and malfunctioning organs of the body is the apparent answer. But how to measure it?

One way has been found. It is an inherited factor—a strain such as we seek in horses or cattle. Therefore the ages of one's parents, averaged out, are a significant factor. The statistics bear out the correlation. It has been suggested that if we knew the longevity of our grandparents and parents and divided by six, we would come closer to one's own span of life than medical reports could provide. Even the theory that in the past people succumbed to diseases which are now extinct and therefore not a fair test is offset by the fact that a strong life force overcame those scourges even before antibiotics were discovered. Similarly, even in the case of death by accident, it can be argued that in many cases a vital life force would have overcome broken bones and infections.

Many years ago, my French law partner, Pierre Gide, recommended to me a doctor who claimed that he could measure one's "life force" by a simple sputum test which he had devised. It registered one to ten, somewhat like a litmus test, by color. If you registered five you were average and reasonably safe for a long life. If you were seven or over, you could smoke, dissipate, be obese—nothing would mow you down. It reminded me of the comedian Ed Wynn, who claimed his uncle was so strong that they had to beat his liver with a club for hours after he died to put an end to him.

The doctor also contended that if the sputum test registered one to three, it was certain that the person had a fatal disease, like cancer, even if it had not yet appeared, and would die within a few years. I tried to introduce him to medical authorities who would permit him to test patients in hospitals, as he claimed he had done in France, but he was rejected as a quack and went the Laetrile way. I never heard of him again. Will his name someday be resurrected, like Semmelweis?

Medical books record unexplainable remissions of fatal diseases like cancer and leukemia. On the other hand, strong and healthy individuals have broken under the slightest strain when there was no prior history of weakness.

So Eisenhower's survival and Stevenson's collapse proved only one thing about medical prediction—that it is unpredictable.

The same might be said for most political predictions. It turned out that Stevenson's second defeat did not destroy his opportunity to run again, as I had thought it would. Of course he was not the irresistible choice he would have been had he sat out the second Eisenhower election. More important, he would have been ready and eager to carry the banner in 1960. As it was, he announced firmly that he would not be a candidate a third time and that opportunity ought to be given to others.

This decision was a composite of sincere principle and the horror he had of another maddening campaign effort. But when it seemed that the prize, and this time it was a prize, would fall to a young senator with no distinguished record, and the burden of cracking prejudice against a Catholic, many leaders of the party turned to Stevenson. He had earned a real chance at the presidency. Who couldn't beat Nixon?

Mrs. Roosevelt spearheaded the effort to get Stevenson to change his mind. We all helped. She emerged from a personal conference with him to announce that he would accept the nomination if it were tendered. There was an explosion of elation among the delegates and the people.

Apparently her anxiety to obtain his consent had misled her into interpreting his gratitude for acquiescence. There was an embarrassing contradiction by Stevenson. She had misunderstood him.

The crowds in front of and in the convention hall were ready to stampede the convention for Stevenson. They were confused by the Stevenson-Roosevelt exchange. Many were in tears. But they continued to scream and hope for Stevenson's acceptance. There is little doubt that, despite the excellent groundwork of the Kennedy forces, had Stevenson said "Yes" he would have been lifted on a wave of wild acclaim to the nomination.

When he entered the convention hall, the greatest and only real unorganized ovation greeted him. The rank and file of the party, including many delegates pledged to others were pleading with him to run again. But he stood firm. Kennedy was nominated—and even he, not yet recognized for the great qualities he later exhibited, and with handicaps which no other candidate was burdened with—beat Nixon. There can be little doubt that had Stevenson, like Williams Jennings Bryan, chosen to run a third time, he would have been nominated and elected President by a far greater margin than Kennedy.

Would he have lived out his term or would he have fallen as he did, but in the White House? Who can tell? He had been disappointed in not being designated Secretary of State. He had served his President and country well at the United Nations, but not without misgivings and embarrassment because he was not the recipient of confidences which later grieved him.

He might have lived had he been President. Even more poignant is the virtual certainty that John F. Kennedy would be alive today if Stevenson had not withdrawn. So, fate is a grimaced visage. Both men might have lived had they been defeated in their purpose. Both died when they succeeded.

In political life, pygmies abound—giants are rare. This is not surprising. When the people rule themselves, their representatives reflect them in all their grandeur and ignorance. We abhor an exclusive elite class, but we welcome the elite when they rise from the people. Stevenson came from a distinguished background. His grandfather was Vice-President under Cleveland. Whatever the derivatives of his qualities, they were unique and brilliant. Due to his sensitivity, he may never have emerged on the political scene. A career as professor, or scholarly international lawyer, or writer might have been more natural. He was not built for the turmoil and aggressive scheming of political warfare. He did aspire to serve in the diplomatic arm of the Government. But a turn of fate catapulted him into public office, and then his outstanding gifts came to the nation's attention.

Such men are rare. They are particularly rare in politics. What a pity that they appear so infrequently, and when they do, they do not attain the presidency. We seek men of vision, and when we find them we call them visionaries. Such men would be the answer to the restless quest of all of us, even though the youth movement claims it as its own, for nobler ideals in government, for higher standards of ethics. For greater intellect in creating new means to meet novel problems, and for the purity of purpose and prose to lead the nation to more worthy goals.

The nation should be grateful to Stevenson. He was a breath of fresh air in a morally polluted atmosphere. His qualities shone so brightly that his opponents had to attack his virtues as weaknesses in a tough world. We must learn before it is too late that the idealists are the real pragmatists. Every castle on earth was once a castle in the air. Men like Stevenson can achieve the nation's highest aspirations, and give such moral and spiritual leadership that the "establishment" would be an honored word.

IMPEACHMENT OR CENSURE?

"Mr. Chief Justice and Senators, I rise as counsel to speak for the President. More importantly I rise to defend the Presidency, and the Constitution.

"I shall not ask you to acquit the President. Too much evidence has been presented to you of unworthy conduct to do that. But I do ask that you not remove him from office, and that censure is the appropriate penalty. He has appeared before you in defense of himself. He was contrite. His explanations were not evasions but the candid statement of such ameliorating circumstances as exist. You may be sure there will be no repetition of the conduct which brought about these charges.

"Removal from office is the extreme remedy. It is capital punishment. Not every offense requires the maximum sentence. A resolution of reprimand for certain conduct is humiliating enough. It would fulfill the moral imperative. At the same time, it is consistent with constitutional restraints which I shall analyze.

"Before I do so I hope you will not consider me presumptuous if I call attention to your special role. In view of the fact that this is the first impeachment trial of a President in more than a century, and only the second in our history, there is little experience to guide us.

"The House of Representatives is the only body, under Article I, Section 2, of the Constitution, which has the power to issue an impeachment. It has done so. That impeachment was equivalent to an indictment in a criminal case. A trial was required. The Senate has been designated by the Constitution to try the case. So you are not sitting merely as senators. You have been transformed into a court, and you have taken a special oath as jurors, if you will, in addition to your original oath as senators. That oath is significant. You are to 'do impartial justice according to the Constitution and laws.'

"During this trial, the Vice-President is not presiding as he ordinarily would. The Constitution designated the Chief Justice of the Supreme Court to sit in his place. Here again, your powers are unique. In a criminal trial, the judge's rulings would be binding on you, subject only to appeal to a higher court. But in an impeachment trial, you can by a majority vote overrule the Chief Justice.

"Also, the ordinary rules of evidence do not apply. Even hearsay may be admitted, to be sifted by you for the inherent weakness in such evidence, or accepted by you.

"Most importantly, your decision cannot be judicially reviewed by the Supreme Court. You are the court of last resort. Some scholars differ on this, particularly if the proceeding had not accorded with the directions of the Constitution. As defense counsel I ought not forgo the possibility of an appeal, but as I have said, I am defending the presidency and the Constitution, not merely the President, and I consider the present proceeding punctiliously correct. I can therefore see no right of judicial review.

"This view is supported by tracing the origin of the impeachment clause in the Constitution. The first draft of the Constitution, in 1787, provided that an impeachment trial should be by the Supreme Court. This was changed to substitute the Senate as the trial forum. One of the reasons must have been that the President on trial may have appointed some of the justices. Also, the Supreme Court might have to review a criminal conviction if the President were tried after he was removed from office. The history of the impeachment clause therefore indicates that you are the final arbiters. There is also a common sense reason for this conclusion. If the Senate removed a President from office, and the Supreme Court reinstated him, the confusion during the interim period when no one would be sure who the Commander-in-Chief was, and later the doubtful authority of a restored President, might be fatal to the nation's security. Therefore, you have the responsibility of an irrevocable decision.

"Finally, your role as jurors is unique. Ordinarily, a juror is disqualified if he knows the defendant. Most of you know the President personally. Most of you, like myself, belong to the opposite political party and are therefore opposed to many of his programs. Some of you, like myself, have even spoken and written critically, if not indeed bitterly, about him. A few of you have even expressed in advance your opinion about the issues in this trial. Yet you are not disqualified. You sit as his judges.

"Thus, there is placed upon you an extraordinary responsibility. You have many things to remember. Remember that you are the final court. If you err, there is no appeal to correct your decision. Remember that you must overcome your political partisanship, your possible personal animosity, and that you are sitting as judges of the facts and law, although by usual standards you would be disqualified to do so. You must shed preconceived notions, your bias, the passions of the day, and in the words of your solemn oath, 'do impartial justice according to the Constitution and laws.'

"You must be inspired by the ideals of our Constitution to rise above any prejudice. You must vindicate that Constitution which expected you to act in such a crisis as only men of the highest character could. There is a special call for your conscience to guide you; you are truly acting for the ages and, as you judge, so shall you be judged.

"To put it simply, I plead with you, in the name of our noble Constitution, to keep your minds open. Yes, to keep your hearts open, to what I shall say.

"How shall we decide when a President has so violated his duty that no other remedy but removal from office is necessitated? Under what circumstances may a lesser punishment be given?

"I believe that the test for removal is that the President's continuance in office will imperil the nation. Anything less than that may permit either acquitting him or censuring him. That is in your discretion. But if he is not an immediate danger to the nation's security, you cannot overrule the will of more than two hundred million Americans who elected him. Your disapproval cannot encompass his removal.

"Let me support this conclusion. First we look at the impeachment clause in the Constitution. It gives three grounds for impeaching a President: 'Treason, Bribery and Other High Crimes and Misdemeanors.' The last phrase is vague and requires interpretation. If a President is guilty of maladministration is he impeachable? We can find the answer to this question in the debate on the impeachment clause in 1787. Originally the committee recommended that the only grounds should be 'Treason and Bribery.' It even rejected 'corruption' as a ground for impeachment. Then the following debate took place:

Col. Mason: 'Why is the provision restrained to treason and bribery only?'

He moved to add the term 'maladministration.' James Madison objected. 'So vague a term,' he said, 'will be equivalent to a tenure during the pleasure of the Senate.' Colonel Mason then withdrew the word 'maladministration' and substituted the phrase from English law, 'High Crimes and Misdemeanors.'

"There you have it. Our founding fathers rejected the firing of a President by the Senate even if he had committed sins of maladministration or even corruption. They feared the possibility of the Senate saying what Congressman Gerald Ford later said concerning a proposed impeachment of Supreme Court Justice William Douglas, that 'impeachable offenses are what the House and Senate jointly consider them to be.' They didn't want this body to have the arbitrary power to create its own definition of impeachment. They specified treason and bribery, most horrendous crimes, to be serious enough to throw a President out of office. By adding, 'and *other* high crimes and misdemeanors,' they surely were referring to equally shocking acts. 'Misdemeanor,' in this context, has been held to mean 'felony.'

"The law has rules to construe language. These rules of construction are based on common sense. One such rule is that when specific words are followed by general words, the general words take on the same shades of meaning as the words which they followed. The Latin scholars among you will recognize this rule by its name *'eusdem generis,'* meaning 'of the same kind.' Thus the general words 'high crimes and misdemeanors' related to the preceding specific words, 'Treason and Bribery.' In short, 'high crimes and misdemeanors' meant crimes generally as serious as treason or bribery. So we begin with the proposition that the Constitution lists only the most serious charges as grounds for impeachment.

"Must these charges be crimes, or can lesser misconduct be sufficient for impeachment? No less an authority than Blackstone said that only a crime could justify impeachment. He wrote that an impeachment 'is a prosecution of the already known and established law.' This view was expounded by President Andrew Johnson's attorney, who argued, at the impeachment trial in 1868, that 'no impeachment will lie except for a true crime.'

"I do not agree. I believe you have wider latitude. There may be misconduct which imperils the nation, even though it is not a violation of any law. I stress again that the test is whether the nation is imperiled, not whether there is any common law or statutory dereliction.

"So, for example, if a President announced that he would veto all legislation because of his contempt for Congress; or if he closed all foreign embassies and refused to communicate with nations because he regarded them as selfish or treacherous; or if he became a psychotic, or an alcoholic, and no one knew what military directions he might give; he would not be committing a crime under the criminal code, but he certainly ought to be impeached.

"If impeachment could result only if the President committed a crime, then the Constitutional protections for a criminal trial would have to be observed. A jury trial would be necessary. None exists here. Unanimous agreement would be required among the jury or there could be no conviction. This does not apply here. A two-thirds vote of this body is sufficient for conviction. There would be the right of appeal. There is none here.

"The proper interpretation of your powers is more important for the welfare of our nation than the defense of any particular President. Your authority is larger than narrow constructionists contend. In justice to this President, he is aware of my position and supports my contention for the broad concept, although it puts him in greater jeopardy.

"Does this mean that no matter what crime a President committed, even murder, that his only punishment would be removal from office? No. When he was no longer President, he could be indicted and tried in the regular way in a criminal court. Then he would be accorded all the protections of due process. But in an impeachment trial there is no due process in the traditional sense. He cannot even be sentenced. He can only be removed from office. It is a political process. As Mr. Justice Story of the United States Supreme Court wrote, 'an impeachment is purely of a political nature. It is not so much designed to punish an offender as to secure the state against gross official crimes. It touches neither his person nor his property, but simply divests him of his political capacity.'

"Indeed, if impeachment could only be based on the commission of a crime, then a later criminal trial would be barred, because it would constitute 'double jeopardy.'

"So, I concede, gentlemen of the Senate, that you have the power to remove the President, even if his conduct did not constitute a crime. You could do so if his deeds or lack of action were so serious and dangerous that the nation was in jeopardy from his continuing in authority even another day or week.

"As you will see from this test, the opposite is also true. Just as a crime is not necessary to impeach, so not every crime requires impeachment and removal. For example, adultery is a crime. There are current revelations that several of our most revered Presidents committed this crime repeatedly. Had they been charged while they were in office, would anyone think they should be impeached and removed?

"Suppose a President obstructed justice by deliberately concealing the fact that one of his aides had a supply of marijuana, should be thrown out of office?

"Suppose that the President treated valuable gifts given by other governments as his own or his wife's, should he be removed because the crime of thievery was charged?

"As we go up the scale of crimes, the answers become more difficult. But the test isn't. It remains the same. Does the President's continuance in office imperil the nation? If it doesn't, then he may not be ousted even though he may fall in our regard, fail in his ambition for high historical appraisal, be shunted aside for re-election, or, if he is not eligible for a new term, prejudice his party's continuance in power. The public may eagerly await the coming election to 'throw the rascals out,' but the Constitution does not permit the Congress to usurp that privilege of rejection. It resides in the ballot box. Otherwise there might be horrendous proceedings against almost every President elected.

"You might have had President Franklin D. Roosevelt sitting here in a wheel chair, with ten pounds of steel around his legs, facing the charge that he violated our country's declared neutrality by selling weapons to the Allies and that his Lend-Lease deal, giving England fifty destroyers, was a tricky evasion of the Neutrality Act passed by this Congress. You would hear arguments that such abuse of power risked catapulting the United States into a world war. True, he would have contended that his acts were morally necessary to preserve England from being overrun by the Hun. Such a defense is not entirely dissimilar from President Nixon's claim that the bombing of Cambodia was essential to save the lives of American soldiers placed there by other Presidents. Incidentally, in judging this charge, remember that after you found out on March 27, 1973, about the bombing of Cambodia you waited until August 15 of that year before acting to end it. To what extent was your delay acquiescence, or at least uncertainty?

"Remember also that during the entire Vietnam War, Congress had the power to cut off funds for its continuance, and that you did not do so. I am not arguing the merits of the President's or your actions. After all, three previous Presidents and Congresses were involved in initiating and prosecuting the growing Vietnam War. I merely point out that he who points a finger at someone else has three fingers pointed at himself, and that your judgment must be tempered by your own uncertainty as these events were unraveling.

"You might also have had sitting before you President John F. Kennedy, charged with an invasion of the Bay of Pigs, secretly planned and executed without approval of Congress, which is the only body authorized to declare war. There might have been added the charge that the gross incompetence and failure of the undertaking caused great injury to our nation's standing in the world. And you might have had to pass on a count charging the electronic surveillance of Dr. Martin Luther King authorized by Attorney General Kennedy.

"If brazen lying by a President warranted removal, you might have had sitting before you a grinless President Dwight D. Eisenhower, charged with public denial that a U-2 spy plane had flown over Russia, while unknown to him, the Russians had already captured that plane and its pilot, Gary Powers, and could reveal to the world the plane's extraordinary spy equipment.

"If a claim of personal aggrandizement were enough to bring on an impeachment proceeding, the list of tractors, bulls, and other valuable articles listed by Drew Pearson, an 'investigative columnist,' as having been presented to President Eisenhower for his farm in Gettysburg, would have required him to suffer the anguish of an impeachment trial, although he was universally known to be a man of the highest integrity. Errors of judgment are to be distinguished from venality. If "cover-up" were a fatal charge then we would have been deprived of the lifelong services of a great Supreme Court justice, Hugo Black. During confirmation proceedings, he and his supporters remained silent about the charge that he had joined the Ku Klux Klan. It was deemed unproved and he was confirmed. A month later, an enterprising reporter of the Pittsburgh *Post-Gazette* exposed the evidence that Black had attended a secret Birmingham Klorero. Justice Black then went on the air and said, "I did join the Klan. I later resigned. I have never rejoined." Had President Nixon acted similarly, would he have had to resign?

"I could continue these analogies, but a few will suffice to make my point that we do not expect perfection from our chief executives any more than we do from our executive chiefs in business. To put it another way, we may hope for the best, but not every disappointment permits the punishment of removal from office. Ladies and gentlemen of the Senate, there is no Federal law, such as a few states have, which upon a sufficient number of petitioners requires a special election to recall the elected officer in the midst of his term.

"My plea that removal of the President from office is not the appropriate penalty in this proceeding is supported not only by a study of our Constitution, but by the profound philosophy of our form of government. Let me analyze the governmental design of the Presidency.

"Democratic government has many forms. Generally there are two plans to determine the tenure of the chief executive. The first is the parliamentary system. The second is the definite term approach.

"In the parliamentary system, the premier, as he is usually called, has no specific term. He holds his office only as long as the elected parliament chooses that he should. If it votes 'no confidence,' he must submit himself to a new election. Notice, please, that so must the parliament. It has not the privilege of putting him out and remaining in office itself. The entire government falls. The people are invited to elect new representatives and through them a new leader. England, France, Israel, and many other countries have chosen this form of democracy.

"The second democratic system is the election of the President for a fixed term. Congress cannot by a 'lack of confidence' vote to shorten his term. Even when Congress and the President are at odds, and he vetoes its bills, it can overrule him only by a two-thirds vote, but it has no power to interfere with his office, let alone end his term.

"Similarly, Congress has a definite term. It, too, cannot be 'dissolved.' It cannot under any circumstances be made to stand election before its prescribed term has ended.

"Which is the better system? Each has its advantages and defects. The parliamentary form is sensitive to the public's changes of heart. Under it President Nixon would probably have 'fallen' a long time ago, as have prime ministers in Europe. Then the Vice-President and congressmen and senators would also have to face election.

"The greatest defect of the parliamentary system is that in a turbulent world, the moods of the populace change frequently. This may result in a series of governments within a short period. At one time France had six within two and one half years. It is difficult for foreign governments to deal with a head of government who by ordinary majority may be ousted the next month. How can domestic or foreign policies be adopted in such an atmosphere of uncertainty?

"It has been argued that immediate response to the public's will does not allow the maturing of public opinion. This principle of avoiding precipitous action which one may regret has been applied in other areas. For example, many states have passed laws which do not permit the institution of a divorce suit until the husband or wife has filed notice of intention to sue, and a number of months intervene to permit a cooling-off period. In political life, too, there is precipitous public reaction which may change. Compulsory patience may prove that an unpopular President was right all along.

"You recall that when President Harry S Truman fired General Douglas MacArthur, the public condemnation was so intense that a poll showed the President to be at the lowest ebb in modern times (23 per cent) lower than the present incumbent, despite the tirade of criticism and abuse aimed at him for at least a year.

"Incidentally, there were cries to impeach President Truman at that time. Yet recently, a group of historians ranked Truman the ninth greatest President in our history, and in listing his virtues made special mention of his courage in dismissing the nation's revered military hero, in defiance of public adulation for him. So much for the volatility of public reaction. Perhaps immediate response to public clamor is one of the defects of the parliamentary system. Virtue and fault often interchange position.

"Our founders, having surrendered the advantage of continuous citizen control in favor of stability, imposed upon us the strengths and weaknesses of a fixed term. As a people, we are aware that when we elect a President, we are taking him for better or for worse for four long years. We know that only in the most extraordinary circumstances can we even try to dislodge him.

"We also know that in the coming years of his administration unanticipated problems will arise, concerning which he will have no mandate from us. There can be no advance guidance for the unforeseeable. Therefore in choosing a President, we vote more for his character and judgment than for his position on issues. Indeed, we have learned that Presidents, once elected, have often reversed themselves on issues they had announced as unshakable. This has not been due to treachery or even light-mindedness, but to changing circumstances, or caution which the power to act instills in the theoretician without responsibility, or perhaps access to better advisers, or even a larger perspective of the whole, from the height of the presidency.

"Many Presidents have abandoned the platform on which they rode into office, from Wilson, whose emphatic promise was to keep us out of war, to the President who sits before you, who reversed himself on wage and price controls, détente with Russia, approaches to China, a balanced budget, and more. Flexibility and a ventilated mind may be better than consistency. Certainly we are forewarned by experience that we must depend much more on the kind of man we elect than on the kind of speeches or promises he makes.

"All this has made us searchingly cautious in our choice of a President. The men who aspire to our highest office have faced scrutiny for decades. They have been senators, governors, and in public service all their lives. They have made hundreds of speeches on radio and television, written articles and books, and been dissected by opposition critics. Finally, to achieve the nomination of their party, they have had to trudge across our immense country, submitting themselves in the most intimate way to the view and touch of millions of citizens. It is a test of ruggedness as well as intellect and personability.

"Then, those rare few who achieve the nomination begin a grueling campaign of more than three months, in which they talk to more people in one night than all the religious, political, and military leaders in nineteen centuries reached in a lifetime. Through enlarged visualization which penetrates their skin, every flicker of the eyelid, every involuntary muscle movement of the face, every hoarsening inflection or hesitancy of the voice, we learn about them as if a thousand psychiatrists had given us the benefit of their scientific insights.

"Why do I recite all this, which you know so well? Because our democracy, more than any other, gives us an opportunity to judge the character of the man we elect. The doctrine of '*caveat emptor*,' 'buyer beware,' applies to people as well as to things.

"Therefore, having had the opportunity for evaluation of our chief executive to a greater extent than is afforded by any other government, we must take responsibility for our choice and abide by it for the fixed term, even if we have regrets. I suggest that there is an equation between knowledgeable selection and the right of rejection. The larger the former, the smaller the latter.

"This principle applies with double, nay, triple force to the incumbent President. Not only was he a congressman, a senator, sitting among you, but for eight years he presided over this body as Vice-President. In that capacity he traveled to many countries, thus giving the people further insight into his capacity and character. Yes, and they also were made aware of defects, recounted with paradoxical gleeful anger by political opponents. He was pilloried with rhymed meanness as 'tricky Dick,' and ridiculed as an untrustworthy secondhand car salesman, just as Thomas Dewey was reduced to a pygmy comical role of a bridegroom on a wedding cake. Such is the vituperation our public figures must endure, I suppose on the theory that in a land of free speech, humiliation begets humility, and lightning is the proper precaution against those who think their heads are in heaven.

"The people weighed it all, and he, a Republican, was elected President after eight years of Democratic rule. He was chosen in a three-way race by a minority vote, and even then by a margin so thin it was almost invisible. So he had to prove himself all over again to the American people, at that time deeply divided by its most unpopular war.

"Then, after four years of laser-lighted examination of his every mood and movement, of every word and worth of his pronouncements, of leadership which expanded from national parameters to the free world and even made deep inroads into vast areas previously deemed too hostile or enigmatic for democratic approach, he received the most phenomenal endorsement of a public figure in American history. He won forty-nine of the fifty states. He received five hundred twenty-one electoral votes, almost twice the number required for election. His popular vote total of more than forty-seven million gave him a plurality of eighteen million. From a minority vote in his previous election, he won by a 60 per cent plurality. This was more than a landslide. It was an avalanche. And the roar of approval of the American people must still echo in this chamber today.

"The impeachment process has been heralded as democracy's safeguard, but it must not become the nullifier of the will of the people, the source and strength of democracy itself.

"Frankly, the presidency is not the only branch of our government which is in low estate. Polls indicate that Congress itself is held in less regard than even the beleaguered President. Under these circumstances we must take mutual measures to lift the ethical standards of all representatives, whether they wear legislative or presidential robes. This is not the first administration in which shoddy practices have occurred. Self-criticism leads to necessary reform. It heals, no matter how severe the wrench from accustomed practice. On the other hand, punitive attacks only widen the breach and may give the false impression that democracy itself has failed. At one point during these developments, bumper stickers appeared, reading 'Don't re-elect anybody,' a disturbing jest. We can overcome such cynicism by raising the moral standards of all branches of government. At the same time, we must respect the will of the electorate, even if it errs, unless, in the words of minority counsel Albert Jenner of the Watergate Committee, 'the conduct of the President is so grave that it amounts to a subversion of government.'

"Consider the consequences throughout the world of the removal of the President. American leadership requires stability abroad as well as at home. The world would be shocked by the disgrace and disappearance of the President in the midst of vital treaty negotiations.

"Foreigners are more resigned than we are to human frailty among their leaders. If the President were censured, but maintained in office, other nations would respect our sensitive standards, but not feel that they had been left adrift. If we throw him out, the consequences abroad cannot be foreseen. It might even trigger aggressive action in some part of the world by adversary nations who have in the past seized any moment of weakness to act boldly and swiftly to fill a power vacuum. Can we afford the risk of such a disaster, perhaps even a third world war, when the remedy of censure would leave at the helm a strong President, respected and feared abroad? Continuity has its own momentum. I sit wise to assert our concern with domestic chicanery in such a way that we tempt, almost invite, hostile nations to miscalculate our Constitutional strengths and overestimate our confusion? The remedy of reprimand is safer and better.

"It may be in your minds that censure, too, may so injure presidential prestige that he will be unable to conduct foreign affairs. This might argue for acquittal, particularly since acquittal does not mean approval. It merely means that the charges have not been proven. But as I have said, too much has been demonstrated to claim that the misconduct does not rise to a level requiring condemnation. The question is what form it shall take.

"As to the fear that this President will no longer be able to conduct foreign affairs, the evidence to the contrary should comfort you. Even while the Watergate scandal was our daily headline to be swallowed with our morning coffee; even when the scandal stole the front pages of the press abroad, the President's travels were greeted in foreign lands with unprecedented curb-cheering people. It may well be that this was due in large measure to the world's regard for the office more than for its occupant. This, too, is encouraging. It is another illustration of the advantage of a fixed term. Due to the power and stability of his office, the President's influence can survive even crisis. Indeed, the President has derived so much strength from his trips abroad that his opponents fear he may continue long journeys to overcome the ordeal at home.

"Has he been so distracted by his troubles that he cannot attend to the inundating duties of his office? If so, that might imperil the nation. But the record is to the contrary. While the Watergate revelations were beginning to blaze, the Vietnam War was being wound down and tens of thousands of soldiers brought home; the great wall in China was being scaled, the Iron Curtain in Russia partly lifted, the Middle East hostile forces parted, and the Cyprus melee subdued; the President's declaration that our country would avoid direct military involvement in remote corners of the globe evoked praise from the House and from this body.

"The domestic scene was filled with recommendations of bills, imposition of wage and price controls, the devaluation of the dollar, a new trade policy which imposed a 10 per cent surcharge on most imports, addresses to the nation, and appointments of administrators of new programs, all of which appealed sufficiently to the electorate to evoke a cascade of favorable votes. Whether one approves or disapproves of the administration's policies, it has not been slothful or moribund.

"If you examine the sequelae of removal, it is more likely that the ousting of the President may imperil the nation, than that his retention after reprimand will.

"There is another guideline to determine when an extraordinary remedy, like impeachment, should or should not be applied. For example, an injunction, which is the use of the chancellor's equitable sword, will not be issued unless two tests are met. First, the proof must be overwhelming and beyond ordinary standards. Second, it must be demonstrated that the wrongs are continuing. If there is no real danger of repetition, then lesser remedies may lie, but not an injunction.

"Let us apply these two criteria to an impeachment. I have said that the rules of a criminal trial need not be followed. Therefore it is not necessary to prove the President's guilt beyond a reasonable doubt. But neither should the standard be that of an ordinary civil trial, that a preponderance of evidence is sufficient. We are engaged in a unique procedure of momentous consequences, and the proof required for removing a President should be unusually persuasive, even if not beyond a reasonable doubt. Otherwise public divisiveness would flourish. The awesome power to cancel the deliberate choice of the people must be supported by the strongest kind of proof. This is particularly true where it is charged that the impeachment decision in the House of Representatives was made by a group dominated by the President's political and philosophical enemies. It was just such an accusation which undermined public confidence in the impeachment of President Andrew Johnson. The main charge, that he had removed Secretary of War Edwin M. Stanton without senatorial consent, and Johnson's escape from conviction by only one vote short of the two-thirds majority required were further warning that the passions of the opposition party are not to be trusted, and that public approval must be courted by fair procedure. I would say that unimpeachable evidence is essential to impeachment. Otherwise, the highest court of all, the people, may not accept the verdict.

"Assume that you have winnowed the various charges to eliminate those which are not established by overwhelming evidence, and assume further, as I do, that some remain; is the second test met? Is there a danger of continuing violations? Surely not.

"When a man has achieved the highest and most powerful political office in the world, his ambition turns to historical appraisal. That is why recent Presidents have made plans to construct libraries of their works. So the President would wish to live down his censure, to demonstrate his integrity; to prove that the achievements of his administration will outweigh its desultory aspects; to salvage the President's name and reputation for the history books.

"Far from taking a desperate risk of 'more of the same,' we would be assured that the chastisement of censure would stimulate the President to live up to the highest precepts of his office for the remainder of his term.

"I come now to the most painful aspect of my appeal. Punishment is not and should not be equal for all. This is a common error I hear all about me. If it were so, we would not have probation departments which investigate every facet of a man's life and background, to report to the sentencing judge. If it were so, judges would not have to weigh facts extraneous to the crime itself, to determine whether the punishment should be lenient or severe. If it were so, there would be no wide discretion vested in the judge to impose either a suspended sentence or fine or a long prison sentence for the same crime. We punish the man, not the crime. Men who commit wrongs are as different from one another as nature intended good men to be, too. We must therefore consider the condition of each to make the punishment fit not only the crime but the man who committed it.

"One of the facts which you should weigh, as every judge does, is the suffering which the defendant has already endured.

"I don't think any of us are in a position to evaluate the anguish the

President has suffered. We can only use our imagination, and it too must fail in this instance. Why? Because there is only one person in a world of hundreds of millions of human beings who can be President. He stands alone at the apex of the international complex of nations. We can only truly feel and understand that which touches our experience. And none of you, even though you hold exalted positions yourselves, can grasp the unique feelings of a man who knows in every waking second of his existence as President that he wields unprecedented power, is held in awe by people all over the world, and is destined for history. It is a glory and a responsibility which challenges the sense of reality of the most balanced man. Intimate friends address him as Mr. President. Kings and ministers seek his nod. Trumpets blare and guns salute when he appears abroad. Every word he utters is sent across the world. No matter how prosaic his movement or deed, it is recorded for millions to read. He sleeps in Lincoln's bed. He is surrounded by mementos of George Washington, Thomas Jefferson, and every historic name since then. He is seen and heard by tens of millions of people in the remotest regions of the world, and when electronics are not available, the printing press features his utterances as well as his features in newspapers and magazines wherever they are printed. Even all this is only a glimpse of the Olympian heights on which he resides.

"So when such a man faces disgrace, the hurt is magnified to the same degree that his pre-eminence separates him from other citizens. This is true in lower echelons as well. The more distinguished the defendant, the more painful his fall. But when the man who stands before the bar is the President of the United States, the indignity is almost unbearable—unbearable for our country and unbearable for him.

"The President has suffered the torment of turning his mind backward to make a different choice. It is a painful reliving of events because the outcome cannot be changed by reverie. Such dreams become nightmares of futility. 'If only I had to do it over again' is a self-inflicted penalty, there being no second chance.

"The suffering of the President cannot be alleviated by his intimates. The reflected agony of friends is as difficult to bear as the gloating of enemies. Added to his own burden of guilt is the pain he has caused to those loyal to him. One can see on the President's face this magnification of sorrow.

"And as for his family, I would like to think their grief is private, and not the proper subject for this matter of state. But I cannot. We do not elect the President's wife, but she has been weighed in the public judgment of his choice during her campaign travels. She must be equal to the title of First Lady we confer on her and the ceremonial duties she performs. So her suffering is not irrelevant in considering what she and the President have endured. He must also bear the tears of his lovely Julie. I need not tell you who, by proximity, see the pain etched on their faces and its transference to him.

"The people understand all this. I have heard over and over again that it is a wonder the President can stand this pressure; that it would kill an ordinary man. When Napoleon was defeated, disgraced and exiled, he told an aide that he would 'kill himself.' The aide replied, 'No, Your Majesty could not do that. A gambler kills himself. A king faces adversity.' The President has lived up to the greatness of his office by facing adversity. He knew that an advance estimate of the votes to be cast against him in this chamber would reach the two-third minimum required to remove him from office. But he has come here to express apology and face humiliation bravely. He has been able to do this because he believed that you were open-minded; that some of you would yield to the moral imperatives of the democratic process which elected him; that you would hesitate to destroy the principle of stability which has protected us at home and abroad; that you would weigh his candor and his contrition; that you would not forget his past deeds when you consider his failings; that you would be comforted by the assurance that being recondite there would be no repetition of misconduct; that therefore the nation would not be imperiled by his continuance in office; and most important of all that there is an alternative to removal, namely, reprimand, or censure, and that this would best serve the Constitutional structure.

"If you censure but maintain the President in office, he will never again wield the power he once exercised. Oh, his Constitutional powers will be the same, but that power, which derives from the full trust and affection of the people, will be withheld until he proves himself again worthy of it. Such loss of power is in itself an unendurable death. Francis Bacon wrote, 'Who can see worse days than he yet living, doth follow at the funeral of his own reputation.'

"That march of penance will continue. Its pain is ineradicable. Indeed, it is the true measure of his penalty and you need not fear that a lesser punishment than removal from the Oval Office, will be inadequate.

"The very fact that merciful consideration is extended by you, the members of the opposition party, will attest to its nonpolitical nature. It will soothe the feelings of millions of Americans who, although not condoning his wrongs, would resent the extreme penalty of divestiture of office. It would be healing in a moment when our country desperately needs it. It would provide continuity of authority, in a strife-ridden world, in which the symbol of America's power and influence resides uniquely in the President. It would at the same time be a declaration of high principle, and a warning to this and future Presidents that the President is no king, and that the law is the true majesty.

"I beseech you to abstain from removal or acquittal, and as to those charges which you feel were proven by overwhelming evidence, that you express your condemnation in the form of censure.

"In that way, you will have fulfilled your special oath. You will have served our country best."

Of course, such a summation was never made by any counsel. It was not necessary. Nixon resigned. As he later put it, "I impeached myself."

Whenever public officials quit under fire, they attempt to turn their surrender into noble sacrifice. They declare that they want to spare the public the ordeal of a disrupting contest. Actually, Nixon resigned because the most careful tabulation of votes, after an incessant drive for support, convinced him that he would lose the impeachment trial. Had he had the courage to face his accusers, without dissembling, he might have won them over to a lesser penalty and salvaged his presidency.

I have illustrated in an imaginary exercise this Constitutional and persuasive possibility. But the preconditions for such an appeal required his appearance and testimony with uninhibited forthrightness. It would also require his consent that his counsel should not spare him. His wrongdoing could not be denied, although, of course, it could be stated without unnecessary animus. When a tree is down everyone runs with his hatchet. His counsel had to wield a merciful one. But the catharsis had to be complete. No acquittal could or should have been sought.

If Nixon could have brought himself to such a posture, he would not have been in this dilemma in the first place. So perhaps even strong legal guidance in the right direction would have been of no avail.

This appears to be the fact, because there was a subsequent test. Tempted by money, he emerged from seclusion to explain himself on television in a David Frost interview. I saw three Nixons in that one broadcast. The first continued to evade, quibble about the true meaning of words, claim that the quotations from the tapes were taken out of context, assert his "understanding" of his enemies' motives in a self-pitying way, and suggest conspiracies against him, by "an impeachment lobby," a media "fifth column" and the "peccadilloes" of the CIA—while at the same time disavowing his belief in the conspiracy theory and otherwise disporting himself in the manner which had set the desultory tone of the White House conversations.

Also, he continued to add to the truth, thus really subtracting from it. He added his motives to the facts, thereby subtracting from their true nature, for he failed to distinguish between motive and intent. One may have the motive of a Robin Hood but his intention to rob makes his act a crime nevertheless. Particularly offensive was his attempted justification of his instructions to his assistants, to be sure to utilize the "I don't remember" evasion. He claimed that every defense lawyer instructs his witness not to volunteer if he is not sure. Indeed! The difference between restraining a voluble witness who spouts irrelevancies of which he has no knowledge, and an instruction not to reveal what one knows, is so basic that only moral astigmatism could confuse the two.

The second Nixon who emerged from the broadcast was the one who engaged in what is known in law as confession and avoidance. Under great stress, he conceded that he had lied, "let my country down," "let my friends down," and had "screwed up" the mess (he could not get away from the inelegant language which had flooded the tapes). Yet, having confessed, he sought to avoid the consequences. He insisted that he had not committed a crime or an impeachable offense.

Nevertheless, this second Nixon moved us to compassion. His face quivering with suppressed tears, which his eyes betrayed, one felt the anguish which racked him. The prosecutor of Warren Hastings, who was impeached in Parliament in 1787, expressed the feelings which, nearly two centuries later, many Americans experienced: "To see that man, that small portion of human clay, that poor feeble machine of earth, enclosed now in that little space, brought to that Bar—and to reflect on his late power! . . . What a change! How he must feel it!" Sympathy went not so much to the man as to the tragedy of the great fall.

The third Nixon was one who gave us psychiatric insights to himself. The most revealing was his statement that he had "brought himself down." He said that he had given his enemies a sword and they stuck it into him "and twisted it with relish." Here was the picture of a vicious assailant. Who was he? His next sentence identified him. "I would have done the same in their place." So he really plunged the sword into himself "and turned it with relish," a remarkable revelation of suicidal intent. The continued taping even while the scandal was mounting and the preservation of the tapes were also illustrations of a subconscious desire to be caught and destroyed.

The nation was fortunate not to have suffered worse from the transference of presidential power to a Vice-President who had replaced Spiro Agnew, a felon, and who had therefore himself not been elected to office. The vacuum of authority and a dismayed citizenry might well have invited adventurers abroad, or disorganization at home.

The greatest accolade to democracy is the peaceful transition of power. It is due to centuries of education and a new tradition of graceful acceptance by the defeated. That is why sudden installation of democracy in territory unprepared for it causes a reversion to bullets and conspiratorial coups.

The Nixon resignation tested our constitutional tradition most severely. We had to accept a transition in bitter atmosphere, and where legitimacy was strained. We succeeded. Fortunately, the risk was not enlarged by hostile opportunism abroad. In retrospect, it was fortunate that Nixon had not challenged the extreme remedy of ouster. As it turned out, we were saved the ordeal of a trial, while escaping the dangers to which the abrogation of a fixed presidential term might have subjected us. From a viewpoint of precedent, the result is not cheering. Is there the danger that a partisan legislature may someday seize upon the misdeeds of a President, even if they do not clearly come within the ambit of the general proscription of the Constitution, to force him to resign, rather than face ouster?

The rarity of such a situation, even when Presidents have acted beyond their traditional authority, should limit our fears. Ultimately, it is the common sense of the people which is the true motive power. Consent by the governed also applies to procedures like impeachment, in which they are not directly involved. The genius of democracy is that the people's representatives hear the thunder of election day long before it approaches.

The imaginary defense summary, which I have presented, might really have taken place. Only an accident of time prevented it. Unexpectedly, I became involved in the critical developments.

After the House voted impeachment, I thought that there would be an extensive period of preparation and a trial before the Senate. I had not anticipated Nixon's resignation, especially because he declared over and over again that he would fight to the last. Perhaps I should have learned from Vice-President Spiro Agnew's similar assurances, before he resigned, that the emphasis on resistance to the very death was a ploy to discourage the pursuer and encourage the pursued.

In any event, anticipating a Senate trial, I was troubled and intrigued by the constitutional questions presented in such a proceeding. Having been invited by the *Reader's Digest* to write an article of my choosing, I wrote one entitled, "Impeachment or Censure?" Then I decided it would be more appropriate for the New York *Times Magazine* and might thereafter be reprinted in the *Digest*.

On August 6, 1973, I was on the phone with a Washington client concerning a legal matter. He could not keep his mind on the subject. He was a friend of Julie Eisenhower, and he described her distress, because her father had decided to resign. An announcement was soon to be made on television. He asked my opinion about the clash of views between the President and his advisers as to whether he should stand trial or quit.

"In my opinion," I said, "if he went to trial, and the right argument was made, he might not be removed from office."

The voice at the other end became urgent. "Why?" he asked.

I explained, with appropriate telephone brevity, my theory that the test of removal was nothing less than imperilment of the nation, and that Nixon's wrongs might warrant censure or reprimand and not ousting from office.

"Can you dictate this immediately?" he asked.

"I have already written it as an article."

He pleaded with me to deliver a copy at once to the White House. He would call Julie and arrange for its immediate transfer to the President. "Perhaps it is not too late," he said. To save minutes, my article was Telecopied for immediate delivery to the White House by special messenger. It arrived there shortly before four in the afternoon.

The scene at the White House was chaotic. The die had been cast. Nixon's television announcement of his resignation had been scheduled. Everyone was emotionally drained by the preceding indecision, and numb from the decision itself. In tears and shock, the family and staff were busy packing for the first nonpresidential journey to San Clemente. An article on constitutional alternatives was hardly suitable reading matter in the midst of such a mournful crisis.

At first, I was advised that General Al Haig had shown the article to the President, who had commented, "Why didn't this come two weeks ago?" Later, I was informed that in the stress of events, the article had not been read by Nixon until much later in San Clemente.

In law, we use the phrase "Time is of the essence." It is a peculiar phrase, because time is always precious and the most unrecoverable asset in life. But the legal phrase has a special connotation. Even delay of hours may be fatal. It is possible that, had my article been mentioned earlier to my Washington friend, it would have been received at the White House in time to be evaluated. Then my imaginary summation plea to the Senate might have been made by some attorney. Perhaps history would have been changed.

ILLUSORY SYLLOGISMS

"I know you don't believe in ESP or parapsychic phenomena," said one of my law partners, "but how are you going to explain this?" "This" was almost impossible to explain as a coincidence. The facts come best from a skeptic like me.

One day a lady in distress called from Monte Carlo. Her immensely wealthy husband was acting strangely. He was apparently trying to get rid of her. She was terrified. Could I send someone to meet with her surreptitiously at an appointed place to guide her? My law partner Gerald Meyer, gifted in foreign languages and laws, took off to Monte Carlo on this mission of matrimonial mercy. Later he was joined by my partner Julia Perles. They returned with a bagful of legal problems. The most important was jurisdiction. In what country would her rights to share his wealth (a matter of intense personal concern, euphemistically called community property) be best protected? Where should her suit be brought?

As befits the very rich, they had residences in many lands. Why experience the inconvenience of foreign travel when you can arrange to be at home everywhere? So, they had mansions in Switzerland, England, France, United States, Monte Carlo, and, in addition to some others, South Africa, where they had been married.

The legal research therefore required knowledge of the matrimonial law of South Africa, and if that law was favorable, what other countries would apply the law of the country of marriage, rather than their own? How to find out the matrimonial law of South Africa? To communicate with a law firm there was hazardous to the secrecy required. The husband was so influential that important law firms might well have represented him in his multifarious enterprises (unlike some women, she didn't pronounce it nefarious enterprises). There would be a conflict of interest. They would disqualify themselves, but somehow the husband might learn that his wife was not a complacent sufferer, ready to surrender. So we had to find the law ourselves.

We reasoned that there must be a legal textbook on South African matrimonial law. We were determined to find it, if there was one. Search soon revealed that there was. Its author was Professor H. R. Hahlo. The title was literally precise, *Husband and Wife*. But neither the law libraries of the leading bar associations, the university law libraries, nor the comprehensive public libraries possessed this esoteric book. We called our Washington office and stressed the importance of obtaining Professor Hahlo's work. Researchers who had previously found the thinnest and smallest needle in the largest haystack scoured all possible sources, from the Library of Congress and Copyright Office, to the law libraries of the many law firms in Washington. All to no avail. Calls to lawyer-friends in California and other states ended the same way: "Never heard of it." We began to suspect that Professor Hahlo's publisher had only printed a few copies and confined them to the country of their special interest.

On Thursday, June 17, 1976, the client was to call us for advice at 4 P.M. On an untraceable private phone in Monte Carlo. We would have to confess that we were not ready to guide her.

At 2 P.M. my secretary put upon my desk a huge book (it had 674 pages) with old-fashioned heavy leather black-brown mottled covers. "What is that?" I asked.

"It just arrived without a letter."

I rose from my desk to look at the almost invisible title. It was *Husband and Wife*, by Professor H. R. Hahlo!

On the left inside cover was scribbled a flowery compliment signed "C. K. Friedlander."

We didn't know who the inscriber was or how he came to send this rare book so that it would arrive at the critical hour. The mystery would have remained forever unsolved were it not for a search of a file marked "miscellaneous correspondence" which revealed a letter from C. K. Friedlander, dated April 21, 1976. On the letterhead of the law firm of C. K. Friedlander, Kleinman and Shandling situated in Cape Town, South Africa, he wrote that he had just read my book *My Life in Court* (thirteen years after it was published), and hastened to express his compliments. (That is one of the satisfactions of authorship. The work is never stale to one who reads it for the first time. Books enable us to reach across centuries and touch the reader intimately. Perhaps the arts receive our special homage because they provide this unique possibility of immortality.)

I answered the letter with formal expression of appreciation for his graciousness. (When it is a friend who sends such a note, I can indulge in a light-mannered reply of complimenting him for being a discriminating reader.)

Generally there are two classes of correspondence each day; the worrisome, which requires thought and treatment, and the pleasant, which induces rereading and filing. So this letter was filed.

It was almost a month after that verbal bouquet was filed that the lady in Monte Carlo found herself distraught, and we in equally desperate need for Professor Hahlo's book. Friedlander could not, therefore, have known all this, and certainly could not have known that we had only two hours before the client would seek the answer locked in that book.

We devoured the pertinent contents of the huge book which had just arrived. It described the Dutch-Roman law, a source as remote as the book itself. We were ready with a stream of advice to the lady in distress when she called.

I wonder if she, like me, doesn't believe in telepathy or other mysterious forces of communication?

A similar eye-opening coincidence occurred in the very preparation of this book. Because of its autobiographical nature, Ken McCormick, Doubleday's senior editor, suggested that childhood photographs might be appropriate. Theoretically, as a man gets older he acquires the face he deserves. What was his face before it was molded by his conduct? Also, early photographs of my parents might be instructive. Aside from the quaint outfits they wore in London in 1900, their physiognomies might reveal unseen genetic clues. I had seen a few such memorabilia in the past, but where was one to find them now? My parents were long dead. If there ever were photographs sixty or seventy years old, they had been washed away by the currents of time.

Only Ripley's title *Believe It or Not* is suitable for what follows. Within a week after Hahlo's book on South African law materialized on my desk, a grayish-blue suitcase appeared in my office. Upon opening it, I would have been less surprised to find a treasure of ancient jewels and gold than to see what the contents were: photographs of myself from infancy to adulthood, photographs of my parents, some taken in London, still clear in their somewhat faded sepia color. Where had they been? How had they suddenly shown up?

Like great magic tricks which have simple explanations, mysteries often have obvious solutions. My parents' summer home in Bethlehem, New Hampshire, had a brick path entrance, difficult to traverse because the chrysanthemum bushes on both sides jutted toward each other affectionately, and an orchard of apple and pear trees. Most important for this recital, the house had what is a rarity these days, an attic. My parents had gradually discarded old possessions, but somehow several barrels of things, too sentimental to leave behind, found their way to the attic.

I recall, on one occasion, Mildred and me climbing to the attic on a shaky wooden ladder to explore the unknown region. There, beside albums of old phonograph records, Mildred found in one barrel London dishes ringed with raised gold, issued for the coronation of Edward VII, teacups with a mustache protector (so that a gentleman could drink his tea without wetting his adorned lip), a brass vessel with accompanying brass pestle which druggists used to mash pills, and sundry other items which justify the existence of the word "miscellany." Mildred selected a few to be saved from the strewn confusion, and with care we lowered them in a sling. Some are in our home today.

My parents were astonished at our interest in these items, even after I told them of a sign in an antique shop which read, "If you think this stuff is junk, come in and price it."

This reminds me of a semantic problem which caused Mildred much hurt. The Yiddish word for delicious is antique (with a broad "a"). Used about a person, the idiom is "She is an antique"—a doll. Bragging about her one day, my father resorted to this Yiddish expression. Mildred overheard it. It took a long time to convince her that my explanation wasn't an artful lawyer's device to extricate my father from an insulting reference; although all she had to do was look in the mirror to know that what she heard was not what she thought it meant. "*Interpretare est prodere*"—to translate is to betray.

Our groping in the attic revealed no photographs. When my parents died, I presented the property to the community. Various couples lived there in the next two decades. The present occupants are a Mr. and Mrs. Bressman. A short while ago the admission committee of our law firm had selected a number of young graduates, among them one David Bressman, the son of the Bethlehem occupants. I knew nothing of this relationship or even who the occupants of our former home were. But the Bressmans, aware of the link, and having come across photographs, a tennis trophy I had won in 1933, and other personal items, felt that their son ought to deliver them to his senior. So it was that a suitcase suddenly showed up in my office out of nowhere. I shudder to think that the reader might otherwise have been deprived of the visual nostalgia which surrounds this book.

Another incident hovering between coincidence and mystery occurred on my birthday. It is possible now to trace the disparate facts which converged to create the result.

Scene 1: In Woodstock, New York, a man by the name of Ed Balmer was in the business of building swimming pools. One day when he was preparing a hole for an installation, he accidentally dug up an electrical feed line. He had to repair it at considerable expense. He decided to eliminate such risks in the future by inquiring about devices which could detect metal underground. The most efficient metal detector was produced by the Garrett Company in Texas. He not only bought one but became a dealer for the product. Whenever a new model came out which detected metal at a lower depth, he would test it at Woodstock Recreation Field.

This was a site which the troops of the Revolutionary War used for drilling. Later traveling circuses and carnivals camped there.

It became a favorite place for men in the area to go "treasure hunting" with metal detectors. Balmer had found a silversmith hammer, an old hand-forged stirrup, and an aluminum medallion with a portrait of Lincoln on one side and a motto, "Death to the Traitors," on the other.

Three years ago, his metal detector discovered a fourteen-carat gold charm four inches underground. Imprinted on it was the calendar month of February. The date of the sixth had been drilled through and a tiny amethyst, the stone of Aquarius, shone where the number had been.

Scene 2: A young lady, by the name of Monelle Richmond, became a secretary of one of my associates in our law office in March 1976. Her mother had been an astrologer for twenty-five years and Monelle was therefore interested in horoscopes. Because she worked in our office and had read my books, she wanted someday to prepare a horoscope about my future. She learned that I had been born on February 6, and entered that date on her Rolodex for future use.

Scene 3: Monelle Richmond and her mother had lived in Woodstock for many years. They knew Balmer. Recently he asked Monelle when she was born. She told him February 11. He told her about the February 6 date on the charm. The next day when she returned to New York, as she described it:

"Something snapped in my mind. I looked on my Rolodex, and sure enough! I told him when I next saw him that it was your birthday."

Scene 4: Since February 6 fell on a Sunday, my law partners decided to tender me a birthday luncheon two days in advance on February 4. At twelve-twenty, just as I was leaving for the party at the Park Lane Hotel, a letter arrived from Balmer. It read:

Dear Mr. Nizer,
An unexpected birthday present is always fun, particularly from somebody you never laid eyes on.

He explained the link with Miss Richmond, whom I had also never met, and concluded:

I am old enough to remember that bastard McCarthy and your part in his comeuppance, which is most of the reason you are getting this. Enjoy a very happy birthday with my best wishes!

Enclosed was the beautiful gold calendar charm.

Scene 5: I took it to the luncheon, where I was presented with a Steuben glass decanter with an eagle cover, and more glittering speeches with sentimental covers. After I explained that I had felt uneasy about the event, but enjoyed its warmth so much that I would appreciate semiannual repetitions; and after I commented that my dislike for birthday parties was not because I minded others knowing about my age, but that I did not want to learn about it myself; preferring to cling to my illusion that I was only thirty-five years old, and after telling my family of thirty-eight partners-in-law that growing old is a bad habit which I was too busy to cultivate, I told about the remarkable incident of the unexpected gift from a stranger.

It gave a surprise note of mystery to a warm event.

Even those who believe in mental telepathy may balk at the notion that the dead can communicate with the living. I don't believe in either, yet Aldous Huxley involved me in a message he sent after his death to his widow.

Huxley, brilliant author and extraordinary man, was fascinated with the extensions of consciousness. He experimented with hypnotism (called mental passes) and later with mescaline and LSD. Shortly before he died, he said, "It is a little embarrassing that after forty-five years of research and study, the best advice I can give to people is to be a little kinder to each other."

But that was for the living. Huxley's sense of the cosmos convinced him of a continued consciousness after death. He sought to bridge the gap by psychedelic (a word he used first) experiments which he described in *The Doors of Perception*; by visionary experience, meditation, and deep hypnosis about which he wrote in *Heaven and Hell* and finally synthesized in *The Island*.

His wife, Laura, an author in her own right, has written a remarkable book about him called *This Timeless Moment: A Personal View of Aldous Huxley*. It is a tender, sensitive description of that handsome, gifted man. It has many photographs of him revealing the penetrating eyes, the deep-nostriled nose, and high brow with distinguished gray curved hairline, the small hollow in the cheeks like masculine dimples, and the full lips—all of which constituted a combination of superior intelligence and sensuality. The photographs featured his hands, which were as artistic as his face. Indeed, there was one photograph of only his right hand, with its long slender fingers, above which he had written

"Aldous." It may have been a symbol of his reaching out to the here-after.

Huxley had long preparation for his death. He was afflicted with cancer of the tongue, and after he declined surgery, which would have made him speechless, he recovered. But then his glands developed a new cancer, and for months he knew he was dying.

Although the knowledge of the ultimate end is always with us, its imminence often sets off the terror of dying. Huxley's search for greater consciousness in life led him to the mysteries of survival after death. His poetic sense of purposefulness provided a rationale for each individual's permanence, in spirit if not in flesh. In a letter to his doctor he wrote: "The emphasis, in the last rites, has to be on the present and post-human future, which one must assume—and I think with justification—to be a reality."

A medium, aware of these convictions, advised his wife that "Aldous says that you are going to receive . . . *classical evidence of survival* of the personalty and consciousness—not something that can be explained by telepathy or other theories."

Since Laura Huxley had no predilection toward spiritualism or messages from disembodied spirits, how had the "classical evidence of survival" been given to her?

A young man she identified as K.M.R., who was doing research in parapsychological aspects, had sought her out for a television interview in her home. He discussed mediumship, ESP, and reincarnation. He explained that he was a medium and headed a foundation in Seattle for parapsychological research. Then he offered a reading. She declined in a kindly way, suggesting that she would take "a rain check" until he returned from Europe, where he was headed for more television interviews. But this was not the last of it, as is often the case and intended to be, from vague postponed appointments. He returned. He had obtained a television interview with Bertrand Russell, then ninety-four years old. Russell was a dear friend of Huxley, and the fact that he spared his flagging energies for K.M.R. impressed Laura.

Once more he offered her a private reading. She declined, but when he suggested a group reading for the five guests who had come to dinner, she accepted, probably because it would be an entertaining oddity. The guests were skeptical but curious, and agreed.

He gave each of them a card on which was printed "Direct your billet to loved ones . . . write full names; place questions in center, sign your full name at bottom. Thank you." These cards were placed in sealed envelopes, and given to him unopened. He was thoroughly blindfolded. Then he went into a trance for an hour and a half.

He reported personal messages from disembodied spirits to each of the questioners. They were not merely astonished. They were overwhelmed. The words conveyed intimate information which could not have been known to the medium. For example, Laura asked about an old friend. The medium's face registered suffering and he said that the man had been brutally murdered. This was the fact. He even mentioned Ensenada, a place which Laura and the man had visited, and other details she did not recall, but which photographs taken by a friend later confirmed.

Each guest encountered replies of similar startling information. When incredulity is breached by the inexplicable, there is either confusion or shock. All guests were in this state. The medium told Laura that Aldous Huxley had been present throughout the session and he reminded her of his offer to give her a private reading.

But first, motion pictures of his interviews abroad were to be shown. While threading the projector, the medium suddenly said, "Please give me a pencil and paper. Aldous is saying I must write this down."

He wrote:

17th page
6th book from left
3rd shelf
    or
6th shelf
3rd book from left
23 line

He told Laura that Aldous wants her "to look up those books."

She and a "witness" proceeded immediately to the library. The first book designated was in Spanish. Page 17, line 23, began as follows (translated into English):

Aldous Huxley does not surprise us in this admirable communication . . .

Laura commented that she was "speechless," especially because she was certain Aldous had never seen this soft-cover book in a cardboard container, sent after Aldous had been unable to attend a conference in Buenos Aires.

She decided to make the "book test" again by counting the shelves from the opposite direction. The book so designated was titled *Proceedings of the Two Conferences on Parapsychology and Pharmacology*: Page 17, line 23, read:

Parapyschology is still struggling in the first stage. These phenomena are not generally accepted by science although many workers are firmly convinced of their existence. For this reason the major effort of parapsychological research has been to demonstrate and to prove that they are working with real phenomena.

Once more the quotation was pointedly meaningful. Then Laura writes:

One more book was found that met the requirements of location and page. It was *My Life In Court* by Louis Nizer.

There I described a man six feet five inches tall, which approximated Aldous Huxley's unusual height, and as his wife wrote: "It is as though the intelligence that motivated the two previous events wanted now to give also a physical proof. We were stunned."

The book then concluded with a quotation from Huxley's grandfather that one must "sit down before fact like a little child, and be prepared to give up every preconceived notion . . ."

What shall we make of all this? As a nonbeliever, I nevertheless accept Laura Huxley's assurance that she made "an objective report without opinions or emotions—only facts." This is the classic approach to credibility of the incredible. Not only those engaged in search for truth as she was, but fiction writers use the device of having a character in the book express his disbelief more emphatically than would the most skeptical reader. Later the impossible occurs and breaks down the character's resistance and therefore, the author hopes, the reader's as well.

One thing caught my eye, when I read the instruction on the medium's printed card, "place questions in center." It recalled an experience I had with an entertainer called the "X-Ray Mind." He astonished audiences by reading their minds.

One day he came to see me professionally. Of course, his very presence in my office was disproof of his mental powers. Why would one with his professed gifts need advice? I did not consider my jaundiced view of his telepathic readings to be pertinent, and treated him like any mortal whose brain did not simulate the Roentgen ray.

Somehow his pride was hurt. He needed awe as well as advice. So he opened the subject:

"Have you seen me perform?" he asked.

"Yes." My tone denied him the admiration he sought.

"You don't believe in mental telepathy, do you?"

I did not flinch from the question, put as if it were an accusation. I confessed I did not.

"Well, suppose I give you a reading right here."

I had other things to do, but how could I dodge the challenge and convict myself of closed-mindedness. I agreed.

It was early afternoon. My room was lit bright by copious windows. He continued to make the test severe. "I'll do it right at your desk. I'll use any piece of paper you give me, so you won't think I have something prepared."

There was a small yellow pad on my desk, a printed form to be filled in with data. I tore off a sheet, turned it on its blank side, and handed it to him. He drew a circle in the center and said:

"I'll leave the room until you call me. Write any question you wish in the circle. Fold the paper four times, so no one will know what you have written."

I did, and buzzed my secretary to send him in. He took an ashtray on my desk and put it in front of him. Then he lit a match and held out his hand for the tightly folded sheet. I gave it to him and he set it afire. He watched the smoke intently as it curved upward, while the black ashes fell into the ashtray.

Then he proceeded to answer the question I had put on the folded sheet. There was no doubt that he knew what the question was, although his answer could not be checked at that time.

He gazed at me triumphantly, awaiting my surrender. I told him I was impressed, but I still believed it was a trick, conceding mystification but not the phenomenon of a penetrating X-ray mind. I would give it thought and try to learn how it was done.

He left with a shrug, which meant that obstinacy can make an intelligent man a fool.

Having amateurishly practiced the art of magic, which, despite my lack of dexterity, amused children, I knew that the right way to solve the puzzle, if it could be solved, was to trace back in detail everything that had happened. My mind lit on the circle he drew on the piece of paper and his instruction to write my question within it. Was it possible to burn the folded paper and leave the center palmed in the hand for a quick glance? Indeed it was. I did it myself. A magician told me that there was a shorter cut to the trick. Any skillful magician could palm the entire folded paper and substitute a similar one without detection. The burning of the fake paper would prevent checking its authenticity. I believe the former method was used. That is why the instruction was not simply to write a question, but to do so within a predrawn circle.

The medium's card likewise instructed "place questions in center." But that is as far as I could get in deduction because Laura Huxley told us that she put each card in an opaque envelope, and that the blindfolded medium held the closed envelope in his hand while the disembodied spirits spoke the answers through him. The incident is too remote for further investigation, but the question arises, why in such supernatural goings-on was it necessary to write out a question? Why couldn't the incarnate spirit indulge in the elementary power of reading the questioner's mind? One would think that a mind which could pierce an envelope, and isolate a spirit among billions of dead to reply, would also divine the question without mundane script.

What force is it that draws an intelligent mind to a preposterous belief such as spiritualism? It is the force of logic! Yes, logic so brilliantly deceptive and enticing that its logic is not detected. I call it the illusory syllogism.

It is a series of reasoned steps which seem irresistibly right and which lead to an inevitable conclusion. But it is an illusion. If you spot the error, the syllogism collapses.

Laura Huxley, her bright and talented mind notwithstanding, unwittingly gives us a good illustration. How does she induce the reader to believe in her husband's message from beyond?

The first step in the syllogism is her comment:

A medium is similar to a telephone, he is a channel of communication between different states of consciousness—possibly the living and the dead.

This is a modest statement. It merely states a possibility—fair enough.

The second step is to cite an illustration of disbelief in some other phenomenon which was overcome by miraculous facts: She writes:

If a few telephones had suddenly appeared in the Middle Ages, people would have considered them the work of the devil—and their users burned at the stake. What? Speak to someone in Florence when you are in Sienna? . . . no one can speak *that* loud—it is *impossible!*

Having shown that people who disbelieved were terribly wrong, the syllogism proceeds to analogize the telephone with spiritualism:

What? To be able to communicate between this, our universe, and the invisible universe of the dead—we are not sure it even exists! Exceedingly suspect!

By this time, the logic is pressing hard, the reader is beginning to feel almost ashamed of his skepticism. The next step in the syllogism is to pry the mind open a little more; to weaken resistance to a belief which earlier seemed preposterous. This is done by exploiting a current example, an event which almost everybody considered implausible even to contemplate, and yet happened in front of our eyes:

Suppose we had not been informed, through press, radio and television, of the preparation of the last eight years for trips in outer space; suppose we had not seen on the TV screen the launching of space vehicles. How would we react to a man who showed us a blurry photograph of sands and pebbles and announced, 'This is the moon'? It is easy to predict. We would call him a charlatan or a madman. Now, secure in our knowledge, we all agree that the famous blurry photograph is indeed the moon!

So, we have reached our destination. Discarnate entities may well exist and they speak to us through a medium who is nothing but a telephone communicating the message. If you doubt this, you are guilty of the same error which caused people to reject as a charlatan's claim every great invention before it became a reality. You belong to the embarrassed multitudes who were willing "to bet their heads" that man would never step on the moon. Your mind is closed to the miracles all around you. You are a reactionary, devoid of imagination and prejudiced against cosmic possibilities. You reject the mysterious although life is filled with mystery, being unveiled to us day by day. Etc., etc.

Yet, all this is based on an illusory syllogism. The fundamental gap is that before one can talk of disembodied spirits communicating messages to us through an anointed medium, there must be some evidence that living animals not only survive after death but have all the communicating and other attributes of life except physical embodiment. To merely assume such a conclusion by an analogy with physical phenomena which previously astounded the skeptic is an unwarranted leap. It begs the question. It assumes that the miracle of splitting the atom or computerizing a trip to the moon automatically makes reasonable a belief in discarnate bodies yearning to speak to us. It is an illusory syllogism because it equates the fact that some things did eventuate which we once thought were impossible, with the conclusion that we should believe anything at all. It is an illusory syllogism because it assumes that because we were in error before, we must surrender all judgment and accept everything or we may err again.

The illusory syllogism isn't confined to spiritualism, reincarnation, and such. It has misled us in law, medicine, politics, indeed in any area where reasoning fashions our beliefs.

An illustration of the illusory syllogism in politics is the betrayal of Czechoslovakia. Hitler's voracity would permit nothing but the annexation of the neighboring state. England and France, unprepared to resist and desperate for time and peace, went to Munich and sacrificed

Czechoslovakia to save themselves. Munich became a symbol of the villainy of appeasement. Clearly, this was ignoble, if not indeed treacherous. So, we heard on all sides condemnation of them. "They are no better than Hitler." "They are just as amoral."

The syllogism was false. What was overlooked was the distinction between the aggressor and the amoral conduct of those who should have aided the victim. The murderer who invades a home and threatens to kill is not to be equated in venality with the policeman who is too cowardly to interfere.

The illusory syllogism is active in the arts. Isn't present tolerance of mediocrity and even fakery partly the result of its application? Why do we accept a blue line across a white canvas as a possible masterpiece? Why do we hesitate to condemn it as a hoax? Because prior new directions in painting were ridiculed and later were recognized as the work of genius. Listen, for example, to a respected critic writing about the Impressionists in 1876:

An exhibition has just been opened at Durand-Ruel which allegedly contains paintings. I enter and my horrified eyes behold something terrible. Five or six lunatics, among them a woman, have joined together and exhibited their works. I have seen people rock with laughter in front of these pictures, but my heart bled when I saw them. These would-be artists call themselves revolutionaries, "Impressionists." They take a piece of canvas, colour and brush, daub a few patches of colour on them at random, and sign the whole thing with their name. It is a delusion of the same kind as if the inmates of Bedlam picked up stones from the wayside and imagined they had found diamonds.

Far more savage criticism was written about these Fauvists, whose works now are hailed as unique and beautiful revelations of nature (and, incidentally, turning the critic's sarcastic comment about inmates of Bedlam picking up stones and imagining they were diamonds into a tribute to their imagination). Nevertheless, does it follow that, because many were once artistically blind, we must now see virtue in trash, as if *we* were blind? Only the illusory syllogism pushes us to an abandonment of discretion. Out of fear that we may reveal our ignorance, we see gold raiment where there is only nudity.

The same is true in music. We refrain from holding our ears, and instead listen reflectively to cacophonies of weird dissonant noises (sometimes made by scratching a tin washboard) because we dare not pit our judgment against historical precedent which exposed the most vociferous critics as stupid.

None of the geniuses escaped abuse. Had it come from minor critics it might not have mattered. But they were seared and humiliated by the foremost musical critics of the day. To read these attacks is to appreciate the vitriolic virtuosity of the critics, if not their judgment. Friederich Dionys Weber, the respected musical theorist, considered Beethoven's ninth symphony "pure nonsense." Another famous critic wrote that Wagner's *Tannhäuser* overture was "only a commonplace display of noise and extravagance." Lohengrin was denounced as "a frosty, sense-and-soul-congealing tone-whining." *Meistersinger's* overture was an "ugly rioting of dissonances" whose effect was "caterwauling." *Parsifal* reminded one eminent critic of "piano-tuning with impediments," and another of "The howls of a dog undergoing vivisection."

The famous critic Eduard Hanslick was more comprehensive: he lumped Beethoven, Wagner, and Mozart together and shot them down with one bullet: "There has been nothing of any interest since the classicists."

Of course Stravinsky was an even more inviting target. Appropriately enough his music was compared to the paintings of the Fauvists and called "The music of the Fauve." This was not intended as a complimentary allusion. His works were condemned for their savagery and brutality. The critics' anger spread to the people. At the premiere performance of *The Rite of Spring*, at the Théâtre des Champs-Élysées in Paris, on May 29, 1913, an enraged audience rose in mass, hooting and stamping their feet. Blows were exchanged. One woman spat in the face of a demonstrator. The music was drowned out by noises more dissonant than that which came from the stage.*

So it is understandable that some current critics, knowledgeably indoctrinated by the past, may be slow on the trigger. Who knows, they think, but what grates on their eardrums and offends their minds may soon be recognized as brilliant representation of the discordant times in which we live? Furthermore, it is chic to be avant-garde, to hear into the future, even if one cannot see into it. The result is caution, a lack of confidence to state their true feelings, and sometimes even a struggle to find talent in the very revolutionary formlessness of a creator without the power to create. That is why it is always possible to find somewhere a kind word for rubbish.

The illusory syllogism takes many forms. Here it is expressed in the syllogism that great artists break through traditional barriers; that we are repelled by the unfamiliar; that everything new meets resistance until we educate ourselves to appreciate it; and therefore that we must not scoff at the aberrational or even at emptiness. It is new and when we accustom ourselves to it, perhaps we will learn that it is an ad-

* David Ewen, *The World of Twentieth Century Music*, Prentice-Hall, N.J., 1968. P. 789.

vance in art. Therefore we abandon our discriminating judgment. Don't reject. Don't denounce. Accept with tolerance the possibility that what you believe is trash may turn out to be gold.

As between the risk that posterity will prove us fools and the risk of surrendering our judgments, I prefer the former.

So in matters of the occult—no equivocation. I don't believe in extra-sensory perception, astrology, reincarnation or spiritualism.

If I am wrong, the first words uttered by a medium some future day, when he summons my voice from beyond, will be "I apologize."

LAUGHING AT OURSELVES

A human being is distinguished from all other animals by his capacity to laugh. By this standard, Harry Hershfield was one of the great human beings of our time.

Most comedians have musical identifications, like "Thanks for the Memory" or "Everybody Loves Somebody." Harry's was prose: "He walks with the mighty but has never lost the common touch." Five Presidents of the United States called him their friend. Kings and statesmen, from Winston Churchill and Charles De Gaulle down, paid him tribute. The foremost scientists, writers, and painters honored him. But it was the people who took him to their hearts.

This is a great American tradition, to choose a humorist by popular choice and make him the folk hero of his generation. His duty? To tell us the truth about the mighty and ourselves without offending us. To cleanse the democratic process by making us laugh at ourselves. Hershfield belonged to this long line of aristocracy in our democracy; Mark Twain, Josh Billings, George Ade, Robert Benchley, and Will Rogers.

I had good opportunity to observe his hold on the people. We often ate together at the Algonquin Round Table. Ate is a bad description— we choked and gasped for breath from laughter between bites. On one occasion he had just arrived from Washington, where he had been a guest of President Nixon. He exhibited White House cuff links which had been presented to him. "Mr. President," he had said, "the country doesn't need cuff links. It needs shirts!"

Even his food order sent the waiter into spasms. "Let me have something that will give me heartburn now, not two in the morning."

After lunch, he would walk me back to the office. When we passed the Lambs Club, we would encounter prominent stars, all of whom, men and women, embraced him with enthusiasm out of all proportion to the need for professional recognition. As we continued, the street cleaner raised his brush in salute. The shoeshine boy lit up with a smile brighter than his shine. And sometimes, when we passed the alleyway of the Belasco Theater, a drunken derelict would open his swollen eyes and greet him, "Hello, Harry." I got to imagine that the policeman's horse neighed his greeting too. Harry belonged to all, because he made us all happier.

There are people who carry germs and infect others with disease. Harry was a carrier who infected people with good will. If you were morose or moody, you had to be wary of him. If you carried your business burdens on your shoulders, you had to shun him. You didn't have a chance, if you met him. For whether he was telling a story to one or to 25,000 at Madison Square Garden, his enthusiasm, gaiety, and boyishness infected you. You lost your sad face. You walked away with a stronger back, if not a lighter burden.

You could observe this phenomenon at any of the thousands of banquets at which he presided. A distinguished foreign dignitary, public official, or artist would approach him ponderously. Within a moment, Harry would be telling him a story. You would see a smile and then the explosion—the diaphragm moving violently up and down. The visitor had been infected with good humor. Now he had become a carrier himself. When he returned to his seat, he repeated the story to his neighbors. Thereafter, Harry acted as toastmaster, and the laugh germ spread to the whole audience. For more than seventy years, he spread such epidemics throughout the nation.

In 1955, Mayor Robert Wagner designated Harry officially as "Mr. New York." At a brilliant dinner in the Grand Ball Room of the Waldorf, overflowing to the highest tier, Times Square was designated "Hershfield Square."

Even in appearance Harry represented the conglomerate qualities of the city. He had Irish gray hair, Scandinavian blue eyes, Greek pallor, French vivacity, Italian love of music, Jamaican gaiety, and he was thoroughly, wonderfully Jewish. New York is a huge melting pot and Harry seemed to be standing over it with an enormous stirring spoon pouring humor into it to prevent it from boiling over.

Freud commented on what he called "the peculiarly liberating and elevating effect" of humor. Harry didn't tell jokes because of social consciousness. He simply enjoyed making people laugh. He breathed laughter, as ordinary mortals breathed air.

Harry was born in Cedar Rapids, Iowa, in 1885, two weeks after his parents arrived from Odessa, Russia. His parents were gifted. His father, Michael, was a musician and linguist and head of a "gymnasium" in Russia. His mother, Alta, came from a family of musicians and physicians. Harry was one of thirteen children. He had aspired to become a doctor, but he quit high school because the study of drawing was irresistible. (One of his later lines was "Educated he is, but smart he isn't.") It was his brother Alex who became a distinguished physician in Chicago.

At the Frank Holme School of Illustration, Harry's classmates were the cartoonists, H. T. Webster, Will B. Johnston, and LeRoy Baldridge.

He obtained a job on the Chicago *Daily News* as an illustrator, but was suspended when he retouched a photograph of the Leaning Tower of Pisa to straighten it up.

Harry became not only a repository of stories but a creator of humor. One could tell by his bemused look that a "new" joke someone eagerly told him was one he had invented and used in a Kabibble cartoon a half century earlier.

Unlike most raconteurs, he carefully measured the possible hurt of a story, and his kindliness prevailed over laughter. So he would check with his friends Cardinal Spellman and Bishop Sheen before making a talk at a Communion breakfast. (Is it all right to say that you make holy water by boiling the hell out of it, or that the donkey carrying Mary stumbled and Joseph cried out, "Jesus Christ, he almost fell" and Mary said, "You know, that's a better name than Irving.")

He took more liberty with Jewish groups, as if to cure their hypersensitivity:

"A child brought home a poor report card. Facing the tirade of his parents, he explained, 'The teacher is anti-Semitic. She picks on me.'

"The next morning the irate mother visited the teacher and upbraided her for bigotry. 'It isn't true. Your boy just doesn't know his lessons. Let me prove it to you. Sammy, how much is 10 and 10?'

" 'There she goes, Ma, picking on me again!' "

And so by the thousands, stories poured from him. He was an inexhaustible geyser of humor. For years he demonstrated his prowess on radio and television programs called "Can You Top This?" If anyone doubted the authenticity of his instant recall, all one had to do was be in his presence and witness the spontaneous flood of stories from his computerized brain.

He was an etymologist of jokes and his books on humor developed the theory that basically there were only six stories. He would illustrate professorially. A Mussolini story (a pollster reported to him that 99 per cent of the people were for him, "but I must say I constantly ran into the other 1 per cent") could be used for Stalin, Hitler, or any other dictator. He could illustrate ten offshoots of a basic war story ("Don't be scared. Every bullet has a name on it. If your name is not on, then you're safe." Frightened soldier, "I'm worried about the bullet which has on it 'To whom it may concern,'").

He was a humorist, not a comedian.

The common denominator of virtually all his stories was their meaningfulness. They pointed up the foibles, weaknesses, or surprise ingenuity of the underdog. The point may have been washed away with the first burst of laughter, but then reflection, like the tide, brought it back and we enjoyed the intellectual aftertaste.

Harry had no compulsion to be "on" all the time. He would listen respectfully to serious discussions. He would sit back reflectively, his lips pursed as if he were savoring good wine. It was interesting to watch him as others tried to tell him a "new" joke. Inevitably he knew it, but not once did he embarrass the teller by stopping him. He would listen appreciatively, and comment, "Isn't that wonderful." His tolerance was like that of a lover of opera who can enjoy the same music over and over again. When he was challenged to admit that he had known the story all the time, he would reply, "But I like the way you told it."

His generosity was unlimited. He practiced the greatest exercise of all —to bend down and help someone up. He was the softest touch wherever he was. Although it was his profession to make appearances and entertain either as toastmaster or speaker, he made hundreds of talks without compensation, either because a friend (and who wasn't his friend?) asked him, or because the function was charitable.

He was the quickest draw in the land, in picking up a check at the dinner table. If it weren't for the rule of the Algonquin Round Table that all guests signed their own checks, he would have paid everyone's bill every day.

As a toastmaster, he was overgenerous in introducing others, but his exaggeration was forgiven because it stemmed from his goodness. But when he was introduced, he turned compliments aside jestingly. "I am not as good as you have been told, but I am not as bad as you out there are thinking."

He never told a joke which had daggers in it. He never told an off-color joke in public.

He could be given to pixieish mischievousness, but, as always, it was harmless. Once he presided at a public dinner at which Congressman Sol Bloom was a speaker. The politician glowed in the aura of his appointment by Roosevelt as the head of the George Washington centennial celebration. This made him more verbose than usual. After forty-five minutes, the audience was getting exceedingly restless—a step preceding their abandonment of the speaker to converse among themselves. Harry put a note before Bloom, "Time." Bloom ignored it.

Fifteen minutes later, another note, "Time." Bloom continued with what Harry used to describe as his eighth "In conclusion."

Finally, Harry scribbled another note. Bloom read it, and sat down instantly, hardly finishing his sentence.

We on the dais had watched this. The audience had long before retired. (Harry used to tell of the speaker who looked at his watch, and someone in the audience yelled, "There's a calendar behind you!")

"What did you write on that last note?"

"I just wrote 'Your fly is open!'"

He had been attracted to the theater and tried his hand at it. In 1912 he appeared at Hammerstein's Victoria Theater with Eddie Cantor and Lila Lee. His column "Broadway Unlimited" earned him one of the first appearances in talking pictures, with President Coolidge and Adolph Zukor, in 1926.

He also appeared on the first television program, sent to Times Square from Jersey City, which starred George Jessel and Sid Grauman. At one time he was a theater reviewer on a radio program called "One Man's Opinion."

Nevertheless, the artifices of performing were inimical to his sincerity and simplicity.

Therefore, he did not practice the art of embellishing a story with dialect, elaborate descriptive language, or Thespian skills. To him, the joke "is the thing." He did not wish to dazzle. It was the story which was front stage. The spotlight must be on it. I sometimes thought he practiced economy in the telling, so as to have more time for more stories. Only once did I hear him "stoop" to performing. It was the story of the Jew on line with hundreds milling about the United States Bank, which had closed during the 1929 crash. He was screaming imprecations at the officers of the bank. Harry imitated his hysterics, "Even hanging was too good for such villains!"

A passer-by asked him how much money he had in the bank.

"None—if I had had any money in there, would I be taking it so lightly?"

'He appreciated art. He was a collector and his home and office were filled with fine paintings and sculpture. He was also a collector of memorabilia. I drew dozens of drawings of him on napkins and he saved them all. Once, not realizing his collecting mania, I drew his head on a tablecloth. He insisted on cutting it out and offered payment to the owner.

Although his humor directed him to cartoons (the famous Abe Kabibble, Desperate Desmond, Homeless Hector, and According to Hoyle), he was a good draftsman and could have had an art career. At one time for three years he was a scenario writer for Warner Brothers and, later, editor of animated cartoons for M-G-M. However, to be in Hollywood was like being banished from New York, the great banquets and the teeming excitement which were essential environment to his well being. His constitution could not stand the sun. He needed Broadway electric lights.

He was the author of a serious novel about New York. On the flyleaf, he wrote "Where everyone mutinies and no one deserts."

In his early days he was a sports writer and artist of sports events for the San Francisco *Chronicle*. Among the hundreds of photographs which crowded each other off the walls, onto the tables and floor of his home and office, were poses with every champion boxer of the last sixty years, his slight figure throwing a punch upwards, while his opponent feigned distress. But also there were dozens of photographs picturing his dais companions, the foremost public officials of this country and abroad.

He had unusual eating habits. He could not touch butter or any dairy product. His translucent pale skin revealed his sensitive organism. Captains and waiters in all the grand ballrooms knew of this eccentricity. As the food was paraded to the tables in military file, one waiter would head for the dais with a special Hershfield plate. It was a perquisite of his fame and popularity. For he had entertained them, too, dozens of times and they loved him.

As he neared his ninetieth birthday, he changed in only one respect. He became good-naturedly philosophical. "I have lived and experienced everything. Now I enjoy everything more because I understand better." His phenomenal good nature prevailed over his age and he really believed it was the best period of his life.

He had practiced joyful serenity all his life. He, like everyone else, had suffered tragedy. But he was dauntless. In 1917 he had married Jane Isdell, a beautiful actress whom he met in Chicago, where she was appearing in *The Girl Question*. But she became mentally ill, suffering from all sorts of phobias. He loved and cared for her for a half century, until she died. Few ever saw her. He always appeared alone. No one would have suspected his private anguish.

Even his own illness could not dampen his bubbling spirit and gaiety.

His heart failed and he was desperately ill. No visitors were permitted. But he persuaded the nurse to permit him to take my telephone call.

"Hello, Harry. I'm delighted I can visit you on the phone."

"Oh, Lou, I am so glad, so glad to hear your voice."

"How are you feeling?"

"Lou, I'm too weak to collapse."

He joined me in laughter but his was weak.

"Harry, you're incorrigible. I understand they're going to give you a heart pacer. That should make you feel better."

"Yes, I'll try it for ten years. If it doesn't work I'll throw it out."

"I can hear the nurse telling you to hang up. I'll talk to you again soon. Feel well."

"Don't worry. In a few weeks I'll be back to abnormal!"

Two days later, December 15, 1974, he was dead.

Few people can go through life without making an enemy. The process of achievement is abrasive. To excel is to rise above others reaching for the same pinnacle. We are reared in the tradition of competition—in business, arts, and sports. We try to assuage the loser by honoring "good sportsmanship"—which usually means, to lose gracefully. But the psyche does not yield to slogans.

We envy the victor and often hate him. And it is easy to find or imagine a grievance to justify the violation of the loser's ethic.

Harry was unique not only because of his talents as raconteur, columnist, and artist, but because of his personality.

He combined sophistication, guilelessness, and goodness. He was truly loved and thus he lived a fulfilled life.

Measured by customary standards of greatness, he was not a great man. But he was the foremost philanthropist of our day because philanthropy does not mean giving money. The word is derived from *philo* (love) and *anthropos* (man); to love man.

When one evaluates the joy he brought to millions, the realization grows that this warmhearted man came closer to the mysterious purpose of life than most of us.

PORNOGRAPHY—OBSCENITY

Is pornography or obscenity a crime? It is under certain circumstances, but the Supreme Court of the United States has admitted that it is "an intractable problem." Several dissenting judges have criticized the Court for being "mixed" in definitions of obscenity. Justice Jackson sarcastically referred to his own tribunal as the "High Court of Obscenity," which reviews erotic and scatological material. Other judges have expressed concern that any obscenity conviction violates the First Amendment guarantee of free speech. Yet, the Supreme Court has upheld criminal statutes which make obscenity a crime punishable by jail.

However, the road to this conclusion has had so many detours that one traveling it didn't know whether he was coming or going. The definition of obscenity has been changed time and again. On some occasions a majority of the Court could not be found to reach a decision, there being so many splintered views.

Justice Harlan in the Dallas "censorship" case, which I argued, wrote of "a variety of views among members of the court unmatched in any other course of constitutional adjudication."

The Court has held that free speech requires "breathing room" and any limitation upon it must be made with "sensitive tools." How sensitive? And what is obscenity?

The word derives from the Latin *obscaenus*, meaning filth. My Webster's dictionary defines it as "disgusting to the senses, grossly repugnant to the generally accepted notions of what is appropriate."

Pornography derives from the Greek *porné*, harlot, and *graphos*, writing. Literally it means a description of prostitution, of lewdness, a portrayal of erotic behavior designed to cause sexual excitement.

These are dictionary definitions, but they do not determine the legal test of when the state will consider them criminal.

The reason that this subject so intrigues the public is not only because, like all subjects of sex, it arouses interest, but for more profound reasons. It poses questions of our values, moral, ethical, and philosophical. Is there a point at which permissiveness endangers the structure of civilized society? We are warned that the decline of empires is preceded and accompanied by general licentiousness, and that this is no coincidence. On the other hand, we are also warned that free expression is democracy's strength and ensures the possibility of change while preserving fundamental values. Is there a line which can be drawn between these two precepts without sacrifice of either?

I have argued a number of motion picture pornography cases in the Supreme Court, and have engaged in "debate" with the judges, who initiate and encourage it, in preference to be passive listeners of a prepared speech by counsel. I have participated to some extent in the evolution of the prevailing rule and deign to enter and explore this mined territory.

I begin the journey with a decision in 1957 (Roth case) that obscenity was not protected by the First Amendment. How did the Court justify this apparent encroachment on freedom of expression? Simply by saying that obscenity didn't qualify as the kind of expression worthy of constitutional protection. It didn't rise to the level of ideas, good or bad, which would be shielded by the guarantee of free speech. It was just garbage. This still left the need for a definition. When would the words or scene be deemed obscene? The answer was when the dominant theme appealed to prurient interest (aroused sexual feelings), which an average person, according to community standards existing at the time, would find patently offensive.

Little wonder that these generalities did not put the matter to rest. The Court proceeded to search for a more precise definition. Nine years later in 1966, the Court fashioned one in the famous case of *John Cleland's Memoirs of a Woman of Pleasure* v. *Massachusetts*. Material would be considered obscene if it contained three elements:

One, the dominant theme as a whole appealed to prurient interest in sex.

Two, it was patently offensive because it violated contemporary community standards.

Three, it was utterly without redeeming social value.

The word "utterly" in the third test left a loophole so large that even complete nudity, sexual intercourse, and oral sex could be depicted and still not be condemned as obscene. The reason was that in books or motion pictures where all this was vividly depicted, there were other scenes which were not "utterly without redeeming social value." Resourceful producers had no difficulty beginning a picture with the heroine fully dressed, interviewing men and women in various strata of life about so-

cialism, marriage, children, and politics, and then being frustrated by
their opinions, while the viewers were bored by them, proceeding with
her lover to the bedroom where her resourcefulness could be better illustrated. The first breakthrough picture which used this device was *I
Am Curious Yellow*. In 1968 the Federal Court of Appeals, by a two-to-
one vote, held that it was not obscene; that it came under the protective arm of that phrase, "not utterly without redeeming social value."

The Court expressed its discomfort at its own decision, saying:
"There are scenes of oral-genital activity . . . The film is presented with
greater explicitness than has been seen in any other film produced for
general viewing." But the Court said that it was bound by the definition in the *Memoirs* case.

Judge Friendly agreed, although he argued with himself in the course
of writing his opinion, as brilliant judges often do, by commenting "A
truly pornographic film would not be rescinded by inclusion of a few
verses from the psalms." But he too found some redeeming social value
in the girl's search for her identity. Both judges warned, however, that
if the producer's promise that children would not be permitted to see
the picture was broken, or that if the advertising stressed the sexual aspect of the picture, they would be subject to criminal action such as
sent the publisher Ralph Ginzburg to jail, because he had "pandered"
his wares by offensive advertising and thus refuted his alleged serious
purpose. Judge Friendly concluded by saying, "With these reservations
and with no little distaste, I concur in the reversal." Chief Judge Lum-
bard wrote an indignant dissent: "The participants indulge in acts of
fellatio and cunnilingus. Needless to say these acts bear no conceivable
relevance to any social value, except that of box-office appeal."

A Danish sex film virtually mocked the "redeeming social value" test
by claiming that it consisted of an appeal from the screen by one of the
characters to the audience, to sign a petition which would be supplied
in the lobby, protesting against the prudery which put any limit on sex
depiction. This was, to say the least, an imaginative device of an inverted automatic compliance with the test. If the same resourcefulness
had been applied to the sex scenes, the picture would have been a
greater success.

The "utterly without redeeming social value" requirement pleased
the advocators of absolute First Amendment rights much more than
those who sought to curb pornography, because it was almost impossible to convict under it. In a way there was satisfaction for both sides.
The law condemned obscenity. On the other hand, the definition of obscenity permitted very wide latitude. An uneasy truce descended on the
battleground. As permissiveness gained during the lull, a cry went up
again for restraint.

President Johnson appointed a commission which after lengthy study rendered its report. It found that "society's attempts to legislate for adults in the area of obscenity have not been successful" and that "exposure to explicit sexual material" does not cause criminal behavior among youths or adults insofar as evidence can demonstrate.

By the time this "Report of the Commission on Obscenity and Pornography" was filed, President Nixon was in the White House. He denounced it because he claimed it overstressed freedom of expression instead of recommending restraint. In doing so, he was reflecting public indignation. Of course his strictures on moral rectitude could hardly have come from a less appropriate source:

I have evaluated that report and categorically reject its morally bankrupt conclusions and major recommendations. So long as I am in the White House, there will be no relaxation of the national effort to control and eliminate smut from our national life . . .

If an attitude of permissiveness were to be adopted regarding pornography, this would increase the threat to our social order as well as to our moral principles . . .

American morality is not to be trifled with . . . I totally reject its report.

However, it was not a report or Nixon's views which would control. It was the Supreme Court's search for a definition of obscenity which would be sound enough to obtain concurrence of a majority of the Court. The opportunity arose when a man called Marvin Miller was convicted by a jury of distributing obscene material in California. The case went to the Supreme Court in 1973 and became so famous that it is referred to merely as *Miller*, an intimacy reserved only for landmark cases.

What had Miller done? He had conducted a mass mailing campaign to advertise the sale of four books entitled, *Intercourse, Man-Woman, Sex Orgies Illustrated,* and *An Illustrated History of Pornography,* as well as a film entitled *Marital Intercourse.* The brochures consisted chiefly of pictures and drawings explicitly depicting men and women in groups of two or more, engaging in a variety of sexual activities, with genitals often prominently displayed. A recipient of the brochures and his mother complained to the police. Indictment and conviction followed.

When the case came to the Supreme Court, it said that it had re-examined its earlier decisions. It repeated that obscene material was not protected by the First Amendment, and was a crime. However, it carefully set forth a new definition of pornography or obscenity, which it said would protect the public against smut and nevertheless comply with free speech requirements. The break with the previous rule was complete. Chief Justice Burger, who wrote the majority opinion, conceded that there wasn't a single judge who still supported the *Memoirs* test. Even Justice Brennan, who had written that decision, abandoned it.

The new test substituted for the famous "utterly without redeeming social value" the following: to be obscene a work, taken as a whole, must lack serious literary, artistic, political, or scientific value. If it had any one of these values, it could not be obscene irrespective of what else it portrayed. The serious quality, like an antitoxin, made it immune from attack.

Even if a work failed to have any of these qualities, it could be obscene only if two other conditions existed:

One, would an average person, applying contemporary standards, find that it appealed to prurient interest; and second, did the work depict in a patently offensive way sexual conduct specifically defined in the state statute?

The Court for the first time defined what would be considered "patently offensive":

(a) Descriptions of ultimate sexual acts, normal or perverted, actual or simulated.
(b) Descriptions of masturbation, excretory functions, and lewd exhibition of the genitals.

The decision attempted to still the concern of extreme free speech advocates:

No one will be subject to prosecution for the sale or exposure of obscene materials, unless these materials depict or describe patently offensive "hard core" sexual conduct . . . Today for the first time . . . a majority of this Court has agreed on concrete guidelines to isolate "hard core" pornography from expression protected by the First Amendment.

The villain had been identified. It was "hard-core pronography." It was sheer (to avoid the unfortunate word "pure") smut. Everything else would be exempted from punishment, either because it had literary, artistic, political, or scientific value, or because it was not patently offensive.

Chief Justice Burger anticipated the attacks which would be made on this formulation. He argued that just because no one could define regulated material with "god-like precision" didn't mean that the states or

Congress should not be able to strike at "hard-core" pornography. His opinion did not spare the dissenting members of the Court.

I have always thought that it was unfortunate when, during oral argument, judges of the Court argued with each other. Sometimes they attacked their "brothers" on the bench, by addressing the hapless lawyer, who then received a reply from the "brother," the lawyer becoming an unwilling conduit. The attorney dared not agree with either judge, but had to exhibit the kind of tact which an English solicitor once demonstrated when he said to the Court, "Last month your honors decided a case for the plaintiff, and this week you decided an identical case for the defendant; and may I say, your honors, in both instances, most admirably."

Ordinarily differing opinions would evidence vigorous intellectual discussion. But the Supreme Court has deservedly been held in greater awe than some of our Presidents. Unlike the White House, the Court is visited by people from every part of the nation who observe how it functions during argument. They may not understand the quarreling among the judges. It strips the Court of the aura of infallibility, a psychological, if not realistic, expectation. Clash of views, sometimes angry ones, should be reserved for the conference room. Indeed great Chief Justices have striven to achieve unanimous decisions because dissents weaken the persuasive effect of the majority. For example, the ruling against President Nixon on the production of tapes derived special force from the absence of any dissent.

The obscenity debate, however, was so volatile that the opinions themselves in *Miller* reflected the contentiousness and fiery disagreements which pervaded the conference room. By reading them one could almost hear the bitter exchanges behind the closed door. The Chief Justice took on Justices Brennan and Douglas directly. Mentioning them by name, he wrote:

The dissenting justices sound the alarm of repression. But, in our view to equate the free and robust exchange of ideas and political debate, with commercial exploitation of obscene material, demeans the grand conception of the First Amendment and its high purposes in the historic struggle for freedom . . . Civilized people do not allow unregulated access to heroin because it is a derivative of medicinal morphine.

Justice Douglas, as eloquent as he was extreme in advocating free speech, dissented:

There are no constitutional guidelines for deciding what is and what is not "obscene" . . . What shocks me may be sustenance to my neighbor. What causes one person to boil up in rage over one pamphlet or movie may reflect only his neurosis, not shared by others . . .

The First Amendment was not fashioned as a vehicle for dispensing tranquilizers to the people.

The four dissenting Justices saw "dark days" for America if obscenity was made an exception to the rule that free speech was absolute. They predicted that zealots would raid libraries to remove offensive works, and that motion pictures, which were not hard-core pornography, would nevertheless be attacked.

Soon we would see. It did not take long. Within eight days after the *Miller* decision, the District Attorney of Albany County acted against *Last Tango in Paris*, starring Marlon Brando and Maria Schneider, and directed by Bernardo Bertolucci. This motion picture had been playing for almost two months in the Towne Theater in Albany. It was rated "X" by the Motion Picture Producers Association. The rating code, and how it came about, I shall discuss later. Suffice it to say that the "X" rating merely meant that children would not be admitted. It was no evaluation of the quality of the picture. Indeed, three "X"-rated pictures, *Midnight Cowboy*, *The Damned*, and *Clockwork Orange* had won Academy Award nominations.

The reason that children were barred from *Tango* was that it had scenes of nudity, sexual intercourse, and sodomy.

Curiously enough, most of the coupling was done while fully dressed. This was to emphasize the sudden impulse devoid of personal relationship. Its dehumanizing aspect was accented by the "butter" sodomy scene. It was only later when the man's feelings turned to love that he derived real gratification.

Clearly, the picture had a genuine story in which the sexual scenes advanced the plot rather than dwarfed it. The film took two hours to show, of which time eight minutes were devoted to sex scenes. True, the test is not merely time. A hard-core pornographic motion picture may have the same proportion of actual sex scenes, but they are the dominant characteristic of the film. The rest is flimsy excuse for its real purpose. In *Tango* the reverse was true. Sex was incidental to the story. The film was a study of a man whose wife had committed suicide after betraying him, and who at the age of forty-five found himself tormented and embittered. He met a girl accidentally in an empty apartment which both were trying to rent. Almost without communication, and while fully dressed, they indulged in intercourse while standing up. The erotic relationship continued on his insistence that they should not know anything about each other, not even their names. The impersonal, animalistic nature of their sex relationship "leaves no room for lying, deceit or treachery," but it turned out to be unsatisfactory. What began as a quest for the assertion of male mastery moved on to love. She wanted to be free of him and when he pursued her she killed him. As one literary expert testified, if the film was considered in its entirety, the plot was the coat. The sexual scenes were the buttons. Clearly the film had serious literary value.

The *Christian Century* described it as "a parable of man seeking release from inner anguish through sexual catharsis and finding that love, not sex, is the answer." When *Tango* was shown at the New York Film Festival at Lincoln Center, New York, Pauline Kael, the film critic of the *New Yorker*, equated its impact on cinema with the effect of Igor Stravinsky's *Rite of Spring* upon modern music.

The critic of the New York *Times*, Vincent Canby, called it a "beautiful, courageous, foolishly romantic and reckless film . . ."

Judith Crist, the distinguished critic, wrote that "Tango is not about sex . . . it is about the things man lives by."

Lavish praise came from all sections of the country. As if anticipating the impending struggle, Max Lerner, teacher and author, wrote: "No one will dare to ban 'Last Tango' and get away with it. The critical audience won't let them, and that is what counts."

But, critical audiences don't fight legal battles.

The prosecutor, believing that *Miller* gave him an opportunity to strike at the hard-core pictures in the Albany area, and confusing *Tango* with *Deep Throat* and its lurid progeny, because they all had an "X" designation, summoned theater owners to his office. He gave them a summary of *Miller* to read and announced that all "X" films would be submitted to the grand jury for possible prosecution.

So there it was. The District Attorney went fishing for pornography and *Tango* was caught in the net.

The exhibitor who was playing *Tango* was told that if he ceased playing the picture, the subpoena would be withdrawn. He "pulled" the picture immediately even though under his contract with United Artists it had many weeks to run. The result was that all other bookings of *Tango* were jeopardized. Why should a theater owner risk criminal involvement? There has never been an abundance of martyrs (even though it has been said that martyrs should not be pitied because they liked their job). The expense of a legal test would be severe. The case might have to be taken to the Supreme Court. There were many other pictures available. This was a perfect example of the "chilling effect" so often bespoken by those who argue that encroachment on free expression frightens off others from expressing themselves.

United Artists, however, decided to test the issue. As its counsel, I rushed to Albany to argue before a three-judge panel which we had demanded, because of the constitutional question involved. After some skirmishing, *Tango* triumphed and continued its unmolested career.

In reflective terms, the dissenters in *Miller* could point to *Tango* to support their prophecy that repressive efforts would follow that decision. The majority could reply that that effort had failed, and that the beneficent effect of curbing hard-core pornography must not be sacrificed because of misguided application of the law. In a sense, it was a standoff. Soon, however, there was a more severe test which would come before the Supreme Court in 1974. Then it could look at its handiwork empirically. How did the clashing theories really work out in the field?

The motion picture involved was *Carnal Knowledge*. It boasted the combined talents of some of America's leading contemporary artists. It was directed by Mike Nichols; written by Jules Feiffer; acted by Jack Nicholson, Candice Bergen, and Ann-Margaret, who won an Academy Award nomination for her performance in this very picture; and produced by Joseph E. Levine. Even the cost of the picture, $9 million, distinguished it from the $25,000 to $100,000 budgets of most of the skinflicks.

Carnal Knowledge had played to seventeen and a half million people in some five thousand theaters, including cities in Georgia, enjoying popular and discriminating acceptance.

However, during an engagement in a theater in Albany, Georgia, the local sheriff seized the film. The manager, Billy Jenkins, was arrested on the charge of "public indecency." The case was tried by a jury. No doubt it was shocked. Words not generally bandied by men except in the proverbial smoking car (I wonder what has happened to this release of profanity now that people fly) emanated from the screen to the mixed audiences sitting in the dark theater. There was a youthful petting scene in which he pleaded to touch her breast and then guided her hand to himself. There were obvious scenes of intercourse, and a final scene in which the impotent "hero" engaged in a fantasy with a woman so that she could talk him into turgidity.

The jury, ignoring all the rest of the film, found Jenkins guilty. He was sentenced to one year's probation and fined seven hundred fifty dollars.

This decision caused little stir because it was the finding of a local jury, which probably would be corrected. Jenkins' lawyers took an appeal to the Supreme Court of Georgia. When that court upheld the conviction by a vote of four to three, an alarm arose throughout the creative world. If a theater manager could be criminally convicted for showing *Carnal Knowledge*, how could anyone dare to produce anything but "kiddy" pictures? Who knew but that some other local jury might find a passionate kiss or a deep-shadowed cleavage a crime? One of the judges of the United States Supreme Court had said "that distributing books should not be a hazardous occupation." The same applied to motion pictures. But now it clearly was.

Also private interest had been placed in jeopardy. What would happen to future bookings of *Carnal Knowledge?* Would other theaters risk exhibiting it in the face of the warning by the highest court of one of our states that it was criminal to do so? Was this multimillion dollar project to be mummified as a historic example of the fate of unconventional artistic effort?

The clashing opinions of the majority and minority of the Georgia Supreme Court were like jagged lightning flashes preceding the thunder in the world of creative artists.

The majority of four judges rested on the foundation laid down by the United States Supreme Court that "obscenity is not within the area of constitutionally protected speech or press." It pointed out that the Georgia legislature had enacted a statute which adopted the *Memoirs* test of "utterly without redeeming social value." The *Miller* case had come down since then and actually provided a more restrictive test. But *Miller* had also held that a jury "can consider State or local community standards 'in lieu of national standards.'" The jury therefore had the right to evaluate the local standard according to which the picture was obscene.

The majority wrote in stentorian tones reserved for conclusions from on high:

We hold the evidence in this record amply supports the verdict of guilty by the showing of the film "Carnal Knowledge" in violation of the definition of distributing obscene material under our Georgia statutes.

The decision added moral justification for the jury's verdict. The showing of an obscene picture, it said, "involved the welfare of the public at large since it is contrary to the standards of decency and propriety of the community as a whole."

It referred to the "legitimate interest" of the state to regulate commerce in obscene material. In this way, "states' rights" and "public welfare," like pepper and salt, were added to the brew.

The minority opinion was legalistically phrased, but Judge William Gunter could not disguise either his emotions or acerbity. *Carnal Knowledge* had been shown to all seven judges of the court. Four thought it was "obscene, pornographic material, unprotected by the First Amendment." Three thought it was not obscene and therefore constitutionally protected as free expression. He then quoted Chief Justice Burger's retort to the minority of his own court:

The dissenting Justices sound the alarm of repression . . . Their doleful anticipations assume that Courts cannot distinguish commerce in ideas, protected by the First Amendment, from commercial exploitation of obscene material.

Could they? Judge Gunter didn't think so:

My experience with this case teaches me that the "alarm of repression" was validly sounded.

To think that judges could distinguish ideas from commercial exploitation of obscenity was, he said:

a too optimistic assumption. The Jenkins case is the proof of the pudding: material is pornographic and unprotectected in the subjective mind and senses of one judge; and the same material has serious literary or artistic value in the subjective mind and senses of another judge.

He referred to an old saw which mocked the Supreme Court. That court's decision is not final because its members are infallible. It is infallible because it is final. For good measure, he sounded a louder alarm of repression than even Justices Douglas and Brennan:

"If the motion picture 'Carnal Knowledge' is not entitled to judicial protection under the First Amendment's umbrella, then future productions in this art form utilizing a sexual theme are destined to be obscenely soaked in the pornographic storm."

The alarm was heard. Authors, book, magazines and newspaper publishers, motion picture producers, directors, actors, theater owners, television companies, unions in the art industry, libraries and others expressed their determination to join in the battle to reverse the Jenkins conviction.

I was requested by the Motion Picture Association of America Inc. to represent Billy Jenkins. With his consent and that of his lawyers, I undertook to appeal and argue the case in the Supreme Court of the United States.

But first, that court's permission to appeal had to be obtained. It had refused to do so in some twenty obscenity cases, sending them back to the state courts to comply with the new standards of the recently decided *Miller* case. The Jenkins case had also preceded *Miller*, but we nevertheless filed a petition (*certiorari*, it is called) requesting the Supreme Court to hear our appeal. This was opposed by the State of Georgia.

The Supreme Court announced that our petition was granted. We were delighted to have passed the first hurdle. *Carnal Knowledge* would be the first case argued and reviewed by the Supreme Court since its *Miller* decision.

Intense preparation and brief writing began. Dozens of obscenity cases were dissected to derive every nuance. Articles on the confused law of pornography which had appeared in the law reviews of leading universities were analyzed for their errors as well as insights. Hundreds of pages of preparatory legal data were reviewed. Our briefs went through the critical process of more than a dozen lawyers, and their suggestions were weighed for acceptance or rejection.

Although only Tony H. Hight, counsel for the District Attorneys Association of Georgia, would argue for the State of Georgia, and I for Billy Jenkins, many briefs were filed by organizations not parties to the controversy but having a large stake in the outcome. These are called *amicus curiae* briefs, submitted "as friends of the court." It is a quaint phrase because one must obtain permission from the Court to be its "friends." The reality is that amicus curiae briefs are intended to aid one of the litigants. In this case, the Court granted petitions to listen to its "friends" on both sides. So briefs were filled by the Authors League of America, Inc.; the Directors Guild of America, Inc.; the National Association of Theater Owners; the American Publishers, Inc.; Magazine Publishers Association, Inc.; American Booksellers' Association, Inc.; the National Association of College Stores, Inc. All these supported Jenkins' position.

The State of Georgia was supported by only one friend-of-the-court brief, filed by Charles H. Keating, Jr. founder of Citizens for Decency Through Law. The plethora of briefs indicated to the Court the enormous concern in many quarters about the case.

Each of these briefs, as well as our own, had a different color for identification. They were like warning flags. The shades of opinions in them were as different as the covers.

One of my tasks was to cajole excellent counsel for these organizations to be consistent with our strategy in the case. Otherwise, as has not been unknown, your ally may do you more injury than your opponent. For example, the brilliant dissenters in the Georgia Supreme Court had lined up with the dissenters in *Miller*. They sounded an alarm of repression. They contended that the *Miller* majority was wrong. We welcomed the dissent of Judge Gunter in favor of Billy Jenkins, but should we too attack Chief Justice Burger and the majority which voted with him?

I thought this was wrong strategy. On principle as well as persuasive wisdom, we ought to agree with *Miller* that hard-core pornography should be ruled out. Our position ought to be that *Carnal Knowledge* was not hard core, and that the majority of that court ought to give emphatic warning that the true meaning of its decision could not be debased. Such a trumpet call denouncing those who stretched and distorted the *Miller* decision would dissuade district attorneys from instituting futile prosecutions. *Miller* needed a follow-up, not a chastisement. Such an approach would not antagonize the majority, and might even win over some judges on the minority side.

Also this would be consistent with the position of the leading motion picture producers, none of whom made or approved hard-core films.

Some of our *amicus curiae* friends were purists. They wished to see *Miller* destroyed. They wanted to point up its failure in the Jenkins case and to predict the inevitability of other repressions.

It took as much energy to unify our comrades as to prepare our own briefs. A lawyer, particulary when he deals with eminent co-counsel, whose talents and achievements warrant strong egos, must be a consummate diplomat.

What else must he be? He must be an archaeologist who exhumes evidence; a psychologist who strengthens his client and weakens his enemy; a paragon of patience to withstand the unreasonableness of troubled clients; a man of endurance to withstand the strain of the most arduous profession; an optimist in the darkest hours and a pessimist in the brightest, so that momentum doesn't slacken; a historian of the law so that he can better predict its future; an idealist in the service of justice and a practical man who may forgo litigation in his client's interest; a precisionist who must draft documents which defy ambiguity; a negotiator who makes deals not breaks them; an administrator who can recommend corporate efficiency and achieve it in his own office; a pleader whose eloquence is harnessed by sincerity; a scholar who is not confused by his learning; a lover of the law so that sacrifice for it becomes a selfish act; a visionary who uses legal tools to sculpt a better society; and a realist who knows that it is impossible to attain any of these except to a small degree but who never stops trying.

Well, many of these attributes were needed the night before the argument in the Supreme Court. Gathered in the huge living room of a suite in the Hay Adams Hotel in Washington were more than twenty lawyers and some executives to help prepare the argument for the morrow. I sat behind a desk with briefs and pads to make final notes, while around me swirled a brilliant coterie of experts unhesitant about their suggestions. Present were Jack Valenti, the president of the Motion Picture Association of America, Inc., who appeared before congressional committees frequently, to argue as well as to observe, and who sat with lawyers continually in the problems that beset his worldwide industry; who traveled in all directions of the compass whether to the Shah of Iran, the Soviet Union, South America, to the heads of state in Europe, with sufficient peripatetic zeal to qualify him to be Secretary of State; Sidney Schreiber, general attorney of the Association, who was a storehouse of motion picture law and lore; James Bouras on his staff; my law partners Gerald Phillips and Gerald Meyer, who had worked on the brief with me; Tench Coxe, Atlanta counsel and his associate, attorneys who had submitted *amicus curiae* briefs, and other executives and wives who wanted to share what might be a historic moment, and who looked to me like people who were not content to see the meal offered up but wanted to watch the chef as he prepared it.

To be helpful, everyone anticipated questions which the Court might put to me, so that we could review the proper answers and cite the appropriate authorities. Naturally, there were differences of opinion concerning the right reply, sometimes very vehement ones. I drank it all in, making up my own mind in silence. The exercise was useful because it paraded every conceivable attack which the judges, differing among themselves, might launch, but one could not decide what tack the answer should take by argument with a committee. That would be more wearing on my throat and energy than was advisable. As the clock hands stiffened at midnight, the group thinned out. Finally at about 2 A.M. only a few stalwarts were left. I packed my voluminous notes, knowing that if they had not been stored in my mind, they would be useless in the give and take of oral argument, and we retired.

The next morning, I had breakfast in bed, as always while reading a newspaper. This was not an ice-in-veins demonstration. I simply function better if I awake without shock of an alarm bell, and slowly recapture consciousness. Even if I have been up through the night working on a case, I eat breakfast leisurely, and deliberately read the morning news in the same way as when there is no anxious court engagement. It is a discipline helpful to me because it eases tension. Just as there is an erosion limit to listening, so there is an erosion limit to strain. The longer it is delayed, the more effective one is. When contrasted with the sleepless witness or his nerve-racked counsel, the advantage is enlarged.

This, of course, is not an equation applicable to judges, for they "don't know what side they are on," and their tension is of a different character. It is one of concern about true performance of duty. I recall a judge of the highest court of a state consulting me about his unbearable headaches. He felt it was due to his misgivings about decisions he had rendered. Doubt tormented him day and night.

"I have watched you in court, Lou; and observed your equanimity. How do you do it? Is it a born trait, or can you learn it? If I don't, I may have to resign from the bench. I simply can't stand it any more."

I told him that it was not an inherited characteristic at all. It was the result of persuading oneself (call it self-hypnosis if you wish) of the stupidity of a worrisome disposition.

Self-control comes from perspective. It can be trained like a muscle. It banishes fear and induces calm. Freud discovered that learning why we are neurotic is itself a catharsis which eliminates the neurosis. Similarly, learning that we exaggerate our fears eliminates them. I advised the learned Judge to render judgment on himself; to recognize that he was inducing migraine headaches by overblown fears about his decisions; that he was enervating his function as a judge, which required a steady, confident mind, by torturing himself into inefficiency, ill health, and resignation.

"You don't need advice from the outside," I said. "You are intelligent enough to give yourself a lecture and wise enough to accept it."

I do not know whether our talk was responsible or his headaches ran their course and stopped (doctors always claim credit for cures of coincidence, so why shouldn't lawyers?), but he became well and continued to serve on the bench with great distinction.

In this spirit of self-induced calm, I arrived in the Supreme Court. A lengthy line of visitors from many areas of the nation were waiting for admission to the two hundred seats. It would have been wise if the architects of the fairly recent courthouse had provided thrice that number. Like airports which become obsolete before they are finished, we underestimate people's interest in their government, particularly the Supreme Court. Many were turned away in disappointment.

Counsel who are scheduled to argue are led by attendants to front row desks on which are pads and inkwells with feather quill pens. This reminded me of the Congressional Room preserved in Philadelphia where the Constitution was enacted, and where stood similar desks and inkwells with quill pens. There is also on each desk a card indicating by squares the names of the judges as counsel faces the bench. This is about as necessary as the identification letter Lindbergh presented when he landed at Orly in Paris. More useful is an instruction of how to address the Court: "Mr. Chief Justice, may it please the Court." The Chief Justice acknowledges this greeting by nodding and greeting counsel by name. It is the first time the lawyer is sure that he is not speaking to the photograph in his office.

There is also instruction about the light signals on the podium, white to indicate that only three or five minutes are left in accordance with advance request to the Clerk, and the red light, which requires immediate completion of the sentence and withdrawal. Counsel is admonished not to inquire of the Court how much time is still available. Furthermore, time used to answer questions by the Court is not deductible. It is part of the argument and not deemed by the judges an intrusion of counsel, as he may feel. However, if the Chief Justice feels that the lively questioning by the justices may have been too pervasive, he will volunteer to counsel that a few more minutes are granted him. This is a matter of mercy on the part of the Chief Justice, although many a lawyer would be better off without his beneficence.

There was a low-keyed buzz in the room, which disappeared into frozen silence when a gavel descended loudly three times. There followed the deep somber voice of the clerk, "The justices of the Court."

The burgundy-red plush curtain behind the bench quivered and one by one the nine judges emerged to stand in front of their seats, the most recent appointees at the end, and the others according to their seniority on the bench nearer to center on both sides of the Chief Justice. The effect was not dissimilar to that which occurred when the lace curtains on the balcony window in Castel Gandolfo fluttered and the Pope in white satin splendor stepped forward.

The Clerk, his voice now stronger and tinged with emotion, announced, "Oyez! Oyez! Oyez! All persons having business before the honorable, the Supreme Court of the United States, are admonished to draw near and give their attention, for the Court is now sitting. God save the United States and this honorable court." This ceremonial opening did not help to release the voice of counsel, already locked in his throat.

Our case was called. I stepped up to the podium, which was equipped with a microphone and light gadgets. In the preliminary description of the case, I stressed that children under the age of eighteen had not been admitted to see *Carnal Knowledge*, and also that there was no "obstrusive exhibition to unwilling persons." This was to eliminate other problems which bedeviled consideration of pornography and to which I shall address myself later. I quickly isolated the issue and put it in the simplest form.

The *Miller* decision had expressed sensitive regard for First Amendment rights by clearly announcing that "hard-core pornography—*and only hard-core pornography*—may be suppressed." Would this Court now permit its decision "to be stretched and grievously misinterpreted so as to strike down a work of serious literary and artistic achievement, such as *Carnal Knowledge?*"

I attempted with economy of words to describe the apprehension which had swept through all the creative elements of our nation "from producers who fear to risk production; to theater owners who fear to exhibit on pain of criminal involvement; to book publishers who fear to print beyond the safe norm; to authors who fear to be innovative; and most important of all, the public which may be deprived of access to athletic diversity which flourishes best when the artist is not reined in and must conform to the lowest common denominator of safe presentation."

I spoke not only of *Carnal Knowledge* but of the visible and subtle encroachment—chiefly self-censorship—induced by uncertainty.

So very early in the argument our position was not critical of *Miller* or of the majority which had passed it, but rather a condemnation of the Georgia decision, which would have "a chilling, indeed a freezing effect on the First Amendment right of expression, unless the Supreme Court vigorously renounced that holding. I asked the Court to repeat and emphasize that hard-core pornography was "the sole exception to the protective shield of the First Amendment."

The motion picture print of *Carnal Knowledge* had been deposited with the Clerk and the Court would later view it—all but Justice Douglas, who believed that the Constitution protected even hard-core pornography from molestation and therefore saw no purpose in viewing the picture. But for the rest of the justices it was nevertheless necessary to summarize the film, so as to give meaning to my statement that "it is unthinkable that this picture should be confused with hard core pornography."

I gave a frank word picture of its contents.

"The film depicts the lives of two college students over a span of thirty years. They grow older, but they don't grow up. They are preoccupied with sex, but the picture isn't. It does not bombard the senses with erotica driving all other ideas out of the mind (which is characteristic of hard core pornography).

"The picture deals with the human predicament resulting from the enthronement of impersonal detachment, the inability to love, and the sequellae of cruelty and psychic illness.

"It is an artistic treatment of a problem which has beset this decade and has evoked many social and philosophical studies. It has been the subject of plays from Strindberg to Tennessee Williams."

I followed this thumbnail sketch with thumbnail quotations from the reviews. The New York *Times* called it "profound"; the *Saturday Review,* "mature," the Atlanta *Journal,* "One of the best films in a long time," and the Catholic *Film Newsletter,* despite some reservations, "a perceptive and brilliant put-down of a certain style." The many critics throughout the nation who shared these views couldn't all have been fantasizing.

I believe that every argument should be punctuated with a telling sentence which by its forcefulness becomes an exclamation point. Having concluded that the dominant effect of the film was of a sincere and earnest effort to create a literary and artistic work, the exclamation point was:

"To confuse this picture with pornographic imbecility is cultural illiteracy!"

I was going along swimmingly. The Court was attentively silent. Then it came. The Chief Justice unerringly put his finger on the most vulnerable spot in our armour.

Chief Justice Burger: "Mr. Nizer, we are dealing here with a jury's finding of obscenity. Hasn't it been recognized that the jury represents the conscience of the community? If so, do we not have to accept its judgment rather than impose our own?"

Mr. Nizer: "Mr. Chief Justice, I fervently believe in the jury system. I think jurors have seven senses, not five—they add horse and common. But there is a distinction between ordinary facts and what this Court has called constitutional facts.

"Here we are dealing with First Amendment rights which involve constitutional facts and this Court has stated that in such a case, the Supreme Court will reserve to itself independent review . . . If a jury decided that Michelangelo's statue of "David" would be obscene unless a fig leaf was used, this Court would be heard from.

"In short, your Honor, in the ordinary commercial world, we give special weight to the common sense of the jurors, but when we are dealing with the precious rights of the First Amendment and a constitutional question is involved, this Court should not hesitate to express its paternal care of the constitution which is exclusively vested in it."

I turned to another error in the Georgia decision. It assumed that just as one tests offensiveness by community standards, one can test literary value the same way. Here again was our friend, the "illusory syllogism." I argued that this wasn't so. Even if a majority of people in a community thought otherwise, Chaucer, Boccaccio, Rabelais, and Fielding still had literary value. The test was quality, not popularity. Then the exclamation point sentence:

"A literary work survives even the illiteracy of its reader."

Carnal Knowledge had literary value and therefore had the impregnable shelter of the First Amendment. Even if it hadn't, it did not meet the two other tests of pornography; its appeal was not to prurient interest, nor was it patently offensive. It was not designed to exploit sex for its own sake. The camera was almost always on the faces of the characters, not below. The camera angles were deliberately discreet, picturing the least, not the most, and avoiding explicitness. Sex was treated as a sometimes baffling and exasperating part of life, but without lewdness or lasciviousness.

MR. JUSTICE WHITE: "Mr. Nizer, assume that a work is pornographic, do you see any other inquiry that we are required to make under the Miller decision?

MR. NIZER: "If a work has literary, artistic, scientific or political value, it cannot be obscene no matter what else is in it. The Constitution protects it even if it offends the public, because the right of free expression is not limited to those who approve.

"Therefore, I would put it this way: that the inquiry ends when it is found that the work has literary or artistic value. It must enjoy the protection of the First Amendment.

"If the work has no literary or artistic value, then it still may not be obscene unless it has explicit sexual scenes which are patently offensive and appeal to prurient interest. So, in such a situation where there is no literary value, the inquiry doesn't end. We must still examine the other two tests which may make it obscene."

Soon, the argument lost its unilateral character, and became a question-and-answer period, if not indeed a debate. The transformation was caused by a geographical consideration. How large must the community be whose standard governs? Was it local, statewide, national?

Miller had rejected the national test because "our nation is simply too big and too diverse" to permit a standard for all fifty states in a single formulation. It accepted the state as an appropriate unit for determining the community standard. Even then, it held it would not be error if a local standard was applied.

Motion picture producers and book publishers were alarmed by this. They had to make a product for national distribution. How could they risk running the gamut of local prejudice? They couldn't make different versions to meet the views of various sections of the country. During the preceding evening's preparation, this question caused the longest and loudest differences. Some thought I should boldly argue for a national standard. Others replied heatedly that in view of the express language in *Miller* rejecting it, "You will have your head torn off if you try that." Others urged that I should attempt to sway the Court to rule out "local standards" and plump for a state standard. Still others contended that I should leave it alone. "It's too hot a potato." I resolved not to ask affirmatively for a national standard, but, if the opportunity arose, to test the waters. But no one had foreseen how the argument would develop.

When the argument reached this sensitive area, I attacked the "local standard" test of the Georgia decision. Did "local" mean county, city, or neighborhood? It was a void test because it was constitutionally vague.

Furthermore, there were 78,200 separate political subdivisions in the fifty states. There were almost 15,000 theaters and many more bookstores which were situated in areas which overlapped. There would be a crazy quilt of conflicting standards if the local standard was applied. This would put an intolerable burden on the dissemination of communication. It was not feasible to prepare different versions of books and films for different parts of each of the states.

This loosed a barrage from the Court.

MR. JUSTICE REHNQUIST: "Wouldn't you have the same problem if we decided that the state, not the local community, should be the geographic unit to determine community standard?"

MR. NIZER: "No, your Honor. There would be a decided difference in degree and that is very important in this matter because we are not dealing with absolutes. We must apply a rule of reason. A State is a natural sovereignty with well-recognized boundary lines. The confusion which would result from barring overlapping local areas would be avoided to a very large extent if the State were the required area."

MR. JUSTICE MARSHALL: "Would you have the rule of one state determine the rights of another State?"

MR. NIZER: "No, your Honor. I am talking about state statutes and each state would determine the community standards of the entire State in deciding what is patently offensive.

"Where there is a State statute isn't it more reasonable to insist upon a State standard, thus also avoiding the constitutional burdens of continuous query to this Court whether the varying fragmented hodgepodge of local areas constitutes a constitutionally viable standard?"

MR. JUSTICE STEWART: "Mr. Nizer, if we adopted a state standard and this Court upheld a decision by a state court holding the picture obscene, wouldn't the theaters in other states be just as much inhibited from playing the picture as you say they would be within the state if we upheld an obscenity decision of a local community?"

MR. NIZER: "Psychologically, the States are sufficiently jealous of their own sovereignty not to be overly impressed with a standard set by another state. But if the highest court in a state upholds a con-

376 Reflections Without Mirrors

viction in one of its localities, it is unlikely that other localities in the same state will test their own standards. They are more likely to consider the announcement of their highest court conclusive upon them.

"There are illustrations of this, your Honor. When "I Am Curious Yellow" was decided to be obscene in Maryland, other states nevertheless played the picture and many upheld it.

"We are dealing with imprecise factors, but the rule of reason would indicate greater safety for First Amendment rights if state standards are adopted."

MR. JUSTICE REHNQUIST: "But legally it would be no inhibition either upon the local community or on another state to make their own test, would there?"

MR. NIZER: "No, your Honor, that is why I used the word 'psychologically.' This Court said in the Freedman case that it is very easy for an exhibitor not to play a picture. The fact that the situation is imponderable does not give comfort to this Court, which is concerned with the free access to commerce and thought."

MR. JUSTICE STEWART: "Mr. Nizer, you recognize however, don't you, that it is more difficult for a jury to determine a community's standards for a State than it is for its own locality."

MR. NIZER: Mr. Justice Stewart, we leave to juries more difficult tasks than this every day in the courts. In a certain sense, the struggle of the jury to discover the State community standard causes it to avoid too narrow a view."

I felt that these questions by the justices had opened the door to a try for a national standard. Since it was supposd to be a forbidden subject, I trod softly. But despite the warnings the night before, an advocate must feel his way in the maze of argument. So continuing my answer to Mr. Justice Stewart, I said:

"Indeed, the question may arise why not a national standard? Your Honors have held that a national standard is inappropriate because our country is too big and diverse for such a standard. If this court would entertain any reconsideration of that holding, I would respectfully suggest three reflections:

1. There is a technological equalizer which reduces the national diversity. Television, the same columnists in different newspapers, national magazines like 'Time' and 'Newsweek', the ease of travel, have made for homogeneity.

2. Such diversity as survives is not much different from that which exists within a State.

3. And most important, the larger the circumference of geographical parameters, the less likely an infringement of First Amendment rights.

"After all, we are dealing with a national constitution, and national standards accepted in Federal Obscenity Statutes such as Customs, Interstate Transportation, Mailing, Broadcasting ought with the same ease be applied here."

There was no vocal reaction from the Court. My "head was not torn off" because I had dared to request a reconsideration in favor of national standard. However, silence was not agreement, as we shall see.

Then in two brief sentences, I sought to gain the next best result:

"Coming back to the need for at least a State standard, as against a local standard, I would point out that a Balkanized application of the Constitution would make impossible a uniform standard of criminal justice."

The white warning light flashed.

"Time no longer supports me and I must lean on our brief for due process deprivations which abound in this case.

"We request this Court to make doubly clear that only hard core pornography may be suppressed and that such works as "Carnal Knowledge" were not intended to be caught in the net of obscenity."

An angry red light told me I had one sentence left before retiring:

"Only thus can we preserve the Constitutional rights of free commerce in ideas; the right to communicate them and the right to receive them."

I sat down, removing my papers and water alongside the podium to make room for my adversary's equipment.

Mr. Hight, who argued for the State of Georgia, had the advantage or disadvantage, depending on the angle of prejudiced sight, of the Court's comments on the chief point he was about to argue. That was, that a jury had heard, and in this case seen, the evidence, and decided the case. That decision involved a fact. Was *Carnal Knowledge* obscene? No appellate court should interfere with factual findings of a jury. It would only review errors of law. He insisted that the jury's decision, upheld by the highest court of his state, was final. It should not be tampered with.

The Chief Justice had anticipated this contention by a question to me, perhaps only to explore this vital issue. Echoing still was the answer that constitutional considerations raise certain facts to a constitutional level which *would* be reviewed. As in flashbacks in motion pictures, I hoped the words would come back, that if a jury found that Michelangelo's statue of David was obscene because it lacked a fig leaf, the Supreme Court would not be precluded from reviewing such a decision. Professor Alexander Bickel of Yale University had once written that if a jury found the calf of a woman's leg obscene, the Supreme Court "would be heard from."

Mr. Hight also contended that the question of obscenity was not before the Court, because it had not been properly raised in the lower court. One of the judges disposed of this with asperity:

"Counsel, I see on one page of your brief the word obscenity five times."

Finally the impartial red light signaled him too that his argument time, if not his argument, had expired.

The next case was called. Clerks appeared behind the judges carrying new sets of briefs, and removing our multicolored ones on which some judges had written their notes. Hopeful counsel stepped up as we hurriedly gathered our papers and tiptoed out.

In an alcove outside the building were television cameras and Fred Graham of CBS. I declined to be interviewed. When a matter is pending before the Court, I do not consider it fair for either or both counsel to condition the public to his view. Only if the rule is violated by opposing counsel is it permissible to reply, in order not to be at a disadvantage. Also, outside I met Billy Jenkins for the first time. This also was strange. Usually counsel "lives" with his client for weeks, and sometimes months, in a legal struggle. Here the issue was abstract. Jenkins had become a mere symbol of a constitutional battle.

Two and a half months later, the Supreme Court's decision came down. It unanimously reversed the conviction and held that *Carnal Knowledge* was not obscene. The reasons for the reversal, however, still differed.

Justice Douglas reversed because he refused to recognize any limitation of free speech, including hard-core pornography.

Justice Brennan reversed because he agreed with Justice Douglas except that he would recognize the right of the Supreme Court to interfere where children were involved, or where "unconsenting adults" were subjected to "obtrusive exposure." Otherwise he rejected the doctrine of "Constitutional fact," which required the Court to review, case by case, every obscenity decision. He argued that this placed an undue "institutional stress upon the judiciary." Two other justices agreed with this view. They were Mr. Justice Stewart and Mr. Justice Marshall.

Five justices, Chief Justice Burger, White, Blackman, Powell and

Rehnquist reversed because they upheld *Miller*, and found *Carnal Knowledge* not obscene.

Mr. Justice Rehnquist wrote the opinion. He quoted the *Saturday Review*'s description of the picture, which he considered accurate:

Nicholson has been running through an average of a dozen women a year but has never managed to meet the right one, the one with the full bosom, the good legs, the properly rounded bottom.

This was hardly comstockian language. It reminded me of Federal Judge John Munro Woolsey's description of the Betty Boop doll which we claimed had been infringed. "She has the most self confident little breasts," he wrote. It must not be assumed, as some fighters for free speech do, that judges are old fogies, or, as in the case of Mr. Justice Rehnquist, young fogies.

In denying patent offensiveness, he pointed out that although there were "ultimate sexual acts" in the picture, the camera did not focus on the bodies of the actors at such times. "There is no exhibition whatever of the actors' genitals, lewd or otherwise. There are occasional scenes of nudity, but nudity alone is not enough to make material legally obscene under the *Miller* standards."

Writing for the majority of five, Mr. Justice Rehnquist rejected the argument that the jury verdict was not subject to review because it dealt with a question of fact which was final. There was no hedging. Juries have not "unbridled discretion" where First Amendment rights are involved. The Court embraced tightly the doctrine of "Constitutional facts," which require "the appellate courts to conduct an independent review." The Court substituted another illustration for my Michelangelo statue argument. It would not "uphold an obscenity conviction based upon a defendant's depiction of a woman with a bare midriff."

As to the "community standard," the Court said the jury had the right to consider the national, or state, or even local area. No geographic area had to be specified. The trial court had the right simply to instruct the jury to apply "community standards" without more. If a state legislature, as in *Miller*, prescribed a state standard, that was permissible.

Although at first blush this might appear indecisive, or an evasion of the national vs. state or local test, it actually gave the creative world much comfort. It really meant that, irrespective of what geographic standard was used, a finding of obscenity would be reviewed by the Supreme Court. It would not be deemed beyond its protective arm, even though it involved a fact decided by a jury. First Amendment rights had to be guarded. They were too precious to be precluded by a jury verdict.

The Court's over-all conclusion was sounded in resonant terms:

We hold that the film "Carnal Knowledge" could not, as a matter of constitutional law, be found to depict sexual conduct in a patently offensive way, and it is therefore not outside the protection of the First Amendment . . ."

It repeated the *Miller* admonition that "no one will be subject to prosecution . . . unless the materials . . . describe patently offensive hard core sexual conduct . . .

"We reverse the judgment of the Supreme Court of Georgia."

Before considering the effect of this discussion on the general problem of pornography which persists, I turn to a unique development in which the cultural industries sought to deal with permissiveness outside of the courts.

The motion picture industry was the first to do so. When Jack Valenti was installed as president, and I as general counsel of the Motion Picture Association of America, Inc., we encountered the changing tides of public tolerance. Gone was the Hays Code, which limited the number of seconds a kiss could be shown on the screen, the strict limitations of cleavage exhibition, the prohibition of words such as "virgin," which caused a denial of a Code license for the picture *The Moon Is Blue* and United Artist's withdrawal from the Association the insistence that all villains be punished, abolishing thereby the antihero.

Permissiveness was on the march. Yet as I look back, hardly the first tentative step had been taken. The first picture which confronted the new president was *Who's Afraid of Virginia Woolf?*, starring Elizabeth Taylor and Richard Burton. The dialogue was unprecedented. "Screw you," "frigging," "son-of-a bitch," "goddamn," and "hump the hostess," a game bitterly announced by the betrayed husband, assaulted our ears from a screen which had never before yielded to such verbal realism. Valenti and I were shocked. Would there not be a public revolt against excessiveness in motion pictures, particularly in the Bible Belt and Midwest.

Our reaction was not personal sensitivity. Valenti had been on Capitol Hill, where swearing was a grand tradition coming from Benjamin Franklin and the other founding fathers, and carried on by no less than Abraham Lincoln, Andrew Jackson, and our later Presidents. Legislators were not to be outdone by their historic ancestors.

As for myself, how could an active lawyer escape the bruises of foul language on all sides?

Our concern was censorship. To anyone dedicated to free speech, that word is anathema. It was one thing to have the courts deal with offensive material. There would be a trial, judicial review, and appeals. That was due process. But to have a private censorship board cut into the flesh of a book or picture was an atrocity.

So we concluded that self-restraint by our own companies was necessary; or censorship boards, goaded by religious organizations, would multiply like viruses in a conducive environment. Valenti felt that unless he asserted his captaincy at once, the ship would zigzag uncontrollably into rocky waters. At this time there was no rating system. A seal was issued by the MPAA or refused. If a picture was not granted a seal, many theaters might not wish to book it for fear of offending their patrons.

Warner Brothers was the producer of the film *Who's Afraid of Virginia Woolf?*, Jack Warner was a personal client. I would appeal to him in the larger interest of the industry's defense against censorship, to make some cuts. The picture would still remain powerful. The furious, drunken, hate-love quarrels between husband and wife would still be there. Warner, who disguised his large vision and pioneering achievements behind a clownish exterior, was not too difficult to convince. However, he felt that he could not undermine his general sales manager, Ben Kalmenson, and that we ought to have his consent too. When we met with him, he told us in choice four-letter words, which were part of his vocabulary even in friendly discussion, what we could do with ourselves. He was adamant. He raised technical problems of recalling all the prints out in the field, the alignment of the music track with the dialogue, all of which was not only costly but would delay bookings contracted for and submit his company to hundreds of suits. All this was punctuated with expletives which made us grateful for the few in the picture. Suppose Kalmenson had written the entire script? Indeed, judging by the dialogue in pictures released years later, maybe he was the disguised author of all of them. Valenti stood his ground. Warners agreed to delete "screw you" and "frigging" but not the other objectionable words pleading that it was impossible to reshoot the picture with fitting music track, contract violations, and all the rest. A seal was refused.

The procedures permitted an appeal. The Appellate Board was composed of producers, independent producers who were not members of the Association, and theater owners, who would have to take the brunt of criminal proccedings and were, therefore, highly sensitive. When they viewed the picture, they thought it was an artistic work of the highest order. It was based on a play by Edward Albee which had won the New York Drama Critics Award and played throughout the country. Warner offered to insert a clause in its contracts with theater owners prohibiting children under eighteen from attending.

The Appellate Board granted a seal on the express condition that this was not to be a general precedent which would apply to "a film of lesser quality . . . This exemption does not mean that the floodgates are open for language or other material. Indeed, exemption means precisely the opposite. We desire to allow excellence to be displayed and we insist that films, under whatever guise, which go beyond rational measures of community standards will *not* bear a seal of approval."

The picture played throughout the country and was an enormous success. No lightning flashed from distant territories to strike dead those responsible for the desecration of the screen. But the intended limitation could not be isolated. Other works had artistic merit too, and now they were condimented with audacious dialogue. The threshold of permissibility was lowered, or should I say raised to public acceptance. Perhaps the "floodgates" were not opened, but the trickle breached the dam, letting through an ever-broadening stream until it reached torrent proportions in which restraints on language were swept away.

This was not impeded by Supreme Court rulings, which gave special protection to use of words no matter how much they violated previous norms of public expression.

For example, in one case a writer with the implausible name of Kois wrote a "Sex Poem" giving a detailed account of his experience and sensations during intercourse. It was completely uninhibited, including vulgarisms which expressed passion's candor. His style was as affected as its content. The writing ran in vertical columns, like Chinese script, one word under the other, often repeated three or four times to simulate the rhythm of thrusting.

In 1971, he was indicted and convicted under a Wisconsin statute which forbade dissemination of "lewd, obscene or indecent written matter." He was sentenced to one year in jail and one thousand dollars fine. The highest court of Wisconsin upheld the conviction.

The Supreme Court of the United States reversed. It acknowledged that the poem was "an undisguisedly frank, play-by-play account of the author's recollection of sexual intercourse. But sex and obscenity are not synonymous." The Court thought that the poem had "some of the earmarks of an attempt at serious art" even though "the author's reach exceeded his grasp."

Still publishers and authors feared criminal prosecution under the various state statutes. They did not look forward to legal struggles which would require the Supreme Court to free them from jail.

When John O'Hara submitted his script of A *Rage to Live* to his publisher, Random House, in 1948 they were advised by their counsel that the bedroom description of the wedding night would subject the publisher and O'Hara to possible criminal charges under the New York statute. They cited cases. O'Hara was asked to eliminate some of the vivid detail. He refused. In desperation, Bennett Cerf, the president of Random House, turned to me. He thought that, as O'Hara's attorney, I might overcome his artist's principled stubbornness. After all, he urged, O'Hara didn't want to go to jail.

O'Hara sent me a mound of his typewritten yellow sheets of A *Rage to Live*. The wedding night was described in lyrical, erotic terms, which, like his other descriptions, whether of the silverware on the table, the furniture in the room, or the clothes of the characters, omitted not a single detail. This was one of his gifts. He saw and noted everything, so that trivia fitted into a mosaic which ultimately gave the reader a sense of presence and the very feel of the atmosphere. In the same way, the bed scene was so realistic that the reader almost felt every touch, heard every sigh and cry, and experienced the waves of passionate love that came from the pages. O'Hara was persuaded to eliminate some phrases, on the ground that his original script was selective too. He had not included everything that took place. Therefore, the issue was not really an artist's integrity, but rather the degree of selectivity. Perhaps a little more shading might enhance the effect and still satisfy the frightened publisher. As one can still see by reading the slightly cut published version, the intended impact remained. Actually, O'Hara, by economy of words, achieved the emotional effect which Ernest Hemingway (his greatest hero, whom he compared with Shakespeare) did in The Sun Also Rises: when the heroine says she must leave her lover for another man, he protests. She says:

"Do you still love me, Jake?"

"Yes," he said.

"Because I'm a goner," she said, "I'm mad about the Romero boy. I'm in love with him, I think."

"Don't do it."

"I can't stop things. Feel that?" Her hand was trembling. "I'm like that all through."

Still, in later years, before O'Hara had to give up drinking, when we sat at the bar of Dune Deck, near his Quogue home, we would laugh at the recollection of the furor about the bed scene in A *Rage to Live*, in view of what the current books contained.

Despite the liberal view of the courts toward "offensive" language, motion pictures were mass enertainment, and there were sufficient thousands, perhaps millions, who vocally resented it. The larger the audience, the greater the risk that it will encompass unsophisticates and prudes. Organizations of all kinds, often headed by church and social workers, put pressures on legislatures. Censorship boards grew by leaps and bounds. The board of one city or state would demand certain cuts, another would approve the same scenes but demand other cuts. The inconsistency and confusion of censorship standards wreaked havoc on the industry, not to speak of the expense of submitting films to each board, with all the attendant horrors of delay and bureaucratic application of imprecise moral standards.

The motion picture industry had, together with other art industries, fought censorship for many years. The new standard of permissiveness made this effort a losing one. At times we succeeded. In the United States Supreme Court I argued against the Dallas ordinance which was held to be too vague and therefore unconstitutional. We were sweeping back the ocean of oppressiveness with a broom. However, during the argument of this case, there was the usual exchange with the judges. One of them remarked that if the motion picture industry could protect children, the Court might have less difficulty in upholding works of daring content. This theory of a separate standard for children had been suggested by the Court in other cases. It was called the doctrine of variable obscenity.

Valenti decided to act upon it. He invited all elements of the industry to co-operate in setting up a rating board. No motion picture would be barred from being shown, no matter what its contents were. But a label would be put upon it, so that the public would know what to expect. The label was in the form of initials. "G" meant suitable for all. "GP" suitable but parental guidance suggested. "R" meant restricted, children under seventeen would not be admitted unless accompanied by adults. "X" meant that children would not be admitted under any circumstances. An enormous educational program was projected so that the public would understand the symbols. Theater owners volunteered to display these symbols at their box offices, and bar children when the symbols required.

Was this censorship? Of course not. Government-imposed restrictions of what we may see or hear is censorship. Self-imposed restraint in the interest of protecting children and guiding adults is not. If I am told I may not view a picture or read a book, I am censored. If I decide I would rather not see such a picture or read such a book, that is my privilege, not to be condemned. The rating code merely applied the old doctrine of *caveat emptor*, buyer beware, to motion pictures. It was a label on the bottle, "not suitable for children," or for adults who had prudish inclinations, but the bottle was not barred.

Nor was the rating an evaluation of quality. That was solely for the audience and critics to determine. The rating system was voluntary. A producer who chose not to submit his picture for rating did not have to do so. True, he might then encounter resistance from some theaters which desired to advise their patrons what an impartial rating board had considered was the nature of the picture. Walter Reade, Jr., a distributor of films and a chain theater-owner, did not believe in the rating system and ignored it. He remained a member in good standing in the theater association and his own pictures and others were exhibited. If there was any protest, it had to come from his patrons, who were deprived of information they might have thought helpful for their choice.

The public appreciated the classifications, which the rating system provided. Furthermore, the effectiveness of the rating system as an antidote to censorship can be judged by the fact that since 1968 not one of the many proposed censorship statutes passed any state legislature. Nor have the bills for classification (mimicking the industry's rating system) passed in any state except Rhode Island; and that has never been implemented.

We knew that sooner or later the legality of the Rating Code would be tested. There are always those who believe that no limitation of any kind of free expression, even to "protect" children, should be countenanced. They are purists and undoubtedly believe in their hearts that any compromise, no matter how modest or reasonable, destroys principle. It is to my mind another example of the "illusory syllogism"; free speech is good, therefore any exception, no matter how mild and morally pragmatic, violates it and must be fought. It does not matter that the shielding of children by voluntary action helped also to defeat censorship, the real enemy of free speech.

Soon the test came. It was made by the motion picture producer of Henry Miller's *Tropic of Cancer*. The book had been considered by many a classic and variously by the courts, when it sought entry into the United States. One court described it as "a kind of grotesque, unorthodox art form," and another, "a filthy, cynical, disgusting narrative of sordid amours." Now it had been brought to the screen.

Paramount Pictures had contracted to distribute it. When it was submitted to the Rating Code administration, it was designated "X." There was no doubt in Paramount's judgment or those of theater owners that children under sixteen ought not to be admitted to see the film. The language was Milleresque, that is to say, completely uninhibited. Nudity and fornication gave visual support to the words and vice versa. Scatology abounded, from vermin to turds. It was an adult picture if ever there was one. This did not mean that it was hard-core pornography. It was a serious description of Henry Miller's early days in

Paris, when he starved for food and sex, and gratified the latter more than the former. While Miller's experiences crackled in words, the visualization of them had a double impact. Some were harmlessly ingenuous. For example, behind the titles, one saw a beautiful fountain. As the camera focused to detail, the fountain turned out to be a bidet.

In 1970 the producing corporation sued Paramount and the Motion Picture Association of America, Inc., for having designated the picture "X," claiming that the Rating Code was an illegal group boycott and that the producers and exhibitors who participated in it were guilty of violating the antitrust laws. Treble damages were demanded. An injunction was sought in a Federal court. The battle to legitimize the Rating Code had begun.

I took the testimony under oath of the able producer and director of the film, Joseph Strick. In order to demonstrate the extremity of his position, I developed that he had objected to deletions which Paramount had made in the advertising trailers shown in theaters. In one scene, the character was about to make love to the girl depicted with nude breasts. Paramount deleted her comment, "Did I tell you I have the clap?" Similarly, he objected to the deletion from the trailer of "fuck you" and "hard-on." In another scene Miller was shown teaching a class of young children and he said, referring to a whale, "This noble beast has a penis two feet long." Paramount's deletion of this line was strenuously protested.

What made the producer's insistence in these matters bizarre was that some of these phrases were not in Miller's book. "They were dialogued in," the witness explained.

So, for example, Miller in the book had a "reverie" about animals, but the scene was transposed in the picture to a schoolroom and made the subject of an illustrated lecture.

I asked, "In the Henry Miller book, that reference to the whale and his prodigious qualification are a general reverie, but in your picture you inserted that line when he was talking to the children in the classroom, right?"

ANSWER: "I would say the young adults."

QUESTION: "Some look 10 and 12?"

ANSWER: "I would say 12 to 14."

. . .

QUESTION: "In other words, you felt that since Miller made a general comment, not even in Miller's Milleresque terms of four-letter words, but referring to the fact that when he taught children he didn't bar any subject . . . that you would use the dramatic license to fill in at that point something that he had mentioned in reverie about a huge penis of an animal and have him tell that to the children, that is what it amounts to, in a transposition?"

ANSWER: "In effect, yes."

. . .

QUESTION: ". . . it is a scene which by transposition is different from what Miller wrote about that particular whale?"

ANSWER: "That's correct, sir."

QUESTION: "And you do recognize that if I transposed words from one scene to another, I can change the content of the subject matter very easily, this is commonly done, isn't it?

ANSWER: "That is quite so, sir."

QUESTION: "And who was it that made the decision to transpose the reverie statement about the whale into the classroom, you?"

ANSWER: "Yes, sir."

The theory that the rating system was an illegal restraint of trade was false for two reasons: First, there was no restraint. No picture was barred. It was merely labeled. Second, not all restraints of trade are illegal. Only unreasonable ones are. Every contract restrains trade. It automatically limits the contracting parties' dealings with others. But that is not unreasonable. Also, there are beneficent combinations to hold fire drills, contribute to charity, or protect children from adult entertainment. These are not unreasonable restraints of trade, and therefore legal.

When the injunction application was argued before the Federal court, I pointed out that this principle had been upheld when Howard Hughes tested the right of the Motion Picture Association of America, Inc., to refuse a seal to his picture. The court upheld the right of the Association to maintain such a system in the public interest. It was a reasonable restraint of trade. This, of course, was more true of the rating system which did not bar pictures no matter what their content. Judge Morris Lasker candidly wrote that the objective of the rating system was to make possible the exhibition "of films dealing frankly with sexual matters, and at the same time wishing to avoid what they felt might constitute an onslaught of legislative censorship."

The Court denied a temporary injunction, adding for good measure that the plaintiff had not demonstrated a probability of success. The Judge also commented that the television networks' refusal to book the picture was due to its contents, not its rating. The rest of the opinion was so devastating that the suit was dropped "with prejudice," meaning it could not be reinstituted. The Rating Code had been legitimized and has been in effect every since.

So, the struggle for artistic freedom has fared well, even though it has suffered setbacks. Persistence and ingenuity have overcome the efforts of well-intentioned protectors of morals who would delimit expression because it was offensive to some. The same vigilance necessary to protect political liberty must also be exercised to protect artistic liberty. But this does not mean that the line between excessive (some won't recognize this word at all) permissiveness and freedom of expression has been accepted generally.

It is argued that morals can't be legislated. But we do. Adultery becomes a test for the dissolution of marriage. So does homosexuality or lesbianism. Even the refusal to bear children is a ground for annulment under certain circumstances. Also, we forbid exposure of genitals, fornication in public, or intercourse with animals. Indeed, moral considerations are the basis of all laws, from Sunday closings to child welfare. The real question is what quality of life and what kind of a society we prefer. Absolute freedom of expression was supposed to enhance social and intellectual progress. I fervently believed this. But now we find that it protects pornography, which blights entire neighborhoods, fills them with massage parlors, "adult" bookstores, "adult" movies, prostitutes, pimps, live sex acts, drug addicts, narcotic pushers, simulated homosexual rape, co-ed wrestlers engaging in sodomy, lewd magazines, all of which attracts mob control of a foul billion-dollar industry.

Even the contention that those who disapprove need not participate is no longer valid. The blazing neon signs, the advertisements, the handbills handed out on corners, the pervasive invasion of large areas such as famous theater or fine restaurant districts where audiences still wish to visit, make it impossible to escape the obscene pollution. The Supreme Court's denunciation of the intrusion of pornographic material on unconsenting families applies equally to the intrusion of physical presence in public streets of the pornographic plague. This is no isolated evil. From Times Square, New York, to the Barbary Coast in San Francisco, and almost every city, large and small in between, the infestation of smut has driven out decent enterprises, despoiled living conditions, increased crime, corrupted the law-enforcing authorities, and achieved an antisocial result. Where are we heading? If someone was willing to commit suicide on a stage, or if consenting adults agreed to fight to the death, should society be indifferent to the brutalizing entertainment? We forbid cockfighting and bearbaiting not only because of cruelty to animals, but because it debases us.

Must we, in the name of an abstract principle, close our eyes to the ugly view, and our noses to the stench? Or shall we, by modest interpretation, which declares that hard-core pornography is not protected by the First Amendment, or by zoning which isolates the evil to limited territory, sweep back the filth which inundates us?

I have observed previously that when logic leads me to a conclusion which offends my sense of rightness, I am alerted to re-examine the intellectual process for some unobserved flaw; to search for the illusory syllogism. The pornography question is such an instance. Intellectually, it is difficult to resist the contention that free expression must not be compromised, no matter what the consequence. Someday it can be argued that what we thought was offensive may turn out to be acceptable and even desirable. "One man's vulgarity is another man's lyric." Perhaps, it is contended, it will be proven that pornography provides a healthy sexual outlet and properly breaks down sexual taboos. Nevertheless, the reality is that today the injury to our society and the moral order which is essential to it (or else crime and anarchy will take over) justifies the Supreme Court's exclusion of hard-core pornography from constitutional protection. It is a reasonable limitation in the interest of a healthier social structure.

I believe that such a limitation will not affect the very broad area of free expression, sexual or otherwise. A work which has any literary, artistic, or scientific value will enter the "market place" of ideas, no matter what else it contains. By localizing our blows to hard-core pornography, we not only limit its antisocial impact, we protect freedom of speech generally from indiscriminate attacks. This is the real danger. Provocation begets countermeasures, which unintentionally injure liberty itself.

FOREIGN AGENT

A criminal case involved me with President Kennedy and Attorney General Robert Kennedy. It gave me insight to their characters and personalities from a rare vantage point. One of the fascinations of law is that almost every case radiates beyond its natural boundaries in the most unexpected ways. Such was the situation in the indictment of Igor Cassini, for failure to register as a foreign agent.

Cassini was a columnist for Hearst newspapers under the name of Cholly Knickerbocker. It was a newsy gossip column, with an unlimited range of social events, unsocial marriages, data of who was dating whom (expecting the reader to supply the appropriate inference) and who was just expecting (where no inference was necessary), inside revelations, called news if it was national, and intrigue if it was international, exploits of the jet set, a phrase Cholly had coined to denote speedy living, although bore set might have been more accurate, and much more, which Cholly would call "gutsy." The large circulation, which the column enjoyed, transformed its popularity into commercial value. But even though Cassini had a public relations firm called Martial and Company, there was no correlation between the names in the column and the clients of Martial. Ethical conduct has its rewards. When a crisis arose, I was able to demonstrate that fact to Bill Hearst, and maintain Cassini's position in the newspaper during the proceedings.

Igor, who was called Ghighi, was married to Charlene, the daughter of a prominent social family, the Wrightsmans. Joseph Kennedy and his clan (a favorite column description) were next estate neighbors of the Wrightsmans, and visited each other. John F. Kennedy had once dated the beautiful Charlene.

Joe Kennedy had been fond of Igor Cassini and his talented brother Oleg, and had become their adviser and intimate friend. Later, Oleg became the clothes designer for Jacqueline Kennedy when she became the first lady of the land.

Allen Dulles was the Wrightsmans' lawyer, and when Kennedy became President, he was made head of the CIA. The President, Igor Cassini, and Allen Dulles played golf at Palm Beach. One of Igor's friends was Porfirio Rubirosa, who had become an aid of Generalissimo Rafael Trujillo, the dictator of the Dominican Republic, and married his daughter. He had been ambassador from the Dominican Republic to Cuba, Belgium and held other important posts for that island. His diplomatic career was not so exacting that it prevented him from achieving a reputation as the leading playboy in the world.

One day, Igor recalled, Rubirosa confided in him that there was danger of a coup against Trujillo, and the seizure of the island by troops supported by the Communists. According to him, another Cuba was in the offing. The Cassini family, which had to flee Russia when the Communists took over, continued to be implacable enemies of its tyranny. They apparently had a sharpened sense of foreboding. Igor had denounced Castro as a Communist, before he was recognized as such by many who were taken in by his sweet, democratic intentions when he spoke in the United States. So when Igor was alerted by as close a source as Rubirosa that the Dominican Republic might turn Communist, he reported this to his friend Joseph Kennedy.

The White House took due note. It designated Robert Murphy, former ambassador and Under Secretary of State for Political Affairs under Eisenhower, to visit Trujillo, the dictator of that island, secretly and find out whether he would install certain democratic reforms, so that the United States might improve its relations with him. The implication was that if he would voluntarily curb his powers by permitting a free press and elections, President Kennedy could throw a protective arm around him. Was it not better for Trujillo to be an eagle with clipped wings rather than a dead bird?

The designation of Murphy for this task was natural and admirable. He was then an executive of Corning Glass, but he had once performed a heroic military mission which would not have been expected from a man in striped pants. During World War II, he had been landed in dark of night by submarine off the Normandy coast to meet the French underground chiefs in a deserted old house in preparation for the invasion. The Nazis had become suspicious, and sent a few soldiers to investigate the candlelit house on the shore. Murphy and the French leaders hid in a cellar, while the French family held off the investigators. Below they stood ready to shoot it out if the Nazis decided to make a search. Yes, movie scenarios are not always fiction.

Joseph Kennedy advised Igor Cassini that, in view of his close friendship with Rubirosa, the President wanted him to accompany Murphy. So it came about that a society columnist was designated on a confidential, international mission.

Murphy and Igor urged upon the dictator the admission of foreign correspondents and their right to file uncensored reports, as a beginning to his new role of elder statesman. They reported to President Kennedy that Trujillo was giving some thought to the matter of democratic reform since it would not affect the enormous wealth he had improperly accumulated. However, less than three months later, in May 1961, Trujillo was ambushed on a visit to his mother. He was assassinated by General Juan Tomás Díaz and his troops.

Two years before this, in 1959, Trujillo, probably on the recommendation of Rubirosa, had offered Igor's company, Martial and Company, a contract to render public relations services in the United States for the Dominican Republic. Igor was about to accept, but when, as always, he consulted Joseph Kennedy, he was advised to reject the offer. The reason was that Martial and Company represented a number of South American countries, and they might resent such a liaison. Igor had more to lose than gain by representing a country hostile to his other clients. He refused.

He so advised his attorney, Paul Englander. Their relationship was unique. Englander not only represented Igor and Oleg legally, he was their sponsor and intimate friend. He had their power of attorney to pay their bills, even household expenses. He was a wealthy man and lent them moneys. He was over seventy years of age and treated the Cassinis as if they were his sons. The relationship was one of complete trust. It was Englander who had suggested to Igor that he open a public relations company.

It was, therefore, natural for Igor to suggest that, rather than have another public relations firm inherit the $160,000 Dominican account, why didn't Englander take it? He did, organizing a corporation called Inter-American Company, hired several South American specialists, and registered the company and his manager as foreign agents.

Englander offered Igor a finder's fee, but he refused it. Englander had been his benefactor too long to modify a long overdue gesture of appreciation. However, Trujillo would not accept an unknown agency and Igor had to recommend Englander's new company to the dictator. In order to persuade him, Igor assured him on a letterhead of Martial and Company that the service would be excellent. He did not anticipate that a copy of his letter of recommendation would later be used by the FBI and prosecutor to claim that it was really Cassini's company which was the principal, and Englander's company was merely a blind. If Igor was the real owner, then it had been his duty to register Martial and himself as foreign agents. Since he did not do so, it was claimed he had violated the statute. The innocent color of events glows guiltily when subjected to a dark light from future developments.

To make things worse, after Trujillo had met the fate of tyrants, and democratic reforms were in the offing, Igor anticipated recognition of the new regime by the United States. This would enable him to accept a contract from the new government without conflict of interest with his other South American clients. So he arranged a contract with the new regime in the name of Englander's company to await the happy event. Then he would take over. Again he didn't register.

In 1962, Senator Fulbright's committee, incensed by "the sugar lobby," began an investigation of foreign agents and their reported payments to American officials. The matter had no relationship to the Cassini situation, but Martial and Company and Inter-American Company came under inquiry. Newspapermen saw an opportunity for an exposé. Bobby Kennedy, as Attorney General, was given data which seemed to implicate Cassini at least on the technical charge of not registering. Bobby was driven not only by duty, but by fear that if he did not act, it might appear that because of the Cassinis' friendship with the President and the Kennedy family, he was being treated favorably.

Joe Kennedy learned that Igor was under investigation. He called him to ask whether he had received money from the Dominican Republic while he was on the diplomatic mission with Murphy. Igor assured him that he had not received a cent.

Now Bobby was convinced Igor was lying, because he had evidence of moneys passing from Englander to Igor. These were part of the general loans from Englander to Igor which were repaid, but without explanation they seemed incriminating.

Bobby dispatched an army of FBI agents who swooped down on every employee of Inter-American and Martial, their bank accounts, and even Oleg's bank accounts, much to his embarrassment.

Word spread that the charges would soon be submitted to a grand jury, and Igor would be indicted. Failure to register as a foreign agent was a felony punishable by a long jail sentence.

Igor retained me to defend him. While my staff was digging into the facts and law, the grand jury indicted him on four counts. The press reported "the item" in sensational style, often featuring an old smiling photograph of Igor, as if he took the matter lightly. Actually he was distressed to the point of panic. He knew that the struggle would be destructive even if he won. He immediately offered his resignation from the Cholly Knickerbocker column to Dick Berlin, the head of the Hearst organization. William Randolph Hearst, Jr., who was married to Igor's second wife, "Bootsie," and Berlin refused to accept it. However, it was just a matter of time. He was suspended until he could be cleared.

His clients in the Martial Company began to melt away. How could a public relations company be effective in exploiting its good will and influence when it was under a cloud of a criminal charge itself?

The condition at home reflected the disaster. Charlene, too frail under any circumstances to withstand pressures, was particularly vulnerable at the time. She had sustained a fracture of her leg in a skiing incident. Before it healed, she fell and suffered a concussion. Her mother had died within twenty-four hours after an inconsequential quarrel with her. Her ski instructor and friend had committed suicide. She was taking psychiatric treatments.

Suddenly there was added to this pyramid of misfortune Igor's "disgrace," the cutting off of his earnings, her father's request that she and Igor not visit him when the Kennedys might drop in, and, worst of all, their son, Alexander, coming home from school in tears because children taunted him about his father.

I suggested that I talk to Charlene. Perhaps it would give her confidence and strength. I have found this a useful and often necessary legal "therapy" for a man who is in deep trouble. The suffering of his loved ones add to his distress and thereby increase their concern. A circle of anguish is set up, growing constantly as it feeds on mutual reactions. So I have frequently invited the wives and children of a client to visit me, and I spend hours analyzing the case fairly, and reducing their fears to proper perspective, and, whenever I can, expressing confidence in the outcome. It is especially interesting to observe the reaction of children, some of them in their teens, asking pertinent questions and registering relief because of better understanding. The circle of suffering is then reversed. Hope and an occasional smile light up the intense faces. One realizes then that it is the impact of the tragedy which must be overcome as much as the tragedy itself.

I arranged a dinner meeting at the Forum of the Twelve Caesars Restaurant for Charlene, Igor, Mildred, and myself. I did my utmost to assure Charlene that Igor would be completely vindicated. I should have been successful because I was absolutely certain of this, based upon the research we had by then completed. I shall describe the reasons below. But I watched Charlene's placidity (not to be confused with serenity), and I knew that while she smiled and was charming, nothing was reaching her. Her malaise was deep and rooted, and although her love for Igor made the instant crisis unbearable, its removal would not leave her in peace.

Later, Igor sent me a copy of Charlene's handwritten letter to the President. She apparently had decided to solve Igor's problem by direct action rather than through legal channels. She began the letter, "Dear Mr. President," but before she was through, she was calling him "Jack."

March 31, 1963

Dear Mr. President,

I have hesitated writing you before, but now I feel I must appeal to you. I don't know if you fully realize what have been the repercussions of Ghighi's indictment. Brushing aside the personal embarrassment it has caused our family—it has completely ruined us financially. Ghighi has not only lost his job at the newspaper, but his public relations company has completely disintegrated. And this just at a moment when there are staggering lawyers bills to meet. My father hasn't made a gesture to help us, and if it were not for Oli who lent money, Ghighi couldn't even have afforded a lawyer for his defense.

I tell you this simply because this alone should satisfy Bobby, who seems to be hell-bent in punishing Ghighi. I cannot tell you how surprised and shocked I have been by Bobby's harsh and punitive attitude. We always considered ourselves good friends of the Kennedys, and Ghighi still cannot understand why the son of a man whom he considered one of his closest friends for 17 years, and who so often advised him in all matters, should now be determined to bringing him down to total ruin.

I realize, of course, that Bobby as Attorney General has duties to perform that take precedence over his loyalty to friends. But my husband is not an arch-criminal, and whatever mistakes he may have made they don't warrant the kind of investigation he has been subjected to—with dozens of F.B.I. men scurrying around and harassing all his employees and friends for weeks, and all sorts of people, some who hardly knew Ghighi were called before the Grand Jury—the leaks to magazines and newspapers that have but already totally destroyed him, and finally the staggering preparations being made for the trial by the Justice Department. Frankly, I don't think the Justice Department could have acted with more vigor if the entire Communist Party had been involved!

It has come back to us directly that Bobby has stated that Ghighi and his co-defendant Paul Englander, are going to get the "full treatment", and that the Government is out for a win and that special counsel will be hired by the Government to prosecute this case. You would think that Ghighi was another Hoffa, or that he had conspired for the overthrowing of the United States Government. The reason for this massive retaliation, we have heard again and again from Bobby's friends is Ghighi lied to Bobby and, therefore, he should be punished.

Ghighi had no chance to lie to Bobby because he never talked to him. What happened is that one day Oli came back from Washington and told him to send a memorandum of his Dominican activities to Bobby.

In this memo, Ghighi explained his relationship to Englander and explained about the 1959–1960 contract that he had helped Englander secure. He omitted saying anything about the 1961 contract because that was well known to your father—in fact your father advised Ghighi and complimented him for the great assistance he had given Bob Murphy during that entire period—and Ghighi naturally believed that this was well known to you and Bobby. Besides, Ghighi was still under the impression that Bobby wanted to help him, and he didn't realize that this document was going to be turned over to a Grand Jury and used against him!

I have been told that you believe that Ghighi was offered a chance to come forth and tell his story but he refused. That is not so. Ghighi was told he could go before a Grand Jury, that had been convened expressly to indict him, and his lawyers did not permit him to do so, although he himself was most anxious to tell the whole truth.

I am not trying to say that Ghighi did not make some foolish mistakes. Evidently he did, otherwise he wouldn't be in the trouble he's in now. Certainly he surrounded himself with people who later betrayed him in order to cover their own guilt. And the Government gave these people immunity in order to indict Ghighi.

But no matter how you look at it, Ghighi's mistakes do not warrant such punitive measures. He has registered for other Governments, and if Dean Acheson can be an agent for Communist Poland, and Franklin D. Roosevelt, Jr. could be an agent for Trujillo, Ghighi would have done so had he been so told or advised. Instead he was made to understand it was not necessary. That is the crime he's accused of.

If you think it is advisable, I will be glad to go and speak to the Attorney General and appeal to him directly, for evidently he had taken this as a personal matter. I know it is up to the Government to take either a harsh or lenient attitude. Therefore, it's entirely up to the discretion of you and Bobby to what extent you want to go against Ghighi.

I hope, Jack, that you will not resent my writing you this letter. We've been friends for so many years, and in this terrible moment in which our family needs help, I appeal to you.

                                                          Sincerely,
                                                          Charlene

The President was moved by this letter. I received word that he wanted to see me. He was warm and gracious.

He quickly told me that, of course, he would not interfere with the Attorney General's duty to enforce the law. But that formal statement having been made, he showed his deep feeling for the Cassinis' plight. He wanted to know what my view was of the case. As briefly as possible, I told him that Igor and his company had previously registered when they represented Brazil and Italy. There was, therefore, no reason why he would not register again, had he undertaken the representation of the Dominican Republic. Due to a conflict of interest, he did not accept the Dominican offer, and had turned it over to Englander and his company, Inter-American, which had registered.

I knew Robert Murphy, and had recently talked to him, and he would assure the President that Igor had been helpful and loyal in his mission. Allen Dulles would do so too. It was a matter of discretion whether Bobby should have sought indictment in such a technical matter. No prosecutor can act on all the violations brought to his office. He must choose those cases for prosecution which will best serve the public interest. I could not understand why there had been such concentration on a matter of such little consequence and, in my opinion, which could not be won by the Government.

"You don't think the Government has a good case?" he asked.

"No, Mr. President, there isn't a jury in the world which will convict under these circumstances, with Murphy, Dulles, Rubirosa, and others testifying for Ghighi. However, in the meantime, Charlene and Ghighi have already been punished as if a serious crime was involved."

He suggested that I should see the Attorney General and have a talk with him. I, of course, agreed to do so.

I had a psychological block about John F. Kennedy. I never really believed he was President. I thought of him as a young, handsome Hollywood star who was playing the role, like Jimmy Stewart being a senator in his early pictures. This impression continued as I saw him behind Franklin D. Roosevelt's and Dwight Eisenhower's desk in the White House. His blue eyes, abundant hair giving off red tints from the bright light, his large white smile which searchlighted his face long before Jimmy Carter tried it, and his surprising height and slimness when he arose, all added to my illusion that he was too young and handsome to be President.

But his Lincolnesque compassion during our talk brought me back to the reality of his position. In the midst of all the problems which fill the President's office, it was obvious that he was suffering for Charlene and Igor and was trying to correct an overzealous attack upon them.

The very next day, I received a call from the office of the Attorney General to come to see him. An immediate appointment was arranged.

The physical layout of that office is more impressive than even the President's. Whoever originally constructed it wanted to express the majesty of the law more earnestly than those who built the Supreme Court building. A large anteroom leads into an office so enormous that couches and stuffed chairs galore abound to avoid the embarrassment of size. The architects must have envisioned that no one less than basketball center size would ever hold the post.

So when one entered and found the small figure of Robert Kennedy almost blocked out of view by the high desk except for the feet perched on it, coatless, sleeves rolled above his elbows, tie hanging inches below an opened collar, and an unruly lock of hair over his forehead, the incongruity of the office and the occupant was plain. President Carter was not the first to install informality in Washington.

He greeted me as a friend without reservation. He was interrupted during our talk by a telephone call. "Check whether they'll have lights on tonight," he said. Then, "Louis, do you want to go ice skating with us tonight?" I declined with thanks, curbing my impulse to make a smart comment about skating on thin ice.

When we turned in earnest to the case, his demeanor changed to sheer ugliness. He cussed and denounced Igor and I had to retort sharply that the facts did not warrant his anger. The most charitable view I could take of his personal venom was that he resented the Kennedys being drawn into the matter. He must have known that his father was responsible in the first instance for Igor's designation to the diplomatic mission. Also, the President must have told him how concerned he was about Charlene if not Igor. On the other hand, a Senate investigation and newspaper stories compelled him to act. At one point, he expressed his frustration when he yelled, "Do you think I like this? Do you think the President should be bothered with this? It's a pain in the ass!"

He was getting angrier by the minute. I thought I read his fears, and assured him with utmost sincerity that I would try the case on the merits. No extraneous references to the family friendship would be mentioned. He could hardly hide a look of relief on his face.

In the less bitter atmosphere, I struck hard with the most persuasive argument which can be made to any prosecutor. "You can't win this case," I said, and developed some of the reasons. There were two objectives in the Registration Act: one to ensnare spies or informers for hostile governments; the other to register any representative for friendly governments. The statute should never have confused the two. It ought to be redrawn. In Igor's case, we were dealing with a technical requirement of an innocent service. Almost every large law firm in Washington was registered as a "foreign agent." Igor had done so when he sought publicity for other governments. At worst, his failure to do so for the Dominican Republic was an innocent oversight, even if the Government was right that he should have registered. I told him why, in our opinion, he was not obliged to register at all. After reviewing the law, I said:

I have not come here with hat in hand asking for a favor. I am here because the President asked me to see you. If you feel you cannot drop this matter, very well, we'll try it.

As the discussion continued, I could not help but remind him that the Government had lost an infinitely stronger case against Roy Fruehauf of the Fruehauf Trailer Company, who gave a huge loan to Dave Beck of the Teamsters Union. But because Fruehauf's moral position was sound, he not having received a single benefit in his labor contract, the jury acquitted him. That decision had come down only a short time before, and I knew Bobby's deep disappointment. I reminded him that I had to try that case under the handicap of having Dave Beck, the predecessor of Jimmy Hoffa, brought into the courtroom daily from prison, where he was serving a sentence for another crime. How in the world could the Government prosecutor expect to prove Igor guilty beyond a reasonable doubt on the hocus-pocus technicality with which he was being charged?

Bobby would not yield. He had to do his duty. Igor was not worth consideration. He had lied to him. He would think about it, which meant to me that he would report to the President, but I sensed it would be a negative recommendation.

The contrast between the two brothers was startling. Jack had responded with heart. Bobby with bile. Both were honorable, but feelings are part of honor. Even a judge who does not leaven his interpretation of the law with considerations of human frailties becomes an automaton. Heartlessness is not an essential ingredient of judicial or executive objectivity. A great official or judge must first be a noble man, and there can be no nobility without compassion.

The great crisis was still to come.

I had urged Igor to continue his social activities as if nothing had happened. Psychologically, the withdrawal of a man under charges calls attention to his plight and gives the impression that he is immobilized because he is weighted with guilt. So Igor put on a smiling face and continued the rounds and parties, which were part of his professional life. Charlene, however, was not strong enough to engage in charades. I observed this the evening we met for dinner. She smiled, but her eyes remained sad.

On April 8, 1963, the Cassinis were to attend a birthday party. Charlene begged off, as she had on other occasions, but insisted that Igor should go. She had a better excuse than usual. It was Academy Award night on television. She and their fourteen-year-old daughter, Marina, preferred to have the Hollywood party visit them in their bedroom than venture out. Igor yielded. Later he telephoned just to be sure everything was all right.

After Marina's nurse had retired, Charlene sent Marina to the drugstore to fill a prescription. The nurse had been under instructions not to do so, but the child obeyed. When she returned with the bottle,

Charlene went into the bathroom. After a long while, she emerged and lay back again in bed. Her gasps alerted the child. She could not waken her mother, and called the doctor in alarm. He summoned an ambulance and dashed to the house, arriving almost simultaneously with Igor's return. An empty bottle which had contained thirty sleeping pills left no mystery as to the cause of her unconsciousness.

Through the night the customary emergency treatments were applied, and she responded well to them. In the morning, the doctors who were reporting the gradual progress to Igor appeared again. It was a final report. Her heart had given out. Charlene was dead.

If only we could have as true a perspective of human struggle as death imposes on us. How puny and unnecessary the strife over a technical registration seemed when beautiful Charlene, thirty-eight years old, did away with herself.

The shock reached into the White House. I received another call to visit the Attorney General. But now I was to receive another kind of shock.

After my first meeting with Bobby, I had reported to Igor on my private telephone. I had explained the President's sympathetic reaction and Bobby's stubbornness. He exploded. Between stuttering expletives, he threatened to tear the robe of respectability from Bobby, and proceeded to give me a bill of particulars. I interrupted him. I knew that his outburst was to relieve the pressure within him, like the primal scream healers advise. It was not a serious program of retaliation. Nevertheless, I told him firmly that his idea was unthinkable, and that if he really meant it, he would have to get another lawyer. "We will win this case on the merits," I assured him, and added that I understood his resentment. He quieted down and we discussed the hiring of accountants to analyze Englander's accounts with him and Oleg and other preparations for the trial.

When I visited Bobby after Charlene's suicide, I had expected that tragedy to be the opening fulcrum for our discussion. I was, therefore, taken back when instead he launched a bitter attack on Igor.

"Now you have found out," he said, "that your client is a blackmailer at heart." He combined this condemnation with praise for my rectitude in curbing him. It was clear that my telephone talk with Igor had been tapped. I was stunned by this violation of law by the Attorney General in the course of trying to prove a violation by Igor. I grew more sullen when his reference to Charlene was merely another jumping-off place for his berating Igor. I had to curb my impulse to tell him just what I thought of his tactics and venom. But always in such moments, the lawyer's thoughts must be of his client. I would injure Igor if I "broke" with Bobby. A lawyer can afford to be emotional on behalf of his client, but not to his injury.

Also, the President was behind these appointments. I could not expect him to continue his benign influence if I defied his brother. So I suffered in silence. He must have observed my mood, because he changed his tone abruptly. He suggested that he would set up an appointment for me with Assistant Attorney General Nicholas Katzenbach, to determine whether the case could be resolved without trial.

Katzenbach was summoned. Bobby said, "See if you can get together with Nizer and straighten out the Cassini matter." I arranged to meet with Katzenbach and Kevin T. Maroney, the Government attorney in charge of the case, at Katzenbach's home. I had permission to bring my Washington law partner, Lawrence Lesser, with me. We met at eight-thirty in his living room in front of an active fireplace and talked until midnight.

Katzenbach's and Maroney's integrity and fairness warranted letting down my guard. I virtually tried the case before them, revealing factual and legal points which ordinarily a defense advocate would not present to a prosecutor.

There is a saying in law that one should go "for the jugular." This ugly phrase, suitable for military warfare, is an unhappy allusion in law, where the objective is justice, not death to the enemy. Nevertheless, the principle is sound that if an argument which is the basis of other contentions can be destroyed, the whole case collapses.

I began with such a legal argument. The Government assumed that it was Igor's duty to register. I surprised its counsel by arguing that under the statute Igor was exempted from registering. Why? Because the statute said that it was not necessary to do so if the foreign country is deemed by the President "vital to the defense of the United States." I contended that the Dominican Republic met this test. In 1936, the Buenos Aires conferences had established the principle of hemispheric solidarity. In 1940, the Act of Habana provided that an aggression against one American state should be considered an aggression against all.

When the bombardment of Pearl Harbor catapulted the United States into World War II, the Dominican Republic, faithful to its commitment, declared war on the Axis powers, and became an ally of the United States.

Furthermore, whether the President "deems" a country vital to our defense may be determined by whether he enters into defense treaties with it. My research showed that on January 1, 1962, there existed 139 bilateral and multilateral treaties between the United States and the Dominican Republic. They covered such defense matters as atomic energy, the Atlantic Charter, GATT (General Agreement on Tariff and Trade), the Organization of American States, and one actually called "Defense."

I pointed out to Katzenbach, and he agreed, that it was not a violation to represent a foreign country. The only wrong was not to register. But the Dominican Republic was one of the exceptions which did not require registration. I predicted that the indictment would be dismissed.

Sometimes the legal escape route is like a thin string which is too feeble to hold a man, but if it is attached to a thicker and thicker cord, ultimately a defendant can climb out of his dilemma on a sturdy rope.

There was a continuation of the logical cord which lent strength to the argument. Suppose it was contended that the Dominican Republic, being a dictatorship and for other reasons, was not a country vital to our defense, despite its proximity and strategic position. Who would decide whether it was or not? The statute made the test subjective. It was what the President, and only the President, thought that counted. The language is, "If the President deems the defense of the foreign country vital to the defense of the United States . . ."

How could a citizen find out whether the President "deems" it so or not? There was no declaration to which anyone could point. The President's intention did not appear in the Federal Register, where sometimes similar matters are recorded. A citizen would, therefore, not be sure whether he had to register or not. He would have to guess. Such vagueness in a statute made it unconstitutional. Katzenbach and Maroney were familiar with Supreme Court decisions which had so decided.

Under our law, no person may be put to the risk of interpreting an ambiguous statute and find himself guilty of a crime if he guessed wrong. That would be entrapment. Criminal laws must be clear and precise so that an ordinary citizen would know what he may or may not do. If they are vague they are held to be unconstitutional. So, for example, a statute which forbade the carrying of a three-inch knife was held not to apply to a three-inch razor. If the legislature intended to include razors, it should have said so. A citizen should not have to guess or interpret on pain of committing a criminal act. Similarly, a statute against pornographic "writings" was held not to include a private pornographic letter. An indictment against the letter writer was dismissed. True, a letter is a "writing," but if the legislature intended to bar private communications, it could have said so explicitly. We do not slap people into jail if the prohibited conduct is not clearly expressed.

How was Igor to know whether the President "deems" ("Notice the present tense," I said) the Dominican Republic vital to our defense? If he guessed it was, he did not have to register. The statute was too vague to be the basis of a criminal charge.

I cited Italy as an illustration. In 1942, it was an ally of Hitler and at war with us. In 1944, Italy made peace with the United States and became our ally. Surely a President would "deem" Italy differently in those years. Suppose, as has been feared, Italy became a Communist country. Again, the President would "deem" it differently in making this test. The need for current reappraisal made the statute even vaguer. One could not guide himself by the past attitude of the President, even if it had been recorded, for example, in the Congressional Record, which it was not.

Katzenbach suggested that Cassini should have resolved the doubt by registering. But the law placed no such burden on the citizen. The Government would have to prove "beyond a reasonable doubt" that he had violated the law, not that he could have avoided the problem by doing what he was not obliged to do.

At one point, Maroney asked whether I had copies of all the letters Igor had sent. The inference was that there was an incriminating one, and I suggested that in the spirit of mutual revelation, he show it to me, rather than hoard it for a day which might never come. He looked at Katzenbach, whose impassivity was consent and pulled out a huge folder. He turned to a letter dated April 27, 1961, signed by Igor and addressed to "His Excellency and the Dominican Republic," in which he urged the acceptance of Englander's Inter-American Company for public relations services. Maroney stressed the word "we" in the letter to indicate that Cassini was really the principal and, therefore, evidence that the moneys derived from the contract were coming to him and his Martial Corporation.

It was easy to demolish this contention. The accountants' records which I submitted to him showed that Cassini did not receive one cent from the Dominican Republic account directly or through his company. He had even refused a finder's fee from Englander.

True, there were checks from Englander's special account to both Igor and Oleg, but these followed the same pattern which had existed from 1947, fourteen years before the Dominican contract. Igor and Oleg had given all earnings to Englander, who invested for them. He sent them checks for their needs. When they were short of funds, Englander lent them moneys, and repaid himself when there was a surplus. It was an unusual lifetime, paternal relationship. However, the checks from Englander to Igor and Oleg had no relationship to the Dominican matter. The amounts were the same as previously and their innocent purpose had been identified by an accountant's study. Katzenbach freely admitted that this showing was impressive and might well undermine the Government's theory.

Besides, I asked him not to forget that the issue was not whether Igor received moneys from the Dominican contract, but whether he had a duty to register. The legal point, that he did not have to do so, superseded any factual argument. The Government might seek to color its claim at the trial with irrelevant money considerations. "If color was going to be the order of the day," I said, "let us not overlook Igor's two battle stars, for his services in the war and his and Oleg's impeccable record."

After midnight we left. Katzenbach and Maroney were to report to the Attorney General and we would hear.

It was too late to return to New York. I stopped at the Mayfair overnight and called Igor to report the developments. Before meeting with Katzenbach, I had told Igor at dinner that his phone had previously been tapped, and cautioned him to keep his feelings to himself lest what he said in anger might again be misunderstood. So after my midnight report, he remained eloquently silent.

Having thus tried the case before a jury composed of prosecutors didn't mean that we could sit back and await their verdict. There was a real jury verdict still to be won. We continued our preparation for trial.

Although Trujillo had disappeared in a flash of bullets, there was one knowledgeable link to him still available to us. It was Porfirio Rubirosa, his former son-in-law and for thirty years an ambassador for the Dominican Republic. I wanted vital testimony from him. He was a friend of Igor, but would he come forth in his hour of need? Rubirosa was a traveler and not easy to track down, but we found him, of all places, at Frank Sinatra's home in Palm Springs, California.

I called Sinatra, who had retained me several times to protect his ex-wife, and others—typical of his expansive friendship. He was pleased to invite me for the weekend, but cautioned me to bring my golf clothes. His home was on the fairway, in this case, a sign of new preoccupation, like the tennis or golf novice who is outfitted with the finest equipment. Naturally, specially crafted clubs and a "limousine" golf cart would not be enough for Sinatra learning the game. A home on the course was indicated.

Rubirosa was heavily built but trim. He was a two-goal polo player and moved with ease and grace. The sun had emphasized his swarthiness and given it a glow. He exuded vitality. A quick snack ushered the three of us right onto the golf course. The legal work could wait. Rubirosa, poor man, thought he could transfer his athletic skill to golf. If he could hit a speeding ball with a mallet while riding full speed on a pony, plunging against other ponies, how ridiculously easy it would be to strike a stationary ball from a standing position, while no one harassed him. He couldn't believe it when he failed to make contact at all, swinging right over the mocking ball (Sam Goldwyn used to explain that his home course was two inches higher than the one he was playing on). Soon he was jumping up and down and screaming in exasperation. It was quite a picture of the glamorous playboy, former husband of Danielle Darrieux, Doris Duke, and Barbara Hutton, squealing and carrying on like a petulant child.

When the nine holes with the two great lovers were finished (something I thought would never happen, what with balls finding their way into forests and lakes and everywhere else than on the green), we proceeded to the magnificent nineteenth hole, which Sinatra called home. Finally, we got down to the purpose of my visit.

Rubirosa's recollection of events was a complete refutation of the Government's case. I wrote out his statement and he signed it unhesitatingly. After explaining that he had made many visits to the United States over a period of ten years and would have knowledge of any arrangements or contracts between the Dominican Republic and any public relations firm or individual through the period of 1959 to 1961, he asserted:

To my knowledge, neither Messrs. Igor Cassini nor Martial Corporation, directly or indirectly represented the Dominican Republic in the United States or elsewhere. I can also state that to my knowledge neither Igor Cassini nor Martial Corporation directly or indirectly received any money or other compensation from the Dominican Republic for any representation or for any other service whatsoever.

It was part of Rubirosa's duties to be familiar with efforts to improve the image of his country in the United States. He was, therefore, able to say:

I know that Igor Cassini recommended Mr. Englander's firm, Inter-American, as the representative for the Dominican Republic; that a contract was made between the Dominican Republic and Mr. Englander's firm for one year; and that later when Cassini recommended a renewal of this contract, such renewal was not made.

His final paragraph would have served as an excellent summation to a jury:

I can sum it all up this way: that to my knowledge, Mr. Igor Cassini and his company (Martial) never represented the Dominican Republic

406

Reflections Without Mirrors

in the United States, or performed services for the Dominican Republic, or received any compensation from the Dominican Republic.

How could the prosecutor overcome such testimony from the only other party to the claimed contract with Igor? Also, Rubirosa was well and favorably known to Bobby and the President. He and his wife, the beautiful French actress Odile Rodin, had been guests at the White House on more than one occasion. His diplomatic standing qualified him, and his playboy reputation apparently didn't disqualify him. Who knows, perhaps it made him more attractive and adventurous to the Kennedys.

To think how star crossed they all were, the President and Bobby assassinated, and Rubirosa killed in a car crash shortly thereafter.

When I reviewed our preparation, I knew that our confidence in winning was justified both on the facts and the law. More important, I believed the prosecutor knew it too. The problem was how he could retreat. If he dismissed the indictment, would it not appear that Igor's and Oleg's friendship with Joe Kennedy, the President, Jackie, and Bobby was responsible? In politics and law, appearance can be as deadly as reality. I knew we were all trapped by the very friendship which should have assisted us. We would have to go through with a trial.

I was wrong. The President, Bobby, and Katzenbach came up with an idea. The prosecutor would drop three counts of the indictment and press only one, the technical charge of failing to register. Igor would plead *nolo contendere*, which meant that he would stand mute. He would not plead guilty or not guilty; he would simply remain silent. He would not contest the charge. The prosecutor would not request a jail sentence. Under such circumstances, the chances for a mere fine were overwhelming. That is how the whole matter would be resolved.

It was now up to us to decide whether to accept this offer and change the "not guilty" plea to *nolo contendere.* It was an agonizing decision. Igor, Oleg, and we as counsel weighed the advantages and disadvantages of the plan. The most serious negative aspect was that *nolo contendere* was equivalent in law to a plea of guilty insofar as the Judge's power to sentence was concerned. I did not want to alarm Igor, but I had in mind a case in the Midwest in which the president of a corporation pleaded guilty to a criminal charge of violating the antitrust law. He did so on the express promise of the prosecutor that no prison sentence would be imposed and that the prosecutor would recommend only a fine to the Judge. The prosecutor lived up to his promise, but the Judge disagreed, and sentenced the defendant to five years in jail. The defendant fell dead at the counsel table.

I had related this lurid story to Bobby, but was assured that such rejection by the Judge was extraordinary and would not reoccur, especially on the limited charge which would be asserted in our case. More important, the President felt the same way.

Another objection to *nolo contendere* was that it deprived Igor of full vindication. True, it was less offensive than a plea of "guilty," although even if the plan required such a plea, it would be worthy of consideration.

There were a number of arguments in favor of accepting the plea of *nolo contendere*. Such a plea, when accepted by the prosecutor, was, as Attorney General Herbert Brownell once said, "an admission by the Government that it has only a technical case at most and that the whole proceeding was just a fiasco."

Also by withdrawing the three more serious counts in the indictment, the Government eliminated the risk, no matter how infinitesimal, of a maximum penalty of twenty years in jail. Newspapers always liked to give importance to a story by asserting the top figure of incarceration if found guilty. They would be deprived of an impressive number.

The acceptance of a *nolo contendere* plea would avoid a long and costly trial, and above all emotional exhaustion. One who has not experienced the tension of facing a trial, or been sufficiently involved with the participants, either as counsel or family, cannot feel the nerve-tearing strain involved. The witness knows he will be questioned endlessly by friend and foe. Can he hope to be letter perfect in his recollections? Will he with one slip of the tongue destroy the case on which so much depends?

Having dealt with actors, I am aware of their desperate fear of blotting out on their memorized lines. Even those who can hold an audience enthralled with confident declaimer become nervous wrecks if asked to speak impromptu at a luncheon. Think then of the witness who cannot seek the shelter of well-memorized fiction but must hold his own against a cunning cross-examiner hurling questions at him in rapid succession to disorganize his defenses. The risk of making a fool of himself in the presence of an audience is as frightening as losing the case itself. Even the lowliest of us doesn't want to be marked stupid. Notice how often the ignorant protest, "Do you think I'm an idiot?" Fortunately they are spared a frank answer.

Since a confused answer may send a defendant in a criminal case to jail, his fear grows, further disorganizing his thought processes, and increasing the percentage of error which he is struggling to reduce. Thus is set up a circle of confidence erosion. The more one considers the hazards, the more they are likely to occur.

Being aware of this, I do everything possible to overcome the distress which I know is building in the witness. First there is thorough, thorough preparation. Every letter, every document, every date, every conversation and act is patiently reviewed, over and over again, until the witness has relived the past so often that it has become the present. Then I drill him in cross-examination. After he has withstood the bolts from my merciless questioning, he feels more competent to deal with the attack of an opposing lawyer, which often turns out milder than what he has experienced with me. This mental device is not dissimilar to the physical one of swinging a heavy club, so that a normal one will feel light. Finally, I assure him that even if he slips, it will not be fatal. There is redirect examination, which can rehabilitate him.

Nevertheless, despite all this, I know that as the day of battle approaches, he sleeps fitfully, eats mechanically, and worries continually. Yet he must be driven to approach witnesses, so that through personal contact their reluctance will be overcome, and to review developments into the early hours of the morning. The trouble with the formula for success is that it is the same as for a nervous breakdown.

All this was present in Igor's case, and, added to it, the sentence, inflicted in advance, of his suspended job, his upended public relations firm, and his never-ended tragedy at home. The temptation of relieving him of the ordeal of trial was therefore great, especially because the plea was comparatively innocuous. I had to tell him that the chances of a dismissal of the charge, without his even taking the stand, were good. But in view of the virtual certainty that only a fine would be imposed (which would be much less than the cost of a trial) and that there was no moral turpitude involved in the reduced charge, I would not oppose his wish to accept a *nolo contendere* plea. He registered relief.

I can only guess that Bobby Kennedy received this decision with relief, too. He was under pressure from the President and probably from his father (who by that time had suffered a stroke), to dispose of the matter mercifully, and without too much fanfare. After all, despite my determination to try the case strictly on the merits, one could not prevent the newspapers from drawing the Kennedys into it. They knew that the President had designated Igor for the diplomatic mission to the Dominican Republic. They also knew of the intertwining relationships of the Cassinis, the Wrightsmans, and the Kennedys. The suicide of Charlene would not go unnoticed. Rubirosa, a true original, always made good copy. The case was bound to create a field day in the press. From a legal viewpoint, Katzenbach's report must have dimmed Bobby's enthusiasm for a successful prosecution.

Under the new plan, the indictment would not be dropped entirely, and thus the prosecutor would be "vindicated." Yet for all practical purposes, Igor would be let off. Also, the President's heartfelt impulse to do something, no longer for Charlene but in her memory, would be achieved.

The details were worked out. On October 8, 1963, Igor appeared before Chief Judge Matthew F. McGuire in the Federal District Court in Washington, D.C. He pleaded *nolo contendere* to the single charge. The prosecutor approved the special plea and the Judge accepted it. Sentence was scheduled for January 10, 1964, three months later, to allow the Probation Department to prepare a presentence report, and also to skip the intervening holiday season.

We used the time effectively, meeting with the probation investigators to submit the facts of Igor's impressive background. A probation official's duty is to be nosy. He learned that Igor had been born thirty-nine years before in Sebastopol, Russia; that he was a member of the Russian Orthodox Church; that after fleeing Russia he had attended the University of Florence, in Florence, Italy, for three years, and had thereafter attended law school at the University of Perugia in Perugia, Italy, for another three years; that he had served as sergeant in the United States Army in the Battle of the Rhine and Nuremberg, and had received the European Theater Medal with two campaign stars; that he had three marriages and other scars such as from an appendectomy; that he held newspaper posts on the *Times-Herald* in Washington, D.C., and on the *Journal-American* for eighteen years; that he was proficient in golf, tennis, and skiing, and on endlessly.

We obtained letters of commendation for Igor from people whose opinions would carry special weight. Allen W. Dulles was so eager to be of assistance that he overcame his reticence as a former director of Central Intelligence to write that he was "quite prepared to talk to the probation officer" and he confirmed Robert Murphy's views about Igor's service during their visit to Trujillo. Murphy had written an uninhibited letter of praise for Igor. Other telling letters were submitted by Richard Berlin, president of Hearst Corporation; J. Kingsbury Smith, publisher of the New York *Journal-American*; Franklin D. Roosevelt, Jr., Under Secretary of Commerce; Robert Lehman, investment banker; Earl E. T. Smith, former Ambassador to Cuba; Ray Stark, motion picture producer; Vincent Garibaldi, president of Fiat Corporation; Father George Grabbe, priest of the Russian Orthodox Church; Liz Smith, columnist; Clyde Newhouse, art dealer, and many others.

"Too bad," I teased, "that we can't submit letters from Joe Kennedy, the President, and Jackie."

A presentence report is addressed to the wide discretion which a sentencing judge must exercise in the degree of punishment. One who has committed a crime, no matter how serious, is entitled to the consideration of the ameliorating circumstances of his life. If it is his first "fall from grace," he should be treated more mercifully than if he is a recidivist. Also, his previous good works and normal, crimeless life are a consideration in judging the public's safety if he is returned earlier to society. The presentence report strikes a balance of good and evil, not unlike the compassionate balance which religion teaches will be struck in the hereafter in determining how much angel and devil was in each of us.

Came the day. Igor stood before Chief Judge McGuire. The Court invited me to address it on the subject of sentence. It was an opportunity to reduce the charge to the technical triviality which was involved. Contrasted with the minor aspect of the accusation was the major punishment already suffered by the defendant; the loss of his wife, his profession, his business. I believe the Judge, too, felt the enormity of the disproportional grief already imposed on Igor. He imposed a fine of $10,000 and a six-month probation period.

Igor walked out free. His ordeal had ended. But Charlene could not be restored to life, nor even could his column nor his public relations firm.

Igor has since written an autobiography entitled *I'd Do It All Over Again*. I could suggest a slight amendment or two which would interrupt the inexorable repetition of his life, and save him from unnecessary anguish. Couldn't we all stand such an amendment?

Every case is unique. Like human beings, there are no replicas. This one unexpectedly buffeted me from the President to his brother, the Attorney General. It preceded Kissinger's shuttle diplomacy to create a new genre, "shuttle advocacy."

TYCOONS

The business tycoon is a growing American phenomenon. He has replaced the Alexanders and Napoleons to conquer new worlds—industrial worlds. Governments have set up defenses against him—to no avail. Theodore Roosevelt began the major assault against "the malefactors of great wealth." Antitrust laws were enacted. Political platforms uniformly promised to curb business "predators." Franklin Roosevelt created a Maginot Line of legal obstructions from the SEC to the Federal Trade Commission. President Truman seized one of their plants illegally and had its president removed from office. Kennedy became so angry with one of the tycoons who raised steel prices despite White House appeal that he lost his verbal elegance and called him a "son of a bitch."

What do the tycoons desire? Wealth? Not entirely, because after they have amassed uncountable millions they redouble their efforts if that is possible. Power? Not entirely, because after they have built industrial empires, they drive on to create conglomerates, absorbing unrelated industries in their original companies. Ego satisfaction? Not entirely, because many, like the old Rockefeller, Harriman, Carnegie, Gould, Morgan, and Howard Hughes, are shy men avoiding publicity and genuinely seeking anonymity.

Yet, it is all of these in some way or other, but with no terminal point. The game never ends. The struggle persists, lending credence to the theory that the strife and excitement in the course of achieving are the goal itself.

What makes all this more curious is the sacrifice gladly made for an objective so ephemeral that it is difficult to define.

Every tycoon, without exception, gives complete dedication to his task. There are not enough hours in the waking day, so sleeplessness is gladly endured. The luxury rewards of money and power are either eschewed entirely or are not enjoyed. They are workoholics, accepting slavery willingly. They surrender more than their freedom. They give up their health, suffering ulceration, heart disease, and mental breakdown, but they will not stop. They cannot stop. They are builders who cannot put down the hammer. I knew one such man who in his spare time, as if there were any, literally built houses on his estate. Without cease, he built a "doll's house," as he called it, for his wife; one for himself; a large one where both could live; a playhouse for the children; a bowling alley for the grownups; a boathouse on the lake; dressing rooms at the pool; a game room; and on and on. His estate later became a resort, it never having been a home.

Arde Bulova did the same in his Connecticut estate. After he had built guesthouses and a four-hole golf course, he constructed a large adjoining open-aired dining platform. He wanted the outdoor pool to be covered by a huge Plexiglas dome for use in winter. But the dome had to be on rails, so that it could be moved over the dining area. However, in cold weather, the steam heat would cloud the Plexiglas, cutting off the view outside. So he created air currents which kept the glass clear and permitted us to see the trees shadowed white with snow, while we swam and enjoyed the orchid plants on the inside.

I have noticed that some of these driven men lose their restlessness and high-tensioned tantivy when they are on water. The transformation is extraordinary. Put some tycoons on a boat and they calm down as if sedatives had been administered. Perhaps it is the feeling, as the boat takes off, that the world has moved away from the stationary object on which they sit, leaving them isolated in outer space. There is nothing but lonely water—nothing to conquer. The horizon is empty. The challenge has disappeared and a new perspective has taken its place.

Tycoons have been changed by social evolution. Once they were ruthless in their climb. "The public be damned" was their motto. I recall representing Robert Young, the railroad magnate, who gathered in department stores and motion picture companies. I was to make a plea to a congressional committee for tax relief so that roadbeds could be rebuilt and the American railroads freed from palsy type rides accompanied by deafening staccato noises as the cars jumped over the gaping cracks in the rails. I suggested a memorandum which would emphasize public convenience. "Say it, if you want to," he said, "but actually I don't give a damn about that. We are interested in a decent return on our investment and we are entitled to it, just as much as a public utility is." This was in the 1950s. It was an echo from the early tycoons who were not abashed by the adjective "ruthless."

Those who sought to conquer a rugged continent had to be as roughhewn as the "enemy" they were determined to subdue. They had a worthy adversary. Nature fought back. Railroads built around the curves of mountains were attacked by rock slides. Forests cut down to create passageways summoned up nature's fecundity and overran the cleared area. Rainstorms washed away embankments and swelled streams which hurled themselves against the dams and broke them. Mines resisted being disemboweled, caving in on their invaders and crushing them.

But the tycoons won the desperate battle. Only personal tragedy could daunt them. They were human after all. Young's severity accompanied his quiet frenzy. But he softened in the presence of his beautiful wife and daughter.

His daughter went up in a private plane with her fiancé and both were killed in a crash. Young seemed to take even that blow stoically. But a year later, he blew his brains out with a gun. Financiers sought an explanation in possible hidden reverses of his financial empire. There were none. He died extremely wealthy, but impoverished by deprivation of the joy of conquest.

Tycoons had to be brilliant, as well as determined, to earn the title. This brings me to the social evolution I mentioned. New generations set new standards. A business could not succeed unless the good will of the public was earned.

Telephone companies sponsored concerts and operas on television even though their excellence kept people away from telephones. Oil companies spent millions to tell the people how they spend billions to find oil and provide cheaper power. Huge corporations sponsored television specials on public issues, often warming the hearts of their liberal antagonists with civil rights contents. (In 1975, Xerox produced a two-hour television special of the John Henry Faulk trial, which eliminated blacklisting. In support of this drama it published one million educational booklets for schoolchildren. It was presented on CBS network, which had been involved originally in the blacklist.) Manufacturing companies advised the public of their concerns about pollution and their huge expenditures to protect the environment.

Symphonies, ballets, modern dance teams, instrumental soloists, like Heifetz, Menuhin, and Horowitz, singers like Beverly Sills and Robert Merrill, all were brought before huge TV audiences by commercial enterprises which sought nothing more than recognition for their public spiritedness. Why don't stockholders who sue management at the drop of a financial statement attack the enormous expenditures for such projects which often do not even describe their product, let alone extol it? Because the good will of the public is money in the bank. It is a real asset created by the awareness of the buying public of new values. From "the public be damned" we have come to "the public is our first concern."

This evolutionary process is startlingly illustrated in the labor field. Tycoons used to consider unions illegal, radical intrusions upon their sacred property rights. They felt fully justified in organizing counterforces to quell the workers' insurrections. As public reaction to strikebreaker goons and scabs mounted, sales were affected. The evolutionary process of making the tycoon conscious of customer good will accelerated.

Today, almost every large corporation installs a vice-president in charge of labor relations. He often comes from union ranks, understands the workers' psychology and needs, and negotiates contracts with union leaders on a sophisticated brotherly basis.

Not only that, but it is deemed advantageous to employers to install pension plans, health programs, escalated vacation periods, bonuses, stock acquisition plans, coffee breaks in leisure rooms, lecture and promotion programs, severance pay, etc. The good will of the worker is sought as eagerly as that of the customer, because often the two are the same.

But although evolution changed attitudes, it didn't change human nature. The arrogance which accompanied employers' power was just as evident when employees became dominant. Exceptions of course abounded in both. In the so-called "needle industry," unions made loans to employers so that they could survive and give employment. Unions accumulated hundreds of millions and even billions of trust funds. They retained economists to make financial studies and guide them just as employers did. They lobbied in Washington just as traditionally employers had always done. There was no greater virtue, efficiency, or farsightedness in one group than in the other. Even the selfish manipulations of corporate management which the Securities and Exchange Commission was created to curb, found its counterpart in corrupt practices of union leaders.

The fact that neither honor nor evil is a monopoly of any class is the idealist's tragedy. He needs a clearly defined enemy to overcome; some thing and some one to sacrifice for; the satisfaction of destroying oppressive forces. But when what he lances against is found also in his own midst; when, as he triumphs, he absorbs the enemy and his iniquity, he is frustrated and confused.

Resignation is not the answer. A tolerant understanding of man's imperfections is. Then one can be a reformer and not an absolutist. Then one can try to better the world and not become a fanatic. Then one can fall short of the goal and not be disillusioned.

We might learn from scientists who, despite the miracles of technology, allow tolerance for all instruments. If we similarly allowed tolerance for human frailty, we would not suffer disappointment so often. We would be less neurotic and wiser.

I have represented and studied businessmen of all types. The most remarkable businessman I have ever met is Dr. Armand Hammer.

His life touches so many distant shores of excitement, involving legendary personalities and events, that a mere mention of them defies credibility. Born poor on the East Side of New York, he became a millionaire while attending Columbia (by acquiring a bankrupt pharmaceutical company and guiding it to success in spare evening hours). He gave up a possible musical career as a concert pianist to become a doctor (he was designated "the most promising" in his graduating class).

While he was in medical school an incident occurred which could have changed the course of his life. It involved obstetrics. Seniors were required to put their studies and observations to actual test by delivering several babies. They were moved into the New York Nursery and Child's Hospital for Women, near the medical school. There they could treat women as outpatients during pregnancy and ultimately deliver their babies.

One midnight, a nurse woke him and gave him a card which directed him to a woman in labor at Sixtieth Street and Tenth Avenue. He took his bag of instruments and rushed for his first delivery. Climbing several flights of the tenement located in the poor Italian neighborhood, he was ushered to the bed by a distraught husband. Although his instruction card recited a normal pregnancy, the woman was screaming from pain.

Hammer put on his gown and rubber gloves and after extensive examination discovered that he was confronted by an unusual condition, a breech delivery. The child was upside down. The feet would emerge first instead of the head.

There had been a lecture on breech deliveries, but his preoccupation with his pharmaceutical enterprise had caused him to miss it. However, he had had the foresight to pack a textbook, Cragin's *Obstetrics*, with his instruments. He rushed into the bathroom with the book, indexed it to the section on breech deliveries, and saw the illustration of the technique. He also learned that when the labor progressed to the point of expulsion, that unless the head, the largest part of the body, could be released immediately, the infant would be strangled.

He dashed back to the woman and found that meconium (feces) was being released. This meant that he only had minutes to save the child and perhaps the mother. Following Cragin's instructions, he inserted the index and middle fingers of his right hand into the womb and into the child's mouth. With this grip, he rotated and slid the head gently in one direction and then the other until he swiveled it out of the womb. He cut the umbilical cord, washed the protective coating from its body, slapped it, and heard the most pleasant noise of his twenty-two years on earth. As he placed the child next to the exhausted mother, the father and neighbors who had gathered burst into song and dance. A great breakfast was prepared, but incongruously, wine, not coffee, was served. His ears ringing with praise, Hammer left and returned to the hospital. It was four in the morning. He arose hours later to attend Professor Loeb's class in pharmacology.

Word had spread that Hammer had successfully made a breech delivery. He was congratulated by the students. They called him "Professor" and good-naturedly teased him about doing things "ass backwards."

While in the classroom a message arrived that the dean, Dr. Samuel Lambert, wanted Armand Hammer to come to his office. When Hammer arrived, he found many members of the faculty seated alongside the dean. He was about to put on his modest manner—"Really, I don't deserve all this"—when he was startled by Dr. Lambert's announcement: "Mr. Hammer, you have been summoned here to answer why you should not be expelled." "Expelled?" The thud from the sudden descent stunned him. He sat speechless.

"You risked the lives of a child and its mother in a dangerous situation. You should have called for a staff doctor or a member of the faculty. How dared you undertake a breech delivery without any experience."

The injustice of it all shocked him into articulateness.

"The diagnosis and treatment card given to me gave no indication that this was not a normal pregnancy."

Dr. Lambert waved this excuse aside irately.

"But when you discovered it was a breech you should have called for help at once."

"There was no telephone. Besides, I realized that there was no time. The child would have strangled before anyone could arrive."

"You could have found out much sooner that this was a breech case. Then you would have had time to call for an experienced obstetrician."

"Dr. Lambert, this woman was treated by your staff here for months." He took a long look at the judges sitting before him.

"If they couldn't discover that the baby was in an abnormal position during this long period, how do you expect a novice like me to do so on a moment's notice?"

He had achieved a logic breech. It was the dean and his staff who were on the defensive. They dismissed the charge and sent him back to his studies.

What they did not know was that they had almost cost the college millions of dollars. How could they know? It was a half century later, in 1977, that Dr. Hammer arranged with my partner Arthur Krim (who in addition to being a special adviser to Presidents had by then become chairman of the Board of Trustees of Columbia University) to give a $5 million gift to Columbia Medical School.

At the age of twenty-three, Dr. Hammer decided to visit Russia, which was famine-ridden and in need of medical services. The pragmatic aspects of this startling decision were that he could do his internship on a large scale, and try to collect moneys due him for pharmaceutical sales. He brought with him a $100,000 World War I surplus field hospital stocked with medicines and instruments, and also a $15,000 ambulance. The daring of such a trek to the hostile Bolshevik country which was still in the agony of a revolution can only be compared to that of pioneers who headed west into Indian territory. He encountered mass starvation (one Russian was chopping wood for his own coffin in anticipation of his death). Hammer broke through the European economic blockade, and imported a million bushels of wheat in a barter deal. The feat came to the attention of Lenin, who invited the young American doctor to see him.

Thus began a friendship as warm as it was bizarre between the five-foot-three, bald, brown-eyed founder of the new Russian state and an American capitalist. Lenin talked English fluently. Incredibly his affinity with Hammer was in the economic realm. Lenin picked up a scientific American magazine and urged that American technology and know-how were what Russia needed. He saw no reason why the two countries couldn't do business together. He appointed a committee for concessions and gave Hammer the first concession of asbestos. Later Lenin wanted to confer on his friend another concession. Hammer surprised him by requesting the pencil concession, because "I know you will want to wipe out illiteracy, and everybody will need pencils." Lenin was warmed by the gesture. In the papers left after his death, he wrote about Hammer fourteen times.

Hammer persuaded Henry Ford, as bitter an enemy of Bolshevism as could be found on the globe, to sell tractors to Russia. Hammer then became the agent for thirty-seven other companies which sought entry into the virgin market, including U. S. Rubber, Allis-Chalmers, Ingersoll-Rand, Underwood (typewriters), and Parker Pen. Later Ford actually built a plant in Russia which turned out 100,000 cars a year.

When the first Ford tractors arrived, Hammer climbed on one of them and led the parade into Novorossisk. The people mistook them for tanks and the Communist guard was called out. When it was explained that these were friendly machines which would make possible more food, cheers and tears replaced their fears.

In 1922, Lenin suffered a severe stroke. His right side was paralyzed: Lenin doggedly conquered his aphasia and learned to speak again. His right hand was dead. He learned to write with his left. But two years later he died.

Hammer also met Leon Trotsky, but found him cold and unlike Lenin. Due to the killing of twenty members of the Moscow Communist Committee, by a bomb thrown through a window, Trotsky's windows were covered with steel netting. He sat in a darkened room, with only an electric light over his head. He conversed with Hammer in German. He, too, following Lenin's lead, wanted to interest American capital, contending that investments there were safer because the revolution had already taken place, whereas it was yet to come to the United States. It was one of those inverted arguments like the cynical jest that it is better to re-elect a corrupt politician because he has already taken his graft.

What came through Hammer's experience, supported in part by Lenin's writings, was that had he lived longer, he might have set Russia on a path of amity with the Western world, deriving economic strength from capitalism, to buttress his impoverished people. Perhaps he would have been content with that achievement, without exporting Communistic revolution by force of arms and infiltration. There might have been true détente. Who knows, revolutionaries are fanatics and unpredictable.

After the Stalin freeze, Russian leaders, Khrushchev, Kosygin, and Brezhnev, all greeted Hammer eagerly and dealt with him. The fact that he was a friend of Lenin was a unique passport which pierced all reserve and suspicion of a noted capitalist. Brezhnev announced on an NBC documentary, while standing next to his friend, "Armand Hammer has expended considerable effort. I help him, he helps me. It is mutual. We do not discuss secrets—just business." That business involved a $20 billion deal in which superphosphoric acid would be shipped to Russia in return for ammonia, urea, and potash. Also, natural gas was to be shipped from Siberia enough to heat two million American homes for thirty years, while a hundred-million-dollar trade center with offices for American firms would be erected in Moscow.

The hope was that trade coexistence might lead to military and political coexistence.

What a triumph that would be for capitalism. The Communist prophecy of the collapse of capitalism would be defeated by Russia's need to utilize the efficient productivity of the system it hated. On the other hand, Communist states could point to the triumph of socialist policies adopted by capitalistic countries which paternalistically cared for the masses. One is reminded of President Franklin Roosevelt's observation that Russia was moving toward capitalism and the United States toward socialism, and the two would meet midway.

One of the chief architects of the former has been Armand Hammer, who, due to his friendship with the George Washington of the Russian state, now deemed god-like by its mystically inclined people, has bridged the commercial chasm.

A man's life is colored by the dye of his imagination. Hammer's ventures in other directions were no less challenging than his "Russian connection." Roosevelt's secretary, General "Pa" Watson, once told the President that he ought to use Hammer because "The man is just plain lucky." This was a superstitious imprimatur, which might be more flattering than the prosaic explanation of imagination harnessed by hard work. Roosevelt assigned Hammer to Harry Hopkins, with whom he developed the fifty-destroyer lend-lease for Great Britain in return for some bases. This broke the U-boat stranglehold, and might well have saved the Allies.

Hammer's "luck" included staying out of the stock market in 1929, turning a rotting Maine potato surplus into alcohol, and later selling out his liquor business to Schenley for six and half million dollars cash, discovering phosphate in northern Florida, where none had been found before, combining it with sulphur, by buying the Jefferson Lake Sulphur Company in Texas to create a leading fertilizer company, accidentally becoming interested in breeding bulls, which resulted in his acquisition for $100,000 of the world's prize black Angus bull, Prince Eric (whose picture is next to Lenin's autographed photograph on Hammer's shelf and whose one thousand calves in three years, by means of artificial insemination, resulted in $2 million profit); and buying the Mutual Broadcasting System, signing Walter Winchell and Kate Smith and selling it one year later for $1,300,000 profit.

"The most versatile tycoon of the century," as Hammer has been called, demonstrated his imaginative flair, in the most dangerous of all enterprises—oil. He had retired at the age of fifty-eight, to devote his time to his art gallery and the gathering of masterpieces for gifts to museums, $25-million bequest to the Los Angeles County Museum and drawings to the National Gallery in Washington, D.C.

A tax accountant suggested oil investment because the inevitable dry holes would provide tax relief (one of the curious consequences of a high tax bracket). So he bought into a defunct little company called Occidental Petroleum Corporation, worth $34,000, with three employees, and built it into the twentieth largest corporation in the United States, with thirty-five thousand employees, three hundred thousand stockholders, six billion dollars annual revenues, and an after-tax profit of several hundred million dollars.

What kind of alchemist is this who turns everything he touches into gold? Like all tycoons he is tirelessly dedicated to his venture, whatever it be. Like all achievers he spouts energy in greater bursts than his oil gushers. There are other attributes and the usual faults.

His nervous system is protected by mental shock absorbers which enable him to be serene in the midst of turmoil. He can talk in sequence to ministers, kings, and business royalty in distant countries at hours normal there and appropriate for sleep here, read reports, write shorthand notes, all without nervous strain. He increases his capacity by avoiding tension. But how eliminate stress when so much is at stake? One way is to take a ten- or fifteen-minute nap in the midst of work, I learned the signal. When during a hectic conference, he asked for a private room to telephone, he would be given an office with a couch. In a few seconds he was sound asleep. He would return shortly, refreshed, and eager for the fray with less rested adversaries.

Reflective calm is another antidote to the wear and tear of activity. Those upon whom others lean for decision must not waver. Confidence in their wisdom brings out the best in them, and gives impetus to execution, which often makes a questionable instruction come out right. Hammer, like all tycoons, has this quality of decisiveness.

His personal habits are sound. Every morning, there is the one-half-hour naked swim in his indoor pool followed by five hundred stomach contractions, rubdown, and cold shower. Then to bed for breakfast. He eats moderately and drinks less. But when travels abroad require feasts, he returns to a strict diet regimen, until the bulges disappear.

However, concentration, like that of most tycoons, is directed with laser beam narrowness to the particular venture he is guiding. He will listen and even participate in general discussion but his heart isn't in it and his eye is dull. It is only politeness which prevents him from revealing his boredom. But mention his enterprises and animation sweeps across his face and body. This one-trackedness can freeze a man but in his case it is relieved by a readiness to laugh and a capacity to enjoy.

He has had three wives. The first was Baroness Olga Vadina Von Root, a blue-eyed beautiful daughter of a Czarist general whom he met in Moscow. She was a concert singer. She bore him a son. The marriage was stormy and unsuccessful. A second marriage, to a beautiful society girl with a weakness for drink, also failed, but his third, to Frances Tolman, has been one of rare complementary affinity. They share common interests in finance, art, and joy of achievement. She gladly suffers the 300,000 miles of travel a year to all corners of the earth, to be near him, and he feels at home whenever she is beside him.

Hammer's serious demeanor, made somewhat forbidding by the knowledge of his accomplishments, changes to charm when he is on a persuasive tear. He is irresistibly insistent. He could have been a fine advocate. I know. I have been the target of some of his pleas.

Once Mildred and I were on vacation in Monte Carlo. Hammer called. His soothing solicitous voice warned me that an unusual request was coming. There was an important case scheduled for trial in Midland, Texas. He set forth the complicated facts pithily to demonstrate how just Occidental's cause was. He wanted me to try the case.

"When?" I asked.
"Tuesday."
"Today is Friday. That is impossible. I never try a case without thorough preparation. You have prominent Texas counsel. Why not proceed with them?"
"They'll collaborate. This is a case you must try. Please, Lou, do this for me."
"Can you adjourn it?"
"No, and besides it is important to us not to delay it."

So the conversation continued. When I pleaded that I could not even get a reservation on a plane on such short notice, the reply was that he would send his plane. The result: I flew to Midland, studied the files for forty-eight hours without sleep, and tried the case. Lest this be deemed a demonstration of low resistance by me, I can report that I have seen tough executives lured to hazardous posts abroad; others cajoled into deals they had forsworn, by the persistence, charm, and pleas to which they were subjected from the same source.

On the other hand, if he feels he has been wronged, he is no respecter of powerful forces arrayed against him. He is unabashedly litigious. He has started suits against the mighty and earned their enmity. He has dared as an "independent" to challenge the giants, and it has taken a long while for some of them to accept him as a fellow giant, or at least an independent not to be tampered with. In the meantime, we had fought successfully various legal battles, one of five years' duration against Armour & Company over a patent infringement involving superphosphoric acid, another against Standard Oil Company of Indiana, which had attempted a take-over of Occidental, one against Tenneco, and a number of others.

In the course of Occidental's growth, Hammer has left strewn behind him many adversaries. They have not hesitated to injure him public relations-wise whenever they could. He is vulnerable because he has President Johnson's sensitivity to criticism. So he fights back with threats of libel suits and corrective letters to the publications.

In view of his optimism and enthusiasm, his anticipatory claims, while sincerely made, are not always realized.

There is no reluctance in many quarters to pounce upon "his exaggeration" and try to discredit him. Ultimately, in almost every instance, he has exceeded his promise, but his "enemies" have no desire to be patient. So it came about that probably the most gifted businessman of our time, who has earned unprecedented accolades, has also been subjected to embarrassing skepticism. There is only one way to avoid criticism: to say nothing, do nothing, and be nothing. Anyone who violates all three cannot escape the lash.

I have referred to the tycoons' gratification from battle, as much as from victory. Hammer qualifies. Like Al Smith, who was known as the happy warrior, Hammer has the joy of combat. He and only one other person, in all my experience, are eager to testify. I have seen men who risk their lives readily but quail at taking the stand to face cross-examination. It takes a special kind of courage akin to super-self-confidence salted and peppered with an arrogance and conceit to face a trained cross-examiner. The lawyer's scalpel which cuts into the mind is painful enough, but to have the surgery performed in the presence of a judge, jury, audience, and worst of all a gloating adversary is purgatory to most people. Yet Hammer looks forward to taking the stand. As in his business deals, he prepares thoroughly. Hours mean nothing. I have been called "slave driver" by many clients (the first to so dub me was Harold Lloyd), but Hammer doesn't understand why we quit at three in the morning. He studies every fact, every date, and the principles of law involved. Then in a quiet way, hiding his exultation, he corrects the examiner on some misstatement, parries every point, frequently referring to a document by memory, which proves him right and embarrasses the less prepared attacker. He comes close to being the perfect witness; politely devastating and disarmingly persuasive. And he enjoys every minute of it, particularly the postverdict reminiscences of the verbal thrusts which felled the enemy.

Being intrepid himself, he despises lawyers who are nay sayers because they see the dangers and wish to avoid the risks. Lincoln used to bemoan the timidity of his generals, until he found Grant, whiskey and all. Eisenhower and Bradley appreciated the daring Patton, neuroses and all. There is a time to settle and a time to fight, and sound judgment in making the choice is an invaluable attribute of an adviser. But Hammer has a nose for sniffing out advice motivated by fear and supported by a catalogue of possible disasters, to which every important controversy lends itself. He would endorse the great Elihu Root's statement that the function of a lawyer is not to tell you that it can't be done, but how you can do it legally. In short he glories in resourcefulness as much as in the goal it achieves.

When principle is involved, he rejects compromise. No matter how prudent it might be to make a settlement which would be "a premium on an insurance policy against an enormous risk," he insists on a verdict to vindicate his position. It does not matter how great the gamble. I shall cite one example which engaged us in an eight-year litigation. At stake was a quarter interest in Occidental's great oil strike in Libya. The damages sought against Occidental were "in excess of a hundred million dollars" and an accounting which might well increase the claim to a quarter of a billion dollars. A defeat would be a crippling blow to Occidental.

Yet Hammer, feeling that Occidental's honor had been impugned, because he was charged with welshing on a written contract, refused to settle. As his trial counsel, I agreed, although the responsibility of advising and supporting his stubbornness was a burden which kept me sleepless beyond preparation necessity. The litigation war was fought before fourteen Federal judges and took us to Italy, Switzerland, England, Germany, and Belgium.

The author of the *Arabian Nights* could not have provided a more engrossing scenario. We were engaged in a fascinating struggle, filled with mystery, intrigue, forged documents, and miracles, such as the discovery of an ocean of water beneath the Libyan desert. Naturally, then, Hammer enjoyed the drama while hiding his anxiety, while I, as lawyer, shared the anxiety without appreciating the drama.

It all began in 1964 when the highly regarded Allen brothers (Charles and Herbert), heads of one of the foremost investment companies, advised Hammer that a friend of theirs, Ferdinand Galic, could be very helpful in obtaining oil concessions which were about to be granted in Libya. Galic said that he was a friend of General de Rovin, who was represented to be in the good graces of the Libyan Government. A meeting was arranged in London. A draft of an agreement between Hammer and the Allens was drawn, granting them a 25 per cent interest in any concession which "Galic turned up." Costs and profits were to be shared in the same proportion.

The Allens did not wish to subject themselves to costs which might run to millions of dollars and wind up with a dry hole. So after consultation with their lawyers, they inserted, in ink, after the word "costs," "to be mutually agreed upon."

In returning the letter for Hammer's signature, Allen referred to this insertion as a "major change," as indeed it was. It was known that two American oil companies each had expended $50 million exploring previous concessions in Libya without getting a single barrel of oil. A French company had a similar experience to the extent of $25 million. The Allens knew, as they later acknowledged in cross-examination "that hundreds of millions could be sunk into the ground in a vain search for oil." As prudent businessmen, they wanted to have a veto on how much risk they would take. The condition they inserted gave them this protection.

Hammer accepted the condition which permitted the Allens to be let out if they so chose. He signed. With uncanny instinct he took the burden for Occidental alone of millions of dollars for seismograph and other expenses, and later enormous drilling costs, without assurance that there would be a barrel of oil.

Then came the first melodramatic incident. It was discovered the General de Rovin was an impostor. He was no general. He was a notorious crook with a long criminal record. Galic, too, had no real standing in Libya. Besides, it was learned that the concessions were not to be granted by negotiation. They were to be awarded on sealed competitive bids, so that influential negotiations were not necessary.

Hammer decided to get rid of the disreputable promoters who had been foisted on him. He terminated their representation. Since Galic would therefore no longer be in the picture, he could not "turn up" any concessions and the letter agreement with the Allens also fell. Hammer so wrote them. They never protested this cancellation in writing. Not until eighteen months later, when one of the greatest oil gushers in the region's history flooded the sands, and floated Occidental's stock upwards, did they decide that they were 25 per cent partners, although they had not put up a cent of risk capital.

In the meantime, how had Occidental obtained two choice concessions, which many of the one hundred twenty sealed bids sought? Imagination and resourcefulness carried the day. Libya requested that bidders offer not only money, but other considerations called "preferences."

Occidental submitted unique preferences in the form of sheepskin diplomas rolled and bound with silk ribbons of red, green, and black, the national colors of Libya.

The wrapping caused the Libyan minister who opened the sealed bids in public to comment that he hoped the inner contents were as interesting. They were. The suggestions were so intriguing that he asked Occidental's representative, Richard H. Vaughan, to explain them out loud.

Occidental offered to earmark 5 per cent of its net operating profits derived from oil exploitation in Libya for the agricultural development of Kufra, which was King Idris' birthplace and where his father was entombed. (The King has not yet been overthrown by Qadaffi.) Later the King, in appreciation of the redemption of Kufra, offered to change its name to "Hammer," but with self-abnegation suitable to the occasion, Hammer declared this would be "too much of an honor" and suggested that the newly discovered oil site be called Idris Field. The King, not wanting to hurt Hammer's feelings by rejecting his suggestion, overcame modesty and consented.

Also, Occidental offered to build an ammonia plant in Libya to manufacture fertilizer. This structure would cost $30 million and would be spent even if oil was not discovered in the concession area. In addition, Occidental offered to use its Oxytrol process for the transportation of vegetables and produce over long distances without spoilage. Finally, it offered to use modern technology to search for water in the desert.

The total offer was so appealing in its mixture of economic advantage, national pride, and general welfare that one of the competitors was heard to remark, "Why didn't we think of something like that?"

All councils of the King and finally the King himself approved the grant of two highly promising concessions to Occidental.

After $5 million of drilling there was only a dry, a very dry hole. Then, near the very sight where Mobil had previously abandoned hope, a rare, geological phenomenon occurred. A reef was punctured. It contained so much encapsulated oil that it would flow almost indefinitely without the use of pumps. A single well produced 72,000 barrels of the finest quality of low-sulphur oil a day. Hammer immediately ordered a crash $150 million pipeline, one hundred and thirty miles long, capable of transporting a million barrels of oil a day.

When the first oil reached the sea, Occidental arranged a celebration attended by eight hundred Cabinet ministers, robed local chieftains, diplomats, a United States senator, and many others. The King presided proudly in a specially built air-conditioned building in the desert. Flowers flown from abroad decorated the entire region. Food was imported. The party cost $1 million.

Occidental stock took wings and soared to one hundred dollars a share. After splitting amoeba-like three for one, the stock still climbed to fifty-five dollars a share in 1968. Those who believed in Hammer's luck, from servants to friends, became millionaires.

The Allens could not resist the temptation to lay claim to some of this wealth. They had been there at the conception, even though Occidental had made an earlier application for Libyan oil concessions. They brought suit in the Federal Court in New York.

Still Occidental's position appeared invulnerable to attack. The Allens had avoided the risk of investment. They had not protested Occidental's cancellation notice until a year and a half later when the Libyan sands were drenched black with oil. The cancellation was not frivolous. Notorious crooks had been interposed as agents and Hammer had the right to get rid of them.

All looked well for a victorious defense. But was there ever a suit in which a surprise witness or document didn't suddenly appear to upset all calculations?

The Allens produced such a document. It detonated in our midst and almost drove us to surrender. Then we recovered our stance and fought on more determinedly than ever.

What was it? Nothing less than a letter from the Minister of Petroleum Affairs of Libya, Fuad Kabazi, on the official stationery of the Libyan Government, addressed to Ferdinand Galic and indicating their intimate relationship and Kabazi's reliance on the Allens' financial ability. He advised Galic that Occidental would receive two concessions. The letter could not have served the Allens better if it had been prepared by them to create a perfect claim against Occidental. That was the trouble with it. It was too pat.

When we had recovered our breath, we launched a counterattack to demonstrate what we suspected, that Kabazi, who no longer was a minister, had backdated his letter to aid Galic and the Allens in winning their suit and probably share in the result.

The Allens' counsel sought to take Kabazi's testimony in advance of trial. The court designated London as the site of the deposition. We welcomed a chance to get at him. We might as well know whether we could survive his damaging testimony.

The examination took place in the American Embassy building so that the American Consul could swear in the witness and preside, if necessary, over formal matters, acting as an extension of the United States courts.

Kabazi was a handsome, academically bearded man, with eyes which could have qualified him as a hypnotist. He prided himself on being a poet, which he announced frequently to offset his difficulties with the commercial issues. He had not the slightest idea of Anglo-Saxon judicial procedure. He did not understand the function of cross-examination and considered my questions an insult to his integrity. He had previously been interviewed by the Allens' lawyers, in a friendly manner. He kept chiding me for not being as courteous, by which he meant believing, as "the other lawyers."

Cross-examination is often effective when its purpose is not discernible, and the witness readily steps into traps. Only later does he discover his predicament. So, for example, Kabazi testified that he was in Tripoli when he typed the letter. It seemed to be an innocuous statement. He was sure of it. In much later testimony, unaware of any contradiction, he testified that he had attended Council meetings in Beida (seven hundred miles from Tripoli) on dates which included the very day of the letter's date.

Similarly, he said that he had always communicated with Galic in

Italian, addressing him "Dear Ferdo," and received replies in French. English was never used. He overlooked the fact that the questioned letter, was in English, and addressed Galic, "Dear Sir.—"

He conceded that neither Galic's name nor the Allens' was mentioned in Occidental's application, and that the attached letter of the Chase Manhattan Bank in support of financing was satisfactory, and yet his letter claimed he was relying on Allens' financial standing. The internal contradictions in the letter escaped him. There was a more subtle contradiction. His testimony was in broken English, the kind one speaks when he must mentally translate Italian, in which he thinks, into a language and grammar of which he is unsure. But the letter, which he claimed he personally typed, was in perfect English.

When the cross-examination became really cross, and I confronted him with a section of the Libyan criminal law which would send him to jail for six months, for leaking the grant of concessions in advance, as he had done in his letter, he rose in mighty indignation at the insult to his honor, and stormed out of the room.

I moved to strike his entire testimony, if the witness did not return to complete his examination in accordance with the Court order. This caused the Allens' lawyers to join with the American Consul in pleading with Kabazi to continue. He finally returned, sulking in his chair as if it were a tent. He continued to make speeches about his being an artist and resenting the insinuations against his honor. But as admissions were wrung from him (such as that he could not have voted as he claimed for Occidental concessions in the Council meeting because he only had a vote if there was a tie and there was none), his protestations of a poet's honor began to sound more and more hollow.

We were moving closer to our conviction that Kabazi had dated back a letter bearing the imprimatur of Ministry of Petroleum Affairs to make it appear that Galic's friendship with him was responsible for the award of concessions to Occidental. In short it was a forgery. It was neatly constructed to prove that Galic, through his influence, had "turned up" the concessions.

Like the conceited counterfeiter who was finally caught because he put his own face on the twenty-dollar bill, Kabazi had left the stamp of his perfidy on every word of his testimony. He claimed that he typed the letter on his portable Olivetti typewriter. Where was the typewriter? He fumbled around, resentful of the probing questions, and finally said he had given it as a gift to a friend in Rome, whose name he could not remember. Did he think we would stop there? We retained an expert, Ordway Hilton, who provided objective evidence that the type on the letter was not that of an Olivetti. Even plaintiffs' experts, including one brought in from Scotland, conceded this fact. So both sides condemned Kabazi as a liar on this point.

Kabazi claimed that he had made a copy of his letter and filed it in the Ministry of Petroleum Affairs. We obtained an authenticated statement from the ministry that no such copy was found in its files.

Furthermore, we challenged his statement that he had made a carbon copy at all. It was necessary to submit the original letter to experts for microscopic and ultraviolet-ray tests to determine whether any traces of carbon could be detected in the indentations caused by the keys striking the paper. The plaintiffs' attorneys refused to surrender the letter to us for such purpose, claiming we might mutilate an important exhibit. We battled before three judges before we could wrench the letter from the plaintiffs' hands.

A court-appointed expert, J. Howard Haring, reported that no carbon copy had ever been made. The plaintiffs brought an expert from Texas to give another view.

Thus the legal contest raged to overcome the surprise Kabazi document presented by the Allens. But the shock of newly discovered documents was not ended. This time it was Occidental which provided the surprise.

A rumor had reached us that "General de Rovin" and Galic had split. The thieves had fallen out. Galic, we learned, had obtained a 10 per cent interest in any judgment which the Allens would recover in the suit. De Rovin apparently felt he was entitled to part of the loot. This was denied to him and the betrayer felt betrayed. I asked my partner Neil Pollio to visit de Rovin in Italy to find out whether his bitterness could be turned to our advantage.

De Rovin was so eager to do Galic in that he delivered to us his personal file of correspondence with him. When we read its contents, we could not believe our eyes. There, set forth in Galic's own handwriting, was a detailed description of the fraudulent arrangement to make it appear that Galic had "turned up" the concessions through his association with Kabazi, and thus give substance to the Allens' suit. I do not believe the Allens were participants in this scheme. They had blind faith in their personal friend Galic, and he deceived them too, in order that they would win and he and Kabazi could share in the bonanza of tens of millions of dollars.

Trial lawyers dream of a future invention which would enable them to lift out of the airwaves words spoken years before, a sort of automatic recording, so that truth could be accurately reconstructed. That wish was fulfilled in this instance by words inscribed by Galic himself.

Armed with Galic's letters, we laid a deep trap for him. I examined him for days, as if I did not have his writings, which were hidden, like explosives, under the table. He felt free to paint a fictitious picture of his intimacy with Kabazi and the way he was responsible for everything good which had happened to Occidental. I actually encouraged him to do so, each question being phrased closer and closer to the contradictions in his own handwriting, which I had memorized.

Then when the examination seemed to have been exhausted, and opposing counsel asked whether we would be through in an hour or so, I began all over again. But this time, after quoting his previous days' answers (from stenographic minutes delivered overnight), I confronted him with his letters to de Rovin. They were in French and each had an English translation, which he conceded was accurate. His own words gave the lie to almost every answer he had made. Instead of "palship" with Kabazi while he was minister, he wrote to de Rovin that he had tried to arrange a meeting with Kabazi twice but that he would not see him.

Instead of learning in advance from Kabazi that Occidental's concessions would be awarded Occidental, he confessed knowing nothing and suggesting that perhaps someone else might find out for him.

At one point, he wrote ruefully, "I wanted to be the first to announce to Dr. Hammer but I see he is informed before everybody. I do not know from where. . . . He is always in advance of anybody."

In another letter he said he had learned that "Kabazi did nothing at all" to obtain the concessions.

The most embarrassing of all was Galic's letter to de Rovin, revealing the Allens' predicament. Galic wrote:

I relied on your [de Rovin's] statement that the concessions could be obtained by negotiation and then it was by tough bidding. This is what Mr. Allen reproached me yesterday. You could have avoided that. That will be the weak point in my lawsuit.

As he was confronted with these devastating letters, Galic's face seemed to turn the colors of the Libyan flag. Then in order to salvage his prior testimony, he condemned his own letters as lies, "all lies." After a while, he got tired of calling himself a liar, and shifted to "baloney." He stuttered and fumed as his words struck him.

More revealing than Galic's disintegration was his lawyer's conduct. He put a wood pencil in his mouth, and as the letters unfolded, he actually chewed the pencil in half.

Federal Judge Edward Weinfeld, who is recognized throughout the nation as a scholar, concluded in his forty-seven-page opinion that Galic's testimony "is belied by his own statements in letters and cablegrams sent to de Rovin. Caught in a web of falsehood by this cor-

respondence, Galic sought to extricate himself by testifying that he lied
to de Rovin to mislead him and keep him out of the deal. But there is
more than this perfidious conduct which mars his testimony. His glib
and facile explanations of falsehoods and contradictions are implausible. A careful word-by-word reading of the record compels the conclusion that Galic's testimony is utterly lacking in credibility."

Kabazi, who was also impaled by Galic's lies, fared no better in the
court's opinion. The Judge found his testimony replete "with inherent
contradictions and implausibilities." Much worse, the court condemned
the Kabazi letter as "deliberately contrived and written some time after
the awards were announced, predated, and sent to Galic in an effort to
aid Galic in a contemplated lawsuit against Occidental."

The cross-examination of both Allens consumed a large part of the
three-week trial. They suffered not only from the Galic-Kabazi debacle,
but from their own inconsistent conduct.

When Occidental floated a $61 million debenture issue, its friends,
the Allens, were one of the underwriters. As such, Allen & Company,
Inc., had to sign a statement to reveal whether it had any financial
interest in Occidental. Had they believed that they had a 25 per cent
interest in Occidental's Libyan concessions, they would have so stated.
But they answered that they had no "material relationship" with
Occidental. This, we argued, demonstrated that they had accepted
Hammer's cancellation letter, and did not consider themselves partners.
Also, in reports filed with the SEC the Allens did not list any assets or
contingent liabilities involving Libyan concessions.

So it always is. The truth is a thicket for prevaricators. Past conduct
of no special significance becomes an accusing finger of inconsistency.
The court rejected the Allens' testimony.

The court also found that "The proof is overwhelming that by their
acts and conduct they acquiesced in and consented to the termination
of the claimed agreement with Occidental," and further that Occidental
had the right to cancel the agreement.

As in every case there was an equitable principle at the core. Can one
lie in wait to see how a risky enterprise turns out and then announce
that he was a partner all the time? The courts have dealt with many
such cases, particularly in mining, where millions may be lost or won.
One judge expressed this age-old principle in colloquial terms: "Heads I
win and tails you lose, cannot, I fancy, be the basis of an equity." Judge
Weinfeld put it another way: The Allens "sought the best of two
worlds. If oil was struck they could claim a 25% profit in the joint venture; if it turned out to be a dry hole, it could disavow liability for 25%
of the loss, pointing to Occidental's termination letter. The Allens cannot have it both ways."

There was an appeal and the Court of Appeals, composed of three judges, unanimously affirmed the judgment.

Above all, from Hammer's viewpoint, he had taken an enormous risk involving approximately a quarter of a billion dollars, in order to be vindicated. He was.

So the drama ended. Occidental struck a great oil gusher. Libya received something more precious than oil income. Occidental had taken a drilling rig and crews five hundred miles across the burning desert, and 250 feet below the surface found an underground ocean of beautiful clear spring water larger than the flow of the Nile for two hundred years. Hammer immediately ordered miles of aluminum irrigation pipes, sprinklers, and chemical fertilizers. Occidental planted alfalfa and it grew as if planted in rich soil. The desert bloomed.

So did Occidental's wealth, which Hammer utilized to buy Island Creek Coal Company, the third largest in the United States, for a mere $150 million. It had annual sales of almost that much, with reserves of over three and half billion tons of coal. Its profit in 1976 alone was approximately $100 million.

After other triumphs and acquisitions like the Jefferson Lake Sulphur Company, Hammer's star had risen so that he was as honored as he was feared as a business adversary.

He lavished his attention and money on public interest and artistic endeavors. He made a $5 million grant to the Salk Institute for Biological Studies to seek a solution for cancer, as immunization had solved polio.

He has not lacked recognition. President Truman appointed him to the Citizens' Food Committee, President Eisenhower to the Council for the Study of Peace in the World, and President Kennedy to the Eleanor Roosevelt Memorial Foundation. Rulers of many nations have welcomed and decorated him.

At this point of his life, nearing the age of seventy-eight, he was struck with disaster. A criminal charge was made against him by Watergate Special Counsel. He faced the possibility of losing command of the company he had built, and the high regard of distinguished friends all over the world. Much worse, he faced the possibility of spending his final years in jail.

His vaunted fighting spirit was undiminished. He felt he was innocent and insisted upon a trial so that he would not end a creative life in disgrace. But the strain of this totally unexpected threat was too much for his heart. He collapsed, and was put in a hospital. His very life was imperiled.

What was the charge which had caused such havoc? Hammer, who had made beneficences in the tens of millions, was accused in a matter involving $54,000. The charge grew out of a contribution to the Nixon campaign. It was a purely technical claim. Campaign gifts after April 7, 1972, could not be anonymous. Hammer was accused of making such a gift without revealing his name. He claimed he had made it before April, and, therefore, did not have to announce his name. There was no moral turpitude involved. Were it not for the Watergate aspect, I doubt that any prosecutor would have given the matter much attention. But Watergate prosecution was the great news of every day. Any prominent name added to the sensationalism which justly filled the Washington air, and floated speedily throughout the nation.

Like most tragedies, the beginning was uneventful. One of Occidental's vice-presidents was Tim Babcock, Governor of Montana from 1962 to 1968, a leading Republican figure, well known to President Nixon.

When Nixon's second campaign got under way, an intense drive for funds was conducted as if a desperate election struggle, rather than a sweep, was impending. Maurice Stans was the generalissimo of the insistent sell. Executives were called in and were virtually told, rather than asked, what their financial duty was to re-elect "a great President." Babcock was assigned by Stans to hit Hammer. An appointment was arranged in Washington. Hammer had reported his Russian deals to Nixon. He had resolved to make a $50,000 contribution from his personal funds. Stans thought $250,000 was more appropriate for one of his standing. Hammer didn't appreciate the compliment. Under pressure, he agreed to increase his contribution to $100,000. He paid $50,000 immediately to Babcock, on March 31, and promised to pay the balance when he arrived in Los Angeles a few days later.

It had been widely announced in the press that, due to a new statute, Section 440, any campaign contribution *after* April 7 would have to bear the donor's name. Hammer knew this. He wished his substantial contribution to Nixon to be anonymous because he himself was a Democrat.

The opposite number to Babcock in his company was Marvin Watson, former Postmaster General in Johnson's cabinet. Hammer had contributed more to Nixon than he had anticipated and did not want the Democrats to seek similar largesse. He, like many executives who contribute to both political parties, preferred no publicity about his dual gifts. In general, I have found that many important entrepreneurs avoid publicity like a plague. It is not their modesty but their instinct for self-preservation which motivates them. They fear provoking tax authorities, kidnapers, charity seekers, and jealous competitors. Anonymity achieves the same protective coloration that animals use to avoid predators.

So Hammer hied himself to his vault in Los Angeles on April 3, as the record there shows, to obtain the balance of the payment and deliver it to Babcock before April 7.

However, Babcock later contradicted Hammer. He insisted that he had received the balance of the contribution after April 7. At first, he thought it was July and later August or September. If so, it would be claimed that Hammer had violated Section 440 by not revealing his name as donor. If Hammer's recollection was right there was no violation. He had the right to give his contribution without a name.

But it wasn't as simple as that. Whenever it was that Babcock received the money, he did not pay it over immediately, as he should have, to the Republican Campaign Committee. He only turned over the first $46,000. The rest of the $100,000 he paid in three installments over a period of many months, the last so late that the election was over.

Investigation later revealed that Babcock had suffered severe losses in his business enterprises in Montana. He was sorely pressed for money. Could it be that he had utilized Hammer's money to satisfy creditors, instead of turning it over immediately to the Campaign Committee?

Babcock had a different explanation. He said he was delayed because he was seeking friends who would give their names to the contributions. He would pretend that he had loaned them money to make the contributions. Then, when he feared that the FBI would inquire where he had obtained the money to lend to his friends, he arranged through an associate in Occidental to obtain a fictitious loan for which he gave a note. Hammer claimed that he knew nothing of this silly charade, but now the original charge had grown to include the deadly word "cover-up."

To conform to the new statute, questionnaires were sent by the Senate Select Committee to investigate Presidential Campaign Practices, called the Ervin Committee, to donors to state the amount of their campaign contributions. Hammer had previously received a letter from Stans's office advising that he had made a $46,000 contribution. That is how he learned that Babcock had not delivered the additional $54,000 he had given him. So he answered the questionnaire by adopting the figure supplied by him by the Committee, namely $46,000.

Had he answered $100,000, would it have been correct, when only $46,000 was registered as his contribution? At worst, this was an ambiguous matter. Yet, the prosecutor added the charge that Hammer had lied to the Senate committee, violating Section 1001 of the Criminal Code. A minor matter involving a date had grown, like Topsy, into a series of felony accusations, made more ominous by the inflamed Watergate atmosphere.

The central issue still was whether Hammer had delivered the

$54,000 before or after April 7. I thought of a lie detector test. Like many courts which will not admit it in evidence, I had doubts about its infallibility. But the psychological significance of a willingness or fear to take the test was real. Would Babcock take it?

I called Hammer long distance and asked him whether he would submit himself to such a test. He almost flew across the wires in his eagerness to consent. There was no doubt that he sincerely believed that he had complied with the law. Why should he not have? Certainly, he was not lacking the money to make the contribution. He knew it had to be made before April 7 if it was to be anonymous. What reason did he have to delay and involve himself in a criminal charge?

We retained Scientific Lie Detection, Inc., an outstanding company whose president, Richard O. Arthur, had headed the polygraph examiners of New York State, taught 1,800 polygraphists, and coauthored a leading book, *Lie Detection and Criminal Interrogation*. He had a reputation for integrity and objectivity.

Hammer answered questions while the levers recorded his pulse variations. As Mr. Arthur reported, "In order to verify the consistency of the polygraph reactions, Dr. Hammer was requested to return the following day for additional tests. This was agreeable to Dr. Hammer."

The written report gave the following conclusions:

On April 3, 1972, did you give Tim Babcock that $54,000?
ANSWER: Yes.
By April 7, 1972, had you then already actually given Tim Babcock that $104,000?
ANSWER: Yes.
On September 6, 1972, did you give Tim Babcock $54,000?
ANSWER: No.
On both examinations there were definite indications of truthfulness when Dr. Hammer answered the same pertinent test questions.

During one of our conferences with the special prosecutor, I gave this report to him and offered to have him select any polygraphist of his own to repeat the test, and to invite Babcock to do so. We heard nothing more from him on this subject.

While searching his mind for proof that he had delivered the money before April 7, Hammer recalled a visit to the White House several months after that date, on July 20, 1972. He had just returned from Russia with his first trade agreement and was invited by Nixon to report on the event. At the end of the conference, as he was leaving, Hammer said, "Mr. President, I am glad to tell you that I am a member of the $100,000 club."

Now that it was learned that everything was taped, could not his comment be proved? Would this not indicate that he had already delivered the $100,000? If, as the prosecutor charged, and Babcock claimed, he completed the contribution months later, in September, it was unlikely that he would have made the comment, which could be so easily checked, to the President.

We asked the prosecutor to review the tape to confirm the incident. He did, and Hammer was borne out by it. But, whatever impact it made was not revealed to us any more than that of the polygraph test.

On the contrary, the prosecutor was preparing to present the matter to a grand jury. Then if indictments were handed down, the story would break for the first time in the press. Hammer wanted to volunteer to appear before a grand jury and tell his story. He was convinced that he could persuade the jury that he was telling the truth and that it would not indict him. It was our painful duty to forbid him to do so. Why? Because experience had shown that when a prosecutor wants an indictment, a grand jury will almost always hand one down. If the target of the indictment testifies, and others like Babcock in this case, contradict him, the prosecutor can add a perjury charge to the original accusation. And he often does. For example Maurice Stans and John Mitchell offered to appear and testify before a grand jury. They were then indicted for perjury. The trial took place in New York and they were acquitted by a jury, but they had to defend themselves on a felony charge of perjury, which their voluntary appearance before a grand jury made possible. (The defects in the grand jury system are another example of how a noble procedure may become ignoble in practice. The grand jury was created to avoid the tyranny of a king, but over the centuries it has become tainted by another kind of tyranny, the power of overambitious prosecutors. In too many instances, the grand jury becomes a rubber stamp for a prosecutor who sheds his obligatory neutrality and seeks indictment.)

Hammer did not yield readily to our precautionary advice. His self-confidence was buttressed by his certainty that he was innocent. He distinguished other cases from his own. He had not used one cent of corporate money in making his contribution. He had used his personal funds only. This was in accordance with his general principle of personally absorbing most corporate expenses when he traveled. He felt that a grand jury would not submit him to a criminal charge in so technical a matter, but this was one time our insistence overcame his.

In the meantime, Babcock had sought mercy from the prosecutor by pointing a finger at Hammer. He entered into a plea bargain which involved him only in a misdemeanor charge. He was advised by his counsel that his punishment would be limited to a fine. This appeared sound enough, especially since the prosecutor agreed to make no contrary recommendation. But when Babcock appeared before Federal Judge George L. Hart, Jr., in Washington, everyone was stunned when the court sentenced him to four months in jail. The Judge held forth as follows:

"Mr. Babcock, in your case, you were not some untutored underling who had to dance to the tune of the boss. You are independently wealthy, you were decorated for bravery at Remagen Bridgehead, you could have told Hammer that you had no intention of assisting him in breaking the law, and been impervious to any penalty of any sort that would have meant anything."

Thus Hammer, who had not yet been charged with anything, had not appeared in any court, or had an opportunity to defend himself, was condemned by the court!

The press and media prominently carried the story. Often it was Hammer's picture, not Babcock's, which accompanied it.

It was an unbelievable and unjust blow. Almost everything about the pronouncement was incorrect. Babcock was not "independently wealthy." He was in a severe financial bind. He had solicited $5,000 from Hammer for senatorial campaigns. Four thousand dollars of this sum was deposited in his own corporate account in the Commerce Bank in Helena, Montana, as was verified by the prosecutor. As Hammer later wrote to the probation officer, "The fact is, I was the victim, not principal."

Now we had to overcome another burden. Would not the jail sentence to Babcock put a psychological burden on any court to do likewise? Only an acquittal could avoid the danger. It made a trial inevitable. I was convinced that he would be acquitted, even by a Washington jury understandably drenched with deep feelings about any Watergate charge. (This was before Edward Bennett Williams demonstrated this possibility when he represented Governor Connally.)

Hammer was ready for the fray. But his heart wasn't. We were advised by two eminent cardiologists who had to be called in that he could not stand the strain of a criminal trial. We were forced to reveal our dilemma to the prosecutor, requesting that he designate his own cardiologist to verify the finding. He selected Dr. Meyer Texon, who in two reports confirmed the medical condition of Dr. Hammer.

Babcock appealed his prison sentence. He appeared to have a cogent argument that a misdemeanor precluded anything but a fine, and that the prosecutor had so understood the consequence of his plea. Suddenly Hammer found himself rooting for a victory for Babcock, who had been hoisted on his own sword, the point of which, however, was also thrust into Hammer.

We faced a new dilemma. Our client insisted that he was innocent and yet he could not stand trial. The doctors forbade it. We were not going to risk his life, although he was recklessly willing to do so. What was the solution for such an impasse?

The law, in its wisdom, provided one. It is called "The Alford Plea." It permitted a defendant to assert that he was innocent, but that he was willing to plead guilty in order to avoid the ordeal, expense, and uncertain outcome of a trial. It was the perfect instrument to extricate us from our predicament. But it required the agreement of the prosecutor, and then the approval of the court. The prosecutor would not accept such a conditioned plea. We were left with one alternative, to negotiate a plea of guilty for the smallest offense possible. It would have to be a misdemeanor. Under no circumstances would Hammer consent to a felony plea. If it came to that, we might have to yield to Hammer's insistence for vindication by trial, even if we had to bring him into court on a stretcher. But it was not yet necessary to face this agonizing decision. We were just perplexed about how a technical dispute about a date had cancerously enlarged itself into a life and death struggle.

After long negotiations with the special prosecutor, a plea bargain was struck, whereby Hammer would plead guilty to three misdemeanors involving the campaign contribution by him of $54,000 without revealing that he was the donor. He also had to accept a prejudicial, historical recital of the surrounding events, even though it was stated they were not relevant to the charges to which he pleaded.

There would be no grand jury hearing; no indictment. It would all be processed by the filing of a mere information, suitable to the minor nature of the charge. Furthermore, as some protection against any punishment, except a fine, the prosecutor agreed not to ask for a jail sentence and to recommend to the court that it "should take into consideration as a relevant factor in imposing sentence" the medical opinions concerning Hammer's ill health.

With heavy heart, physically and psychologically, Hammer agreed to this agreement. It was not easy for us, as counsel, to recommend it. In preparation for a trial, before the deterioration of Hammer's health, I had written more than twenty briefs demonstrating that even as pure legal matter there were no violations. For example, even assuming a lie in the questionnaire sent to the Ervin Committee, it was not a criminal violation under Section 1001. Not every misstatement is a crime, or a large part of the population would be in jail. The test is one of perjury, the strict standards of which could not be diluted. So Judge Gerhard

Gesell, in Washington, later ruled in another case involving a lie to an FBI agent.

Similarly, even the giving of a campaign contribution anonymously after April 7, was not a crime, because a fictitious name did not accompany the gift. It was later supplied by Babcock's friends. I demonstrated in a brief that the gift and false name must be simultaneous, or there was no violation. I found authority for this argument in a case where an elected senator who had not yet been sworn in was charged with bribery. His conviction under the public official section was reversed. He had not yet become a senator, and his subsequent swearing in could not be referred back to constitute a crime. The prosecutor could not "retroject." We had the same defense under the doctrine of "retrojection."

These and other arguments might be deemed by a layman technical defenses, but could there be anything more technical than the charge; before April 7—valid, after April 7—a crime? In dealing with men's liberties, the burden of proving the specific accusation "beyond a reasonable doubt" lies heavy on the prosecutor. Also, he had to rely on Babcock as his chief witness, and he knew that we would welcome a test of credibility between him and Hammer.

Our client had carefully read my briefs. He was persuaded that we even had a chance for a directed verdict in his favor at the end of the Government's case. Then it would not be necessary for him to testify at all.

However, health considerations prevailed over everything else. The mere pendency of the proceeding was a pressure on Hammer's nervous system which communicated itself to an arrhythmic heart. We persuaded Hammer to take the misdemeanor plea.

So Hammer appeared before Chief Judge William B. Jones in the Federal Court in Washington to plead guilty. The court, in accordance with required procedure, questioned him closely to be certain that he knew the possible consequences of his plea. He wanted Hammer to understand that the court could sentence him to jail, even though only a misdemeanor was involved. Hammer protested that he had been advised by counsel that the only punishment was a fine. The judge insisted that although he was not saying that he would impose a jail sentence, he had the power to do so. Hammer grew more edgy. The court recognized his dilemma and suggested a recess for a half hour so that he could consult with his counsel in a private conference room.

The scene that followed was chaotic. The majority of counsel agreed with Hammer that he should plead not guilty and stand trial. The minority vociferously opposed. Washington counsel Edward Bennett Williams interpreted the letter agreement with the prosecutor as to require a plea of guilty without reservation and threatened to withdraw from the case (later he did). The argument grew so strident that a court attendant bade us to lower our voices, because they could be heard in the adjoining courtroom.

When I looked at Hammer, pale-faced and shaken by divided counsel and knowing the doctors' forebodings, I shifted my position. I advised that the plea of guilty be taken. I felt that nothing was more important than to accelerate the end of the proceeding. It was desirable to have a vindicated client but only if he was alive. Hammer announced that he would follow my advice. He returned to the courtroom and answered every question docilely. The court then accepted the plea, and adjourned for another date so that he would receive the probation officer's report before imposing sentence.

At last we thought we were nearing the end of the struggle. Little did we know that it had just begun. Extraordinary intervening events made everything that preceded a mere interlude.

Hammer was interviewed by the probation officer, James Walker, in Los Angeles. He was invited to open his heart and his mind and set forth fully all the circumstances surrounding the events which led to the misdemeanor plea. This and any other statements about his background, age, health, achievements, and the opinions by others about his character were solicited, so that Judge Jones would have before him a full history upon which to exercise his discretion in meting out punishment.

Probation reports are based on the theory that not all the same crimes should be punished equally. It is a common misconception that they should. The law punishes the individual, not the crime. One who has lived an exemplary life and has strayed under unusual circumstances should not be punished equally with one who has previously been an enemy of society and who has no redeeming record to warrant mercy.

Thus invited, Hammer wrote a letter which was virtually a stream of consciousness.

Did my intention to make the payment before April 7 become confused with the actual deed? In the hectic life I lead, with problems of global scope often engaging me day and night, this matter could conceivably have been overlooked although I had it checked off in my mind as done. I know that such memory quirks can occur—for example have we not all had the experience of being sure of having sent a letter, when it turns out that the intention to dictate it was never executed?

In view of his illness he was willing to resolve all doubts in favor of the prosecutor and plead guilty

Judge Jones was angered by this letter. He did not consider it "the outpouring of the heart of a very troubled man," but rather a protestation of innocence inconsistent with the plea of guilty. He directed Hammer to appear under oath and reaffirm the answers he gave when the plea was taken.

Hammer's condition had grown worse, and a trip from Los Angeles to Washington was not advisable, but we imposed on Dr. H. J. C. Swan, past president of the American College of Cardiology, and professor of cardiology at U.C.L.A., to come with him. The doctor, having no authority to practice in Washington, took the precaution of retaining a heart specialist in the capital to attend, in the event that some incident occurred, in the courtroom. Also Arthur Groman, Hammer's able California counsel, who had participated from the start and knew his condition best from daily observation, and conferences with the physicians, flew in to present the medical evidence to the Judge.

Dr. Hammer volunteered to take the stand under oath to confirm his plea. The court refused to hear him. The court also refused to permit Dr. Swan to testify, "The continued strain could easily produce . . . a catastrophic illness in Dr. Hammer." The physician designated by the Government had agreed.

The court ruled that "I am unable to find a factual basis for the plea of guilty." Even though neither the prosecutor nor defense counsel sought to change the plea, the court on its own motion (*sua sponte*) vacated the guilty plea, entered a "not guilty" plea for Hammer, and set the case down for trial.

Thus forced to a decision which, except for Hammer's health, we would have welcomed, we sought the doctors' views about the risk. The prosecutor ended our indecision. He announced that, the plea bargain having been set aside, he was convening a grand jury and would indict Hammer on two felonies to be added to the misdemeanors which had been set down for trial. This was too much.

We immediately applied for a stay which would enjoin the prosecutor from indicting Hammer. We appealed from Judge Jones's decision and requested that the plea bargain be reinstated. The prosecutor moved to dismiss our appeal and argued that a stay could not be granted which would enjoin a law enforcement agency from pursuing a criminal prosecution.

The Court of Appeals, composed of three judges, granted a stay until argument could be heard. We faced a new crisis. At the argument the judges indicated their perplexity as to why Judge Jones had been so offended by the letter to the probation official. It was obviously intended, like so much other material, to aid the court in deciding the degree of punishment. I offered to withdraw the letter. The judges directed that the plea be reinstated, thus forbidding the prosecutor from seeking felony indictments. I was asked how soon Hammer could appear before Judge Jones to complete the procedure. I commented how eager we were, for reasons of his health, to expedite the matter. I would try to have him appear within three days. So it was ordered.

I telephoned the good news to Hammer, who was elated with the reversal. We were confident Judge Jones would recognize the conclusive findings of five leading heart specialists, including the Government's, which ruled out any jail sentence particularly for a misdemeanor.

This time we were sure we were nearing the end. What else could happen? The worst of all. Judge Jones issued an order transferring the case to another judge. He designated Judge Hart, who had previously condemned Hammer when he sentenced Babcock to jail! It appeared that we had not been cast from the proverbial frying pan into the fire, but directly into jail.

A lawyer cannot afford to surrender to either physical or emotional exhaustion. Hammer had heart disease, but we could not be disheartened. Our adrenalin was flowing freely. We had learned of Judge Jones's order at 4:00 P.M. I asked the staff of my Washington office to stay through the night. We dictated a motion to disqualify Judge Hart from sitting in the case, and supported it with affidavits and briefs recounting the tormented history of the case. We asked in the alternative to transfer the proceedings to California.

At 6:00 A.M., the voluminous papers were typed and bound. Two attorneys were assigned to wait at the prosecutor's office to serve them at 8:30 A.M., and then to file them in the courthouse immediately thereafter. If Judge Hart refused to disqualify himself (recuse himself, is the legal phrase), we had also begun preparation for an appeal.

An hour later, when Judge Hart ascended the bench, I was ready for argument, any dishevelment of appearance offset, I hoped, by the stimulation derived from the effort.

"May I say at the outset—and with great sincerity, and not as lip service, that it is a great honor to appear before Your Honor, and I am grieved that my application must be made to recuse, but a lawyer's duty to his client often requires very embarrassing tasks."

THE COURT: "Well, don't be embarrassed. Just give me your point of view."

MR. NIZER: "Very well, I will, sir."

I quoted his previous condemnation of Hammer.

Then I read from the statute that a judge should recuse himself when "his impartiality might reasonably be questioned." I emphasized that it was not partiality which was the test but the appearance of partiality which had to be avoided.

"How can the defendant feel when the Judge before whom he comes has already condemned him with respect to matters which our affidavit now shows were incorrect?"

The Judge assured me that he had no personal knowledge of the disputed facts:

THE COURT: "Counsel, what you are arguing is something that, in the event that the plea was accepted, and he comes up for sentence, you could argue in connection with the sentence but it has nothing to do with this matter so far as I can see."

I urged again that:

"in the interests of this court and generally, that there be no punishmen of Dr. Hammer, at your hands, in the light of your prior condemnation of him."

Furthermore, I contended that if Judge Jones wanted to transfer the case, the rules required that the new judge be selected at random from a revolving wheel. It had been improperly assigned directly to him.

Despite the sensitivity of my requests, the argument had proceeded with admirable professional objectivity. Judge Hart was known for his fairness and he accepted my contentions with tolerance. But suddenly I realized that he was riled, not by my challenge of him, but what he understood was my challenge of Judge Jones:

THE COURT: "Mr. Nizer, this is a fifteen Judge Court. Normally, whenever a defendant asks me to disqualify myself I am inclined to do it, but let me ask you a question: Did you or did you not ask the United States Court of Appeals to remove Judge Jones from this case?"

I explained that Judge Robb in the Court of Appeals had commented that apparently Judge Jones had felt imposed upon by Hammer's letter, which he thought repudiated his plea. I replied that "we had the greatest regard and respect for Chief Judge Jones" but that if he felt imposed upon by the defendant, the court might consider sending the case back to another judge, as was the practice, for example, in the Second Court of Appeals, so that a judge who was reversed might not harbor resentment. The issue was the same—the avoidance of the appearance of partiality. So I concluded my answer to Judge Hart, saying that I had not volunteered my request about Judge Jones, but responded to a statement that he might feel resentment. "To that extent I made the application."

Judge Hart was not appeased.

"I certainly have no desire to have this case; I would be very happy to get rid of it, but I have a duty to take it.

"I have a duty to see that judge-shopping is not permitted, and I will therefore not disqualify myself in the case."

MR. NIZER: "I assure your Honor with the greatest earnestness that we are not judge-shopping.

"On the contrary, we think that inadvertently the assignment of this case, not in the regular manner by random choice was much closer to the selection of a Judge than anything we wished to do, and we would respectfully submit that we wish any Judge who was impartial and might not give the appearance, no matter what the fact is, of partiality to sit in a matter of this kind.

"So I respectfully except to your Honor's ruling."

This exchange was an example of confrontation, which sometimes occurs between counsel and the court, in which daggers fly, disguised though they be in courteous sheaths.

The bitter exchange having ended, Judge Hart immediately addressed himself dispassionately to the medical problem, with equal concern for Hammer's health and the prosecution's rights. This, despite my provocative statement (necessary to protect our client) that I would proceed, "but we do not thereby wish in any way to acquiesce in Your Honor's sitting in the matter ultimately."

The Judge's duty also had to be performed without rancor.

THE COURT: "Well, you have your remedy there, if you wish to pursue it."

An appeal to a higher court was in the air again. But in the meantime we were invited by the court to discuss Hammer's physical condition and our motion to transfer the case to California.

Groman, who had again flown in with the latest sad tidings, submitted an affidavit of Dr. Rexford Kennamer, who for seventeen years had been Hammer's personal physician. He described an attack his patient suffered at ten in the evening, two days previously, which required him to be brought to the Los Angeles Hospital. His condition was diagnosed as preinfarction angina, congestive heart failure, and disturbance of his cardiac rhythm. The affidavits of three other pre-eminent cardiologists and one selected by the prosecutor attested to the seriousness of Hammer's condition.

The prosecutor suggested that the Judge appoint an independent physician to examine Hammer and report. I said that "we would welcome that."

Judge Hart announced that he had selected four "outstanding" cardiologists, and he would designate any two that the prosecutor and I agreed upon. It was time for a grand gesture;

"We will consent to any doctor that the prosecutor selects—do that blindly—he doesn't have to consult me because I know what the tragic facts are."

The heated session came to an end on a hopeful note.

MR. NIZER: "Perhaps Your Honor might still consider in the light of the health situation, the advisability of transferring the matter to California."

THE COURT: "That could be. It would depend on the physical situation, I guess."

The prosecutor selected from the Judge's list Dr. George A. Kelser, Jr., director of cardiology of the George Washington University Medical Center, and Dr. Ross D. Fletcher, chief of cardiology of the Veterans Administration Hospital in Washington, D.C. They flew to California, submitted Hammer to the most rigorous examinations and tests, and filed a seventeen-page report.

Judge Hart set another hearing. He bade us present the medical evidence. I put his appointed physicians on the stand. Their findings confirmed in every detail those made by five other outstanding cardiologists including one previously designated by the prosecutor. Hammer was "threatened with acute myocardial infarction due to coronary artery atherosclerotic disease." Surgery might be necessary.

The very pending of the proceeding "contributed significantly to a life-endangering situation." The unanimous conclusion was that:

The nature of his disease is such that he will need to remain close to his physicians for an indefinite period of time. If feasible, consideration should be given to possible arrangement of transfer of the court appearance to Los Angeles when the acute phase of his illness has abated.

The prosecutor accepted the doctors' report. Judge Hart was fully convinced by the independent judgment of his own designated physicians, as well as those of the pre-eminent cardiologists who had treated Hammer.

The Judge issued an order transferring the case to the Federal Court in Los Angeles County, and indicated his solicitude for Hammer's survival, by directing that his order be expedited "forthwith" so that the proceeding there could be hastened, thus relieving Hammer as soon as possible of the anxiety which worsened his condition.

The motion to disqualify the Judge became obsolete.

In Los Angeles, the turn of the court wheel designated Judge Lydick. He was a severe disciplinarian, insisting on precise conformity with the rules. He refused to accelerate the proceeding by holding court in Dr.

Hammer's hospital room, as some judges had, in their discretion, done in other cases. There was fretting delay. Finally Dr. Hammer was taken to the courtroom, wired invisibly with telemetered electrocardiographic equipment, so that he could be monitored secretly in an adjoining room.

The court not only had before it the voluminous medical reports forwarded by Judge Hart, but questioned Dr. Swan under oath. He accepted Hammer's plea.

Then he weighed the appropriate sentence. He considered the probation report, and the more than one hundred letters which had been sent to Judge Jones recommending the greatest consideration for Dr. Hammer. These letters came from men in the highest stations in all walks of life, from clergymen like James Francis Cardinal McIntyre, Rabbi Edgar Magnin, and Norman Vincent Peale (who called him "one of the most creatively inspirational persons I have ever met"), to public officials like Secretary of the Treasury William E. Simon (who wrote that "Hammer is a man of the highest character and integrity who would not consciously or knowingly violate our laws"), six United States senators, presidents and deans of universities, ambassadors, Federal judges and two former presidents of the American Bar Association, publisher Arthur Ochs Sulzberger of the New York *Times*, public figures like Lady Bird Johnson, Henry Ford II, Lowell Thomas, and Bob Hope, business executives, and many, many others.

The outpouring of high regard and good will for Hammer offset the anguish of the occasion to some extent. It was a gratifying by-product of a criminal charge. How else could a man solicit such letters? Like flattering obituaries of ourselves, we would like to read them, but are pleased to forego the pleasure.

The Judge fined Hammer $3,000, and provided for one year probation. Hammer was free.

Then occurred the most startling of all developments. Within weeks, Hammer was dismissed from the hospital forty pounds lighter from his regimen there. He began his exercises to tone his muscles (a musical reference as if the body would sing). Sing it did.

He took vigorous charge of his business duties. He began to fly across the globe, although he diminished the risks by an oxygen tank and a resuscitating machine in his private plane, the three pilots trained in its use, catnaps on a comfortable bed, and for a while a doctor alongside him. Even the visual change was remarkable. He looked ever younger, as if his age retreated with the lost hours of his far-flying travels. He resumed his around-the-clock schedule.

Lest this be confused with mere nervous energy, the medical reports confirmed what the doctors considered an impossible recovery. They were astounded. Understandably, laymen and readers of his continued exploits became skeptical of the prior prognoses, particularly in the midst of a criminal proceeding.

Due to several experiences I had witnessed of litigation neurosis caused by stress, I was not as mystified. I had seen a young woman with a clutching hand (called syndactilism), diagnosed as permanent by opposing insurance company doctors, open her hand a week after a verdict. I had seen men and women in matrimonial and other disputes, seriously ill from bleeding ulcers, high blood pressure, diabetes, paralysis, and even dangerous tumors, recover when their problems were solved. We simply have not sufficiently evaluated the effects of "stress"; the cruelties it can inflict and the miracles resulting from its banishment.

The Thirteenth Report, No. 275, of the World Health Organization asserts that 70 per cent of all patients currently being treated by doctors are suffering from conditions which have their origins in stress (*Stress Disease*, by Peter Blythe).

Dr. Hans Selye, in his book *The Stress of Life*, has traced many diseases directly to stress, particularly cardiovascular disease. Predisposition to a disease increased the vulnerability to stress. This factor existed in Hammer's family history. His father and one brother had died of heart attacks, and his younger brother had suffered a stroke and had undergone carotid endarterectomy. We do suffer the ills of our fathers.

Also, studies have revealed that in evaluating the intensity of over forty types of "life-stress" events, the fear of a jail term ranked first, death in the immediate family second, and divorce third. So the "miracle" of Hammer's recovery was not as mysterious as it seemed, in the light of science's discovery of litigation stress.

But the "miracle" of his "luck" in developing new enterprises remained. After his heart and honor were rehabilitated, he devoted himself largely to solving the energy crisis, not through conventional oil drilling and coal, but by means of a new technology.

Nature has endowed the United States with more oil than exists in the entire Middle East. It is located in the Rocky Mountains. In three states, Colorado, Utah, and Wyoming, there exist one trillion, eight hundred billion barrels of oil, two and a half times the entire oil reserve of the world, and sufficient to supply the needs of the United States for one hundred forty years at its 1973 rate of consumption.

Why had this "black gold" not been tapped? Because the oil is encased in shale rock and the former method of extracting it was uneconomic. The technique was to dig into the mountain, excavate tons of shale, reduce it to rubble, heat it to release the oil, and then cool it with water. This was known as aboveground shale oil mining. It was not only prohibitively expensive but left surface shale debris, offensive to any ecologist. To produce fifty thousand barrels of oil a day by the aboveground method would require moving twenty-five million tons of shale rock a year to a plant for refining. Thereafter, the spent shale rock would have to be transported to a dump. Veritable mountains would have to be moved.

Some years ago, Hammer became interested in a new technology to extract shale oil. The mining took place inside the mountain. It was called in situ (in place) mining. The process was to dig a chamber, called a retort, and fragment the shale by use of explosives. Then the shale rubble was lit with a gas flame so that the heat separated the oil from the shale, which then flowed to the bottom of the chamber. From where it was pumped to the surface and sent to a refinery. This method cut the cost in half and made it competitive with imported oil. It avoided the ecological effect of shale mounds left on the surface, and it did not require the large use of water.

Hammer acquired the technique for Occidental, obtained nine patents on the process, and has spent approximately fifty million dollars to develop it. Three agencies of the Government have passed on the new development. The Department of Interior, the Federal Energy Administration, and the Energy Research and Development Administration have reported that "Occidental Petroleum has developed the modified in situ process that offers economic and environmental advantages over conventional processing techniques."

With characteristic flair, Hammer offered this technology to the United States Government for defense purposes at no cost. He offered to license private firms at a reasonable fee, namely 3 per cent of the selling price of the oil. He also suggested a national plan like GOPO (Government Owned Private Operated), which President Roosevelt developed to meet the rubber crisis during World War II.

There are other potential sources of energy. After all, it was American ingenuity which turned the barren sands of Arabia into a rich oil reserve. We may learn to send solar energy by laser beams from outer space, as one astronaut told me could be done. Energy from the sun captured on the "beads" of windmill-like arms of Skylab provided the power upon which it operated while in earth orbit. In addition to nuclear, coal, wind, and water power, we may even get free and abundant energy from the air itself, or from the sea. A national concentrated effort, similar to the one that produced artificial rubber or the atomic bomb, could tap the vast resources of oil beneath the Rocky Mountains.

In the meantime, a tycoon who had to fight for his freedom may have made possible energy independence for the United States.

MIRROR WITHOUT REFLECTIONS

Many people fear to make their last will and testament. Family and business planning look to future living. Wills look to death. The subconscious evasion of that uncertain certainty is pierced by every word in a will, from the customary provision that funeral expenses shall be paid first, to the painful disposition of assets. The older one is, the greater the reluctance. It appears to be, as a child said of his grandmother reading the Bible, "preparation for the final exam." To rationalize their fears, some people turn to superstition: "It is a bad omen to make a will." Picasso, for example, who died at ninety-one, and therefore must have anticipated the need for a will to dispose of his $750-million fortune, refused to make one. He shrank from the mere mention of death. The same was probably true of Howard Hughes.

In a sense, an autobiography, even a semiautobiography such as *Reflections Without Mirrors*, presents the same problem. The implication is that a final summary of one's life is being written.

Well, I don't feel that way. The gifts of vitality, I have previously bespoken, are overflowing.

There is a custom followed in many religions that upon death mirrors are covered or turned to the wall. Presumably this is to defeat the vanity of those who come to pay condolences.

As I end *Reflections Without Mirrors*, I have no thought of writing "finis." There are many cases I will still try, many landscapes I will paint, music I will write, and more books within me to release before the final day of that mirror without reflections.

INDEX

A.B.C. Company, 54
Academy of Music (Brooklyn, N.Y.), 39–40
Acheson, Dean, 396
"Acid in the blood" philosophy, 52–53
Acquisition departments, law firms and, 96
Actors (acting), 44–45. *See also* Celebrities; specific individuals
Adams, John, 9
Ade, George, 349
Adjective law, 77–78
Adolescents (*see also* Children): suicide as second leading cause of death among, 175–76, 177
After Dark (magazine), 143
Agnew, Spiro T., 331, 332
Agriculture, technology and, 28
Ah, Wilderness (O'Neill), 44
Airglow, astronauts and navigation by, 223
Air pollution, 27, 74
Alabama, University of, 264–65
Albee, Edward, 382
Alcohol (liquor), use of, 28; Sholem Baranoff on, 250
Aldrin, "Buzz," 230, 231
Aleichem, Sholem, 241
"Alexander's Ragtime Band," 32
"Alford Plea, The," 437
Algonquin Hotel, Round Table at, 106–7, 349–50, 352
Ali, Muhammad, 229
Alicoate, Jack, 50, 51, 106
Alienation, 176, 179
Alleghany Railroad Company, 4
Allen, Charles and Herbert (Allen & Company, Inc.), 423–24, 425–26, 427, 428, 429, 430–31
American Arbitration Association, 269
American Jewish Congress, 71
American Legion, Adlai Stevenson address on patriotism to convention of, 299
Amherst College choral group, 211–12

Amicus curiae briefs, 367
Amnesia, instant, credibility of witnesses and, 214
Anders, William, 224, 230
"Anniversary Song, The," 32
Ann-Margret, 364
Anti-Semitism: in Russia, 204, 210–11; in U. S. State Department, 285–86
Antitrust laws and suits, 96, 99–100, 411. *See also* Monopoly, law of
Antiworlds (play), 209
Apollo space missions, 223, 224, 225, 226, 230–31
Appeals, judicial, 88, 89, 91, 92ff., 188ff., 267 (*see also* specific aspects, cases, courts, developments, individuals); children as witnesses and, 192ff.; and child sex abuse cases, 188ff.; new evidence and, 191–92
Appellate Division (New York State), 88
Arabs, 165 (*see also* specific countries, individuals); and Israel, 285–86, 287, 288–89, 290, 292–93, 294
Arbitration system and boards, motion picture industry and, 98–99
Armstrong, Neil, 229
Arnold, Benedict, 112
Arnold, Horace L., 112
Arnold, Matthew, 112
Arthur, Richard O., 434
Artists (*see also* Arts, the), suicide among, 157, 178
"Art of a Jury Trial, The," 105
Arts, the, freedom of expression and (*see* Freedom of expression; specific artists, works); illusory syllogism and, 346, 347–48
Arvey, Jacob, 301
ASCAP (American Society of Composers and Publishers), 42
Associated Press, 265
Astronauts, 220–33; casualties among, 226; and contract problems, 227–29; preparation and training of, 221–24,

225, 226–27; requirements for, 221–22; varying and unique personalities among, 229–30, 231

Attlee, Clement R., 284, 287

Augustine, St., 169

Austin, Warren, 289

Babcock, Tim, 432, 433, 434, 435, 436, 437, 438, 441

Bachrach, Burt, 32

Bacon, Francis, 329–30

Baker, Phil, 32

Balaban, Barney, 95

"Balance of spheres" theory, marriage and divorce and, 173ff., 178, 180, 181

Baldridge, LeRoy, 351

Balfour Declaration, 286, 288

Balmer, Ed, 337–38

Balzac, Honoré de, 124

Baranoff, Lisa, 240, 253, 255

Baranoff, Sholem, 238–57; dedication of "The Baranoff Theater" to, 254–55; health and food theories of, 239–57 *passim*

Bar Association of the City of New York, 92; building of, 65

Bar examinations, 77, 78, 79

Barrett, Rona, 158–61

Baskakov, V., 208

Bassuck, Jacob, 82, 83

Bateman (John) case, 182–95

Beck, Dave, 218, 399

Beck, Walter, 542–43

Beethoven, Ludwig van, 88, 124, 347

"Bei Mir Bist du Schoen" (song), 35

Benchley, Robert, 349

Ben-Gurion, David, 290

Benjamin, Robert S., 100

Benny, Jack, 45

Bercovici, Konrad, 106

Bergen, Candice, 364

Beria, L. P., 198

Berle, Milton, 48

Berlin, Irving, 32

Berlin, Richard (Dick), 393, 409

Berry, "Chuck," 224

Berryman, John, 178

Bertolucci, Bernardo, 362

Bethlehem, N.H., 33, 295, 336

Bible, the, 168–69

Bickel, Alexander, 378

"Bicycling," transportation of motion

picture prints and, 99

Billings, Josh, 349

Biological (genetic) engineering, 26, 261. *See also* Molecular biology

Bishop, Mr. (L.N.'s math teacher), 14, 15–16

Black, Hugo, 281, 321

Blackmun, Harry A., 378

Blacks (*see also* Race problems), Fiorello LaGuardia and, 71

Blair, William M., Jr., 301

Block, John, 47

Bloom, Sol, 352–53

Blythe, Peter, 446

Board of Education (N.Y.C.), 102, 103, 104

Bodne, Ben, 106

Bolshoi Ballet, 205

Books (literature), obscenity and pornography laws and suits and, 357–58, 359ff., 365, 374, 375ff., 382–83, 384–85; literary value test and, 373–74

Borman, Frank, 224, 229, 230

Bouras, James, 369

Boys High School (Brooklyn, N.Y.), 14

Bradley, Omar N., 228, 422

Brain: memory storage and, 2–3, 25–26; research on learning and, 24–26

Brando, Marlon, 362

Brennan, William Joseph, Jr., 360, 361, 366, 378

Bressman, David, 337

Brezhnev, Leonid I., 418

Broderick, Vincent, 162

Bromfield, Louis, 283

Bronx Home for the Aged, 72

Broun, Heywood, 56, 140

Brown, Jerry, 283

Brown, Paul A., 164

Brownell, Herbert, 407

Bryan, William Jennings, 119, 313

Bryant, "Bear," 264–65

Buber, Martin, 178

Bugging, in Moscow, 197

Bull Moose Party, 52

Bulova, Arde, 412

Burger, Warren E., 360–61, 368, 373, 378–79

Burke, Edmund, 266

Burnett, George, 265

Burton, Richard, 380

Mikoyan, Anastas, 198
Milk drinking, Sholem Baranoff on, 249–50
Miller, Henry, 385ff.
Miller (Marvin) case, 359–62, 363, 364, 365, 367, 368, 371, 372, 374, 379, 380
Miniaturization, space program and development of, 233
Minimum hourly wage, 117
Minow, Newton, 301
Mississippi, University of, 265
"Mr. District Attorney" (television program), 281
Mitchell, Edgar, 231
Mitchell, John, 435
Moiseyev Dancing Ensemble, 205
Molecular biology (molecular neurology), 24–26, 28
Monnier, Alexandre, 25
Monopoly, law of, 96 (*see also* Antitrust laws and suits); motion picture industry and, 99–100
Monroe, Marilyn, 178
Moon Is Blue, The, 380
Moon space flights, 229, 230
Moot court trials, law schools and, 105
Morality: obscenity and pornography laws and, 359, 388, 389; science and humanism and, 26–29; sexual abuse of children cases and, 182–95
Morgan, John P., 282, 411
Mormons, 110
Morros, Boris, 56
Moscow, 196–212; film festival (1967), 206; film festival (1971), 196ff.; Jews in, 210ff.; Kremlin, 200, 201, 202; Lenin's tomb, 198–99, 200–1; L.N.'s trip to and observations on, 196–212; Moskva (hotel), 196–98; Pushkin Museum, 209; Red Square, 198, 199, 200; Rossiya (hotel), 197; St. Basil's Cathedral, 199–200; subway, 203; swimming pool, 202; Taganka Theater, 209
Mosel, Tad, 208
Moses, Robert, 63
"Mother Machree" (song), 40
Motion Picture Association of America, Inc. (MPAA), 3, 154, 196, 362, 366, 369, 380–82; and seal and Rating Code, 362, 381–82, 384–88

Motion Picture Club, The, 62; Entertainment Division for Fiorello LaGuardia, 62
Motion picture industry, 98–100, 131, 132ff. (*see also* specific companies, developments, films, individuals); libel suits and Hollywood stars, 139, 145–47; obscenity and pornography laws and suits and, 357ff., 362ff., 380–89 *passim*; and Russia, 196ff., 206ff.
Mozart, Wolfgang Amadeus, 8, 110, 347
Muckraking, freedom of the press and, 275–77
Mulligan, Robert, 208
Munich, as a symbol of appeasement, 345
Murphy, Robert, 391–92, 393, 396, 397, 409
Music, 347 (*see also under* Nizer, Louis); illusory syllogisms in criticism of, 347; L.N. and Jewish tradition and training in, 30, 31–41 *passim*
Mussolini, Benito, 5, 64, 202, 351
"My Country 'Tis of Thee," 33
My Life in Court (Nizer), 1, 101, 335, 342

Nagel, Conrad, 42
Namath, Joe, 229
Napoleon, 154, 329
NASA (National Aeronautics and Space Administration), 220, 227, 228, 231, 233
National Labor Relations Act, 117
Nature of the Judicial Process, The (Cardozo), 89
Nazis (Nazism), 71, 113, 147, 165, 177, 199, 282, 391 (*see also* Hitler, Adolf); creation of Israel and, 286–87; rally in Madison Square Garden of, Fiorello LaGuardia and, 67–69; suicides in concentration camps of, 176–77
Negative pregnants, credibility of witnesses and, 215
Nelson, Donald, 159
Nervous gestures (nervousness), credibility of witnesses and observation of, 214
New Deal, 117

New Dyckman Theatre (N.Y.C.), 132
New evidence, as basis for appeals,
  191–92
Newhouse, Clyde, 409
Newspapers. *See* Press, the; specific
  developments, newspapers
New York Film Board of Trade, 93,
  107, 131, 135
New York *Herald Tribune*, 147
New York Law Journal, 81
New York *Times*, 152, 162, 205,
  263–64, 285
New York Times Company v. Sullivan,
  263–64
New York *World Telegram*, 247
Nichols, Mike, 364
Nicholson, Jack, 364, 379
Nietzsche, Friedrich W., 8
Nixon, Richard M., 42, 140, 153, 289,
  304, 309, 359, 361; and Armand
  Hammer and illegal campaign
  contributions case, 431–32, 433, 434;
  and David Frost interviews, 330–31;
  Harry Hershfield and, 349; and
  impeachment, 315–33 *passim*; and
  John F. Kennedy debates, 60, 271;
  and public speaking, 42, 127;
  resignation of, 321, 330, 332, 333;
  Adlai Stevenson and, 309, 312–13;
  and Watergate, 269 (*see also*
  Watergate charges and revelations)
Nizer, Louis: as attorney for the
  astronauts, 220–33; award-winning
  address on capital punishment as
  Columbia University student, 124;
  award-winning address on
  disarmament as Columbia University
  student, 122; on Sholem Baranoff's
  health and food theories and practices,
  238–57; birth in London, emigration
  with parents to the United States,
  1–2ff.; and capital punishment, 124,
  168–72; cases where his life was
  threatened, 130–37; childhood and
  early recollections, 1–7, 29–42, 116ff.;
  closeness to death following dentistry,
  234–38; as coxswain on Columbia
  crew, 41; on credibility of witnesses
  (*see also* Credibility of witnesses),
  213–19; early employment prior to
  law practice, 80–82; early experiences
  in public speaking, 116–29 *passim*;

entry into Columbia College, 41; first
  law case, 77ff., 82ff.; founding of law
  firm of Phillips and Nizer, 93–94; on
  freedom of expression and individual
  rights, 262–80 *passim* (*see also*
  Freedom of expression; Libel law and
  suits); on humor and Harry
  Hershfield, 349–55; and Igor Cassini
  and the Kennedys, 390–410; joins
  Louis Phillips' law firm, 93–94, 95;
  on the judicial process (*see* Judicial
  process and system); and
  Kennedy-Keating senatorial contest,
  269–73; and libel law and suits,
  138–68 (*see also* Libel law and suits;
  specific cases, individuals); on
  marriage, divorce, and the family,
  172–81; and motion picture industry,
  98–100 (*see also* Motion picture
  industry; specific cases, companies,
  individuals); and music, 30, 31–41, 42
  (*see also* Music); on Richard Nixon
  and question of impeachment or
  censure, 315–33; on obscenity and
  pornography laws and suits, 356–89;
  and parents, 2, 3, 6, 7, 8, 30, 31, 32,
  33, 81, 82, 88, 93, 118, 122, 123,
  124, 130, 236, 240–41, 295, 336, 337;
  passes bar examination and is sworn in
  before Appellate Division, 79–80; on
  politics and Adlai Stevenson,
  296–314; on the practice of law (*see*
  Law practice); and predictions on the
  future of mankind, 258–61; on
  preparation and research for court
  trials, 78–79, 84–85, 111–12; on
  public speaking, 111–29; on refusal of
  judicial posts and politics, 267–69;
  Russian trip and observations,
  196–212; on sexual abuse of children
  cases and justice, 182–95; as song
  composer, 42; on spiritualism,
  parapsychology, and illusory
  syllogisms, 334–48; teaches English to
  foreigners in night school, 102–5; and
  teaching of law, 105; on Harry
  Truman and Israel, 281–95; wins
  Curtis Oratorical Medal Award twice,
  122
Nizer, Mildred (Mrs. Louis Nizer),
  53–54, 109, 152, 156, 172, 236,
  267–68, 294, 295, 336–37, 394, 421